UNEQUAL RIGHTS

The LAW AND PUBLIC POLICY: PSYCHOLOGY AND THE SOCIAL SCIENCES series includes books in three domains:

Legal Studies—writings by legal scholars about issues of relevance to psychology and the other social sciences, or that employ social science information to advance the legal analysis;

Social Science Studies—writings by scientists from psychology and the other social sciences about issues of relevance to law and public policy; and

Forensic Studies—writings by psychologists and other mental health scientists and professionals about issues relevant to forensic mental health science and practice.

The series is guided by its editor, Bruce D. Sales, PhD, JD, University of Arizona; and coeditors, Stephen J. Ceci, PhD, Cornell University; Norman J. Finkel, PhD, Georgetown University; and Bruce J. Winick, JD, University of Miami.

***

Unequal Rights

DISCRIMINATION AGAINST PEOPLE
WITH MENTAL DISABILITIES
and the
AMERICANS WITH DISABILITIES ACT

Susan Stefan

AMERICAN PSYCHOLOGICAL ASSOCIATION

WASHINGTON, DC

Published by
American Psychological Association
750 First Street, NE
Washington, DC 20002

Copies may be ordered from
APA Order Department
P.O. Box 92984
Washington, DC 20090-2984

In the U.K., Europe, Africa, and the Middle East, copies may be ordered from
American Psychological Association
3 Henrietta Street
Covent Garden, London
WC2E 8LU England

Typeset in Times Roman by EPS Group Inc., Easton, MD

Printer: United Book Press, Baltimore MD
Dust jacket designer: Berg Design, Albany, NY
Technical/Production Editors: Allison Risko and Amy J. Clarke

The opinions and statements published are the responsibility of the authors, and such opinions and statements do not necessarily represent the policies of the American Psychological Association.

Library of Congress Cataloging-in-Publication Data
Stefan, Susan.
  Unequal rights : discrimination against people with mental disabilities and the Americans With Disabilities Act / Susan Stefan.
    p.   cm.
  Includes bibliographical references and index.
  ISBN 1-55798-681-9 (cb : acid-free paper).
  1. Discrimination against the mentally ill—Law and legislation—United States.   2. Mental health laws—United States.
  3. United States. Americans With Disabilities Act of 1990.
  I. Title.
  KF480.S684 2001
  342.73'087—dc21   00-036204

British Library Cataloguing-in-Publication Data
A CIP record is available from the British Library.

Printed in the United States of America
First Edition

Every human being needs earth, air, and light to survive.
To my mother Gabrielle Stefan, my friend Jamie Elmer,
and my husband Wes Daniels, who are my earth, air, and light.

If all else perished, and they remained, I should still continue to be; and if all else remained, and they were annihilated, the universe would turn into a mighty stranger: I should not seem a part of it.

CONTENTS

ACKNOWLEDGEMENTS

Behind every book like this there are a phalanx of cheerful, competent, patient, and unheralded librarians. I would like to first thank the University of Miami School of Law's library staff, including tireless reference librarians Clare Membiela, Carlos Espinosa, Janet Reinke, Tica Stanton, and Virginia Templeton. No medal or award could sufficiently repay "Interlibrary Loan Heroines" Sue Ann Campbell and Barbara Cuadras.

The University of Miami School of Law gave me summer grants to conduct the research and perform the writing necessary to complete this book over a 3-year period. Dean Rick Williamson was particularly supportive during moments of crisis, when his background in diplomacy was evident. I was assisted in researching the book by Alan Jockers, Katrina Barcelona, Beth Wolt, David Daniel, Alan Poppe, Ben England, Marc Rothenberg, Larry Brown, Annie Fox, Alex Asuncion, Beth Nagle, Christine Giovannelli, and Oswaldo Rossi. I would particularly like to acknowledge Travis Godwin, a law student who volunteered his time to help me when I lost research assistance 1 month before this manuscript was due. I am also grateful to the University of San Diego and Grant Morris for their hospitality to finish the last chapter of this book. Finally, I would like to thank Lisa Daniels for her help at the end.

This book is the product of the contribution and support of many people. I have been blessed by the generosity and mentorship of Professor Bruce Winick, whose kindness and encouragement to me have spanned almost 10 years and who is a model of what an academic colleague should be—I thank him.

I also thank all the people who took the time to complete the survey that is at the heart of this book. The survey itself could not have been distributed without the help of David Oaks of Support Coalition International; the New York Commission on Quality of Care for the Mentally Disabled; Joseph Buffington of Florida State Hospital; Karen Milstein of the GrassRoots Empowerment Project in Madison, Wisconsin; Judy Lavine of the National Association of Rights Protection and Advocacy; and Tim Ravitch, a law student at the University of Miami School of Law. Nancy Frost compiled the survey results and did the computer wizardry that makes no sense to me. Joanne Manees was absolutely crucial in the final push to the finish line.

I am indebted for the assistance of Susan Ridgely of RAND Corporation and Michelle Kunkel of the Florida Mental Health Institute in helping with the research for chapter 5 and to Dr. John Pandiani for his patience and scholarly assistance with chapters 4 and 6.

My husband Wes Daniels was patient and gave much substantive editorial assistance. Professors Michael Perlin, Marc Fajer, Tom Baker, Michael Fischl, and Clark Freshman helped me throughout the years with difficult intellectual struggles; I appreciate very much having first-rate scholars as pals.

There are many people whom I have never met but who have inspired me with their humanity and understanding. I would like to thank and acknowledge the leaders of the disability community, who have consistently refused exclusionary pressures from those in power and stood by people with psychiatric disabilities, especially under strong pressure from Congress at crucial moments in the Americans With Disabilities Act debate. I would also like to thank Oliver Sacks, Robert Coles, Bob Hayman, and Judge William Wayne Justice, for whom I had the honor to serve as a law clerk, all of whom are models of service, humanity, and compassion.

I have also been fortunate to meet many people while doing work with and for people with psychiatric disabilities who have impressed me with their courage, compassion, and integrity, including Mary Auslander, Susan Mann, and Diana Rickard. There are so many people who have devoted amazing amounts of time and energy to fight the good fight, people from whom I have learned tremendously: Len Rubenstein, Andy Blanch, Ira Burnim, Tim Clune, Becky Cox, Joel Dvoskin, Bob Factor, Bob Fleischner, Mary Gallagher, Jim Green, Diane Greenley, Debbie Hiser, Steve Schwartz, Ellen Saideman, Al Smith, and Cliff Zucker.

I acknowledge and honor my clients, all of whom inspired me, in particular Jennifer W. I mourn always the clients who died, especially Elizabeth. You are not forgotten.

Finally, there are people that Laura Ziegler describes as truly "down with us" —Nancy Bowker, David Oaks, and Steve Gold—people who beyond their time and energy have committed their lives and souls to fighting the injustices that damage and kill people who are perceived as "crazy." Some of these people I am fortunate enough to call my friends, my community, and my inspiration: Tom Behrendt, Laura Cain, Peter Cubra, Emmett Dwyer, Beth Mitchell, Laura Prescott, Rae Unzicker, and Laura Ziegler. Thank you.

INTRODUCTION

This is a book about how people with psychiatric disabilities or diagnoses experience discrimination and how antidiscrimination law protects (or does not protect) them. One of the problems with discrimination against people with psychiatric disabilities is that it is often not even recognized as discrimination. In 1983, I was a law student working at the San Jose Mental Health Advocacy Project. My first client was a young woman in her 20s—about my age—and I will never forget her. She had been at a psychiatric facility for 1 week and had been told she would be discharged. I was being shown around the ward when I overheard an aide tell her that the doctor had decided to keep her another week for observation. She protested that she had to get back to her job, she had to pay the rent, she had to leave today—the doctor had promised.

"The doctor changed his mind," said the aide. The young woman began to cry, asking to see the doctor. "You can see the doctor later," said the aide, adding, "You calm down, or we'll have to put you in restraints." The woman cried out, "It's not fair!" Her voice rose as she talked about her job, her apartment. I saw the aide look around, motion with his head. Other aides began to converge on the young woman. "Don't!" she shrieked. "Don't touch me! I'll walk—I'll walk!" By this time, I was frozen, watching and listening.

Aides surrounded her, grabbed her arms and legs, and carried her off, struggling and crying out. I burst into tears. The third-year law student who was showing me around took me to the courtyard and comforted me as I sobbed. She was my first client, although she never knew it. I had to turn her case over to someone else because I was not allowed to return to the facility where I had disgraced myself. I had behaved inappropriately because I could not control my tears. But no one put *me* in restraints. I did not even understand our situations as comparable, or the event as one involving discrimination, until years later.

My most recent client was about the same age as my first client. She was a law student who went to the emergency room because she took too much over-the-counter pain medication after a fight on the telephone with her father right before Christmas. She was kept for 3 days for observation. When she left, she began to worry about her pending applications to the Florida and Georgia bars and her attempts to get health insurance. She asked to see the records of her treatment and was initially turned down (although both bars were entitled to receive the full records). At that time in Florida, there was an absolute statutory right to examine one's own medical records. There was an equally definitive exemption for mental health treatment records: A person could be turned down for no reason at all. The hospital attorney told her that she would have to sue, and she did. She sued under the Americans With Disabilities Act (ADA), which prohibits state statutes that discriminate on the basis of disability.

The ADA was signed on July 26, 1990, amid ceremony and celebration, by

President George Bush. He promised that "with today's signing of the landmark Americans with Disabilities Act, every man, woman and child with a disability can pass through once-closed doors into a bright new era of equality, independence and freedom."[1] Although the passage of the ADA represented a victory for all people with disabilities, it was a particularly significant victory for people with mental disabilities because some in Congress had attempted to exclude them entirely from the act's protections.[2] It is only because of the advocacy of those with more socially acceptable disabilities and the support of key legislators that people with mental disabilities were included in the ADA at all.

The attempt to exclude people with mental disabilities from the protection of the ADA was not because they did not need its protections. At the time of passage, the federal government, state governments, the private sector, and the general public discriminated against people with mental disabilities both officially and indirectly. People were discriminated against on the basis of mental disability in ways that would be unthinkable if based on race, gender, or physical disability. For the most part, these practices continue unabated to this day. Presently, there still exist

- laws that prohibit marriage based on mental illness[3]
- laws that permit states to deny people professional licenses as dental hygienists, social workers, and veterinarians if they voluntarily admit themselves to mental institutions[4]
- laws that permit divorce based on mental illness[5]
- laws that permit the termination of parental rights based on a parent's mental illness[6]
- laws that give people with mental illness fewer rights in the execution and enforcement of advance directives[7]
- laws that give people with mental illness fewer rights in guardianship proceedings[8]
- laws that give people who have received mental health treatment fewer rights of access to their treatment records[9]
- workers' compensation laws that cover workers' physical injuries on the job but not emotional injuries, such as the reaction to a sexual assault on the job or witnessing the violent death of a coworker[10]
- laws that permit evidence of psychiatric treatment to be introduced in court to attack a witness's credibility[11]
- laws that permit the denial of the right to vote based on mental disability[12]
- laws that toll statutes of limitations for people who are incompetent or disabled, with the single exception of people who are incompetent or disabled because of mental illness.[13]

This list includes only those instances of intentional discrimination in statutes. It does not include the vast amount of discrimination in policies and programs carried out by the public or private sectors, or both. This kind of discrimination is reflected in

- the provision of differential insurance coverage to employees for psychiatric and physical disabilities[14]

- the denial of insurance to people because they have seen a therapist in the past 2 years[15]
- policies that limit or exclude people with psychiatric disabilities from receiving organ transplants[16]
- policies of state professional licensing boards inquiring into mental health treatment, even 10 years ago, and requiring access to treatment records before a person can be licensed[17]
- the policy of the military to turn down applications from any potential recruits who have been on medications such as Ritalin or antidepressants.[18]

Finally, some of the most damaging and painful discrimination comes about not by statute or policy but simply by pervasive and uncontested practice, including the discrimination against people with psychiatric disabilities

- in emergency room settings[19]
- in medical treatment[20]
- in higher education.[21]

Discrimination against people with psychiatric disabilities is pervasive throughout American society. For many people, it creates barriers to employment, to insurance coverage, and to education and decent health care; threatens the custody of their children; and undermines meaningful relationships with others. None of this includes the most pervasive statutory scheme that intentionally differentiates between people with mental disabilities and the rest of American citizens: involuntary civil commitment because of mental disability.[22] Up to a third (at the least) of these commitments do not require institutionalization, even according to treatment professionals. These people are routinely denied the rights accorded to other citizens to refuse treatment and medication regimens that they do not want.

Most readers of this book would probably not consider institutionalization or involuntary psychiatric treatment to be "discrimination." More than race or sex discrimination, disability discrimination law raises questions about what exactly constitutes discrimination and even what constitutes disability. These questions are particularly acute in the area of psychiatric disability.

The law constructs mutually exclusive categories and demands that individuals fit into one category or the other: disabled–not disabled, competent–incompetent, mentally ill–not mentally ill. The very nature of psychiatric disability is that it is episodic and may be triggered or exacerbated by environmental or interpersonal factors. A person may be simultaneously severely impaired and brilliantly productive. Psychiatric disability eludes categorization and varies far more dramatically than, for example, paraplegia. Psychiatric disability is about people who struggle, and the law, with its rigid categories, is extraordinarily unreceptive to the process of struggle.

Discrimination is not only occasioned by psychiatric disability. Discrimination can cause disability; it is like an infection striking an already vulnerable and struggling soul. When the person who was thrown out of school or denied a job breaks down, the discriminatory prophecy fulfills itself. The connection between the discrimination and the breakdown is lost. The severity and impact of discrimination against people with psychiatric disabilities is hardly reported and does not really seem to exist as a concept in the American mind.

This is because little effort has been made to explore the perspectives of the people personally familiar with and deeply damaged by discrimination, the people on whose behalf the antidiscrimination laws were written and the cases are litigated. This book, therefore, reflects the voices of people who have psychiatric diagnoses or who have been regarded as mentally disabled by others—people in institutions, people with highly paid and demanding jobs, people on disability benefits, people in graduate school, people in day programs and halfway houses. I have drawn from their books, articles, and testimony before Congress and state legislatures.

I also conducted a survey to get specific information about people's experiences with discrimination.[23] Clearly the survey was only completed by those who chose to complete it—a process of self-selection. Equally clear is the fact that I make no claims of statistical training or expertise; however, no one with statistical training or expertise has undertaken this kind of survey,[24] and I could not write a book about discrimination against people with diagnoses of mental illness without seeking as much information as possible from the people the ADA was supposed to protect.[25] In fact, the personal responses revealed a world of discrimination unavailable by simply reading case law or scientific articles.

Case law and social science research has missed a lot about what discrimination means, its devastating effects on people, and what matters to people who are regarded or who regard themselves as having a mental disability. This book is an attempt to persuade the public and policymakers of this reality and the terrible damage caused by discrimination against people with psychiatric disabilities. Chapter 1 provides an overview of the way discrimination presses in at every corner of a person's life whose psychiatric disability is known to others. Chapter 2 looks at the way discrimination is created and communicated by the language of mental health professionals and the law and how drastically different that language is from the self-descriptions of people with psychiatric disabilities. Chapter 2 also proposes that people with psychiatric disabilities divide into two groups whose experiences of discrimination are almost entirely different: (a) people who "pass," who live in the community with jobs and families and whose struggles with their disability are discounted, and (b) people who are part of the public mental health system, whose strengths and abilities are erased. In part, this is because many of the latter group receive government benefits, and many Americans believe that there is a dissonance or contradiction between receiving disability benefits and having disability rights. Chapter 3 discusses this issue in the context of an overview of federal disability benefits programs and rights laws as well as provides a history of the change in consciousness that led to the disability rights and mental health rights movement.

The two different groups of people mentioned above also have different concerns when it comes to their legal rights. For people in the public mental health system, the crucial issues are civil commitment, institutionalization, the right to refuse treatment, and government benefit programs, such as Supplemental Security Income (SSI) and Medicaid. Chapters 4 and 5 look at these issues, whereas chapters 6 and 7 are oriented to the principal discrimination concerns of the second group of people, whose psychiatric diagnoses are less public: discrimination in the provision of private insurance and in professional education, licensing, and discipline. Employment discrimination is addressed in a companion volume to this book, tentatively titled *Hol-*

low Promises: The American With Disabilities Act and Employment Discrimination Against People With Mental Disabilities.[26]

For all people with disabilities, ending discriminatory treatment by state governments is important, but for people with mental disabilities, it is crucial. Just before this volume went to press the U.S. Supreme Court agreed to review the constitutionality of the ADA's application to actions challenging discrimination by state governments. The legal arguments at the heart of this controversy are summarized in chapter 3; the impact of a decision that the federal government does not have the power to prohibit state governments from discriminating against people with disabilities is discussed in chapter 4.

This is the first book devoted to the examination of discrimination against people with psychiatric disabilities and the impact of antidiscrimination laws on their lives. I have tried to make it informative, readable, and useful to the general public, lawyers, policymakers, and mental health professionals. Of course, some chapters may be more readable than others. There may be an author out there who can make a detailed exposition of Medicaid or insurance law into a lively and playful reading experience, but I am not that author.

Although I have tried to cover disability discrimination law in its many myriad applications (insurance, child custody, institutionalization, professional education and discipline, and other categories), there are a number of omissions from this book. I have not included discrimination on the basis of alcoholism or substance abuse, and I have excluded two huge groups that endure brutal discrimination on the basis of mental and emotional difficulties: children and adolescents, and prisoners. Each of these deserve an entire volume of their own.

At the end of this book, I hope the reader will take away from it the understanding that discrimination is not just a matter of misunderstanding or well-meaning paternalism. Discrimination kills people outright, from the 15-year-old girl who died in restraints because she did not want to surrender a picture of her family, to the mentally ill man killed by police. Discrimination robs people of their lives, year by year, in isolated institutions. Discrimination saps people's strength and their ability to struggle through each day—hence causing the very depression, hopelessness, anxieties, and suspicions that become the basis for further discrimination.

Laws that prohibit much of this discrimination have been passed; it is up to all of us to learn them, understand them, take them seriously, and enforce them. These laws will not eradicate discrimination, but we must at least try to hold this country to the promises embodied in its laws.

A Word About Terminology

Names and labels are always potent, and nothing illustrates this more than the ongoing battle over the appropriate terminology to use when describing the condition that serves as the basis for some of the most potent discrimination in U.S. society.

I have often used "crazy" in the past because, like Stephen Morse and Judi Chamberlin, I believe that "for legal purposes it is more descriptive and carries fewer connotations about disease processes that beg important questions about self-control."[27] As the title to Morse's article indicates, some people use "mental disorder" and others use "mental illness," "emotional disorder," or "behavioral disorder." Descriptively, I marginally prefer the language of disorder to the language of disease, but overall I believe that "disability" captures the truth better than "illness," "disorder," or "disturbance." Many (although far from all) people who have or are perceived as having these conditions agree that the "disability" language is less offensive than the "disease" language.

Still, we are not out of the woods. How do you characterize this disability? The Equal Employment Opportunity Commission, the Department of Justice, and most major researchers in the field of discrimination law describe it as "psychiatric disability." The American Psychological Association resists this terminology as having unwarranted biological connotations and suggesting that these disabilities are solely classified and treated by psychiatrists. I have therefore agreed to use "mental disability," which I believe to be somewhat problematic because of its lack of specificity embraces mental retardation, developmental disability, and organic problems. However, "mental disability" seems to be the least controversial of terms, so I have used that one.

There has also been considerable debate among legal academics regarding whether to capitalize the words *black* and *white*. I understand why respected scholars, such as Lucie White and Kimberle Crenshaw, capitalize the former but not the latter. Yet I agree with Barbara Flagg that "the terms 'white' and 'black' should be treated equivalently, since we otherwise risk reinforcing the idea that blacks, as 'the other,' have a race, while white ethnicity becomes the hidden norm." [28] I choose to capitalize neither word because capitalizing *white* is what white supremacists do in their writing and because I agree with Jennifer Rosato that capitalizing *black* and *white* "symbolically adds to the bipolarism endemic to our society." [29]

Endnotes

1. Remarks by the President during a ceremony for the signing of the ADA (July 26, 1990).
2. See chapter 1, this volume.
3. Discussed in chapter 1.
4. 59 Okl. St. 328, 33 (g)(1999) (dental hygienists); 63-23-106 (7), TENN. STAT. ANN. (1999) (social workers); 63-12-124 (24), TENN. STAT. ANN. (1999) (veterinarian). In Florida, a woman wishing to be a masseuse had to engage a lawyer to obtain her license, which was being held up because she had been diagnosed with depression; interview with Ellen Saideman of the Advocacy Center for Persons With Disabilities, Hollywood, FL (Mar. 1994).
5. Discussed in chapter 1.
6. Discussed in chapter 1.
7. Discussed in chapter 4.
8. *See* chapter 4. For example, a Vermont statute permits anyone "who desires assistance with the management of his or her affairs" to petition for a "voluntary guardian," unless he or she is mentally retarded or mentally ill, in which case guardianship can only be imposed involuntarily; 14 U.S.A. § 2671 (1999).
9. Discussed in chapter 4.
10. Discussed in chapter 5.
11. *See* Susan Stefan, "Impact of Law on Women With Diagnoses of Borderline Personality Disorder Related to Childhood Sexual Abuse," in Bruce Levin, Andrea Blanch, and Ann Jennings, Eds., *Women's Mental Health Services: A Public Health Perspective* (Thousand Oaks, CA: Sage, 1998) at 246–249.
12. Discussed in chapter 1.

13. Kumar v. Hall, 423 S.E.2d 653 (Ga. 1992).
14. Discussed in chapter 6.
15. *See* chapter 6.
16. Discussed in chapter 5.
17. Discussed in chapter 7.
18. Bob La Mendola, "Certain Drugs Can Bar Entry to Service: Ritalin, Given for Attention," AUSTIN–AMERICAN STATESMAN (Dec. 29, 1996):A14; Gary Kane, "Ritalin Use Puts Military Service Off-Limits," PALM BEACH POST (Nov. 24, 1996):A1.
19. Discussed in chapter 5.
20. Discussed in chapter 5.
21. *See* chapter 7.
22. Other groups who are civilly confined involuntarily include people with mental retardation, substance abusers, and sexual offenders, and a few people with active cases of tuberculosis who refuse to accept treatment. Civil confinement—segregation—is a pretty good measure of society's most despised groups. It is on the decline for people with mental retardation, and on the rise for sexual offenders. The vast majority of involuntarily committed people, however, continues to be people diagnosed with mental illness. Although the Supreme Court has held that mental disability cannot justify commitment in the absence of dangerousness, Kansas v. Hendricks, 521 U.S. 346, 358 (1997), state courts have shown remarkable flexibility in describing acts as "dangerous," *see, e.g.,* In re Verda C. R., 218 Wisc. 2nd 168 (1998) (respondent who piled up her belongings outside of her apartment door, "spent hundreds of dollars on clothing which she then gave away," "interject[ed] herself into conversations between others in an intrusive manner," and "complain[ed] about persons breaking into her apartment and stealing things" was considered dangerous on the basis of her actions).
23. The questions on the survey are presented in Appendix A at the back of this book.
24. There have been several well-known polls of people with disabilities in general. To my knowledge, only two comprehensive surveys of people with psychiatric disabilities have been conducted: one in the United States and the other in England. In the United States, Jean Campbell and Roy Schraiber's *The Well-Being Project: Mental Health Clients Speak for Themselves* (Sacramento, CA: Network of Mental Health Clients, Summer 1989) is a comprehensive survey that has several questions related to discrimination (*e.g.,* Q31: "Have you ever been discriminated against because you were or are a mental health client?," to which 52% answered yes; 41% answered that people treated them differently "all of the time" or "most of the time" when they found out they had received mental health services or been psychiatrically diagnosed) and discusses issues of discrimination at 90–92. In England, Ann Rogers, David Pilgrim, and Ron Lacey's *Experiencing Psychiatry* (Basingstoke, England: MacMillan, 1993) reports on interviews conducted with 516 people who had experienced at least one episode of inpatient hospitalization and contains some discussion of discrimination in the form of stigma and its effects. Apparently, none of the 240 questions specifically addressed experiences of discrimination (the authors do not publish the questions in the survey).
25. From now on, references to "the survey" or "survey respondents" are references to this survey.
26. Susan Stefan, Washington, DC: American Psychological Association (in press).
27. Stephen J. Morse, "A Preference for Liberty: The Case Against Involuntary Commitment of the Mentally Disordered," *California Law Review* 70 (1982):54, 58, note 14.
28. Barbara J. Flagg, "'Was Blind But Now I See': White Race Consciousness and the Requirement of Discriminatory Intent," *Michigan Law Review* 91 (1993):953, 955, note 7.
29. Jennifer L. Rosato, "A Color of Their Own: Multiracial Children and the Family," *Brandeis Journal of Family Law* 36 (1997–1998):41, note 2.

UNEQUAL RIGHTS

Chapter 1
THE LANDSCAPE OF DISCRIMINATION TODAY

The minute I got the diagnosis people stopped treating me as though what I was doing had a reason. (Tani, a survivor of both severe childhood abuse and the diagnosis of multiple personality disorder)[1]

Prevalence of Discrimination Against People With Psychiatric Disabilities

Many people who have received mental health treatment have stories to tell about their experiences with discrimination. Their stories are of different experiences, told with very different voices. One person wrote about

> being involuntarily committed to a psychiatric unit because school faculty believed I was behaving in an excessively eccentric manner. Subsequently, I was not allowed to live in student housing, even though I was in no way endangering myself or anyone else. When I tried to enter my dormitory in order to remove my possessions, I was stopped and campus safety was called to escort me out of the building. I was treated as though I was going to massacre everyone in the building, even though I only wanted to gather my belongings! . . . Afterwards, I was watched like a hawk, and any "out-of-the-ordinary" behavior was viewed as being dangerous or disruptive. I felt as though I had to completely alter my personality in order to appear "sane" and "normal." . . . Is a blind person expected to act as though they have 20/20 vision?![2]

As another wrote,

> One December, my landlord came for my rent, and while I was getting it, she told us we had to move, because she was afraid my mental illness would cause me to start fires. I had to get out before Christmas.[3]

Some people are angry at how they are treated; others are baffled. For many, this treatment simply seems to be a fact of life. One woman wrote that she had

> been called names by people like "crazy." Most of what I remember about my teenage years was being cold, tired, ignored, or yelled at. [I] was forced to do time in Marion County Pathways Program by [my] husband where emotional abuse was rampant by staff and patients . . . had a case worker who would speak sweetly to my husband and then speak very rudely to me when we were alone. I was told I was a failure because I wasn't making any points in the program. I was bored there and offended by the way I and other patients were treated. . . . [At a job interview, the interviewer] kept talking about how he didn't want "weeds in the garden."[4]

Some people manage to be wryly amused:

> Head Start refused to hire me because I had a psychiatric label. They gave me the Parent of the Year award and I volunteered once a week at the local center, but [they]

turned me down as a teacher's aide because they didn't want a manic–depressive in the class. I was still allowed to volunteer.[5]

Some of the stories are ironic, signs of the times:

> This past summer I applied for and was accepted into the U.S. Army Reserves . . . .
> I withheld that I had any type of history with depression and other "mental illness" so I could pass their medical. I passed it with flying colors, but kept wondering how I'd take meds (anti-depressants and mood stabilizers) into BT [Basic Training], without being discovered, and how I'd somehow or another get more sent in to me. The unit I would have been assigned to was "tactical" and "highly mobile" which means they get shipped out regularly for 9 months at a time. I couldn't figure out how I'd keep my meds a "secret" without being discovered. I finally gave up . . . got myself discharged under the DON'T ASK, DON'T TELL policy, saying . . . how politically active I'd been re HIV/AIDS and . . . [lesbian/gay/bisexual] politics in '92 during Bill's campaign.[6]

Discrimination pervades the lives of people with psychiatric diagnoses. They are excluded or disadvantaged in employment, education, the health care system, insurance, the media, and—most painfully—in family and romantic relationships, friendships, and everyday personal encounters. This book is about attempts to combat this discrimination through the legal system. Although neither the Rehabilitation Act of 1973 nor the Americans With Disabilities Act (ADA) of 1990 can change the behavior of families, friends, and strangers, both laws enable people with mental disabilities to challenge for the first time the limitations and exclusions that have barred their paths in education and employment and have literally barred the doors of institutions and psychiatric facilities. Some of the worst discrimination is beginning to be addressed, but despite the broad language of the Rehabilitation Act and the ADA, neither has worked well so far to prevent or remedy discrimination against people with mental disabilities.

One reason for this failure is that the legal system limits the ways in which claims of discrimination can be presented and described. The law sees discrimination as a self-contained event, an aberration, not an accumulation of interrelated and exhausting experiences. From the legal point of view, a potentially blameworthy person or entity, the defendant, is charged with specific prohibited behavior, discrimination on the basis of a protected characteristic. In the eyes of the law, the employer is different from the landlord, who in turn is different from the dean of the college and the doctor, and they may not be sued together.[7]

For those who have lived and experienced discrimination, however, the events are cumulative and interrelated. It is not only that people are rejected by their family and shunned by their friends; dismissed from school; scrutinized uneasily or fired at work; patronized by doctors and refused coverage by insurance companies; denied custody of their children by judges; and threatened by family, friends, and doctors with institutionalization, but also that all of these things happen in interrelated and long-term ways. The extraordinary difficulty of coping with all of these accumulated losses and burdens day after day, year in and year out, is precluded from evidence and thus never described in case law, rarely considered in social science research, and never reflected in public discourse. Even more complex is the degree to which all of these pressures are intertwined with related but different pressures, such as poverty, violence, and other kinds of discrimination.

Thus, individual acts of discrimination combine and continue to have an effect on the individual that is far greater than the sum of its parts: exclusion from a graduate program or college on the basis of a diagnosis affects family relations, health care, employment, and self-confidence; loss of employment affects health care, housing, and self-confidence; each of these affects the other in a continuing cycle. This picture of discrimination is consistent with race and gender discrimination as well: the accumulation of burdens and bitterness and doubts about one's self and one's place in the world. But when discrimination is based on mental disability, those who have the power to give comfort, help, and support may be part of the problem. The family relationships of people receiving mental health treatment are often problematic and filled with pain. The professionals who are supposed to help are sometimes feared and dreaded for the treatments that they force on unwilling recipients. Lawyers are wary of such socially discredited clients and often steer clear of them, making it difficult to rectify real injustices.

Many people who have been diagnosed or hospitalized for mental health treatment and who have succeeded in life hide their past and distance themselves from people whose diagnoses are public. The distancing of family members is also felt by many people who are gay. Many people with physical disabilities also have difficulties with the professionals and experts in rehabilitation. The final experience of discrimination against people with psychiatric disabilities that is unique, and uniquely painful, is that if the pressures and burdens of discrimination cause breakdowns, despair, or anger, they are attributed to the person's condition, confirming the family's dire predictions or the college's or employer's wisdom in dismissing the person. The role of the interacting discriminations and accumulated pressures of the person's life in causing the breakdown or despair or anger is erased.

The diagnosis becomes the central, overwhelming aspect of the person's social identity in a way that does not permit any other part of that person's story to be told, the lens through which all accounts are viewed, the frame to every self-portrait. Many efforts by people with psychiatric diagnoses to help themselves are labeled as symptoms of their illness. Attempts to give accounts of ill treatment are ignored or disbelieved. Anger at discrimination or exploitation is construed as loss of control. When an individual diagnosed with a mental disorder actually does lose control or make mistakes, the social reaction is a tide that carries away all previous successes. Everything is subsumed under symptomatology—from the effects of discrimination that may have led to defeat and breakdown, to anger at the discrimination and individual efforts to combat it. If, against all odds, the person struggles to a reasonably successful life, the common assumption is that he or she never really had a serious mental disability anyway.

This is the landscape of discrimination that people with mental disabilities face. Social science research confirms that mental illness is one of the most—if not the most—stigmatized of social conditions. State and federal statutes continue to explicitly discriminate against and disadvantage people with mental disabilities, despite prohibitions against such discrimination by the ADA.

The cumulative anger, weariness, frustration, and pain of discrimination are eloquently borne out in the stories of people who have or are perceived to have psychiatric disabilities.[8] People who have been diagnosed with mental disabilities have much to say about discrimination, where and how they experience it, and how it affects their lives.

Testimony in Support of the ADA and the Congressional Response

Some of what people with mental disabilities have to say can be found in the testimony in support of the ADA. Those who testified[9] about their lives and experiences,
or about the experiences of those they knew, talked about adversity in almost every
area of life. In order of frequency and emphasis, their testimony reflected the following:

1. Problems associated with institutional settings, both psychiatric institutions[10]
    and nursing homes.[11] In psychiatric institutions, these included client
    deaths,[12] restraint,[13] aversive therapy,[14] and the overuse of psychotropic med-
    ication.[15] In addition, deaths in institutional settings were attributed to the
    same kind of discrimination in medical care as is described in (4).[16]
2. Discrimination in employment, including questions about psychiatric history
    in applications and during interviews,[17] and discrimination by unions.[18]
3. Discriminatory housing and rental practices,[19] as well as the lack of afford-
    able housing.
4. Denial of care by medical professionals, who construed medical complaints
    as psychiatric symptomatology,[20] and denial of mental health care because
    therapists would not accept Medicaid.[21]
5. Discriminatory treatment by educational institutions.[22]
6. Discrimination in government programs, including vocational rehabilita-
    tion.[23]
7. Discrimination by public accommodations such as restaurants,[24] banks,[25] and
    movie theaters.[26]

Although only one witness on behalf of people with psychiatric disabilities testified
regarding discrimination by insurance companies,[27] it might be misleading to conclude that this was not a major concern, because testimony by Bill Dorfer, another
witness at the hearing, regarding insurance practices, was explicitly discouraged by
Rep. Major Owens (D-NY),[28] and this may have influenced the testimony presented
by other witnesses.

The testimony was eloquent and urgent about the need for the ADA. The witnesses did not know that a major battle was going to be fought over whether people
with mental illnesses even deserved to be covered.[29] One senator wanted to exclude
from coverage under the act anyone with a condition defined in the *Diagnostic and
Statistical Manual of Mental Disorders* (*DSM*) of the American Psychiatric Association.[30]

Mental illness[31] was the only disability[32] that was subject to attack on the floor
of Congress during the debate over the ADA.[33] Although members of Congress were
appalled at the mistreatment of people with mobility impairments,[34] cerebral palsy,[35]
and arthritis,[36] Sen. William Armstrong (R-CO) articulated clearly that congressional
disapprobation of discrimination did not necessarily extend to people with psychiatric
disabilities:

> I came to work this morning thinking that we are going to vote on a bill to help the
> handicapped, and I would certainly be very sympathetic to that. I would not think
> you would have to be very smart to know that the ideals of our country certainly call
> upon the Senate to do whatever it can to be helpful to people in wheelchairs or who

have some kind of a physical disability or handicap of some sort and who are trying to overcome it. . . . What concerns me is the thought that this disability might include some things which by any ordinary definition we would not expect to be included. . . . Mental disorders, such as alcohol withdrawal, delirium, hallucinosis, dementia with alcoholism, marijuana, delusional disorder, cocaine intoxication, cocaine delirium, disillusional disorder [*sic*]. . . . I could not imagine the sponsors would want to provide a protected legal status to somebody who has such disorders, particularly those who might have a moral content to them or which in the opinion of some people have a moral content.[37]

The equation of psychiatric disability with moral defects was repeated in a number of congressional comments and colloquies, including the following exchange between Sen. Jesse Helms (R-GA) and Sen. Tom Harkin (D-IA):

Mr. Helms: Does an employer's own moral standards enable him to make a judgment about any or all of the employees identified in our previous question?

Mr. Harkin: Are you talking about transvestites?

Mr. Helms: Pardon?

Mr. Harkin: Are you talking about transvestites?

Mr. Helms: Right, or kleptomaniacs or manic–depressives. You said they are covered and that schizophrenics are covered as well. How far does your covered list of individuals go in denying the small businessman —so often referred to on this floor—the right to run his company as he sees fit?[38]

Another item in the legislative record leading to the passage of the ADA that reflects common attitudes about mental illness is a letter from the U.S. Department of Justice responding to a series of questions put by Sen. Dan Coats (R-IN). Although most of Sen. Coats's questions were aimed at excluding drug abusers from ADA protections, his 10th and 11th questions illustrate many of the stereotypes of violence associated with mental illness:

10. Assume that a patient with a history of violence and child molestation is released from a mental institution. As such he is considered not to be a direct threat to the health and safety of others. Should he then apply for a job at a day care center, will this former mental patient be afforded rights to employment under the ADA? Under the ADA, how does a day care center act prudently if it does not wish to hire a person with this kind of background without violating the law?

11. Doesn't the broad definition of disability in the ADA in effect repeal the provision in Title 18 of the U.S. Code, Section 922(g) prohibiting a person who has been "adjudicated as a mental defective or who has been committed to a mental institution" from receiving or possessing a firearm?[39]

Even the comments of members of the U.S. Congress sympathetic to the ADA help illustrate the ways in which stereotypes of mental illness are ingrained in American culture and discourse. When Rep. Donald Payne (D-NJ) argued that some business owner's objections to the ADA were built on worst-case scenarios unlikely to occur, he pointed out that "a handicapped, wheelchaired person" wasn't likely to be found doing construction work on a second-story beam. After all, he concluded, "because you are handicapped, it doesn't mean you are mentally ill also."[40]

Later in the same hearing, Rep. Major Owens (D-NY) interrupted a dialogue between witness Arlene Mayerson of the Disability Rights Education and Defense Fund and Rep. Steve Bartlett (R-TX). Rep. Bartlett had been inquiring at some length about the feasibility of inserting language in the ADA to specifically exclude homosexuality as a covered disability. Asking Bartlett to yield, Rep. Owens tried to make an ironic point:

Mr. Owens: Do you think we should put a statement in that this Act does not cover devil worship as a form of mental illness?

Mr. Bartlett: I hadn't thought about that [laughter].[41]

But Ms. Mayerson apparently did not understand that Rep. Owens was speaking rhetorically and, despite his brushing away his own comment, endeavored to answer:

Ms. Mayerson: I am sorry, Mr. Owens. I didn't understand the question.

Mr. Owens: Should we take care of devil worship? Devil worship may be a mental illness. Should we say that this Act doesn't cover devil worship? You don't have to—thank you very much.

Ms. Mayerson: I am afraid I don't really know that devil worship stems from in terms of disability [sic]. I mean, schizophrenia? I don't think we can go so far as to say schizophrenics are not covered by the Act.[42]

All of these remarks reveal the different associations that people make with mental illness: mental illness as moral failing; as triggering violence; as lack of judgment; and, of course, as the very incarnation of evil: child molestation and devil worship. The above dialogues reflect attitudes that are national in scope and deeply embedded in U.S. society.

Social Science Research

For most Americans, "real" disabilities are considered visible, permanent, and beyond the control of disabled individuals,[43] even though the disability may have been caused by morally "faulty" behavior (e.g., driving while drunk). Although the social stigma associated with visible physical disability is high, the stigma associated with nonvisible disabilities, such as mental illness, is even higher. Study after study shows that people would rather work with convicted felons than with people diagnosed with mental illness, would rather live near a prison than near a halfway house for people with mental illness, and would rather meet almost anyone rather than someone with a diagnosis of mental illness.[44] In a recent Harris Poll, 59% of Americans reported being "very comfortable" when meeting someone in a wheelchair. Only 47% were comfortable meeting someone who was blind. When asked if they would be comfortable meeting someone who was known to have a mental illness, only 19% said that they would.[45]

A study of professionals and managers in key decision-making positions regarding employment showed that while they were willing to work with people who had heart disease, cancer, diabetes, a stroke, polio, epilepsy, cerebral palsy, or paraplegia, they were not willing to work with (in order of increasing unwillingness) gay men or lesbians, ex-convicts, people with mental illness, juvenile delinquents, alcoholics,[46] and drug addicts. The only thing unusual about this study is that there were three groups more highly stigmatized than people with mental illness; of all stigmatized groups, people with mental disabilities are generally considered among the most stigmatized.[47]

Health care providers share these attitudes. When nurses were asked to list categories of patients for whom they disliked providing care, psychiatric patients were at the top of the list,[48] along with AIDS victims and seriously ill children. The nurses cited feelings of frustration and helplessness ("I hate to see them waste their lives on emotional problems")[49] as well as stress, fear, and lack of training ("I don't know anything about psychotropic drugs").[50] Another study of physician attitudes noted, "Dislike of a patient by the physician may be a clue to serious psychiatric impairment [of the patient]."[51]

One reason for these attitudes is that in the case of blindness, deafness, and paraplegia, society does not blame the disabled person for his or her condition or believe that it is controllable by him or her.[52] For psychiatric disabilities, substance addictions, and HIV infection, however, the social discomfort arising out of disability is compounded by the belief that this disability is within the control of the individual. A recent poll showed that 47% of Americans think that depression is caused by the weak character of the sufferer.[53] A plethora of research studies confirm the finding that "individuals with mental–behavioral stigmas were perceived as being responsible for their condition, were rated relatively low on liking, evoked little pity and relatively high anger, and elicited generally low judgments regarding the receipt of personal assistance and charity."[54]

Clearly a flash point of social discomfort with the concept of mental illness comes when attempts are made to explain antisocial behavior as being caused by or attributed to mental illness. This is true even when those attempts come in the form of apologies or remorse. In a recent case, an apology from a criminal defendant diagnosed with paranoid schizophrenia evoked an angry response from the sentencing judge. The letter from the defendant reads as follows:

> Now that I look back I know I was wrong and I am very ashamed because I could not control my illness and I am sorry I did not continue the treatment that was necessary to bring me back to reality. I understand now that the refusal to continue the treatment was part of my illness. I would like to apologize to the teller . . . and to my family, and everyone involved in this case. I was found guilty by the jury and am now prepared to face the consequences of my actions.[55]

The judge said the man "did not and perhaps does not even now accept responsibility in the moral sense. He essentially blames what occurred on his illness, and now I don't think that's acceptance of responsibility."[56]

Psychiatric disability is considered the result of voluntary choice, and this choice is seen as reflecting character defects associated with a failure of responsibility and

willpower—being unwilling, rather than unable, to conform to the norm. Thus, the
deep discomfort that people without disabilities associate with disability in general
is compounded by resentment that this discomfort is being fraudulently foisted on
the nondisabled person. There is a deep belief that the person claiming a psychiatric
disability could, if he or she only tried hard enough, not be disabled at all.[57]

Social attitudes toward psychiatric disabilities, however, encompass a muddle of
stark contradictions. Opposing assumptions coexist without discomfort in people's
minds, courts' decisions, and statutory provisions. In addition to generally thinking
that people with psychiatric disabilities could control their behavior if they wanted
to, people and courts also (inconsistently) believe that a psychiatric diagnosis means
that an individual is uncontrollably unpredictable and dangerous.[58] The fear of people
who have a mental illness also reflects a social belief that mental illness is real,
uncontrollable, and scary. As one review noted,

> It would seem from these studies that the greatest stigma is attached to conditions
> that make behavior unpredictable, with a component that in lay terms might be de-
> scribed as "lack of willpower." It has been suggested that one cause of such rejection
> is an instinctive fear of the unfamiliar or strange [citation omitted].[59]

The discomfort associated with difference and the resentment arising from the perception that the discomforting difference could be remedied by the individual with
the disability are further compounded by the perception that the difference results in
the person being dangerous, unpredictable, and—worst of all—unpredictable in a
dangerous way. One of the main problems with being considered unpredictable is
that almost no amount of consistent "good behavior" can erase the stereotype, because the very nature of unpredictability involves good behavior with intermittent,
unpredictable, dangerous outbursts.

Thus, the fact that mental health problems are episodic, highly responsive to
context and environment, and exist along a spectrum, which could theoretically be
cause for hope—people with mental disabilities are frequently strong, talented, competent, and capable, and their environments can be structured in a way to support
and increase their strengths, talents, competence, and capabilities—ends up being
seen as almost wholly negative. If people are strong, it must mean that either their
disability was malingered or that they are about to fall apart at any minute. Society
is most comfortable with disabilities that are permanent and chronic; either one is
disabled or one is not. Even people with physical disabilities who sometimes have
to use a wheelchair find themselves regarded with skepticism and suspicion bordering
on hostility.[60]

There is, in addition, the almost completely unrecognized effect of mutually
magnifying multiple stereotypes: Many claims of discrimination on the basis of mental disabilities are made by women, members of minority groups, and women who
are members of minority groups.[61] Many people with mental disabilities also have
serious health problems or physical disabilities. Some are older Americans. Stereotypes of race, gender, and physical disability interact with and reinforce stereotypes
of mental disability. Black men who are perceived to be mentally ill are also perceived to be much more dangerous.[62] Women who are considered mentally ill are
considered much less able to care for themselves and much less likely to be competent;[63] minority employees with disabilities are deemed lazy malingerers trying to
take advantage of the system for "extra benefits," and so on. This phenomenon,

which is recognized in legal scholarship under the name "intersectionality" but has very rarely been recognized by the courts, is discussed at greater length in chapter 2.

People with a mental illness are considered to have no control over their behavior—and are therefore frightening and dangerous—yet they are also viewed with contempt and punished for not controlling their behavior. They are considered completely unpredictable and likely to lapse into psychosis without warning and at the same time chronically and unremittingly ill. The lapses of mental disability are considered character lapses, yet spouses flinch from having children because of the fear that these character defects will be inherited.[64] Society views psychiatrists as easily fooled by malingerers, yet it trusts their "expert" judgment in parental rights termination, child custody, forced medication, and civil commitment proceedings affecting hundreds of thousands of people every year. Images of violence, moral deviance, unpredictability, lack of control, and weak character abound in social discourse and public opinion polls and, as was shown earlier in this chapter, even on the floor of Congress.

Finally, in addition to society's discomfort with difference, profound uneasiness with unpredictability, and condemnation of the voluntary nature of the disability, the most profound source of hostility and discrimination is a blurring of boundaries between mental illness and issues of character and morality. This blurring is not necessarily completely a product of ignorance or bigotry. Some of the survey responses raised these issues. One respondent answered a question about the way in which her disability limited her life activities by writing "I can't be happy within a relationship, nor can I keep my mate's needs in mind when I make a decision. (In other words, I am quite selfish, more than normal.)"[65] Sen. Warren Rudman (R-NH), a more thoughtful man than either Sen. Helms or Sen. Armstrong and a cosponsor of the ADA, made this point in the Senate debate:

> While our knowledge of psychiatry has greatly improved in recent years, the fact remains that a diagnosis of mental illness is frequently made on the basis of a pattern of socially unacceptable behavior and lacks any physiological basis. In short, we are talking about behavior that is immoral, improper, or illegal and which individuals are engaging in of their own volition, admittedly for reasons we do not fully understand. . . . In principle, I agree with the concept that the mentally ill should be protected from infidious [sic] discrimination just as the physically handicapped should be. However, people must bear some responsibility for their own actions. In addressing this conflict, we found a few years ago, following the attempted assassination of President Reagan, that the law had been allowed to swing too far away from holding people accountable. . . . I am afraid that, in a civil rights context, we may be making the same mistake now.[66]

Sen. Rudman is right that "a diagnosis of mental illness is frequently made on the basis of a pattern of socially unacceptable behavior and lacks any physiological basis." In fact, unless people voluntarily seek help on their own for their own emotional troubles and discomforts, diagnoses of mental illness are made solely on the basis of a pattern of socially unacceptable behavior. As social acceptance of behavior changes, so do diagnoses of mental illness.[67]

Likewise, the common public perception that people with mental illness are dangerous is partly due to the media's automatic underscoring of any mental health treatment history associated with someone accused of violence.[68] Mental health professionals have also contributed to the blurring of boundaries between character and disability. The popular press and the U.S. courts entertain the views of highly questionable "experts" and credit many ersatz "diagnoses" not endorsed by reputable mental health professionals, from "success neurosis" to "spoiled child syndrome."[69] The resulting media stories help create stigma, discrimination, and skepticism for people with psychiatric diagnoses.

Thus, it is not surprising that mental illness or treatment for mental illness is frequently grouped with convictions for crime, moral turpitude, and dishonorable discharge from the military.[70] Since the ADA took effect, there has been an enormous backlash specifically directed at people with mental health problems and phrased in explicitly moral terms. People who assert that they have emotional difficulties are portrayed as lazy malingerers in Alan Dershowitz's *The Abuse Excuse* and Walter Olson's *The Excuse Factory: How Employment Law Is Paralyzing the American Workplace.*[71] When the Equal Employment Opportunity Commission issued its enforcement guidance on the ADA and psychiatric disabilities[72] for workers with psychiatric disabilities, *The New York Times* reported the story with the headline "Breaks for Mental Illness: Just What the Government Ordered" and posed the "deceptively hard question" of "Are sex addicts and sadists supposed to have their illnesses accommodated at work?"[73]

Millions of people have psychiatric diagnoses, however, and headlines like that ensure that they will conceal those diagnoses at all costs and not ask for "breaks" that might help them be more productive. Those whose diagnoses become known will face the aversion, fear, contempt, and disbelief of others that cause enormous suffering in their lives. This suffering is clear from articles, books, interviews,[74] and from my survey.

Survey of Experiences of Discrimination

To get specific information about people's experiences with discrimination, I sent out a survey to hundreds of people and organizations interested in mental health issues.[75] I asked whether people had experienced discrimination in the areas mentioned by witnesses in support of the ADA: institutionalization, employment, higher education, treatment by the medical profession, insurance, housing, and public accommodations such as stores and restaurants. I also added three categories: treatment by others, courts, and other. In addition, I asked in what area they experienced the worst discrimination and asked them to describe the events and their impact.

Many (74%) of the people who responded to the survey said they had experienced discrimination (although some indicated that they had experienced discrimination on the basis of race, gender, sexual preferences or age, and *not* on the basis of disability). This high percentage is not surprising because people who had experienced discrimination would have a greater incentive to fill out the survey.

What *was* surprising were the responses relating to discrimination in everyday "treatment by others." "Treatment by others" opened up a vast reservoir of pain that the ADA cannot hope to address except by changing attitudes over the long run: daily personal interactions with family, friends, neighbors, fellow students or churchgoers, and strangers on the street; 65% of the respondents felt that they had been discriminated against in treatment by others.

The next highest discrimination category was employment (55%), followed by institutional settings (34%), educational institutions (30%), medical care (29%) and insurance (29%), the court system (24%), housing (23%), and stores and restaurants (9%). Almost all respondents marked more than one category, but few needed to use the "other" category.

When asked where they had experienced the *worst* discrimination, respondents clearly identified employment (33%) and treatment by others (30%) as the two areas that led the rest. Sixteen percent of respondents identified the treatment they had received in mental institutions as the worst discrimination they had experienced, and 6% identified discrimination in educational settings.

Discrimination in Everyday Life

These statistics conceal the devastation and pain of discrimination, which I have tried to reflect throughout this book. But the necessity of separating the book—like the statistics—into chapters that discuss in depth the major categories where people experience the worst discrimination means that the totality of discrimination is also separated into categories. People do not live their lives or experience pain in "major" and "minor" categories, however, and the next part of this chapter attempts to give the reader an idea of some of the many other areas in addition to institutional settings, higher education, insurance, disability services, and medical care in which people with face discrimination.

Family, Loved Ones, and Friends

For many years, having a family member with mental illness or mental retardation was a source of shame. The child was not spoken about, hidden from view (sometimes literally, in attics or cellars or institutions). Although social attitudes have improved, the survey reflects that some of the old attitudes still remain. One respondent wrote, "My father was so ashamed of my psychiatric treatment and hospitalization that he didn't tell most members of my family except my mother and sister, who originally committed me."[76] A surprising number of responses to the question "Please give examples of the *worst* discrimination you have encountered" mentioned the responses of family members to their diagnoses.[77] Perhaps this is because, as one person wrote, "I expect them to understand and not treat me differently, but they don't. They were never wary before my diagnosis and medication."[78] One person wrote that the most painful discrimination was "[n]ot [being] invited to family affairs because I couldn't dress properly because I was too poor to buy appropriate clothing. Maybe I would say something embarrassing."[79] Another wrote cryptically, "I was sad that I had to be locked up for more than a year, and then I remembered what home was like."[80]

Other people mentioned the reactions of friends.[81] When asked to give examples of the worst discrimination, respondents wrote "friends who have abandoned me."[82] Another wrote simply, "I'm sick of losing friends."[83] One question in the survey tracked the definition of "disability" in the ADA, asking if the individual's impairment substantially limited him or her in major life activities and, if so, in what way.

One respondent wrote "yes" and in the section to explain the substantial limitation on life activities wrote "no job, no friends."[84]

Other respondents drew no distinction between family and friends in terms of the worst discrimination they had encountered. For example, one respondent reported that the worst discrimination he had suffered because of his disability was "family and friends saying I would never amount to anything."[85] Another wrote about being "called names by people like 'crazy.' Most of what I remember about my teenage years was being cold, tired, ignored, or yelled at . . . my family wanted nothing to do with me."[86] Survey respondents reported that their complaints about poor treatment were attributed to their disabilities, as in this case:

> When I was in an abusive relationship, when I finally forced myself to articulate some of the abuse . . . this was equated (only once, but that was enough) by this individual with "paranoid schizophrenia." . . . More than once someone who was relating to me in an exploitative/abusive and dishonest way invoked that history [psychiatric treatment] to invalidate my identifying what they were doing as abusive/dishonest.[87]

This lack of credibility, especially in personal and family relationships, is cited over and over again as one of the most painful aspects of having a psychiatric diagnosis, despite a recent study by some of the most respected mental health professionals showing that even when people are in the process of being institutionalized, their accounts of what happened are as accurate as those of the mental health professionals or family members involved in the institutionalization.[88]

Other people recounted painful instances of rejection and even harassment by people in their neighborhood: "Neighborhood children picked up views of their parents after I returned from Winnebago State Hospital for 11-month observation. They would shout 'psycho' at me. Once they circled me in the alley on their bicycles."[89]

On the other hand, understanding and supportive family, friends, and community probably make the greatest difference between a difficult but bearable life in the so-called American mainstream and the lonely neglect of an institutional ward. It would be difficult to overstate the pivotal importance of the support of family and friends.[90] As one woman wrote,

> a few years after my illness I met someone who permitted me to talk about my hospitalization. As I described the experience, I cried. A gentle touch that said, "It doesn't matter; we can still be friends" was worth years of therapy. That moment was an emotional breakthrough for me.[91]

Churches

One particularly good reason to do surveys on the impact of discrimination on people with psychiatric disabilities is that the surveys illuminate some of the forms of discrimination that usually remain hidden and undiscussed: they are not the subjects of litigation, because the discriminators are insulated by law. There are no *60 Minutes* or *20/20* segments on them because the people who were discriminated against would be unwilling or ashamed to publicly tell their stories.

Thus, I was unprepared for the outpouring of disappointment and grief from survey respondents about their treatment by church congregations.[92] The number of

responses referring to discrimination by churches leaders or congregations was astonishing, especially because that had not been listed as a choice on the survey.

In response to the question "Please give examples of the *worst* discrimination
you have encountered," one respondent wrote that

> working for a Roman Catholic church—[the] Priest knew I was bipolar—all is well
> —then a few of his church women recognized me as having had local mental health
> services and he was pressured to get rid of me. . . . I was very hurt—Really liked the
> priest and surprised he bent under.[93]

Another respondent, writing of the pain of feeling rejected by members of a church,
wrote, "they said my 'voices' were 'demons.' "[94] As one person recounted,

> The situation with the church was extremely painful. I had been very active in this
> church for more than 20 years, had worked there for 9 years. I was fired from my
> job [when her previously hidden psychiatric symptoms became obvious] and felt great
> shame. No one reached out in any way—no calls, visits, cards, as is usually done
> there when people are ill.[95]

The degree to which the official church bureaucracy subscribes to modern psychiatric expertise is quite surprising, especially because the indifference of many
mental health professionals to the spiritual concerns of their patients reflects that
respect, in this instance, is not a two-way street. Robert Coles, a psychiatrist, tells
of

> all the letters I've written, over the years to bishops in the Catholic Church or the
> Episcopal Church—certifying one person's or another's "mental stability" or "nor-
> mality" or "psychological health." Had I ever known my fellow psychiatrists to ask
> the clergymen what they thought of the character, the moral makeup of this or that
> would-be doctor or psychiatric trainee? Put differently, why is it that psychiatry now
> has so much intellectual, and yes, moral authority among the clergy?[96]

However, church leaders and their congregations who are welcoming and
friendly are clearly factors of enormous importance and sustenance to people with
diagnoses of mental illness. In response to a question about whether the respondent
feels like part of a community, many who answered affirmatively specifically referred
to being active in their churches.[97] Churches, when they are accepting, can provide
a tremendous community and support for people with mental disabilities.

Higher Education

Many respondents described experiences with college, graduate school, and professional schools as their worst experiences of discrimination. Often, when the student
was discharged from the hospital, the school refused to permit the student to return
to his or her dormitory:

> I was thrown out of college after being hospitalized for five days. I had called the
> University's Health Center, which was closed. It gave an emergency number, which
> happened to be the police. . . . While I was in the hospital, I received word that I
> would not be allowed to go back to any dorm on campus. Since this was in Boston,

> I could never afford the rent off-campus. . . . The university's health insurance denied
> my claim for that five-day hospital stay. I am not sure what to do about the $15,000
> bill yet. I certainly can't pay it. . . . Only after we contacted a lawyer, whose fee was
> very high, and said we would sue unless they returned our thousands in tuition in full
> did we get that money back.[98]

In other cases, being on medication,[99] receiving psychotherapy,[100] or being informed of a diagnosis was enough to trigger exclusions or limitations, even when
the student was doing exceptionally well in school. One respondent was not permitted to finish student teaching when the school learned that she was on medication.[101] Another noted dryly that the worst discrimination was "[w]hen I wanted to
study linguistic structure of schizophrenic speech and made [the] mistake of saying
why I was interested. I had 3.8 average, but suddenly the university said it was not
an area of study they could support."[102]
Even schools specializing in the arts, long viewed as a haven for creative ec-
centrics, came up in the survey responses. In reporting his worst experience of discrimination, one individual wrote that

> being told, upon completion of my audition for Julliard, that I deserved to be accepted
> but that the then-head of the Acting Program was going on 70, had never worked
> with a disabled actor before, and wasn't about to start now. As I pondered this, I was
> told that since Julliard did not receive federal funds at the time, I had no grounds on
> which to bring a lawsuit.[103]

It is particularly distressing to read about the unhelpful and damaging responses
of colleges and universities to the emotional difficulties of their students when so
many people with mental disabilities identify college as the time of their lives when
what had previously been a vaguely experienced oddness or difference or sadness
exploded into crisis. This is a time when support, not pathologizing or rejection, is
desperately needed. Too often, it seems that the reactions of college and university
administrators add to the damage rather than alleviate it.

Housing

A variety of forms of housing discrimination emerged from the survey results, span-
ning all class and income levels. More affluent respondents reported the inability to
obtain loans for mortgages or to rent expensive apartments.[104] Poor respondents complained that landlords refused to accept the applications of people with Section 8
housing certificates if the applicants were perceived as mentally ill.[105]
Stories involved eviction even though the individual was continuing to pay
rent.[106] One respondent was evicted from an apartment after being hospitalized, even
though the rent was paid.[107] This respondent reports successfully suing the apartment
complex.[108] In another report, a landlord refused to let a tenant move into a better
apartment after learning that the tenant was taking Prolixin, even though the tenant
paid the rent and was quiet and orderly.
When people who are already in the mental health service system receive housing, they are often seen more as patients than as tenants. Often, the right to continue
to reside in housing—whether group home, supported living, or even an "independent" apartment—is tied to compliance with treatment programs and, in particular,

to medication. Although theoretically the individual may retain the right to refuse medication, the reality of this right may seem illusory if the cost of exercising it renders the individual homeless. Some have suggested that such bundling of mental health services and housing may violate the ADA.[109]

Related to this argument is the contention that using group homes when many individuals would be able to live in more independent settings in the community itself violates the ADA. Because the act requires services to be provided in the most integrated setting appropriate to the needs of the person, the use of group homes, which require people with disabilities to live together, is a form of segregation that is not applied to other people with disabilities who receive housing assistance. In fact, of all people in American society who receive housing assistance, only people with psychiatric disabilities, mental retardation, and substance-abuse problems or who are elderly live in group settings with people with similar diagnoses or characteristics. Whereas advocates for people with substance-abuse problems have argued that these group living situations are beneficial to recovering substance abusers, no such argument has been made for people with mental illness.

It is clear from both interviews and survey responses that citizens, including lawyers, do not understand that the Fair Housing Amendment Act of 1988, not the ADA, is the legislation under which almost all discrimination in housing must be pursued. Various respondents reported anger and frustration at reporting housing discrimination to the ADA division of the Department of Justice, only to be told that the division did not handle such complaints. Perhaps the DOJ could take steps to have this distinction publicized more clearly.

Discrimination by the State: A Sample of Statutes and Practices

One recurrent image of disability discrimination in the United States is that discrimination is the result of ignorance, misinformation, and paternalistic stereotypes that simply need to be shaken off for disabled people to take their true place in society. For example, the U.S. Supreme Court wrote that discrimination on the basis of disability is more often the "result of thoughtlessness and indifference—of benign neglect."[110] This has been repeated by lower courts, commentators,[111] and legal scholars.[112]

Yet to this day, intentional differentiation and disadvantaging of people with psychiatric disabilities are explicitly articulated in state and federal statutes. Although statutes or rulings that denied parental rights to a child because the parent was physically disabled would be considered unjust,[113] statutes exist today that permit judges to deny parental rights on the basis of mental illness,[114] and these statutes are invoked with extraordinary frequency in terminating the parental rights of mothers with psychiatric disabilities.[115] Statutes restricting such basic activities as voting and marriage on the basis of physical disability are equally unthinkable, yet statutes that mandate those exclusions on the basis of psychiatric disability exist today.[116] These statutes—and analogous policies, programs, and practices in business, academia, and the professions—are not the products of "benign neglect and indifference." They are the result of purposeful and ongoing discrimination.

In almost every state in this country, statutes prohibiting discrimination on the basis of mental disability coexist with statutes that embody such discrimination.

These latter statutes are not archaic leftovers, unenforced for years. When these statutes have been challenged, states defend them[117] and courts uphold them.[118] The same is true, to a lesser extent, of the federal government.

The government continues to discriminate on the basis of psychiatric disability. Discrimination is written into statutes that disadvantage people explicitly on the basis of their status as people with psychiatric disabilities. These statutes are enforced. The following is a sample of the ways in which people with psychiatric disabilities are singled out for differential and adverse treatment by statute.

Right to Vote

Although a number of states explicitly provide that the right to vote is not lost on admission to a psychiatric facility,[119] and others make provisions for absentee ballots for people who are institutionalized or are mentally disabled,[120] many state constitutions still explicitly exclude people with mental disabilities from the right to vote.[121] Although some states have mitigated the impact of these constitutional prohibitions,[122] others have recently taken steps to enforce them. For example, in 1997 Maine passed an initiative denying the right to vote to people under guardianship because of mental illness (but not to those under guardianship for any other reason).[123]

Driver's Licenses

For years, people with or indications of mental illness such as hospitalization had difficulty obtaining and keeping driver's licenses. Several responses to the survey on discrimination mentioned issues relating to driver's licenses that appeared to be largely historical: "If you answer questions on mental illness truthfully [on application for driver's license in New Jersey] like I did years ago, you will have a provisional license";[124] one respondent "had to get psychiatric approval to get a driver's license in Virginia in 1969";[125] another recalled "most of the problems occurred when I was younger. . . . [I was] denied the right to have a driver's license."[126] Attempts to challenge these requirements on constitutional grounds generally failed.[127] In some states, requirements for the immediate suspension of a driver's license on admission to a mental hospital were successfully challenged, although in each case the statute was overturned not because the court disagreed with the substantive requirement but because insufficient procedural protections were provided.[128] States have generally (although in some cases belatedly)[129] reformulated these provisions, denying licenses to people adjudicated incompetent[130] and giving the Division of Motor Vehicles (DMV) discretion to investigate people who, by reason of physical or psychological impairment, may be a hazard to public safety.

Problems still exist. At least one state still requires a court to report to the DMV "any person adjudged to be afflicted with or suffering from a mental disability or disease."[131] The Bazelon Center on Mental Health Law fielded a complaint from an individual who was denied a driver's license because he used his car to transport people with mental disabilities.[132]

Challenges to these remaining obstacles have had mixed results. Courts are more sympathetic to procedural due process claims—revoking a license without giving the driver an opportunity to be present at a hearing[133]—than to substantive claims that psychological or physical impairments should not be associated with inability to drive.[134] Courts may be skeptical of blanket limitations or exclusions on the basis of disability, but they support individualized inquiries and investigations prompted by the existence or report of a disability. For some people, having to submit to a psychiatric examination to retain a driver's license may be burdensome and even traumatic.

An emerging battle is between medical and bureaucratic decision makers. If the driver's doctor certifies that he or she can safely drive, is the agency still entitled to impose requirements in the name of safety? Courts have reached conflicting results. The 1st Circuit held in favor of the DMV, whereas the Connecticut Supreme Court, finding that governmental classifications and decisions on the basis of disability were subject to strict scrutiny under its state Constitution, struck down a requirement by the Connecticut DMV that a man with epilepsy who had three seizures in 33 months had to submit medical reports every 3 months for 3 years to retain his driver's license.[135] The court found that the Connecticut DMV had no medical basis for this requirement and had not tailored the requirement as narrowly as possible to meet the DMV's legitimate safety concerns.

Neither the medical nor the bureaucratic model helps the individual who may appear mentally ill but has no supportive doctor, whether he or she is too poor, is not in treatment, or does not like mental health professionals. The commonsense solution would be to treat all individuals equally and make decisions regarding their licenses on the basis of driving records and objective driving tests.

Marriage Laws

When the Civil Rights Commission issued its groundbreaking report on discrimination against people with disabilities in 1983, it noted that a substantial number of states restricted the rights of people with disabilities to marry[136] or to adopt children.[137] Although many states have repealed these prohibitions, some states still prohibit people with mental disabilities from marrying.[138] In some states marriages of people of unsound mind are voidable;[139] in others they are illegal.[140]

Divorce Laws

Although most states permit no-fault divorce, in some states in which a spouse seeking divorce or annulment must allege grounds for it, mental illness remains a basis for divorce.[141] Statutes singling out psychiatric conditions, which usually also refer to some period of institutionalization, in relation to the termination of a marriage operate in two ways.

In the majority of statutes, "incurable mental illness" is simply another ground for divorce or annulment. These statutes are discriminatory, because incurable physical illness and hospitalization for such illness, or even being in a coma, are not grounds for divorce. A trial-level state court in New York refused in 1998 to consider a challenge to this statute under the ADA, and the decision was upheld by the appellate court, even when 12 amicus organizations joined to ask the appellate court to review the statute's legality under the ADA.[142]

However, in states such as North Carolina, the separate provision in divorce law for people who are "incurably insane" can be seen as an attempt to protect people with psychiatric disabilities by making it more difficult for the spouse of the "incurably insane" person to obtain a divorce than would otherwise be the case under state law and providing for possible lifetime maintenance of the "incurably insane" spouse.[143]

In all states, mental illness can be taken into account in establishing permanent or rehabilitative alimony.[144] Recently, an appellate court in Maryland reversed a trial courts' finding that a woman could not petition for an increase in alimony unless she was willing to take psychotropic medication. The appellate court found that because such a ruling implicated the woman's right of informed consent, it could only be made if "the expert testimony regarding mental illness and treatment [is] highly reliable and particularized to the individual whose health is at issue."[145] In most states, "cruelty" sufficient to provide grounds for divorce includes mental cruelty or causing significant emotional suffering. One ground for divorce on the basis of cruelty is the attempt, not made in good faith, to commit a spouse to a mental institution.[146] However, courts usually find that these attempts were made in good faith.[147]

Child Custody

Discrimination in decisions relating to child custody was explicitly mentioned as one of the major areas of discrimination in the 1983 report *Accommodating the Spectrum of Individual Abilities*. This was true across all disabilities: "Child custody suits almost always have ended with custody being awarded to the nondisabled parent regardless of whether affectional or socioeconomic advantages could have been offered by the disabled parent."[148] Whereas higher courts sometimes reversed the discriminatory decisions of the lower courts,[149] higher courts have always supported custody awards to the nondisabled parent when the disability was psychiatric.

Issues of child custody emerged in the survey results,[150] with family and spousal discrimination given the weight of judicial enforcement. One man wrote that the worst discrimination he ever encountered was when "My ex-wife (who was a major cause of my depression) began divorce proceedings against me while I was in psychiatric hospital, and tried to use my efforts to get help to prevent me from seeing my son (while she collected child support)."[151]

Research shows that parents can lose custody or visitation rights simply on the basis of diagnosis, hospitalization, or treatment for mental illness, without any disturbing behavior.[152] Survey respondents confirm this. "I lost custody of my daughter when she was very young because (in the words of the judge in Massachusetts) 'Someone who has had ECT should not have custody of a child.'"[153]

Termination of Parental Rights

Custody decisions are made between parents; the termination of parental rights usually involves the invocation of state statutes against abuse and neglect and results in the state assuming legal custody over the child.

Some of the least chronicled and most heroic struggles against discrimination on the basis of mental disability are made by women trying to keep their children.

Their struggles are against bureaucracy, legal obstacles, and outright discrimination by the child welfare system.[154] Almost always, their efforts do not bring back their children. Often their efforts are cruelly recast and distorted by social workers, mental health professionals, and the courts. For example, one woman who faithfully followed the program set out by the agency, doing all that was required of her, heard her compliance with the requirements characterized as symptoms of mental illness and herself reduced to a diagnosis:

> During the termination proceedings, Dr. Wunderman opined that the mother was "addicted" to the termination proceeding, and that she had completed the required parenting course, visited her children at the scheduled times, and appeared in court "as a means of escaping a feeling of tremendous emptiness, tremendous loneliness, tremendous nothingness that the borderline personality disorder does feel."[155]

Children are often the key motivation for parents with mental disabilities to keep their lives organized, and the loss of a child is a bitter desolation. Yet poor women who seek mental health treatment in an effort to organize their lives risk losing their children.[156] After a child is taken away, rather than assist parents with reunification services, some state laws permit judges to specifically exclude parents with mental illness from receiving reunification services at all.[157] Even where the law requires the agency to assist parents with psychiatric disabilities, courts sometimes have to order agencies to provide this assistance. For example, a court had to order the Arkansas Department of Human Services (DHS) to pay for one woman's Prozac prescription and the cost of the bus tokens to go to family counseling sessions ordered by the department.[158] The DHS fought this order, which cost less than $42 a month, all the way to the Arkansas Supreme Court (where it lost the case).[159]

Because state child welfare agencies are public entities under Title II of the ADA, their programs, benefits, and services cannot discriminate on the basis of disability. There are a number of ways in which these child welfare agencies can be subject to charges of discrimination under the ADA. For example, some state agencies remove children from parents perceived as psychiatrically disabled—often within days after birth—and seek the termination of parental rights without making any attempts at reunification.[160]

A number of state and federal courts have heard challenges under the ADA to the process by which the parental rights of parents with mental disabilities were terminated or to the lack of reasonable accommodations for parents with mental disabilities. Although all courts agree that the ADA applies to the general policies and procedures of child welfare agencies,[161] courts are split as to how ADA challenges can be brought: whether in the context of an individual termination proceeding or raised in a separate proceeding.[162]

Courts give various reasons for precluding the use of the ADA in an individual termination proceeding: the most cogent is that juvenile courts lack jurisdiction to provide the requested remedies against the state;[163] the least coherent is that "in the context of a termination of parental rights case, it is the conduct of the respondent that is the focus of the court's inquiry, not the disability."[164] The reason that most misapprehends and misconstrues the law is that "parental termination proceedings are not 'benefits, services or programs' under Title II of the ADA."[165]

Many courts that rule that the ADA cannot be used to assist parents in termination proceedings also cite the ADA provision that people with disabilities cannot be made to accept accommodations under the ADA when parents are not cooperative with state agencies or reject certain services.[166]

In addition to discriminatory practices by state agencies, state statutes singling out parents with mental illness for disadvantageous treatment are also subject to attack under Title II of the ADA. These laws have also been challenged under state and federal constitutional provisions. A number of states have laws that permit the termination of parental rights on the basis of mental illness or disability if the disability renders the parent incapable of caring for the needs of the child.[167] Not long ago, mental illness alone was sufficient to terminate parental rights.[168]

Utah's statute permitting the denial of reunification services on the basis of mental illness was upheld by an appellate court against an equal protection challenge.[169] The court found that parents with mental illness were not "singled out" by the statute, which also permitted the judge to omit reunification services for parents who could not be found, who had severely abused their children, or who had been previously found to neglect or abuse other children. This is an example of the "lists" on which mental illness appears, and it seems to reinforce rather than mitigate the discriminatory nature of the statute.

Police Practices

Intrusion in the Home: Search and Seizure

Although the U.S. Supreme Court has limited police intrusions, requiring a warrant to arrest someone at home[170] and limiting arrests at homes to arrests for felonies and intrusions at night to emergencies, police routinely take people—most of whom have no idea that this is going to happen—at night to hospitals for psychiatric detention and examination. Some state laws explicitly authorize this.[171] This practice comes to the public attention on those occasions in which the individual refuses to come out, and the police surround the house, sometimes for over a month at a time.[172]

It is rare for police to surround a house for lengthy periods of time. More often the police simply break down the door.[173] At least some state laws authorize them to do so. In one case, a psychiatrist signed a paper authorizing the police to bring a 64-year-old Holocaust survivor, whom he had never met, to a hospital for psychiatric observation. Ruchla Zinger had no idea any of this had happened when the police kicked in the outside apartment house door, then

> proceeded upstairs to [her] apartment. The officers knocked and announced their presence, received no response, and began to kick in [her] apartment door. Ms. Zinger began screaming, "Why are you kicking in my door?" then cracked it open. . . . The officers pushed their way into her apartment . . . [and] forced her to the floor on her stomach and handcuffed her hands behind her back. She lost control of her bladder. . . . She was carried to the stairs, then dragged down one step at a time . . . . At the bottom, the ambulance crew strapped her on the stretcher, face down. By this time, she had stopped screaming, and the officers noticed that her hands appeared blue and that she was bleeding from the mouth. Ms. Zinger was pronounced dead on arrival at the hospital.[174]

If Ms. Zinger had been suspected of having committed a crime, even a felony, the police could not have entered her apartment without a warrant, but the 1st Circuit ruled that the city policy permitting forcible warrantless entries of private residences to enforce involuntary civil commitment laws did not violate Ms. Zinger's constitutional rights.[175]

In another case, Becky Moore was taking a shower when the ambulance arrived to take her in for psychiatric observation because the night before she had alarmed her therapist in a talk on the telephone. She also had no idea what was happening as she was dragged naked into the street. The paramedics refused her friend's request to let her have a towel or get dressed.[176]

Some of the most widely lauded community mental health programs are based on the PACT model,[177] which has succeeded in substantially lowering rates of institutionalization. It does so, as its acronym suggests, by "assertive" community treatment, which includes showing up at the apartment or house of an individual. A number of survey respondents mentioned this as something that caused them great fear.[178]

Police have wide discretion to take people to psychiatric hospitals.[179] In many states, the only people with the authority to require someone to be taken involuntarily to a psychiatric facility are one or more mental health professionals, after examination of the person; a judge, after hearing evidence; or the police, who do not have to do either. As one survey respondent wrote,

> I'd gone for a walk in the light rain in May. I was barefoot and had on a light colored longish dress with the hem let down, and a conventional long dull green poncho. . . . [A] cop pulled over and asked where I was going. I said (I think) "to the library" unless it was "home"—and his response was "In that getup? Get in the car." . . . Someone I knew years later was locked up at her landlord's instigation after a barefoot walk in spring drizzle—the cops said, "O.K. lady, let's go." She had a psych history and no shoes on. This was also on Long Island.[180]

Under these circumstances, even though a person has not committed a crime, disturbed the peace, or been the subject of public complaint, that person has little choice other than to accompany the police to the hospital. Otherwise, as discussed below, the person may be subject to serious physical assault or abuse.

Harassment and Hostility

In addition to intrusion in the home, police have frequent dealings with people with psychiatric disabilities. For one thing, people with psychiatric disabilities are arrested at a greater rate than the general population.[181] This is not because, as a whole, people with psychiatric disabilities are much more violent than the general population.[182] Rather, people with psychiatric disabilities are arrested more often for petty offenses, often associated with homelessness—loitering or urinating in the street. One respondent wrote, "Because of my label I was jailed for yelling at a cop."[183] Sometimes police are understanding and kind, but inappropriate arrests of people with disabilities by police were of sufficient concern to Congress that the arrests were specifically referred to in the ADA legislative history.[184] When DOJ did not write regulations explicitly requiring police to be trained in how to deal with disabled people, both individuals and organizations complained vigorously.[185] DOJ declined to require training, noting that discriminatory arrests and brutal treatment are already unlawful police activities. The general regulatory obligation to modify policies, practices or procedures requires law enforcement to make changes in policies that result in discriminatory arrests or abuse of individuals with disabilities. Under this section law enforcement personnel would be required to make appropriate efforts to determine whether perceived strange or disruptive behavior or unconsciousness is the result of a disability.[186]

Criminal records, including records of arrest, have a tremendous impact on people's lives, because employers and government housing programs, among others, often explicitly base a refusal to hire or provide housing on an individual's criminal record. The exclusion of people with mental illnesses from community housing on the basis of a criminal adjudication without an individualized determination of whether the person is currently dangerous has been challenged successfully as a violation of the Fair Housing Act.[187]

To compound the problem, people with mental disabilities who are subject to these discriminatory arrests are beginning to be routed through special "mental health courts," in which compliance with treatment is exchanged for dropping criminal charges that never should have been brought in the first place, such as the theft of a single pack of gum, or of two cigars. These courts were started by well-meaning people frustrated with the lack of access to mental health treatment services in the community and the overflowing and brutal conditions in county jails; however, any time society starts having "special courts" for disfavored populations where virtually all of the cases are poor and lower-class people, we should be concerned. It is highly unlikely that people like the president of American University or the chief judge of the highest court in New York, who were arrested for making obscene telephone calls and writing obscene letters, respectively, and who both asserted they were suffering some form of mental illness, would be routed to any mental health court.[188]

Police arrest of people with psychiatric disabilities under circumstances in which nondisabled people would not be subject to arrest is only one manifestation of misunderstanding of people with psychiatric disabilities. Another is the frequency with which people with diagnoses are shot, even killed,[189] by police, even when they are unarmed. Although comments on police practices were not specifically mentioned in the survey, several people raised incidents where friends or people they knew had been shot by police.[190] Protection and advocacy lawyers also reported police shootings of their clients.[191] There are a number of cases involving rough treatment by police in the process of taking a person to an emergency room, including cases charging assault and excessive force.[192] Courts are divided about the extent to which Title II of the ADA covers police conduct.[193]

Conclusion

Most people who do not have much experience with discrimination imagine it as a discrete event rather than as overlapping, interacting burdens and rejections that ultimately create a set of expectations in a person's mind of how he or she will be treated.[194] The more deeply structural, embedded, and nondiscrete the discrimination is, the less it is recognizable or remediable as discrimination. As one survey respondent wrote, "the discrimination hides inside the law, which is interpreted so narrowly it doesn't address the social issues."[195] Structural discrimination—the life that many people lead—is contributed to by many actors, none of whom can fairly be held responsible for the whole, but whose actions nevertheless combine to create the miserable and debilitating life that many people struggle through every day. The remainder of this book is an extended chronicle of the landscape of discrimination: in legal and psychiatric imagery of mental disorders, case law, medical care, the mental health system, government assistance programs, private insurance, and the medical and legal professions. It is pervasive and crushing, yet people struggle, survive, and even manage to flourish in it. The following chapters recount the odds that they face.

Endnotes

1. Judith Herman, *Trauma and Recovery* (1992) at 128.
2. Survey No. 145.
3. Survey No. 178.
4. Survey No. 179.
5. Survey No. 11.
6. Survey No. 69.
7. I am not suggesting that the doctor should be liable for the discrimination of the landlord. My principal complaint here is one relating to the rules regarding the admissibility of certain kinds of evidence and the joinder of parties that make it more difficult for a plaintiff to present the context and underlying reasons for his or her behavior and reactions.
8. This literature is discussed at greater length later in this chapter and in chapter 2.
9. Written or oral testimony (or both) principally involving the impact of the ADA on people with mental disabilities was submitted to the Subcommittee on Select Education of the House Committee on Education and Labor. Much of this testimony was submitted at a hearing on H.R. 4498 (the ADA of 1989), held at the Lafayette Hotel in Boston, MA, on Oct. 24, 1988, although a substantial amount of testimony was also taken in Washington, DC. Witnesses included Bill Pyle; Marilyn Levin, supervisor, occupational therapy, Department of Mental Health, Boston, MA, testifying on behalf of Edward Murphy, director of the Department of Mental Health; Kevin Preston, Department of Mental Health, Boston, MA; William Cavanaugh, executive director, Ad Lib, Berkshire County, MA; Eleanor Smith; Ilona Durkin; Elizabeth Lyons; Lelia Batten; Patricia Deegan; Eleanor Blake; Laurence Urban; and Deanna Durrett on behalf of Josef Reum, commissioner of the Indiana Department of Mental Health, Indianapolis. Witnesses who spoke about issues relating to disabilities in general, which included significant points about discrimination against people with mental disabilities, included Arlene Mayerson of the Disability Rights Education and Defense Fund, Oakland, CA; Stan Koslowski (spelled different ways in different places in the record), Connecticut Office of Protection and Advocacy for Handicapped Persons, Hartford; James Brooks, a paralegal, Disability Law Project, Boston, MA; and Eileen Healy Horndt. This testimony was compiled by the law firm of Arnold and Porter and is available on the Internet (http://web2.westlaw.com/, search under the following categories: federal, legislative history, Arnold & Porter, and ADA). The citations to the testimony that follow are to the page numbers of the Arnold and Porter materials.
10. Testimony of William Cavanaugh, A&P Comm. Print 1990 (28B)*1067; testimony of Lelia Batten, A&P Comm. Print 1990 (28B)*1191–1204; testimony of Eleanor Blake, A&P Comm. Print 1990 (28B)*1260; testimony of Ilona Durkin, A&P Comm. Print 1990 (28B)*1080, 1081; written testimony of Laurence Urban, A&P Comm. Print 1990 (28B)*1232, 1233; testimony of Patricia Deegan, A&P Comm. Print 1990 (28B)*1251.

11. Testimony of Elizabeth (Lisa) Lyons, A&P Comm. Print 1990 (28B)*1157; testimony of Eleanor Smith, A&P Comm. Print 1990 (28B)*1161.

12. Testimony of William Cavanaugh, *id.* at note 9; testimony of Lelia Batten, *id.* at note 9.

13. Testimony of Lelia Batten, *see* note 9; testimony of William Cavanaugh, *see* note 9.

14. Testimony of William Cavanaugh, *id.*

15. Testimony of Lelia Batten, *see* note 9; testimony of William Cavanaugh, *see* note 9; testimony of Patricia Deegan, *see* note 9; testimony of Stan Koslowski, A&P Comm. Print 1990 (28B)*926.

16. Testimony of Lelia Batten, *see* note 9.

17. Testimony of Lelia Batten, *see* note 9; written testimony of Laurence Urban, *see* note 9; statement of Eleanor Blake, *see* note 9; testimony of Marilyn Levin, A&P Comm. Print 1990 (28B)*1161–1162.

18. Testimony of Eileen Healy Horndt, A&P Comm. Print 1990 (28B)*1117 (people with mental retardation and emotional disabilities are asked to become dues-paying members of a union and then not allowed to vote).

19. Testimony of Lelia Batten, *see* note 9; written statement of Laurence E. Urban, *see* note 9; testimony of Stan Koslowski, *see* note 15; testimony of Bill Pyle, A&P Comm. Print 1990 (28B)*1520–1522. Many practices complained of were illegal under the Fair Housing Amendments Act of 1988, which prohibits discrimination in housing on the basis of disability, including psychiatric disability. The ADA has also been used to attack discrimination in housing.

20. Testimony of Patricia Deegan, *see* note 9; statement of Lelia Batten, *see* note 9; statement of William Cavanaugh, *see* note 9.

21. Testimony of Lelia Batten, *see* note 9.

22. Written statement of Laurence Urban, *see* note 9 (an interview of the applicant to nursing school was "progressing very satisfactorily until she revealed that she had previously had two hospitalizations for mental illness. The interviewer then immediately informed her that there was no way she would be admitted to nursing school since nursing was a very stressful profession and her psychiatric history would indicate that she would not be able to deal with stress. . . . [S]ince that interview . . . this person has obtained a BA in Liberal Arts and a Master's in Social Work from Boston University"); statement of Eleanor Blake, A&P Comm. Print 1990 (28B)*1260.

23. Testimony of Lelia Batten, *see* note 9; testimony of Elizabeth Lyons, *see* note 9.

24. Written statement of Laurence Urban, *see* note 9 (because one member of a day-treatment center acted badly in a restaurant, the owner later told other members that no one from the day-treatment center could be served in the restaurant).

25. Testimony of James Brooks, paralegal at the Disability Law Project, A&P Comm. Print (1990)*1259; an older couple with mental illness were denied a home interest loan on the basis of their disability.

26. William Cavanaugh, a witness with a history of psychiatric disability, testified that when he went with a friend of his who had cerebral palsy to a movie theater, the friend was denied entrance, *see* note 10 *1068.

27. Statement of William Cavanaugh, *id.* Note that a number of practices that were complained about by other witnesses with disabilities, or pervade the interviews and writings of people with psychiatric disabilities, were not mentioned or rarely mentioned in testimony before Congress. These practices included police misconduct toward people with psychiatric disabilities, the stark prevalence of people with mental illness in prisons and jails, and discrimination against mothers with psychiatric disabilities in parental rights termination and child custody proceedings.

28. *See* chapter 6 for further discussion.

29. *See* later in this chapter and chapter 2.

30. 135 *Cong. Rec.* S11173, 101st Cong., 1st Sess. (the *Cong. Record* identifies these remarks as inserted into the record rather than spoken on the floor of the Senate).
31. Although exclusionary arguments were framed in terms of "mental disabilities," people with mental retardation were not subject to the same attacks on the floor of Congress —in fact, stories about children with Down's syndrome were received with sympathy and approbation.
32. It was clear that attacks on HIV were attacks directed at a subset of those who have this illness: lesbians and gay men. More to the point, Congress made it explicit in page after page of the *Cong. Record* that the ADA was intended to protect people who tested HIV positive. Defenders of people with mental illness—notably Sen. Pete Domenici and Tom Harkin—were few and far between.
33. Note that a bipartisan group of senators also defended the inclusion of people with mental illness in the ADA, including Sen. Tom Harkin, Dennis DeConcini, and Alan Simpson. The latter two senators noted that they had family members with mental illness. Sen. Harkin, who became a leader in Congress championing disability rights after Sen. Lowell Weicker was defeated in his campaign for reelection in 1988, has a brother with mental retardation.
34. Statement of Sen. Edward Kennedy, 135 *Cong. Rec.* No. 112, S10718 (daily ed. Sept. 7, 1989) (recounting Judith Heumann's testimony of being removed from an auction house because she was "disgusting to look at" and being excluded from a movie theater because she could not transfer out of her wheelchair); statement of Sen. Albert Gore, *Cong. Rec., id.*, at S10753 (recounting the testimony of a woman who had to crawl up stairs to go to the bathroom at an orchestra performance); statement of Sen. John Kerry, *Cong. Rec., id.,* at S10801.
35. Statement of Sen. Kennedy, *id.* (recounting the story of a child with cerebral palsy who was excluded from a classroom because his appearance produced a "nauseating effect" on his classmates).
36. Statement of Sen. Kennedy, *id.* (recounting the story of a woman with arthritis excluded from a job because "normal students shouldn't see her").
37. Statements of Sen. Armstrong, 135 *Cong. Rec.* No. 112, S10753 (daily ed. Sept. 7, 1989).
38. Colloquy between Sen. Tom Harkin and Jesse Helms, 135 *Cong. Rec.* No. 112, S10765 (daily ed. Sept. 7, 1989).
39. Letter from John P. Mackey, deputy assistant attorney general, Office of Legislative and Intergovernmental Affairs, Department of Justice, to Sen. Dan Coats, July 13, 1989, reproduced in G. John Tysse, Ed., *The Legislative History of the Americans With Disabilities Act* (Horsham, PA: LRP, 1991) at 828, 845, 846. The Department of Justice duly responded that an employer need not hire anyone who was a "direct threat to the health and safety of others" and that the ADA was not intended to interfere with legislation designating crimes.
40. Cong. Donald Payne, A&P Comm. Print 1990 (28B)*1655.
41. Cong. Owens and Bartlett, A&P Comm. Print 1990 (28B)*1653.
42. Exchange between Cong. Owens and Bartlett and witness Arlene Mayerson of the Disability Rights Education and Defense Fund, *id.*
43. Courts repeatedly, in the course of ruling against plaintiffs claiming other disabilities, compare those conditions unfavorably with blindness, deafness, and paraplegia: High cholesterol "is wholly unlike blindness or paraplegia or the other conventional disabilities that trigger the protection of the ADA," Christian v. St. Anthony Medical Center, 117 F.3d 1051 (7th Cir. 1997), *cert. denied,* 523 U.S. 1022 (1998); Runnebaum v. Nationsbank of Maryland, 95 F.3d 1285, 1297 (4th Cir. 1996) (*en banc*) ("determinations of disability must be made on a case-by-case basis. . . . [B]lindness and deafness will always substantially limit the major life activities of blind and deaf individuals").
44. Bernard Weiner, Raymond Perry, and Jamie Magnusson, "An Attributional Analysis of

Reactions to Stigmas," *J. of Pers. and Soc. Psychology* 55 (1988):738, 741; Bertram Black, *Work and Mental Illness* (Baltimore: Johns Hopkins University Press, 1988); Bruce G. Link, "Understanding Labeling Effects in the Area of Mental Disorders: An Assessment of the Effects of Expectations of Rejection," *Amer. Soc. Rev.* 52 (1987):96–112; Bernard Weiner, "On Sin Versus Sickness," *Amer. Psychologist* 48 (1993):957, 960 ("Medical doctors, then, generally treat those perceived as not responsible for their plights, whereas mental health practitioners assist those considered personally responsible for their condition"); Bruce G. Link, "Mental Patient Status, Work, and Income: An Examination of the Effects of a Psychiatric Label," *Amer. Soc. Rev.* 47 (1982):202–215; A. Weber and J. D. Orcutt, "Employers' Reactions to Racial and Psychiatric Stigmata: A Field Experiment," *Deviant Beh.* 5 (1984):327–336; K. M. Goldstein and S. Blackman, "Generalizations Regarding Deviant Groups," *Psychological Reports* 37 (1975):278; Clifford Schneider and Wayne Anderson, "Attitudes Toward the Stigmatized: Some Insights From Recent Research," *Rehab. Counselling Bull.* (1980):299, 301. In an older study, employers were asked to rank various groups in the order in which employers in general would be most likely to hire a member of that group. The groups included people with physical disabilities, people with mental disabilities, members of minority groups, older people, prison parolees, student militants, whites, and Canadians. The researchers found that "physical disability groups were clustered together and ranked lower than all minority groups and older people [as well as ranking lower than prison parolees and student militants]." However, the groups with physical disabilities ranked higher than all groups with mental disabilities; James N. Colbert, Richard A. Kalish, and Potter Chang, "Two Psychological Portals of Entry for Disadvantaged Groups," *Rehab. Lit.* 34 (1973):194–202.

45. Louis Harris and Associates, *Public Attitudes Towards People With Disabilities* (1991), Study No. 919028, conducted for the National Organization on Disability.

46. One irony of these findings is, of course, that these managers probably work with more people who abuse alcohol than with any other group listed in the study.

47. S. J. Harasymiw, M. D. Horne, and S. C. Lewis, "A Longitudinal Study of Disability Group Acceptance," *Rehab. Lit.* 37 (1976):98; J. L. Tringo, "The Hierarchy of Preference Toward Disability Groups," *J. of Spec. Educ.* 4 (1970):295; R. L. Jones, "The Hierarchical Structure of Attitudes Towards the Exceptional," *Exceptional Children* 40 (1974):430.

48. Helen Lippman Collins, "The Patients Your Colleagues Hate to Nurse," *RN* 50(12) (Dec. 1987):46.

49. *Id.*

50. *Id.*

51. J. M. Goodwin, J. S. Goodwin, and R. Kellnen, "Psychiatric Symptoms in Disliked Medical Patients," *J. of the Amer. Med. Assn.* 241 (1979):1117–1120.

52. Even as to people with physical disabilities, there is a more intangible blaming buried below the surface. One poll found that 54% of Americans believe that "people get the suffering they deserve"; R. Wurthnow, *Acts of Compassion* (Princeton, NJ: Princeton University Press, 1991). A British soccer coach was recently reported as saying that people were born disabled as a result of "karma from another lifetime. . . . What you sow, you have to reap"; "Coach Asked to Explain His Remarks About the Disabled," MIAMI HERALD (Feb. 1, 1999):C3.

53. "Group Urges Expanded Mental Health Insurance," ARIZONA REPUBLIC (Feb. 3, 1996): A4.

54. Bernard Weiner, Raymond Perry, and Jamie Magnusson, "An Attributional Analysis of Reactions to Stigmas," *J. of Pers. and Soc. Psychology* 55 (1988):738, 741; *see also* Bernard Weiner, "On Sin Versus Sickness," *Amer. Psychologist* 48 (Sept. 1993):957, 960 ("Medical doctors, then, generally treat those perceived as not responsible for their plights, whereas mental health practitioners assist those considered personally respon-

sible for their condition"); K. M. Goldstein and S. Blackman, "Generalizations Regarding Deviant Groups," *Psychological Reports* 37 (1975):278; Clifford Schneider and Wayne Anderson, "Attitudes Toward the Stigmatized: Some Insights from Recent Research," *Rehab. Counselling Bull.* 23 (1980):299, 301.

55. United States v. Reno, 992 F.2d 739 (7th Cir. 1993).

56. *Id.*

57. An interesting illustration of this point is the tremendous hostility directed toward deaf individuals who refuse on behalf of themselves and their children to receive cochlear implants that would improve or restore their hearing, *see, e.g.,* Harlan Lane, *The Mask of Benevolence: Disabling the Deaf Community* (New York: Knopf, 1992); Edward Dolnick, "Deafness as Culture," *Atlantic Monthly* 272 (Sept. 1993):37; Laurie Lucas, "Bitter Dissent Over Hearing Implants," RIVERSIDE PRESS-ENTERPRISE (Dec. 19, 1993): E1; Amy Elizabeth Brusky, "Making Decisions for Deaf Children Regarding Cochlear Implants: The Legal Ramifications of Recognizing Deafness as a Culture Rather Than a Disability," *Wis. Law Rev.* 1995 (1995):235.

58. In the recent U.S. Supreme Court case of Kansas v. Hendricks, 521 U.S. 346 (1997), the court considered the situation of Leroy Hendricks, who had been repeatedly convicted of molesting children. Criminal conviction is synonymous with responsibility and the ability to control one's behavior, yet Leroy Hendricks's subsequent commitment to a mental hospital after his criminal sentences expired because the Supreme Court found that he had a "mental abnormality" that so substantially impaired his volition that he could not control his actions. If this were true, he should have been found not guilty by reason of insanity rather than convicted for his crimes.

59. Clifford Schneider and Wayne Anderson, "Attitudes Toward the Stigmatized: Some Insights From Recent Research," *Rehab. Counselling Bulletin* 23 (1980):299, 302.

60. *See* Shapiro v. Cadman Towers, 51 F.3d 328, 332, 333 (2nd Cir. 1995); interviews with Laura Prescott (Nov. 1997) and Barbara Kornblum (Apr. 1997).

61. This is probably not coincidence but due to the cumulative effect of the living conditions for minorities, women, and people with physical disabilities in this country, who have the greater likelihood of living in poverty, surrounded by violence, or subjected to greater stresses and economic hardship.

62. *See* Susan Stefan, "Women and Ethnic Minorities in Mental Health Treatment and Law," in Bruce D. Sales and Dan Shuman, Eds., *Law, Mental Health and Mental Disorder* (Pacific Grove, CA: Brooks/Cole, 1996) at 254.

63. *See* Susan Stefan, "Silencing the Different Voice: Competence, Feminist Theory and Law," *Univ. of Miami Law Rev.* 47 (1993):763.

64. Joshua Logan, *My Up and Down, In and Out Life* (New York: Delacourt Press, 1976) at 153.

65. Survey No. 24.

66. Statement of Sen. Warren Rudman, *Congressional Record* 135(112), S10796 (Sept. 7, 1989).

67. The classic example is homosexuality, which was regarded as a mental illness until 1973 for no reason other than that it was a pattern of socially unacceptable behavior lacking any known physiological basis. Equally well known are past diagnoses of women who wished to work outside the home as suffering from mental illness because they "wanted to be like men."

68. The mental health treatment history of Naomi Judd, Rod Steiger, Michael Wallace, Ted Turner, William Styron, Earl Campbell, Patty Duke, Buzz Aldrin, Oliver North, and Lawton Chiles, among others, is rarely highlighted in the stories lauding their accomplishments; *see* Jolie Solomon, Claudia Kalb, and Carla Power, "Breaking the Silence," *Newsweek* (May 20, 1996):20–22.

69. One attorney subjected to discipline produced an expert to testify that he had a mental disability called "success neurosis" that caused his misconduct, People v. Goldstein,

887 P.2d 634, 638, note 1 (Colo. 1994) (*en banc*); "Loophole That Lets Killers Off the Hook," *Spectrum, Scotland on Sunday* (Aug. 31, 1997):4 (the aversion and hatred of homosexuals are also a medical condition; a "diagnosis" of "homosexual panic," "a medical condition" that caused a man to "lose control when propositioned by a homosexual," resulted in a finding of manslaughter rather than murder when a gay man was savagely beaten to death in Great Britain in the late 1980s).

70. *See, e.g.*, the grounds for divorce in a number of states include "incurable mental illness" along with "cruel and inhuman treatment" and "confinement in prison," N.Y. C.L.S. DOM. REL. Sec. 170(1)–(3) and 140(f), 141 (permitting a marriage to be voided or annulled on grounds of incurable mental illness); the questions on the applications for professional licensure, which include treatment for mental illness along with the questions about the records of arrest or fraud, *see* chapter 7. Statutes that criminalize libel about candidates for political office consider certain statements libel per se, including the statements regarding the conviction of a crime involving moral turpitude, dishonorable discharge from the military, and "whether the candidate has received treatment for mental illness," NEB. REV. STAT. ANN. Sec. 294A.345(d).

71. Walter Olson, *The Excuse Factory: How Employment Law Is Paralyzing the American Workplace* (New York: Free Press, 1997); Alan Dershowitz, *The Abuse Excuse and Other Cop-Outs, Sob Stories, and Evasions of Responsibilities* (Boston: Little, Brown).

72. Equal Employment Opportunity Commission, *EEOC Enforcement Guidance: The Americans With Disabilities Act and Psychiatric Disabilities* (Washington, DC: Author, 1997).

73. Sheryl Gay Stolberg, NEW YORK TIMES (May 4, 1997):Sec. 4, p. 1, col. 2.

74. In the course of writing this book, I interviewed many people with psychiatric diagnoses, including professors, law students, lawyers, doctors, secretaries, and people in institutions and community day programs.

75. The text of the survey is reproduced in Appendix A along with a discussion of the methodology used in distributing the survey and compiling the results. A more detailed explanation of the survey can be found in the introduction to this book.

76. Survey No. 186.

77. Survey No. 143 ("The worst [discrimination] has been from my family. For years my sisters did not communicate with me because of my perceived mental illness. Now my daughter herself avoids me"); Survey No. 154 ("family members have resented my activism in mental health reform movement").

78. Survey No. 153.

79. Survey No. 103, on file with the author. *See also* Survey No. 116 ("My family turned against me after I became ill and my sister didn't speak to me for five years").

80. Survey No. 128.

81. Survey No. 160 ("As my disability has become known, I've lost half my friends"); Survey No. 162 ("I've lost friends over this who were too afraid of how I would affect them. That maybe I was contagious or just unpredictable and therefore threatening or unreliable").

82. M. E. C. Survey.

83. Survey No. 17.

84. Survey No. 67.

85. Survey No. 140. *See also* R. B., Survey No. 1 ("[My] college dorm roommate moved home after I told him I'd been on a psych ward. Both [my] father and mother declined to leave me any significant tokens (*i.e.*, inheritance) upon their passing."); J. W., Survey No. 107 (the worst discrimination was "Friends and family ask 'What do you do with your time?' as if I can still work or have no limitations. They act resentful, they tell me, 'I have to get up and go to work.'"); P. H., Survey No. 135 ("family and friends can be [the] cruelest"); Survey No. 171.

86. Survey No. 179.

87. Survey No. 204.

88. Charles Lidz, Edward Mulvey, Steven Hoge, Brenda Kirsch, John Monahan, Nancy Bennett, Marlene Eisenberg, William Gardner, and Loren Roth, "The Validity of Mental Patients' Accounts of Coercion-Related Behaviors in the Hospital Admission Process," *Law and Human Beh.* 21 (1997):361–376.

89. Survey No. 334.

90. *See* chapter 2.

91. Joan F. Houghton, "First Person Account: Maintaining Mental Health in a Turbulent World," *Schizophrenia Bull.* 8 (1982):548, 551.

92. Survey No. 17; Survey No. 3 (N. D. B.); Survey No. 22 (J. E.); Survey No. 41 (K. A. C.); Survey No. 160; No. 196 (M. R.).

93. N. D. B. Survey.

94. K. A. C. Survey.

95. Survey No. 196.

96. Robert Coles, "Psychiatric Stations of the Cross," in Robert Coles, *The Mind's Fate: A Psychiatrist Looks at His Profession* 2nd ed. (Boston: Little, Brown, 1995) at 114.

97. S. M., Survey No. 95; Survey No. 92 ("I have a strong faith community").

98. Survey No. 130, *see also* Survey No. 145, quoted at the beginning of this chapter); N. J. C., Survey No. 112 (the student was not permitted to return to graduate school); Survey No. 158 ("[I was] denied the right to go to college"); and Survey No. 162 ("I was expelled from the college I loved dearly because they didn't want the liability of having me around"). Cases against colleges, graduate schools, and professional schools are an increasing part of the caseload of protection and advocacy agencies. One agency, the Center for Public Representation in Massachusetts, sued a college that did not permit a woman who had been hospitalized to return to her dormitory under the Fair Housing Act and successfully settled the case.

99. Survey No. 115.

100. Survey No.186 ("[I was] once denied entrance to [the] graduate psychology program shortly after [my] interview with [the] department head when I openly mentioned I had psychotherapy").

101. Survey No. 115.

102. Survey No. 131.

103. Survey No. 144.

104. A. F., Survey No. 70; Survey No. 160.

105. P. W. Survey ("Potential landlords don't want to rent to someone who has a mental illness, and is on Section 8 subsidized housing because of the stereotypes about mental illness and them not wanting to do the paperwork involved in Section 8"). Section 8 is a government program providing federal housing subsidies to low income people by the government paying part of the rent to the landlord. One case attempting to argue that the refusal of landlords to accept Section 8 certificates constituted discrimination on the basis of disability under the Fair Housing Act failed, Salute v. Stratford Greens Garden Apartments, 136 F.3d 293 (2nd Cir. 1998).

106. Survey No. 178; *see also* Surveys No. 95 and No. 197 (B. R.).

107. S. M., Survey No. 95, on file with the author.

108. *Id.*

109. *See* Michael Allen, "Separate and Unequal: The Struggle of Tenants With Mental Illness to Maintain Housing," *Clearinghouse Rev.* 29 (1996):720.

110. Alexander v. Choate, 469 U.S. 287, 295 (1985).

111. U.S. Civil Rights Commission, *Accommodating the Spectrum of Individual Abilities* (Washington, DC: Author, Sept. 1983) quoted "some authorities" as describing discrimination against people with disabilities as "first and foremost a result of 'simple thoughtlessness' and 'primarily a matter of oversight.'"

112. *See, e.g.,* Michael A. Rebell, "Structural Discrimination and the Rights of the Disabled," *Georgetown Law Rev.* 74 (1986):1435, 1451–1452 ("in the handicapped context, how-

ever, where *invidious animus* is often not the predominant cause of discrimination");
Theresa E. Cudahy, "Federal Statutory Requirements for Accommodating Handicapped
Students in School Choice Programs," *Univ. of Chicago Law Forum* 1991 (1991):293,
304, made a representative statement when she wrote that "the disparate impact standard
is useful in cases, like disability, where discrimination is more often the product of
neglect than malice." This comment is particularly inapt in a piece about education
because federal legislation was required to correct the well-documented intentional exclusion of children with disabilities from school on the basis of their disabilities; there
was no "neglect" about the failure of schools to admit handicapped children. Note, first,
that none of these authors gave any citations to support these statements and, second,
that this viewpoint is held principally by nondisabled people. When disabled people
write about their own experiences and perceptions of the world, they rarely describe
themselves as the "subjects" of neglect or indifference; rather, they emphasize experiencing vicious and intentional discrimination.

113. In re Carney, 598 P.2d 36 (Ca. 1979); *see also* Michael Ashley Stein, "Book Review:
     'Mommy Has a Blue Wheelchair': Recognizing the Parental Rights of Individuals With
     Disabilities," *Brooklyn Law Rev.* 60 (1994):1069.

114. *See* p. 22 *infra; see also* Susan Stefan, "Impact of the Law on Women With Diagnoses
     of Borderline Personality Disorder Related to Childhood Sexual Abuse," in Bruce Levin,
     Andrea Blanch, and Ann Jennings, Eds., *Women's Mental Health Services: A Public
     Health Perspective* (Thousand Oaks, CA: Sage, 1998) at 249–257.

115. *See, e.g.,* In re T. J. and M. D. and C. J., 666 A.2d 1 (D.C. 1995) (in which the previous
     judge explicitly used the "mental illness" portion of the statute rather than a finding
     that the child was without proper care, control, subsistence, or education because he
     found that "the mother always ensured that someone would provide for the child's
     needs"); In re B. K. F., 704 S.2d 314 (La. App. 1998).

116. *See* pp. 18–19, *infra.*

117. Doe v. Stincer, 990 F.Supp. 1427 (S.D. Fla. 1997).

118. Anonymous v. Anonymous, 677 N.Y.S.2d 573 (N.Y. App. 1998) (finding "no merit" to
     the claim that a law permitting divorce on the grounds of "incurable insanity" violates
     the ADA).

119. COLO. REV. STAT. Sec. 1-2-103; FLA. STAT. Sec. 394.459(7); PA. STAT. ANN. Sec.
     961.502(4).

120. O.C.G.A. 37-3-144, 37-4-104, 37-7-144; R.I. GEN. LAWS Sec. 17-9.1-9.1.

121. ALASKA CONST. Art. V, Sec. 2 (listing as the only people who cannot vote in Alaska
     those who have committed felonies involving moral turpitude and those judicially de-
     termined to be of unsound mind); KANSAS CONST. Art. 5, Sec. 2; KENTUCKY CONST.
     Art. 145 (prohibiting "idiots and insane persons" from voting); NEW MEXICO CONST.
     Art. VII, No. 1 ("legally insane"); MAINE CONST. Art. II, Sec. 1; WEST VA. CONST.
     Art. IV, Sec. 1 ("unsound mind"); R.I. CONST. Art. II, Sec. 1.

122. In West Virginia, a series of opinions by the attorney general of the state clarified that
     the constitutional denial of the right to vote to people of "unsound mind" did not deny
     the right to vote to people who had merely sought treatment or to people who had been
     involuntarily committed to a mental institution; W. Va. Op. Atty. Gen. No. 57 (Mar. 28,
     1980). In Kentucky, a series of opinions by the attorney general clarified that a person
     declared incompetent but not insane was not necessarily barred from voting, Op. Atty.
     Gen. 73-700, 76-549; Alaska repealed a statute prohibiting voting by people of unsound
     mind in 1996, 49 ch. 86, S.L.A. 1996, repealing ALASKA STAT. Sec. 15.050.040.

123. 21-A MAINE REV. STAT. ANN Sec. 115(1).

124. N. D. B. Survey, on file with the author.

125. J. B. F. Survey.

126. Survey No. 158.

127. Jones v. Penny, 387 F.Supp. 383 (M.D.N.C. 1974) (rejecting substantively the equal

protection challenge to North Carolina statute under which people who were involuntarily committed were subjected to an investigation by the Division of Motor Vehicles, but those who voluntarily admitted themselves to an institution were not).

128. Gargagliano v. Secretary of State, 233 N.W.2d 159 (Mich. App. 1975); Jones v. Penny, 387 F.Supp. 383 (M.D.N.C. 1974). More recently, in Commonwealth v. Clayton, 684 A.2d 1060 (Pa. 1996), a man with epilepsy successfully challenged on constitutional grounds a requirement that a person's driver's license must be suspended for 1 year if he or she has had a seizure.

129. Alabama removed references to "insane and feeble-minded persons" from its statutes regulating driver's licenses in 1996, see notes to ALA. CODE Sec. 32-6-7 (Michie 1998).

130. See, e.g., ARK. CODE ANN. Sec. 27-16-604 (Michie 1997); FLA. STAT. ANN., Sec. 322.05(7); OHIO REV. CODE ANN. Sec. 4507.161; VA. CODE ANN. Sec. 46.2-314 (Michie 1998).

131. Alaska Stat. Sec. 28.15.191(e).

132. Ira A. Burnim, "'Equal Treatment' and 'Special Treatment': Considerations in ADA Implementation," in Clarence Sundram, Ed., *Choice & Responsibility: Legal and Ethical Dilemmas in Services for Persons With Mental Disabilities* (New York: New York Commission on Quality of Care for the Mentally Disabled, 1994) at 245, 247. The chapter does not say what happened.

133. See cases listed in notes 127 and 128 and Aurelio v. R.I. Department of Administration, 985 F.Supp. 48 (D.R.I. 1997).

134. Theriault v. Flynn, 162 F.3d 46 (1st Cir. 1998) (dismissing in a footnote a facial challenge to a regulation listing "physical or mental impairments" as a basis for the belief that an applicant for a driver's license might be a hazard to public safety), see also Strax v. Commonwealth of Pa., 588 A.2d 87 (Commonwealth Ct. 1991) (refusing on grounds of mootness to reach a challenge to procedures that singled out visibly disabled drivers).

135. Daly v. Delponte, 624 A.2d 876, 883 (Conn. 1993).

136. U.S. Civil Rights Commission, *Accommodating the Spectrum of Individual Abilities* (Washington, DC: Author, 1983):40.

137. *Id.* at 167.

138. KY. REV. STAT. Sec. 402.020 (marriage is prohibited and void "(1) with a person who has been adjudged mentally disabled by a court of competent jurisdiction"); 23 PA. CONS. STAT. Sec. 1304 ("no marriage license may be issued if applicant is weak minded, insane, of unsound mind").

139. ALASKA STAT. Sec. 25.24.030.

140. Washington, DC 30-103 (the marriage of a person "adjudged to be a lunatic" is illegal; as is "any marriage either of the parties to which shall be incapable, from physical causes, of entering into the married state").

141. ALA. CODE Sec. 30-2-1-8 (permits a divorce if a spouse is "hopelessly and incurably insane" as evidenced by confinement to a mental hospital for 5 successive years); ALASKA STAT. Sec. 25.24.050(8) (1997) (permits a divorce for incurable mental illness when a spouse has been confined to an institution for at least 18 months prior to the institution of the proceeding); ARK. CODE ANN. Sec. 9-12-301-7(A) (authorizing a divorce if spouses have lived apart for 3 years by reason of the "incurable insanity" and institutionalization of the spouse); GA. CODE ANN. Sec. 19-5-3(11) (providing for divorce on grounds of incurable mental illness only if the spouse has been judged mentally ill by a court or certified by two physicians and has been confined in an institution or under continuous treatment for 2 years, and only if the superintendent of the institution or a competent physician appointed by the court certifies under oath that the spouse "evidences such a want of reason, memory and intelligence as to prevent the party from comprehending the nature, duties and consequences of the marriage relationship and that in light of present day medical knowledge, recovery of the party's mental health cannot be expected at any time during his life"); IDAHO CODE Sec. 32-501(3) (a mar-

riage may be annulled if either party was of unsound mind at the time of the marriage); MISS. CODE ANN. Sec. 93-5-1(8) (a divorce may be granted on the grounds of "insanity or idiocy" of either party at the time of the marriage; N.Y. DOM. REL. Sec. 7(5) (permitting the annulment of a marriage if one spouse has been "incurably mentally ill" for a period of 5 years or more); N.C. GEN. STAT. Sec. 50-5.1 (permits the divorce of an incurably insane spouse after a separation for 3 years; otherwise North Carolina law permits divorce after separation of 1 year). Other states used to have these provisions, e.g., CONN. GEN. STAT. Sec. 7327 (requiring at least 5 years confinement) and IOWA CODE Sec. 598.17.

142. Anonymous v. Anonymous, 677 N.Y.S.2d 573 (N.Y. App. 1998).
143. Scott v. Scott, 442 S.E.2d 493, 495 (N.C. 1994) (a separate divorce statute when one spouse is "incurably insane," requiring 3 years separation rather than the 1 year required when a sane spouse petitions for divorce from an incurably insane spouse and providing for the possibility of the lifetime maintenance of the insane spouse).
144. *See, e.g.,* Kunzweiler v. Kunzweiler, 698 S.2d 1251 (Fla. App. 1997).
145. Baer v. Baer 738 A.2d 923, 930 (Md. Sp. App.).
146. Gerk v. Gerk, 158 N.W.2d 656, 662 (Iowa 1968).
147. *See* "Charge of Insanity or Attempt to Have Spouse Committed to Mental Health Institution as Grounds for Divorce of Judicial Separation," 33 A.L.R.2d 1230.
148. Carolyn L. Vash, *The Psychology of Disability* (New York: Springer, 1981) at 155.
149. The most famous case in this regard is In re Carney, *see* note 113.
150. Survey No. 175, No. 176.
151. Survey No. 175.
152. *See* Susan Stefan, "The Impact of the Law on Women With Diagnoses of Borderline Personality Disorder Related to Childhood Sexual Abuse," in Bruce Lubotsky Levin, Andrea K. Blanch, and Ann Jennings, *Women's Mental Health Services: A Public Health Perspective* (Thousand Oaks, CA: Sage, 1998) at 257–259.
153. S. C., Survey No. 143.
154. *See, e.g.,* In re J. P., 633 N.E.2d 27 (Ill. App. 1994).
155. Samantha Simms v. State of Florida, 641 S.2d 957, 963, note 2 (Fla. App. 1994) (Jorgensen, J., dissenting).
156. *See* Deborah Belle, *Lives in Stress: Women and Depression* (Beverly Hills, CA: Sage, 1982) at 201 ("The most alarming barrier to mental health treatment was the fear women expressed that their children would be taken away from them if it became known [they] had emotional problems. . . . One woman who lost her child after she sought treatment explained: 'If you have a breakdown, it will follow you faster and further than a prison record' ").
157. *See, e.g.,* CA. WELF. & INST. Sec. 361.5(b)(2); UTAH CODE ANN. Sec. 78-3a-311(3)(b)(ii) (1996) (the court may order that reunification services need not be provided if it finds by clear and convincing evidence that "the parent is suffering from a mental illness of such magnitude that it renders him incapable of utilizing reunification services . . . based on competent evidence from mental health professionals establishing that, even with provision of services, the parent is unlikely to be capable of adequately caring for the child within twelve months").
158. Arkansas D.H.S. v. Clark, 802 S.W.2d 461 (Ark. 1991).
159. *Id.*
160. In re Jennilee T., 3 Cal. App. 4th 212 (1992); In re of the Welfare of S. Z., 536 N.W.2d 37 (Minn. App. 1995).
161. State child welfare and family services agencies are public entities that must provide their benefits, programs, and services in a nondiscriminatory way, pursuant to Title II of the ADA, 42 U.S.C. 12132.
162. Courts that have held that the ADA cannot be raised in the context of an individual parental rights termination proceeding include In re Antony B., 1998 WL 285848 (Conn.

Super. May 21, 1998); In re Maryia R., 1997 WL 178082 (Conn. Super. Apr. 1, 1997); In re of Torrance P., 522 N.W.2d 243 (Wisc. App. 1994); In re B. F. K, 704 S.2d 314 (La. App. 1997); In re B. S., 693 A.2d 716 (Vt. 1997); and Stone v. Davies County, 656 N.E.2d 824 (Ind. App. Oct. 17, 1995). Courts that have held that the ADA could apply in an individual parental termination proceeding (although in each case the court concluded that the ADA did not apply in the particular proceeding before it) include in re John D., 934 P.2d 308 (N.M. App. 1997); In re Caresse B., 1997 WL 133402 (Conn. Super. Mar. 11, 1997); In re A. J. R., 896 P.2d 1298 (Wash. App. 1995); In re C. M., 526 N.W.2d 562 (Iowa App. 1994); In re Angel B., 659 A.2d 277 (Me. 1995); In re Penny J., 890 P.2d 389 (N.M. App. 1994); and J. T. v. Arkansas Department of Human Services, 947 S.W.2d 761 (Ark. 1997).

163. In re B. S., 693 A.2d 716 (Vt. 1997).

164. In re Antony B., 1998 WL 285848 (Conn. Super. May 21, 1998). For a discussion of the conduct–disability dichotomy in public and judicial discourse, *see* chapter 3.

165. In re B. K. F., 704 S.2d 314 (La. App. 1997). Of course, the point that the parents were trying to make in these cases is that the reunification services and programs in parenting assistance are geared toward parents without disabilities; it is the services of the agency, not the termination proceeding itself, that are the subject of the claim. In any event, Title II of the ADA prohibits discriminatory practices in general and in "benefits, programs and services"; *see* Crowder v. Kitagawa, 81 F.3d 1480 (9th Cir. 1996).

166. In re Matthew S., 1999 Conn. Super. LEXUS 1909*27 (Conn. Super. July 16, 1999); In re of John D., 934 P.2d 308, 315 (N.M. App. 1997).

167. ILLINOIS COMP. STAT. Sec. 40-1501-D-p; MONT. CODE ANN. Sec. 41-3-609(2).

168. In re of J. L. B. 594 P.2d 1127 (Mont. 1979).

169. L. R. v. Utah, No. 971369, 1998 Utah App LEXIS 97 (Oct. 22, 1998). The court applied the "rational basis" test, rejecting the argument that the passage of the ADA required the use of strict scrutiny. The court also found that the statute would pass muster even under strict scrutiny.

170. Payton v. New York, 445 U.S. 573, 583-590 (1980).

171. *See, e.g.*, FLA. STAT. ANN. Sec. 394.463(2)(c) ("a law enforcement officer may serve and execute such order on any day of the week at any time of the day or night").

172. "A Paranoid With Real Cause for Fear," CHICAGO TRIBUNE (Oct. 29, 1997):22 (noting that police surrounded Shirley Allen's house for 38 days, fired tear gas into it, ringed it with ultrasensitive listening devices, drove over her lawn in all-terrain vehicles, and tried to send a dog in. Allen was alone in the house and did not want to be taken for a psychiatric evaluation.

173. *See, e.g.*, State *ex. rel.* Children, Youth and Family Department v. John D., 123 N.M. 114, 121, 934 P.2d 308 (N.M. App. 1997) ("the police broke into her home to forcibly remove her" and take her to a mental hospital); DiCola v. Fulmele, 1993 U.S. Dist. LEXIS 8825 (E.D. Pa. July 2, 1993).

174. McCabe v. Lifeline Ambulance Services and City of Lynn, 77 F.3d 540 (1st Cir. 1996).

175. *Id.*

176. Moore v. Wyoming Medical Services, 825 F.Supp. 1531, 1535 (D.Wyo. 1993).

177. PACT stands for the Program for Assertive Community Treatment. Developed in the late 1960s, it features 24-hour community services and workers who visit a client's residence, *see* A. J. Marx, Mary Ann Test, and Leonard I. Stein, "Extrahospital Management of Severe Mental Illness," *Archives of Gen. Psychiatry* 29 (1973):505–511. Although it has been shown to keep mental health clients out of the hospital, many clients have feelings of ambivalence about the program.

178. V. B. Survey.

179. Oregon v. Johnson, 843 P.2d 985 (Ore. App. 1992) (the police found a woman in the

cold and took her to a hospital where she was civilly committed on the basis that she could not meet her shelter needs).

180. Survey No. 204.

181. Psychiatric patients are arrested at a rate of 12.03 per thousand, compared with the nonpatient arrest rate of 3.62 per thousand, Rael J. Isaac and Virginia C. Armat, *Madness in the Streets* (New York: Free Press, 1990) at 272; H. Richard Lamb and Linda Weinberger, "Persons With Severe Mental Illness in Jails and Prisons: A Review," *Psychiatric Services* 49(4) (1998):483–492; Linda A. Teplin, K. M. Abram, and G. M. McClelland, "Prevalence of Psychiatric Disorders Among Incarcerated Women: I. Pretrial Detainees," *Archives of Gen. Psychiatry* 53 (1996):505–512.

182. John Monahan study.

183. Survey No. 182.

184. "For example, persons who have epilepsy, and a variety of other disabilities, are frequently inappropriately arrested and jailed because police officers have not received proper training in the recognition of and aid for seizures. Often, after being arrested, they are deprived of medications while in jail, resulting in further seizures. Such discriminatory treatment based on disability can be avoided by proper training," Committee on the Judiciary, H.Rep.101-485, Pt. III at 50.

185. "A number of commentators asked that the regulation be amended to require the training of law enforcement personnel to recognize the difference between criminal activity and the effects of seizures or other disabilities such as mental retardation, cerebral palsy, traumatic brain injury, mental illness, or deafness. Several disabled commentators gave personal statements about abuse they had suffered at the hands of law enforcement personnel," Department of Justice, 28 C.F.R. Title II, Interpretive Guidance to Sec. 35.130.

186. *Id.*

187. In re J. W., 672 A.2d 199, 202 (N.J. App. 1996).

188. *See* further discussion of this issue in chapter 2.

189. Russo v. City of Forest Park, 953 F.2d 1036 (6th Cir. 1992).

190. Survey No. 153; Survey No. 157 (the respondent gave a presentation on police misconduct toward people with psychiatric diagnoses at the National Tribunal on Police Brutality and Misconduct; several friends also testified).

191. Communication from Stephen Yelenosky, Advocacy Inc., Austin, TX, Feb. 3, 1999 ("we've had two people with mental illness shot [by police officers] when the situation might have been handled differently").

192. Anderson v. Village of Forest Park, 606 N.E.2d 205 (Ill. App. 1992); Fields v. Dailey, 587 N.E.2d 400 (Ohio App. 1990); DiCola v. Fulmele, 1993 WL 246092 (E.D. Pa. June 29, 1993).

193. Not surprisingly, people with physical disabilities have fared better than people with mental disabilities in these cases; *cf.* Gorman v. Baitch, 152 F.3d 907 (8th Cir. 1998) and Lewis v. Truitt, 960 F.Supp. 175 (S.D. Ind. 1997) with Gohier v. Enright, 186 F.3d 1216 (10th Cir. 1999) and Hainze v. Richards, 207 F.3d 795 (5th Cir. 2000).

194. *See* Bruce Link, "Understanding Labeling Effects in the Area of Mental Disorders: An Assessment of the Effects of Expectations of Rejection," *Amer. Soc. Rev.* 52 (1987):96.

195. Survey No. 189.

Chapter 2
IMAGES OF MENTAL ILLNESS

But never let it be doubted that depression, in its extreme form, is madness. The madness results from an aberrant biochemical process. (William Styron)[1]

* * *

Part of our condition is to feel despair. . . . Women and men have looked down into the pit that is themselves and that is life and questioned the meaning and mourned the futility of it all. . . . This was not an illness. I was not being sick and having symptoms . . . they were me and not my sickness. (Janet Gotkin)[2]

* * *

Q: How do you know that you are disabled?
A: The (health) director told me.
Q: Do you think you are disabled?
A: I think I am doing real well. . . .
Counselor (interrupting): That's right. Yes, Trudy, you are doing better than I have seen since I have been here.
Q: Do you feel better?
A: I thought I was fine but I am glad I (am) improving. (to Counselor: Do you really think I have improved?) (interview with Trudy B.)[3]

* * *

Q: How do you know you are paranoid?
A: Because I take medicine for it, and everybody else here is (paranoid). . . .
Q: What if you didn't take the medicine? Would you still be paranoid?
A: If I was still coming [to the Community Mental Health Center] I guess so. (interview with Yolanda H.)[4]

These are the words of people who have received diagnoses of mental illness. William Styron has no doubt that there is a condition called depression, that it is biologically based, and that he has been correctly diagnosed with it. Janet Gotkin rejects the diagnosis and the profession that invented the word *schizophrenia* entirely. Trudy B. and Yolanda H. believe that they have schizophrenia simply because that is what they have been told.

Although William Styron and Janet Gotkin disagree completely about the nature of mental illness, they have more in common with each other than with Trudy B. or Yolanda H. Those like Gotkin, who reject the identity of mental illness imposed on them, defy the experts and professionals, and rely on their own judgment and experience, are rare. Yet those like Stryon who, after careful consideration and reliance on their own experience and judgment, concur with the experts and professionals and accept the diagnosis of mental illness are also rare. Many people are like Trudy B. and Yolanda H., simply taking the word of experts for their conditions rather than searching for their own answers and defining their experiences in their own terms.

We all take the word of experts to identify our conditions—conditions that experts do not have and have not experienced themselves. Clearly, oncologists do not have to have had cancer to treat cancer, but it may help to have had cancer to treat the cancer patient. Much of this is a matter of language and attitude. Experts in all kinds of diseases and disabilities use different language to describe those diseases and disabilities than the language used by the people who have them. This has led to an explosion of literature by people diagnosed with various kinds of illness, trying to name and create their experiences with their own language—language that is more meaningful to them.[5]

Although the language of doctors is undoubtedly different from the language of patients, the language of mental health professionals is even more different from the language of people with mental illness. The complaint about medical experts is that they are too neutral: They describe the horrors of tumors, lesions, and hemorrhaging with objective, detached language. By contrast, the language of psychiatry is filled with an overt hostility not often seen in other fields of experts. Dr. Karl Menninger described many psychiatrists who "use words like 'sick,' 'pathological,' or 'abnormal' with flagrant imprecision, with condescension, with malice; any disagreement with their findings is evidence of 'sickness,' for which, of course, the dissenter needs something called 'treatment.' "[6] Patients have been called "mistresses of manipulation" and one of the most standard mental health phrases used to describe patients with depression is "hopeless and helpless."[7] The language of the two psychiatrists in *Villanova v. Abrams* is fairly typical:

> [The patient] presents today with tangential irrelevant responses to inquiries. He is superficially oriented, quite grandiose, and has delusions of thought projection. Insight is lacking and judgment is poor.

> [Patient] displayed inappropriate blunted to flat affect.... He is extremely guarded and evasive and appears to have a great deal of underlying hostility.[8]

It could be argued that all medical language deals with defects and deficits, and psychiatric language only appears hostile because the defects and deficits being discussed are more personal: characterizing a person as having deficits in judgment or insight, the cornerstones of character and identity, has different connotations than describing a person as having 20/100 vision or a low T-cell count or a restricted range of motion.

Emotional and cognitive difficulties can be described precisely and without condescension, however. People who have been diagnosed with psychiatric disabilities have poured out a description of their conditions in a rich literature. The difference is not that they describe their experiences positively, but that their self-descriptions cry out with pain, sorrow, and terror. The accounts and language of mental health professionals, on the other hand, often seem completely alienated from the suffering and pain of their patients. As one woman diagnosed with a mental illness said dryly in an interview, "I've never known anyone with schizophrenia describe themselves as having 'blunted affect' or 'poverty of thought.' "[9] Rather, these "symptoms" are described in terms of numbness, exhaustion, wariness, or pain so extreme that, as Emily Dickinson noted, it creates a blank.[10]

Courts, especially appellate courts who never hear anyone but the lawyers in the case, draw almost all of their language and imagery about mental illness from the testimony of experts. This testimony is phrased in terms that can easily be interpreted as derogatory toward the individual rather than descriptive of the diagnosis. Legal images of mental disability, drawn from statutes and court decisions, are even more judgmental and less nuanced than those of mental health professionals. In case law, the voice of the person whose fate is being decided has often been completely silenced, the pain erased from the account in the case and the person's story told by the judge and the mental health professionals. In *Alphonso v. Charity Hospital*, Lori Jean Alphonso was raped twice while institutionalized. She later received a letter from her rapist indicating his "intention to ravish her" (he had obtained her home address through the "negligence of hospital personnel"). She was denied medical expenses as damages because a psychiatrist testified that "schizophrenics may have atypical responses to a trauma such as rape, and the rape trauma syndrome may not be as severe, and the posttraumatic stress disorder may be less."[11] Lori Jean Alphonso is not quoted; her only testimony in the case is the judge's observation that she "slashed most of her body—neck, chest, legs and abdomen—with a razor, to prevent the rapist from recognizing her and to make herself sexually unattractive to the rapist if she were recognized."[12] Lori Jean Alphonso did not get to tell her story in any way but this one.

Legal Images of Psychiatric Disability

The history of society's views of mental illness can be seen in its legal terminology. Like geological layers, the language of laws passed many years ago gives glimpses of assumptions and perspectives of the day, and the changing language of the laws over time reflects changing attitudes.

Some language has not changed. There are only 16 terms that Alabama considers important enough to define for its entire legal code. The fifth definition provides that "the words 'lunatic' or 'insane' or the term 'non compos mentis' shall include all persons of unsound mind."[13] Statutes still in force today permit divorce from a spouse who has been in a mental hospital for 5 years and is "hopelessly and incurably insane."[14] Virtually every state has a statute permitting the dissolution of a partnership if one of the partners is of "unsound mind" because that is the language of the Uniform Partnership Act.[15] Statutes regarding contracts often distinguish between someone of unsound mind, whose contract is only voidable, and a person "entirely without understanding," whose contract is void.[16]

Some language has changed only recently. In 1988, Alaska changed its banking code to substitute "incapacitated person" for "lunatic, idiot, person of unsound mind, or habitual drunkard."[17] In 1984, the Mississippi State Legislature adopted the following definition of *feebleminded,* which it uses to this day:

> The term . . . shall apply to persons such a degree of mental inferiority from birth . . . that they are unable to care for themselves, profit by ordinary public school instruction, to compete on equal terms with others, or to manage themselves and their affairs with ordinary prudence, and consequently constitute menaces to the happiness and safety of themselves or of other persons in the community. These persons . . . comprise those commonly called idiots, imbeciles, and morons, or high-grade feebleminded persons.[18]

This definition is notable for its explicit articulation of what lies beneath the surface of much of U.S. social policy: that people who cannot compete or take care of themselves are inferior, and not only inferior but actual "menaces to the happiness and safety of themselves or of other persons in the community." This definition underscores the importance of ensuring that people with disabilities have opportunities for employment and may explain the increasing public willingness to accept people with diagnoses of serious mental illness, such as Ted Turner or William Styron, as long as they are otherwise successful or "managing themselves and their affairs with ordinary prudence" (whatever that is).

The Mississippi legislation also contains to this day the instruction that "all care of such feeble-minded females must secure their protection and segregation. It shall be the first duty of boards of supervisors in extending care and protection to feeble-minded persons, to prevent the propagation of the feeble-minded."[19] Lest the reader suspect that only Mississippi retains such terminology, the state of California regulates leaves of absence from state hospitals for "defective or psychopathic delinquents,"[20] whereas Colorado provides "whenever the terms 'idiot,' 'feeble-minded person,' 'mental defective' and 'mentally deficient person' are used in the laws of the State of Colorado, they shall be deemed to mean and to be included with the term 'person with a developmental disability,' as defined in Sec. 27-10.5-102(11)(b)."[21]

Most legal terminology about mental conditions is less jarring to the ordinary ear. Laws define "mental illness" for the purpose of involuntary civil commitment, "insanity" for the purposes of criminal defenses,[22] "incompetence" either to stand trial[23] or as justifying guardianship or conservatorship, and "disability" for applicants to receive government disability assistance[24] and vocational rehabilitation programs,[25] or for protection against discrimination.[26] Managed care plans of the modern era refer to "behavioral health."

Sometimes the same terms are used across different legal categories with different legal meanings. For example, "unsound mind" may be used in contract law to determine whether a contract is voidable,[27] in evidence to decide whether a witness may testify,[28] and to suspend the statute of limitations for a particular legal claim.[29] It is clear that "unsound mind" means different things in each of these contexts. For example, in Arizona, to suspend the operation of the statute of limitations, an *unsound mind* means an "inability to manage ordinary daily affairs";[30] however, to preclude a witness from testifying, the same term means "deprived of the ability to perceive the event or of the ability to recollect and communicate with reference thereto."[31]

Within a given legal category, however, different terms generally mean much the same thing. Some states may refer to "incompetence to stand trial" and others to "insanity,"[32] but the standards for deciding whether an individual is competent to participate as a defendant in a criminal trial—can the individual understand the charges and assist his or her counsel—remain nearly the same.[33] States have elaborately different definitions of "mental illness" for the purposes of civil commitment, but basically the same people are civilly committed regardless of the definition used. This is true even when a state changes its own definition.[34]

In some cases, even modern judges quote or use dated and inapposite terminology. In a 1997 decision in federal court in Connecticut, a judge quoted the following comments interpreting the Restatement of Torts in considering whether the employee of a nursing home could sue a woman with Alzheimer's who had hit her:

> If mental defectives are to live in the world, they should pay for the damage they do ... their liability will mean that those who have charge of them or their estates will be stimulated to look after them, keep them in order, and see that they do not do harm.[35]

In another recent case, the judge referred to a plaintiff who "had a manic fit," although the plaintiff "did not become violent or rip his clothes off."[36] Judges' ideas about the meaning of mental illness also vary according to the case before them even when the diagnosis is the same. Thus, for example, posttraumatic stress disorder (PTSD) is unquestioned as a diagnosis when the issue is whether a veteran is entitled to benefits; however, courts have expressed doubts as to the validity of the diagnosis in disability discrimination cases or in cases involving prisoners or criminal defendants.[37]

Many other diagnoses have different meanings in different contexts. Borderline personality disorder is considered a serious, lifelong diagnosis in disability discrimination,[38] civil commitment,[39] and parental termination cases.[40] One court overturned a substantial jury award of damages for rape to a woman with a diagnosis of borderline personality disorder, citing in part the testimony of medical experts describing borderline personality disorder as characterized by "perverse fantasies, as well as behavior that is impulsive, manipulative, aggressive, and controlling."[41] Judges treat borderline personality disorder as a far less serious condition when it is advanced as a defense in the criminal context, quoting experts for the proposition that "borderline personality disorder is very common in the general population and is not considered a disease."[42]

Although the legal contexts vary tremendously, the one thing they all have in common is that if a person's mental state is at issue, courts turn to mental health experts for advice and answers. Psychiatrists and psychologists are called on systematically to answer what Ben Bursten called the "sick or _____" questions: "sick or criminal? sick or sinful? sick or unwise? sick or lazy? sick or manipulative? sick or merely unpleasant? sick or inexperienced?"[43] As Bursten pointed out, the answers to these questions implicate culture and deeply held moral values that mental health professionals are not necessarily qualified to answer. Yet framing these questions as "sick or _____" means that mental health professionals are asked to answer them all.

A better way of understanding mental health issues in law is to break them down into four core concepts. However varied the subject of the cases and the terminology applied, almost all mental health law can be broken down into questions about present or predicted volition, cognition, functionality, and treatability.

Volition involves the question of whether a person's actions are voluntary or beyond his or her control. If they are not within the person's control, he or she cannot be held legally responsible for them. However, to lose legal responsibility for one's actions is to risk losing the legal rights that accompany society's core assumption that every adult is responsible for his or her actions. Whether a mental illness rendered a person unable to control his or her behavior so that he or she can assert an insanity defense and the Supreme Court's recent limitation on commitment of sexual offenders to those who cannot control their behavior are both examples of legal concerns with volition.[44]

Cognition is the question of the individual's awareness or understanding of his or her circumstances and choices. People who are significantly out of touch with what we regard as reality are considered "cognitively impaired"; again, this may result in losing the rights whose exercise requires some ability, however limited, to reason from recognized facts. Whether a person can understand the benefits and drawbacks of medical treatment, the difference between right and wrong, the provisions of his or her will, and the charges against him or her in a criminal proceeding are all inquiries into cognition.

Functionality is an increasingly important aspect of inquiry into the legal meaning of mental impairments. For many years, the existence of mental illness was itself sufficient to negate functionality for legal purposes. The ability to assist legal counsel, the ability to be gainfully employed, and the question of whether a person's mental impairment substantially limits major life activities are all questions about how a mental impairment affects a person's ability to function in the world.

Treatability is a focus in a number of statutes involving parental termination, involuntary civil commitment, and divorce. Many state commitment statutes and a number of cases address the issue of whether a person may be civilly detained if there is no treatment available for his or her condition. Some state statutes permit the termination of parental rights if there is no prospect that treatment will benefit a parent with a mental illness.[45] Many states permit a spouse to petition for divorce if the other spouse is "incurably" insane.[46]

Obviously, these four categories are sometimes interrelated. The question of a person's functionality may vary depending on the answer to his or her treatability ("Could this person survive in the community if he or she took medication?"); and questions about functioning may be implicitly about volition ("Does the depression *really* make him or her unable to work?").

The point of breaking down legal issues relating to a person's mental state into these four categories is twofold. First, if courts ask questions in these terms, they may steer legal rhetoric away from overreliance on diagnoses that often serve as inexact proxies for them. Second, it assists in clarifying the boundaries of expertise of mental health professionals to advise the courts.

Although cognition is and treatability may be within the realm of the mental health professional, he or she has little expertise to answer questions of volition and functionality. There are no psychological tests to measure the level of willpower or control one has over one's behavior. Whereas mental health professionals may describe how a particular condition makes it difficult to function, there is a range of functioning among people with a particular diagnosis that professionals cannot generalize in helpful ways. Whether a person actually does function or not can be testified to and described by laypeople, and often laypeople do just that in Social Security and workers' compensation hearings.

Medical Images of Mental Illness: Diagnoses

If we see a patient who puzzles us, we can avoid the mystery and challenge of the unique through readily available diagnostic categories.[47]

Like the law, the medical and rehabilitation communities have a plethora of terminology, including "impairment," "handicap," and "disability." Confusion also arises in these communities because different entities define the same word differently. For example, the World Health Organization (WHO) defines "impairment," "disability," and "handicap" as three distinct concepts. An *impairment* is "any loss or abnormality of psychological, physiological, or anatomical structure or function."[48] Examples might include a broken or missing finger or depression. A *disability* is "a restriction of ability or lack of ability to perform an activity considered normal for the person."[49] A person with the impairment of a broken finger might have a disability of being unable to lift certain objects or catch a basketball; a person with depression might be disabled in his or her ability to concentrate or sleep. A *handicap* is "disadvantage for a given individual, resulting from a disability or impairment, that limits or prevents fulfillment of a role that is normal for that person."[50] If the broken or missing finger meant that the individual could not play sports or the depression led to an inability to work or go to school, that would be a handicap.

In the United States, under the American Medical Association's *Guides to the Evaluation of Permanent Impairment*,[51] the definition of *impairment* tracks that of the WHO: "a deviation from normal in a bodily part or organ system and its functioning."[52] Americans, however, often blur the WHO's concepts of "handicap" and "disability,"[53] using *disability* to mean what the WHO means by *handicap*. Americans used to use the word *handicap* but have stopped because people with disabilities find it offensive. A *disability* is "an alteration of an individual's capacity to meet personal, social, or occupational demands or statutory or regulatory requirements, because of an impairment."[54] *Impairment* is seen as a purely medical judgment, whereas the *disability* created by the impairment is context specific, "subjective and value laden."[55] Ellen Smith Pryor argued persuasively that *impairment* is also subjective and value laden.[56]

Although many mental health professionals evaluate people for impairments and disabilities, the bottom line for most courts, as well as for the ubiquitous third-party reimburser, is the diagnosis. A number of respected psychiatrists and psychologists have expressed frustration and impatience with diagnosis as an obstacle rather than an assistance to treatment,[57] but the diagnosis is crucial to reimbursement and to the legal system and, as it turns out, is central to the process of discrimination.

Epidemiological studies confirm that many people—a majority in fact—who are considered to have major mental illnesses never receive either a diagnosis or treatment. (The same studies show that a fairly significant number of people who do not meet diagnostic criteria have been diagnosed and treated for major mental illnesses, including some who were institutionalized at the time of the study.) This phenomenon enables researchers to examine whether discrimination is based on the disability and its manifestations, as opposed to simply having a diagnosis. For example, pioneering work by Bruce Link showed that people with "treated (labeled) cases of psychiatric disorder have less income and are more likely to be underemployed than similarly impaired untreated (unlabeled) cases with comparable background characteristics."[58] This is underscored throughout society: Exclusionary laws, policies, and regulations are often simply based on diagnosis or history of treatment rather than on conduct;[59] licensing boards in the professions consider treatment an unfavorable rather than favorable reflection on an individual's character;[60] insurance companies deny coverage based on treatment rather than ongoing symptoms of disabilities; and medical professionals approach patients differently if the patient reveals a history of mental health treatment.[61]

Conditions referred to as "mental disorders" in one way or another run the gamut from caffeine and tobacco addiction[62] to deep depression[63] and psychoses.[64] Although mental illness is an amorphous and changing concept, one of the points that are not in dispute is the burgeoning number of diagnoses. The first time data about mental illness in the population were collected by the U.S. Bureau of the Census, the bureau relied on the New England Psychological Association's seven categories of mental illness: mania, melancholia, monomania, paresis, dementia, dipsomania, and epilepsia.[65] The first edition of the American Psychiatric Association's *Diagnostic and Statistical Manual of Mental Disorders* (*DSM*), published in 1952, had 60 diagnoses. By the time the 4th edition was published in 1994, its 866 pages contained 374 diagnoses.[66]

Disorders are occasionally subtracted as well. Homosexuality was deleted from the *DSM* in 1974 by a vote of 5,854 to 3,810.[67] However, the additions far exceed the deletions. Thousands of people are diagnosed with borderline personality disorder and PTSD, diagnoses that were not even in the *DSM* until 1980. *Neurosis* is no longer in the nomenclature, although the term is still widely used by insurance companies in making coverage decisions. Even today, the American mental health community uses a different set of categories of mental disorder[68] than the rest of the world.[69]

It would be unlikely for the United States to use a different set of categories for cancers than Europe. "Traditional" disabilities such as blindness or paraplegia are recognizable by laypeople and experts alike. These are generally visible, and their existence (as opposed to their consequences on an individual's ability to function) is usually not subject to dispute. Indeed, there are a few mental conditions that have been described for centuries and are described internationally: depression ("melancholia"),[70] schizophrenia ("dementia"), and bipolar disorder or manic depression ("mania" for the manic phases).

Even for relatively consistent diagnoses, the attribution of cause and the consensus on treatment have varied tremendously. Theories about the causes of depression and psychoses have alternated regularly over the years between attribution to biological causes and attribution to social causes.[71] Historically, apart from escaping the notion that insanity was a punishment for sin,[72] theories about causation have not progressed or developed much. The divisions between those who favor biological causation and those who look to social or environmental context have raged for 300 years:

> The division between William Battie and John Monro in the mid-eighteenth century, and that between "physicalists" such as Thomas Mayo and George Nesse Hill and "mentalists" such as Andrew Harper and Alexander Crichton at the turn of the nineteenth, hinged on whether madness was at root an organic disease or a psychic disorder—a debate which had a long future ahead of it, as has been made clear in Bonnie Blustein's and Michael Clark's analyses of late Victorian debates over mind and brain, psychiatry and neurology in America and Britain.[73]

In the early- and mid-18th century, "doctors considered madness a thing of the body."[74] By the end of the 18th century, with the advocacy of "moral treatment," it was considered a matter of mind and spirit. Sixty years later, the new consensus was that "all mental illness is brain disease."[75] Freud and his followers put an end to that theory until the 1980s. In 1990, President George Bush declared that the 1990s was the "Decade of the Brain." The debate about the origins of mental illness has been going on consistently for centuries. Followers of each school believe with great certainty that their answer is the final one, and they attack any opposition with virulence.

There are political and social consequences to many of the posited causes of mental illness. Biological models may contribute to the erasure of the conditions and context in which psychiatric disability occurs—the conditions and contexts, regardless of causation, that are associated or correlated with it. For example, for over 20 years, literally hundreds of studies associated serious mental disabilities with unemployment, a history of childhood sexual abuse, and battering and domestic violence. The public picture of mental illness, however, is biological, a disease of the brain. The decision as to whether mental illness is "biological" or "environmental" or a combination of both has major legal consequences. For example, as seen in *Alphonso v. Charity Hospital*, Lori Jean Alphonso's own treating psychiatrist testified that "her schizophrenia, a biological disease caused by chemical imbalances, was not and could not be aggravated by the trauma of rape."[76]

The erasure of connections between health problems and national social policies, business interests, and environmental conditions is hardly unique to psychiatric disabilities. The connection between deadly lung diseases and asbestos was purposely concealed for decades, as was the link between cancer and hazardous waste, nuclear testing, and smoking.[77] Social values collude in these concealments, preferring to see weakness, illness, and debility as localized in the individual or even the fault of the individual. We are suspicious and contemptuous of victims and are so caught up in individualism that the interconnectedness of health, environment, and violence is still a relatively new concept.

Although we are not willing to look to social causes for the origins of mental health problems, we are more than willing to look to mental health professionals for the answer to social problems and then to condemn them for their answers. The juggernaut of adolescent institutionalization[78] is in part the result of parents seeking to hand off difficult adolescents to professional caretakers.[79] Arguments rage over whether psychiatric diagnoses unduly pathologize normal behavior,[80] embody cultural and social stereotypes,[81] or unjustifiably medicalize and therefore operate to excuse immoral behavior and character defects.[82]

An example of a diagnosis often considered to pathologize normal behavior is oppositional defiant disorder, which is a "disorder of infancy, childhood, or adolescence."[83] The diagnostic criteria require a finding that a child or adolescent engages in

> a pattern of negativistic, hostile, and defiant behavior lasting at least six months during which four (or more) of the following are present:
>
> (1) often loses temper;
> (2) often argues with adults;
> (3) often actively defies or refuses to comply with adults' requests or rules;
> (4) often deliberately annoys people;
> (5) often blames others for his or her mistakes or misbehavior;
> (6) is often touchy or easily annoyed by others;

(7) is often angry or resentful; or

(8) is often spiteful or vindictive.[84]

As anyone who has a child or can be objective about his or her own childhood knows, this describes many adolescents, and the 6-month time requirement does not narrow the field. Although the diagnostic criteria specify that a criterion is met "only if the behavior occurs more frequently than is typically observed in individuals of comparable age and developmental level," this caveat is so subjective as to be almost useless. Similar controversies rage over the diagnosis of attention deficit hyperactivity disorder (ADHD) in children and the use of the drug Ritalin to control them. Is a child very active, or does he or she have ADHD? Are these two ways of describing the same child, each embodying a different kind of value judgment?

Some of the same questions that plague jurisprudence plague mental health studies. Do mental health professionals "create," "discover," or "interpret" mental illness in the way that judges are said to "create," "discover," or "apply" the law? When the Supreme Court held that the Constitution protects extended families against zoning regulations that would preclude their living together "precisely because the institution of the family is deeply rooted in this nation's history and tradition,"[85] the court transformed certain social traditions and phenomena, such as extended families living together, into the language of legal rights. Are psychiatrists and psychologists doing something analogous when they translate certain social phenomena into medical conditions?

Sometimes, interpreting social phenomena as psychological symptomatology is seen as helpful. It helps to explain the behaviors of soldiers returning from Vietnam, of refugees from wartime atrocities, or of children with histories of sexual abuse, and understanding their experiences and reactions may help society treat them with more compassion.[86] It is not entirely clear why these explanations have to come in medical terms, except that medical (especially psychiatric) terminology has assumed special credibility in society for explaining social phenomena.[87]

Other times, the psychiatric profession is seen as inappropriately medicalizing behavior for which people should take responsibility or behavior more appropriately described in nonmedical terms, such as "road rage," which may be destined for entry in the next edition of the *DSM*;[88] caffeine addiction; or child molestation. Profound differences exist as to whether addictions, sexual psychopathy, paraphilias, sociopathy, or personality disorders represent psychiatric disorders or issues of moral character. The dichotomy itself is revealing.

Examples of diagnoses that have been criticized as reflecting cultural and social stereotypes are current diagnoses of borderline personality disorder, premenstrual stress disorder, and histrionic personality disorder.[89] Although the *DSM-IV* states that there is similar prevalence in the latter disorder among female and male individuals, it also describes individuals with this diagnosis as people who, "without being aware of it, . . . often act out a role (*i.e.*, 'victim' or 'princess')."[90] Women, including mental health professionals, successfully fought the inclusion in the *DSM* of diagnoses such as self-defeating personality disorder.[91]

Personal Accounts From People With Psychiatric Diagnoses

The voices of those who have received diagnoses of mental illness are there to be heard. There is a vast, generally little known, and growing body of literature about the personal experiences of people who have had experiences in the mental health system. This includes authored books,[92] edited collections of accounts,[93] and first-person accounts that appear in each issue of *Psychiatric Services* (formerly *Hospital and Community Psychiatry*),[94] each year in the *Schizophrenia Bulletin,* and occasionally in other professional journals.[95] Although relatively more difficult to obtain, there are also hours of testimony before state legislatures and Congress, including testimony supporting the Americans With Disabilities Act (ADA) of 1990, and there are bulletins and newsletters produced by various groups of people with psychiatric diagnoses. Although they are rarely polled as a group, there have been a few surveys of people with psychiatric disabilities.[96] There is also a growing body of literature by relatives of people with psychiatric disabilities that offers additional insights on a level more personal than either the professional or legal literature.[97]

One of the first questions in my own survey asked people if they considered themselves to be substantially limited in one or more major life activities as a result of their diagnoses and, if so, to describe the limitations in their own words. The descriptions were strikingly similar. Although a few simply listed their diagnosis,[98] survey respondents of different occupations and income levels described problems with concentration and focus,[99] memory,[100] lack of energy,[101] exhaustion,[102] and difficulty sleeping.[103] Some described mood surges, fluctuations, or attacks of anxiety and panic. Several described hearing voices[104] or having hallucinations;[105] some said they were afraid;[106] and over and over again, people described their problems in terms of the inability to deal with stress.

Written accounts by people who had received mental health treatment used imagery to describe how their disabilities affected their lives—imagery that was strikingly different from the language of symptomatology and "poverty of thought." They described their conditions in different terms: "It felt as though I was living in a mine field; any additional stress and I would be blown apart,"[107] "a veteran of an unnamed war,"[108] "a soldier with battle fatigue,"[109] and "being sucked under by a powerful undertow."[110] The imagery is filled with metaphors of battle and natural disasters, of overwhelming and powerful forces beyond an individual's control. These metaphors are echoed by some mental health professionals,[111] but they are far from the majority. One survey respondent explicitly differentiated between her own interpretation and the likely interpretation of a mental health professional:

> A psychiatrist would diagnose me as having depression and generalized anxiety disorder. I believe that I have simply had a painful and often frightening life which has left me with realistic pain and elevated fear levels. Because of the fear, sometimes I'm not able to be in places where I might feel trapped (e.g., sometimes crowded rooms, restaurants, conference rooms with lots of people in them). Because of the pain problem, I'm often unable to associate with people in the usual cheerful way. People tend to pick on my mood, telling me to do something about it (either buck up or see a shrink); that makes me feel worse. I also sometimes feel guilty about exposing other people to my pain, which also makes it worse. I'm discriminated against in the workplace because I'm not perky, upbeat and optimistic but am sober and realistic. That makes me feel worse also. And when I feel bad enough, I just can't function at all: have trouble getting out of bed, even caring for myself.[112]

The nature of these experiences, and the question of who has the authority to describe them, has been the subject of debate for hundreds of years. Both people labeled as mentally ill and mental health professionals have questioned whether psychiatric disability has an independent, objective, discernible, factual existence of its own, or whether it is socially created. Regardless of its biological reality, mental illness clearly exists as a social identity. To be considered mentally ill by others— mental health professionals, friends, or the law—leads to an imposed identity that does not resonate with a person's own language or description of his or her experience.

Identity and Disability

One crucial distinction among people with disabilities is the extent to which the disability becomes a source of identity. Although many disability discrimination complaints received by the Equal Employment Opportunity Commission come from people with back problems, there is little indication that people with back problems consider themselves part of an identity group. There are few support groups, newsletters, or societies of people with back pain.

Conversely, some disabilities do become a source of personal identity. Among these, there is a further distinction to be made between people whose shared experience of disability is almost entirely negative and those for whom the disability is a source of positive identity. A decade ago, Susan Sontag remarked that people with cancer "evinced disgust at their disease and a kind of shame."[113] People with AIDS, amyotrophic lateral sclerosis, or cancer generally experience their conditions as wholly negative, as encroachments on their identity rather than a part of their identity, and want desperately to be cured. This is generally the case with disabilities that are commonly identified as "illnesses."

By contrast, some people who are deaf, who have mobility impairments, or who have received mental health treatment have made it clear that they do not want to be "cured" and fade into the mainstream. Instead, they want to be accepted and appreciated, to have society make room for them as they are.[114] For these people, social obstacles rather than disability are the primary source of suffering. Buttons and slogans, such as "Deaf Pride" and "Mad Pride," are displayed and worn. What is clear is that what is "disability" to some is an integral part of the identity of others. Even some who regard their psychiatric disabilities as illnesses to be controlled still describe the illnesses as central to their identity, with certain positive features that are difficult to surrender.[115]

At the same time, unlike people who are deaf or mobility impaired, the identity shared by some people who have been diagnosed with psychiatric disability comes from rejecting the diagnosis rather than embracing it. Although people who are actually deaf or mobility impaired may disagree with the social view that they should be "cured" or with the damaging stereotypes associated with being deaf or in a wheelchair, they do not deny that they are deaf or in a wheelchair. They have the same perception of their condition as the rest of society, if not of the social consequences of being this way. Their dispute is with the meaning ascribed to being deaf or mobility impaired, not with the existence of the category itself.

It is clear that throughout history, some people who have been diagnosed as mentally ill have rejected this imposed identity and the treatment that accompanies it. The rejection has taken the form of recasting what others label as illness as an emotional or spiritual experience, or as extraordinary stress, of resisting diagnosis as explanatory of experience, and especially of insisting that one's identity is more complex and far-reaching and that one's behavior, beliefs, values, and passions can have a source other than mental illness and express more than mental illness. The passionate resistances and insistences have in turn been used, both clinically and legally, as proof of the validity of the clinical and legal determination of mental illness: "patients" who "lack insight" into their mental illness are by definition the most ill of all, afflicted with a brain imbalance whose tragic consequences include the inability to recognize their own condition.

Whether mental disability is an identity imposed by others or claimed proudly and defiantly, it is clearly a far more socially encompassing and engulfing identity than that created by many other disabilities. It defines a person in a way that back problems[116] do not. As noted in chapter 1, mental illness includes negative associations about morality and character in a way not shared by other identity-establishing disabilities such as blindness, deafness, and mobility impairment. And whereas having AIDS or being HIV positive also is a socially encompassing identity with negative connotations, mental illness is considered amorphous, elusive, and capable of faking and malingering, which are not problems associated with a diagnosis of AIDS.

Race and Gender

It is also clear that unlike deafness, mobility impairment, or HIV seropositivity, race and gender play significant roles in how people experience psychiatric disability and in determining whether people will be perceived and treated by others as mentally ill. The ways in which women, African Americans, Hispanics, and Asians express and manifest what is called "craziness" speak eloquently to the political pressures and tensions of being female, black, Hispanic, or Asian in contemporary American society.

These stories appear as fragments in case studies, interviews, or essays in newsletters of former patients, but considered together they tell much about the interrelationship among race, gender, and ascriptions of craziness in society. For example, the authors of a letter to the *American Journal of Psychiatry* noted that

> while interviewing patients on the "homeless" ward of a hospital, we noticed an interesting similarity among the delusions exhibited by five psychotic African American patients: [one claimed he was actually "white" while the others] all recognized that they were black but each claimed to have been born white and then somehow transformed.[117]

Both the results of the survey and case law illustrate in innumerable ways the impossibility of abstracting disability discrimination from race or gender issues. One survey respondent with bipolar disorder wrote, "I am white and married to an Afro-American which in some weird way added to misconception of my psychiatric disability."[118] Interviews with black women at a community mental health center illustrate the poignancy of the battle against stereotypes. One woman's "symptoms" of schizophrenia included painting her face with "war paint." She explained why she did this, saying because I am at war with them. They see me on the streets late at night and they think I am a prostitute or something. But, I try to show them and explain that I am not, though they think I am.

Q: How does putting paint on your face change that?

A: I don't know, but then I don't look like a hooker. I get to explain that I am not what they think.[119]

Another woman at the same mental health treatment center was asked about her reactions to being discriminated against because of her skin color and being discriminated against because of her diagnosis. Her responses show a striking difference in her perceptions of herself and the nature of difference and discrimination:

Q: Do you ever get upset when people ... call you "black" in a bad way?

A: Yes ... but [that is] ignorant of them. I am no different "cause of my skin."

Q: Do you ever get upset when people call you "mental"?

A: Yes. I can't do anything about that except take my medicine and come [to the community treatment center.][120]

One discrimination case involved a white woman whose black supervisor called her "crazy" for wanting to date black men and for wanting to have a black child while in her 40s and who told coworkers that the white woman had been psychiatrically hospitalized because she had a fetish for black men.[121]

Much of the work in mental health practice is about adjustment and adaptation to the norm, even when the norm is outdated. One common complaint from women who have received mental health treatment is the extent to which adherence to old-fashioned feminine ideals is equated with mental health: "It was very sexist, like: she's wearing makeup today! Two thumbs up!"[122] I took a deposition in a case in which a female psychiatrist who said she did not have time to teach staff how to look for the warning signs of tardive dyskinesia ran a "group" for women patients on how to match their skin tones to the color of clothing they should be wearing.[123] One treatment plan in Alabama in the 1990s had as its only goal to teach a woman with a mental disability to use makeup, noting as one of the treatment "problems" that the woman did not like using makeup.[124]

For women, issues of childhood sexual abuse and adult sexual harassment are frequently inextricably intertwined with diagnoses of mental illness. For many, childhood sexual abuse seems to be connected with severe emotional difficulties later in life. For others, the desperation, neediness, and vulnerability of emotional disabilities translate into a willingness to trade exploitation and abuse for human contact. For others, being heavily medicated or in restraints clears the way for sexual assault.[125]

Some women are involuntarily committed for being in abusive relationships, no matter how they react to those relationships. If they stay in them, they may be committed. For example, one therapist admitted that she involuntarily committed a woman (very much against the will of the woman) because the woman's husband was abusing her, and the therapist believed that the woman was not taking sufficient steps to protect herself.[126] In another case, however, a husband arranged for his wife to be involuntarily committed because she left and took her children to a shelter for abused women.[127]

One conclusion became inescapable as I read literally hundreds of articles, survey responses, books, and essays by women who were diagnosed with mental disabilities. One of the most potent predictors of being able to "overcome" mental disability for a woman was that she had *not* suffered sexual abuse in childhood. The autobiographies of women with mental disabilities who "succeeded" in this society's terms, many of whom also adopted the medical model and portrayed their mental health professionals as helpful, described supportive families or, at least, not physically abusive families. The accounts of women who had been subject to repeated hospitalizations, many of whom are now receiving disability payments, who rejected the medical model and were skeptical if not terrified of mental health professionals often reflected a background of abuse at home. This "two-world" pattern is reflected in many other ways throughout the survey responses and is worth exploring at length.

Two Worlds: The Social Paradigm of "Cripples" and "Overcomers" Among People With Psychiatric Diagnoses

Although some of the survey respondents echoed themes and concerns identical to the people who testified before Congress, other respondents reported entirely different concerns. In contrast to people who testified before Congress, who complained that overfocusing on mental disability led to an underestimation of their abilities, a substantial number of survey respondents felt the opposite: that discrimination manifested itself in a refusal to accept that they were in fact struggling with real and devastating problems. The surveys, interviews, and books I studied led me to the conclusion that people with psychiatric disabilities within the United States are divided into two worlds and that Americans discriminate against one group in markedly different ways than they discriminate against the other.

The largest group of people with diagnoses of mental illness—even so-called "serious" mental illness like depression and bipolar disorder[128]—have primary identities, both self-perceived and confirmed by the world around them, that do not revolve around their psychiatric diagnoses. In fact, they may be among the vast majority of Americans whose psychiatric disability has not been diagnosed or treated.[129] For the most part, although not universally, people in the first group keep their diagnoses and treatments secret or at least private.[130] They "pass,"[131] often holding positions of enormous responsibility, sometimes treating, representing, sentencing, or committing people who are more publicly identified as mentally ill. Survey respondents included lawyers,[132] an engineer with a master's degree,[133] a university professor,[134] a certified public accountant,[135] several psychologists,[136] social workers,[137] and a former police officer.[138] The fact that people pass does not mean that they do not suffer immensely. For the most part, these people conceptualize their problems as primarily medical. They have an illness that although crucial in their lives, does not constitute their identity, which is constructed around profession, family, and life in the larger community. Although they may experience considerable discrimination or (more likely) constrain their conversation and actions out of fear of discrimination, they rarely construct these events as part of a larger political picture and almost never publicly join groups or organized movements designed to expose injustice and discrimination against people with mental disabilities. They are grateful to their treatment professionals and describe their families as supportive.

The second group of people are socially and publicly identified primarily through the label and experience of being a "mental patient." This category includes people who live in state psychiatric institutions, often because they have nowhere else to go, or in group homes or assisted-living facilities in the community; people who are supposed to receive mental health services and are officially recorded as clients of the state mental health system; people who receive state and federal disability benefits; and people who identify themselves as "consumers" of psychiatric services or "survivors" of psychiatric hospitalization. Paradoxically, the second group includes people who, after experiencing the identity of being a mental patient, have devoted their lives to rejecting that identity for themselves and others. For the most part, although far from universally,[139] these people lead marginalized lives in poverty, sometimes cycling miserably through institutions, jails, community facilities, and the streets. They are either ignored or treated with contempt, fear, or pity by the rest of society.[140]

For this second group of people, parsing out those aspects of their behavior, condition, and the way they are treated that are attributable to mental disability, as opposed to poverty, stigma, violence, marginalization, racism, and lack of medical care, is difficult. Many of the injustices that they suffer are a result of intertwining racism, disability, and poverty-based discrimination. For example, research repeatedly confirms that people with psychiatric disabilities who are members of ethnic or racial minorities have far greater employment difficulties than white people with psychiatric disabilities or people of color without psychiatric disabilities,[141] have much more difficulty obtaining basic health care,[142] and are treated far worse by the police.[143] Each of these difficulties—with employment, health care, and the police —is the subject of individual research studies, but for the people who live them, the unemployment, lack of health care, and police harassment combine to create an overwhelming social reality of cumulative, daily, exhausting difficulty.

The confluence of all of these prejudices not only requires much more strength and perseverance and resilience to survive on a daily basis but also serves to eliminate rather than support legal relief. A judge in a police discrimination or brutality case, for example, would not be interested in knowing that the plaintiff was in pain because she could not access medical care or had been denied treatment at the emergency room and could not afford medical care because she could not get a job. None of these things would be relevant to making out a case of discrimination against the police, even though the plaintiff's poverty, clothing, demeanor, and living situation might be crucial to the attitudes and conduct of the police. The law gives its remedies in particularized ways: race discrimination, age discrimination, disability discrimination. Neither race discrimination by itself nor disability discrimination by itself, however, adequately captures the situation of Junius Wilson, "a deaf black man [who] was accused of rape in 1925, castrated and locked up in a state mental hospital for 69 years . . . at some point state authorities realized he was neither mentally ill or retarded."[144] If Wilson had been black but not disabled, he might have been lynched or executed rather than institutionalized; if Wilson had been white and disabled, he would probably not have been charged with the crime in the first place and certainly would not have been castrated. It is the intersection of Wilson's race and disability that explains his fate, but there is still no race–disability discrimination claim under the law.

Neither gender discrimination nor disability discrimination alone accounts for the story of Terri Nichols, a deaf–mute employee of the U.S. Postal Service who was forced to submit to sex by her supervisor, the only supervisor where she worked who could sign.[145] As her distress over the sexual harassment and her fear of communicating the situation grew,[146] her marriage fell apart, and she broke down. Her supervisor made her submit to sex as a condition of granting her leave to deal with her emotional and marital problems.[147] The 9th Circuit Court's struggle to decide whether her breakdown was an injury due to sex discrimination or a health condition caused by work remediable only through the equivalent of workers' compensation was because her claim grew out of the intersection of sexual harassment and disability discrimination, an intersection the law is ill equipped to handle (although it describes the truths of many women's lives). Despite all that she had been through, Nichols was back at work two years later, a single mother with custody of her two children.[148] The strength, humor, resilience, and eloquence of people who have struggled with despair, terror, and death pour out in the case law, in responses to my survey, and in a remarkable and little-appreciated body of literature.

Although members of both the first and second groups write of their struggles with mental disability and society, the accounts are distinctly different. Robert Lowell,[149] William Styron,[150] Kay Jamison,[151] and others in the first group[152] have written individual accounts of their own experiences with illness. These accounts hardly ever include shared experiences of being a mental patient with identified other mental patients. Janet Gotkin,[153] Judi Chamberlin,[154] Huey Freeman,[155] and others in the second group[156] also write articulate accounts of how they and others like them, named and described, were treated as patients in the mental health system.[157] When people in the first category describe their experiences as patients, they distance themselves from other patients. The people who matter to them are those in the world they came from and to which they know they will return, not those in the mental patient world in which they have been forced to spend a temporary and usually extremely unpleasant interval. Thus, their identities have remained tied to their families, prior lives, and accomplishments, not their diagnoses.

Economic Class and Childhood Experiences

People in the second group, on the other hand, are in the "mental patient" world for the long haul. They identify the social contexts of poverty, racism, and the arrogance and cruelty of the mental health system and professionals as responsible for a great deal of what others believe to be symptoms of their mental illness and for the conditions of their lives in general. They are far more likely to place their personal circumstances in a political and social context and to see the need for civil rights laws protecting them from discrimination on the basis of disability than do people in the first group.

It is easy to conclude that these two categories simply mirror class and economic divisions in society. It is true that people who are upper-middle class and rich can keep their diagnoses private more easily, can buy certain kinds of accommodations so that they do not have to ask for them, and are more likely to have their aberrant behaviors interpreted in benign and nonpathological ways than can poor people. Their diagnoses are often voluntarily revealed after they have reached certain stature in society.[158] If they are extremely wealthy, they may avoid the mental health system altogether,[159] unless they commit criminal acts[160] or are perceived as wasting their presumptive heirs' inheritance.[161]

By contrast, poor people lead lives that are more publicly examined by social workers, welfare workers, police, and passersby. Behavior that middle-class people can hide in their houses becomes grounds for state intervention and labeling, and this labeling in turn produces stigma and discrimination that will pursue, hamper, and limit them for the rest of their lives. The inability to secure employment or housing because of a psychiatric record can produce stress and breakdown leading to further hospitalization, and so on, in a disastrous cycle that terminates finally in bleak poverty on the disability rolls. It is impossible to understand discrimination on the basis of mental disability without understanding how this issue is enmeshed in those of class, race, and gender.

To conclude that the difference between the two worlds is simply an economic or class division, however, would be misleading. The class explanation is not all encompassing. Janet Gotkin, Judi Chamberlin, Doug Cameron, Leonard Roy Frank, David Oaks, and other writers in the second group[162] were children of the middle class. One of the most famous writers in the second group is Kate Millett, who wrote *The Loony Bin Trip*[163] about her experiences in the mental health system. In fact, most people who seek radical reform or abolition of institutions and civil commitment come from middle- or upper-class backgrounds, from Mrs. Packer and Clifford Beers[164] to the present day. It is likely that expectations created by their class status fueled their outrage at the way they were treated, and middle-class assumptions may permit them to believe that their writing and political activism can and will lead to change. For example, David Oaks, a prominent activist and clearly a member of the second group, was in his senior year at Harvard when he went to Phillips Brooks House, "which is a social service agency for Harvard students. I said, 'Look, you should have something about mental patients' rights in here. It's terrible in those places.' One of the women said, 'Let's meet for lunch,' which we did. . . ."[165] In addition, the fact that a substantial number of children of upper-middle-class and wealthy families end up in the second category, institutionalized or in board or case homes or on disability benefits, was the catalyst for the formation of the powerful National Alliance for the Mentally Ill.

Furthermore, many poor and lower-middle-class people "pass," despite enormous internal suffering and behavior, which, if discovered, would surely result in commitment. For example, many people who cut or burn themselves on a regular basis are employed as teachers, insurance salespeople, and clerks.[166]

The dichotomy between the two categories can be considered in part a dichotomy based on class. However, it may also be explained in part by the different childhood experiences of people in the two groups. Family and personal relationships are pivotal in everyone's lives, but they seem to be even more crucial in determining the life paths of people with mental disabilities. Kay Jamison, a psychiatrist with bipolar disorder and coauthor of the most respected text on bipolar disorder, dedicates her book to her mother, as someone who gave her life not once but countless times;[167] Tracy Thompson, a successful journalist who struggled with depression, writes that visitors to her family were struck by "the degree to which I played a starring role, by how much the father I adored also doted on me."[168]

On the other hand, women with the same diagnoses whose life stories involve repeated institutionalizations, suicide attempts, substance abuse, and generally being enmeshed in the mental health system often report treatment in childhood so grotesque, violent, and chaotic[169] that a psychiatric subspecialty has developed to support therapists who are traumatized simply by hearing these stories.[170] Far from being doted on by her father, one woman told the following story from her childhood:

> I was only six, I think, when he started coming in my room at night. One day I tried to fight back and he took my puppy and bashed in his head with a rock and told me that if I didn't shut up he'd do the same thing to me.[171]

This theme is repeated in other accounts:

> I saw my father kicking the dog across the room. That dog was my world. I went and cuddled the dog. He was very angry. There was a lot of yelling. He spun me around and called me a whore and a bitch. . . . He put me against the wall. Things went white. I couldn't move. I was afraid I'd break in two. Then I started to go numb. I thought: you really are going to die.[172]

What is odd is that the women with diagnoses of mental illness who report horrors from their past are frequently disbelieved, although such child abuse is reported virtually daily in the newspapers and it is confirmed in cases involving termination of parental rights[173] and domestic abuse.

"Overcomers" and "Cripples"

Whatever the origins of the dichotomy, it clearly exists, as reflected in surveys, literature, and case law. It can be usefully analogized in some respects to two categories referred to in the disability rights movement: cripples and overcomers.[174] The *overcomer* "learns to deny her disability and frequently disassociates herself from her own disability or from other people with disabilities."[176] Because mental disabilities are not visible, most overcomers with diagnoses of mental illness keep them private, so they are neither regarded as "inspirational" nor "applauded for not giving in to personal constraints and for 'conquering' handicaps" in the same way as are people with visible physical disabilities. In the case of overcomers who reveal their diagnoses, the response is often either that the person could not have been very disabled or that the person has been "cured" by the very psychiatric community that some overcomers credit and others criticize harshly.

The *cripple* is "assumed to be unable to work, and her subsequent failure to produce is interpreted as proof of her inferiority. She engages in little social activity, bears what is seen as a bleak existence, and is socially devalued."[175] The difference between the physical disability model of the cripple and the corresponding psychiatric disability model is that the physical cripple is "not morally blamable" for her circumstances, and society rarely questions that "Jerry's kids" are indeed disabled ("Come on, you could throw those crutches away and play rugby if you just put your mind to it"). In fact, as reflected in telethons and the March of Dimes, society often mixes its revulsion for people with severe physical disabilities with pity and charity, two attitudes rarely expressed toward people with severe psychiatric disabilities.

The Common Experience of Discrimination

As a society, American attitudes and reactions reinforce both of these categories. Society treats the second group, the "cripples," as though their episodes of disability are permanent and chronic, often fulfilling a social prophecy by not permitting people in this group the opportunity to prove otherwise. Rather, they are institutionalized because of a lack of community housing, and attempts to provide community housing are fought bitterly by neighborhoods. Jobs are scarce, and vocational rehabilitation is patronizing and absurd.[177] The complaint of those in the second world is that people intervene too quickly, giving them no chance to "weather the storm," to recover for themselves. When asked "What do you want other people to know about psychiatric disability, perceptions of psychiatric disability, discrimination, or law that I should include?" one respondent answered that for many people, "Crisis intervention is not always welcome, needed, or appreciated. Make sure there is truly a CRISIS with the 'psychiatrically disabled' person before taking extreme action!"[178] People in the second group feel that society overlabels them and damages their chances of navigating the storm by pathologizing both them and the storm, by medicating them into oblivion, and by institutionalizing them. The talents and potential of these individuals are ignored and denied. Survey respondents repeatedly told of being actively discouraged by mental health and vocational professionals and staff from setting their sights too high, saying

> the people who are the LEAST sympathetic, surprisingly, are the workers in the hospitals I have been in. They openly make fun of the patients right in front of us. They have told me, "Why are you even trying to go to college? You will never make it." I have been told I would never get a job, so I should just go on disability. I have been holding this current job for over three months, and I held down the previous job for over six months (the previous one was a seasonal job).[179]

* * *

> My vocational rehabilitation program . . . refused to let me take a civil service exam for a para-professional position that I was interested in and overqualified for [respondent is a certified public accountant].[180]

For people in the second group, the disability obscures all other social judgments about them. Society sees only the diagnosis and not the struggle, with its victories and setbacks; every behavior, emotion, and expression becomes a "symptom" of one kind or another, and the human being who is happy, sad, angry, hopeful, or discouraged is lost.

On the other hand, society treats the first group, the overcomers, as though their success and achievement are also permanent and chronic, erasing or minimizing both their episodes of disability and the struggle that they undergo to reach those achievements. One of the most consistent themes in the accounts of the first group is that their friends and colleagues and sometimes even their families ignored, denied, or were silent about their clearly manifested symptoms, discouraged them from identifying those symptoms as mental illness, and even tried to keep them from seeking treatment.[181] One survey respondent wrote that the reactions of her friends and family to a diagnosis of bipolar disorder, which required "many different medications to stop crying, feelings of self-hatred, worry, and fear" was to tell her to "just shake it off," or "get busy, you will feel better."[182] Another wrote that

> when my husband was unable to work due to mental health problems his family refused to acknowledge his inability to hold a job and at one point requested that I

threaten to leave him so that he would go to work. When I refused, they became angry at me. . . . There were several incidents where family and my therapist encouraged me to leave my husband because of his mental health problems. I felt isolated and abandoned myself. Eventually I became clinically depressed myself.[183]

One of the most striking aspects of the survey responses was the percentage of people who described themselves as disabled but said that other people did not regard them as so, saying things such as "even the people who know of my psychiatric history do not know what a struggle it is for me to maintain my balance."[184] Another wrote "Friends and family—they don't understand my illness/disability—they think I am getting away with something—that there is nothing wrong with me."[185]

Some people in the first group recognize that their family and friends were trying to save them from a descent into the shame and stigma of the second group but believe that the resulting delay in seeking help might have jeopardized their jobs and even their lives. The overcomers, once they do seek treatment or are dragged into treatment, complain consistently about the infantilizing, paternalistic way that they are treated. A recurring theme is to criticize mental health professionals who see them as or are actively trying to convert them into members of the second group, which they emphatically reject, and to praise mental health professionals who "save" them from the world of institutionalization and lifelong disability and dependence. They do not pause to consider that their own generalizations about the people in the second group might also be mistaken.

Both groups have a lot in common. Both emphasize the role that discrimination plays in causing emotional breakdowns. For both, the damage and discrimination arise from society's assumption that mental disability is a static condition. Mental disability is constructed as preexisting, ongoing, and unvarying; discrimination is conceptualized as a reaction to manifested conduct or symptoms. Survey responses challenge this model. First, discrimination is a reaction to the knowledge that someone has a diagnosis or is taking medication, not to behavior or conduct. Second, the discrimination causes real emotional devastation. Over and over, people who were struggling and coping are pushed over the edge into a breakdown by acts of discrimination.[186] One woman whose medication was not working, making her slower at work, was fired as she was changing medications: "I was devastated. I ended up in the hospital psych isolation room on a suicide watch."[187] Another respondent who was not permitted to student teach after it was discovered that she was taking medication wrote, "I had a breakdown after they wouldn't let me student teach. Thought I would never be anything—hopeless—lasted 1½ years."[188] In the case law, there are repeated references to the deterioration in plaintiffs' mental states after being fired,[189] and in a number of cases, the plaintiff's treating professionals urgently recommended a return to work as soon as possible as being the best course for the individual's mental health.[190]

The harmful, damaging, and destroying effects of discrimination are swallowed up by the psychiatric diagnosis; this is all too evident in case law as well. All damage, whatever the cause, is attributed to the disability rather than to events in the person's life. I heard a psychiatrist assert that an 18-year-old girl who was removed from her parents' custody at the age 10 because her father began raping and beating her when she was 3 years old had a personality disorder that was biologically "hardwired" by the age of 2 and that the abuse was essentially irrelevant to her disorder.[191]

The first group of people is making substantial strides at overcoming disability discrimination because they conform to general social expectations in identifying their mental disability as primarily medical and located in themselves alone. As discussed in the chapters ahead, if mental disabilities are not identified as primarily medical or biological or if they are described in terms of personal interactions, they are rarely seen by courts as disabilities at all.[192]

People in the second category are doing better in the courts. Because plaintiffs in these cases are often institutionalized, their identities as "disabled individuals" are more stable and accepted. As long as they stay within the legal, political, and rhetorical boundaries of the social ghettoes that have been created for them, they can get legal relief for the worst aspects of their treatment.[193] At the same time, most other aspects of their lives are deteriorating: Legal services have been cut drastically, welfare ended, housing programs slashed, and Supplemental Security Income and Medicaid threatened with cuts.

That may be one reason why the people who testified in favor of the ADA were all from the second group—people whose primary social identification revolved around their mental disability.[194] The Ira Magaziners,[195] Mike Wallaces, and Patty Dukes of America did not step forward to testify in favor of the ADA. This was in marked contrast to people with physical disabilities, who came forward from all classes and categories to testify in favor of the ADA. One of the most moving personal testimonies relating to experiences of discrimination on the basis of disability was given by Rep. Tony Coelho (D-CA), who has epilepsy and was shamed and discriminated against as an adolescent because of it.[196] Although Sen. Lawton Chiles (D-Fla.) had struggled with depression before leaving the U.S. Senate, he did not come back to tell his colleagues about it.[197] Although Chiles was elected governor of Florida after revealing that he had taken Prozac for depression, the Republican candidate for lieutenant governor publicly raised questions about his stability and warned that Chiles might commit suicide in office.[198]

The reality that unifies the people in both groups, and comes through in the books, the testimony, and the survey results, is that psychiatric disability involves episodes of crisis and inability to function, alternating with much longer periods of genuine functioning, achieving, and existence indistinguishable from most other people's existence. As one survey respondent summed up,

> some people think I'm crazy (psychiatric labels). Some of my friends think they're crazier than I am (true) and people at work think I'm about as crazy as they are (I think some of them are crazier). I think our civilization drives everyone crazy and it's best to regard everyone with caution.[199]

One central truth of psychiatric disabilities is that, for most people, crisis alternates with productive functioning. Another truth is that for perhaps even more people, crisis coexists with what society would call productive functioning. Our classmates, colleagues, and cousins may be suicidal, or cutting themselves, or hearing voices, and are continuing to go to work, be mothers and fathers, and get good grades.[200] People understand fairly well the possibility of alternating or coexisting crisis and functioning.

Yet when a person is taken to the emergency room or the psychiatric ward or when an employer or college dean discovers this has happened, these private crises receive a public label, and depending on what happens at the emergency room or the psychiatric ward and depending on how the employer or dean reacts, the person starts on the road that leads to membership in the second world as a client of the mental health system or a recipient of disability benefits. It does not have to be this way. It would be nice to think that the ADA and the Rehabilitation Act of 1973 would protect the person from the stereotypical assumptions of the employer and the dean, but often, the judge does not understand either.

The economic, mental health, and legal structures, however, cannot accommodate the central truth of alternating or concurrent crisis and functioning at all. The U.S. legal system, mental health system, and labor market are marked by a static and dichotomous vision: One is either disabled or not, and once identified as disabled, residence in the category is presumed permanent. There is no place for the complexities and contradictions of people's real lives. As one survey respondent wrote when asked what he would want other people to know about mental disability, "I don't know, give us a break, but I don't want a break all the time . . . just when I need it . . . so how could anybody know?"[201]

If "they" who are socially identified as mentally ill, the people in the second group, struggle toward inclusion as "we" or resist being categorized as "they," the social, legal, and mental health systems are unforgiving. Victories and progress in the struggles with sadness or mania are either punished as proving that the struggle was faked or the problems illusory or nonexistent,[202] or bring on social expectations that the struggle is over—the disability benefits are cut off, the Section 8 housing benefits ended. Defeats, by the same token, are also not seen as temporary but as permanent. One bad episode can mean the termination of parental rights, an involuntary commitment, or involuntary medication. It is all or nothing in American society's concept of mental disability, and people who try to insist that they are both badly damaged and very competent are not heard.

Conclusion

The people in both groups endorse the description of life as a complex mixture of competence and incompetence, strength and vulnerability, that is always a struggle. The people in the first group see it as their personal task to fit in with the world. The people in the second group, when they have the strength and the voice, construct the problem as social and contextual, related to poverty and violence, and ask that the social, mental health, and legal systems accommodate themselves to that reality rather than squeeze the individuals into the dichotomy of complete fitness or utter debilitation.

Disability discrimination law, with its requirements of "reasonable accommodation," represents the beginning of a social understanding of how disability discrimination operates. We are beginning to realize that inviting mobility-impaired people into our buildings may involve changing the building by adding a ramp; arranging to meet them at the building requires having buses with lifts or adapted vans or taxis willing to pick up a disabled person. If we assure deaf people that we want them to participate in the political process, we must have interpreters or learn sign language ourselves. Society is just beginning to reach these understandings when it comes to physical disabilities (and the most socially acceptable ones, at that). We have little or no understanding of the corollary social adaptations that are necessary to fully integrate people with mental disabilities into our society. This is because the dominant languages of the mental health profession and the law make it difficult to conceptualize people with mental disabilities in any other way than as dysfunctional, disconnected, symptomatic individuals whose diagnosis promises little hope for recovery, at best amelioration through medication.

What are the equivalents of ramps and sign language interpreters for people with mental disabilities? How can we adapt our society to welcome them as full citizens? Necessary social adaptations involve changing isolation and exclusion into connection—ending segregation in institutional settings; transforming the loneliness of board, care, and community residential facilities into homes where people can live with their loved ones and families; and understanding that for women, especially, ties to children should not be ruptured because of a diagnosis or hospitalization. These kinds of lessons about inclusion and connection begin in childhood, not only with parents teaching that it is wrong to mock others who are different but with schools paying more than lip service to the concept. Instead, schools themselves try to exclude students who are different, and some are slow to punish the athletes and others who are bullies and tormentors.

We need to accompany the biological rhetoric of mental illness with examinations of social context. A woman who cuts herself may seem appalling until you understand that her father did much more appalling things to her. The language of denigration and objectification of people as "borderlines" or "chronics" translates into the practice of coercion and force when mentally disabled people are restrained in institutions, shot by frightened police, and medicated involuntarily. Like curb cuts (small concrete ramps at sidewalk–street intersections), these accommodations might benefit many people in society beyond those who have mental disabilities by enhancing our respect for humanity and permitting us to slow down enough to appreciate it.

Endnotes

1. William Styron, *Darkness Visible* (New York: Random House, 1990).
2. Janet and Paul Gotkin, *Too Much Anger, Too Many Tears* (New York: Quandrangle Books, 1975).
3. Trudy B. (personal communication, Mar. 5, 1998). Trudy B. is a member of Fellowship House, Coral Gables, FL. Permission to interview and tape obtained. Transcript on file with author.
4. Yolanda H. (personal communication, Mar. 22, 1998). Also a member of Fellowship House. *See* note 3.
5. One of the first of these books, and still one of the most famous, was Susan Sontag's *Illness as Metaphor* (New York: Farrar, Straus & Giroux, 1978), which was prompted by her own diagnosis with cancer. At about the same time, Stewart Alsop's *Stay of Execution* (Philadelphia: Lippincott, 1973) was published. Oliver Sacks's *A Leg to Stand On* (New York: Harper & Row, 1984) is a neglected classic. *See also* Allen Widome, *The Doctor the Patient: The Personal Journey of A Physician With Cancer* (Miami, FL: Editech, 1989).
6. Robert Coles, "The Way of the Transgressor," in *The Mind's Fate* 2d ed. (Boston: Little, Brown, 1995):35.
7. Richard Schwartz, Peter Cohen, Norman Hoffman, and John Leeks, "Self-Harm Behaviors (Carving) in Female Adolescent Drug Abusers," *Clin. Ped.* 28 (1989):340–346.
8. Villanova v. Abrams, 972 F.2d 792 (7th Cir. 1992). Judge Posner scolded the plaintiff's lawyers for making fun of these reports, saying that the language was no more "un-

lovely" than legal language. Legal language is awkward and complex but rarely so hurtful.

9. S. M. (personal communication, Sept. 1998).

10. Many of Emily Dickinson's poems parallel the writings of women who have been in the mental health system. She wrote "Pain . . . has an element of Blank. . . . / It cannot recollect when it begun" (Poem 650) and "There is a pain . . . so utter . . . / It swallows substance up . . . / Then covers the Abyss with Trance / So Memory can step / Around . . . across . . . upon it" (Poem 559). These poems echo the words of women who have been diagnosed with dissociative identity disorder. *See also* Poems 642, 937, and 967, Emily Dickinson, *The Complete Works of Emily Dickinson* (Boston: Little, Brown, 1924).

11. Alphonso v. Charity Hospital, 413 S.2d 982, 988 (La. App. 1982).

12. *Id.* at 984. A number of sources discuss self-injury as a language for women who have been silenced by physical or sexual abuse.

13. ALA. CODE Sec. 1-1-1(5) (Michie, 1998). Note that all of these statutes are currently applicable, despite the date of publication of the volume in which the statute appears. Statutory changes appear in cumulative supplements, which have also been checked. In addition, the statutes have been checked against computer databases on LEXIS. Georgia defines 24 terms at the beginning of its legal code; the 9th term also defines *lunatic, insane,* and *non compos mentis* to mean "persons of unsound mind," O.C.G.A. 1-3-3(9) (1999).

14. ALA. CODE Sec. 30-2-1-(a)(8) (Michie, 1989); N.C. 5.0-5.1 (1999).

15. The Uniform Partnership Act is a model statute regulating partnerships and developed by the National Conference of Commissioners on Uniform State Laws, which has been adopted by every state except Louisiana. Section 32(a) permits dissolution by decree of the court if a partner "has been declared a lunatic in any judicial proceedings or is shown to be of unsound mind." *See, e.g.,* M.R.S. 312-A(1)(A); MD. REV. STAT. 9-603(A)(1); MASS. GEN. LAWS ANN., ch. 108A § 32(1)(A) (West, 1999).

16. MONT. CODE ANN., Sec. 28-2-203 (West, 1999).

17. ALASKA STAT. Sec. 06.05.180, Banking Code, Powers of Trustee, LEXIS Law (1998). The legislature retained the word *spendthrift* from the previous statute.

18. MISS. CODE ANN., Sec. 99-13-1 (West, 1999). This statute was passed in 1984.

19. MISS. CODE ANN., Sec. 41-21-43 (West, 1999).

20. CAL. WELF. & INST. CODE § 7294 (1999).

21. C.R.S. 27-10.5-135(2) (1999).

22. The Model Penal Code provides that

"(1) a person is not responsible for criminal conduct if at the time of such conduct as a result of mental disease or defect he lacks substantial capacity either to appreciate the criminality of his conduct or to conform his conduct to the requirements of the law; and

(2) as used in this Article, the terms 'mental disease or defect' do not include an abnormality that is manifested only by repeated criminal or otherwise antisocial conduct."

Section 4.01, Model Penal Code (American Law Institute, 1985). *See also* Ford v. Wainwright, 477 U.S. 399 (1986) (holding that the 8th Amendment prohibits the execution of someone who is insane without defining *insanity*).

23. The test for incompetence to stand trial is whether the person is able to understand the charges against him or her and to assist counsel in his or her defense, Dusky v. United States, 362 U.S. 402 (1960).

24. An individual must have "a physical or mental impairment of such severity that [he or she] is not only unable to do previous work but cannot, considering age, education and work experience, engage in any other kind of substantial gainful work which exists in the national economy," 42 U.S.C.A. Sec. 1382c(3)(B) (1999, suppl. pamphlet). The

impairment must be one that will either result in death or be expected to last for a continuous period of not less than 12 months, 42 U.S.C.A. Sec. 1382c(3)(a) (1999, suppl. pamphlet).

25. To receive Social Security disability benefits, an individual must demonstrate "an inability to engage in any substantially gainful activity by reason of any medically determinable physical or mental impairment," 42 U.S.C.A. Sec. 423(d)(1)(A) (1999; Cum. Annual Pocket Pt.).

26. The ADA defines *disability* as a physical or mental impairment that substantially limits one or more major life activities, a record of such an impairment, or being perceived as having such an impairment, 42 U.S.C.A. Sec. 12102(2) (1995).

27. Deering's CA. CIV. CODE Sec. 39(a), 40 (LEXIS Law, 1999, pocket suppl.); IDAHO CODE Sec. 32-107 (Michie, 1996); MONT. CODE ANN. Sec. 28-2-203 (West, 1999).

28. State v. Griffin, 570 P.2d 1067 (Ariz. 1977).

29. Florez v. Sargeant, 917 P.2d 250 (Ariz. 1996).

30. *Id.*

31. State v. Griffin, 570 P.2d 1067 (Ariz. 1977).

32. *See* Jackson v. Indiana, 406 U.S. 715, 720, note 2 (1972) (Indiana's use of the term *insane* refers to "incompetence to stand trial").

33. Dusky v. United States, 362 U.S. 402 (1960); Pate v. Robinson, 383 U.S. 375 (1966).

34. Mary L. Durham and John Q. Lafond, *Back to the Asylum: The Future of Mental Health Law and Policy in the United States* (New York: Oxford University Press, 1992).

35. Colman v. Notre Dame Convalescent Home, 968 F.Supp. 809, 812 (D. Conn. 1997).

36. Miller v. Runyon, 77 F.3d 189 (7th Cir. 1996).

37. Freeman v. City of Inglewood, No. 96-55270 (9th Cir. May 16, 1997) (at a pretrial conference, the judge asked for a briefing on the issue of "whether, as a matter of fact, a so-called post traumatic stress disorder [PTSD] is a disability within the ADA, which is also a question of law"); Al-Jund v. Oswald, 1997 U.S. District, LEXIS 15431 (W.D. N.Y. Oct. 2, 1997); *see also* Venezia v. United States, 884 F.Supp. 919, 924 (D. N.J. 1995) (referring to the "so-called" PTSD in rejecting ineffective assistance of the counsel claim for counsel's failure to explore the defendant's incompetence due to PTSD).

38. Doe v. New York University, 666 F.2d 761, 771 (2nd Cir. 1981) ("Borderline personality disorder is a serious psychiatric problem that is extremely difficult to cure"). This case is discussed at greater length in chapter 7.

39. In re Rosell, 547 A.2d 180, 182 (D.C.App. 1988); In re Elizabeth M., 514 N.W.2d 424 (Wisc. App. 1993).

40. Matter of Guynn, 437 S.E.2d 532 (N.C.App. 1993). ("Borderline personality disorder is an emotional illness which has significantly and detrimentally affected her ability to care for her daughter. . . . This illness will continue throughout the daughter's minority and as a result the mother will never be able to provide a stable home for her child.")

41. Tardi v. Henry, 571 N.E.2d 1020 (Ill. App. 1991).

42. People v. Eckhardt, 509 N.E.2d 1361, 1374 (Ill. App. 1997); U.S. v. Wood, 628 F.2d 554, 568 (D.C. Cir. 1977) (the dissenting judge quoted testimony of a psychiatrist that Wood had a "severe borderline personality disorder" and "was on the boundary between personality disorder and mental illness").

43. Ben Bursten, *Beyond Psychiatric Expertise* (Springfield, IL: Charles C Thomas, 1984) at 7. Bursten was not the first psychiatrist to warn of the dangers of social dependence on psychiatrists to answer what are basically social questions. The most famous book of this kind is Jonas Robitscher's *The Powers of Psychiatry* (Boston, MA: Houghton-Mifflin, 1980). More recently, Dr. Peter Kramer raised similar questions in *Listening to Prozac* (New York: Viking Press, 1993).

44. Kansas v. Hendricks, 521 U.S. 346, 358 (1997).

45. 10 OKL. ST. 7006-1.1(A)(13) (1999).

46. ALA. CODE 30-20-1(8) (Michie, 1989); Deering's CA. CODE ANN., CA. FAM. CODE 2312 (1999); MD. FAMILY CODE ANN. 11-112 (1999); N.Y.C.L.S. DOM REL. § 141 (1999).

47. Robert Coles, "A Young Psychiatrist Looks at His Profession," in *The Mind's Fate: A Psychiatrist Looks at His Profession* 2nd ed. (Boston: Little, Brown, 1995).

48. *International Classification of Impairments, Disabilities, and Handicaps* (ICIDH) (New York: World Health Organization, 1980) at 47.

49. *Id.* at 143.

50. *Id.* at 183.

51. A. Engelberg, Ed., *Guides to the Evaluation of Permanent Impairment* 3d ed. (Chicago, IL: American Medical Association, 1988). This all-important book is used to determine workers' compensation and disability awards in most states. For a fascinating review of the *Guides, see* Ellen Smith Pryor, "Book Review: Flawed Promises: A Critical Evaluation of the AMA's Guides to the Evaluation of Permanent Impairment," *Harvard Law Rev.* 103 (1990):964.

52. This definition is found in the *Guides'* glossary and defines *impairment.*

53. For example, the *Guides* also define *impairment* as "an alteration of an individual's health status that is assessed by medical means," *id.* at 2.

54. *Id.*

55. Deborah Stone, *The Disabled State* (Philadelphia: Temple University Press, 1984) at 110.

56. *See* note 51.

57. Joel Dvoskin, former director of Forensic Services and former acting director of the Office of Mental Health in the State of New York, wrote a short and powerful essay questioning the utility of personality disorder diagnoses, particularly in the prison setting. Joel Dvoskin, "Sticks and Stones: The Abuse of Psychiatric Diagnosis in Prison," *J. of the Calif. All. for the Mentally Ill* 20 (1997):20–21. He is in good company. Robert Coles wrote that there is simply not enough knowledge to use terms such as *disease* and *illness,* saying that "in the face of such uncertainties and ambiguities, modesty on the part of psychiatrists and a certain hesitation to talk about 'diseases' and their 'causes,' as other doctors are wont to do, might even be 'therapeutic' for beleaguered patients and their relatives, who deserve more than nervously authoritative fiats, and for those clinicians who have to contend with what are, finally, life's complexities," Robert Coles, "The Case of Michael Wechsler," in Robert Coles, *The Mind's Fate: A Psychiatrist Looks at His Profession* 2nd ed. (Boston: Little, Brown, 1995). Sandra Bloom, another psychiatrist, noted that "we had termed these patients 'borderlines' [and] 'hysterics'— all a way of saying that our helping efforts were thanklessly frustrated," *Creating Sanctuary: Toward a Sane Society* (New York: Routledge, 1997) at 136.

58. Bruce G. Link, "Understanding Labeling Effects in the Area of Mental Disorders: An Assessment of the Effects of Expectations of Rejection," *Amer. Soc. Rev.* 52 (1987):96, citing to Bruce G. Link, "Mental Patient Status, Work, and Income: An Examination of the Effects of a Psychiatric Label," *Amer. Soc. Rev.* 47 (1982):202.

59. *See* the Introduction and chapter 1. This includes laws and regulations relating to voting, driver's licenses, security clearances, acceptance into the military, and gun ownership.

60. *See* chapter 7.

61. *See* chapter 5.

62. The diagnosis of "caffeine intoxication" is in section 305.90 of the *Diagnostic and Statistical Manual of Mental Disorders* 4th ed. (*DSM-IV*; Washington, DC: American Psychiatric Association, 1994). The diagnosis of "nicotine dependence" is found in section 305.10 in the same manual.

63. The coding for major depressive disorder is somewhat complex: General information is found at section 296.3x; explanations for how the therapist fills in the fifth digit are found elsewhere in the *DSM.*

64. The section concerning "Schizophrenia and Other Psychotic Disorders" comprises pages 273–315 of the *DSM*.

65. Center for Mental Health Services, *Speaking With a Common Language: Past, Present and Future Data Standards for Managed Behavioral Healthcare* (July 1995) at 1. These categories correspond roughly to bipolar disorder, depression, obsessive–compulsive disorder, organic brain damage, schizophrenia, alcoholism, and epilepsy. Individuals with epilepsy were committed to psychiatric institutions until well into the 1960s and early 1970s in this country, *see, e.g.,* Heryford v. Parker, 396 F.2d 393 (10th Cir. 1968).

66. *DSM* (Washington, DC: American Psychiatric Association, 1952); *DSM-IV* 4th ed. (Washington, DC: American Psychiatric Association, 1994).

67. Paula J. Caplan, *They Say You're Crazy* (Reading, MA: Addison-Wesley, 1995) at 56. The diagnosis was replaced with "ego-dystonic homosexuality," which means that homosexuality was still a mental illness if the homosexual individual was unhappy or uncomfortable with his or her sexual preference, *id.*

68. *DSM-IV* (American Psychiatric Association).

69. The general manual used throughout the world and in some U.S. studies is the *International Classification of Diseases and Related Health Problems* (*ICD*), currently in its 10th edition. It has been approved by the 190-member nations of the World Health Organization and consists of 21 chapters that deal with different groups of medical conditions. Mental and behavioral disorders are classified in chapter 5. Many researchers in the United States use these classifications.

70. "Depression, for example, was studied quite systematically in fifth century B. C. Greece," Charles Kiesler and Celeste G. Simpkins, *The Unnoticed Inpatient Majority in Psychiatric Patient Care* (New York: Plenum Press, 1993) at 12; Roy Porter, Ed., *Medicine: A History of Healing* (New York: Barnes & Noble, 1997).

71. Roy Porter, *id.*; Sandra Bloom, *Creating Sanctuary: Toward a Sane Society* (New York: Routledge 1997) at 136.

72. W. F. Bynum, Roy Porter, and Michael Shepherd, Eds., *The Anatomy of Madness: Essays in the History of Psychiatry* Vol. I. (London: Tavistock, 1985) at 8–9. ("They [physicians] regarded as the greatest leap forward their specialty had ever made the view, gaining ground amongst doctors from the late Renaissance, that witchcraft and 'possession' were not, after all, authentic acts of the devil, but rather symptomatic of bodily or mental disease.") This attribution of mental illness to possession and sin had been a dominating viewpoint for many centuries. The New Testament appears to refer to a person with epilepsy or mental illness as possessed by evil spirits. In the early Middle Ages, the equation of madness with sin was most prominently reflected in the publication of "Malleus Malificarum," which attributed madness to control by the devil.

73. *Id.* at 12.

74. Roy Porter, *id.* at 147.

75. *Id.* at 151.

76. 413 S.2d 982, 987 (La. App. 1982).

77. *See, e.g.,* Susan Griffin, *A Chorus of Stones* (New York: Doubleday, 1995); Mitchell Lathrop, "Tobacco-Related Litigation: How It May Impact the World's Insurance Industry," *Conn. Ins. Law Journal* 3 (1996):305, 313; Paul Brodeur, *Outrageous Misconduct: The Asbestos Industry on Trial* (New York: Pantheon Books, 1995); Jonathon Harr, *A Civil Action* (New York: Random House, 1995).

78. *See* Louise Armstrong, *And They Call It Help: The Psychiatric Policing of America's Children* (Reading, MA: Addison-Wesley, 1993); Joe Sharkey, *Bedlam: Greed, Profiteering and Fraud in a Mental Health System Gone Crazy* (New York: Thomas Dunne/St. Martin's Press, 1994); and Lois A. Weithorn, "Mental Hospitalization of Troublesome Youth," *Stanford Law Rev.* 40:773 (1988). The rate of institutionalization of adolescents rose fourfold between 1980 and 1984, *id.*

79. Many of the first-person accounts of the trauma of institutionalization are by women who were institutionalized as adolescents by their parents: Susanna Kayren, *Girl, Interrupted* (New York: Random House, 1993); Daphne Scholinski, *The Last Time I Wore a Dress* (New York: Riverhead Books, 1997). *See also* Hannah Green, *I Never Promised You a Rose Garden* (New York: Holt, Rinehart & Winston, 1964).

80. Joe Sharkey, "You're Not Bad, You're Sick. It's in the Book," NEW YORK TIMES (Sept. 27, 1998):Sec. 4, p. 1.

81. Phyllis Chesler, *Women and Madness* (New York: Doubleday, 1972); Kate Millett, *The Loony Bin Trip* (New York: Simon & Schuster, 1990); Susan Stefan, "Issues Relating to Women and Minorities in Mental Health Treatment and Law," in Bruce Sales and Dan Shuman, Eds., *Law, Mental Health and Mental Disorder* (Pacific Grove, CA: Brooks/Cole, 1996).

82. In Milner v. Apfel, 148 F.3d 812, 814–815 (7th Cir. 1998), for example, Judge Posner made it clear that people who are found not guilty by reason of insanity can be appropriately subject to moral judgment and condemnation; *see* this discussion in chapter 5.

83. Found at section 313.81 in the *DSM*.

84. *Id.*

85. Moore v. East Cleveland, 431 U.S. 494 (1977).

86. *See* Judith Herman, *Trauma and Recovery* (New York: Basic Books, 1992).

87. John Monahan and Laurens Walker, Eds., *Social Science in Law* 3rd ed. (New York: Foundation Press, 1994). They discussed PTSD, rape trauma syndrome, and "involuntary subliminal television intoxication." *See also* Susan Stefan, "The Protection Racket: Rape Trauma Syndrome, Psychiatric Labeling, and Law," *Northwestern Law Rev.* 88 (1994):1271.

88. Joe Sharkey, *see* note 80.

89. *DSM-IV,* section 301.50.

90. *Id.*

91. *See* Paula Caplan, *They Say You're Crazy* (Reading, MA: Addison-Wesley, 1995), for an account of this battle.

92. The best known of these are Hannah Green's *I Never Promised You a Rose Garden* (New York: Holt, Rhinehart & Winston, 1964) and, thinly disguised as fiction, Mary Jane Ward's *The Snake Pit* (New York: Random House, 1946) and Sylvia Plath's *The Bell Jar* (New York: Harper & Row, 1971). Many people are aware of Cifford Beers's *A Mind That Found Itself* (originally published in 1903; reissued New York: Doubleday, Doran, 1944) or the account of F. Scott Fitzgerald on his breakdown, *The Crack-Up* (originally published in 1936 reissued New York: Laughlin, 1945 and with William Styron's *Darkness Visible* and Janet Frame's *Faces in the Water* by Asheville, NC: Pegasus Press, 1961). Less familiar are Barbara Field Benziger's *The Prison of My Mind* (New York: Walker, 1969), Wilfrid Sheed's *In Love With Daylight: A Memoir of Recovery* (New York: Simon & Schuster, 1995), Mark Vonnegut's *The Eden Express* (New York: Praeger, 1975), and Joshua Logan's *My Up and Down, In and Out Life* (New York: Delacorte Press, 1976). Kenneth Donaldson, the plaintiff in the U.S. Supreme Court case of O'Connor v. Donaldson, wrote *Insanity Inside Out* (New York: Crown, 1976). Earlier works include A. Graves, *The Eclipse of a Mind* (New York: Medical Journal Press, 1942); John Custance, *Wisdom, Madness, and Folly: The Philosophy of a Lunatic* (New York: Farrar, Strauss & Cudahy, 1952). Two older books of great value are Judi Chamberlin's *On Our Own* (New York: Hawthorne Books, 1978) and Janet and Paul Gotkin's *Too Much Anger, Too Many Tears* (New York: Quadrangle Books, 1975); others include Huey Freeman's *Jury, Judge and Executioner* (Urbana, IL: Talking Leaves, 1986), Persimmon Blackbridge and Sheila Gilhooly's *Still Sane* (Vancouver, British Columbia, Canada: Press Gang, 1985), and Doug Cameron's *How to Survive Being Committed to a Mental Hospital* (New York: Vantage Press, 1980). More recently,

books on this subject include Susanna Kaysen's *Girl, Interrupted* (New York: Random House, 1993), Tracy Thompson's *The Beast: A Reckoning With Depression* (New York: Putnam, 1995), and Elizabeth Wurtzel's *Prozac Nation* (New York: Riverhead Books, 1994). Although people tend to associate first-person accounts of psychiatric disabilities with poets and authors, a substantial number of mental health professionals have also written accounts of their mental health problems, usually with titles indicating their professional status; *see, e.g.,* Norman Endler, *Holiday of Darkness: A Psychologist's Personal Journey out of His Depression* (Toronto, Ontario, Canada: Wall & Thompson, 1990); Martha Manning, *Undercurrents: A Therapist's Reckoning With Her Own Depression* (San Francisco: Harper, 1994); although *see* Kay Redfield Jamison, *An Unquiet Mind: A Memoir of Moods and Madness* (New York: Knopf, 1995).

93. Dale Peterson, Ed., *A People's History of Madness* (Pittsburgh, PA: University of Pittsburgh Press, 1982); Roy Porter, Ed., *The Faber Book of Madness* (London: Faber & Faber, 1991); Michael Susko, *Cry of the Invisible* (Baltimore: Conservatory Press, 1991); Seth Farber, *Madness, Heresy, and the Rumor of Angels: The Revolt Against the Mental Health System* (Chicago: Open Court, 1993); Maxine Harris and Jeffrey Geller, Eds., *Women of the Asylum* (New York: Anchor Books, 1994); Janine Grobe, *Beyond Bedlam: Contemporary Psychiatric Survivors Speak Out* (Chicago: Third Side Press, 1995).

94. Jeffrey Geller, a psychiatrist, has done an enormous amount to publicize the voices of people with psychiatric disabilities. He is the coeditor of a book of accounts by women who were institutionalized; Jeffrey Geller and Maxine Harris, Eds., *Women of the Asylum: Voices From Behind the Walls* (New York: Anchor Books, 1994). As editor of the "Book Review" section of *Psychiatric Services*, he has both reviewed books by people within the mental health system and asked ex-patients to write book reviews.

95. *See, e.g.,* "Manic Depressive Illness," *Lancet* 8414 (1984):1268.

96. Much of the work in this area was pioneered by Jean Campbell. *See* accounts in chapter 1 of my survey and others.

97. Jay Neugeboren, *Imagining Robert* (New York: Morrow, 1997); Danielle Steele, *His Bright Light* (New York: Dell, 1998). For an account presented as fictional that resonates with truth, see Wally Lamb's *I Know This Much Is True* (New York: HarperCollins, 1998).

98. Survey No. 64 ("borderline personality disorder").

99. Survey Nos. 5 and 11.

100. Survey Nos. 1 and 5.

101. Survey No. 11 ("fluctuations in energy").

102. Surveys Nos. 5 and 12.

103. Survey No. 12.

104. Survey Nos. 44 and 45.

105. Survey No. 49.

106. Survey No. 40.

107. Tracey Dykstra, "First Person Account: How I Cope," *Schizophrenia Bulletin* 23 (1997): 697.

108. Laura Prescott, presentation (unpublished), Human Rights Conference of the Massachusetts Department of Mental Health (1995).

109. Tracey Dykstra, *id.* at note 107.

110. Martha Manning, *Undercurrents: A Therapist's Reckoning With Her Own Depression* (San Francisco: HarperCollins, 1994).

111. *See* especially Judith Lewis Herman, *Trauma and Recovery* (New York: Basic Books, 1992); Sandra Bloom, *Creating Sanctuary: Toward a Sane Society* (New York: Routledge, 1997) at 136.

112. Survey No. 37.

113. Susan Sontag, *AIDS and Its Metaphors* (New York: Farrar, Strauss & Giroux, 1988) at 12.

114. Kenny Fries, Ed., *Staring Back: The Disability Experience From the Inside Out* (New York: Plume, 1997); John Hockenberry, *Moving Violations: War Zones, Wheelchairs and Declarations of Independence* (New York: Hyperion, 1995); Irving Zola, *Missing Pieces: A Chronicle of Living With a Disability* (Philadelphia: Temple, 1982); Steven Shapiro, *No Pity: People With Disabilities Forging a New Civil Rights Movement* (New York: Times Books, 1994).

115. Kay Redfield Jamison, *A Mind Apart* (New York: Knopf, 1995); Elizabeth Wurtzel, *Prozac Nation* (New York: Riverhead Books, 1994) at 248. ("Yes, there was a certain beautiful honesty to my depressed state—I miss it sometimes now. I miss having so little stake in the status quo that I could walk out of rooms in tears at times that other people would have deemed inappropriate. I liked that about myself. I liked that disregard for convention").

116. Until recently, the Equal Employment Opportunity Commission reported that the largest number of disability discrimination complaints were filed by people with back problems. People who fit into the category of psychiatric disabilities now file the greatest number of complaints of any individual category.

117. Adam S. Levy, Rebecca M. Jones, and Craig Olin, "Distortion of Racial Identity and Psychosis," *Amer. J. of Psychiatry* 149 (Letter to the Editor) (June 1992):845

118. N. D. B., Survey Response No. 3, on file with author.

119. Trudy B. (personal communication, Mar. 5, 1998). Trudy B. is a member of Fellowship House, Coral Gables, FL. Permission to interview and tape obtained. Transcript on file with author.

120. Yolanda H. (personal communication, Mar. 22, 1998), also a member of Fellowship House.

121. Merrifield v. Beaven Interamerican Co., 1991 U.S. Dist. LEXIS 12128 (N.D. Ill. Aug. 30, 1991).

122. Diana Rickard (personal communication, Aug. 1998).

123. Ihler v. South, Deposition of Dr. Virginia Hill, on file with the Bazelon Center for Mental Health Law, Washington DC.

124. Treatment plan from the *Wyatt* case on file with author. I am indebted to Shelley Jackson of the Bazelon Center for sharing this plan (with the identity of the patient redacted) with me.

125. Judith Musick, "Patterns of Institutional Sexual Assault," *Responses to Violence in the Fam. and Sexual Assault* 7 (1984 May–June): 3; Daphne Scholinski with Jane Meredith, *The Last Time I Wore a Dress* (New York: Riverhead Books, 1997).

126. James v. Grand Lake Mental Health Center, 1998 U.S. App. LEXIS 23916*7 (10th Cir. Sept. 24, 1998), note 1 ("Ms. James says Ms. Vella's decision to commit her was intended as punishment. Ms. Vella claims she was concerned because Ms. James appeared to be unable to take precautions to protect herself from her abusive husband").

127. In re of J. P., 574 N.W.2d 340, 342 (Iowa 1998).

128. I do not believe these conditions are not serious; I do, however, believe that conditions such as PTSD and dissociative identity disorder are equally serious.

129. Lee N. Robins and Darrel A. Regier, Eds., *Psychiatric Disorders in America* (New York: Free Press, 1991) at 340–342 (only 18.2% of people with a mental disorder have sought mental health treatment).

130. A *Newsweek* article described businessmen who borrowed their secretaries' cars to go to appointments with their therapists, or paid in cash, to avoid any possibility of tracing the fact that they were visiting a therapist, Jolie Solomon, Claudia Kalb, and Carla Power, "Breaking the Silence," *Newsweek* (May 20, 1996):22.

131. Several survey respondents used this terminology. One wrote "I 'pass' for normal— very well until I get into an intimate relationship such as a lover or a work relationship or a roommate. So I guess the world at large doesn't see the disability," Survey No.

188; "Because I 'pass' as a normal whenever I can, I feel as much a part of my community as anyone else," Survey No. 198. An article in *Newsweek* quoted a best-selling author with obsessive–compulsive disorder in his 40s who left his apartment 20 times in 1 evening to check the lights and locks on his car. He described himself as an "expert" in "passing" and said "he plans to do it for the rest of his life," Jolie Solomon, Claudia Kalb, and Carla Power, "Breaking the Silence," *Newsweek* (May 20, 1996): 20–22.

132. Survey Nos. 70, 39, and 43 (2nd-year law student).

133. Survey No. 171.

134. Survey No. 174.

135. Survey No. 108.

136. Survey No. 186.

137. Survey Nos. 151 and 189.

138. Survey No. 321.

139. Some notable exceptions include Dan Fisher, a former psychiatric patient and now a psychiatrist who is one of the directors of the National Empowerment Center, a national center run by people who have experienced the mental health system as patients and devoted to education and training about mental health issues, especially in the areas of recovery and managed care; and Scott Francis, former president of the National Association for Rights Protection and Advocacy and director of the Francis Family Foundation in Kansas.

140. *See, e.g.,* Susan Sheehan, *Is There No Place on Earth for Me?* (New York: Vintage Books, 1983); and John La Ford and Mary Durham, *Back to the Asylum* (New York: Oxford University Press, 1992).

141. Edward H. Yelin and Miriam G. Cisternas, "Employment Patterns Among Persons With and Without Mental Conditions," in *Mental Disorder, Work Disability and the Law,* Richard Bonnie and John Monahan, Eds. (Chicago: University of Chicago Press, 1997).

142. There are hundreds of articles on the disparities in access to health care and quality of health care by individual disease, that is, cancer, heart disease, and so forth. Some of the more general studies include J. Z. Ayanian, "Race, Class and the Quality of Medical Care," *J. of the Amer. Med. Assn.* 271 (1994):1207; D. P. Rice, "Ethics and Equity in U.S. Health Care: The Data," *Intl. J. of Health Services* 21 (1991):637; and D. W. Baker, C. D. Strauss, and R. H. Brooks, "Determinants of Emergency Department Use: Are Race and Ethnicity Important?" *Annals of Emer. Med.* 28 (1990):677 (this study concludes that "after adjusting for age, health insurance coverage, regular source of care, and *barriers to health care,*" there is no difference between black and white usage of emergency rooms (emphasis added).

143. *See* "Developments in the Law—Race and the Criminal Process," *Harvard Law Rev.* 101 (1988):1472, 1494–1498; Richard H. McAdams, "Race and Selective Prosecution: Discovering the Pitfalls of Armstrong," *Chicago–Kent Law Rev.* 73 (1998):605, 652–655; Tracey Maclin, "Black and Blue Encounters—Some Preliminary Thoughts About Fourth Amendment Seizures: Should Race Matter?" *Val. Univ. Law Rev.* 26 (1991):243. A University of Florida study by nationally prominent sociologist Joe Feagin shows that of 130 reported cases of police brutality in a 2-year period, 97% involved black or Latino victims and 93% "centrally involved" white policemen. In only 2 of the cases was the sole victim white. The study also shows that blacks were "more likely to be victims of police brutality if they were disrespectful in their demeanor toward the officers than if they posed a deadly threat." *See* "National Study Reports White Cops' Beatings of Blacks Reveal 'Dirty Secrets of Racism,' " *Jet* 84(1) (May 3, 1993):14.

144. "North Carolina Atones for Theft of Man's Best Years," SARASOTA HERALD-TRIBUNE (Feb. 2, 1996):A5. *See* Wilson v. North Carolina, 981 F.Supp. 397 (E.D. N.C. 1997), and a further discussion of this case in chapter 4.

145. Nichols v. Frank, 42 F.3d 503, 506 (9th Cir. 1994).

146. She and her husband had just bought a house, and she was afraid if she lost her job, they would lose the house. She was afraid if she told her husband, he would divorce her and "take my children"; *id.* at 507, "And so I was just stuck . . . as time progressed, I was getting crazier." Terri Nichols tried to kill herself as a result of her situation and was ultimately diagnosed with PTSD.

147. *Id.*

148. *Id.*

149. Robert Lowell, *Collected Prose* (New York: Farrar, Straus & Giroux, 1987) at 286.

150. William Styron, *Darkness Visible* (New York: Random House, 1990).

151. Kay Redfield Jamison, *An Unquiet Mind* (1995), see note 92.

152. Tracy Thompson, *The Beast: A Reckoning With Depression*, see note 92; Wilfrid Sheed, *In Love With Daylight*, *see* note 92; Elizabeth Wurtzel, *Prozac Nation*, *see* note 92.

153. Janet and Paul Gotkin, *Too Much Anger, Too Many Tears*, *see* note 92.

154. Judi Chamberlin, *On Our Own* (1978), *see* note 92.

155. Huey Freeman, *Judge, Jury and Executioner* (1986), *see* note 92.

156. Doug Cameron, *How to Survive Being Committed to a Mental Hospital*, *see* note 92.

157. Estroff et al. suggested that in the days of deinstitutionalization, "receipt of disability benefits has replaced long term hospitalization as a crucial social factor shaping the course and direction of disablement"; Sue E. Estroff et al., "Pathways to Disability Income Among Persons With Severe Persistent Psychiatric Disabilities," *Milbank Quarterly* 75 (1997):495, 521. Although receipt of disability benefits clearly reshapes an individual's perception of him- or herself and at least one person reported being treated with suspicion and contempt when she applied for disability benefits, *id.* at 502, receipt of disability benefits does not occasion the hierarchy, intrusion, coercion, and outright violence reported and resisted as part of being a "patient." The ex-patient literature reflects despair at the indignities and deprivation of poverty forced on an individual by trying to live on about $400 a month, but it is devoid of the kind of rage associated with the experience of institutionalization.

158. Lawton Chiles, Kay Jamison, Ira Magaziner, Rod Steiger, Mike Wallace, Roseanne Barr, Patty Duke, Jonathan Winters, and professional golfer Bert Yancey are all celebrities who revealed diagnoses of serious mental disabilities after proving they could succeed in their chosen careers.

159. Howard Hughes is the classic example of a man who, had he had fewer resources, would certainly have been committed. For example, he was obsessed with the search for a perfect bacteria-free environment, but he sought it in Nicaragua, where all papers had to be handled with gloves and held in Kleenexes; *see* Glenn Garvin, "Quake Got US Tycoon Carried Away," MIAMI HERALD (Jan. 29, 1998):A12.

160. For example, John Dupont was recently charged with murder; Ezra Pound was charged with treason; Chief Judge Sol Wachtler of the New York Court of Appeals spent 16 months in federal prison for harassing his mistress and her daughter; Richard Berendzen, the former president of American University, made obscene phone calls. Both Wachtler and Berendzen wrote books about their experiences: Wachtler's is entitled *After Madness: A Judge's Own Prison Memoir* (New York: Random House, 1997), and Berendzen's is entitled *Come Here: A Man Overcomes the Tragic Aftermath of Childhood Sexual Abuse* (with Laura Palmer; New York: Villard Books, 1993). Wachtler has been teaching law at Tauro Law School in New York, and Berendzen returned to American University as a professor.

161. Improvident marriages often prove the undoing of wealthy and successful men and women of uncertain psychiatric status, for example, Sir Rudolph Bing; *see* "Rudolph Bing Fights Annulment," CHICAGO TRIBUNE (May 22, 1987):C4.

162. Lorelee Stewart, "Testimony," in Jeanine Grobe, Ed., *Beyond Bedlam: Contemporary Women Psychiatric Survivors Speak Out* (Boston: Third Side Press, 1995) at 153.

163. Kate Millett, *The Loony Bin Trip* (New York: Simon & Schuster, 1990).

164. Clifford Beers, author of *A Mind That Found Itself* (originally published in 1903; reissued New York: Doubleday, Doran, 1944) and founder of the mental hygiene movement in the early 20th century, had been a successful salesman and businessman.

165. Seth Farber, *Madness, Heresy and the Rumor of Angels: The Revolt Against the Mental Health System,* see note 93 at 106. David Oaks is far from the only Harvard University student to have been psychiatrically diagnosed and treated; *see* Laurie in Jeanine Grobe, Ed., *Beyond Bedlam, see* note 93; Robert Lowell, *Collected Prose* (New York: Farrar, Strauss & Giroux, 1987); and Elizabeth Wurtzel, *Prozac Nation* (1994), *see* note 92.

166. Armando R. Favazza, "Why Patients Mutilate Themselves," *Hosp. and Comm. Psychiatry* 40 (1989):137, 139–140, describing a waitress who engaged in "cutting, burning and poking needles into my arms," a secretary who cut her wrist, a registered nurse who scraped her vagina with a fish scaler, a 19-year-old clerical worker who cut herself, and a 28-year-old librarian who said, "sometimes I think a dose of the good things— loving, hugging—would do it, but it's simpler to reach for a razor blade."

167. Kay Jamison, *An Unquiet Mind: A Memoir of Moods and Madness* (1995), *see* note 92.

168. Tracy Thompson, *The Beast: A Reckoning With Depression* (New York: Putnam, 1995) at 52.

169. *See, e.g.,* Maxine Harris and Chris Landis, Eds., *Sexual Abuse in the Lives of Women Diagnosed With Severe Mental Illness* (Amsterdam, The Netherlands: Harwood, 1997); Judith Herman, *Trauma and Recovery* (New York: Basic Books, 1992).

170. Judith Herman, *id.*

171. Sandra Bloom, *Creating Sanctuary* (New York: Routledge, 1997).

172. Judith Herman, *Trauma and Recovery.*

173. *See, e.g.,* in re Cassandra B., 1997 Conn. Super. Ct. LEXIS 2925*5–6 (Conn. Super. Ct. Nov. 1997) (in the recounting history of the mother whose rights were terminated, the court noted that after revealing to her mother that the mother's boyfriend had sexually abused her, she "slept in a doghouse with the family St. Bernard, who was her 'protection' until her mother's boyfriend shot and killed the dog").

174. Jonathan C. Drimmer, "Cripples, Overcomers and Civil Rights: Tracing the Evolution of Federal Legislation and Social Policy for People With Disabilities," *UCLA Law Rev.* 40 (1993):1341, 1352.

175. *Id.* citations omitted.

176. *Id.* at 1353.

177. "One gentleman I knew, before his illness, had received a PhD in chemistry, was sent to Goodwill to sort socks as a part of his training and testing," Testimony of Lelia Batten to the U.S. Congress in Support of the ADA, Arnold and Porter, A&P Committee Print 1990 (28B)*1190–1191.

178. Response of A. M. D., Survey No. 145.

179. S. S., Survey Response No. 130.

180. Survey Response No. 108.

181. *See* note 92 the following authors: William Styron, John Custance, Norman Endler, and Tracy Thompson; *also see* G. H. Survey; C. B. W. Survey.

182. Survey Response No. 91.

183. Survey Response No. 92.

184. Survey No. 70 (respondent was identified as a lawyer).

185. Survey No. 107.

186. Survey Nos. 114, 115, 130, and 188.

187. Survey No. 114.

188. Survey No. 115.

189. In Lee v. Publix Supermarkets, 1998 U.S. Dist. LEXIS 8921 (N.D. Fla., March 16, 1998), for example, although the plaintiff had been very depressed prior to losing his job, he developed bipolar disorder after being fired. His treating physician was quoted by the court as concluding that the "precipitating causes seem predominantly to do with the fact that he was fired" from Publix, *id.* *13.

190. Breiland v. Advance Circuits Inc., 976 F.Supp. 858, 861 (D. Minn 1997); Ralph v. Lucent, 135 F.3d 166, 169 (1st Cir. 1998).

191. Comments of Ted Lawlor, who was then medical director for the Massachusetts Department of Mental Health, Western Mass. region.

192. Susan Stefan, "You'd Have to be Crazy to Work Here: Worker Stress, the Abusive Workplace, and the ADA," *Loyola L. A. Law Rev* 31 (1998):795.

193. Michael Perlin, "Where the Winds Hit Heavy on the Borderline: Mental Disability Law, Theory and Practice, 'Us' and 'Them,'" *Loyola L. A. Law Rev.* 31 (1998):775.

194. One possible exception is Patricia Deegan, a PhD psychologist who was diagnosed with schizophrenia. Deegan, however, who is codirector of the National Empowerment Center, strongly self-identifies as a person with a psychiatric label and probably is best described as a voluntary member of the second category.

195. In 1989, when Congress was taking testimony on the ADA, Ira Magaziner had not yet identified himself as a person with bipolar disorder.

196. Testimony Before the House Committee on Select Education and Senate Subcommittee on the Handicapped, S. Hrng. 100-926 (Sept. 27, 1988) at 15.

197. Although Lawton Chiles was struggling with depression throughout the debates on the ADA, he did not begin to take Prozac until December 1989.

198. Bill Moss, "Gustafson Draws Praise, Raises Eyebrows in Race," ST. PETERSBURG TIMES (Aug. 28, 1990):B6. The candidate for lieutenant governor was quoted as saying, "I don't want to have a suicide during [Chiles's] term of office or during the election. I don't know if he's that bad and you don't either."

199. Survey No. 150.

200. *See, e.g.,* Elizabeth Wurtzel, *Prozac Nation*; Tracy Thompson, *The Beast*; Kay Redfield Jamison, *An Unquiet Mind*, all at note 92.

201. Survey No. 176.

202. In employment discrimination litigation, proof that the plaintiff secured other employment is cited to show that he or she is not really disabled; in one opinion, a judge held that because a plaintiff had made it through law school, she could not be disabled; Clark v. Virginia Board of Bar Examiners, 861 F.Supp. 512 (E.D. Va. 1994). The judge withdrew this opinion, but it is emblematic of the presumption that truly disabled people cannot successfully compete in any but the most menial professions.

Chapter 3
DISABILITY BENEFITS OR DISABILITY RIG[

The contrast between the federal government's attitude toward people with mental disabilities and its attitude toward people with physical disabilities helps to explain the different ways in which the two groups became politically mobilized and the different uses they have made of the legal system. People with physical disabilities and those with mental disabilities have historically had different concepts of the kinds of rights that they needed, which resulted in different paths to achieving those rights.

In some salient ways, however, the major obstacle to civil rights for people with disabilities is the same for both groups: the perceived tension between governmental benefits based on disability and the government's prohibition of discrimination based on disability. Whereas people with disabilities argue that discrimination leads to an underestimation of their actual abilities and Congress proclaims that discrimination keeps people from employment, the federal disability benefit rolls keep rising, even after the passage of the Americans With Disabilities Act (ADA). This chapter examines the ways in which the federal government's provision of disability benefits both undermines and complements the goal of disability rights. It examines the history of the federal government's policy toward people with disabilities and shows how that policy was transformed when people with disabilities began to name their own experiences in their own language. These experiences led them to concentrate on access to the community.

To gain access to the community, people in mental institutions had to first get out of the institution. Although for 20 years the organization and strategies of people with physical disabilities were distinct from those of people who had been in the mental health system, both movements came together in their support of the ADA and its mandate that all people with disabilities be integrated into American society. As this book goes to press, the ADA has been challenged in the U.S. Supreme Court. This chapter discusses the consequences of the challenge to disability rights in the 21st century.

Disability Benefits as Undermining the Right to Equal Protection

In 1985, the U.S. Supreme Court heard its first case raising the claim that discrimination against people on the basis of disability in a civil setting violated their constitutional rights to equal protection under the 14th Amendment.[1] The case of *City of Cleburne v. Cleburne Living Center*[2] involved the rejection of a zoning request that would have permitted a group home for people with mental retardation to locate in the city of Cleburne. Attorneys for the group home argued that the court should examine disadvantageous classifications of people based on mental retardation with the same "strict scrutiny" with which it examined categorizations based on race. The Court of Appeals for the 5th Circuit had held that people with mental retardation were entitled to heightened—but not strict—scrutiny. This meant that state decisions disadvantaging people on the basis of mental disability would be subject to the intermediate level of scrutiny that the Supreme Court had deemed necessary in examining categorizations based on gender, illegitimacy, and age.[3]

The U.S. Supreme Court rejected the 5th Circuit Court's analysis, holding that disadvantageous decisions based on the category of mental retardation were entitled to no special level of scrutiny. Justice Bryon White, writing for the majority, cited two principal reasons for this holding.[4] Both reasons reflect popular American perceptions about people with disabilities—especially mental disabilities—and explain much about why people who are generally sympathetic to race and gender discrimination laws may be skeptical or even hostile to disability discrimination law.

First, the Supreme Court held that the equal protection clause only forbids differential treatment of people who are "similarly situated."[5] Laws cannot disadvantage people based on factors "that generally provide no sensible ground for differential treatment,"[6] such as gender. Of course, this raises the question of what in society constitutes a "sensible ground for differential treatment." A prior Supreme Court decision on gender discrimination differentiated "sex from such nonsuspect statuses as intelligence or physical disability" on the grounds that "the sex characteristic frequently bears no relation to the ability to perform or contribute to society."[7] Because the Supreme Court identified "the ability to perform or contribute to society" as a crucial, organizing value in this country,[8] differences in the ability to perform or contribute to society justify differential and disadvantageous treatment. Therefore, the Supreme Court held because "those who are mentally retarded have a reduced ability to cope with and function in the everyday world . . . they are thus different, immutably so, in relevant respects."[9]

The Supreme Court is asserting is that it is legal, and even natural, to disadvantage people on the basis of their "reduced ability to cope with and function in the world." This obviously has an ominous ring for people with all kinds of disabilities, not to mention elderly people[10] and children. Although the Supreme Court recognized that these characteristics might serve as a justification for benefiting people as well as treating them disadvantageously, it used this recognition to provide its second justification for not requiring heightened scrutiny of disadvantageous categorizations based on disability.

The Supreme Court pointed out that Congress and the states had passed a number of statutes designed to benefit people with mental disabilities. The court reasoned that these statutes demonstrated that there was no "continuing antipathy or prejudice"[11] toward people with mental disabilities. Their presence reflected society's good will toward people with mental retardation and, therefore, eliminated any "corresponding need for more intrusive oversight by the judiciary."[12] Unfortunately, by the time of the *Cleburne* decision, the Supreme Court's own "intrusive oversight" resulted in a substantially weakened interpretation of each statute that the court cited.[13] Even worse, the Supreme Court is now poised to invalidate a crucial portion of the most significant statute—the ADA—ever passed to protect the rights of people with disabilities.

On April 17, 2000, the Supreme Court agreed to hear two consolidated cases in which the state of Alabama challenged the validity of Title II of the ADA, which prohibits discrimination by public entities, including state governments.[14] The question posed by these cases is "Does the 11th Amendment bar suits by private citizens in federal court under the ADA against nonconsenting states?" Although the 11th

Amendment grants states immunity from suits by citizens, the 14th Amendment gives the U.S. Congress the power to subject states to liability under federal law if the law—such as the ADA—was passed to protect rights guaranteed by the 14th Amendment, such as the right to equal protection of the laws. Congress must have evidence that the states have violated citizens' rights and the law must be "congruent and proportional" to address the violation of rights without undue intrusion on state sovereignty.[15]

States have in fact discriminated against people with mental disabilities in virtually every aspect of their lives from residential segregation such as that in *Cleburne* to unnecessary institutionalization,[16] to denials of the right to vote and to marry, to exclusions from public buildings and transportation, to discrimination by police and state emergency services. Because many states cannot be sued for discrimination by their own citizens in state court, a holding by the U.S. Supreme Court that the ADA could not be applied to the states would permit a range of exclusion and discrimination, with no legal remedy available to disabled citizens.

It is possible that the Supreme Court will strike down some portions of Title II of the ADA and uphold other portions. Both cases before the court present issues of employment discrimination; one involves reasonable accommodation, and the other involves exclusion from employment on the basis of an inability to meet allegedly discriminatory employment criteria. Some commentators have suggested that whereas the ADA may prohibit discriminatory exclusions and segregation such as that at issue in *Cleburne,* it may not require the states to provide reasonable accommodations in employment or at all.[17] Reasonable accommodations are, however, necessary to remedy discriminatory exclusion: The ramp to the polling site, the waiver of the zoning exclusion, and the provision of interpreters for deaf jurors are all reasonable accommodations.

The great irony of the challenge to the ADA is that it is facilitated by the Supreme Court's decision in *Cleburne* that people with mental disabilities did not need any special protection under the 14th Amendment of the U.S. Constitution. In coming to this conclusion, Justice White pointed to a number of federal statutes protecting people with disabilities (the ADA had not yet been enacted). Now, the fact that people with disabilities are entitled to no special constitutional protection may be used as an argument to strike down the federal statutory protection of the ADA. It is difficult to believe that the Supreme Court will consign people with disabilities to lives of dependency, segregation, and exclusion because of a jurisprudential "Catch-22."

It is true that in this society, people receive benefits and entitlements based on disability. It is completely incorrect to conclude, however, that no protection to be free from discrimination is required for people with disabilities. Indeed, society's skepticism about according rights against discrimination to a category of people who receive benefits based on that category is one of the chief stumbling blocks to public understanding and support of disability discrimination law.

One way to understand the existence of benefits statutes is that they provide support to people who could work but are excluded from doing so because of discrimination. Congress passed the ADA in part on the argument that people with disabilities who could and wanted to work collected benefits because they were the victims of employment discrimination. This may represent a partial truth, but it is hardly the whole story. For example, many people who could work choose not to because Congress itself has linked crucial Medicaid and Medicare benefits to disability benefits. In addition, because Congress has also refused to mandate health benefits unless people are impoverished and disabled or impoverished and formerly on welfare, disabled people who want to work must risk their health if they take jobs that do not provide health benefits. Others choose not to work because of Congress's repeated refusal to raise the minimum wage and to provide the kind of subsidies for public transportation and child care that are common in Europe, meaning that any meager income from minimum-wage jobs would be eaten up by transportation, child care, and other work-related costs, which are even higher for people with disabilities than for those without. Still others could not work because of a complex intersection of different kinds of discrimination. As one commentator pointed out, many people who receive disability benefits are middle-aged or older people with limited job skills who probably would not be able to get a job whether they had a disability or not.[18] This is due partially to age discrimination, partially to disability discrimination, and partially to the failures of our vocational rehabilitation system and the lack of successful job training programs.[19]

In other words, employers never get the chance to discriminate against people with disabilities because the social and economic structure that Congress has created or refused to change has made it rational for disabled people to avoid employment, even when they desperately want to work. Whether this is discrimination or not depends on one's definition of discrimination.

Disability benefit laws are, for the most part, creatures of the 20th century; disability discrimination law is barely more than a quarter-century old. The coexistence of disability discrimination laws with disability benefit laws has created a complex legal environment, including situations in which many different disability benefits programs have been challenged as discriminatory.[20]

Disability rights and disability benefits are theoretically complementary under a number of models. One suggests that disability rights enable people who can work to be free from unjustified discrimination, whereas disability benefits enable people who cannot work to live a reasonably dignified existence. Another model notes that an ADA claim that a person can do a job only if he or she receives reasonable accommodations may be consistent with a disability benefit claim that he or she cannot work in the absence of those accommodations.[21]

Although the disability benefits and disability discrimination regimes are theoretically separate, they collided early on. Because the ADA requires plaintiffs to be "otherwise qualified" for employment, employers have argued that an employee who applied for disability benefits could not be otherwise qualified yet totally unable to work as required to qualify for disability benefits. Many courts appeared outraged that a person would both apply for disability benefits and sue under the ADA, chastising plaintiffs for bringing claims for employment discrimination under these circumstances, stating that "plaintiff cannot have it both ways"[22] and accusing the plaintiff of "speak[ing] out of both sides" of his or her mouth.[23] A number of courts took the position that an individual who applied for disability benefits should be judicially estopped from suing under the ADA or at least subject to a presumption that he or she was not otherwise qualified under the ADA.[24] In fact, the fourth ADA case taken by the U.S. Supreme Court involved the question of whether someone who had applied for disability benefits should be subject to a presumption that he or she was not otherwise qualified under the ADA.[25] The Supreme Court rejected this position, holding that "pursuit, and receipt, of SSDI [Social Security disability income] benefits does not automatically estop the recipient from pursuing an ADA claim. Nor does the law erect a strong presumption against the recipient's success under the ADA."[26]

A close look at discrimination cases in which plaintiffs file for disability benefits finds people in excruciating real-life dilemmas. Under the ADA, a person must wait 6 months to file a discrimination claim in court.[27] By the time an employment discrimination case wends its way through the court system, a person could easily have lost his or her living situation and health care benefits. Often the plaintiff is older, and his or her job prospects are not hopeful, in part because of the disability itself. For people with depression or anxiety problems, the loss of employment itself can make a previously bearable burden unendurable, so that the experience of discrimination is what is disabling.

In many cases, the period of time between a person's termination and filing for benefits suggests that the individual had searched unsuccessfully for other employment and filed for benefits simply because he or she needed a source of income and perhaps also health care. Or as suggested above, the lack of employment and the uncertainties of searching for employment may have exacerbated the psychological condition of the individual to the point where he or she could not work.

Another frequent explanation is that the person might be able to work but is unable to find employment because of a combination of age, disability, history of termination, and perhaps sex or race discrimination. To preclude a person in any of these situations from claiming that he or she was terminated due to discrimination on the basis of disability seems to be asking that individual to choose between justice and survival. As the 9th Circuit commented,

> her case illustrates the problems faced by a worker in her position. Her employer concluded that she could not perform her job, and placed her on unpaid leave. She disagreed with her employer's determination and unsuccessfully challenged it. Then, without pay because of her asserted disability, she applied for temporary disability benefits and received them. What else was she to do?[28]

In fact, there is no necessary contradiction between claiming to have lost one's job due to discrimination and filing for disability benefits. The law providing disability benefits itself assumes that some people receiving disability benefits can work; people receiving disability benefits can engage in a "trial work period" for up to 9 months without losing their benefits,[29] and after that they may work without receiving benefits for up to 3 years,[30] during which time they can resume receiving benefits at any time without any new determination that they are disabled. In addition, some conditions, such as blindness or HIV seropositivity, are presumed by social security regulations to be totally disabling, yet many people who are blind or HIV positive are capable of working and do so.

This certainly fits Deborah Stone's theory that disability benefits in part serve as a way for employers to get rid of marginally employable workers in times when there are plenty of workers in the labor market.[31] Disability benefit claims are higher among groups that are historically discriminated against in employment: older workers, people of color, and women.[32]

Numerous commentators have discussed the tension between disability benefits and disability rights models.[33] In a revealing comment, one senator described the ADA and federal benefits programs for disabilities as "a schizophrenic national disability policy."[34] In general, commentators forecast that the apparent incongruity will lead to a tightening of the requirements to qualify for disability benefits, usually predicting that the ADA provisions will be woven into eligibility for benefits.[35] However, although a substantial number of disability discrimination claims have included issues about applications for disability benefits, only a few disability benefit cases have discussed the implications of the ADA.[36]

Society's perception that a tension exists between disability benefits and disability rights is especially problematic because the ADA's prohibition of employment discrimination has not translated into meaningful protection for people with disabilities, in general, and has been next to useless for people with mental disabilities, in particular.[37] In addition, one of the very real sources of employer hesitation to hire people with disabilities—and one of the principal reasons that people with disabilities hesitate to seek employment—is the cost and coverage of health care needs. This may be partially ameliorated by the recent passage of the Ticket to Work and Work Incentives Act of 1999.[38] This statute provides, among other things, that SSDI beneficiaries may retain Medicare coverage for up to 8½ years after they begin working and permits disabled people to receive Medicaid coverage if their salaries are up to 250% of the federal poverty level.

The fact is that the apparent tension between the theory behind disability benefits —that disabilities prevent people from working—and the theory behind disability rights—that discrimination prevents disabled people from working—obscures the true situation, which is that much of the behavior of disabled people and their potential employers is driven by concerns about the availability and cost of health care. Many more disabled people could work and many more employers would be willing to hire them if this threshold issue were satisfactorily addressed. It remains to be seen whether the Ticket to Work and Work Incentives Act will be helpful in addressing these concerns. Of course, the extension of Medicare coverage is not as helpful for people with mental disabilities as for those with physical disabilities because Medicare coverage of mental health problems is significantly narrower than its coverage of other health problems.

The History of Federal Laws Relating to People With Disabilities

The history of disability benefits law itself is one more aspect of the history of discrimination against people with mental disabilities. In almost every federal statute conferring disability benefits, benefits for people with mental disabilities were added at a later date, added in a weakened or diluted form, or excluded altogether. This kind of discrimination continues to this day. Although people with diagnoses of mental illness constitute a far greater proportion of people with disabilities than those with "traditional" disabilities such as blindness or deafness, the proportion of federal expenditures on programs to provide assistance, education, and advocacy to people with physical disabilities is far higher than appropriations to equivalent programs for people with diagnoses of mental illness.

Disability Benefits and Vocational Rehabilitation

Federal legislation regarding people with disabilities is as old as the nation itself. At the founding of the country, Congress provided health care for sick and disabled seamen.[39] During the Civil War, Congress created a disability system for the military.[40] Near the end of World War I, the federal government moved beyond income support and replacement to provide vocational rehabilitation to assist disabled veterans.[41]

These early programs, however, excluded the general civilian population. In response to public demand, soon after World War I Congress passed the Fess–Kenyon Act, which extended vocational rehabilitation to any citizen "disabled in industry or in any legitimate occupation."[42] Initial eligibility for these programs was limited to those with physical disabilities, and there was no funding for rehabilitation or treatment to diminish the effects of the disability. During World War II, Congress made significant changes to the 1920 act. Among these was that vocational rehabilitation was made available for the first time to people with mental disabilities.[43]

In 1948, discrimination on the basis of physical disability was outlawed in civil service hiring,[44] and in 1950 President Harry Truman attempted to establish a federal disability insurance program under the Social Security Act. Although the U.S. Senate rejected this proposal,[45] it did establish Aid to the Permanently and Totally Disabled, (APTD),[46] which provided federal assistance to people with disabilities while allowing states to determine who qualified as disabled. There was one significant exception to this program; it categorically prohibited the distribution of any federal funds to people in "institutions for the mentally disabled."[47]

Meanwhile vocational rehabilitation was being expanded. Congress passed the Vocational Rehabilitation Amendments of 1954, which provided that its purpose was to aid "physically handicapped individuals," defining them as people "under a physical or mental disability which constitutes a substantial handicap to employment."[48] Thus, people with mental disabilities were confirmed as entitled to vocational rehabilitation.

In 1956, in the face of the vehement opposition of the Republican administration[49] and the American Medical Association,[50] Congress finally enacted the nation's first disability insurance program. Hardly a radical program, it was available only to workers between ages 50 and 64 who had been employed for at least 20 quarters prior to their impairment. Mental and physical disabilities were covered, but only disabilities that prevented "any substantial gainful activity" and were "expected to result in death or to be of long-continued and indefinite duration."[51] President Dwight Eisenhower reluctantly signed the bill into law.[52] Over time, the SSDI program expanded (as its opponents had feared it would), and it presently covers any worker who becomes disabled after working for 10 years.[53]

As part of President Lyndon Johnson's Great Society, in 1965 Congress passed the Medicaid program,[54] which was intended to provide medical assistance to people who were too poor to afford it themselves. Like APTD, Medicaid prohibited federal reimbursement for services provided to people in institutions for mental disabilities, (called "IMDs") unless they were older than 65.[55]

Thus, by the early 1970s, a substantial array of federal programs provided income security and rehabilitation to people with disabilities, including generalized income replacement programs, such as SSDI; some disability-specific programs, such as those to assist people who were blind or who had contracted black lung disease;[56] many occupation-specific programs, such as the Railway Labor Act of 1926[57] and the Railroad Retirement Act of 1974,[58] the Federal Employers' Liability Act of 1908,[59] and the various military disability programs;[60] and needs-based assistance for people with disabilities through the Supplemental Security Income (SSI) program, which was established in 1972 and implemented beginning January 1, 1974.[61] There were also federal vocational rehabilitation programs[62] and, most important, programs providing health care and medical assistance for people with severe disabilities that were tied to the income support programs.[63]

Indeed, there is a plethora of statutes whose operation has a significant impact on people with psychiatric disabilities. There is a veritable alphabet soup of such statutes on the federal level alone, including Employee Retirement Security Act of 1974 (ERISA), Emergency Medical Treatment and Active Labor Act (EMTALA), Civil Rights of Institutionalized Persons Act (CRIPA), Protection and Advocacy for Individuals With Mental Illness (PAIMI), Protection and Advocacy for the Developmentally Disabled (PADD), Patient Self-Determination Act (PSDA), Consolidated Omnibus Budget Reconciliation Act (COBRA), Family and Medical Leave Act of 1993 (FMLA), and the SSI and SSDI programs of the Social Security Administration (SSA). These statutes are enumerated and summarized in Appendix B.[64]

It is often the case that an individual with a mental disability is better off seeking a benefit or remedy under statutes of general application rather than statutes aimed specifically at people with mental disabilities. For example, whereas federal courts have been hostile to claims for leaves of absence as a reasonable accommodation under ADA,[65] the FMLA requires that such leaves be granted for up to 12 weeks.[66]

Today, the funding of programs providing benefits for people with disabilities continues. In addition to the large programs of medical care and income replacement discussed above, the federal government continues to fund Gallaudet College, the National Technical Institute for the Deaf, the Helen Keller National Center, and the American Printing House for the Blind. The total budget for these programs for 1997 was $136 million.[67] By comparison, the federal government spends less than 1% of this total on private programs designed to provide assistance and information to people with psychiatric disabilities; in 1997, it funded two technical assistance centers[68] with a total budget of $800,000. The federal government also funds a number of federal commissions dealing with issues related to both physical and mental disability.[69]

From Medical Condition to Minority Status

By the early 1970s, people with disabilities were beginning to redefine their identity.[70] The 1960s civil rights movement focused attention on concepts of discrimination, stereotyping, and unequal treatment based on unfounded assumptions of inferiority arising from membership in a disfavored group. Black people and later women challenged this treatment and reclaimed their identity as a source of pride. This precedent provided inspiration to people with disabilities.

The transformation of disability from medical diagnosis to political identity proceeded separately for people with physical and psychiatric disabilities. People with physical disabilities coalesced around the Independent Living Movement, while people who had been hospitalized because of diagnoses of mental illness formed a number of groups in Northern California and on the East Coast.[71]

Although individuals had written for many years of horrifying experiences in psychiatric institutions,[72] these had generally been calls for reform of psychiatric treatment in institutions. The new movement was a collective identification of people with psychiatric diagnoses as a minority group subject to discrimination in all spheres of life.

The change from a medical model describing functional limitations in an ostensibly objective way to the minority group model that conceptualized limitations as created by society acting on its own myths and stereotypes[73] was fueled by sociological theories such as labeling theory and the sociology of deviance. Some of the critique came from psychiatrists themselves;[74] the best-known author of the time questioned whether mental illness existed at all.[75] Feminists joined the debate, sharply questioning both Freudian theory and the general psychiatric view of women.[76]

In 1972, Bruce Ennis and Charles Halpern formed the Mental Health Law Project, the first public-interest law firm devoted to securing the rights of people diagnosed in the public mental health system. Although the Mental Health Association had existed for years, advocating for better care and treatment of people with mental illness, the Mental Health Law Project reformulated the request for charity as a demand for rights.

These lawyers and the writers who preceded them, although political, were not ex-patients themselves. The literature soon began to be written by people who had lived the experiences that Szasz, Chesler, and Ennis wrote about. Ex-patients began producing newsletters such as *Madness Network News*. By 1975, Janet Gotkin and her husband Paul had written a harrowing first-person account of treatment in the mental health system,[77] which remains one of the finest books of its kind today. In 1978, Judi Chamberlin published *On Our Own*,[78] calling for patient-run alternatives to the traditional mental health system. This consciousness of a political identity and identification of injustices committed by others on the basis of that identity was a necessary precondition for enactment and enforcement of federal antidiscrimination laws.

Mental Health Law and Disability Rights Law

The evolution of the law regarding the rights of people with disabilities is complex. Mental health law can be seen as evolving from a constitution-based, due process model to a statute-based, antidiscrimination model. This has been proposed as the natural progression of all civil rights law relating to disfavored groups.[79] The law relating to people with disabilities, however, is not so much a progression as the parallel development of two models, the mental health law model and disability rights model. These models resulted in different approaches, litigated from different perspectives, framed in different ways, and—until recently—seeking different goals.

Mental Health Law

The mental health law model had its origins in civil rights law and the civil rights movement of the 1960s. Modern mental health law cases[80] were first brought by lawyers representing prisoners, not mental patients.[81] This is logical, because prisoners came from a system in which people had lawyers—the criminal justice system —and in which the concept that substantive and procedural due process has to be observed in depriving them of liberty was assumed. It took almost 10 years for the Supreme Court to issue its first decision involving the rights of patients outside the criminal justice system. In 1975, the Supreme Court decided *O'Connor v. Donaldson*,[82] holding that the state could not constitutionally commit someone solely on the basis of mental illness.

As in prisoner's rights litigation, the chief adversary in mental health law was the state, which took away an individual's liberty and his or her rights through civil commitment. The goal, initially, was substantive and procedural protection against the loss of liberty represented by involuntary commitment. Lawyers worked to ensure that people could not be committed simply because they were eccentric or even because they needed treatment. Although some argued that commitment could be justified if the state provided treatment,[83] for the most part advocates worked to ensure that substantive standards for commitment required dangerousness, manifested by recent overt acts or the imminent threat of harm. Procedurally, lawyers fought for the right to a hearing, representation by counsel, and the cross-examination of witnesses.[84]

Concurrently, other concerns arose, such as the length of time between initial detention and hearing; the right to refuse to speak to examining psychiatrists, or at least to be warned that anything said to the psychiatrist would be used in the commitment hearing; the right to be free from psychotropic medication at the time of the hearing; the right to a hearing in a courthouse, rather than a hospital; the right to wear one's own clothing at the hearing; and the right to independent expert witnesses paid for by the state.[85]

The chief legal tool to achieve these goals was the due process clause of the Fourteenth Amendment to the U.S. Constitution; the chief forum was the federal court, which was initially sympathetic to claims brought on behalf of people with mental disabilities. Indeed, in 1972, Justice Harry Blackmun virtually invited lawyers to file such cases.[86]

Soon the focus shifted from the commitment process to its aftermath: institutions and the conditions in which institutionalized people were forced to live. The goal was initially formulated as establishing a right to treatment. Mental health lawyers seized on an article written by Morton Birnbaum, a medical doctor, which was published by the *American Bar Association Journal* in 1960. Birnbaum proposed that if the state took away a person's liberty on the premise that he or she needed treatment, the state must in fact provide that treatment.[87] Rights in institutions that were the subject of litigation included, at first, the right to racially integrated treatment settings and to a racially integrated work force; the right to be free from unreasonable seclusion and restraint; the right to safety; and the rights to send and receive private mail, to retain and wear one's own clothing, to have visitors, to receive compensation for work performed at the institution,[88] and even to fresh air and exercise.[89]

Then, as lawyers began to listen more clearly to the people formerly and currently in institutions and to respond to their concerns, the right to refuse medication and to refuse electric shock treatment gained ascendancy. Lawyers also began to work not only at improving conditions in institutional settings but also at moving people out of those institutions and securing for them the housing and support services that they needed in the community.

Again, the chief legal tool to achieve these goals was the due process clause of the 14th Amendment. Building on previous constitutional doctrine in other areas, the concept that treatment in the "least restrictive alternative" setting was required as a matter of constitutional law gained a brief ascendancy in case law. Although it was later repudiated by the courts, the concept found its way into both federal regulations[90] and the psychiatric standard of care.[91]

In the wake of the increasing conservatism of the federal courts and the Supreme Court's explicitly articulated desire to remove federal courts from the task of monitoring state institutions,[92] some advocates began turning to state constitutional guarantees and state statutory rights—most of which had been enacted in response to previous activity and judgments in federal courts[93]—to achieve victories in mental health law.[94]

Because mental health law was chiefly based on federal and state constitutional guarantees and in some rare cases on the statutory rights of service recipients of state mental health systems, defendants in mental health law cases were state actors.[95] To this day, the principal mental health law treatises[96] and law textbooks[97] concentrate on issues relating to the incarceration and commitment of people on the basis of mental illness, their right to treatment, and their right to refuse treatment in both institutional and community settings.

The principal decisions by the Supreme Court now suggest that although a person may not be civilly committed to a mental institution without a finding by clear and convincing evidence[98] of mental problems impairing the ability to control dangerous behavior,[99] a great deal of latitude will be given to states in defining the mental problems sufficient to support commitment. The Supreme Court has long been dubious about the abilities of psychiatrists to define, diagnose, or treat mental illness, and more than one opinion has explicitly articulated the need to keep constitutional requirements loose enough that the psychiatric profession will be able to meet them.[100] Whether the condition of mental illness must be treatable for commitment to be constitutional remains an open question. It is clear that the Supreme Court is more concerned about the dangerousness prong of the constitutional requirement than the question of which mental problems suffice to support involuntary commitment.

Once a person is involuntarily committed to a mental institution,[101] he or she has a right to food, clothing, shelter, safety, freedom from undue bodily restraint, and minimally adequate treatment.[102] Under Supreme Court interpretation, however, the content and contours of these rights are determined by mental health professionals under the "professional judgment" standard. If an institutionalized person claims that his or her rights have been violated—any kind of rights, from the 1st Amendment right to free speech to the 4th Amendment right to be free from unreasonable search or seizure—the person can prevail only if the deprivation of the right constituted a "substantial departure from professional judgment." Although this standard makes sense if the person is claiming a right to treatment, it makes little sense in other contexts, such as religious freedom, search and seizure, and associational freedom.[103]

The professional judgment standard is particularly unhelpful in cases in which the plaintiff seeks to establish his or her right to reject professional judgment: generally cases involving the refusal of psychotropic medication, electric shock, and aversive behavior-control techniques, and the use of seclusion and restraint. In these cases, the plaintiff asserts a right that arguably transcends professional judgment—just as the right of a Christian Scientist to refuse a medically necessary blood transfusion transcends the medical judgment that he or she should have it or the right of students to learn in an integrated school or to refuse to salute the flag transcends the education professional's decision that segregation is educationally preferable and saluting the flag is a prerequisite of school discipline.

The Supreme Court's jurisprudence on the right to refuse psychotropic medication has developed in the criminal context,[104] and it is difficult to say how those decisions would be altered in the civil arena. At the very least, the court recognized a significant liberty interest in the refusal of mind-altering medication, but it has nevertheless held that (in the criminal context) such medication may be forced on a competent individual if it is in his or her medical interest and if he or she is dangerous without it. Lower federal courts have been notably deferential in permitting involuntary psychotropic medication. Many courts have adopted the Supreme Court's standards developed in the criminal context to the civil environment.[105]

Disability Rights Law

While mental health law was advancing through the courts, simultaneously but separately people with physical disabilities were organizing around issues relating to autonomy and independence, principally related to transforming disability benefits to remove disincentives to work, increasing funding for vocational rehabilitation, creating independent living centers, moving funding from nursing homes and institutional care into the community, and assuring accessible transportation.

The disability rights movement was unlike the mental health law movement in many ways. Whereas mental health law focused on individual liberties against the intrusions of the state, the disability rights movement decried neglect by the state and underscored the importance of integration and assimilation. People wanted their disabled children to be educated with other children in a regular classroom—and those who were disabled wanted admission to a regular classroom themselves. People with mobility impairments wanted to be able to use buses and airplanes and trains to travel around their cities and the nation.

The methods of the disability rights movement also differed considerably from those of mental health law. Disability rights advocates concentrated on reforming legislation and regulations rather than on court challenges involving constitutional rights. While mental health lawyers were working to create new constitutional rights to treatment and to refuse treatment, the disability rights movement was promoting federal legislation on accessible transportation and working on extending the scope of the Rehabilitation Act's prohibition on discrimination against people with disabilities.[106]

The disability rights movement organized their constituencies. No one ever took over, or even contemplated taking over, a mental institution, but when the U.S. Department of Health, Education and Welfare (HEW) dragged its feet on issuing regulations for the Rehabilitation Act, people with disabilities took over Secretary Joseph Califano's office in Washington, DC; visited his home at night for a candlelight vigil; and occupied HEW's regional office in San Francisco. They did not leave the office in San Francisco for almost a month. In the wake of the protests and an order by a federal judge,[107] an extremely reluctant Califano promulgated the regulations.[108]

Disability rights activists lobbied Congress, negotiated with government officials, and became known to the national political community. As a result, they began to be appointed to political office. Ed Roberts was appointed by Governor Jerry Brown to head California's Department of Rehabilitation. The late Evan Kemp was Chairman of the Equal Employment Opportunity Commission (EEOC) under President George Bush. When Bill Clinton was elected president, he appointed Judy Heumann, once the scourge of Joseph Califano, as Deputy Secretary of Education. Paul Miller was appointed to the Civil Rights Commission.

Mental health lawyers, known in the legal rather than the political community, became judges[109] and law school professors and deans,[110] but they have generally not been appointed to political office. Many have gone on to other careers in the law[111] or other careers in the public interest world.[112] Ex-patients have been politically active in some states, notably California. However, to say that there has not been any major effort to appoint people with diagnoses of mental illness to high positions in state or federal government would be an understatement.

The Rehabilitation Act of 1973 and Its Amendments

Given the tension between disability benefits and disability rights, it is ironic that the first major federal prohibition on disability discrimination law came as part of a disability benefits law. In the early 1970s, Congress first became concerned with discrimination on the basis of disability—or handicap, as the terminology was then. In 1972, Sen. Hubert Humphrey (D-MN) and Sen. Charles Percy (R-IL) introduced a bill to amend the Civil Rights Act of 1964 to prohibit discrimination on the basis of mental or physical handicap in federally assisted programs. A similar bill was introduced in the House of Representatives by Rep. Charles Vanik (D-OH).

Opposition to these bills came not from conservatives but rather

> apparently came from those who were committed to protecting the groups already covered by Title VI of the Civil Rights Act, notably blacks. . . . Civil rights advocates were concerned that any significant broadening of the scope of the Civil Rights Act would necessarily distract from, and thus diminish enforcement of, existing provisions.[113]

No hearings were ever held on these bills, nor were they ever voted on in the committees to which they were referred, but the same year saw greater legislative progress through a different approach. In 1972, a one-sentence prohibition on discrimination on the basis of handicap was attached to legislation appropriating funds for vocational rehabilitation. That legislation, the would-be Rehabilitation Act of 1972, was a sweeping measure intended to redesign vocational rehabilitation,[114] principally directed at expanding vocational rehabilitation services, research, and training to reach people with the most severe disabilities, who had been drastically underserved.

The story of how a prohibition against discrimination on the basis of handicap by federal agencies and entities receiving federal funds came to be added to this bill has been researched by Richard Scotch, who found that

the idea for including an anti-discrimination prohibition in the Rehabilitation Act occurred toward the end of a meeting held in late August [1972] to discuss revision of
the marked-up rehabilitation bill. . . . Staff members felt that the final goal of the VR
[vocational rehabilitation] program, getting disabled people into the mainstream of
society, was being blocked by negative attitudes and discrimination on the part of
employers and others. Someone suggested that language be included in the Rehabilitation Act proscribing discrimination against handicapped people in federally assisted
programs. Such a provision would be comparable to the provisions of Title VI of the
Civil Rights Act of 1964, and to Title IX of the Education Amendments of 1972, but
would not involve amending those statutes. Roy Millenson of Senator Javits' staff had
been involved in the development of the Education Amendments, and he ran out of
his office and brought back language from Title VI. The language was adapted and
inserted at the very end of the Rehabilitation Act.[115]

The Rehabilitation Act was passed by Congress. President Nixon pocket vetoed
it, labeling it as wasteful government spending. By this point, people with physical
disabilities were organized well enough to demonstrate against the veto in several
cities, including New York City.[116] After the elections, Congress reintroduced the
same legislation and held hearings on it. One witness noted and applauded the antidiscrimination provisions.[117] In April 1973, Congress passed the bill, but President
Nixon once again failed to sign it into law. Congress attempted but failed to override
the veto.

The Rehabilitation Act was introduced for the third time in the spring of 1973,
with concessions to President Nixon's concerns about cost. In the fall, the Rehabilitation Act of 1973 was passed, with identical language pertaining to discrimination,
and President Nixon finally signed it into law.[118] Under the act, any person with a
physical or mental handicap was eligible for benefits and entitled to protection
against discrimination as long as their condition caused a "substantial handicap to
employment" and the individual "could reasonably be expected to benefit in terms
of employability."[119]

In 1974, Congress passed extensive amendments to the Vocational Rehabilitation
Act. The legislative history to these amendments contains Congress's first explanations of what it wished to accomplish by prohibiting discrimination on the basis
of handicap. Noting that its prior prohibition of discrimination had been read to
prohibit only discrimination in employment, Congress clarified its intent to prohibit
all discriminatory actions by recipients of federal funds instead of solely prohibiting
employment discrimination. Congress also extended discrimination protection further, stating that people who were not in fact handicapped but who were discriminated against because they were perceived to be handicapped or who had a record
of handicap were also protected from discrimination. In the prohibition of discrimination on the basis of a perception of disability, the legislative history of the bill
specifically analogizes this prohibition on discrimination against people with disabilities to legislation prohibiting discrimination against minorities embodied by
Titles VI and VII of the Civil Rights Act of 1964. President Gerald Ford vetoed this
bill,[120] but Congress overwhelmingly overrode the veto.

Title VI, which Congress considered to be analogous to Section 504 of the
Rehabilitation Act of 1973, prohibited discrimination on the basis of race by entities
receiving federal funds.[121] Title VII prohibited employment discrimination on the
basis of race or gender by any private employer of 15 individuals or more[122] and

was considered to be the model for Section 501 of the Rehabilitation Act, which prohibited discrimination on the basis of handicap by the federal government, and later for Title I of the ADA, which prohibits discrimination on the basis of disability in employment generally.

Unlike race or gender, however, employers and others might mistakenly attribute a handicap where none in fact existed and still discriminate on the basis of a perceived handicap. Therefore, Congress modified its definition of "handicapped" solely for the purpose of the antidiscrimination provision. After 1974, handicapped individuals were defined as "any person with a physical or mental impairment that substantially limits one or more of such person's major life activities or an individual with a record of such an impairment or who is regarded as having such an impairment."[123]

This definition has remained essentially unchanged for 25 years and has been used to define disability in a number of subsequent statutes, including the Fair Housing Amendments Act of 1988,[124] prohibiting discrimination on the basis of disability in housing; the Air Carrier Access Act of 1986,[125] prohibiting airlines from discriminating against passengers on the basis of disability; and the ADA.

Despite the clarification of the meaning of "handicap," however, the single sentence prohibiting discrimination in the Rehabilitation Act proved singularly hard to interpret. Congress had mandated that HEW write interpretive regulations, but this took far longer than expected and had dramatic political ramifications.

The Rehabilitation Act Amendments of 1974,[126] which altered the definition of *handicapped* became law on December 7, 1974, and proposed regulations were drafted by HEW and ready for promulgation by July 1975.[127] However, the new Secretary of HEW, David Mathews, was concerned about "the appropriateness of including alcoholics, drug addicts and mentally ill people within the definition of handicapped person."[128] The publication of the draft regulations in the *Federal Register* for notice and comment was delayed until disability activists demonstrated in Secretary Mathews's office and threatened to picket the upcoming National Republican Convention. The proposed regulations were then published.[129] However, they were not finally adopted unitl court challenges and the office takeovers of 1977 forced the Carter Administration to act.

The Rehabilitation Act was amended in 1978 to extend Section 504's coverage to all programs and activities conducted by federal executive agencies.[130] Crucially, the 1978 amendments also defined for the first time the legal remedies for violations of Section 504. Until then, there had been considerable debate in the courts as to whether a private right of action even existed under Section 504—that is, whether individuals could bring suit to enforce their right to be free from discrimination under the act. The 1978 amendments made it clear that all of the remedies of Title VI of the Civil Rights Act were to be applicable to Section 504 of the Rehabilitation Act as well. The 1978 amendments also saw the first introduction of the concept of "direct threat," which was applicable at the time only to alcoholics or drug abusers.

In 1985 the Supreme Court held in *Atascadero v. Scanlon*[131] that states could not be sued under the Rehabilitation Act because Congress had not made its intent to abrogate the states' 11th Amendment immunity sufficiently clear. Congress acted promptly to rectify the situation and passed the Rehabilitation Act Amendments of 1986,[132] indicating that states could indeed be sued under the Rehabilitation Act, and the U.S. Department of Justice supported this conclusion.[133]

Additional strengthening of the Rehabilitation Act was provided in 1987 by the

Civil Rights Restoration Act,[134] which made it clear that "recipients of federal funds" were to include not only the direct, initial recipients of federal funds but also those eventually receiving the funds.[135] For example, although the New York State Board of Law Examiners does not directly receive federal funds, it cashes vouchers from New York state vocational rehabilitation agencies to pay for their clients to take the bar examination, and those agencies in turn use federal funds to pay for the vouchers. Under these circumstances, the New York State Board of Law Examiners is a recipient of federal funds under the law and regulations.[136]

The Americans With Disabilities Act

By the mid-1980s, however, it was becoming increasingly apparent that the Rehabilitation Act of 1973 was not sufficient to guarantee the rights of people with disabilities to be free from discrimination. The Rehabilitation Act was problematic as a tool for remedying discrimination against people with disabilities in a variety of ways: its language was limited to discrimination solely on the basis of disability,[137] its coverage was limited to entities receiving federal financial assistance, it was not well enforced,[138] and its judicial interpretation was inconsistent.

Those problems helped prompt a renewed call for the direct expansion of the Civil Rights Act of 1964, and the Civil Rights Commission in 1983 called for federal legislation to add *handicap* to the act's title.[139] A bill was introduced to accomplish this in 1985, but it was not successful.[140] The National Council on the Handicapped recommended in 1986 that legislation be passed to ensure that people with disabilities would be protected against discrimination.[141] The council drafted the legislation in 1988, and the ADA was first introduced in Congress in 1988. It failed and was reintroduced in 1989. Congress held a total of 14 hearings at the Capitol and 63 field hearings on the ADA, and it accepted hundreds of "disability diaries" submitted by people with disabilities about their experiences of discrimination. The ADA was passed by Congress and signed by President George Bush on July 26, 1990.

The ADA is divided into five titles. Title I prohibits discrimination against people with disabilities by employers.[142] The federal agency in charge of enforcing Title I is the EEOC. It has received more complaints of discrimination from people with psychiatric disabilities than any other group of people with disabilities.

Title II forbids discrimination by public entities, namely, state and local governments and their agencies.[143] The U.S. Supreme Court is currently considering two consolidated cases, *University of Alabama v. Garrett* and *Alabama Department of Youth Services v. Ash*,[144] that argue that Congress exceeded its authority under Section 5 of the 14th Amendment when it made the states subject to liability under the ADA. By the time this book is released, the Supreme Court should have rendered its decision. If the Supreme Court agrees with those who challenge Title II, states will not be subject to litigation seeking money damages but will still be subject to litigation seeking prospective injunctive relief. Title II also regulates transportation, with detailed directions intended to make the nation's systems of transportation accessible to people with disabilities.

Title III prohibits discrimination by public accommodations, such as restaurants, hospitals, movie theaters, doctor's offices, and private universities. Whether Title III subjects insurance companies to liability for discriminatory provisions in their insurance coverage is the subject of considerable litigation and is discussed at length in chapter 6. Both Titles II and III are enforced by the Department of Justice.[145]

Title IV sets out detailed standards for telecommunications designed to make communications in the United States accessible to people who are deaf. These provisions are enforced by the Federal Communication Commission.[146]

Title V is a mixed bag of miscellaneous provisions, such as the abrogation of state 11th Amendment immunity at issue in *Garrett* and *Ash*,[147] and compromises that were required to win passage of the ADA. It includes a safe harbor provision for insurance companies,[148] discussed at length in chapter 6. It also contains an interesting list of society's most despised classifications, explicitly excluded from coverage (even though there is some doubt that they would have met the definition of disability in any event) at the insistence of Sen. Jesse Helms (D-NC) and others as the price of passing the ADA: "compulsive gamblers," "kleptomaniacs," "pyromaniacs," "exhibitionists," "pedophiles," "transsexuals," "voyeurs," and of course "homosexuals," "lesbians," and "bisexuals."[149] For some reason, which is not entirely clear, "transvestites" were excluded from the definition of disability in a separate section of Title V.[150]

Although one of the principal goals of the ADA was to enable Americans with disabilities receiving government disability benefits to secure and maintain employment by giving them the tools to fight employment discrimination, many in Congress have now realized that prohibiting discrimination is not enough to accomplish this goal. Lack of health care benefits from employers often forces people who could work to stay on disability simply to ensure coverage of health care costs. The Ticket to Work and the Work Incentives Improvement Act of 1999,[151] signed by President Clinton on December 17, 1999, would permit disabled people receiving Medicaid and Medicare to work without losing health care coverage. This legislation is at least as necessary as the ADA in enabling Americans with disabilities to work.

Conclusion

The interplay between disability benefits and disability rights is a complex one. The concept expressed by some courts that Americans must choose between benefits on the basis of disability and the right to be free from discrimination on the basis of disability is itself a result of stereotypes about disabilities. Certainly U.S. society is replete with groups of citizens that receive both benefits and freedom from discrimination on the basis of the same status. Veterans and members of the military receive substantial educational, housing, employment, and health care benefits on the basis of their status and are also protected from discrimination on the basis of their status.[152] Pregnant women receive attention from federal health programs and are protected from employment discrimination by the 1978 Pregnancy Discrimination Act.[153] Older Americans are entitled to Medicare and to be free from discrimination on the basis of their age under the Age Discrimination in Employment Act of 1967.[154] Children may receive social security benefits for being disabled, and few question their right to be free from discrimination in the school system on the basis of disability.[155]

The perceived tensions between disability benefits and disability rights may be due to the different presumptions and approaches of the different statutes. Social security presumes that some conditions are disabling, whereas the ADA has been held to require individualized inquiry. Social Security does not look into the possibilities of individualized accommodations; the ADA mandates such inquiries. The Social Security Act's presumptions and practices serve the goal of efficiently administering a huge system affecting millions of people and involving billions of dollars. The individualized inquiry of the ADA is intended to maximize justice and minimize presumptions and stereotypes. The individualized approach may operate at the cost of efficiency, but Americans do not like to think of justice as mass produced or of judges as bureaucrats.

Disability benefits, the ADA, mental health litigation, and disability litigation all serve one underlying and unifying purpose: to enable people with disabilities to live integrated, independent lives in the community rather than isolated, segregated lives in large institutions. From mental health litigation, which focused on making commitment more difficult and later on enhancing treatment in the community, to disability litigation, which focused on accessible transportation and enforcing disabled children's right to education, to Social Security benefits, which provide limited income support so that people can live in the community, disability benefits and disability rights are aimed at limiting segregation and enhancing the individual's ability to live and learn in the community. Disability benefits programs and disability rights seek inclusion,[156] integration, and nondiscrimination.

The bridge between mental health law and disability law—between disability benefits and disability rights—is the current use of the ADA, the home- and community-based waiver provisions of the Social Security Act, and the Ticket to Work and Work Incentives Improvement Act of 1999, to fight the segregation of disabled individuals in institutional settings—nursing homes, psychiatric institutions, and institutions for people with mental retardation and developmental disabilities—and to permit people to live with families and friends in the community.

Endnotes

1. The first equal protection claims involving people with mental illness were brought by prisoners and pretrial detainees. The reason for this particular development in the law is discussed in detail below.
2. City of Cleburne v. Cleburne Living Center, 473 U.S. 432 (1985).
3. Cleburne Living Center v. City of Cleburne, 726 F.2d 171, 173 (5th Cir. 1984).
4. City of Cleburne v. Cleburne Living Center, 473 U.S. 432, at 440–443.
5. *Id.* at 439.
6. *Id.* at 440.
7. *Id.*
8. *Id.* at 440, 441.
9. *Id.* at 442.
10. Since this passage was written, the U.S. Supreme Court decided Kimel v. Board of Regents, 120 S.Ct. 631 (2000), which holds that the Age Discrimination in Employment Act is unconstitutional when applied to state governments.
11. City of Cleburne v. Cleburne Living Center, 473 U.S. at 443.
12. *Id.*
13. The Supreme Court cited three statutes as examples of legislative concern for people

with mental retardation: Section 504 of the Rehabilitation Act, the Developmental Disabilities Assistance and Bill of Rights Act, and the Education of the Handicapped Act. By 1979, the court, in its first opinion interpreting Section 504 of the Rehabilitation Act, has significantly weakened it; Southeastern Community College v. Davis, 442 U.S. 379 (1979). The Supreme Court ignored the contrary position of the Department of Justice in Southeastern Community College v. Davis; the department filed an amicus brief in support of Davis. In its first opinion interpreting the Developmental Disabilities Assistance and Bill of Rights Act, the Supreme Court held significant provisions of the act to be "merely precatory" and unenforceable; Pennhurst v. Halderman, 451 U.S. 1 (1981), and in its first interpretation of the Education for the Handicapped Act, the Supreme Court held that its guarantee of a "free, appropriate public education" was satisfied when a deaf girl could only understand 58–59% of communication in the classroom because the act entitled her only to a program "reasonably calculated to enable her to receive education benefits"; Rowley v. Board of Education, 458 U.S. 176, 206, 207 (1982).

14. University of Alabama at Birmingham Board of Trustees v. Garrett, consolidated with Alabama Department of Youth Services v. Ash, No. 99-1240, 68 U.S.L.W. 3654 (Apr. 17, 2000). Both cases involve employment discrimination claims against the state; in one case the plaintiff had breast cancer, and in the other the plaintiff had respiratory difficulties; Jonathan Ringel, "Supreme Court Update," LEGAL TIMES (Apr. 24, 2000): 8.

15. City of Boerne v. Flores, 521 U.S. 507 (1997); Kimel v. Board of Regents, 120 S.Ct. 631 (2000).

16. Olmstead v. L. C., 119 S.Ct. 2176 (1999), as discussed in chapter 4.

17. James Leonard, "A Damaged Remedy: Disability Discrimination Claims Against State Entities Under the Americans With Disabilities Act After Seminole Tribe and Flores," *Arizona Law Rev.* 41 (1999):651.

18. Matthew Diller, "Dissonant Disability Policies: The Tensions Between the ADA and Federal Disability Benefits Programs," *Texas Law Rev.* 76 (Apr. 1998):1003, 1009.

19. *See* chapter 5.

20. These are primarily related to workers' compensation statutes, Cramer v. Florida, 885 F.Supp. 1545 (M.D. Fla. 1995), *aff'd,* 117 F.3d 1258, (11th Cir. 1997); Harding v. Winn-Dixie, 907 F.Supp. 386 (M.D. Fla. 1995), Brown v. Campbell County Board of Education, 915 S.W.2d 407 (Tenn. 1996), but also include challenges to the state administration of the Social Security Plan for Achieving Self-Support (PASS) Program, Vaughn v. Sullivan, 83 F.3d 907 (7th Cir. 1996), and to state disability-assistance programs, Does 1-5 v. Chandler, 83 F.3d 1150 (9th Cir. 1996), Weaver v. New Mexico Human Services, 945 P.2d 70 (N.M.1997), and Rodriguez v. DeBuono, 44 F.Supp. 2nd 601 (S.D. 1999), *rev'd,* 197 F.3d 611 (2nd Cir. 1999).

21. Cleveland v. Policy Management Systems Corp., 143 L.Ed.2d 966 (1999).

22. Miller v. U.S. Bancorp, 926 F.Supp. 994 (D. Ore. 1996), *aff'd*, 139 F.3d 906 (9th Cir. 1998).

23. *Id.,* at 971, quoting Reigel v. Kaiser Foundation Health Plan of N.C., 859 F.Supp. 963, 970 (E.D. N.C. 1994).

24. McNemar v. Disney Store, Inc., 91 F.3d 610 (3rd Cir. 1996); Harris v. Marathon Oil, 948 F.Supp. 27, 29 (W.D. Tx. 1996), *aff'd,* 108 F.3d 332 (5th Cir. 1997); Cleveland v. Policy Management Systems, 120 F.3d 513, 518 (5th Cir. 1997), *rev'd,* 142 L.Ed.2d 966 (1999).

25. Cleveland v. Policy Management Systems Corp., 119 S.Ct. 1597, 143 L.Ed.2d 966 (1999).

26. *Id.* at 1600. The Supreme Court nevertheless emphasized that the plaintiff "must explain why that SSDI contention [of total disability] is consistent with her ADA claim that she could 'perform the essential function' of her previous job, at least with 'reasonable accommodation.' "

27. Title I of the ADA, which prohibits employment discrimination, follows the procedural requirements of Title VII of the Civil Rights Act of 1964, 42 U.S.C. §12117 (1999), which requires a person to first make a complaint to the EEOC or the state equivalent of this agency. The person may not go to court until the agency acts in some way on his or her complaint, which it has up to 180 days to do.

28. Fredenburg v. Contra Costa County, 172 F.3d 1176, 1179, 1180 (9th Cir. 1999).

29. 20 C.F.R. 404.1592(a).

30. *Id.*

31. Deborah Stone, *The Disabled State* (Philadelphia: Temple University Press, 1984) at 181, 182.

32. Deborah Stone, *The Disabled State, id.*

33. *See* Susan Stefan, "The Americans With Disabilities Act, Mental Disability, and Work," *Psychiatric Services* 48(12) [Book review] (Dec. 1997):1595; Christopher G. Bell, "The Americans With Disabilities Act, Mental Disability, and Work," in Richard Bonnie and John Monahan, Eds., *Mental Disorder, Work Disability and the Law* (Chicago: University of Chicago Press 1997) at 218; Matthew Diller, "Dissonant Disability Policies: The Tensions Between the ADA and Federal Disability Benefits Programs," *Tex. Law Rev.* 76 (Apr. 1998):1003, 1006.

34. 142 *Cong. Rec.* S8472 (daily ed., July 22, 1996) (statement of Sen. Jeffords).

35. Bell, at note 33; Diller, at note 33.

36. *See, e.g.,* Harris v. Chater, 998 F.Supp. 223, 229 (E.D. N.Y. 1998) (noting that "full integration of these two sets of laws—the SSA and the ADA—has not yet occurred").

37. Susan Stefan, tentatively titled *Hollow Promises: The Americans With Disabilities Act and Employment Discrimination Against People With Mental Disabilities* (Washington, DC: American Psychological Association, in press).

38. P. L. 106-170 (1999).

39. Chapter 77, 1 Stat. 635, July 16, 1798, reproduced in Robert B. Stevens, Ed., *Statutory History of the United States: Income Security* (New York: Chelsea House, 1970) at 32–34. The Marine Hospital Service, which operated the first facilities for these seamen, was reorganized in 1902 as the Public Health and Marine Hospital Service and was later renamed the Public Health Service; Richard Scotch, *From Goodwill to Civil Rights: Transforming Federal Disability Policy* (Philadelphia: Temple University Press 1984) at 17.

40. 12 STAT. 287 (1861), quoted in Major Chuck R. Pardue, "The Grenada Intervention: Military Disability in a Nutshell," *Mil. Law Rev.* 109 (Summer 1985):149–151.

41. The Smith–Sears Veteran's Rehabilitation Act was originally passed to assist returning soldiers, 40 STAT. 617 (1918).

42. Act of June 2, 1920, ch. 219, 41 STAT. 735. Although many law review articles refer to this law as the Smith–Fess Act, *see, e.g.,* Lisa A. Montanaro, Comment, "The Americans With Disabilities Act: Will the Court Get the Hint? Congress' Attempt to Raise the Status of Persons With Disabilities in Equal Protection Cases," *Pace Law Rev.* 15 (1995):621, 637; Ron L. Findley, "Handicap Discrimination in the Workplace: Winning a Rehabilitation Act Section 504 Claim by Contemporary Standards in the Eighth Circuit," 53 *U.K.M.C. Law Rev.* 411, 414 (1985), it is referred to as the Fess–Kenyon Act in the United State Code Annotated Popular Name Table.

43. P. L. 78-113, 57 Stat. 374 (1943).

44. P. L. 80–617, 62 Stat. 351 (1948).

45. The U.S. Senate relied in part on the strong objections of the American Medical Association, which predicted that people would malinger and that such a program would set the nation on the road to a "compulsory sickness program," Statement of the American Medical Association, Senate Hearings on H.R. 6000 before the Senate Finance Committee, 81st Cong., 2nd Sess. (Jan. 1950), quoted in Stevens, note 39, at 365.

46. 64 STAT. 558 (1950).
47. The statute prohibits "any individual (a) who is a patient in an institution for tuberculosis or mental diseases, or (b) who has been diagnosed as having tuberculosis or psychosis and is a patient in a medical institution as a result thereof" from receiving benefits; 64 STAT. 558 (1950). This exception, which became known as the Institution for Mental Disease exception, is discussed at greater length in chapter 5.
48. Vocational Rehabilitation Amendments Act of 1954, P. L. 565.
49. During the Senate hearings, Secretary of Health, Education, and Welfare Marion Folsom opposed disability insurance on the grounds that it would lead to fraudulent claims and "discourage individual rehabilitative efforts"; *Congress and the Nation* (Washington, DC: *Congressional Quarterly,* Inc., 1965) at 1251.
50. The American Medical Association charged that disability insurance was "a specific threat to good medical care through government interference with medical practice," *id.*
51. 70 Stat. 815 (1956).
52. President Eisenhower remarked on the day he signed the bill that "we are loading on the Social Security system something I don't think should be there, and if it is going to be handled, should be handled another way," *Congress and the Nation* at 1251.
53. Before 1978, benefits were calculated in terms of quarters of coverage, and employers reported earnings every 3 months. Starting in 1978, employers report earnings once a year, and a worker receives credits based on how much was earned in that year. In 1997, a worker received one credit for each $670 of covered annual earnings, up to a maximum of four credits per year, Social Security Administration, "Your Personal Earnings and Benefit Estimate Statement" (1997) at 5.
54. 79 Stat. 343. The Medicaid Program is found at Title XIX of the Social Security Act.
55. 42 U.S.C. 1396d(a)(1); 42 U.S.C. 1396d(a)(4)(A); 42 U.S.C. 1396d(a)(15) (1999).
56. 30 U.S.C. § 901–945 (2000) (Black Lung Benefits Act).
57. 44 Stat. 577, 45 U.S.C.A. § 151 (1999).
58. P. L. 93-445, 45 U.S.C.A. § 231 (1999).
59. 35 Stat. 65, 45 U.S.C.A. § 51 (1999).
60. These include veterans' compensation for service-connected disabilities, 38 U.S.C. Secs. 310, 331, 1101, 1131; compensation for non-service-connected disabilities, 38 U.S.C. Secs. 1511, 1512, 1521; vocational rehabilitation for disabled veterans is found at 38 U.S.C. Sec. 3102. Housing for disabled veterans is subsidized, 38 U.S.C. Secs. 2101–2106, as is the purchase of prosthetic and other devices, 38 U.S.C. Sec. 1162 (providing for the replacement of prosthetic devices).
61. 86 Stat. 1465, codified at 42 U.S.C. Secs. 1381 *et seq.* The SSI program took the place of the previous Aid to the Permanently and Totally Disabled Program and other federal assistance to blind and disabled people, which, as noted above, had granted states far greater latitude in defining disability and determining levels of support. The new SSI program federalized the program and, by associating it with the Social Security program, removed much of the stigma associated with the previous program, which had been more closely associated with welfare. This destigmatization was one of the purposes of creating SSI; Matthew Diller, "Entitlement and Exclusion: The Role of Disability in the Social Welfare System," *UCLA Law Rev.* 44 (1996):361, 434.
62. 29 U.S.C. Sec. 701. This is a federal–state program, with the federal government picking up 80 cents of every dollar spent.
63. All of these programs continue today, along with additional programs intended to assist people with disabilities, such as the Targeted Jobs Tax Credit Program, which was part of the Tax Reduction Act of 1977, P. L. 95-30, providing employers with tax credits for hiring disabled employees, and Sec. 190 of the Internal Revenue Code, which gives tax

credits for removing architectural barriers in the workplace; and programs providing advocacy for institutionalized people with psychiatric disabilities who are or have been institutionalized within the past 90 days, 42 U.S.C. Secs. 10801 *et seq.* (1995) (Protection and Advocacy for Individuals With Mentally Illness [PAIMI]), and advocacy for people with developmental disabilities, 42 U.S.C. Secs. 6000 *et seq.* (1995; PADD, 1995), and advocacy for people with disabilities who do not fit into either the PAIMI or PADD programs, 29 U.S.C. Sec. 794e (Protection and Advocacy for Individual Rights [PAIR]).

64. A more complete listing of federal disability-related legislative initiatives, describing 63 statutes relevant to people with all different kinds of disabilities, including blindness, deafness, mobility impairment, and mental retardation, can be found at http:// www.dol.gov/dol/_sec/public/programs/ptfead/rechart/sat5PTFEADfinalwp-19.htm.

65. Susan Stefan, "Delusions of Rights: Americans With Psychiatric Disabilities, Employment Discrimination, and the Americans With Disabilities Act," *Ala. Law Rev.* 52 (in press).

66. 29 U.S.C. § 2612 (1999).

67. *Budget of the U.S. Government, Fiscal Year 1997* (Washington, DC: U.S. Government Printing Office, 1996) at 402–404.

68. The National Empowerment Center, 800/POWER-2-U, 20 Ballard Road, Lawrence, MA 01843; and the National Mental Health Consumers' Self-Help Clearinghouse, 800/553-4539, 1211 Chestnut Street, Philadelphia, PA 19107. Their web site is http://www.mhselfhelp.org. The federal government has funded a technical assistance center for "family members" of people with psychiatric disabilities. This itself is an act of disrespect toward people with psychiatric disabilities: no federal funding is given to centers for family members of people who are blind, deaf, or mobility impaired or have other physical disabilities.

69. These include the extremely effective National Council on Disabilities, the President's Commission on the Employment of People With Disabilities, the President's Committee on Mental Retardation, and the U.S. Commission on Civil Rights.

70. For an excellent summary of the formation of the disability rights movement for people with physical disabilities, *see* Joseph Shapiro, *No Pity: People With Disabilities Forging a New Civil Rights Movement* (New York: Time Books, 1993). The web site is http://www.npr.org/programs/disability/ba_shows.dir/revoluti.dir.

71. These include Project Release in New York, the Network Against Psychiatric Assault in California, and the Mental Patients Liberation Front in Massachusetts.

72. Clifford Beers's, *The Mind That Found Itself* (Garden City, NY: Doubleday Doran, 1944 [reprint]) and Sylvia Plath's *The Bell Jar* (New York: Harper & Row, 1971) are the most famous examples. Many of these older writings can be found in Jeffrey Geller and Maxine Harris, Eds., *Women of the Asylum: Voices From Behind the Walls 1840–1945* (New York: Anchor Press, 1994).

73. Harlan Hahn, "Antidiscrimination Laws and Social Research on Disability: The Minority Group Perspective," *Behavioral Sciences and Law* 14 (1996):41–59.

74. Although he was surely the most prolific, Thomas Szasz was not the only well-known psychiatrist who questioned the power that society has assigned to psychiatrists. Thomas Szasz, *The Myth of Mental Illness* (New York: Harper & Row, 1961); *Law, Liberty and Psychiatry: An Inquiry Into the Social Uses of Mental Health Practice* (New York: MacMillan, 1963); *Psychiatric Justice* (New York: Collier Books, 1965). *See also* Jonas Robitscher, *The Powers of Psychiatry* (Boston: Houghton Mifflin, 1980); Ben Bursten, *Beyond Psychiatric Expertise* (Springfield, IL: Charles C Thomas, 1984); Seymour Halleck, *The Politics of Therapy* (New York: Science House, 1971). Even Fuller Torrey was, in his earlier writings, a skeptic about psychiatry, see *The Death of Psychiatry* (New York: Penguin Books, 1975).

75. Thomas Szasz, *The Manufacture of Madness* (New York: Harper & Row, 1970); *see also* Bruce Ennis, *Prisoners of Psychiatry* (New York: Harcourt Brace Jovanovich, 1972).

76. Phyllis Chesler, *Women and Madness* (Garden City, NY: Doubleday 1972); Kate Millett, *Sexual Politics* (New York: Doubleday, 1970).

77. Janet and Paul Gotkin, *Too Much Anger, Too Many Tears* (1975, reissued New York: HarperPerennials, 1992).

78. New York: Hawthorne Books (1978).

79. *See* James W. Ellis and Maureen Sanders, Romer v. Evans, 517 U.S. 620 (1996); Amicus Brief submitted on behalf of the American Association of Mental Retardation et al. (1995).

80. There are a few earlier Supreme Court cases that could be described as mental health law cases, including Buck v. Bell, 274 U.S. 200 (1927); Minnesota *ex. rel.* Pearson v. Probate Court of Ramsey County, 309 U.S. 270 (1940) (upholding the commitment of "sexual psychopaths"); and Greenwood v. U.S., 350 U.S. 366 (1956). However, there was no area of law commonly called "mental health law" until the late 1960s.

81. The first mental health law cases to reach the Supreme Court concerned the intersection of criminal law and mental health law, Baxstrom v. Herold, 383 U.S. 107 (1966) (a prisoner cannot be committed to a mental hospital after his sentence is served without the same due process protections given to nonprisoners); Specht v. Patterson, 386 U.S. 605 (1967); Humphrey v. Cady, 405 U.S. 504 (1972); and Jackson v. Indiana, 406 U.S. 715 (1972).

82. 422 U.S. 563 (1975).

83. *See* a discussion in Susan Stefan, "Leaving Civil Rights to the 'Experts': From Deference to Abdication Under the Professional Judgment Standard," *Yale Law J.* 102 (1992): 686–692.

84. *See, e.g.,* Lynch v. Baxley, 386 F.Supp 378 (M.D. Ala. 1974) (3-judge court); Doremus v. Farrell, 407 F.Supp. 509 (D. Neb. 1975) (3-judge court); Stamus v. Leonhardt, 414 F.Supp. 439 (S.D. Iowa 1976).

85. This issue is still being litigated, Goetz v. Crosson, 967 F.2d 29, 34, 35 (2nd Cir. 1992) (there is no constitutional right to the aid of a psychiatrist in civil commitment hearings); Goetz v. Crosson, 41 F.3d 800 (2nd Cir. 1994) (holding that a delay of up to 6 weeks in the hearings because of a lack of availability of psychiatrists in Dutchess County did not violate the U.S. Constitution), *cert. denied,* 516 U.S. 821 (1995).

86. Jackson v. Indiana, 406 U.S. 715, 736, 737 (1972): "Considering the number of persons affected, it is perhaps remarkable that the substantive constitutional limitations on this power have not been more frequently litigated."

87. Morton Birnbaum, "The Right to Treatment," *Amer. Bar Assn. J.* 46 (1960):499. This was later dubbed the "quid pro quo" theory.

88. Until quite recently, most institutions relied on unpaid or grossly underpaid patient labor for maintenance, cooking, laundry, and cleaning; Bayh v. Sonnenburg, 573 N.E.2d 398 (Ind. 1991) (reversing a multimillion dollar award to the patients for unpaid labor); Souder v. Brennan, 367 F.Supp. 808 (D.D.C. 1973) (minimum wage and overtime provisions apply to patient workers at nonfederal hospitals, homes, and institutions for people with mental retardation and mental illness); Weidenfeller v. Kidulis, 380 F.Supp. 445 (E.D. Wisc. 1974) (the patient complaining about forced labor stated that his claim was under the Fair Labor Standards Act, 13th Amendment, and constitutional right to treatment). *See also* M. Greenblatt, "Psychiatric Rehabilitation: Some Personal Reflections," *Psychiatry Annals* 13 (1983):530. In Alabama in the early 1970s, the only black patients who were permitted in white institutions were the patients who did all of this work, Marable v. Alabama Mental Health Board, 297 F.Supp. 291, 293, 294, but these patients were housed separately from the white patients, *id.*

89. Jean D. v. Cuomo, 1993 WL 276067 (S.D. N.Y. 1993) (a discovery dispute).
90. *See, e.g.,* 28 C.F.R. Sec. 549.43 (regulating involuntary psychiatric medication given to federal prisoners); 20 C.F.R. Secs. 404.1537 and 416.937 (defining "appropriate treatment" for drug addiction and alcoholism as "treatment that serves the needs of the individual in the least restrictive setting consistent with the treatment plan"); 45 C.F.R. Sec. 135.21 (foster care).
91. Although it is more conventional to perceive the law as giving deference to clinical concepts, in a number of cases clinical concepts are developed in response to legal decisions. Thus, the concept of least-restrictive alternative is now seen as clinically beneficial, American Psychiatric Association, "Guidelines on the Treatment of Schizophrenia," *Amer. J. of Psychiatry* 154 (1997):1–63.
92. Youngberg v. Romeo, 457 U.S. 307 (1982).
93. *See* Alan Meisel, "The Rights of the Mentally Ill Under State Constitutions," *Law & Contemp. Prob.* 45 (1982):7; Michael L. Perlin, "State Constitutions and Statutes as Sources of Rights for the Mentally Disabled: The Last Frontier," *Loyola L. A. Law Rev.* 20 (1987):1249. More recently, *see* Antony B. Klapper, "Finding a Right in State Constitutions for Community Treatment of the Mentally Ill," *Univ. of Pa. Law Rev.* 142 (1993):739.
94. Arnold v. Arizona Department of Mental Health, 775 P.2d 521 (Ariz. 1989); Goebel v. Colorado Dept. of Institutions, 830 P.2d 1036 (Colo. 1992); Rogers v. Commissioner of the Department of Mental Health, 458 N.E.2d 308 (Mass. 1983); Rivers v. Katz, 495 N.E.2d 337 (N.Y. 1986).
95. The U.S. Constitution protects citizens from certain kinds of deprivations of liberty by the state or federal governments U.S. Constitution, Amendments V and XIII.
96. Michael L. Perlin, *Mental Disability Law: Civil and Criminal* Vol. 1–3 (Charlottesville, VA: Michie, 1989).
97. Perlin, *id.*; Ralph Reisner and Christopher Slobogin, *Law and the Mental Health System* 2nd ed. (West, 1990); Spring, Lacoursierre, and Weissenberger, *Patients, Psychiatrists and Lawyers: Law and the Mental Health System* 2nd ed. (Cincinnati, OH: Anderson, 1997).
98. Addington v. Texas, 441 U.S. 418, 433 (1979), requires that the standard of proof be clear and convincing evidence.
99. O'Connor v. Donaldson, 422 U.S. 563, 564 (1975); Foucha v. Louisiana, 504 U.S. 71, 85 (1992); Kansas v. Hendricks, 521 U.S. 346, 358 (1997). Although both *Foucha* and *Hendricks* arose in noncivil situations, the discussions of the Supreme Court bear largely on civil commitment requirements.
100. Addington v. Texas, 441 U.S. 418, 429 (1979).
101. In DeShaney v. Winnebago County, 489 U.S. 189, 199–200 (1989), the Supreme Court suggested that people who were not involuntarily in the custody of the state did not have affirmative constitutional rights, such as the right to treatment. The extent to which "voluntariness" is defined solely by legal status rather than by the actual circumstances of people's lives remains a contested issues in the court, *see, e.g.,* Thomas S. v. Flaherty, 699 F.Supp. 1178, 1185 (W.D. N.C. 1988) (looking to people's actual circumstances to determine whether they are "voluntary").
102. Youngberg v. Romeo, 457 U.S. 307 (1982).
103. Susan Stefan, "Leaving Civil Rights to the Experts: From Deference to Abdication Under the Professional Judgment Standard," *Yale Law J.* 102 (1992):639.
104. Washington v. Harper, 494 U.S. 210 (1990); Riggins v. Nevada, 504 U.S. 127 (1992).
105. Hightower v. Olmstead, 959 F.Supp. 1549, 1570–1571 (N.D. Ga. 1996); Jurasek v. Utah State Hospital, 158 F.3d 506, 510 (10th Cir. 1998).
106. National Council on the Handicapped, *Toward Independence* (Washington, DC: Author, 1986) at 19–21, 35–39.

107. Cherry v. Matthews, 419 F.Supp 922 (D.D.C. 1976).
108. Joseph P. Shapiro, *No Pity* (New York: Times Books, 1993) at 66–69.
109. Patricia Wald, formerly of the Mental Health Law Project, is now a judge on the DC Circuit Court.
110. Charles Halpern, one of the founders of the Mental Health Law Project, was also the founding dean of the City University of New York Law School and is now president of the Nathan Cummings Foundation. Michael Perlin, who brought a number of ground-breaking cases to trial when working for the Office of the Public Advocate in New Jersey, is now a law school professor, as are Jim Ellis and Jan Costello, formerly Mental Health Law Project attorneys. Many professors continue to be involved in mental health law, writing Supreme Court briefs and serving as expert witnesses.
111. Bruce Ennis became a partner at Jennen & Block, and Joel Klein is now better known for his work with the Antitrust Division of the Department of Justice.
112. Norman Rosenberg and Len Rubenstein, both former directors of the Mental Health Law Project, now direct the New Israel Fund and Physicians for Social Responsibility, respectively.
113. Richard K. Scotch, *From Good Will to Civil Rights: Transforming Federal Civil Rights Policy* (Philadelphia: Temple University Press, 1984) at 44, 45.
114. The Rehabilitation Act of 1973 repealed the Vocational Rehabilitation Act in its entirety, 1973 U.S.C.C.A.N. 409, 449 (1972).
115. Richard Scotch, *From Goodwill to Civil Rights,* at 51, 52.
116. *Disabled Tie Up Traffic Here to Protest Nixon Aid-Bill Vote,* New York Times (Nov. 3, 1972):43, col. 1.
117. That witness was John Nagle of the American Federation for the Blind, *id.* Scotch, note 113 at 54.
118. The Vocational Rehabilitation Act of 1973, P. L. 93-112, passed on Sept. 26, 1973.
119. The Vocational Rehabilitation Act of 1973, P. L. 93-112, 1973 U.S.C.C.A.N. (87 Stat.) 409, 414.
120. The President claimed that the veto was a pocket veto (which cannot be overridden by Congress) because Congress was in a brief election recess at the time, while Congress insisted that the veto was a traditional veto and voted to override it. Rather than face a prolonged dispute over the character of the veto, Congress passed a similar bill, and the President signed it into law, S. Rep. No. 93-1297 at 1974, reprinted in 1974 U.S.C.C.A.N. 6373, 6374.
121. 42 U.S.C. 2000(d) (1994) ("No person . . . shall on the grounds of race, color, or national origin, be excluded from participation in, be denied the benefits of, or be subjected to discrimination under any program or activity receiving Federal financial assistance.")
122. 42 U.S.C. 2000(e-2) (1995).
123. 29 U.S.C. Sec. 706(6).
124. P. L. 100-430, 42 U.S.C. 3601 (1999).
125. P. L. 99-435, 49 U.S.C. 41705 (1994).
126. P. L. 93-516.
127. Scotch, note 113 at 87.
128. Scotch at 87, 88.
129. *Id.*
130. P. L. 95-251; the amendment took effect on Nov. 6, 1978.
131. 473 U.S. 234 (1985).
132. P. L. 99-506, codified at 42 U.S.C. Sec. 2000d.
133. Letter of John R. Bolton to Sen. Orrin Hatch, 132 Cong. Rec. S1 5100 (daily ed. Oct. 3, 1986).
134. P. L. 100-259, 29 U.S.C. 794(b)(1).
135. This part of the Civil Rights Restoration Act is codified at 29 U.S.C. Sec. 794.

136. *See* Bartlett v. New York Board of Law Examiners, 156 F.3d 321, 330 (2nd Cir. 1998), *vac.* on other grounds, 119 S.Ct. 2388, 144 L.Ed.2d 790 (1999).

137. Congress purposely eliminated this requirement from the ADA and explained at considerable length in the legislative history its reasons for doing so; Sen. Rep. 101-116, 101st Cong., 1st Sess., at 44–45 (Aug 30, 1989). Therefore, the occasional court decisions that have held that the ADA requires that discrimination be "solely" on the grounds of disability have no basis in the statute and are simply wrongly decided.

138. Compare executive agency enforcement of the Rehabilitation Act with current actions by the EEOC and the Department of Justice to enforce the ADA.

139. U.S. Commission on Civil Rights, *Accommodating the Spectrum of Individual Abilities* (Washington, DC: U.S. Government Printing Office, 1985).

140. H.R. 370, 99th Cong., 1st Sess. (1985).

141. National Council on the Handicapped, *Toward Independence* (Washington, DC: Author, 1986).

142. 42 U.S.C. § 12111 (1999). The impact of Title I is the subject of the second book; *see* Susan Stefan, tentatively titled *Hollow Promises: The Americans With Disabilities Act and Employment Discrimination Against People With Mental Disabilities* (Washington, DC: American Psychological Association, in press).

143. 42 U.S.C. § 12132 (1999).

144. 120 S.Ct. 631 (2000); 120 S.Ct. 1003 (2000); 68 U.S.L.W. 3654 (Apr. 17, 2000).

145. 42 U.S.C. § 12181 (1999).

146. 47 U.S.C. § 225 (1999).

147. 42 U.S.C. § 12202 (1999).

148. 42 U.S.C. § 12201(c) (1999).

149. 42 U.S.C. § 12211.

150. 42 U.S.C. § 12208 (1999).

151. P. L. 106-170, 42 U.S.C. 13206-19 (1999).

152. *See* Personnel Administrator of Massachusetts v. Feeney, 442 U.S. 256 (1979) (the preference in state employment to veterans does not discriminate on the basis of gender); CAL. MIL. & VET. CODE 394 (Deering 1999) (it is a misdemeanor to discriminate on the basis of membership in the military); La.R.S. 29:402(B) (protecting veterans from discrimination on the basis of their status).

153. P. L. 95-555, 92 STAT. 2076, 42 U.S.C. § 2000(k) (1999).

154. P. L. 90-202, 29 U.S.C. 621 et seq. (1994 ed. and Suppl. III). This act still applies to private employers, but the U.S. Supreme Court recently held in Kimel v. Board of Regents that Congress acted unconstitutionally in adopting this statute. However, many states continue to prohibit discrimination on the basis of age in employment, 120 S.Ct. 631 (2000).

155. The Education for All Handicapped Children Act of 1975 (P. L. 94-142), now known as the Individuals With Disabilities Education Act (P. L. 101-476), guarantees a "free appropriate public education" to disabled children. This is somewhat different from a right to be free from discrimination as a conceptual matter, but the Supreme Court has held that the act forecloses equal protection claims against schools under the U.S. Constitution by providing the exclusive remedy for such claims; Smith v. Robinson, 468 U.S. 992, 1009 (1984).

156. Stephan Haimowitz, "Americans With Disabilities Act of 1990: Its Significance for Persons With Mental Illness," *Hosp. and Comm. Psychiatry* 42 (1991):23 ("The act . . . establishes a legal and social principle of inclusion").

Chapter 4
THE AMERICANS WITH DISABILITIES ACT AND ITS IMPACT ON MENTAL HEALTH SYSTEMS

One of the most crucial provisions of the Americans With Disabilities Act (ADA) for people with mental disabilities is Title II, which forbids "public entities" from discriminating on the basis of disabilities. Public entities include all arms of state and local governments, and all state agencies and entities, including the police, mental health system, judiciary and other state agencies, who have profound impact on the lives of people with mental disabilities.

Historically, many of the most crushing forms of discrimination against people with psychiatric disabilities, from forced sterilizations to prohibitions on marriage, from segregation in remote institutional settings to exclusionary zoning, have been actions by the state. Many facially discriminatory state statues exist to this day, in areas including divorce, termination of parental rights, and professional licensing, and discriminatory state practices continue in areas as significant as voting, health care decision making, and the granting and revocation of drivers' licenses. Police practices, specifically mentioned by Congress in its legislative history of ADA, are of particular concern to people with psychiatric disabilities, who are killed and injured by the police at an astonishing rate. Congress considered it vital to the success of the ADA to include Title II's prohibition on discrimination by public entities and included explicit language in the ADA to abrogate state immunity from suits under the ADA.

Challenges to the Constitutionality of Title II of the ADA

As this book goes to press, the U.S. Supreme Court has agreed to hear two consolidated cases raising the question of whether Congress acted constitutionally in imposing the requirements of the ADA on the states.[1] Although both *University of Alabama v. Garrett* and *Alabama Department of Youth Services v. Ash* involve claims of employment discrimination,[2] the resolution of these cases will decide whether an individual can sue a state for damages under the ADA in any circumstance. The cases do not implicate local governments, such as those of counties or cities, or private entities, such as private hospitals or managed care organizations. It is important to note that no matter how the Supreme Court resolves these cases, the outcome will not affect claims against states under the ADA for injunctive or declaratory relief.[3]

However, *Garrett* and *Ash* will have profound symbolic and political significance. In deciding whether Congress validly abrogated state sovereign immunity, the Supreme Court will use a legal standard that will necessarily result in a decision with language involving judgments about the significance of discrimination by the states against people with disabilities and, by implication, the significance of discrimination suffered by people with disabilities.

This is because the second part of the Supreme Court's legal standard[4] to determine whether the ADA validly abrogates state sovereign immunity involves a judgment of whether the ADA is reponsive to or designed to prevent unconstitutional behavior and whether it is "congruent and proportional" to the unconstitutional conduct sought to be prevented. To decide these questions, the court must assess how much of the voluminous record of discrimination before Congress amounted to unconstitutional discrimination and whether the ADA was a congruent and proportional response to this discrimination. If the court decides that Congress acted constitutionally, it will necessarily underscore the brutal excesses of state efforts to segregate and sterilize people with disabilities and to deprive them of fundamental civic rights, such as the right to vote, to reproduce and raise children, to serve on juries, to drive, and to hold employment. If the court decides that Congress exceeded its constitutional limits, it will necessarily downplay the record of discrimination,[5] labeling it rational and therefore constitutional. By doing so, the court will add tremendous fuel to the fire of backlash in this country against the ADA. The stigma of disability and of social hostility to claims of disability discrimination will increase, undermining whatever protections the ADA has left to offer.

Although many states have their own statutes prohibiting discrimination on the basis of disability, the number of those statutes that have abrogated state sovereignty is much lower. State court judges might be less sympathetic to suits against the state than federal court judges and less willing to sustain the kinds of challenges to state statutes and practices that have arisen under the ADA.

Overview

This chapter examines the ways in which the ADA affects the practices of institutionalization, civil commitment, the right to refuse treatment, determinations of competence, imposition of guardianship, experimentation, and associated practices of state mental health agencies and professionals.

When the ADA was first passed, one attorney for a state mental health system described it as being "primarily concerned with changing business practices" rather than "changing a disability service system."[6] The attorney declared that changing disability service systems was accomplished by mental health law rather than by disability laws such as the ADA.[7] Yet witness after witness testifying before Congress in support of the ADA spoke powerfully of suffering and death in psychiatric institutions, making it clear that they saw a connection between the remedies offered by the ADA and the problems they described.

History has revealed that the predictions of the attorney for the state mental health system were wrong and that the expectations of the witnesses are, at least in part, being fulfilled. In fact, the first claims filed following the effective date of Title II of the ADA included claims challenging inappropriate institutionalization.[8] Although the earliest claims were not successful, later cases did succeed and have proven to be the most significant application of the ADA for people with mental disabilities. The U.S. Supreme Court recently recognized that "unjustified placement or retention of persons in institutions . . . constitutes a form of discrimination based on disability."[9] This is the very essence of "changing a disability service system."

The fourth ADA case heard by the Supreme Court involves the question of whether inappropriate institutionalization is discrimination under the act.[10]

Within the mental health system itself, the ADA has been invoked with mixed success to challenge several statutes, including one differentiating between psychiatric patients and other citizens in the area of advance directives[11] and one precluding people in the criminal justice system from being civilly committed.[12] The ADA has also been invoked to challenge decisions relating to civil commitment,[13] emergency room (ER), and detention treatment,[14] mental health services offered to a woman with mental retardation,[15] retention of individuals and classes of people in institutions and nursing homes,[16] and decisions to close certain treatment units,[17] to privatize state mental health treatment functions,[18] to terminate residency or participation in community programs and housing,[19] and to deny a patient access to her mental health records.[20]

In related areas, the ADA has been raised in cases involving guardianship and the right to die. It is only a matter of time before the ADA is applied to experimentation on people with mental disabilities and the right to refuse medication, seclusion, and restraint in psychiatric facilities. Lawsuits challenging state statutes or the decisions or actions of state mental health systems are brought under Title II of the ADA, which prohibits discrimination by a *public entity,* which means "any State or local government, any department, agency, special purpose district, or other instrumentality of a State or States or local government."[21] Every activity of a public entity is subject to the prohibition against discrimination on the basis of disability.[22] The definition of discrimination makes clear that a public entity will be held responsible for the discriminatory actions of other entities with which it contracts, even if they are not public entities themselves.[23]

Private psychiatric hospitals, doctors' offices, and mental health clinics qualify as public accommodations under Title III of the ADA.[24] So far, there has been little disability discrimination litigation directed at private psychiatric hospitals or doctors.[25] Because in recent years more and more admissions to private hospitals are paid for by government funds,[26] plaintiffs in states that contracted with private hospitals to provide care to state clients could presumably choose to sue either the private hospital itself under Title III or the funding state entity under Title II, which prohibits state entities from discriminating through their "contractual, licensing, or other arrangements,"[27] or by using "methods of administration" that subject individuals with disabilities to discrimination,[28] or by assisting entities that discriminate.[29]

Plaintiffs are still probably covered by the Rehabilitation Act of 1973,[30] which applies to all entities receiving federal funds.[31] Almost all hospitals receive federal funds, usually in the form of Medicaid or Medicare dollars.[32] Even if the federal funds are not used for a particular patient's care, they still operate to make the health care entity a recipient of federal funds under Section 504.

Testimony Before Congress on the ADA and Mental Health Systems

As early as 1983, Christopher Bell and Robert Burgdorf, who were instrumental in helping draft the ADA, wrote for the Commission on Civil Rights that institutionalization "almost by definition entails segregation and isolation."[33] In discussing "major social and legal mechanisms, practices and settings in which handicap dis-

crimination arises,'' they specifically cited as examples institutionalization, commitment standards and procedures, institutional abuse and neglect, and the absence of
community alternatives.[34]

The people with psychiatric diagnoses who testified and wrote in support of the
ADA also expected it to have a major impact on the delivery of state mental health
services.[35] Much of the testimony given to Congress by witnesses with psychiatric
disabilities related to abuses suffered in mental institutions. Witnesses spoke with
clarity and anguish of deaths, forced medication, restraint, disrespect and devaluation,
neglect, and the absence of treatment. In hearings held by Rep. Major Owens (D-
NY) in Boston, one witness told the panel that

> state hospitals in the State of Maine are notorious for using medication for controlling
> the behavior of clients and not for treatment alone. . . . This summer, four deaths
> occurred in one of our State hospitals. At least one person experiencing medical
> problems from the heat was treated as if it was a symptom of his psychiatric illness
> and put in restraints where the client died.[36]

As another witness testified,

> I have been a consumer of the mental health system in the State of Massachusetts
> and I have been a past patient of Northampton State Hospital. While a resident of
> this psychiatric institution, I witnessed on a daily basis abuses and day-to-day treat-
> ment that only in the mildest terms would be referred to as discriminatory. . . . One
> such incident that comes to mind is that of a Mr. Vincent Veletia who suffered from
> a debilitating form of mental illness.[37] In desperation, his guardians admitted Vincent
> to a private psychiatric institution that often used adverse therapy techniques as a
> treatment response to certain behaviors. Vincent suffocated and died when a full sen-
> sory deprivation hood was placed over his head. Attached to the hood were earphones
> which emitted constant white static noise. Vincent's hands were handcuffed behind
> his knees, forcing him to remain bent over at the waist. Authorities saw this act not
> as murder, but as an authorized treatment procedure that failed.[38]

Witnesses' concerns about conditions and treatment in mental institutions were
the dominant theme of their testimony,[39] but they also spoke of exclusion from
housing, employment, restaurants, and health care.[40] It should be emphasized that
witnesses who took positions adversarial to their state Departments of Mental Health
were not the only witnesses who expressed concern about the institutionalization and
segregation of people with disabilities. Witnesses on behalf of state mental health
agencies also addressed institutionalization and segregation and described them as
damaging and harmful to people with mental disabilities:

> People with mental disorders have been herded into jail-like asylums along with the
> poor and criminals. . . . Mental patients have been isolated, chained and beaten, and
> abused. . . . Our clients face exclusion from jobs, housing, and the basic rights that all
> citizens enjoy. Due to discrimination and lack of resources, many of our mentally ill
> citizens are among the growing number of homeless.[41]

The testimony of Deanna Durrett for Josef Reum, the Indiana Commissioner of
Mental Health, was pointed and eloquent:

> But we—and now I am speaking as a person with a life-long disability—have never
> been recognized as full citizens. We have had to endure segregation in much the same

way people of color and women have endured discrimination and segregation until recently, and, sadly, even today. But the segregation and stigmatization of people with certain disabilities has been even greater. For people with disabilities such as mental retardation, cerebral palsy, mental illness . . . we have been institutionalized. We have been sheltered. . . . In protesting the right not to be segregated we also encourage the opportunity for integration and learning.[42]

Institutionalization and segregation were not seen as issues that concerned only those with psychiatric disabilities. For example, as Ed Preneta, the Director of the Connecticut Developmental Disabilities Office, said

> the next powerful movement is the rising up of people with mental retardation locked up in institutions and sheltered workshops. . . . The Americans with Disabilities Act will provide a tool for already-existing activists, encouragement for the downtrodden, and an opportunity to reach the most segregated members of our society.[43]

Phil Campbell, the Director of the Massachusetts Department of Mental Retardation, testified that people with mental retardation had, because of discrimination, been "relegated to segregated congregate facilities."[44] A witness on behalf of people with traumatic brain injuries referred to their being inappropriately medicated in psychiatric institutions.[45] Other witnesses spoke in similar terms of institutionalization in nursing homes, referring to the isolation,[46] dependence,[47] and depression[48] bred in many nursing homes, as well as their enormous cost.[49] Committee reports identify such witnesses as "W. Mitchell from Denver, Colorado, who uses a wheelchair" or "Dan Piper, an eighteen-year-old with Down Syndrome" and included "Mary Linden of Morton Grove, Illinois, who lived in an institution."[50]

Finally, it is clear not only that people with psychiatric disabilities considered institutionalization relevant to the ADA, but that members of Congress recognized the link between institutionalization and segration as well. Rep. Owens asked Lelia Batten, a witness who had testified about institutionalization,

> I have a question for Ms. Batten. Has discrimination against the mentally ill, in your opinion, kept people in the hospital longer than they needed to stay in the hospital? And is this a great waste of money?
> *Ms. Batten*: Yes it is . . . if they would ask the clients and listen to what the clients have to say about what treatments are necessary for them, the people would get out of the hospitals sooner.[51]

The ADA was clearly seen by Congress as prohibiting segregation. The Senate Labor and Human Relations Committee observed that "one of the most debilitating forms of discrimination is segregation imposed by others."[52] Analogies were made in both the legislative history and on the floor of Congress between the segregation experiences of people with disabilities and those of African Americans. Former Senator Lowell Weicker, the original sponsor of the ADA, testified before Congress about the impact that the legislation would have on segregation in institutional settings:

> For years, this country has maintained a public policy of protectionism toward people with disabilities. We have created monoliths of isolated care in institutions and segregated educational settings. It is that isolation and segregation that has become the basis of the discrimination faced by many disabled people today. Separate is not equal. It was not for blacks; it is not for the disabled.[53]

Similar statements were made by others equating discrimination, segregation, and institutionalization: "It has been our unwillingness to see all people with disabilities that has been the greatest barrier to full and meaningful equality. Society has made them invisible by shutting them away in segregated facilities."[54] A task force appointed after the passage of the ADA recommended as one of the pivotal areas for implementation that "government must join with the private sector to establish a continuum of affordable, universally available computer-connected programs designed to liberate all people with disabilities from inappropriate institutionalization and dependency."[55]

It is clear that the drafters of the ADA, the witnesses who testified in support of its benefits, and members of Congress all saw a connection between the passage of the ADA and relief from institutionalization, segregation, and the conditions described in institutions and nursing homes. The language of the ADA itself notes that "discrimination against people with disabilities persists in such critical areas as . . . institutionalization."[56]

The ADA's Prohibition of Unnecessary and Improper Institutionalization

Before I built a wall I'd ask to know
What I was walling in or walling out,
And to whom I was like to give offense.[57]

The area in which the ADA has been used most successfully is to challenge the inappropriate institutionalization of people who could otherwise live in the community. Although mental health professionals and government committees had decried brutal conditions in institutions almost since the first one was built,[58] disability professionals' recognition that institutionalization itself had a damaging impact on people and their own and society's perceptions of their identities first appeared in the professional literature in the 1950s.[59] This dawning realization on the part of the professionals was long preceded by the protests and complaints of people subject to institutionalization. "Patients . . . have complained throughout the entire history of mental hospitals that institutions themselves bred attitudes and behaviors amongst staff that robbed patients of their essential humanity, and thereby thwarted any possible constructive psychiatric achievement."[60] These complaints continue unabated to this day and appear with vivid urgency in many current surveys and articles.

Even people who believe that they have a mental illness and that their illness is a biological brain disease are clear that institutionalization on any kind of sustained basis makes things worse rather than better. For people who never perceived themselves as having a mental illness in the first place, hospitalization is even worse. One thing is certain: Thousands of people are forced to live in congregate institutions with little privacy and the inflexibility that accompanies institutional life primarily because there are no available places for them to live in the community.[61]

There is a growing consensus that national disability policy should promote the independence and integration of people with disabilities into the community, which is reflected both in the ADA[62] and in the findings of distinguished panels of disability professionals, government agencies,[63] and scholars.[64] The increasing emphasis on integration is accompanied by a recognition that institutions are both segregating and damaging, even a contributing factor of disability themselves.[65]

Integration is not entirely new to the courts either. A number of cases brought under Section 504 of the Rehabilitation Act of 1973 raised claims challenging institutionalization as segregation.[66] Although in most cases courts did not rule on the substantive claims because state defendants raised only procedural objections,[67] in *Homeward Bound v. Hissom*, the court agreed that unnecessary institutionalization was segregation, violating both the equal protection guarantee of the Fourteenth Amendment of the Constitution and Section 504 of the Rehabilitation Act.[68] *Hissom* was the first decision embodying the recognition by Justices Thurgood Marshall, William Brennan, and Harry Blackmun in 1986 that far from being beneficently motivated, many institutions for people with mental disabilities were

> massive custodial institutions [that] were built to warehouse the retarded for life; the aim was to halt reproduction of the retarded and "nearly extinguish their race." . . . Lengthy and continuing isolation of the retarded has perpetuated the ignorance, irrational fears, and stereotyping that long have plagued them.[69]

Although the *Homeward Bound* decision was never published and remains largely unknown to this day, it was the inspiration for a series of cases culminating in *Olmstead v. L. C.*, the U.S. Supreme Court's recognition that unnecessary institutionalization constitutes discrimination prohibited by the ADA.[70]

State Institutions as Residential Facilities

Two distinct roles for psychiatric institutions or hospitals should be clarified at the outset. One role is the provision of active, intensive treatment for people in acute stages of emotional distress. A separate role is as a residential placement (usually of last resort). The concept that merely residing in an institutional setting is itself therapeutic—known as "milieu therapy"—has been generally discredited for almost 25 years.[71]

There are debates about the treatment role of institutions—some have argued that institutions are needed for acute treatment of psychiatric crisis, whereas others contend that even acute treatment could be accomplished in the community. The argument about the appropriate locus of active treatment is a useful debate, but not one I propose to enter here. I do not address this debate because institutional settings generally become places of discriminatory segregation when they serve as residential facilities for people with nowhere else to live. Some people live for years,[72] decades, and even their entire lives[73] in institutions.

Most of us are willing to exchange privacy and control over our lives for intensive, acute treatment in hospital settings because we know that when the treatment is complete, we will go home. Few would want to call a hospital home or imagine a hospital as a place to live out any substantial part of life. In the days of managed care, this is hardly a problem in the general medical setting. Yet that is what happens to thousands of people in state institutions, often far away from their families, relatives, friends, or even a town or city of any size.[74]

Although the problem of the revolving-door patient has become a staple of psychiatric rhetoric, and like most rhetorical devices contains some truth,[75] it is easier to get into a psychiatric hospital than out of one. Once more than a few weeks have passed, it becomes difficult to keep up payments on an apartment or room or to persuade a community agency starved for resources to keep an empty bed available for the person's return. Once housing in the community is lost, both hospitals and judges are reluctant to order discharge of a patient until housing can be found. Most states have inadequate community residential facilities, and case managers and social workers often do not try to obtain independent housing through Section 8 certificates. Even when they do, many landlords will not accept them.[76] The hospital is allowed to keep most of a person's social security benefits,[77] so the person cannot save to pay a security deposit and first-month's rent anywhere.

Employment is lost, and the addition of psychiatric hospitalization makes it much more difficult to regain. In the case of some criminal acquittees, the difficulties of getting the person out may be political as well, or the hospital staff may be reluctant to discharge someone who must face criminal charges on release. Some people have dual diagnoses,[78] are elderly,[79] or have complicated medical problems, which make them even more difficult to place in the community. This does not make the continued institutionalization of these people any less problematic[80] any more than failing to release people from prison after their sentences are complete because they have nowhere to go is legal.[81]

Living one's life in an institutional setting obviously has profound consequences for every aspect of existence. Not only is it segregated housing—segregated in that the only people who live together are people with mental disabilities—but it also results in segregation in employment, health care, socialization, transportation, recreational programs, and dining opportunities. People are separated from significant others—their families, friends, pets, and communities—from the places they sought out for peace—their churches, public libraries, baseball parks, and bicycle paths—and from anything else whose familiarity might have provided them comfort. Residents of institutions must use "patient's" bathrooms, whereas staff, visitors, and the public use other, superior facilities. If the institutionalized person is age 18 or younger, education is provided in a segregated setting.[82]

When institutions are described as the only alternative to prisons, jails, or the streets, they are being described as residential alternatives. When ex-patients describe the institutions as resembling prisions and jails, they are making residential comparisons. Most of the defenders of institutionalization as a residential alternative are not particularly enthusiastic advocates of institutionalization. Instead, they portray the institution as the lesser evil among unappetizing alternatives. People with mental disabilities, many of whom have experienced homelessness as well as the penal and the mental health systems, are notably more ambivalent as to which is the worst.[83] Many judges in cases involving conditions in institutions make specific and sometimes adverse comparisons between the institutions and prisons and jails.[84]

For people with psychiatric disabilities, the clearest and most eloquent priority expressed in writings, interviews, and testimony is that they not be forced to live in an institutional setting. Some—especially those who are more economically well-to-do—acknowledge the necessity of occasional hospitalizations for acute care, but no one wants to spend his or her day-to-day life in an institution.

The dichotomy between institutions as hospitals providing treatment for acute conditions and institutions as quasipenal residential facilities may become more stark in the face of two modern trends. The first is the flood of legislation permitting sex offenders to be institutionalized when their sentences are over.[85] The second is the states' growing movement to contract their mental health services to managed care companies. If managed care companies do their job and approve only medically appropriate institutional stays, the absence of appropriate, available, inexpensive housing in the community for previously institutionalized people will become even more obvious. However, if even a fraction of the people who are subject to the new sexual predator laws are committed, state institutions will be bursting at the seams with untreatable residents—medically inappropriate residents that will put managed care companies in untenable economic and political positions.

Currently, about 237,133 people are in psychiatric institutions (including inpatient psychiatric treatment at general hospitals, veterans' hospitals, federally funded community mental health centers and residential treatment centers for children with emotional disturbances) on any given day.[86] However, over 2 million people are admitted to these psychiatric institutions each year. It is difficult to accurately measure lengths of stay for psychiatric patients.[87] In 1982, the average length of stay in a state or county psychiatric hospital (measured by the discharge day rather than by the inpatient day) was 143 days—just under 5 months.[88] More recently, a survey of nine northeastern states over 9 years showed that between 40% and 70% of patients have been institutionalized longer than 1 year.[89] In a recent study of Oregon's Western State Hospital, the mean length of stay for extended care on the adult psychiatric unit was 6 months; on the geriatric unit, it was 3 years.[90] Anecdotally, many survey respondents from state psychiatric hospitals mentioned their lengths of stay in passing—"my hospital stay of more than ten years."[91]

Children, adolescents, and older Americans have much longer lengths of stay in institutions, because Congress has created federal fiscal reimbursement structures that reward institutions for keeping children and elderly people with psychiatric diagnoses in institutional settings[92] but has provided relatively less incentive for keeping Americans with psychiatric diagnoses between ages 21 and 65 in institutional settings.[93] When federal and state agencies tighten requirements for nursing home admissions, geriatric admissions to psychiatric institutions increase.[94] About 1½ million Americans with disabilities live in nursing homes, and that number is expected to double in the next 30 years.[95]

Mortality, Injury, and State Institutions

The research that is available[96] suggests that people who reside for any length of time in a psychiatric institution die far earlier than the people who live in the community.[97] Between 1993 and mid-1998, 212 people died in state psychiatric hospitals in Virginia.[98] This is not simply a function of earlier mortality associated with psychiatric disability itself. More than one quarter of the deaths in Virginia were identified as resulting from something other than natural causes.[99] The mortality of institutionalized people is higher than the mortality of people with similar disabilities in the community,[100] although studies have produced mixed results in terms of whether the mortality of people with psychiatric disabilities in the community is higher than that of people without such disabilities.[101] At least one study has related higher mortality to low income level rather than to mental status.[102]

The reported mortality rate in state and county mental hospitals is so much greater than that in private psychiatric hospitals that it cries out for explanation. Government figures for "first-day census" (as in a tally conducted on January 1) for state and county mental hospitals are 75,636 compared with 24,914 for "private psychiatric hospitals": The former reported 1,756 deaths, whereas the latter reported a single death.[103] Possible explanations include the failure to report deaths in private psychiatric hospitals, a far higher geriatric population in state and county hospitals, or a greater likelihood of death when residential rather than acute care is provided. Another striking anomaly is that broken down by state, the deaths in state and county hospitals do not correlate with the populations of states: Georgia reported 227 deaths, whereas California reported 65 (only 1 more than Alabama).[104] This may be explained by Georgia's far higher rate of institutionalization.

The "natural" causes of death in institutions are often pneumonia and other respiratory diseases and "cardiac arrest,"[105] both of which merit further investigation for different reasons. Pneumonia and respiratory complications are prevalent in institutional settings for two principal reasons: (a) They are associated with a growing population of elderly people who are inappropriately institutionalized but have nowhere else to go,[106] and (b) they are associated with psychotropic medication.[107] In addition, with few exceptions,[108] people under intensive medical supervision should not die from pneumonia, an illness that can usually be treated if caught soon enough, which should happen when people live in a supervised setting.

Cardiac arrest is a familiar "explanation" to anyone who has investigated the sudden deaths of otherwise healthy people in institutional settings.[109] It is also associated with psychotropic medications, such as Clozapine:[110] "Most unexpected deaths are believed to be caused by cardiac arrhythmic changes. Phenothiazines and other psychoactive drugs are known to cause a variety of electrocardiographic changes."[111] Cardiac arrest is also associated with deaths while in physical restraints.[112] Citing cardiac arrest, by itself, as the cause of death of a previously healthy individual is so widely considered to be medically unacceptable that it has even made it into popular fiction.[113]

Institutionalized people also die of accidents,[114] suicide,[115] homicide,[116] and disease[117] at a far greater rate than that of people in the community. Although staff are supposed to protect them, individuals in institutions are injured more than are people in the community,[118] in part because in institutions people can be tied down in restraints, and a number of deaths, assaults, and maimings in institutional settings occur while people are in seclusion rooms or in restraints.[119] One woman who died in a Virginia psychiatric hospital had been tied to her bed for 485 hours of the last two months of her life.[120] Thomas R. Harmon of the New York Commission on Quality of Care for the Mentally Disabled testified that

> each year the Commission receives, reviews, and where necessary directly investigates . . . over 2,000 reports of consumer deaths . . . . We have investigated over 200 deaths where restraint or seclusion was a factor . . . . In our casework we've seen people die or be abused in restraints because a simple request for a second cup of coffee was denied; or a request for a sweater on a very cold day was ignored by staff.[121]

Sometimes people are injured, assaulted, or killed by the staff that are supposed to protect them.[122] People are raped and sexually assaulted more in institutional settings than in the general community.[123]

Defining an Institution

Finally, it should be clear that *institutions* are not defined simply by their size. Many institutions, located in what is called "the community," exercise equally complete regulation and control over the lives of the people who live there, sometimes even more control than in larger institutions. Some community facilities accomplish "integration" into the community by ejecting their residents in the morning and locking the doors, reopening them in the evening, leaving residents to wander aimlessly with no private space of their own.

Institutional living is defined not by size but by the measure of control an individual retains over his or her own life and the most basic decisions about how to live it: when to go to sleep and get up in the morning, when and what to eat, the decorations of one's room, and the choice of one's companions. Thus, integration of previously institutionalized people in the community is a necessary but not sufficient condition of autonomy or of having a range of choices and the power to make them. The opposite of institutionalization is not community living but *independent living,* which the National Council on Disability defined as "control over one's life based on the choice of acceptable options that minimize reliance on others in making decisions and in performing every day activities."[124]

Independent living in this sense is the ultimate goal for which we all strive. Rarely, there is a conflict between the twin goals of autonomy and independent living. Sometimes other values in a person's life, such as affiliative and associational values, lead to an autonomous choice for institutional life over more community living: for example, a man with mental retardation might prefer life in a nursing home because his mother, to whom he is strongly attached, is also there.[125] Preferably, both he and his mother could live together in their own home with help.

It should also be underscored that the problem with segregation in institutional settings is not simply that it impedes integration in the community. As Americans discovered in the aftermath of passing the Fair Housing Act in 1968,[126] banning *de jure* segregation does not necessarily produce meaningful integration.[127] People with disabilities may be segregated in the community as well as in institutional settings. Excluding people from the opportunity of integrated life in the community by forcing them to live in institutions is wrong, but it is not the only reason that segregation in institutions is wrong.

Harm of Segregation in Institutional Facilities

Society should try to guard against the involuntary separation of members of disfavored groups in locked central facilities for several reasons. First, the premise of antidiscrimination law is that mental disability, as a characteristic like race and gender, does not tell us very much about the human being with that characteristic and that society's exaggerated and negative focus on the characteristic has obscured the individuality and humanity of the people so characterized to the detriment of everyone. Blacks, Hispanics, and women are not "all the same"—people of the same race or gender are heterogeneous; race or gender is not a homogenizer that trumps individuality. "Prejudice distorts social relationships by overemphasizing some characteristic such as race, gender, age or handicap."[128] To involuntarily group people on the basis of the very characteristic that society is already prone to exaggerate virtually guarantees that the individuality and humanity of the person will be obliterated under the perceptions of disability.[129] This has been confirmed by studies showing that although contact with people with disabilities in social and employment settings may engender positive attitudes toward them by people without disabilities, contact with people with disabilities in medical or institutional settings leaves people without disabilities feeling more negatively toward them.[130]

In addition, having members of a stigmatized and disfavored group all together in one institution is a moral hazard for society. As a matter of historical record, on almost every occasion that the state has acted in an organized way to kill, injure, or endanger people with mental disabilities, it has aimed its policies at people in institutional settings.[131] When states set up programs of involuntary sterilization of men and women on the basis of mental illness or mental retardation, by far the majority of people were sterilized while in institutional settings.[132] When states experimented on children with mental retardation by feeding them irradiated food, the experimentation was done on institutionalized children, not on those in the community.[133] When the Central Intelligence Agency joined forces with psychiatry to investigate brainwashing techniques, the people who were experimented on without their knowledge or consent were in institutional settings.[134] When incompetent people with disabilities were proposed as sources of organ transplants to which they had not consented, this often took place in institutional settings.[135]

I am not suggesting that today's institutions routinely carry out such practices, but neither do I concede that these are simply historical anecdotes. Indeed, variations on these themes continue today. At this minute, the vast majority of experiments carried out on mental patients, and all of the nontherapeutic ones, take place in institutional settings. Today, the use of four-point restraints, which former patients describe as one of the most frightening and traumatizing aspects of institutionalization,[136] happens almost exclusively in institutional settings, as (for the most part) does the increasing use of psychosurgery. The use of these interventions, largely experienced as damaging by the people who receive them, is virtually confined to institutional settings.

It is true that institutions are monitored more easily than are community settings. It is also true that theft, abuse, fraud, and even murder happen to people with mental disabilities in community settings (although these also occur in institutions despite the closer security and monitoring); however, the scant research that has been done tentatively suggests that people live longer outside of institutions. More important, every piece of available data—every study, book, survey, and article—shows that every time anyone asks them, people with disabilities say they that do not want to live in psychiatric institutions.[137]

Olmstead v. L. C.: *Inappropriate Institutionalization Violates the ADA*

One of the explicit missions of the ADA is the integration of people with disabilities into the community,[138] thereby ending their isolation and segregation. After recognizing that over 43,000,000 Americans have disabilities,[139] the very first finding made by Congress in enacting the ADA was that "historically, society has tended to isolate and segregate individuals with disabilities and, despite some improvements, such forms of discrimination against individuals with disabilities continue to be a serious and pervasive social problem."[140] Congress found that discrimination continues to "persist" in "such critical areas as . . . institutionalization."[141] These findings were to prove crucial to the Supreme Court's decision in *Olmstead v. L. C.*,[142] holding that unnecessary institutionalization constituted impermissible discrimination under the ADA.[143]

Since the passage of the ADA, inappropriate institutionalization has been successfully challenged in the lower courts.[144] The Supreme Court held in 1999 that the "unjustified placement or retention of persons in institutions . . . constitutes a form of discrimination based on disability."[145] The court partially affirmed and partially vacated the judgment of the 11th Circuit in *L. C. v. Olmstead*,[146] a case involving two people with dual diagnoses of mental retardation and psychiatric disorders who had histories of repeated and ineffective psychiatric hospitalizations. At the time the case was filed, both were being inappropriately held in psychiatric institutions because the state claimed that insufficient funds existed to provide them with appropriate community placements.[147]

The 11th Circuit rejected Georgia's argument that because its failure to place the two individuals in community settings was due to lack of funds, it could not be discriminating against them on the basis of disability. The court formulated a model of discrimination that framed community services as a reasonable accommodation to the disabilities of the plaintiffs. To achieve equal access to the benefits of community living, the majority reasoned, people with serious mental disabilities must receive some accommodations in negotiating the demands of living in the community, especially those who have been unnecessarily segregated for years in the confines of institutions.[148]

The 11th Circuit remanded the case for the district court judge to take evidence on the issue of whether the state could make out a defense that providing the plaintiffs with community services would constitute a fundamental alteration in the state's mental health program.[149] To succeed in this defense, Georgia would have to show that "requiring it to [expend additional funds to provide L. C. and E. W. with integrated services] would be so unreasonable given the demands of the state's mental health budget that it would fundamentally alter the service [the state] provides."[150]

Although the case had been remanded to the district court, the Supreme Court granted *certiorari* on the question of

> whether the public services portion of the federal Americans with Disabilities Act compels the State to provide treatment and habilitation for mentally disabled persons in a community placement, when appropriate treatment and habilitation can also be provided to them in a State mental institution.[151]

As reformulated by Justice Ruth Bader Ginsburg, the question before the Supreme Court became "whether the proscription of discrimination may require placement of persons with mental disabilities in community settings rather than institutions." The court answered this question "yes," but as Justice Ginsburg made clear, it is a "qualified yes."[152] Nevertheless, even a qualified yes reflects an enormous achievement on behalf of citizens with disabilities in beginning to dismantle segregation that comes from institutionalization. When *Homeward Bound v. Hissom* was decided a little over a decade ago, even sympathetic advocates were skeptical that courts could be persuaded that unnecessary institutionalization was discriminatory segregation.

Why Is Unnecessary Institutionalization Discrimination?

The Supreme Court ruled that unnecessary institutionalization constitutes segregation for two reasons. First, "institutional placement of persons who can handle and benefit from community settings perpetuates unwarranted assumptions that persons so isolated are incapable or unworthy of participating in community life and cultural enrichment."[153] Second, "confinement in an institution severely diminishes the every day life activities of individuals, including family relations, social contacts, work options, economic independence, educational advancement, and cultural enrichment."[154]

Interestingly, these two explanations do not depend on or vary with the quality of institutional care. Inappropriate institutionalization is discrimination regardless of whether the patient resides in a "snake pit" or the newest and fanciest facility. In addition, the emphasis placed on access to normal community activities raises questions about whether some community placements segregate as much as institutional placements.[155]

The dissent strongly disagreed, arguing that a finding of discrimination required "a showing that a claimant received differential treatment vis-à-vis members of a different group on the basis of a statutorily described characteristic."[156] The dissent articulated an older concept of discrimination, which used to be conceptualized as treating people in a protected class less advantageously than others who are not in a protected class. Thus, Georgia argued in *Olmstead* that the plaintiffs were not subject to discrimination on the basis of disability "because 'discrimination necessarily requires uneven treatment of similarly situated individuals,' and L. C. and E. W. had identified no comparison class, i.e. no similarly situated individuals given preferential treatment."[157]

This interpretation of discrimination, rejected by the majority in *Olmstead*, is a historical legacy of the first prohibitions of discrimination based on race. It arises from the premise that discrimination is based on distinctions that are irrelevant; therefore, the discrimination is irrational. For example, the premise of laws prohibiting race discrimination in schools and employment is that race is irrelevant to academic merit, job skills, or productivity; therefore, exclusion on the basis of race is irrational. The consequence of this premise is that if the disfavored characteristic was construed as relevant, then different and disadvantageous treatment is rational and permissible.[158]

Women forcefully challenged this concept of discrimination. Just as people with disabilities have some actual differences from people who do not have disabilities (although often not the differences popularly assumed and often not to the magnitude popularly assumed), women are different from men in a variety of ways. Women get pregnant and give birth, live longer, and are, on average, shorter and lighter. These differences, although relevant in a variety of ways, do not necessarily justify disadvantageous treatment, even when no comparison group appears available. Thus, gross underfunding of breast cancer research was denounced as discrimination against women without a showing that more research was being funded for breast cancer in men.[159] Requirements that an individual charging rape produce witnesses, submit to psychiatric examination, or answer questions about past sexual history were seen as discriminating against women without requiring women to prove that men who brought rape charges were treated differently.[160]

The premise of disadvantageous treatment based on an irrelevant characteristic has not even been followed with regard to race discrimination. Race is actuarially relevant in predicting life span and poor health, but insurance companies are not permitted to charge black people higher rates on the basis of race. Only black people get sickle-cell anemia, but if state programs that treated sickle-cell anemia did so only in institutional settings, few people would argue that this could not be discrimination because white people did not receive medical treatment for sickle-cell anemia and therefore did not receive preferential treatment. Rather, people would argue that institutionalization was not necessary for the treatment of sickle-cell anemia. Institutionalization is also not necessary for the treatment of the vast majority of people with mental illness.

Oppressive and disadvantageous practices based on a disfavored characteristic are actually most likely to occur when only people with the disfavored characteristic will be hurt. A person with a disability struggling to stay in his or her own home might be just as hurt by a law ending the home mortgage deduction as by the underfunding of home- and community-based programs for people with disabilities, but the latter is much more probable than the former. Practices affecting people in a disfavored group are increasingly more likely to be oppressive and disadvantageous the more that the disfavored characteristic is relevant, even crucial, to the practice.[161] For example, it may be unconstitutional to discriminate on the basis of alienage in employment because alienage is irrelevant to qualifications for employment. But because only aliens want green cards and citizenship, the Immigration and Naturalization Service can get away with treating people in ways that beleaguered IRS employees can only dream about.

In fact, oppressive and disadvantageous treatment based on a disfavored characteristic becomes virtually invisible to the extent that there is no comparison group. If Congress passed legislation explicitly excluding people with disabilities from receiving the home mortgage deduction, this would be greeted with horror. However, totally defunding programs providing assistance in paying heat and electricity bills for people with disabilities would barely be publicized and would never cause a reaction of the same magnitude. The presence of a comparison group provides the opportunity for empathy. The more closely linked the disfavored characteristic is to the oppressive practice, the less likely a member of the favored group would feel empathy for the disfavored person. That, after all, is the essence of discrimination: dislike, rejection, and loathing of a person based on a certain characteristic rather than empathy based on shared humanity.

In a paradoxical sense, some form of rudimentary integration is necessary before there can even be discrimination in the sense of differential treatment of people with disabilities compared with people without disabilities. Total separation and segregation preclude differential treatment because people with disabilities do not even have the opportunity to attempt to gain access to goods and services available to people without disabilities. If institutionalized people have no access to the community—to the grocery store, doctors' offices, movie theaters, and restaurants

—then there will be no question of refusal of entry, inferior seating, or the denial of medical treatment.

The Supreme Court majority in *Olmstead v. L. C.* held that actions could be discriminatory without the need for a comparison class. The court simply underscored Congress's findings that identified "unjustified 'segregation' of persons with disabilities as a form of discrimination" without reference to a comparison class. Over dissent by Justices Clarence Thomas, William Rehnquist, and Anthony Scalia, the majority made it clear that the identification of a nondisabled comparison class receiving preferential treatment was not a prerequisite to a determination of discrimination. "We are satisfied," wrote Justice Ginsburg, "that Congress had a more comprehensive view of the concept of discrimination."[162] In a footnote, the court referred to a number of discrimination decisions involving race, sex, or age that make it clear that an individual can prevail in a discrimination claim without having to show that others without the disfavored characteristic were treated better.[163] For example, the court decided that a plaintiff can make out an age discrimination claim without having to show that the individual who was awarded the job was not in the protected class.[164]

Despite holding that no comparison class was necessary, the court majority suggested—and Justice Anthony Kennedy in concurrence makes clear his preference for—the possibility that such a class in fact exists. People without mental disabilities do not have to be locked away from the community to receive needed medical care, whereas people with mental disabilities do. The practical problems of proving such a case clearly worry Justice Kennedy, and the majority underscores that these comparisons are not necessary to establish discrimination.

The comparison class might also be identified as those to whom the state also provides housing, without isolating or segregating them from the surrounding community. Institutions are actually residential settings for a substantial number of people, with thousands of them living in these settings for many years at a time.[165] The fact that the state provides institutionalized people with additional treatment such as medication along with the housing does not excuse segregation, because the segregation is not necessary to provide the medication. States provide housing as well as health and therapy services for homeless people, battered women, and others in the community without the segregation and locked wards of institutional facilities.

When Is Institutionalization Unnecessary or Inappropriate?

To benefit from the holding in *L. C.*, however, one must be "inappropriately" placed in an institution. None of the courts in the decisions involving inappropriate institutionalization have equated the mere fact of institutionalization with segregation. Lower courts have explicitly rejected the notion that these cases mandate "deinstitutionalization"[166] or funding of community services.[167] It was also clear to the Supreme Court that institutions will be the appropriate placement for some people at some times. "The ADA is not reasonably read to impel States to phase out institutions, placing patients in need of close care at risk."[168] The court went so far as to state that for some people, "no placement outside the institution may ever be appropriate."[169]

It is clear from *L. C.* that just because an individual may have been initially appropriately institutionalized does not mean that his or her current institutionalization is permissible under the ADA.[170] Also, the cases do not contain any suggestion that the individual's legal status is controlling in deciding whether he or she is being illegally segregated under the ADA.[171]

Most acute psychiatric care—investigating possible medical causes of aberrant behavior, checking side effects of medication, and adjusting medication or dosage —can be performed in less than 2 weeks,[172] and many people do not spend more than that time in psychiatric institutions. It is, for the most part, those people who stay more than 2 or 3 weeks in an institutional setting who begin to raise issues of segregation.[173] This does not mean that segregation of an individual for under 2 or 3 weeks is appropriate under the ADA[174] or that any stay beyond that point is discriminatory per se.[175] It merely suggests that the point at which the treatment functions of an institution begin to blur into housing and residential functions is a good benchmark for inquiry into whether services are being "administered in the most integrated setting appropriate to the individual's needs."[176]

An individual challenging his or her continued institutionalization under the ADA must be "qualified" for a community setting by "meeting the essential eligibility requirements" of the community setting. The most common way that an individual qualifies for a community setting is by the state's professionals recommendation for placement in such a setting, although both case law before *Olmstead* and *Olmstead* itself suggest that an individual may be able to show that he or she is qualified in the absence of a professional recommendation or in the face of recommendations made by professionals that the individual remain institutionalized.

The Supreme Court ruled that the "state generally may rely on the reasonable assessments of its own professionals in determining whether an individual meets the essential eligibility requirements for habilitation in a community-based program."[177] A "reasonable" assessment, based on earlier lower-court rulings, is one by a professional with appropriate credentials, knowledge of the patient and his or her condition, and knowledge of the programs that are available in the relevant community. In *Charles Q. v. Houstoun,* plaintiffs Charles Q. and Joseph K. disagreed with the state's evaluations.[178] The court granted summary judgment in favor of the plaintiffs with regard to Charles Q. and to the defendants with regard to Joseph K.

The court's approach in *Charles Q.* suggests that the parties focus first on the client's individual needs and describe them specifically. For example, both Charles Q. and Joseph K. initially had problems related to polydipsia (excessive drinking of water) and needed supervision to comply with hygiene requirements. Charles Q. also had inappropriate sexual behavior and was verbally aggressive; Joseph K. had problems related to assaultiveness and elopement.

The court then focused on whether the defendants had made any efforts to identify programs and services available in the community that could meet each client's needs. In addition, the court looked to evidence of people living successfully in the community with the same diagnoses, behaviors, symptoms, and needs. In doing this, the court looked to the state's professionals for specifics rather than simply relying on generalized conclusions as to whether an individual could be placed in the community. It required defendants to both identify the plaintiff's behaviors and symptoms that presented problems and show that they had searched for community placements that could handle those behaviors and problems.

A different approach was followed in *Kathleen S.*,[179] in which plaintiffs raised questions about an entire class of individuals that state professionals had deemed inappropriate for community placement. Plaintiffs argued that the state had failed to "properly assess their needs and their readiness for community placement . . . [and had failed] to plan for the necessary community-based services" that they would need as they became ready for placement.[180]

This is a crucial issue. In many cases, an individual who is ready to be discharged from a psychiatric institution becomes so frustrated, demoralized, or depressed at being forced to stay when he or she wants to go and is ready to go that often deterioration and decompensation take place. The professionals then deem the person unready to leave, causing further frustration and deterioration. This is reflected in numerous cases that have been litigated on behalf of people in psychiatric institutions.[181] Those cases might form the basis for damage actions under the integration mandate of the ADA.[182]

In *Kathleen S.*, the court noted that "both stipulations by DPW and evaluations by Plaintiff's expert identified members of Subclass C for whom the community, not a state hospital, is the most integrated setting appropriate to their needs."[183] The court ordered that an independent expert be chosen to evaluate all subclass members about whom plaintiffs and defendants disagreed.

Although constitutional litigation is not equivalent to ADA litigation, interpretations in those cases may help shed light on what is an "unreasonable" professional conclusion regarding a client's "qualifications" to be in the community. Patients in institutions are unconstitutionally treated if their treatment is a departure from professional judgment, standards, or practice.[184] Under the professional judgment standard, courts have held that recommendations that are not based on individual assessments of the client in question are not reasonable.[185] Professional assessments that are based solely on what is available, or that respond solely to cost, are not reasonable.[186]

It is clear under the ADA that the professional's assessment must be based solely on the individual's condition and not on the availability of community placements —lack of placements for the individual (in the context of a comprehensive, effective placement plan) is part of the state's affirmative defense, not part of the decision of whether an individual is "otherwise qualified" to be placed in the community.

The Supreme Court made equally clear, both in the majority opinion and in Justice Kennedy's concurrence, of its disapproval of the attempt by state professionals to offer one of the plaintiffs a placement in a homeless shelter.[187] Justice Kennedy warned against states' attempting to comply with *Olmstead* "on the cheap . . . integrated settings devoid of the services and attention necessary for . . . [the individual's] condition."[188] It appears that the plaintiffs could agree with defendant professionals' judgment that they need not be institutionalized and thus had a right to integrated community services, while challenging as "unreasonable" the choice of services offered by the defendant—as indeed occurred in *Olmstead v. L. C.* itself at the trial level[189] and has occurred in other cases.[190]

What About "Voluntary" Segregation?

The ADA orders states to provide services in the most integrated settings appropriate to the person's needs.[191] This is because "integration is fundamental to the purposes of the Americans with Disabilities Act. Provision of separate accommodations and services relegates people with disabilities to second-class status."[192] The Supreme Court, however, made it clear that the state could not be obligated under the ADA to force a person in the community who opposed such a placement.[193]

The ADA permits states to establish separate, segregated programs "in limited circumstances"[194] when it is providing a program or benefit to people without disabilities, and the separate programs are necessary to ensure equal access to the benefit by people with disabilities.[195] Even so, the regulations and commentary underscore that the state may not force an individual to choose a segregated program if that individual prefers to accept services in an integrated setting:

> Even when separate programs are permitted, individuals with disabilities cannot be denied the opportunity to participate in programs that are not separate or different. This is an important and overarching principle of the Americans with Disabilities Act. Separate, special, or different programs that are designed to provide a benefit to persons with disabilities cannot be used to restrict the participation of persons with disabilities in general, integrated activities.[196]

This is true even if the segregated programs provide better services than do the integrated programs.[197] The degree to which the state must provide accommodations to an individual who prefers the integrated setting is left to be decided on a case-by-case basis,[198] but "the starting point is to question whether the separate program is in fact necessary or appropriate for the individual."[199] It is obvious from both the statutory language and the interpretations of the courts that it is the person's preference for integrated services that governs, rather than either the voluntary nature of the program or the person's own legal status as a voluntary or involuntary recipient of services. It may not be appropriate for some involuntary recipients of services to receive them in a fully integrated setting, but that would be because of consequences of their disability, such as dangerousness, not simply because of their legal status as involuntary patients.

The language of the ADA, its regulations, and case law, including most recently the Supreme Court's decision in *Olmstead v. L. C.,* also make it clear that people with disabilities can voluntarily choose to participate in segregated programs necessary to provide them with benefits equivalent to those provided to people without disabilities if they themselves make the judgment that this is their preference.[200] However, disabled individuals do not have the right to be institutionalized under the ADA. In *Richard C. v. Houstoun*[201] the court rejected this argument by proposed intervenors, holding that

> the Supreme Court clearly stated that it was considering the circumstances under which the ADA requires the placement of institutionalized disabled persons into community-based treatment programs. Contrary to the assertion of [proposed intervenors], it does not logically follow that institutionalization is required if any one of the three *Olmstead* criteria [including consent to community placement] is not met.[202]

The language of *Olmstead* and the regulations make clear that the preference is for integration. The assumption is integration; the assumption shifts only if the client opposes it.[203] In other word, attorneys may not force the state to place an individual in the community over that individual's opposition, but the state may make the decision to place a person in the community over his or her (or more likely his or her parents') objection.

This raises the potentially troublesome legal issue of whether legal guardians of people who have been adjudicated incompetent may voluntarily "choose" to have their wards segregated, even if this segregation is unnecessary and inappropriate. The same question arises in the contexts of minors whose parents wish to hospitalize them, a practice that is increasingly common.[204]

There is considerable precedent for the proposition that the public interest in minimizing or eliminating segregation takes precedence over private preference. Certainly any preference that black parents might have had for racially segregated education was subsumed to the public interest in integration. There is even more precedent on both the federal and state level that precludes guardians from substituting their voices for those of their wards in cases involving institutionalization.[205] These cases and statutes suggest that guardians may not institutionalize their wards over the voiced objections of the wards and that accession to such institutionalization on the part of the state might constitute a violation of Title II of the ADA.

What Are Defenses to a Claim of Inappropriate Institutionalization?

Unlike Titles I and III, Congress established no affirmative defenses for Title II claims; however, this is mostly likely due to the brevity of the language of Title II. Congress left it to the U.S. Department of Justice (DOJ) to craft regulations to implement the prohibition against discrimination by public entities, including the articulation of appropriate defenses.

Congress did not leave the DOJ completely without guidance as to the scope of defenses under Title II. The legislative history is exceptionally clear about the availability of defenses under Title II. It is worthwhile to quote the House Judiciary Committee report at some length:

> The purpose of Title II is to continue to break down barriers to the integrated participation of people with disabilities in all aspects of community life. . . . While the integration of people with disabilities will sometimes involve substantial short-term burdens, both financial and administrative, the long-range effects of integration will benefit society as a whole. [citation omitted]. . . . The general prohibitions set forth in the Section 504 regulations [citation omitted] are applicable to all programs and activities under Title II. *The specific sections on employment and program access in existing facilities are subject to the "undue hardship" and "undue burden" provisions of the regulations which are incorporated in Section 204. No other limitation should be applied in other areas.* As with Section 504 of the Rehabilitation Act, integrated services are essential to accomplishing the purposes of Title II. . . . Separate-but-equal services do not accomplish this central goal and should be rejected. The fact that it is more convenient, either administratively or fiscally, to provide services in a segregated manner, does not constitute a valid justification for separate or different services under Section 504 of the Rehabilitation Act, or under this title. Nor is the fact that the separate service is equal to or better than the service offered to others sufficient justification for involuntary different treatment of persons with disabilities. (emphasis added)[206]

The reference to "program access in existing facilities" refers to structural barriers for people with mobility difficulties. The Report of the Committee on Energy and Commerce did suggest that the direct threat defense should be available in Title

II actions.[207] No other committee discussed Title II public-entity defenses, although all committee reports devoted considerable space to Title I and Title III defenses.

The DOJ regulations set out more defenses than were directed by the Judiciary Committee. The regulations directly provide for only two defenses. First, the regulations permit a defense to claims of failure to make "reasonable modifications in policies, practices and procedures" that such modifications would "fundamentally alter the nature of the service, program or activity."[208] This is the only claim for which a fundamental alteration defense seems to apply. Second, a public entity may defend either eligibility criteria for its programs or the creation of separate or different "aids, benefits, or services" for people with disabilities by proving that the criteria are necessary to provide the service being offered or that the creation of separate programs "is necessary to provide individuals with disabilities with aids, benefits, or services that are as effective as those provided to others."[209] It is absolutely clear, though, that the entity may not require individuals with disabilities to use those separate aids, benefits, or services.[210]

Although these are the only defenses permitted in the regulations, the DOJ's Interpretive Guidance spends considerable time defining and outlining the defense of direct threat.[211] It also contains, as a passing reference in an example about reasonable accommodation requirements on public accommodations, a comment that requiring a museum to furnish additional sign language interpreters to accommodate people with hearing impairments who do not wish to avail themselves of a museum tour for people with hearing impairments may be an undue burden.[212] This is, however, the only reference in the regulations or the Interpretive Guidance to either undue hardship or undue burden.

Until the Supreme Court decision in *Olmstead,* courts followed the mandate of Congress and the regulations and made it clear that defenses were to be interpreted in extremely narrow ways.[213] Although the court in *Olmstead* sided with the plaintiffs on the question of whether inappropriate and unwanted institutionalization constituted discrimination under the ADA, it also provided defendants with an interpretation of the fundamental alteration defense that appears to give states more leeway than Congress contemplated. In doing this, the court does not relieve states of their obligations to place inappropriately institutionalized people in the community; it simply does not require them to discriminate in favor of litigating plaintiffs when making placement decisions.

Placement in the community and its effects on state programs. The Supreme Court, like the 11th Circuit, permitted states to affirmatively defend a claim to integration in the community through the "fundamental alteration defense"; however, the court construed the fundamental alteration defense more broadly than the 11th Circuit:

> In evaluating a State's fundamental alteration defense, the District Court must consider, in view of the resources available to the State, not only the cost of providing community-based care to the litigants, but also the range of services the State provides others with mental disabilities, and the State's obligation to mete out those services equitably.[214]

This defense does not permit the state to deny community placement to inappropriately institutionalized individuals. It does, however, simply permit the state to deny inappropriately institutionalized plaintiffs immediate placement ahead of other inappropriately institutionalized clients but only if all clients are served according to a comprehensive and effective state plan. Thus, the majority explains that

> sensibly construed, the fundamental alteration component of the reasonable modifications regulation would allow the State to show that in the allocation of available resources, *immediate* relief for the plaintiff would be inequitable, given the responsibility the State has undertaken for the care and treatment of a large and diverse population of persons with mental disabilities.[215]

The state, however, cannot simply point to other people who are being haphazardly or randomly placed in the community as an excuse for its failure to provide a plaintiff with a community placement. The court indicated that a state must "demonstrate that it had a comprehensive, effectively working plan for placing qualified people with mental disabilities in less restrictive settings, and a waiting list that moved at a reasonable pace not controlled by the State's endeavors to keep its institutions fully populated."[216] The ramifications of these potential defenses are discussed below.

State resources and costs of community placements. The majority opinion directs courts to consider the cost of providing community-based services to the litigants "in view of the resources *available* to the State."[217] This is crucial, because many—if not all—states have resources available to them from the federal government to accomplish the goal of providing integrated services to individuals with mental disabilities; the states simply do not take advantage of these available resources.[218] For example, Congress provided a mechanism for states to fund the transfer of institutionalized people into community placements. The Medicaid Home- and Community-Based Services Waiver is a program that permits states to use Medicaid funding for services provided in the community that would otherwise be provided in institutional settings at equal or greater cost. This program, which permits states a great deal of freedom in designing services to enable people to live and be served in community settings, was created because of the recognition

> that many individuals at risk of institutionalization can be cared for in their homes and communities, preserving their independence and ties to family and friends, at a cost no higher than that of institutional care. The Social Security Act specifically lists seven services which may be provided: case management, homemaker services, home health aide services, personal care services, adult day health, habilitation and respite care. Other services, such as transportation, in-home support services, meal services, special communication services, minor home modifications, and adult day care, may be provided, subject to HCFA [Health Care Financing Administration] approval. States have the flexibility to design each waiver program and select the mix of waiver services to best meet the needs of the population they wish to serve. Waiver services may be provided state-wide or may be limited specific geographical subsections.[219]

The waiver program is underused.[220] At least one federal court has held that it is discriminatory under the ADA to underuse or underfund the program, because it compels institutionalization and takes away meaningful choice from people with disabilities.[221] All states have applied for at least one home- and community-based waiver program.[222] At least one case, *Duc Van Le v. Ibarra*, decided under Section

504 of the Rehabilitation Act of 1973, suggests that a state's failure to apply for funds under the waiver program for people with one disability may be discriminatory if it has applied for waivers to serve most other groups qualified to receive services under the program.[223] Application to use available federal funds to finance integrating institutionalized people into the community is such an universal practice among states that it is highly unlikely to constitute an undue burden.[224]

Requiring states to apply for available federal funding could thus be characterized as a reasonable accommodation or a reasonable modification to accomplish the integration of people with mental disabilities into the community. Because the state has no limit on the portion of its Medicaid funds that it can devote to a waiver program, funding exists to desegregate a substantial proportion of inappropriately institutionalized people into the community. In the Title I context, no undue burden defense can be made if funds are available through federal sources that would pay for a requested reasonable accommodation.[225]

So far, the states that have argued that they could not afford to transfer institutionalized people into the community have not made full use of their Medicaid waiver allotments. For example, in *L. C. v. Olmstead*, Georgia could have received federal funding for up to 2,100 transfers from institutions into the community and had actually used funding for only 700 transfers.[226] In *Travis D. v. Eastmont*, Montana was authorized federal dollars to serve 1,666 people with developmental disabilities in the community but only used funds for 930 people.[227] In *Rolland v. Celluci*, a case involving people with mental retardation and developmental disabilities in nursing home settings, plaintiffs alleged that Massachusetts had received federal approval to serve 12,000 people in its home- and community-based services program but used only 8,000 of those slots.[228] In *Cramer v. Chiles*, the plaintiffs also alleged to the underuse of Medicaid waiver slots.[229] It is difficult for defendants to argue that they do not have sufficient resources to accomplish integration when they have not used resources that are readily available.

In addition, states may free existing resources simply by altering some of their administrative procedures. The methods by which state agencies administer their programs contribute a great deal to the degree to which institutions are used in a given state. For example, the methods by which a state finances institutional and community care can have an enormous impact on the utilization of institutional resources. If counties have to pay to provide community care, but the state pays the bill for institutionalization in a state facility, then counties will more readily send their citizens to state facilities. Wisconsin and Ohio reduced the use of their state hospitals simply by requiring counties to pay for the cost of institutionalizing their citizens in them.[230] Another crucial administrative component to the ability to accomplish integrated treatment in the community is that of the mental health agency to transfer funds between line items of their budgets for funds appropriated for the treatment of a person in the hospital to accompany that individual into the community.

There are numerous other examples of state administrative methods that result in keeping individuals with mental disabilities segregated in institutional settings when they could be served in the community. In *Kathleen S. v. Department of Public Welfare*,[231] the court found that the defendants had violated the ADA by failing to "adequately plan for and develop the facilities needed to treat [people in psychiatric facilities who no longer needed institutionalization] in the community."[232]

Significantly, the DOJ underscored that by "methods of administration" the regulations referred not only to "official written policies of the entity" but also to "the actual practices of the public entity."[233] It is an entity's actual practices that often maintain unnecessary segregation despite written policies that endorse treatment in the least restrictive alternative setting.

The failure to adopt these and other administrative mechanisms should be used to challenge any state claim that it does not have sufficient resources to place inappropriately institutionalized people into the community. The failure to use available resources to maximize integration is hardly the result of intentional discrimination but has the result of perpetuating segregation when, without fundamentally altering their programs, mental health agencies could minimize it. The claim of discriminatory methods of administration is a useful tool to educate a judge about the ways in which a state agency could accomplish the provision of community services to inappropriately institutionalized people, and it is a useful counterbalance to any defense relating to lack of funds.[234]

The question of how to measure costs presents interesting issues. Whereas it is true that in the long run it is somewhat less expensive to provide services to people in the community,[235] it is dangerous to base the preference for community services on cost because that will encourage cost cutting in community settings to the detriment of clients, and it is true that a state undertaking to move people responsibly from institutions into community settings will probably experience some period of time during the switch from institutional to community-based care during which both systems are running concurrently at greater cost. After the change is made, the state will recoup the extra cost. Whether an undue burden defense can be made because of elevated short-term costs if the entity will save money in the long run is not clear. If money will be saved over a 5-year period, should an undue burden defense based on money expended in a 1- or 2-year period be permitted?

It is better social policy to permit a reasonably long-term view of expenses in the case of state governments. The undue hardship may simply be imported from Title I, where employers face the prospect of "going out of business." Because states are unlikely to go out of business, steps that save money over a reasonable period of time—5 to 10 years—should not be subject to undue hardship defenses.

It is also unclear just how much more integration can cost before the additional costs can be asserted as a viable defense. Congress obviously expected compliance with the ADA by public entities to entail additional costs:

> While the integration of people with disabilities will sometimes involve substantial short-term burdens, both financial and administrative, the long range effects of integration will benefit society as a whole. . . . The fact that it is more convenient, either administratively or fiscally, to provide services in a segregated manner, does not constitute a valid justification for separate or different services under Section 504 of the Rehabilitation Act, or under this Title.[236]

It might be useful to compare the costs of transforming a state mental health system into one in which people are discharged into community placements when they no longer need institutionalization with the costs of making state facilities physically accessible.[237] In computing these costs, the savings derived from such a system should also be taken into account.

A "reasonable pace" for placement from a waiting list.   As noted above, the Supreme Court held that a state could successfully assert a defense against a plaintiff's claim for immediate placement in the community if it could "demonstrate that it had a comprehensive, effectively working plan for placing qualified people with mental disabilities in less-restrictive settings, and a waiting list that moved at a reasonable pace not controlled by the state's endeavors to keep its institutions fully populated."[238]

Very few states have such plans, and in the states that have done such analyses, the proportion of institutionalized patients who could live more appropriately in the community is substantial. Georgia surveyed its population of institutionalized people with mental retardation in 1980 and concluded that 607 (at least 30%) would be better served in the community.[239] Three years after the report, 525 remained institutionalized—due not to lack of funding, but because $5 million appropriated for community residential services were allowed to lapse, were transferred to other programs, or went unspent.[240]

On an individual level, once a professional has determined that treatment is more appropriate in the community than in an institution, how quickly must this be accomplished? Apparently, the courts of the 1990s will not be satisfied with the "all deliberate speed" with which school desegregation was (or was not) accomplished.

In *Charles Q. v. Houstoun*, the court, having determined that plaintiff Charles Q. was entitled be served in the community, ordered defendants to schedule discharge planning meetings within 4 days of the order, to finalize a discharge plan within 3 weeks, and to place Charles Q. in the community within 60 days.[241] Charles Q. was age 65 at the time of the order and had spent 44 years of his life in confinement.

In *Kathleen S.*, a class-action case, the court rejected the state's proposal that three people be placed in the community per month and found that it was reasonable on the basis of the state's past performance in placing people in the community, to expect the state to place eight people in the community per month. This approach has benefits and drawbacks: basing remedial orders on the state's own voluntarily adopted past schedules may be the most realistic way of determining how fast placements can safely be made. However, the speed at which states make placements is sometimes determined by political and economic considerations rather than the client's best interests and may reward states with poor records of community placement by giving them more time. Finally, the courts' ruling may be seen as inappropriately usurping the state agency's function of deciding how speedily and safely community placements may be made without compromising concerns for the clients. In the absence of a finding of contempt, it may have been premature for the court to reject the state's proposed schedule.

Other Claims Against Institutions Under the ADA

Discrimination on the Basis of Physical Disabilities

A substantial number of people in mental institutions have physical disabilities. They are visually impaired or deaf or have mobility impairments. Older patients in particular have multiple disabilities. Because Medicaid reimburses treatment costs for individuals over age 65 in state mental hospitals, older people are unneccessarily institutionalized in state hospital settings. Under the ADA, the state has an obligation to accommodate its mental health clients with physical disabilities, whether they are institutionalized or in the community.

Given the substantial number of cases brought by prisoners with physical disabilities,[242] there are surprisingly few cases brought by institutionalized people with physical disabilities. It is particularly surprising because whereas correctional facilities do not purport to benefit their residents, psychiatric facilities are ostensibly dedicated to diagnosing and treating people. Thirty years ago, it was discovered that many clients institutionalized for mental retardation did not have mental retardation but were simply deaf. Some of these cases have resulted in litigation.[243] Some clients have both hearing impairments and psychiatric disabilities. The state has an obligation to reasonably accommodate these clients in the provision of treatment for their psychiatric conditions. For example, a client who is deaf is unable to benefit from most traditional treatment modalities and finds it hard to communicate his or her needs and reactions to medication to therapists and staff who do not sign. A judge can readily understand the legal situation of a deaf patient whose treatment plan calls for her to "slow down and listen."[244]

The few cases brought by people with physical disabilities or medical problems against mental health service providers have resulted in victories, or at least partial victories, for the plaintiffs.[245] It is easy to understand the connection between the failure to accommodate disabilities such as deafness and the frustration and deterioration of the client, the likelihood that ineffectual treatment or no treatment at all will lead to unnecessary segregation at the institution and greater length of stay than people without disabilities, and the lack of meaningful access to the services offered by the hospital.

One of the nascent difficult issues raised by situations involving clients who are deaf or speak a different language is that these plaintiffs (understandably) ask for contact with others who are deaf or who speak their language.[246] In fact, states that have addressed these issues have done so by creating units or wards specifically for people who are deaf[247] or who speak Spanish.[248] This raises issues of segregation within a segregated setting.

Such programs, if they are truly voluntary and desired by patients, are probably permissible under ADA regulations; however, what of the deaf patient who asks for integration in a regular ward setting with an interpreter? Is the state required to provide such services? The case law, sparse as it is, strongly indicates that the answer is yes.[249] In fact, in one case, deaf plaintiffs with mental disabilities in the community specifically rejected the state's proffer of interpreters and demanded that they continue to receive treatment from therapists proficient in sign language. The court agreed that plaintiffs had a likelihood of success on the merits of their claim and ordered the state to continue to pay for signing therapists.[250] As the court in *Wilson v. North Carolina* noted, "the issue is not whether there has been sufficient communication to meet the plaintiff's medical, safety, and self-care needs. The relevant issue is whether there has been sufficient communication to provide plaintiff with the same level of services as those received by non-deaf plaintiffs."[251]

It should be noted that Title II of the ADA provides damages as injunctive relief.[252] If clients with physical disabilities have been detained in institutions for inappropriate lengths of time due to the failure to accommodate their disabilities, damages may be an appropriate remedy even when the state belatedly does provide the necessary services.[253]

Discrimination on the Basis of Gender

It is also clear that conditions in psychiatric institutions are particularly unsafe for women, who are raped, sexually assaulted, and sexually harassed in institutional settings. Recently, the 9th Circuit refused to dismiss a constitutional claim against an institution superintendent whose investigations of reported sexual abuse and assault under facility policies and determinations pursuant to those policies were so superficial and formalistic that a jury could find that he was deliberately indifferent to the safety of the women involved.[254]

So far, these cases have sounded in traditional tort, malpractice, and (occasionally) constitutional deprivations of safety. For the first time recently, a case was brought on behalf of a *class* of women subject to rape and sexual assault in an institutional setting that also alleged that indifference of institutional officials to the sexual assault stated both gender and disability discrimination claims.[255]

The failure to credit or believe institutionalized women's accounts of rape or sexual assault in institutional settings, the failure to prevent such attacks, and the failure to appropriately investigate and punish the attacker—especially staff—can be seen as discrimination based on either gender or the intersection of gender and disability.

The facts suggest that disability discrimination is a substantial factor in both sexual assaults on mentally disabled wmen and in the failure to credit or investigate disabled women's reports of sexual assault. First, the rate of sexual assault on women with mental disabilities is far higher than the rate of sexual assault on nondisabled women,[256] attributed by law enforcement officers, mental health professionals, and the attackers themselves to mentally disabled women's greater vulnerability and lower credibility.[257] Second, law enforcement officers take the reports of people with mental disabilities less seriously,[258] and some state prosecutors refuse to investigate allegations of rape in state hospital settings.[259] Third, administrators of these facilities fail to investigate or discipline employees against whom complaints have been made,[260] even when repeated complaints are made against the same employee.[261] One study estimated that 80%–85% of criminal abuse of institution residents never reaches the proper authorities.[262] The very fact that crimes such as rape and sexual assault committed against these residents are called *abuse* rather than *crimes* helps to minimize them.

These issues implicate the constitutional right to safety;[263] most advocates and judges would understand that. But the failure to report, investigate, and prosecute crimes against people with mental disabilities, in general, and women with mental disabilities, in particular, is discrimination so deeply embedded in our society that we sometimes do not even recognize it. Yet the provisions in the settlement of *Caroline C. v. Johnson*,[264] a class action suit charging sexual abuse at an institution, which protect patients from retaliation for reporting rape or sexual assault[265] and prohibit staff members with complaints of sexual molestation pending against them from attending women in restraints,[266] tell a tale of differential and disadvantageous treatment that is repeated in surveys and case law.[267]

Another example of the intersection of disability and gender discrimination is the promulgation of ER or facility policies applicable to people with psychiatric diagnoses that have a differential and particularly damaging impact on women, especially women with histories of sexual abuse. For example, ERs often require complete disrobing in a locked room or require that patients be strapped to gurneys. At least one case has been brought challenging these practices as disability discrimination, and the court refused to grant the defendant's motion to dismiss.[268]

Facilities also have numerous policies that have adverse and differential effects by gender. Women who are on one-to-one observation are often observed by male attendants as they shower or use the toilet. Because many of these women were sexually abused by men, being observed in this way causes substantial deterioration that is less likely in men with no similar history. Women are put in restraints, immobilized, and watched by male attendants. By several weeks into hospitalization, these women are clearly worse off than when they arrived at the hospital. Use of restraints escalates, suicide attempts increase, medication dosage skyrockets, and still no improvement is seen.[269]

These kinds of actions by hospital staff are often punitive and arguably the result of the intersection of disability and gender discrimination. These practices would not be carried out on a woman if she were not disabled or regarded as disabled, and they are clearly carried out predominantly on women. This occurs despite a vast body of treatment literature that has existed for at least a decade warning against the approaches listed above and detailing appropriate treatment options for women with histories of sexual abuse.[270] This literature has for the most part been ignored, although New York, Massachusetts, and Maine are ahead of the country in their recognition of these issues.

Discrimination on the Basis of Mental Retardation

In addition, mental health agencies have an obligation under the ADA to provide mental health services to clients with mental retardation.[271] The lack of treatment for people with dual diagnoses of mental retardation and psychiatric disabilities is hardly a new issue; however, this failure is now being challenged under the ADA as discrimination on the basis of mental retardation. Sometimes the discrimination alleged is overt and intentional: in one recent case, plaintiffs claimed that the state employees had told them that people with mental retardation could not benefit from treatment for their psychiatric problems.[272]

On other occasions, discrimination is related to inappropriate treatment that comes from falling between the cracks of two systems: People with mental retardation in psychiatric settings are inappropriately placed there, whereas people whose mental retardation is compounded by psychiatric disabilities rarely receive treatment for their mental health problems from providers accustomed to serving people with mental retardation.

In other cases, inappropriate psychiatric treatment seems to aggravate the problems of people with mental retardation. This appeared to be the case in *Olmstead v. L. C.*, which involved two people with mental retardation who had behavioral problems and were constantly and inappropriately being committed to psychiatric institutions on a "revolving-door" basis. Only after the litigation was filed did the two plaintiffs receive stable community services. In *L. C.*, the Department of Mental Health paid for their institutionalization, whereas the Department of Mental Retardation paid for community services. This may be true in many states and creates perverse fiscal incentives for mental retardation agencies to transfer their clients to psychiatric hospitals, where the clients' predictable reactions to such inappropriate placements make them even less likely candidates for community placement.

Segregation on the Basis of Severity of Disability

Most of the cases raising issues of discrimination on the basis of severity of disability are cases involving people with mental retardation or developmental disabilities.[273] Some institutions have been accused of placing in the community only those residents who are the most "highly functioning" and present the fewest behavioral or medical problems. This practice has been challenged as discriminatory in a variety of cases.[274]

This raises the question of whether the ADA protects people who are disabled from disadvantageous treatment in relation to other people with the same disability. This is not the same question as whether disability discrimination law protects people with a particular disability from disadvantageous treatment vis-à-vis someone with a different kind of disability,[275] although of course the issue of when a condition is the "same" disability or a "different" disability may blur at the margins.

The majority of courts have held that disability discrimination law prohibits discrimination on the basis of severity of disability.[276] This was one of the earliest claims raised under Section 504 of the Rehabilitation Act of 1973.[277] These holdings are an accurate reading of the intent of disability discrimination law. When Congress passed its first set of comprehensive amendments to the Rehabilitation Act, it made clear that the prohibitions on discrimination were modeled after comparable civil rights protection granted to minorities and women. Congress made the same point even more strongly when it passed the ADA. It has long been recognized under civil rights laws that minorities can file race discrimination claims if they claim disadvantageous treatment in relation to someone of the same race—for example, charges that a light-skinned black employee or applicant was favored over a dark-skinned black person.[278] Prohibition of discrimination on the basis of severity of disability does not exempt plantiffs from having to show that they are "qualified" for a program or prevent defendants from raising the defense of fundamental alteration to their program.

Civil Commitment, Segregation, and the ADA

Involuntary civil commitment is one of the few processes in society whereby citizens who are charged with no crime may be detained against their will.[279] It is certainly the only one in which the detention may be indefinite,[280] even lifelong.[281] It is most likely the only process involving potential loss of liberty for years in which the judge or the person's lawyer can waive his or her presence at the hearing,[282] in which the psychiatric professional who wrote the report recommending commitment often does not appear to testify or be cross-examined, and in which the length of the hearing often varies between 1 and 15 minutes. These are not aberrations in civil commitment; they are the norm.[283] Efforts to change them—to require the psychiatrist to testify or the patient to be present—meet with opposition from judges, mental health professionals, the public defenders who are supposed to represent the individuals, and from the attorneys general of the states involved.

After significant restrictions in the 1970s, the state's civil commitment powers have once again become bloated in response to various public health threats, perceived public health threats, and the inevitable fallout of restricting social and medical care programs. A few states never repealed their statutes permitting the involuntary commitment of people with tuberculosis who would not accept treatment for it, and with the emergence of treatment-resistant strains of tuberculosis, new commitment statutes have been adopted.[284] Attempts to civilly commit or quarantine people with AIDS were fought vigorously and defeated.[285] States have recently been flooded with legislation providing for the involuntary civil commitment of sexual predators.[286] The overwhelming majority of people who are subject to involuntary civil commitment in the United States, however, are people who are perceived to be mentally ill.[287]

Civil Commitment Statutes

It is clearly segregation to be legally mandated to live apart from the rest of society and clearly discrimination to be deprived of one's liberty on the basis of disability.[288] One measure of how entrenched the concept of civil commitment is in society is that only two civil commitment statutes have been challenged as violating the ADA; one of them challenged a state's tuberculosis commitment statute,[289] and the other sought commitment on behalf of an individual.

The latter decision, *McKlemurry v. Hendrix,*[290] challenged a Mississippi statute that prohibits civil commitment proceedings from being pursued against anyone with "unresolved criminal charges" pending against them. Jeremy McKlemurry, who had a long history of involvement with the mental health system, was arrested for drinking a beer, which was a violation of probation requirements for a previous drug possession charge. His grandparents tried unsuccessfully to get him mental health treatment in jail; while he was in jail he twice attempted to commit suicide.

The judge found that McKlemurry was not deprived of mental health treatment, which he could receive through the correctional system, and noted helpfully that he could be civilly committed immediately upon termination of his sentence; indeed, although the judge was uncertain about the legal issues involved, he suggested that commitment proceedings might even begin before McKlemurry's sentence was completed. The Mississippi statute, however, did not violate the ADA because it classified on the basis of the pendency of criminal charges rather than disability, and it did not prevent people from receiving mental health treatment altogether.

The second case is far more substantive. Although *City of Newark v. J. S.*[291] involves commitment for contagious tuberculosis, it has much to offer as a general analysis of the impact of the ADA on commitment laws in general. *J. S.* is a thoughtful and well-reasoned decision and clearly concerned an extremely important issue; little attention was paid to it by mental health scholars or lawyers, however,[292] and it was only released for publication 2 years after it was issued. To this day, it has not been cited by a single court.

The decision is, however, well worth study because it suggests at least a plausible response to the question of whether civil commitment constitutes impermissible segregation under the ADA. The court held that the ADA and substantive due process forbade segregation on the basis of illness alone, stating

> yet for government to try to confine someone based on his or her illness alone is as wrongful an act of discrimination as denying him or her a service from government. If public entities are barred from subjecting disabled persons to discrimination, can it be seriously doubted that they are barred from involuntarily confining them?[293]

The judge found that the only justification for confinement on the basis of disability —and not even a sufficient basis by itself—was proof by the state that the individual met the direct threat exception to prohibitions on discrimination under the ADA.[294]

Title II of the ADA arguably permits a defendant to discriminate against a person with a disability if that person poses "a significant risk to the health or safety of others that cannot be eliminated by a modification of policies, practices or procedures or by the provision of auxiliary aids and services."[295] The reason that the direct threat defense is qualified as "arguable" is that it appears nowhere in the language of Title II or of the DOJ's regulations to Title II. By contrast, Titles I and III of the ADA specifically mention the direct threat defense.[296]

Nevertheless, the DOJ's Interpretive Guidance comments at length on the applicability of the direct threat defense to public entities, defining "direct threat" and elaborating on its interpretation. Unfortunately, it does so in the context of commenting on the definition of "qualified individual with a disability," thereby further obscuring an already nettlesome—and significant—question of whether not being a direct threat is a part of the plaintiff's prima facie case of proving himself or herself to meet a program's essential eligibility requirements in order to be a qualified individual with a disability, as some courts have held, or an affirmative defense, as indicated by Titles I and III of the ADA. The Supreme Court appeared to have settled the question in *Bragdon v. Abbott* in favor of the latter interpretation.[297]

The Interpretive Guidance cautions that determinations of direct threat "may not be based on generalizations or stereotypes about the effects of a particular disability" but rather must be based on "individualized assessment, based on reasonable judgment that relies on current medical evidence or on the best available objective evidence."[298] A decision that a person constitutes a direct threat cannot be made without first specifically identifying the precise risk the disability is thought to pose. Next, the decision maker must take into consideration "the nature, duration, and severity of the risk; the probability that the potential risk will actually occur; and whether reasonable modifications of policies, practices, and procedures will mitigate the risk."[299] Although the ADA is intended to provide protection against discrimination to disabled individuals on the basis of prejudice, stereotypes, and unfounded fears, a state's "legitimate concerns" must also be weighed—specifically, "the need to avoid exposing others to significant health and safety risks."[300]

The court in *J. S.* closely followed this analysis. The judge held that a claim of direct threat required "proof that this specific person (and not similar persons) poses a significant risk to others, a risk that may not be merely speculative, theoretical, remote, or even "elevated" is required."[301] Proof of a direct threat alone, however, would not be sufficient to justify confinement: If the specifically identified risk were amenable to reasonable accommodations, confinement would not be justified. "Only those significant risks that cannot be eliminated by reasonable accommodations can be considered direct threats."[302] In determining whether a person's disability constituted enough of a risk to constitute a direct threat to the health and safety of others, the state would have to specifically identify the nature, duration, and severity of the risk as well as the possibility of harm. The court would have to find that the risk was "probable" in the "reasonably foreseeable future."

In addition, the state would have to articulate precisely what goal it sought to accomplish by confining the individual—the goal could not simply be confinement for its own sake.

> The first step of the individual analysis required here is to define precisely what [the state] seeks. During the active phase of TB, isolation of JS, as opposed to confinement or imprisonment, is what is required . . . . If JS lived in a private home and could be given a private bedroom, confinement to his own home might be appropriate.[303]

Once the state articulated its specific, health-related goal, if the person it sought to confine could suggest an alternative that would meet the same goal, then the state "would have the burden of showing why this less restrictive alternative was not selected."[304]

In *J. S.*, after holding a hearing involving at least seven witnesses,[305] the court interpreted the tuberculosis commitment statute in such a way as to make its substantive and procedural due process requirements consonant with the NJ civil commitment statute for people with mental illness and, therefore, found the tuberculosis commitment statute met the requirements of the ADA.

This does not mean that *J. S.* stands for the proposition that civil commitment statutes pass muster under the ADA and even less for the proposition that these statutes are applied in a nondiscriminatory manner. First, New Jersey's commitment statute is more protective of individual liberties than many other states' commitment statutes,[306] and the New Jersey Supreme Court enforces those protections of citizens' rights.[307] Some state commitment statutes do have provisions similar to New Jersey's; these statutes conform to the ADA as written. However, it is the practice of committing people without taking the statutory requirements seriously that distinguishes most commitment proceedings from ADA cases involving unnecessary segregation. "Involuntary civil commitment cases are routinely disposed of in a matter of minutes in closed courtrooms."[308] The number of civil commitment hearings where the state presents seven or eight witnesses could probably be counted without getting into double digits.[309] Although the length of the hearing is not given in *J. S.* because as the Supreme Court noted, the average commitment hearing takes 9.2 minutes,[310] one can safely assume that it lasted considerably longer.

More important, most people are not civilly committed because they are a direct threat to others[311] but rather because they are a threat to themselves or are "gravely disabled." Generally, people are civilly committed because they have a psychiatric disability and no place to live. But Title II of the ADA does not—as Congress did not—extend the direct threat exception to include danger to self. "Direct threat" applies only to the health or safety of others.

The legislative history of the ADA makes perfectly clear that the direct threat language evolved directly from a provision that would have allowed discrimination if a person were actively contagious. "Direct threat" was substituted for "contagious" in part because this was the language used the by the Supreme Court in *Nassau County v. Arline*. Implicitly, one may assume that the language was substituted precisely to assuage people's fears that the ADA would somehow immunize dangerous mentally ill people, a fear expressed from congressional offices and in newspaper editorials—an unfounded fear that itself reflects the need for both the protection of the ADA and for strict adherence to the narrow exception of the direct threat. This will enable courts to "guard against the risk that governmental action may be grounded in popular myths, irrational fears, or noxious fallacies rather than well-founded science."[312]

Fortunately, the U.S. Supreme Court discussed the direct threat exception and underscored that it must be construed narrowly.[313] The court's analysis suggests a tighter and more scrupulous examination of the precise risk,[314] and the probability of that risk, than is required by many statutes and certainly than exists in the practice of civil commitment across the country. In *Bragdon v. Abbott*, the court applied the direct threat exception under Title III for public accommodations, but Title III's definition of *direct threat* is identical to the DOJ's definition in its Interpretive Guidance to Title II, which is not surprising because the department wrote both sets of regulations. As mentioned previously, this definition does not include danger to self but only danger to others.[315]

Thus, civil commitment cannot under the ADA be justified by reference to disability or need for treatment alone. This is consonant with due process requirements as well.[316] In a sense, substantive due process and the ADA reinforce the same trend: Dangerousness to others rather than disability is the principal support for confinement because disability *qua* disability is almost always more efficaciously treated in integrated settings.

This means that a number of state commitment statutes may be facially invalid under the ADA and certainly as applied to many people who do not pose a direct threat to others. For example, Wyoming's recently amended commitment statute allows commitment of a person who

> evidences behavior manifested by recent acts or omission that, due to mental illness, he is unable to satisfy basic needs for nourishment, essential medical care, shelter or safety so that a substantial probability exists that . . . destabilization from lack of or refusal to take prescribed psychotropic medication for a diagnosed condition . . . will imminently ensue, unless the individual receives prompt and adequate care for this mental illness.[317]

This is far from a requirement of a direct threat to the health and safety of others based on "well-founded science."[318] It also means that an increasing number of outpatient commitment statutes are discriminatory under the ADA to the extent that they single out people for disadvantageous treatment—forced administration of unwanted medications—on the basis of disability alone without requiring proof of direct threat to the health and safety of others.

But the Supreme Court was also—at least until *Hendricks*—equally clear in its insistence that extended civil confinement for dangerousness alone was constitutionally impermissible.[319] One thing is clear. The fabric of illness and treatment in which civil commitment was clothed for years is growing more and more threadbare. This trend is likely to continue until society is forced to face the reality that it is setting up an enormous system of preventive detention for social outcasts,[320] a group that can only grow as the social support systems of the past 30 years are dismantled and the gap between the rich and the poor grows. The number of people in institutions, like the number of people receiving disability benefits, swells in economic hard times and diminishes when things get better. If institutional beds are available, they will be filled by poor people who may otherwise be homeless or in jail. What is completely clear is the social cleanup function served by shelters, institutions, and jails and the totally arbitrary nature of who is in which place.

The ADA forces the social cleanup to be limited—at least in the case of people with disabilities—to people who pose a direct threat to the health and safety of others. Ironically, if the only justification for segregation on the basis of disability is direct threat, and direct threat is only defined by reference to danger to others, then much of the civil commitment system as we know it today is substantially undermined.[321]

Failing to Commit an Individual

At least one case has charged that police discriminated against an obviously ill individual by failing to take him into custody and seek his involuntary commitment.[322] This claim was correctly dismissed by the court. Failing to segregate an individual because of his or her disability should not under any circumstances create a claim under the ADA against police. Nor should it state a claim against hospital officials or county officials unless the person was completely denied services because of his or her disability.

Challenges to Individual Commitment Decisions

Individuals who have been involuntarily civilly committed cannot seek to challenge their commitment under the ADA, although, depending on state law, it may be possible for them to raise ADA issues in their commitment proceedings. Federal courts cannot overturn decisions by state courts in individual cases under the Rooker–Feldman doctrine,[323] and federal courts do not generally interfere in ongoing state proceedings because of abstention doctrines, which counsel federal courts not to interfere with state courts in the conduct of cases before them. One exception to this rule created by at least one court was found in a case which alleged that the civil commitment proceedings were undertaken intentionally in bad faith.[324]

Representation at Commitment Hearings

In many states, the office of the public defender handles both the representation of people charged with criminal offenses and people subject to civil commitment. Although public defenders are often overloaded with more cases than they can handle, they typically approach their representation of criminal defendants with an attitude that is adversarial to the state. The attitudes of the same public defenders toward people subject to commitment are considerably different, and people subject to commitment hearings often receive inferior representation, as measured both objectively —in terms of how much time is put into investigation, how many witnesses are interviewed, and how much time is spent speaking to the client—and subjectively. This difference in attitude is based on the client's disability, or on the attorney's perception of the disability, and is arguably a violation of the ADA.[325]

Empirical research paints a dismal picture of the quality of representation in commitment hearings. Voluminous research over the past 20 years shows that most attorneys are passive at best in commitment hearings, sometimes colluding with the court and the state to ensure that their client is committed.[326] Attorneys in commitment hearings have been described as functioning as "mere bystanders"[327] and as "unwilling to mount anything more than a superficial challenge to the state's evidence for commitment."[328]

Presently, in some jurisdictions a single public defender handles more than 2,000 civil commitment cases a year.[329] The poor performance of attorneys in civil commitment hearings, however, is not simply the analogue of the overburdened public defender in criminal cases; it represents a distinctly different attitude toward both the client and the process. Research shows that attorneys frequently defer to the findings of the mental health professionals. In a recent study in Virginia, "defense attorneys did not question the clinical examiner's conclusions (89.5%), question the admissibility of evidence (97.4%), or question other witnesses (96.8%)."[330] This is true even when attorneys receive special training in cross-examining psychiatric experts; attorneys who received this training persisted in using only superficial cross-examination methods.[331] Attorneys who represent individuals subject to civil commitment often remain uncertain about their appropriate role. Many have never met their own clients.[332] In fact, in cases across the country, the client's own attorney could not pick her out of a lineup, much less adequately represent her in court.[333]

Commitment Hearings of People With Physical Disabilities

Some survey respondents with physical disabilities such as hearing impairments complained that when they were in court they could not hear what was happening, and no accommodations were made.[334] State courts are subject to the regulations of the ADA, although some have been slow in responding to their obligations.

Involuntary Detention Prior to Civil Commitment

There are other kinds of claims involving commitment and the ADA relating to the process by which an individual is detained for examination to determine whether he or she should be subject to commitment. A number of cases involving police practices in this area were reviewed in chapter 1.

Besides the process by which an individual is detained for examination, another area of claims regarding commitment involves the conditions of precommitment hearing detention for people perceived as mentally ill. Some individuals are held in jails prior to their commitment hearings.[335] Even when they are held in psychiatric facilities, they are often denied the opportunity to meet with their families until they "earn that privilege."[336]

In *Roe v. Monongola County*,[337] a man who was picked up on a mental health warrant alleged that he was held for a time in a padded cell, handcuffed and shackled, without receiving proper treatment or a hearing, was not permitted to use the bathroom, change clothes, or eat without handcuffs, all of which denied his right to reasonable accommodation of his disability and violated his right to be free from restraints.[338]

The defendants moved to dismiss the complaint on the ground that the plaintiff was not discriminated against within the meaning of the ADA because he was provided the "care and safekeeping mandated by [West Virginia law] *in the same way that other persons with similar needs are treated, and was not denied access to any program or service*" (emphasis added).[339]

This case provides yet another example of why the ADA must be interpreted to prohibit adverse and disadvantageous treatment on the basis of disability and not simply unequal treatment compared with people without disabilities. People without disabilities (in the sense of people who have no mental disabilities or records of mental disabilities and who are not regarded as being mental disabled) are not subject to mental health warrants. Does that mean that the ADA cannot reach policies dictating the complete segregation and isolation of people subject to mental health warrants? The defendants argued that they had treated Roe exactly as they treated all other people with similar needs and had comported with all the requirements of West Virginia law; therefore, no discrimination had taken place.

The court refused to dismiss the plaintiff's claim, noting his allegations that

he was handcuffed and shackled at all times during his stay with the county defendants, unable to communicate with his family, to attend to personal hygiene, change clothes or even to eat in a proper way. *Thus, even though the plaintiff may have been afforded the due process required by the statute, as in a prompt mental hygiene hearing, he was, in his view, isolated and segregated in a manner that the ADA was designed to prevent.* (emphasis added)[340]

Although Roe presented his case as a claim for reasonable accommodation, it seemed that he was in fact asserting an intentional discrimination claim. His claim was apparently that the county[341] shackled him continuously, isolated him, and prevented him from communicating with his family precisely because they regarded him as being mentally disabled. It is hard to imagine that continuous shackling, isolation, and a ban on communications with family were facially neutral county policies applied to all detainees in the county from which he sought relief on the basis of his disability.

Mental Health Courts and the ADA

One response to adverse treatment of people with mental disabilities by jails and the judicial system has been the creation of a whole new system rather than amelioration or correction of the discrimination in the old system. On June 6, 1997, Chief Judge Dale Ross of the 17th Judicial Circuit Court in Broward County (FL) created by administrative order the first "mental health court."[342] This court was created in response to the county's practice of "repeatedly incarcerating certain people whose only crime was being mentally ill"[343] in jails where they received no mental health treatment, often decompensated, and sometimes died. Now, after being arrested for misdemeanors, some people who appear to be mentally ill are routed to mental health court.

The mission statement of the new court is "to address the unique needs of the mentally ill in our criminal justice system."[344] Rather than being tried for their misdemeanors, they are given mental health treatment. Some are placed in "cottages" on the grounds of South Florida State Hospital for "four to six months"; if people without mental illnesses were arrested for the same offense,[345] they would probably be discharged for time served.[346] Although the Progress Report of the Mental Health Court reports the diagnoses of the defendants, it does not report the misdemeanors for which they were arrested. One witness, however, sitting in on the court for several weeks reported the nature of the arrests that occurred: stealing eight packs of cigars, stealing $3.63 worth of cigars, stealing a watermelon, possessing marijuana, driving without a license, trespassing on a golf course, resisting arrest without violence, drinking in public and, in one case, drinking coffee on the curb outside of a bank.[347] Despite these seemingly outrageous and unfair occurrences, this program has won national awards, despite the reservations of some, including Dade County Public Defender Bennett Brummer.[348]

There are extraordinarily troubling implications about a judicial system and a particular judge getting state and local legislative grants for millions of dollars[349] to do what the executive branch is supposed to be doing—creating housing and treatment for people with mental illnesses whom the judge has the sole discretion to refer to that treatment program.[350]

Does the Broward County Mental Health Court violate the ADA? The state court system that created the mental health court certainly qualifies as a public entity under Title II.[351] Title II provides that "no qualified individual with a disability shall, by reason of such disability, be excluded from participation in or be denied the benefits of the services, programs or activities of a public entity, or be subjected to discrimination by any such entity."[352] Certainly referral to the court takes place "by reason of disability" and results in exclusion from regular court proceedings, which qualify as the court system's "service, program or activities."[353]

It is hard to answer the question of whether the mental health court violates the ADA, in part because it is difficult to determine the legal status of the court. Is it a "diversion" program? Would its creators characterize it as the "reasonable accommodations" of the judicial system for people with mental disabilities? It is clear that isabled people may not be forced to accept accommodations that they do not want,[354] and it is far from clear that any options are presented to the defendants who appear before the court. A true diversion program must present the defendant with the choice of bypassing it and going before the court and going to trial. If the mental health court were truly voluntary, it might pass muster either as a reasonable accommodation or under the ADA exception for "providing benefits, services, or advantages to individuals with disabilities, or to a particular class of individuals with disabilities, beyond those required by this part."[355] The regulations make clear that an individual with a disability need not accept these services, and this is where the mental health court flounders. First, judges and mental health workers refer people to the court unilaterally. They are not told in open court that they have the option not to be in mental health court. No one appears to have ever opted out of the court because he or she did not want to be there. Second, some people who come to mental health court are considered incompetent to be tried for their offenses and, therefore, might be incompetent to choose to be in mental health court.

In addition, there is a question of whether the mental health court provides the defendants with something better than they would have received if they had gone before a regular court. There has been no research on the questions of (a) whether people who do not have mental disabilities are charged and prosecuted for crimes such as shoplifting a box of cigars or stealing a watermelon, and (b) if they are, whether those charges are dismissed. Although there is a consensus among those who established the mental health court that the situation in Broward County prior to its institution reflected enormous systemic mistreatment and disadvantaging of people with mental disabilities, it is no defense to a charge of discrimination under the ADA to claim that terrible discrimination has been replaced with different, less damaging discrimination. The question under discrimination law is not whether people with mental disabilities in the Broward County criminal justice system are receiving better treatment than they did in the past; it is whether they are being disadvantaged in the criminal justice system because of their mental disabilities.

Discrimination in the Community

Discrimination in the Denial of Mental Health Services

There are basically two kinds of discrimination in the denial of health care. The first is denial of health care for one condition because the plaintiff also has another condition, as in the refusal of dentists to treat people who are HIV positive or in the refusal to consider a woman with mental retardation as a candidate for an organ transplant. These forms of discrimination are discussed in chapter 5.

The second is discrimination in providing treatment for the disabling condition itself. Discrimination claims based on the refusal to treat or on the failure to properly treat a person with a psychiatric disability arise in a variety of contexts, such as ERs, mental health centers, and mental health programs. For example, ERs have been charged with mistreating people who seek assistance for psychiatric problems compared with the treatment of others who come to the ER with medical complaints. Some community mental health centers refuse to treat people with certain specific diagnoses. Some mental health professionals are overtly hostile to people on the basis of their diagnosis. Before I consider these issues, a threshold question is whether the ADA prohibits discrimination in the treatment of one's disability.

Does the ADA Cover Discrimination in the Treatment of Disability?

The fact that this is a question at all may surprise some people. Surely hostility toward a person or refusal to treat him or her because of a diagnosis must be discrimination on the basis of disability or perceived disability. What else could it be? Indeed, there would be no question that it was discrimination if practiced by anyone other than a medical or mental health professional.

Discrimination claims against medical or mental health professionals because of their treatment of their clients have a peculiar obstacle arising from the *Baby Doe* cases of the early 1980s. The practice of letting babies born with disabilities die was relatively unpublicized but common before the *Baby Doe* controversy erupted. Indeed, in 1968 the *Atlantic Monthly* published an article in which Joseph Fletcher, a famous theologian, asserted that

> there is no reason to feel guilty about putting a Down's Syndrome baby away, whether it's "put away" in the sense of hidden in a sanitarium or in a more responsible lethal sense. . . . True guilt arises only from an offense against a person, and a Down's is not a person.[356]

Five years later, *The New England Journal of Medicine* published an article contending that 14% of deaths in the special care nursery at a distinguished hospital were due to intentional lack of treatment.[357] These practices finally erupted into public awareness in 1982 when a nurse reported the decision of parents and doctors to forego a routine but lifesaving operation for a baby born with Down syndrome who could have lived a fairly normal life span had the operation been performed.[358]

The federal government and a number of private individuals and organizations made several efforts to thwart this practice, which at first was framed as discrimination on the basis of disability and later was reframed as child abuse.[359] The government's efforts to regulate the treatment of newborns with disabilities were fought vigorously by the medical establishment as incursions on its independence.

Widespread misunderstanding of the meaning of the legal outcomes in the various *Baby Doe* discrimination cases creates questions regarding the viability of litigation challenging discrimination in the delivery of treatment for a person's disability. The key *Baby Doe* decisions raising these questions are the U.S. Supreme Court's decision in *Bowen v. American Hospital Association*[360] and the 2nd Circuit's decision in *United States v. University Hospital*.[361]

Bowen v. American Hospital Association[362] was a plurality decision, and a fragmented one at that. It struck down federal regulations intended to prevent hospitals from denying treatment to handicapped newborns on the narrow grounds that the regulations had been promulgated in violation of the Administrative Procedure Act of 1946.[363] The recurring theme of the plurality decision was that a hospital could not be guilty of discrimination if it failed to treat an infant on the direction of the infant's parents. The hospital was obligated by law to obey the instructions of the parents and to do so could not be considered discrimination. The plurality also stated that "handicapped infants are entitled to 'meaningful access' to medical services provided by the hospital, and a hospital rule or state policy denying or limiting such access would be subject to challenge under Section 504."[364] The plurality reiterated that the case did not involve "a claim that any specific individual treatment decision violates 504"[365] and underscored that it was not deciding whether Section 504 applied to such decisions.

Thus, *Bowen v. American Hospital Association's dicta* stands at most for the proposition that hospitals cannot be charged with discrimination for carrying out the instructions of parents to cease supportive treatment to their disabled infants. Hospitals may not independently seek to terminate the life of a disabled child over the objections of the parents.[366] In addition, *American Hospital Association's* interpretation of Section 504 does not apply in the context of the ADA. The DOJ regulations make it clear that "nothing in this Act or this part authorizes the representative or guardian of an individual with a disability to decline food, water, medical treatment or medical services for that individual."[367]

The 2nd Circuit Court in *United States v. University Hospital* held that the Rehabilitation Act of 1973 did not apply to treatment decisions involving newborns with disabilities on different grounds. First, the 2nd Circuit panel relied on the U.S. Supreme Court's statement in *Davis v. Southeastern Community College*[368]—heavily criticized and later amended by the court itself—that the "otherwise qualified" requirement of the Rehabilitation Act means that a handicapped person must be qualified for a program "in spite" of his or her handicap. Because a person is seeking treatment not in spite of but specifically because of his handicap, the court found that a person could not be "otherwise qualified" in those circumstances. A decision can only be discriminatory "where the handicap is unrelated to, and thus improper to consideration of, the service in question."[369] Thus, the court held that "because where medical treatment is at issue, it is typically the handicap itself that gives rise to, or at least contributes to, the need for services . . . 'the otherwise qualified' section of 504 cannot be meaningfully applied to a medical treatment decision."[370] The court found that "the phrase 'otherwise qualified' cannot be applied in the comparatively fluid context of medical treatment decisions without losing its plain meaning."[371]

First, this entire analysis relates to the requirement of "otherwise qualified," a requirement that has been removed entirely from Title III of the ADA, which applies to private hospitals. There is no requirement that a plaintiff be "qualified" or "otherwise qualified" to receive medical services under Title III of the ADA.[372]

More important, however, the concept that failing to provide medical treatment for the disabling condition itself could never constitute discrimination is deeply troubling. The most pernicious discrimination against people with disabilities has been to consider them unworthy of life because of their disabilities. Under the 2nd Circuit's logic, it is not discrimination to deny people with a disability treatment specifically because of antipathy toward their disability.

As in so many other cases, the outcome depends on whether the focus is on the plaintiff's "qualifications" or the defendant's actions and motivations. In addition, the breadth or specificity with which the services provided by the defendant are defined can control the framework of the case. Children are permitted to die because they are disabled. If they were not disabled, they would not be permitted to die. This is the second most extreme form of adverse treatment on the basis of disability. Affirmatively killing the children because they had a disability would be more extreme, and the Second Circuit might recognize this as disability discrimination. As testimony from the Nazi era reveals, however, affirmative killing and "letting die" are easily blurred. In *The Nazi Doctors,* a woman described a hospital tour in Germany where disabled children were being starved. The doctor explained the decision to deprive the children of food:

> We do not kill . . . with poison, injections, etc.; then the foreign press and certain gentlemen in Switzerland would only have new inflammatory material. No, our method is much simpler and more natural, as you see. With these words, he pulled . . . a child from its little bed. While he then exhibited the child like a dead rabbit, he asserted with a knowing expression and a cynical grin: For this one it will take two to three more days.[373]

People with disabilities are "otherwise qualified" to live. In the *Baby Doe* case in Bloomington, the operation to remove the esophageal obstruction was predicted to have a 90% chance of success, and the decision not to pursue it was made because the child had Down syndrome. Had Baby Doe not had a disability, she would have lived. People with disabilities are also, as human beings, "otherwise qualified" to receive medical treatment and are being treated disadvantageously when compared with other human beings by being denied treatment on the basis of their disability.[374]

The 2nd Circuit's decision also leads to illogical outcomes. Courts have held that a person with a disability cannot be discriminated against in receiving medical treatment for any other medical problem or condition, except the disabling condition itself. Even under the 2nd Circuit's logic, it is not medical treatment decisions per se that are insulated from discrimination law but only those decisions related to the disability itself. Thus, to people who are HIV positive, one must provide dental care[375] and care for their ear problems[376] or other medical problems.[377] Under the 2nd Circuit's reasoning, however, a doctor's decision not to treat the HIV infection itself would be insulated. Of course, because HIV infection itself is a condition that permits opportunistic infection, the determination of what was "the disability" and what was "another medical problem or condition" might be difficult to make.

Rather than become drawn into making these kinds of distinctions, many courts have simply rejected the logic of *University Hospital* altogether. Although agreeing that "'otherwise qualified' may not readily transfer to the context of medical benefits," one court concluded that

> in the context of medical benefits a more meaningful "otherwise qualified" standard may be based on the premise that disability alone is not a permissible ground for withholding medical benefits. . . . I therefore conclude that a MHS [managed health care system] participant is "otherwise qualified" for medical benefits if there is no factor apart from the mere existence of the disability that renders the participant unqualified for the benefit.[378]

This is consonant with the findings of the ADA that reflected specific congressional concern that "discrimination against individuals persists in such critical areas as . . . health services,"[379] which arose from the plethora of testimony about discrimination by health care providers.[380] Title III itself lists "professional offices of health care providers" and "hospitals" as places of public accommodation subject to the ADA. Courts have recognized that "disability discrimination by health care providers" is "disturbingly real"[381] and have concluded that the ADA does not protect discriminatory decisions to refuse treatment or give inadequate treatment on the basis of a person's disabilities. Rather, in a wide variety of cases, courts have focused on the basis and effects of the challenged decision. The 11th Circuit recently rejected "the State's argument . . . that Title II of the ADA affords no protection to individuals with disabilities who receive public services designed only for individuals with disabilities."[382] Rejecting this position as contrary to the intent of Congress, the 11th Circuit cited an impressive array of legislative history to support its conclusion that if the adverse action being complained of was due to the plaintiff's disability, that would suffice to state a cause of action under the ADA.

Discrimination in Emergency Room Settings

In 1963, the Community Mental Health Centers Act[383] mandated 24-hour emergency service as an essential mental health service. The Emergency Medical Systems Act

of 1973[384] provided that the ability to provide services for psychiatric emergencies
was a critical component of ER care. Psychiatric emergencies make up about 10%
of all ER visits nationwide.[385] The research literature uniformly finds that ERs are
ill equipped and disinclined to provide quality treatment to people with psychiatric
emergencies. This is attributed to a host of factors:

> First, these patients have a number of features that make them a difficult, challenging,
> and complicated management responsibility. Second, emergency medical technicians
> . . . and the ED [emergency department] staff have problems dealing with psychiatric
> patients. Third, psychiatric personnel also experience difficulty working with emer-
> gency patients. Thus, to a degree the emergency psychiatric patient represents the
> *unwanted patient.*[386] (emphasis in original)

Other literature focuses more on the environmental context of the ER in explaining the poor care provided by ERs to people with psychiatric disabilities: "The
quality of care these patients receive may be jeopardized by any number of factors,
including the fast-paced, medically (as opposed to psychiatrically) oriented environment of the ED itself, which discourages detailed assessment of patients' mental
status."[387]

The combination of these factors results in negative feelings by ER staff toward
clients with psychiatric difficulties. As Gerson and Bassuk explained,

> a more subtle situational factor affecting the [ER] treatment of psychiatric patients is
> the generally negative attitude toward such patients of the [ER] medical staff, the
> senior psychiatric staff, and, often, the therapists themselves. . . . Psychiatric staff and
> patients are often seen as intrusions into the essential business and are at best tolerated.
> This view often results in neglect of and at times even hostile reactions to psychiatric
> staff and patients by the rest of the [ER] personnel. . . . It is no surprise that therapists
> faced with the many pressures of psychiatric emergency treatment perceive their work
> in the [ER] as "onerous and unrewarding" . . . and react with "phobic avoidance
> manifested by long delays in responding to calls, by resentment, and by bitter com-
> plaints." . . . These maladaptive coping mechanisms are often reflected in strong neg-
> ative attitudes and feelings about specific patients or types of patients.[388]

These "strong negative attitudes" about "types of patients," specifically psychiatric
patients, resulting in "neglect" and "at times even hostile reactions" translate in the
language of the law to impermissible discrimination.

Discrimination in ERs can take place on an individual basis or in the form of
discriminatory policies and protocols. Individually, people with psychiatric disabilities and health care providers both acknowledge that so-called "repeat offenders"
—people with psychiatric disabilities who are frequent users of ER services—are
often punished by ER personnel by being ignored, sometimes for hours at a time.[389]
In addition, at least one study shows that more than a quarter of people who seek
ER assistance for psychiatric problems are suspected of malingering.[390]

Many ERs have protocols for treatment of people who come in with complaints
related to psychiatric disabilities that amount to generalizations based on psychiatric
disability. These protocols, including locking people in rooms, removing their clothing, or tying them to gurneys, serve to exacerbate any psychiatric problems rather
than assist the person with his or her difficulties.[391] This treatment leads to a signif-

icant deterioration of the psychiatric condition that led the individual to seek help in an ER in the first place.

Recently, a court refused to dismiss a claim that a hospital policy to "lock all persons who enter the emergency department seeking psychiatric treatment in a seclusion room, search the patient's clothing and remove the patient's clothing from their presence prior to the patient's mental status exam" violated the ADA.[392] When the plantiff refused to remove her clothes, she was told that the two male security officers would "take the clothes off for her."[393] She took off her clothing in the presence of one of the officers and waited naked in a locked room for an hour before the psychiatrist arrived.[394]

The court held that "the plaintiff effectively alleges that her segregation from the rest of the emergency department because she is mentally ill was unnecessary for the provision of effective treatment."[395] The court rejected the defendant's argument that the plaintiff was a direct threat: "The court cannot determine on the facts alleged in the plaintiff's complaint that the plaintiff constituted a direct threat to the health and safety of others."[396]

Policies such as the one in *Scherer v. Waterbury Hospital* reflect intentional discrimination on the basis of psychiatric disability. No one else (except a person in a state of obvious intoxication) who comes to an ER for treatment is locked in a room, tied to a gurney, or made to remove his or her clothing.[397]

These policies stem from concerns that a patient will be violent or suicidal, which, as reflected in *Scherer,* translate in legal terms to concerns that individuals coming into ERs with psychiatric concerns are direct threats. Because ER policies are by definition applicable to all people who seek psychiatric treatment, they are not based on any individualized assessment as required by law. Furthermore, they are not supported by the comprehensive research literature on the relationship between violence and people with psychiatric disability. Although this literature does support caution in the case of people who are intoxicated, this is a separate matter. Taking precautions in the case of a person with psychiatric concerns who was obviously intoxicated would be predicated on the intoxication and not on the psychiatric concerns.

Concerns about suicidal tendencies fall prey to similar problems. They are not based on individualized assessments, and the fact that the person is seeking assistance would seem to indicate a lesser rather than greater risk for suicide—at least at the time that he or she is in the ER, and few if any kill themselves after an ER visit.[398]

Discrimination on the Basis of Diagnosis

As noted above, discrimination on the basis of severity of disability arose in the context of claims involving people with mental retardation and is more suited to that context. People with diagnoses of mental illness may be discriminated against on the basis of their particular diagnosis rather than on the severity of their disability. Sometimes discrimination between diagnoses with a "biological" basis and those that are not regarded as biological has enormous impact. This is especially true in the case of the diagnoses of borderline personality disorder and dissociative identity disorder.

Borderline Personality Disorder

The diagnosis of borderline personality disorder (BPD) was added recently to the *DSM-IV*.[399] Despite the fact that "since its inception, there has been debate about what should be included within the category of borderline personality disorder and whether the category describes a real entity at all,"[400] it has become an increasingly common diagnosis and one that is familiar to the general public. The diagnosis is far more common among women than among men.

Unlike depression or schizophrenia, BPD is a diagnosis that often carries overwhelming connotations of hostility and anger by the professional toward the diagnosed individual.[401] Note the following primary diagnostic technique.

> There are several clues that may lead the family physician to consider the diagnosis of borderline personality disorder. An early clue is a "sinking feeling" of dread or dislike that the physician experiences when the patient's name is seen on the daily office schedule or when the patient enters the examination room.[402]

This "sinking feeling of dread" is analyzed not as the physician's problem but as a key indicator of the client's pathology. The level of anger and rage expressed by the mental health profession toward people with this diagnosis is often framed as reflecting the depth of the individual's pathology or intractability. This kind of blaming of victims of discrimination—the assertion that they deserve the negative treatment because they somehow brought it on themselves—is characteristic and typical rationalization of discrimination.[403]

It is interesting to note that people with the diagnosis of BPD are often very successful in society at large and are only perceived as pathological by the mental health profession. Even when this fact is acknowledged by mental health professionals, it, too, is seen as a result of pathology in that people

> with borderline personality disorder are found in all socioeconomic groups and all income levels. Their superficial social adaptiveness frequently allows them to function reasonably well in structured occupational settings where they can adapt themselves to expected roles. ... Or patients with borderline personality disorder may reflect this instability in their own lives by being "good" in their work situations, which they perform very competently, and "bad" in their interpersonal relationships, in which they are moody, demanding, and unpredictable.[404]

The words *management* and *control* appear in almost every article about people with BPD.[405] Indeed, in combination with the virulent dislike by the physician, management problems are considered diagnostic: "In the inpatient setting, borderline personality disorder emerges in the form of management problems."[406]

A number of mental health professionals have recognized that the diagnosis of BPD is often misused to "express the physician's dislike of a patient, to mask imprecise diagnostic thinking, to rationalize mistakes, to justify acting on feelings toward a patient, [or] to defend against anxiety-provoking topics."[407] One well-regarded mental health professional wrote an article entitled "The Beginning of Wisdom Is Never Calling a Patient Borderline."[408] It has been proposed that a psychiatric resident's desire to diagnose someone as having a BPD be used as a teaching and supervision tool to examine what has broken down in the treatment relationship.[409]

It is interesting to note that it has been impossible to develop a valid instrument or test that can distinguish people with BPD because "relatively little is known about the course of this disorder."[410] Despite the acknowledged paucity of reliable information about this diagnosis, it has enormous significance in the lives of people who receive it, who often experience singular discrimination because of it. For example, people with personality disorders, in particular BPDs, are notoriously treated with aversion and overt hostility by ER staff, mental health professionals, and mental health agencies. Sometimes this is because they are so well known: "Most communities have a few borderline patients who are well known to every mental health facility, ER and physician in town."[411] The mere diagnosis of BPD, however, can lead to disadvantageous and discriminatory treatment. This is shown not only in the experiences of people with this diagnosis but also by a research study as well. In the study, nurses were given the identical information about a patient, but one group of nurses was told the patient's diagnosis was schizophrenia and another group was told the patient's diagnosis was BPD. The latter group was significantly more hostile and punitive toward the patient.[412]

Thus, people with a diagnosis of BPD are clearly regarded as having a disability. Discrimination has been defined as the

> denial of equal opportunities enjoyed by others, based on, among other things, presumptions, patronizing attitudes, fears, and stereotypes. . . . Public entities are required to ensure that their actions are based on facts applicable to individuals and not on presumptions as to what a class of individuals with disabilities can or cannot do.[413]

The diagnosis of BPD leads to numerous kinds of discrimination. In Florida, the Board of Bar Examiners presumes that the diagnosis of BPD raises questions about an individual's character sufficient to flag and further investigate the application of anyone with such a diagnosis. The military precludes people who are discharged with this diagnosis from receiving veterans' benefits. "Expert" witnesses are permitted to testify, with absolutely no scientific or research basis, that "borderlines" lie, cheat, steal, and deliberately make up false accusations, thus turning the diagnosis into an instant form of impeachment[414] of any testimony of a person with the diagnosis.[415]

Dissociative Identity Disorder

A diagnosis recognized in the *DSM-IV,* dissociative identity disorder (including, although not limited to, what was formerly and more commonly known as multiple personality disorder) is the source of sufficient skepticism among mental health professionals that people presenting with this diagnosis may be refused treatment. In society, there is a mocking condescension and hostility toward those who have been diagnosed with this disorder, rivaled only by the mental health profession's attitude toward those it has diagnosed with BPD.[416] Although society publicly disapproves of the stigma associated with mental illness, attacks on certain diagnostic categories —multiple personality disorder and learning disabilities, for example—are part of unquestioned, unrestrained social discourses.[417]

Discrimination by Community Mental Health Programs and Centers

Although advocates and lawyers for people with psychiatric disabilities have long concentrated their efforts on the rights of people in psychiatric institutions and urged that more treatment be provided in the community, simply basing treatment in a community setting is no guarantee of the quality of the treatment or that the client will be treated with dignity or respect for his or her rights.[418] Many community facilities can be as or more exploitative and discriminatory as psychiatric institutions; it is not the location of the facility as much as the attitude of the staff that determines the treatment of clients.

Although the Rehabilitation Act of 1973 covered community mental health services, because nearly all of them receive federal funds, relatively few lawsuits were filed against them alleging discrimination on the basis of psychiatric disability.[419] This may in part have been due to the perception that disability discrimination law did not extend to discrimination in the treatment of the psychiatric disability itself under the Rehabilitation Act, a notion that is not good law under the ADA.[420]

Termination or Refusal of Mental Health Services on the Basis of Disability

Several cases have been brought challenging a community mental health center's decision to terminate its relationship with a voluntary client because he or she is too difficult to serve. In one case, a court issued a restraining order prohibiting a client from seeking the services of a mental health center that he had sued for medical malpractice. He had also allegedly acted in a threatening way toward therapists at the center. After the restraining order expired, the man sought their services and was denied by workers, who believed that the restraining order was still in effect. Although the court held that the man had stated a claim under the Rehabilitation Act, it granted summary judgment to the defendants on the ground that turning him down because of the mistaken belief that the restraining order was still in effect was not a decision "based on his disability."[421]

In another case, *Doe v. Adkins*,[422] a woman receiving mental health services was terminated by the mental health center. The reason given by the center was "because clinical staff could not establish a therapeutic relationship with her" and that she did not meet the eligibility criteria for services because she was too "high functioning." The reasons given by the clinic are questionable in light of the fact that the woman had been served there for 9 years: If the failure to meet eligibility requirements or establish a therapeutic relationship was 9 years old, the client might have a laches-type argument,[423] whereas if previously established therapeutic relationships had been disrupted or damaged, that would change the nature of the situation completely. The court found that the woman had improperly sued the private center under Title II[424] and that in any case nothing in the ADA "prevents an entity from discontinuing program benefits or participation in services in which the handicapped person's actions result in the impossibility of creating or maintaining a doctor/patient relationship."[425]

In a third case, Kathleen Harris's outpatient mental health services were terminated because her depression and BPD were "serious and complex" and "too difficult for a resident to treat."[426] The court concluded that "in essence, Harris' problems exceeded [the defendant's] capabilities."[427] Harris's HMO apparently prohibited the mental health center from making a referral to another psychiatrist.[428] Harris also sued her general practitioner, who was associated with Oregon Health Sciences University, for terminating her treatment after her mental health treatment ended. The court granted summary judgment to the psychiatric defendants on a number of alternative grounds. It held that Harris was not "otherwise qualified" because of the argument based on the *Baby Doe* case law that "absent her handicap, namely her mental illness, Harris would not have been eligible for any treatment."[429] More ominously, the court considered "with deference the assertions by a medical institution that a reasonable accommodation for adequate psychiatric treatment was not available. A medical decision regarding the scope of psychiatric treatment for a particular patient is not an area that should be second-guessed by the court or a jury."[430]

All of these cases raise troubling and difficult issues. It is clear that these people must have been difficult patients, but defendants were agencies that held themselves out as experts in treating the very kinds of difficulties manifested by the plaintiffs. In *Adkins*, the court placed the onus for the failure of the doctor–patient relationship squarely on the patient—it was her "actions that result[ed] in the impossibility of creating or maintaining a doctor–patient relationship."[431] In *Harris,* it is interesting to note the the court permitted Harris's suit against her primary physician to proceed, finding that whereas in most cases it is prudent for a physician and a patient who do not get along to part company, Harris had alleged that their inability to get along arose from her disability.[432] A doctor could no more refuse to treat a patient because she had BPD than because the patient was black.[433] Therefore, the *Harris* court placed the onus for the failure of the doctor–patient relationship at least in part on the primary care physician—something it was unwilling to do in the case of Harris's mental health professionals. In *DeLong*, the court found as a matter of law that the agency's failure to apprise itself of the expiration date of its own restraining order constituted a nondiscriminatory reason for failure to provide treatment to the plaintiff.

A mental health treatment center does have recourse if therapists have real reason to fear a client, rather than simply wishing to rid themselves of an angry, obnoxious, or difficult person. The ADA permits exclusion or denial of services upon proof of a direct threat but makes clear that this is a high threshold to meet. There must be a significant risk that "cannot be eliminated by a modification of policies, practices, or procedures or by the provision of auxiliary aids and services."[434]

The DOJ has taken the position that when a state agency contracts with private individuals to provide group homes for people with mental disabilities, it is the state agency's responsibility under Title II, rather than the group home owner's responsibility under Title III, to ensure that the homes are accessible to people with disabilities.[435]

Other Litigation by and Against Community Mental Health Centers and Group Homes

Although group homes and community mental health centers impose a number of arguably unnecessary restrictions on their residents, they have rarely been sued under the ADA (or, for that matter, under any other law). One case, brought by a woman without benefit of counsel, charged a community mental health center with locking her out of her residence for failing to attend treatment.[436] Rather than following the legal requirement that pleadings presented by citizens without legal training must be construed liberally, the court dismissed the claim on procedural grounds, holding that because the woman had failed to allege that others were treated differently, she had not pled an essential element of a discrimination claim. Even so, the usual practice in such cases would be to permit the woman to refile an amended pleading meeting the requirements of the claim. The court did not permit the woman to restate her claim.

In another case, a state Department of Public Health, which had ruled that an assisted living facility would lose its license unless it evicted two elderly women with Alzheimer's disease, was sued for discrimination.[437] The crux of the women's claim was that they had a right to choose where they wanted to live and that right was being infringed by the state's actions. The court acknowledged that the state was caught between conflicting goals of autonomy and protection but allowed the suit to proceed. While striking a claim for punitive damages under the facts of the case, the court acknowledged that Title II of the ADA permitted damage awards.

In other cases, community residential facilities have sued the state on behalf of their clients. Although most of these cases involve the Fair Housing Act, some include claims under the ADA. As in *O'Neal*, these cases raise the conflicting state goals of autonomy and protection. In *Buchannon Board and Care v. West Virginia Department of Health and Human Resources*,[438] the state tried to enforce a regulation requiring that all board and care residents have the ability to "self-preservation," that is, the ability to physically remove themselves from situations involving imminent danger,[439] by threatening to close several facilities with residents who could not meet these requirements. The court rejected the defendants' motion to dismiss, holding that the ADA applied to the operation of the fire safety code and refusing to hold that the accommodations proposed by the plaintiffs were unreasonable as a matter of law.

Right to Refuse Treatment and the ADA

> People can be treated by other people in ways that look benign but are really destructive. There is a way of helping people that fills their hands but breaks their hearts. What is kindness to the helper can be cruelty to the helped, because helping people mentally is a matter of perspective. . . . The same holds for goodness. Do not ask the supposed benefactor whether he or she is redeeming a life; ask the one who is supposed to be the beneficiary. . . . In many kinds of "help" you must look closely into the eyes of the recipient if you would know whether help has really happened.[440]

Right to Die and Disability Discrimination Law

Some of the most complex issues involving discrimination and people with mental disabilities are raised by legal questions surrounding the right to die. These were underscored in the Supreme Court cases involving the right to die, *Vacco v. Quill*[441] and *Washington v. Glucksberg*,[442] in which some briefs filed by disability advocacy organizations supported physician-assisted suicide, whereas other briefs filed by disability advocacy organizations opposed it. These debates mirrored the furor raised by the case of Elizabeth Bouvia,[443] which pitted traditional civil rights groups, such as the American Civil Liberties Union (ACLU), against disability rights groups, who believed that Bouvia's desire to die was fueled by despair over discrimination and an absence of residential options. Whereas the ACLU believed that respect for Bouvia's autonomy supporting her stated desire to die, some disability groups believe that the appropriate response was not to acquiesce in her desire to kill herself but to supply her with the residential options necessary to make her life palatable.[444]

The distinction between the disability groups who favored the right to die in *Quill* and those who warned that such a right was a euphemism for and precursor to euthanasia generally mirrors the distinction between the two groups of people with psychiatric disabilities discussed in chapter 2. Middle-class disabled people wanted to enforce the right to physician-assisted suicide,[444] whereas those who strongly self-identified as people with disabilities, and were often much poorer, were far more suspicious that the right to die would ultimately be used to try to eliminate their problematic existence.[446] These people even organized substantial demonstrations outside the Supreme Court on the day of oral argument in *Quill* and *Glucksberg*.[447]

It is clear that those suspicions are not unfounded. A number of courts have found that "do not resuscitate" (DNR) orders in institutions are based on the fact or severity of an individual's mental retardation.[448] A federal court in Connecticut granted a preliminary injunction against state agencies, ordering them to cease placing DNR orders in the medical files of residents with mental retardation in institutions who were not even ill.[449] The court found that the agencies had been "basing DNR orders on an individual's mental retardation."[450] DNR orders were affixed, without the knowledge of patients or their families, to the records of psychiatric clients in western Massachusetts who were not terminally ill.[451] Although it is unclear whether other states have policies regarding a DNR order for their disabled clients, there is something chilling about the statement in a recent article in *Psychiatric Services*: "As the state hospital's population declines, approaches to patient care are changing, and patient self-determination policies—the 'right to die' and 'death with dignity' —offer new options to the residual population of older, difficult-to-manage patients with severe medical needs."[452]

However, all the rhetoric about respecting people's rights to make decisions about ending their lives can fly out the window in a civil commitment hearing when a suicidal person is committed against her will as a danger to herself. As one woman wrote,

> the wish for suicide is fodder for many potent tearjerker movies about people with disabilities. . . . "How would you like it if you had to be me?" pleads the character. The rap of the gavel stops the forced feeding or the involuntary medication or respirator or whatever life support treatments are going on. . . . The judge is clear: "If you were a real (whole) person, I would wonder at your sanity, I would think you crazy, but since . . . life with a disability IS worthless, you are not only not crazy, but (YOU) are within your rights to die. Now if you WERE crazy . . . and we are clear that I, a judge and probably a stranger, get to say whether you're crazy, then we, the legal and psychiatric systems, would work really hard and almost certainly prevent you—at any cost—from killing yourself. We have special hospitals, with rooms designed to keep you from hurting yourself. We have mind-altering drugs, brain-damaging shock treatments, unskilled, often brutal attendant/guards who will zealously keep you from killing yourself . . . even if that should take us the rest of your life.[453]

Ironically, one recent article in a psychiatric journal noted that advance directives in the form of DNRs, which it referred to as "death with dignity," would be honored "except for an accident or a suicide attempt."[454] In fact, the argument that giving people the right to die would eliminate the ability of the state to institutionalize people involuntarily for suicide attempts has been used to oppose assisted-suicide statutes and was adopted by the district court in *Lee v. Oregon*.[455]

The DOJ's regulations implementing both Titles II and III explicitly address one part of this controversy. The regulations, which are identical, provide that "nothing in the Act or this part authorizes the representative or guardian of an individual with a disability to decline food, water, medical treatment, or medical services for that individual."[456] The DOJ explains this regulation in its interpretive guidance:

> Some commenters expressed concern that Sec. 35.130(e), which states that nothing in the rule requires an individual with a disability to accept special accommodations and services provided under the ADA, could be interpreted to allow guardians of infants or older people with disabilities to refuse medical treatment for their wards. Section 35.130 has been revised to make it clear that paragraph (e) is inapplicable to the concern of the commenters. A new paragraph has been added . . . [to clarify] that neither the ADA nor the regulation alters current Federal law ensuring the rights of incompetent individuals with disabilities to receive food, water, and medical treatment. *See, e.g.*, Child Abuse Amendments of 1984 (42 U.S.C. Secs. 5106a(b)(10), 5106g(10), Rehabilitation Act of 1973, as amended (29 U.S.C. Sec. 794); the Developmentally Disabled Assistance and Bill of Rights Act (42 U.S.C. Sec. 6042).[457]

This does not answer some of the most confounding questions raised by the issue of the right to die as it applies in the context of the ADA and people with psychiatric disabilities. Without taking any position on the underlying issues themselves, the following resolution of these issues is suggested as consonant with the ADA.

First, if someone with a mental disability has indicated no desire to die or to avoid extraordinary measures of life preservation, any DNR order associated with that person should be regarded as presenting the possibility of disability-based discrimination. If the person is in an institution and not adjudicated incompetent, no DNR order should be affixed to the individual's file in the absence of a written request by the person. A DNR order by a guardian of an incompetent ward should be resisted by the institution, as has been done in the past,[458] leaving a court to decide the issue.

However, if a guardian wishes to continue a ward's life and the facility opposes it, the guardian's wishes should govern in the absence of an advance directive prepared by the individual prior to the adjudication of incompetence. As one court perceptively noted,

> patients or, if incompetent, their surrogate decision-makers, are demanding life-sustaining treatment regardless of its perceived futility, while physicians are objecting to being compelled to prolong life with procedures they consider futile. . . . The problem is not with care that the physician believes is harmful or literally has no effect. . . . This is arguably medical science. Rather, the problem is with care that has an effect on the dying process, but which the physician believes has no benefit. Such life-prolonging care is grounded in beliefs and values about which people disagree. Strictly speaking, if a physician can keep the patient alive, such care is not medically or physiologically "futile"; however, it may be "futile" on philosophical, religious or practical grounds. . . . This matter is further complicated by federal legislation, such

as the [ADA] and Emergency Medical Treatment and Active Labor Act, that preempts state law and does not recognize a health care provider's right to withdraw life-sustaining care deemed medically inappropriate. Mrs. Causey was both disabled and an emergency patient.[459]

The other side of the question is whether a person with a mental disability is discriminated against by being committed for suicide attempts when society believes that such decisions by people with physical disabilities are rational. If a state recognized the right to commit suicide,[460] a person wishing to commit suicide should not be denied that right solely on the grounds of mental disability. People with psychiatric diagnoses, like everyone else, can make decisions about suicide rashly and impulsively or through a rational, deliberate process. Many who empathize with the notion that life with a major physical disability is unendurable do not understand the extent to which life with a psychiatric disability can also be unendurable. The interrelationship between chronic emotional pain and "rational" decision making is not one that courts have considered in any depth. Currently, however, virtually every state has taken a disability-neutral stance against suicide. Whatever opinion one may have of the underlying issue, it does not appear to be one of disability discrimination.

Finally, there is the issue of DNR orders requested by institutionalized people. The Patient Self-Determination Act (PSDA), passed as part of the Omnibus Budget Reconciliation Act of 1990, obligates facilities receiving federal funds to inform patients of their right to refuse treatment under state law.[461] Almost every psychiatric facility has interpreted this to apply only to end-of-life decision making (which itself might be discriminatory, *see* below). A person requesting a DNR order who is being involuntarily medicated on the grounds that he or she is incompetent to make treatment decisions should not be presumed competent to accede to the DNR order.

Right to Refuse Medication

Although the right to die is, in its broadest sense, linked to the refusal of treatment, the right to refuse psychotropic medication has often been considered a separate issue from general refusal of medical treatment. Courts have been increasingly open to the concept that people have the right to refuse medical treatment. For example, the court in *J. S. v. City of Newark*[462] refused the state's request to force J. S. to submit to treatment for his tuberculosis. The court noted that the medications involved were "quite toxic, dangerous, and some required painful intramuscular administration. J. S. is being asked to take many pills causing numerous side effects, including nausea and pain. The efficacy of the drugs will be unknown until receipt of the sensitivity reports."[463] The court reasoned that J. S. retained the right to refuse treatment even if this were medically unwise and even if it led to his continued confinement as a contagious carrier of tuberculosis. However, the court noted that if J. S. cooperated, the city would have a hard time proving he needed involuntary confinement.[464] If J. S. on release refused to take further medication, the court said that

> to fulfill the requirement of using the least restrictive alternative, public health officials will usually have to show that they attempted step-by-step interventions, beginning with voluntary DOT, supplemented by incentives (*e.g.*, food or money as a reward

for taking medication) and enablers (*e.g.*, travel assistance). Commitment is an absolute last resort.[465]

This holding may astonish people with mental disabilities and their advocates, who
have been unsuccessfully resisting forced treatment with medications that sound quite
similar to the medications described in *J. S.* These drugs cause numerous painful
side effects (Prozac has been reported by its maker, Eli Lilly, as causing nausea in
20% of those who take it),[466] they are often administered through intramuscular
injection, and in many cases they compare only marginally more favorably with
placebos.[467]

The right to refuse psychotropic medication raises issues of discrimination that
the right to commit suicide does not. The state opposes anyone's efforts to commit
suicide, but states emphatically support the right of citizens to make decisions regarding their bodies and their medical treatment, except for people with psychiatric
disabilities.[468] In most states, people cannot be forced to accept treatment for any
physical condition, even contagious conditions, but they can be forced to accept
treatment for psychiatric conditions. The rationale for this is that the condition impairs the judgment of the person affected so that they cannot make their own treatment decisions, but the most recent research by the MacArthur Research Network
(discussed below) indicates that psychiatric diagnoses cannot be reliably used as
proxies for incompetence to make treatment decisions. The ADA counts among the
"various forms of discrimination" "overprotective rules and policies,"[469] and the
policies that permit forced medication of people with psychiatric disabilities are, at
best, overprotective and, at worst, experienced as greatly damaging by the people
forced to take psychotropic drugs.

Most states have developed specialized procedures for deciding right-to-refuse
treatment cases, often taking place on the grounds of the institution with quasi-
judicial (at best) decision makers. The ADA should require that if people with psychiatric disabilities are alleged to be incompetent to make treatment decisions, then
they must be judged by exactly the same standards, and be entitled to exactly the
same procedures, as anyone else in the state who is alleged to be incompetent. These
procedures are generally vastly different and far more protective than the procedures
accorded to people with psychiatric disabilities.

For example, in Florida, if a person has a psychiatric disability, a court on
commitment may appoint a guardian advocate if it finds the person incompetent to
make treatment decisions, or a facility may petition for the appointment of a guardian
advocate on the basis of one psychiatrist's opinion. One professional who is authorized to give an opinion in support of a petition for involuntary placement must testify
at the hearing.[470] If the court determines the patient to be incompetent, a guardian
advocate, who must have had 4 hours of training, will be appointed.[471] Although this
is half the training that a guardian under the regular guardianship system is required
to receive, the statute specifically provides that "this training course shall take the
place of the training required for guardians appointed pursuant to Ch. 744."[472]

If a person petitions for the appointment of a guardian for anyone else in Florida,
the court will appoint an examining committee consisting of three members.[473] One
member must be a psychiatrist or other physician, the remaining members must be
a psychologist, gerontologist, nurse, licensed social worker, or other person who—
by knowledge, skill, training, or experience—may advise the court. The statute re-

quires that each member of the committee examine the person[474] and be able to speak in that person's language or obtain an interpreter. The examination must be comprehensive, including a physical, mental health, and functional assessment.[475] Any guardian appointed must have criminal and credit checks and undergo 8 hours of training. In the case of Florida and numerous other states where people with psychiatric disabilities are stripped of their rights to refuse treatment hastily and administratively, these separate procedures are certainly less than equal and should be eliminated as discriminatory under the ADA.

Determinations of Competence, Treatment Decisions, and Disability Discrimination Law

The Impermissibility of Basing Incompetence Solely on Diagnoses of Mental Illness

Sometimes people who have diagnoses of mental illness are deemed incompetent solely on the basis of their denial that they are ill or that they require medication.[476] This is illegal under both pre-existing law and the ADA. The ADA simply underscores the mandate of existing law, which is supported by the best research in the field:[477] a given diagnosis, by itself, or even the fact of involuntary commitment, tells us little about what the person with the diagnosis or who has been committed can or cannot do and what treatment decisions she can or cannot make.

Research lends support to the pre-existing legal obligation not to base a conclusion of incompetence to make treatment decisions on the fact of a diagnosis with mental illness. This obligation is often embodied in state statutes declaring that a diagnosis of mental illness or the fact of commitment do not affect the presumption of competency that is accorded to all citizens.[478]

Thus, for the most part, courts have rejected differential and discriminatory treatment of people with diagnoses of mental illness or people who are involuntarily committed for purposes of determining competence.[479] Some statutes still exist, however, that differentially disadvantage people who are incompetent by reason of mental disability as opposed to incompetence attributable to any other reason.[480] These statutes are probably vulnerable under the ADA but have not yet been challenged.[481]

The most recent research also underscores the extremely dynamic nature of assessments of competence, with the same individuals receiving different scores on the instruments when tested 2 weeks later. This would seem to indicate that court decisions permitting forced medication with 1-year or 6-month reviews are too long an interval and that involuntary medication trials, if permitted, should be for much shorter periods of time.

Incompetence as a Disability

Litigation under the Rehabilitation Act of 1973 and the ADA has raised the possibility that the status of incompetence itself is a disability meriting protection from discrimination under both acts. A number of state statutes forbid discrimination on the basis of adjudication of incompetence.[482] One early case, suing a hospital for mistreatment[483] of an infant born with cystic fibrosis, made it plain that the plaintiffs were not claiming discrimination on the basis of cystic fibrosis but on the basis of incompetence, saying that

> plaintiffs' counsel made plain that it was the incompetence to speak for herself, to react, and to convey feelings and preferences of the infant Erika which is the handicap on the basis of which the defendants . . . are alleged . . . to have developed the policy and practice of treatment which has been described.[484]

The judge appeared to accept this proposition as a general matter[485] but not in the case of the infant on whose behalf the lawsuit was filed because he associated the incompetence described with infancy rather than with the infant's disability.

The concept that patients who are incompetent are, as a general rule, treated less well in institutional settings than those who are competent is confirmed by the MacArthur researchers, who noted the existence of "data suggesting that patients with impaired decision-making abilities run a heightened risk of receiving suboptimal care."[486] Disorganized people or people who are unable to tell their story in an articulate way may well be more vulnerable to theft and worse forms of abuse from both patients and staff. These clients may need extra security and protection that, to the best of the information currently available, they do not routinely receive in an institutional setting. The MacArthur researchers also raised a concern in this area regarding potentially inappropriate medication of incompetent clients, stating that

> assuming a goal of policy in this area is to protect the interests of persons with mental illness who are unable to act on their own behalf, a primary focus on patients who refuse treatment omits consideration of the needs of the majority of impaired patients. . . . Policies targeted only at the small percentage of patients who refuse treatment fail to meet the needs of the larger group of patients, who although impaired in decisional abilities, assent to treatment.[487]

However, a challenge under the ADA to Medicaid regulations that determined residency in different ways for institutionalized people who became incompetent before the age of 21 than for other recipients of Medicaid was described as "too insubstantial to warrant discussion."[488]

Guardianship Statutes as Discriminatory

The ADA may open the way for litigation challenging state statutes differentiating between incompetence caused by mental disability and disadvantaging people incompetent because of mental disability, as compared with people whose incompetence stems from other sources.[489] This is particularly evident in medical malpractice and tort "reform" statutes relating to tolling of the statutes of limitation.

Recently, the Tennessee guardianship statute and the procedures therein were challenged as being violative of the Rehabilitation Act and the ADA.[490] Although the state court of appeals dismissed the allegations, it is not clear that it understood the nature of the claims presented or the arguments made. First, it found that "the [guardianship] statutes do not deny the ward any benefits or programs but transfer control of the ward and his property to a person who can protect the ward when the ward cannot."[491] Furthermore, the court found that wards "do not meet the 'essential requirements' test. When the ward is sick, he is not qualified to maintain himself. If and when a ward does regain capacity, he does not receive a dissimilar treatment by the State because his conservator is discharged."[492] Thus, the court swept away the plaintiff's challenges to the process by which competency is restored, blaming the ward for not arranging his or her own release from involuntary institutionalization, and stating, "The fact that petitioner or anyone else failed to contact the court to request his release does not entitle him to an ADA claim for the time he remained at [the institution] after regaining competency."[493] The court appeared to replicate the assumptions that necessitated the passage of the ADA in the first place, assuming without discussion that people who had been found incompetent were too sick to take care of themselves or make any decisions at all, but that when they regained competency, they would somehow gain both the knowledge and initiative necessary to arrange their own release. Yet as the MacArthur research shows, the question of competency is far more complex and subtle than the court appreciates.

There are other ways in which guardianship statutes may be considered discriminatory under the ADA. For example, in Vermont the state legislature has provided that "any person, at least eighteen years of age, who desires assistances with the management of his or her affairs" may ask for the appointment of a voluntary guardian.[494] The option of voluntary assistance, however, is not open to people who with mental illness or retardation.[495] They cannot petition for the appointment of guardians for themselves. There is no apparent reason to deny people with mental illness or mental retardation the right to seek voluntary appointment of a guardian; the statute requires as a separate matter a finding that the person is uncoerced and understands the "nature, extent, and consequences" of the guardianship. This statute appears to violate the ADA on its face by making a disadvantageous distinction based solely on disability without any rationale.

Advance Directives and Health Care Proxies

Although almost all states have laws permitting their citizens to execute living wills, advance directives, or health care proxies, the status of these documents vis-à-vis mental health care is often unclear. In some states, such as Massachusetts,[496] the health care proxy statute clearly includes decisions about mental health care among the health care decisions permitted by the statute. In other states, such as Alaska,[497] Arizona,[498] Hawaii,[499] Idaho,[500] Illinois,[501] Maine,[502] Minnesota,[503] North Carolina,[504] Oklahoma,[505] Oregon,[506] South Dakota,[507] Texas,[508] Utah,[509] Vermont,[510] and Wyoming,[511] the state has statutes regarding health care proxies and advance directives for all citizens and a different law, often with fewer rights and more restrictions, for people with psychiatric disabilities. For example, unlike general advance directives, advance directives for mental health treatment typically expire after 3 years or 90 days if the person's condition has not improved or can be disregarded in the case of a life-threatening emergency or require an affirmative showing of competence.

These statutes, which on their face single out and treat people with psychiatric disabilities differently and disadvantageously on the basis of their status as people with mental disabilities, are very likely illegal under the ADA. The Vermont law, which requires that an advance directive of someone who is requiring psychiatric medication need only be honored if the individual does not appear to be experiencing "significant clinical improvement," has been challenged as violative of the ADA.[512]

Although the Patient Self-Determination Act (PSDA)[513] requires that all facilities receiving Medicare or Medicaid funds, including almost all psychiatric facilities, inform incoming patients of all of their rights related to advance directives and health care proxies under state law, anecdotal evidence suggests that state psychiatric facilities are following this mandate incompletely, either by selectively informing patients only about their rights to make living wills relating to end-of-life treatment rather than the full panoply of treatment refusal allowed under state law, or by not informing them of their rights at all.[514]

Hospitals that admit only psychiatric patients may be violating the PSDA by not informing patients of their rights. They may also be violating the ADA if they have a blanket policy of failing to inform patients about their rights on the basis of the patients' psychiatric disability. Of course, to the extent that a hospital serving both medical and psychiatric patients applies differential practices to medical and psychiatric patients in the area of informing patients about their rights to refuse treatment and fill out advance directives on the basis of psychiatric disability, that hospital is very likely violating the ADA.

There are some real-life issues associated with the application of the PSDA to the mental health context. First, the statute requires that patients be informed of their rights on admission to a facility. Informing a patient who is being involuntarily detained for suicidality that he or she has a right to die under state law seems paradoxical and likely to make a difficult, emotionally fraught situation even worse. The regulations to the PSDA provide that "if a patient is incapacitated at the time of admission and is unable to receive information (due to the incapacitating condition or a mental disorder . . . then the facility should give advance directive information to the patient's family or surrogate.[515] This may be helpful if implemented in an individualized way, but a blanket generalization that all admissions for mental illness should fall into this category would violate the ADA.

Second, the suspicion and hostility that coercive treatment engenders in many hospitalized patients makes it unlikely that they will view an institution's attempt to encourage them to execute advance directives as a beneficent gesture. Recent research by Jeffrey Geller confirms this: 34 out of 53 individuals at a Massachussetts state hospital with a proxy form in their charts refused to sign it.[516] Some advocates also worry that an inpatient could be subject to coercion to sign a directive that did not comply with his or her true preferences.[517]

The best option is for advance directives and health care proxies to be developed and signed by individuals in the community and kept by the person most likely to remain in contact with that individual if hospitalized. Interpretation problems abound —can an advance directive affirmatively direct treatment or only decline it? Is it void if the individual is dangerous?—but the meager case law suggests that psychiatric advance directives will be honored if enforced by an outsider.[518]

Experimentation

One doctor was doing research on borderline personality disorder and AIDS and high risk behavior . . . They pressured people to be part of the research study if you were on the ward. [He] asked questions about masturbation and how many times you swallowed [semen]. . . . It was very creepy to have him around knowing all these things about you.[519]

Hundreds of experiments are conducted every year on people in institutions and people with mental disabilities in this country. These include "challenge studies," in which psychosis is induced or exacerbated.[520] Some of them have ended in the injury and death of the participants, but the experiments continue. As of the writing of this book, the inadequacies of protections of people with mental disabilities in experimental procedures are finally beginning to receive national attention.[521]

This country's history and many of its continuing practices in the area of human experimentation include a series of squalid and largely unpublicized exploitations of poor people, minorities, and people with mental disabilities. Although many people are aware of the practice of deliberately infecting black men with syphilis at Tuskegee, far fewer people know of the experiments done on institutionalized children, including deliberate infection with hepatitis at Willowbrook,[522] and the nationwide deliberate subjection of institutionalized children with mental retardation to radiation.[523]

Even fewer people know of the collaboration between Ewen Cameron, the one-time president of the World Psychiatric Association, and the Central Intelligence Agency in its brainwashing experiments. Cameron carried out experiments in Canada that involved "particularly intensive electroconvulsive shock, sensory isolation, drug induced continuous sleep for many days" and administration of LSD to unknowing psychiatric patients.[524] Litigation years later by the survivors led to a settlement.[525]

Experiments on people with mental disabilities continue to this day. The government regulations[526] that seek to protect human participants rely for the most part on institutional review boards (IRBs), which until recently have proven wholly ineffectual in preventing nontherapeutic and exploitative experiments on poor pregnant women,[527] children,[528] incarcerated teenagers,[529] and people with mental disabilities.[530]

One of the most crushing examples of the way in which the law's obsession with neat categories results in the denial of relief to people who are subject to multiple, intersecting forms of discrimination is reflected in the case of *Johnson v. Thompson*.[531] Researchers at the University of Oklahoma decided to investigate the effects of treatment on the survival rates of infants born with spina bifida. To further their research, they divided infants born at the hospital with spina bifida into two categories, those who would receive treatment and those who would not—obviously without the knowledge or consent of the parents of the children who did not receive the treatment. The way the children were divided was based on the researchers' perceptions of the parents' ability to take care of their children, so the children of poor, minority parents did not receive treatment, and the children of more economically stable parents did. Virtually every one of the children who did not receive treatment died. Virtually every one of the children who did receive treatment lived.

When the facts surrounding the experiment became known, the parents of the dead children sued. The court ruled that there was no legal claim stated by these facts that could grant them any relief. There was no discrimination based on disability, because some children with spina bifida did receive treatment, and therefore the discrimination was not based on having spina bifida. Quite the contrary, it was clear that the failure to provide treatment was based on the parents' poverty and minority status. The failure of the state to provide adequate health care to the babies of poor and minority parents did not state a due process claim because the 14th Amendment created no affirmative right for health care from the state. There would have been no race-based discrimination claim because poor white parents were also discriminated against.

Poor and minority populations continue to supply fodder to researchers for damaging experiments, especially in the area of mental retardation[532] and psychiatric research. For example, in a notorious series of experiments, researchers at the New York Psychiatric Institute selected 6- to 10-year-old children who were the younger siblings of teenagers deemed to be juvenile delinquents. The children—all of whom were either African American or Hispanic—were administered phenfluoramine—a drug known at the time to have dangerous side effects and later taken off the market —intravenously. Later, it was revealed that the identities of the "juvenile delinquents" and their addresses were obtained through unauthorized release of confidential court documents. The office in charge of protecting human subjects from experimentation investigated and had no objection to this experiment. The distinction between a Mount Sinai experiment and New York Psychiatric Institute experiment was apparently that the former did not recognize that the experiment was "above minimal risk" and the latter did recognize and discuss this issue, and concluded after deliberations that they would continue with the experiment.[533] The family of one of the children in the Mount Sinai experiments has since filed suit.[534]

There are several ways that the ADA may be invoked by experimentation on people with psychiatric disabilities. First, if there is a pattern of approval of experiments on children or adults with psychiatric disabilities that raise greater risks, or that involve less disclosure, or if IRBs are reviewing these experiments less carefully or federal or state monitoring agencies are investigating them less rigorously, any one or a combination of these may state a claim under the ADA. At least one advocate is convinced that this is the case, noting that

> federal oversight agencies, such as [the Office of Protection from Research Risks and] (to a greater extent) the [Food and Drug Administration and the National Institute of Mental Health] do apply different standards in evaluating risks in experimental studies involving this vulnerable group [mental patients].[535]

The National Bioethics Advisory Commission cautioned that people with mental disabilities may be the subject of experiments "simply because they are in some sense more available than others" and recommended against using people with mental disabilities as participants in experiments where the same research can be done with other participants.[536]

Second, there may be an argument that reasonable accommodation of mental disabilities requires experimenters to be held to a higher standard when obtaining informed consent or experimenting with drugs that involve mental, nervous, or emotional conditions. The National Bioethics Advisory Commission recognized this when they recommended "for research protocols that present greater than minimal risk, an IRB should require that an independent, qualified professional assess the potential [individual's] capacity to consent."[537]

First, for some people with psychiatric disabilities, consent to experiments may raise different issues than for other people. If the subjects are or have been institutionalized, there may be factors that induce them to consent that are not present for other subject populations. If they have been forcibly medicated, they may believe that they do not really have the right to refuse to participate in the experiment.

The risks of harm may be higher in psychiatric experiments because harm to one's emotional and mental faculties—already fragile—is a great deal to ask some-one to gamble. Even proponents of the medical and biological model admit that much about the mechanisms of the brain and psychiatric disorders are shrouded in mystery, so psychiatric experimentation may be inherently more risky because rel-atively less is known about the underlying mechanisms that medications may trigger.

Conclusion

Research has shown that discrimination against people with psychiatric disabilities is often a reaction to a known diagnosis or treatment history and not in response to symptoms, which are often interpreted in other ways prior to a diagnosis being made. Congress specifically used mental illness as an example of the need to prohibit discrimination based on a "history of a disability." This creates a dilemma for people who want assistance for emotional difficulties and often results in the avoidance of treatment; it is even worse for a person who is involuntarily diagnosed and then detained for treatment that he or she never sought and does not want after a 15-minute "evaluation" by a stranger. This experience will now hamper and obstruct employment, education, child custody, housing, and social relations.

When diagnoses are imposed rather than sought as explanations for distress and when detention is involuntary, an individual has taken his or her first steps down the path to becoming part of the public mental health world. The option of hiding di-agnoses and treatment becomes increasingly difficult as the person becomes an iden-tified client of the mental health system and the discrimination becomes more per-vasive and difficult to separate from the very structure of life.

It is the mental health system that creates the conditions for the worst discrim-ination of all: the total segregation from society, sometimes for years, that accom-panies institutionalization. This is the ground zero of discrimination, total segregation that does not even permit the kind of discrimination most of us think of as "dis-crimination" because it allows for little or no interaction with people without dis-abilities. Employment discrimination is impossible because no job is possible; no discrimination in marriage, divorce, or parental rights proceedings is possible because no one is allowed to have a family—or even lovers or sex—in an institution. Once the mental health system assumes responsibility for an institutionalized individual, that person is not discharged unless there is a place in the community, and often no such place exists and no urgency exists to create it. A person can be locked in an institution for years, despite professional recommendations that he or she need not be there. This amounts to robbing people of years of their lives, and it is happening right now to thousands and thousand of people. In addition, institutions are fertile breeding grounds for the metasegregation of seclusion and restraint and for discrim-ination in the treatment of people with mental retardation, women, and patients with physical disabilities. The U.S. Supreme Court has now concluded that unnecessary institutionalization constitutes discrimination. This decision sets the stage for what could be a radical transformation of state mental health systems.

It is clear that a substantial percentage of people who are currently in state hospitals need not be there, in the opinion of mental health professionals—probably a sufficient number to make continued operation of the state hospitals in their current format fiscally unfeasable. In addition, even people who are considered appropriately placed by mental health professionals are not, for the most part, a direct threat to others, but simply are unable to take care of themselves. Arguably, the ADA requires that discriminatory segregation be supported by proof that the individual is a direct threat to the health and safety of others. If this is the case, the vast majority of people in institutions are there in violation of the ADA.

The remedy is not to move people from segregated institutions to the segregated community—segregated group homes at night, segregated treatment centers by day. The aspirations of antidiscrimination law and the goals of successful mental health treatment overlap: integrating people into the community—giving them a chance to live in regular housing with regular jobs and to be part of the community with as much control over their own lives as anyone else has, given their incomes and circumstances.

The mental health system is, of course, caught between two mandates: (1) its ostensible mandate, often articulated in the state's statutes, to treat people in the community as much as possible; and (2) social and political pressures, articulated daily in the media, to remove discomforting or strange people from the sight of the community. The mental health system is squeezed between the aspirations represented by the ADA and the reality of fear and discrimination that the ADA was intended to combat.

That fear and discrimination will not dissipate as long as segregation confirms the validity of the fears and the already integrated—people with serious psychiatric diagnoses—in the "first world"—do not come forward with their paradoxical stories of success and excess. Society needs to see the whole spectrum of psychiatric disability, not just the poor and public end of it. The truth is that society tolerates strange and discomforting people fairly well as long as they are not too poor and tolerates poor people better if they are not residing in institutions, group homes, halfway houses, or board-and-care homes.

All of this means that state mental health agencies, legislatures, and advocacy groups should work together to devise funding structures for mental health services that maximize true integration and deter the use of both mental institutions and group homes as residential environments for poor people with mental health problems. Part of this work requires the recognition that to provide mental health services in the most integrated environment has ripple effects on issues related to housing, health care, transportation, child care, and the requirements of basic subsistence. These concerns implicate Supplemental Security Income and other income support payments as well as Medicaid and state health care systems, which are discussed in the next chapter.

Endnotes

1. University of Alabama Board of Trustees v. Garrett, 2000 U.S. LEXIS 2531 (Apr. 17, 2000), and Alabama Department of Youth Services v. Ash (*id.*). The question on which the Supreme Court granted certification was "Does the 11th Amendment bar a suit by private citizens in federal court under the ADA against nonconsenting states?"
2. *Garrett* involves a woman's claim that she was demoted after returning from leave for breast cancer treatment; the plaintiff in *Ash* asked her employer to enforce its own smoking policy because unauthorized smoking by other employees was aggravating her

respiratory problems; Patti Waldmeier, "Justices to Act in Dispute Over States' Rights," FINANCIAL TIMES (London, Apr. 18, 2000):6.

3. This is because of the doctrine established in *Ex Parte* Young, 209 U.S. 123 (1908), that permits an individual to sue a state official for acting in violation of the U.S. Constitution or federal statute. The "fiction" is that the state would never authorize one of its officials to violate federal law, so that such litigation is not really aimed at the state but at the individual state official who is violating the law. In practice, when the state employee is acting in his or her official capacity, such suits are defended by the state and judicial relief runs against the state. The Supreme Court indicated that Ex Parte Young remains a valid law; Idaho et al. v. Coeur d'Alene Tribe of Idaho, 521 U.S. 261, 269 (1997); Seminole Tribes of Florida, 517 U.S. 44, 73–74 (1996).

4. The first part of the test requires Congress to have explicitly abrogated the state's 11th Amendment immunity. This standard is easily met by the ADA, which explicitly strips states of their imunity from suits at 42 U.S.C. § 12202 (2000).

5. When the Supreme Court struck down Congress's attempts to apply the Religious Freedom Restoration Act of 1993 and the Age Discrimination in Employment Act of 1967 to the states, it specifically pointed to the lack of any record of recent discrimination on the basis of religion, City of Boerne v. Flores, 521 U.S. 507, 530 (1997), and branded the application of the ADEA to the states as "an unwarranted response to a perhaps inconsequential problem"; Kimel v. Board of Regents, 120 S.Ct. 631, 648–649 (2000).

6. Steven Haimowitz, "Americans With Disabilities Act of 1990: Its Significance for People With Mental Illness," *Hosp. and Comm. Psychiatry* 42 (Jan. 1991):23, 24.

7. *See* chapter 3 for a discussion of the differences between mental health law and disability law.

8. People First of Tennessee v. Arlington, 878 F.Supp. 97 (W.D. Tenn. 1992); Williams v. Secretary, 414 Mass. 551, 609 N.E.2d 447 (1993). In *People First,* the ADA claim was filed on Jan. 30, 1992, 4 days after the effective date of Title II of the ADA. The claim was that some institutionalized individuals were "being excluded from community services because of the severity of their disability, but that other handicapped persons are receiving such services"; 878 F.Supp. 101. The court dismissed the claims on the grounds that Section 504 and the ADA did not cover claims of "discrimination among similarly handicapped individuals," *id.* This argument is considered more fully *infra* at pp. 213–218. In *Williams,* the court asserted that the purpose of both Section 504 of the Rehabilitation Act and the ADA is to prevent discrimination against handicapped people in favor of nonhandicapped people and, therefore, rejected a claim that the state violated either act when it provided integrated housing to people with certain disabilities and not to others with different or more complex disabilities.

9. Olmstead v. L. C., 119 S.Ct. 2176 (1999), *see* discussion at pp. 110–114 *infra.*

10. Olmstead v. L. C., 119 S.Ct. 617 (Dec. 14, 1998), amended to limit grant to Q1 of petition, 119 S.Ct. 633 (Dec. 17, 1998). This case was argued in Apr. 1999.

11. Hargrove v. State of Vermont, C.A. No. 2:99-CV-128 (D. Vt., filed Apr. 28, 1999).

12. McKlemurry v. Hendrix, 971 F.Supp. 1089 (S.D. Miss. 1997).

13. Greist v. Norristown State Hospital, 1997 U.S. Dist. LEXIS 16320 (E.D. Pa. Oct. 16, 1997); Musko v. McCandless, 1995 U.S. Dist. LEXIS 5911 (E.D. Pa. May 1, 1995); City of Newark v. J. S., 279 N.J. Super. 178, 652 A.2d 265 (1993) (the patient was commited for tuberculosis).

14. Roe v. County Commission of Monongalia County, 926 F.Supp. 74 (N.D. W.Va. 1996); Patricia S. v. Waterbury Hospital, No. CV97-0137073S (Conn. Super. Ct. filed Dec. 9, 1996).

15. Riffenburg v. State of Michigan, 1998 U.S. Dist. LEXIS 15622 (W.D. Mich. Sept. 3, 1998).

16. *See* cases listed at note 144.

17. Jeffrey v. St. Clair, 933 F.Supp. 963 (D. Haw. 1996).

18. Small v. Montana, discussed in chapter 5.

19. Doe v. Adkins, 647 N.E.2d 731 (Ohio App. 1996); O'Neal v. Alabama Department of Public Health, 826 F.Supp. 1368 (M.D. Ala. 1993).

20. Chris Doe v. Stincer, 990 F.Supp. 1427 (S.D. Fla. 1997), *vac.* on other grounds, 175 F.3d 879 (11th Cir. 1999).

21. 42 U.S.C. Sec. 12131(1) (1994).

22. Any lingering doubts as to this point were put to rest by the Supreme Court's decision in Pennsylvania Department of Corrections v. Yeskey, 524 U.S. 206 (1998).

23. 28 C.F.R. Sec. 35.130(b)(1)(v), 28 C.F.R. Sec. 35.130 (3), 28 C.F.R. Sec. 35.130 (5), 28 C.F.R. Sec. 35.130(6) (1999). The private organizations that contract with public entities, however, cannot be sued under Title II, *see* Doe v. Adkins, 674 N.E.2d 731 (Ohio App. 1996), even if virtually all their funding comes from public entities, and must be sued under Title III of the ADA, which covers public accommodations.

24. 42 U.S.C. Sec. 12181(7)(F) (1994) (specifically includes a "hospital" as a category of covered public accommodation under Title III of the ADA).

25. *But see* Chris Doe v. Stincer, 990 F.Supp. 1427 (S.D. Fla. 1997) (the plaintiff sued a private general hospital and private physicians under Title III and the attorney general of Florida under Title II).

26. Ronald W. Manderscheid and Mary Anne Sonnenschein, Eds., *Mental Health* (Rockville, MD: U.S. Department of Health and Human Services, Public Health Service, Substance Abuse and Mental Health Services Administration, Center for Mental Health Services, 1996).

27. 28 C.F.R. Sec. 35.130(b)(1) (1999).

28. 28 C.F.R. Sec. 35.130(b)(3) (1999).

29. 28 C.F.R. Sec. 35.130(b)(1)(v) (1999).

30. 29 U.S.C. 794, P. L. 93-112, 87 STAT. 394 (1973).

31. *See, e.g.,* Grzan v. Charter Hospital of Northwest Indiana, 104 F.3d 116, 118, note 2 (7th Cir. 1997) (the hospital conceded that it received federal funds). Private individuals are generally not subject to liability under the Rehabilitation Act because of the requirement of receipt of federal funds, *id.* at 119–120.

32. *See* the Health Care Financing Administration's web pages for Medicaid, http://www.hcfa.gov/medicaid and http://www.hcfa.gov/medicare. In addition, some hospitals receive research funding from the federal government.

33. U.S. Commission on Civil Rights, *Accommodating the Spectrum of Individual Abilities* 33 (Sept. 1983). The Acknowledgements on p. iii identify Bell and Burgdorf as the authors of this extraordinarily influential monograph. Later, when the National Council on the Handicapped drafted the first version of the ADA to introduce to Congress, Burgdorf and Bell were among the principal drafters of the proposed bill.

34. *Id.* at 165, 166. *Accommodating the Spectrum of Individual Abilities* was repeatedly cited in the legislative history of the ADA, *see* Report of the Senate Committee on Labor and Human Resources, Rep. No. 101-116, 101st Cong., 1st Sess. (Aug. 30, 1989) at 6, 8 (quoting in its conclusion that "discrimination persists in such critical areas as . . . institutionalization"); H.R. 101-485 (Pt. II) at 28, 31 (quoting in its conclusion that "discrimination persists in such critical areas as . . . institutionalization").

35. *See* the testimony of William Cavanaugh, Oversight Hearings on H.R. 4498, 100th Cong., 2nd Sess. (Oct. 24, 1988), Boston, MA, Serial No. 100-109, A&P Comm. Print 1990 (28B)*1067; testimony of Lelia Batten, A&P Comm. Print 1990 (28B)*1191–1204; testimony of Eleanor Blake, A&P Comm. Print 1990 (28B)*1260; testimony of Ilona Durkin (on behalf of people with traumatic brain injury institutionalized in psychiatric institutions), A&P Comm. Print 1990 (28B)*1081; and the letter of Lawrence Urban, A&P Comm. Print 1990 (28B)*1232–1235. Note that the law firm of Arnold

and Porter in Washington, DC, compiled, catalogued, and has made available every item in the legislative history of the ADA. The citations from the record are taken from this source.

36. Testimony of Lelia Batten, A&P Comm. Print 1990 (28B)*1190–1191. This is not an unusual occurrence. *See* "Deadly Restraint," Investigative Report of the Hartford *Courant*, detailing 142 deaths while in restraints: Dave Altimari, Dwight F. Blint, Eric M. Weiss, Kathleen Morgan, and John Springer, "11 Months, 23 Dead" (Oct. 11, 1998); "Hundreds of the Nation's Most Vulnerable Have Been Killed by the System Intended to Care for Them" (Oct. 11, 1998); "Why They Die: Little Training, Poor Staffing Put Lives at Risk" (Oct. 12, 1998); and "From 'Enforcer' to Counselor: With Strong Leadership the Cycle Can Be Broken" (Oct. 15, 1998); http://www.courant.com/news/special/restraint/data.stm. A disproportionate number of these deaths were children and adolescents, including one 15-year-old girl who was put in restraints for refusing to give the staff a photograph of her family. A number of lawsuits have been filed because of deaths in seclusion or restraints, *see* Hopper v. Callahan, 562 N.E.2d 822 (Mass. 1990) (a woman who complained repeatedly of abdominal pain was placed in seclusion where she later died); estate of Cassara v. Illinois, 853 F.Supp. 273 (N.D. Ill. 1994).

37. This testimony appears to refer to the death of Vincent Milletich at the Behavior Research Institute in late July 1985. It is not clear whether the difference in names reflects a confusion in the transcription, the witness's confusion, or some other reason. In any event, the newspaper reports of the facts surrounding the death of Milletich appear to be substantial, as related by Frank Cavanaugh, "Patient Death Renews Controversy Over 'White Noise' Treatment," SAN DIEGO UNION-TRIBUNE (July 26, 1985):A7; "Judge Refuses to Block Closing of Group Homes," UPI (Oct. 9, 1985).

38. Testimony of William Cavanaugh, A&P Comm. Print 1990 (28B)*1067.

39. *See* chapter 1 for a further discussion of the testimony in support of the ADA by people with mental disabilities. This was not the first time that Congress had heard testimony about deaths, abuse, and injury in institutions. The Senate Subcommittee on the Handicapped of the Senate Committee on Labor and Human Resources sent staff members out to investigate conditions in institutions and found

> heavily drugged patients tied to their beds, left in hospital hallways, and soaked in their own urine. Psychiatric patients and mentally retarded residents were regularly observed with cuts and bruises, and one resident was observed bloodying himself during a seclusion period in full view of the staff. There are indications that similar or more severe acts of violence, including beatings of patients and residents by others including staff, exist as an open secret of institution life.

Statement of Sen. Lowell Weicker, "Care of Institutionalized Mentally Disabled Persons," Joint Hearings Before the Subcommittee on the Handicapped of the Committee on Labor and Human Resources and the Subcommittee on Labor, Health and Human Services, Education, and Related Agencies of the Committee on Appropriations, 99th Cong., 1st Sess. (Apr. 1–3, 1985) at 2. Congress heard 600 pages' worth of testimony about the conditions in institutions for people with mental retardation in connection with Sen. Chafee's Community and Family Living Amendments Act of 1983, S.2053.

40. *See* chapter 1 for a further discussion of this testimony.

41. Statement of Marilyn Levin on behalf of Edward M. Murphy, Commissioner of Massachusetts Department of Mental Health, Boston, A&P Comm Print (28B)*1161 (Oct. 24, 1988).

42. Testimony of Deanna Durrett for Josef Reum, Indiana Department of Mental Health, Indianapolis, Subcommittee on Select Education, A&P Comm Print (28B)*1725 (Oct. 6, 1988).

43. Statement of Ed Preneta, A&P Comm Print (28B)*1096 (Oct. 24, 1988) at 250, Doc. 1.

44. A&P Comm. Print (28B)*1223 (Oct. 24, 1988).

45. Testimony of Ilona Durkin, A&P Comm. Print (28B)*1081 (Oct. 24, 1988).

46. Statement of Laura Cooper, 1979, A&P Comm Print (28B)*1982 (Oct. 12, 1988) (she was aware of the isolation and dependence of nursing homes because she was forced to live in one until 1980 because her community was not accessible to her).

47. Statement of Elizabeth H. Lyons, A&P Comm. Print (28B)*1158 (Oct. 24, 1988); statement of Eleanor Smith, A&P Comm. Print (28B)*1161 (Oct. 24, 1988).

48. Statement of William A. Spencer, A&P Comm Print (28B)*1513–1515 (Oct. 6, 1988); statement of Howard Wolf, A&P Comm Print (28B)*1479 (Oct. 6, 1988); statement of Elizabeth H. Lyons, *see* note 47.

49. Statement of William A. Spencer, *see* note 48; statement of Elizabeth H. Lyons, A&P Comm Print (28B)*1158 (Oct. 24, 1988); statement of Howard Wolf, *see* note 48.

50. Senate Committee on Labor and Human Resources at 4; Report of the House Committee on Education and Labor accompanying the Americans With Disabilities Act of 1990, P. L. 101-336, H.Rep. 101-485 (Pt. II) at 5, referring to the testimony given at a joint hearing on Sept. 27, 1988, before the Senate Subcommittee on the Handicapped and the House Subcommittee on Select Education, identifying Mary Linden of Morton Grove, IL, "who lived in an institution." Sen. Paul Simon (D-IL) referred to the testimony of Mary Linden, who was placed in a nursing home at the age of 34; *Cong. Record* 135(112) (Sept. 7, 1989):S10801.

51. A&P Comm. Print (2B)*1213.

52. S. Rep. No. 110-116, 101st Cong., 1st Sess. (1989) at 6.

53. Americans With Disabilities Act: Hearing Before the Senate Committee on Labor and Human Resources and the Subcommittee on the Handicapped, 101st Cong., 1st Sess. at 215 (1989).

54. Statement of Rep. Miller, *Cong. Record* 136 (daily ed. May 17, 1990):H2447.

55. Task Force on the Rights and Empowerment of Americans With Disabilities, *From ADA to Empowerment: The Report of the Task Force on the Rights and Empowerment of Americans With Disabilities* (Washington, DC: Author, Oct. 12, 1990) at 26.

56. 42 U.S.C. Sec. 12101 (a)(3) (2000).

57. "Mending Wall," Robert Frost, *North of Boston* (New York: Holt, 1927).

58. *See* Roy Porter, Ed., *The Faber Book of Madness* (London: Faber & Faber, 1991) at 350–382.

59. *See* Jacobus tenBroeck and Floyd W. Matson, "The Disabled and the Law of Welfare," *Cal. Law Rev.* 54 (1966):809; Erving Goffman, *Asylums: Essays on the Social Situation of Mental Patients and Other Inmates* (Garden City, NY: Anchor Books, 1962).

60. Roy Porter, Ed., *The Faber Book of Madness*, note 58, at 351.

61. A host of cases and literature support this proposition, *see, e.g.*, Ronald Wisor, "Community Care, Competition and Coercion: A Legal Perspective on Privatized Mental Health Care," *Amer. J. of Law and Med.* 19 (1993):145, 156 (a Massachusetts commission by Gov. Weld identified a third of people in Massachusetts's psychiatric institutions as unnecessarily institutionalized); Dan Turner, "Unnecessary Institutionalization: Tragic Isolation of the Disabled," SAN FRANCISCO CHRONICLE (May 11, 1992):A1 ("of the 6,700 people with mental retardation, autism or physical disabilities in the state's seven developmental centers, more than 2,000 don't belong there, according to assessments by their own doctors and social workers"); Wyatt v. Rogers, 985 F.Supp. 1356, 1394 (M.D. 1997) ("some patients' only 'active' problems are the unavailability of community services"); Kathleen S. et al. v. Department of Public Welfare of the Commonwealth of Pennsylvania et al., 10 F.Supp. 2d 476 (E.D. Pa. 1998) (the defendants conceded that 95 people appropriate for community placement were being kept in institutions because

of the unavailability of community placements); Olmstead v. L. C., 119 S.Ct. 2176 (1999) (Georgia acknowledged that two women with mental retardation were kept inappropriately for years in psychiatric facilities because there were no available spaces in the community).

62. Congress made it clear that one of the principal purposes of the ADA was the integration of people with disabilities into the mainstream of American society in the findings of the ADA, 42 U.S.C. Sec. 12101(a)(2) (1999) ("historically, society has tended to isolate and segregate individuals with disabilities, and despite some improvements, such forms of discrimination continue to be a serious and pervasive social problem"); 42 U.S.C. Sec. 12101(a)(3) (1999) ("discrimination against individuals with disabilities persists in such critical areas as . . . institutionalization"); its language; the legislative history, S. Rep. 116 at 20 (1989), H.R. 101-485 (Pt. II) at 50; and in debate and commentary on the floor.

63. U.S. Commission on Civil Rights, *Helping State and Local Governments Comply With the ADA* (Washington, DC: Author, Sept. 1998) at 93–94.

64. *Balancing Security and Opportunity* at 9–10 ("the Panel believes the primary purpose of [the] national disability policy should be the integration of people with disabilities into American society"); Carolyn Weaver, Ed., *Disability and Work: Incentives, Rights and Opportunities* (Washington, DC: American Enterprise Institute, 1991) at 3 ("Since at least the mid-1970s attention has shifted from income support for the disabled to policies designed to promote independence, freedom of choice, and where possible, employment").

65. National Institute on Disability and Rehabilitation Research, "Strategies to Secure and Maintain Employment for People With Long-Term Mental Illness," *Consensus Statement* 1(3) (Sept. 21–23, 1992):4 ("a dramatic shift has taken place [in the perceptions of employment prospects for people with serious psychiatric disabilities]. Contributing factors include: public and professional awareness that prolonged stays in state and psychiatric hospitals can be disabling").

66. Davis v. Buckley, 526 F.Supp. 985, 989 (E.D. Va. 1981); Homeward Bound v. Hissom, No. 85-C-437-E, 1987 WL 27104*20-21 (N.D. Okla. July 24, 1987); *see also* Medley v. Ginsberg, 492 F.Supp. 1294 (S.D. W.Va. 1980).

67. In both *Davis* and *Medley,* the defendants unsuccessfully argued that the plaintiffs had an obligation to exhaust administrative remedies. The cases presumably settled after these arguments were defeated.

68. In Homeward Bound v. Hissom, No. 85-C-437-E, 1987 WL 27104*20–21 (N.D. Okla. July 24, 1987), the court found that the state had violated the Equal Protection Clause by segregating mentally retarded people in institutional settings. Because the segregation was not rationally related to legitimate state interest, it constituted discrimination prohibited by the Equal Protection Clause. The court also held that Section 504 was intended to combat this type of discrimination against handicapped individuals and that the state must take affirmative steps to reverse the effects of the discrimination by providing needed services in an integrated setting.

69. City of Cleburne v. Cleburne Living Center, 473 U.S. 432 (1985).

70. Olmsted v. L. C., 527 U.S. 581, 597 (1999) ("Unjustified isolation, we hold, is properly regarded as discrimination based on disability").

71. Although not embracing milieu therapy, H. Richard Lamb took the position that institutions should provide needed functions of asylum to some people with mental illness. *See* H. Richard Lamb, "The Homeless Mentally Ill," *Western J. of Med.* 151 (Sept. 1989):313 ("state hospitals fulfill some crucial functions for the chronically and severely mentally ill. The term *asylum* is in many ways an appropriate one").

72. Although it is difficult to accurately measure length of stay, a number of studies suggests that federal figures underestimate length of stay in psychiatric facilities (*see* a discussion

later in this chapter). In addition to empirical research, both case law and some survey responses also suggest considerable lengths of stay in institutions, *e.g.,* Charles Q. v. Houstoun, 1996 U.S. Dist. LEXIS 21681 (M.D. Pa. Apr. 22, 1996) and 1996 U.S. Dist. LEXIS 21671 (M.D. Pa. April 22, 1996) (the case involved four plaintiffs: Charles Q., who had been institutionalized continuously since 1952; Joseph K., who had been institutionalized for 6 years; Lisa, who had been in residential services for 15 years and at that particular institution for 6 years; and Daniel, who had been institutionalized for 11 years); Wyatt v. Rogers, 985 F.Supp. 1356, 1394 (M.D. Ala. 1997) ("in the long term unit at Bryce Hospital, the average length of time since the [patients'] last psychiatric assessment was in excess of seven years"); Olmstead v. L. C., 119 S. Ct 2176, 2183 (1999) (noting that one plaintiff was in the hospital for 4 years, during 3 of which the state admitted she did not need to be institutionalized; the other plaintiff was institutionalized for 2 years, although the hospital staff concluded after 1 month that she did not need institutionalization).

73. Clark v. Donahue, 885 F.Supp. 1164, 1165 (S.D. Ind. 1995) (a woman who froze to death in a state hospital room at the age of 35 had lived at the hospital since she was 14 years old); ironically, the people who stay longest in psychiatric institutions are often the people who, all agree, are the least appropriately placed there, namely, those people with illnesses, such as Huntington's chorea, and people with developmental disabilities; Charles Q. v Houstoun, 1997 U.S. Dist. LEXIS 17305*7 (Jan. 15, 1997) ("Charles Q. [a psychiatrically disabled man with mental retardation] has been confined at HSH [Haverford State Hospital for] . . . more than 44 years"); people with traumatic brain injuries, Williams v. Wasserman, 937 F.Supp. 524, 526 (D. Md. 1996); Subacz v. Sellars, 1998 U.S. Dist. LEXIS 15180 (E.D. Pa., Sept. 21, 1998); and most often older people with dementia or organic brain damage, *see, e.g,* Tomassetti v. United States, 853 F.2d 927 (6th Cir. 1988).

74. In the West in particular, state facilities tend to be placed in small towns and form the backbone of the local economy. In Montana, the state legislature openly resisted the efforts of the State Department of Institutions to close its facility for people with mental retardation on the grounds that even if closure would improve the lives of the residents at the institution, people in the surrounding area needed the jobs.

75. The fact that people repeatedly come back to institutions probably has as much or more to do with the inadequate social supports, the pressures of poverty and stress and discrimination, and the lack of employment and adequate housing than with their refusal to take medication, any deficiency in the care received, or the time spent in the institution; *see* Susan Stefan, "Preventive Commitment: Misconceptions and Pitfalls in Creating a Coercive Community," *J. of Health and Human Res. Admin.* 21 (Spring 1989): 459.

76. *See* chapter 1.

77. This has been challenged successfully in several cases; *see* chapter 5.

78. Olmstead v. L. C., 119 S. Ct. 2176 (1999); Charles Q. v. Houstoun, 1997 U.S. Dist. LEXIS 17305 (M.D. Pa. Jan. 15, 1997); Jackson v. Fort Stanton State Hospital, McCartney v. Barg, 643 F.Supp. 1181 (N.D. Ohio 1986); Armstead v. Pingree, 629 F.Supp. 273, 280 (N.D. Fla. 1986); Riffenburg v. State of Michigan, 1998 U.S. Dist. LEXIS 15622 (W.D. Mich. Sept. 3, 1998).

79. *See* In re S. L., 94 N.J. 128 (1983) (when institutionalized patients are entitled to be released, the state must evaluate their ability to survive in the outside world and must not "cast them adrift into the community"; the state's obligation is to continue care in the least restrictive environment and make reasonable efforts to find placements and prepare people for those placements).

80. It is a violation of the ADA, *see* discussion *infra* pp. 110–114. It is also a violation of due process, *see* In re S. L. at note 79. Furthermore, it is a waste of scarce resources. Last but hardly least, it is painful and damaging for the people in question.

81. *See* Tyler Bridges, "Detention Center Apologizes for Delaying Juvenile's Release," MIAMI HERALD 39 (Jan. 8, 1998):B5 (a private company with a contract to run a juvenile detention center apologized for delaying the discharge of juveniles past their release date so that it could collect more money from the state).

82. This is not to say that people with mental disabilities who do not live in institutions are not also subject to segregated socializing, health care, recreation, transportation, and education; however, it is less inevitable, and enterprising individuals can often carve out niches of their own in their community—a possibility that is absolutely extinguished at the admission to an institution.

83. *See* "Michael O.'s Story," in Michael A. Susko, Ed., *Cry of the Invisible: Writings From the Homeless and Survivors of Psychiatric Hospitals* (Baltimore: Conservatory Press, 1991) at 25 ("the streets are better than the [psychiatric] hospital. . . . You don't have needles shot into you. If you run into a tangle on the streets you can move away from it. Here, you can't").

84. Wyatt v. Rogers, 985 F.Supp. 1356, 1378 (M.D. Ala. 1997).

85. The constitutionality of institutionalizing such individuals was upheld by the U.S. Supreme Court in Hendricks v. Kansas, 521 U.S. 346 (1997).

86. Center for Mental Health Services, *U.S. Inventory of Mental Health Organizations,* Table 4.1. Patient Census in 24-Hr Hospital and Residential Care Settings by Type of Organization and Caseload Statistics (Rockville, MD: Author, 1998). The number quoted is the average daily census. The most recent statistics available are for 1994.

87. The most common way that lengths of stay are measured uses the number of inpatient days within a given year divided by the number of times the patient was admitted or discharged. Because length of stay is measured by the year, however, if a patient was admitted prior to the beginning of the year being measured, the only days that would count in calculating the length of stay would be the days he or she was hospitalized during the year being measured. If a person was admitted just before the end of the year, his or her length of stay would end at the end of the year, even if he or she was still hospitalized. Because the inpatient day length-of-stay studies are conducted within the limits of a given year, no patient can ever have a longer length of stay than 365 days, even though some patients have been in institutions for years. True measures of length of stay require following individual patient records and are more difficult to compile. These studies use such terms as "total days," "discharge days," and "days of care"; *see* Charles Kiesler and Amy E. Sibulkin, *Mental Hospitalization: Myths and Facts About a National Crisis* (Thousand Oaks, CA: Sage, 1987) at 83–84.

88. *Id.*

89. John Pandiani, S. M. Banks, S. Borys, J. Campbell, et al., *One MHSIP State Hospital Utilization Project* (Washington, DC: National Conference on Mental Health Statistics, June 1994).

90. Sheku G. Kamara, Paul D. Peterson, and Jerry L. Dennis, "Prevalence of Physical Illness Among Psychiatric Inpatients Who Die of Natural Causes," *Psychiatric Services* 49 (June 1998):788–789.

91. Survey No. 128.

92. Studies show that the occupation of beds in psychiatric institutions by adults varies primarily according to the condition of the economy but that occupation of psychiatric beds by children and older people varies primarily according to availability of beds; J. R. Marshall and D. P. Funch, "Mental Illness and the Economy: A Critique and Partial Replication," *J. of Health and Soc. Beh.* 20 (1979):282–289. *See* chapter 5 for a further discussion.

93. *See* a discussion *infra* at p. 203.

94. *See, e.g.*, Sheku G. Kamara, Paul D. Peterson, and Jerry L. Dennis, "Prevalence of Physical Illness Among Psychiatric Inpatients Who Die of Natural Causes," *Psychiatric*

Services 49 (July 1998):788, 792 (noting that of 179 patients who died at Western State Hospital of natural causes between 1989 and 1994, 41% had been referred to the hospital from nursing homes).

95. Barry Rovner, Pearl German, Larry Brant, Rebecca Clark, Lynda Burton, and Marshal F. Folstein, "Depression and Mortality in Nursing Homes," *J. of the Amer. Med. Assn.* 265(8) (1991):993; Alice M. Rivlin and Joshua Wiener, *Caring for the Disabled Elderly: Who Will Pay?* (Washington, DC: Brookings Institute, 1988) at 6.

96. There is very little research about deaths in institutional facilities compared with deaths in the community. States reported 2,218 deaths in 24-hour psychiatric facilities and residential care settings in 1994, *Inventory of Mental Health Organizations (IMHO) 1994* (Rockville, MD: Survey and Analysis Branch, Division of State and Community Systems Development, Center for Mental Health Services, 1998). The provision of the information is optional, unverified, does not report cause, and may be incomplete (Joanne Satay, Survey and Analysis Branch, personal communication, Oct. 13, 1999). The General Accounting Office indicated that preliminary evidence from a Joint Commission on Accreditation of Healthcare Organizations survey shows that only 16 states have laws that require mental health agencies to report "sentinel events," such as deaths, to a state agency, and only 15 states have any systematic reporting to alert protection and advocacy agencies of deaths in residential treatment settings, General Accounting Office, *Mental Health: Improper Restraint or Seclusion Use Places People at Risk,* HEHS-99-176 (Washington, DC: Author, Sept. 9, 1999) at 5, 14. Of the 1,203 deaths in mental institutions and residential facilities reported to protection and advocacy agencies in Fiscal Year 1998, over two-thirds were reported by 5 states, *id.* at 12. Twenty-eight states did not report any deaths to protection and advocacy agencies, *id.* Most mental health systems do not keep records of deaths by cause of death in institutional settings, and deaths in institutions are not regularly investigated except in the state of New York. The existing databases on mortality in psychiatric institutions represent for the most part the work of researchers and scholars. There is far more substantial research done on mortality in institutions for people with mental retardation than on mortality in psychiatric institutions. There is also far more research done internationally on mortality in psychiatric institutions than in the United States, *see, e.g.,* M. Valenti, S. Necozione, G. Busellu, G. Borrelli, A. R. Lepore, R. Madonna, E. Altobelli, et al., "Mortality in Psychiatric Hospital Patients: A Cohort Analysis of Prognostic Factors," *Intl. J. of Epidemiology* 26 (Dec. 1997):1227–1235 (finding that the best predictors of increased mortality were nondischarge from an institution and increased length of stay in institutional setting but that there is no relationship between gender or diagnosis and mortality); W. Hewer, W. Rossler, B. Fatkenheuer, and W. Loffler, "Mortality Among Patients in Psychiatric Hospitals in Germany," *Acta Psychiatr. Scand.* 91 (Mar. 1995):174–179; R. W. Licht, P. B. Mortensen, G. Gouliaev, and J. Lund, "Mortality in Danish Psychiatric Long Term Stay Patients, 1972–1982," *Acta Psychiatr. Scand.* 87 (May 1993):336–341; L. C. Lim, L. P. Sim, and P. C. Chiam, "Mortality of Public Mental Health Patients: A Singapore Experience," *Aust. and N.Z. J. of Psychiatry* 27 (March 1993):36–41. For further information on mortality in institutional settings, *see* chapter 6.

97. Peter J. Batten, "The Descriptive Epidemiology of Unnatural Deaths in Oregon's State Institutions," *Amer. J. of For. Med. and Path.* 13 (1992):159, 160 (there was a higher mortality rate than among people in the surrounding community of Marion County, but there was no attempt to match county residents with similar disabilities); Sheku G. Kamara, Paul D. Peterson, and Jerry L. Dennis, "Prevalence of Physical Illness Among Psychiatric Inpatients Who Die of Natural Causes," *Psychiatric Services* 49 (July 1998): 788, 791 (there was a higher mortality rate among institutionalized people than in community, but there was no attempt to match with similarly disabled people in the community); John A. Pandiani, *Mortality Rates for People Served by Behavioral Health*

Care Programs in Vermont, prepared for the Vermont MHSIP Indicator Project (Mar. 31, 1997): copies available from the author, call 802/241-2639 (a 5-year follow-up of mortality in institutions and community provides partial support for higher mortality rates in institutional settings).

98. Linda McNatt, "State Taking Steps to Resolve Crisis in Mental Health Care," VIRGINIA PILOT (Mar. 21, 1999):A1.

99. *Id.*

100. John Pandiani, *see* note 97; Bruce B. Dembling, Donna T. Chen, and Louis Vachon, "Life Expectancy and Causes of Death in a Population Treated for Serious Mental Illness," *Psychiatric Services* 50 (Aug. 1999):1036.

101. *Id.* at 1036, 1038 (studying the clients of the Massachusetts Department of Mental Health receiving inpatient, residential, or case-management services between 1985 and 1994 and comparing mortality with the general population, the researchers found that the average age at death of the former population was 66, whereas the average age at death of the latter population was 76).

102. S. P. Segal and P. L Kotler, "A Ten-Year Perspective of Mortality Risk Among Mentally Ill Patients in Sheltered Care," *Hosp. and Comm. Psychiatry* 42 (1991):708–713.

103. *IMHO Reference Tables 1994*, Table 4.1, *see* note 96.

104. See *IMHO Reference Tables,* Table 4.2, *id.*

105. Sheku G. Kamara, Paul D. Peterson, and Jerry L. Dennis, "Prevalence of Physical Illness Among Psychiatric Inpatients Who Die of Natural Causes," *Psychiatric Services* 49 (July 1998):788, 791; Bruce P. Dembling, Donna Chen, and Louis Vachon, "Life Expectancy and Causes of Death in a Population Treated for Severe Mental Illness," *Psychiatric Services* 50 (1999):1036, 1038 (finding disproportionate numbers of female Department of Mental Health (DMH) clients dying from respiratory diseases but finding lower than expected deaths from cardiac causes).

106. Kamara et al., "Prevalence of Physical Illness Among Psychiatric Inpatients Who Die of Natural Causes" at 791.

107. W. J. Weiner, C. G. Goetz, P. A. Nausieda, and H. L. Klawans, "Respiratory Dyskinesias: Extrapyramidal Dysfunction and Dyspnoea," *Annals of Internal Med.* 88 (1978):327–331; J. Modestin, R. Krapf, and W. Boker, "A Fatality During Haloperidol Treatment: Mechanism of Sudden Death," *Amer. J. of Psychiatry* 138 (1981):1616–1617.

108. These exceptions involve either people with virulent (and rare) forms of pneumonia, which course is unusually rapid, or people who are already medically compromised and fragile.

109. P. Anna Clerege, "Sudden Death of Physically Healthy and Vibrant Sister," testimony of Marie Clerege before the National Council on Disability (Nov. 19, 1998) (12 hours after their healthy sister was hospitalized with psychiatric symptoms, the family was informed that she had died of "cardiac arrest"; an autopsy paid for by the family revealed ethanol alcohol in her system that had not been present when she was admitted to the hospital).

110. Jens G. Killian, Kristin Kenn, Christopher Lawrence, et al., "Myocarditis and Cardiomyopathy Associated With Clozapine," *Lancet* 354 (Nov. 27, 1999):1841–1845.

111. Anil Kumar, "Sudden Unexplained Death in a Psychiatric Patient—A Case Report: The Role of Phenothiazines and Physical Restraint," *Med. Sci. Law* 37 (1997):170, 173; D. C. Moir, J. Crooks, P. Sawyer, et al., "Cardiotoxicity of Tricyclic Antidepressants," *British J. of Pharmacology* 44 (1972):371; J. G. Reilly, S. A. Ayis, I. N. Fennien, et al., "QTC–Interval Abnormalities and Psychotropic Drug Therapy in Psychiatric Patients," *Lancet* 355 (Mar. 25, 2000):1048.

112. *See* Anil Kumar, *id.*; Collette Hughes, Paul Durea, and Gretchen Van Dusen, *Report of an Inquiry Into the Death of Marc Keifer at East Bay Hospital* (Sacramento: California Protection and Advocacy, 1993) at 17.

113. As Kay Scarpetta, the state medical examiner in a best-selling Patricia Cornwell series, complains, "damn it, how many times do I have to tell Dr. Carmichael that you don't sign out a death as *cardiac arrest*. You die, your heart quits, right? And he's done the *respiratory arrest* number too, no matter how many times I amend his certificates"; Patricia Cornwell, *Point of Origin* (New York: Putnam, 1998) at 111.

114. Peter J. Batten, "The Descriptive Epidemiology of Unnatural Deaths in Oregon's State Institutions," *Amer. J. of For. Med. and Path.* 13 (1992):159, 160 (the accident mortality rate per 100,000 in Marion County was 30.47 compared with the accident mortality rate of 288.81 during the same period at Oregon State Hospital).

115. *See* the exhaustive review of the literature on suicide in psychiatric hospitals, both in the United States and internationally, in Peter J. Batten, "The Descriptive Epidemiology of Unnatural Deaths in Oregon's State Institutions: A 25-Year (1963–1987) Study, Part III: A 25-Year Overview of Unnatural Deaths in the Mental and Correctional Facilities," *Am. J. of For. Med. and Path.* 13 (1992):159–162 (although suicide rates vary markedly from study to study, all are higher than the community comparison in the Batten study; however, note that in Batten's study, many of the reported suicides of "inpatients" took place when the patients were not physically present on Oregon State Hospital grounds, *id.* at 164, and it is not clear to what extent this is true in other studies); *see also* the study by John Pandiani. For anecdotal accounts, *see* Don AuCoin and Stephen Kurkijan, "DMH Investigates Suicide of Mental Health Patient," BOSTON GLOBE (Oct. 3, 1995): 52; Alison Bass, "Private Hospitals Faulted in Two Deaths: Mental Health Contracts Assessed," BOSTON GLOBE (Oct. 13, 1995):29.

116. Peter J. Batten, "The Descriptive Epidemiology of Unnatural Deaths in Oregon's State Institutions," *Am. J. of For. Med. and Path.* 13 (1992):159, 160 (compare the county homicide rate of 5.47/100,000 between 1983 and 1987 with the institutional homicide rate of 144.40/100,000) (again, note that just over 20% of "inpatient" homicides took place when the patient was not physically on hospital grounds).

117. Kamara et al., "Prevalence of Physical Illness Among Psychiatric Inpatients Who Die of Natural Causes" at 791. Almost every one of the numerous cases brought in this country alleging violations of rights at institutions, and independent investigations of these institutions, documents "outbreaks of shigella, salmonella, influenza, hepatitis, lice, rashes, and gonorrhea"; Homeward Bound v. Hissom, 1987 WL 27104 at 10 (N.D. Okla. July 24, 1987).

118. Again, although it is hard to quantify injuries at state psychiatric hospitals because no one at the federal level keeps centralized records, anecdotal evidence from case law and research suggests a high rate of injury. In Charles Q. v. Houstoun, the court noted in passing that a 36-year-old plaintiff "has to use a wheelchair as a result of an injury suffered while confined at HSH," 1996 U.S. Dist. LEXIS 21671*2 (M.D. Pa. Apr. 22, 1996). At the South Florida State Hospital, "court records showed employees reported an average of five assaults [on patients] a day" and "patients there were dying faster than at any of the state's other three mental hospitals"; "Ill at Ease: Company's Plan to Cut Jobs Hurting Long-Time Hospital Workers," FLORIDA SUN-SENTINEL (June 7, 1998):B10.

119. Judith Musick, "Patterns of Institutional Sexual Assaults," *Responses to Violence in the Fam. and Sexual Assault* 7 (1984, May–June): 3; Hopper v. Callahan, 562 N.E.2d 822 (Mass. 1990) (a woman dies in a seclusion room); in re Estate of Cassara v. Illinois, 853 F.Supp. 273 (N.D. Ill. 1994). *See also* Investigation of the Circumstances of the Deaths of C. C. and K. C. at Patton State Hospital and J. V. at Camarillo State Hospital (California Protection and Advocacy, Sept. 1991), Report of a Review of the Neglect, Restraint and Death of Zohair Jadeed at Napa State Hospital (California Protection and Advocacy, Mar. 1993), New York Commission on the Quality of Care for the Mentally Disabled, Restraint and Seclusion Practices in New York State Facilities (Albany: New

York Commission on Quality of Care for the Mentally Disabled, 1994), the Hartford *Courant* series "Deadly Restraint," see note 36.

120. Linda McNatt, "State Taking Steps to Resolve Crisis in Mental Health Care," VIRGINIA PILOT (Mar. 21, 1999):A1.

121. Testimony of Thomas R. Harmon to the National Council on Disability (Nov. 20, 1998), submitted by the National Council on Disability to the White House Conference on Mental Health (June 7, 1999).

122. *See,* generally, Care of Institutionalized Mentally Disabled Persons: Joint Hearings Before the Subcommittee of the Handicapped of the Committee on Labor and Human Resources and the Subcommittee on Labor, Health and Human Services, Education and Related Agencies of the Committee on Appropriations, 99th Cong. 268–278 (1985) (testimony of Clarence Sundram, dir., New York Commission on the Quality of Care for the Mentally Disabled); Nielsen v. Clayton, 62 F.3d 1419 (table case); 1995 U.S. App. LEXIS 17126*2–4 (Apr. 13, 1995) (affirming an award of over $1 million after mental health administrators conspired to cover up the death of a patient killed by a staff member in a choke hold); Wyatt v. Rogers, 985 F.Supp. 1356, 1377 (M.D. Ala. 1997) ("the evidence reflected that staff improperly used dangerous physical force to restrain children at the center. These included: hammerlocks, bending a child's thumb back while holding the child in a hammerlock, placing forearms against a child's neck while the child is against a wall; using knees in a child's back to pin the child on the ground"). One man who worked in an institution for children was investigated for 13 different instances of abuse, including "slamming a boy into a gym door, throwing a boy against a security screen and rubbing his face against the window[,] . . . and throwing a boy against a wall and twisting his arm behind his back in a choke hold," *id.* at 1375. Gangs were rampant in this institution, *id.* at 1374.

123. Caroline C. v. Johnson, 174 F.R.D. 452 (D. Neb. 1996) (certifying the class of raped women at the institution); high incidences of rape and sexual assault are also found in institutions for adolescents and children, Wyatt, 985 F.Supp. 1356, 1397 (M.D. Ala. 1997) ("incident reports reveal large numbers of incidents of staff abuse of patients, patient-on-patient abuse, sexual abuse, and unexplained injuries").

124. National Council on the Handicapped, *National Policy for Persons With Disabilities* (Washington, DC: Author, 1983).

125. In re Guardianship of Lamoine S., No. 96–1773, 21 MPDLR 373 (Wisc. App. Mar. 4, 1997). I worked on a case involving placing people with mental retardation in the community where an older gentleman did not want to be placed in the community because it involved being separated from his longtime friend, who was not scheduled for placement at that time. Although ideally both would have been placed somewhere together, I believe that his choice to stay with his friend should have been honored.

126. P. L. 90-284, 82 STAT. 73 (1968).

127. Nancy Denton and Douglas S. Massey, *American Apartheid: Segregation and the Making of the Underclass* (Cambridge, MA: Harvard University Press, 1993).

128. U.S. Commission on Civil Rights, *Accommodating the Spectrum of Individual Abilities* (Washington, DC: U.S. Government Printing Office, 1983) at 22.

129. This is not to say that people who share experiences of unjust treatment on the basis of a particular characteristic should be forbidden from voluntary association; from Smith College to the Million Man March to drop-in centers for people with mental health diagnoses run by people with mental health diagnoses, voluntariness is the key here.

130. Patrick W. Corrigan and David L. Penn, "Lessons From Social Psychology on Discrediting Psychiatric Stigma," *Amer. Psychologist* 54 (1999):765–776; U.S. Commission on Civil Rights, *Accommodating the Spectrum of Individual Abilities* (1983) at 44.

131. *See* Robert Jay Lifton, *The Nazi Doctors* (New York: Basic Books, 1986) (explaining that the first step in the killing of psychiatrically disabled people in Nazi Germany was

to send surveys to institutional doctors to describe their patients; the surveys were used to select the patients to be killed. Mentally ill people in the community were not killed unless they were first moved to an institutional setting).

132. James C. Dugan, "The Conflict Between 'Disabling' and 'Enabling' Paradigms in Law: Sterilization, the Developmentally Disabled, and the Americans With Disabilities Act of 1990," *Cornell Law Rev.* 78 (1993):507, 519; Susan Stefan, "Whose Egg Is It Anyway? Reproductive Rights of Incarcerated, Institutionalized and Incompetent Women," *NOVA Law Rev.* 13 (1989):405.

133. Michael J. Loscialpo, "Nontherapeutic Human Research Experiments on Institutionalized Mentally Retarded Children: Civil Rights and Remedies," *N.E. J. on Crim. & Civ. Con.* 23 (1997):139.

134. *See* Orlikow v. United States, 682 F.Supp. 77 (D.D.C. 1988).

135. Gloria J. Banks, "Legal and Ethical Safeguards: Protection of Society's Most Vulnerable Participants in a Commercialized Organ Transplantation System," *Amer. J. of Law and Med.* 21 (1995):45; Strunk v. Strunk 445 S.W. 2d 145 (Ky. 1969); In re Guardianship of Pescinski, 226 N.W.2d 180 (Wisc. 1975).

136. *See* New York Commission on Quality Care for the Mentally Disabled, *Voices From the Front Line: Patients' Perspectives of Restraint and Seclusion Use* (Albany: Author, 1994) at 12 ("I was brutally treated . . . lost consciousness while in a jacket and was gagging on my own saliva. . . . A huge male nurse and two female aides grabbed me and manhandled me"); Stanley M. Soliday, "A Comparison of Patient and Staff Attitudes Toward Seclusion," *J. of Nerv. and Ment. Dis.* 173 (1985):282–286.

137. Paul Carling, "New Service Approaches, Empowerment, and the Future of Involuntary Interventions," in Daniel Creson, Ed., *Involuntary Interventions: The Call for a National Legal and Medical Response* (1994; available from the University of Texas Medical School, Houston); S. M. Goldfinger and R. K. Schutt, "Comparison of Clinicians' Housing Recommendations and Preferences of Homeless Mentally Ill Persons," *Psychiatric Services* 47 (1996):413; Center for Mental Health Services Roundtable, Jean Campbell and Roy Schraiber, *The Well-Being Project: Mental Health Clients Speak for Themselves* (Sacramento: California Department of Mental Health, California Network of Mental Health Clients, 1989). My survey results also confirm this proposition.

138. Presumably with an approximation of the same range of choices and decision making as Americans without disabilities.

139. 42 U.S.C. Sec. 12101(a)(1) (1999).

140. 42 U.S.C. Sec. 12101(a)(2) (1999).

141. 42 U.S.C. Sec. 12101(a)(3) (1999).

142. Olmstead v. L. C., 119 S.Ct. 2176, 2181 (1999).

143. *Id.* at 2185.

144. Helen L. v. Albert Didario, 46 F.3d 325 (3rd Cir. 1995), *cert. den.*, 516 U.S. 813 (1995); L. C. v. Olmstead, 138 F.3d 893 (11th Cir. 1998); Charles Q. v. Houstoun, 1996 WL 447549*7 (M.D. Pa. Apr. 22, 1996) and 1997 U.S. Dist. LEXIS 17305*2 (Jan. 15, 1997); Williams v. Wasserman, 937 F.Supp. 524 (D. Md. 1996); Messier v. Southbury Training School, 916 F.Supp. 133 (D. Conn. 1996) and 1999 U.S. Dist. LEXIS 6992 (D. Conn. Jan. 5, 1999); Martin v. Voinovich, 840 F.Supp. 1175, 1190-92 (S.D. Ohio 1993); Eric L. v. Bird, 848 F.Supp. 303 (D. N.H. 1994); Kathleen S. v. Department of Public Welfare, 10 F.Supp.2d 460 (E.D. Pa. 1998). In one case, the 11th Circuit reversed the decision of the district court judge that an ADA claim could be added to a case that had been resolved by a consent decree, Wyatt v. Fetner, 92 F.3d 1074 (11th Cir. 1996), whereas a judge who refused to consider a plaintiff's initial posttrial ADA claim because Title II did not take effect until Jan. 26, 1992, *see* Jackson v. Fort Stanton State Hospital, 757 F.Supp. 1243, 1249, note 3 (D. N.M. 1990), accepted the plaintiff's Nov. 1993 motion to amend his complaint in Nov. 1993 to add the ADA claims (motions to amend

complaint and memorandum in support of the motion are on file with the author). The *Jackson* ADA claims were successfully settled, as have been ADA claims in similar suits across the country; Chris S. v. Geringer, No. CV-94-311-J (D. Wyo. filed Mar. 10, 1995); Rolland v. Celluci, 191 F.R.D. 3 (D. Mass. 2000). Some ADA cases charging inappropriate institutionalization are currently pending in the courts, Travis D. v. Eastmont, Civ. Action No. CV 96-63-H-CCL (D. Mont. complaint filed Aug. 23, 1996) (on file with the author; for more information, call Montana Advocacy Project at 406/444-3889); Brown v. Chiles, Civ. Action No. 98-673-CIV (S.D. Fla., filed Mar. 24, 1998). The argument that the ADA requires that inappropriately institutionalized people must be treated in community settings was initially rejected in class contexts in People First of Tennessee v. Arlington Developmental Center, 878 F.Supp. 97 (W.D. Tenn. 1992); *Williams,* 609 N.E.2d 447 (Mass. 1993); and Conner v. Branstad, 839 F.Supp. 1346 (S.D. Iowa 1993). No integration mandate case has failed since the success of *Helen L.*

145. Olmstead v. L. C., 119 S.Ct. 2176, 2185 (1999).

146. 138 F.3d 893 (11th Cir. 1998).

147. Although the state does not concede that the institutional placements were inappropriate, it does concede that a lack of funding precluded community placement; Olmstead v. L. C., Brief of Petitioners.

148. This is reminiscent of, but not identical to, the provision of community services as a remedy for years of unnecessary institutionalization approved by the court in Clark v. Cohen, 794 F.2d 79 (3rd Cir.), *cert. den.*, 479 U.S. 962 (1986). It may also bear a resemblance to the sort of integration that the Supreme Court rejected in Lau v. Nichols, 414 U.S. 563 (1974), where Chinese students who could not speak English were "integrated" into school classrooms but could not understand what was being taught and could not benefit from the education provided to the English-speaking students.

149. L. C. v. Olmstead, 138 F.3d at 902.

150. Olmstead v. L. C. 119 S.Ct. 2184, *quoting* L. C. v. Olmstead, 138 F.3d 905.

151. After the petition was granted and a private law firm was hired to write the petitioner's brief, a reference to *habilitation,* a term used in mental retardation, was removed from the question presented and the term *state mental institution* was changed to *state hospital, see* Olmstead v. L. C., Brief of Petitioners. The state's attempt to change the focus of the case from mental retardation to mental illness might have involved a calculation that the justices would be more likely to worry about people with mental illness in the community than those with mental retardation.

152. Olmstead v. L. C., 119 S.Ct. 2176, 2181 (1999).

153. 119 S.Ct. at 2187.

154. *Id.*

155. *See* Christopher Slobogin, "Treatment of the Mentally Disabled: Rethinking the Community-First Idea," *Neb. Law Rev.* 69 (1990):413, 442 ("the problems of institutionalization are often replicated in the community"); Arlene S. Kanter, "A Home of One's Own: The Fair Housing Amendment Act and Housing Discrimination Against People With Mental Disablities," *Amer. Univ. Law Rev.* 43 (1994):925.

156. 119 S.Ct. 2176, 2194.

157. Olmstead v. L. C. at 2186 (1999) (quoting state's brief).

158. *See* City of Cleburne v. Cleburne Living Center, 473 U.S. 432 (1985).

159. Keelyn Friesen, "Non-Passage of the Women's Health Equity Act: Inaction May Lead to Cancerous Results," *Hamline J. of Pub. Law & Policy* 14 (1993):243.

160. United States v. Wiley, 492 F.2d 555 (D.C. Cir. 1973) (Bazelon, J., concurring).

161. *See* Ann Scales, "The Emergence of Feminist Jurisprudence: An Essay," *Yale Law J.* 95 (1986):1373, 1378 ("the 'relevant' differences have been and always will be those which keep women in their place").

162. Olmstead v. L. C., 119 S.Ct. 2176 at 2186.

163. *Id. See* note 10.
164. O'Connor v. Consolidated Coin Caterers Corp., 517 U.S. 308, 312 (1996).
165. *See* p. 107, *supra.*
166. Helen L. v. Albert Didario, 46 F.3d 325, 336 (3rd Cir. 1995); Greist v. Norristown State Hospital, 1997 U.S. Dist. LEXIS 16320*12, note 3 (E.D. Pa. Oct. 16, 1997).
167. Martin v. Voinovich, 840 F.Supp. 1175 (S.D. Ohio 1993).
168. Olmstead v. L. C., 527 U.S. 581, 604 (1999).
169. This is reminiscent of the court's finding in Youngberg v. Romeo that Romeo would never be able to survive outside of an institutional setting; 457 U.S. 307, 317 (1982) ("Respondent, in light of the severe character of his retardation, concedes that no amount of training will make possible his release"). Nicholas Romeo was placed in the community several years later, even before Pennhurst closed. "Former Pennhurst Patient to Get Settlement," UPI (July 25, 1984), available on LEXIS; Nicholas Romeo is now living in a group home in Philadelphia.
170. Charles Q. v. Houstoun, 1996 U.S. Dist. LEXIS 21671*13–14 (M.D. Pa. Apr. 22, 1996) ("It is also irrelevant that the plaintiffs here did require care in HSH initially. It is only material that both sides agree that they can now live outside the hospital setting with appropriate support services").
171. Both L. C. and E. W. were voluntary commitments; Olmstead v. L. C., note 162 at 2183. Idell S. was not committed in *Helen L.,* although one of her coplaintiffs was involuntarily committed. In Charles Q. v. Houstoun, 1996, U.S. Dist. LEXIS 21671*25–26 (M.D. Pa. Apr. 15, 1996), one plaintiff was voluntarily committed and another was involuntarily committed; the court's mode of analysis did not alter because of the difference in legal status. The classes in Kathleen S. v. Houstoun were certified without regard to legal status; Kathleen S. v. Houstoun, 1998 U.S. Dist. LEXIS 2027*2 and *9 (E.D. Pa. Feb. 25, 1998). Initially, the class was all residents of Haverford State Hospital, and the subclass consisted of class members who were residents of Delaware County. Later the court revised the subclass definition to encompass three subclasses: those identified as appropriate for community placement for whom placements had been identified and were imminent, those identified as appropriate for community placement for whom no community placements were available, and those identified as inappropriate for community placement; Kathleen S. v. Houstoun, 10 F.Supp. 2d 460 (E.D. Pa. 1998). What matters in ADA cases is whether people are being served in the most integrated setting appropriate to their needs, not legal status.
172. There are many people who would also argue that even these acute care functions could be performed in the community, obviating the need for psychiatric institutions altogether. This is a more controversial claim than the one I am making here, and I do not pursue it in this book.
173. Many states, in recognition of this fact, require a judicial review of involuntary commitments after 30 days; various model civil commitment statutes do the same.
174. *See* Roe v. County Commission of Monongalia County, 926 F.Supp. 74, 78 (N.D. W.Va. 1996), in which a man brought in on a mental health warrant claimed that the conditions of his confinement constituted unnecessary segregation in violation of the ADA; the court refused to dismiss his claim.
175. In Charles Q. v. Houstoun, the court found that continued confinement of Joseph K, who had been institutionalized for 6 years, did not violate the ADA in view of his aggressiveness and elopement from the hospital; 1997 U.S. Dist. LEXIS 17305*25 (M.D. Pa. Jan. 15, 1997).
176. As a practical matter, the pace of litigation ensures that the plaintiffs who bring these cases have been institutionalized for months if not years. Although it is certainly possible to have unnecessarily segregated services that terminate after 2 or 3 weeks, such a case would have to be brought as a class action or decided after the patient's discharge as

"capable of repetition yet evading review." In addition, focusing on the residential aspect of institutionalization helps to avoid the troubling question of the status of treatment for the disability itself under the ADA (*see* discussion *infra* pp. 136–139).

177. 119 S.Ct. at 2188.

178. Charles Q. v. Houstoun, 1996 U.S. Dist. LEXIS 21671 (M.D. Pa. Apr. 22, 1996).

179. Kathleen S. v. Houstoun, 10 F.Supp. 2d 460 (E.D. Pa. 1998).

180. *Id.* at 466.

181. This is one of the principal assertions of the complaint in Johnson v. Sellars, No. 87-369-CIV-T-24-E (Bucklew) (M.D. Fla. filed Mar. 11, 1987); James K. Green, attorney for the plaintiffs (personal communication, Oct. 22, 1999).

182. Whether damage actions are available against state defendant under the ADA will be decided by the U.S. Supreme Court in University of Alabama v. Garrett, *see* pp. 74–75 and 99–100.

183. *Id.*

184. Youngberg v. Romeo, 457 U.S. 307 (1982).

185. Susan Stefan, "Leaving Civil Rights to the Experts: From Deference to Abdication Under the Professional Judgment Standard," *Yale Law J.* 102 (1992):639.

186. *Id.*

187. Olmstead v. L. C., 119 S.Ct. 2176 at 2189 and 2192.

188. *Id.* at 2192.

189. *Id.* at 2183.

190. Charles Q. v. Houstoun, 1997 U.S. Dist. LEXIS 17305*26 (E.D. Pa. Jan. 15, 1997).

191. 28 C.F.R. Sec. 35.130(d) (1999).

192. 28 C.F.R. Pt. 35.130, App. 35, 130(b)(2) (1998).

193. Olmstead v. L. C., note 187 at 2188. Although no one can assert a right to integrated services on behalf of an individual who does not want these services, that does not confer a right on individuals to remain institutionalized if the state has decided that they belong in the community. *See* text at note 2, *infra*.

194. 28 C.F.R. Pt. 35.130, App. Sec. 35.130(b)(i)(iv), (d) (1999).

195. A public entity may provide "benefits, services or advantages to individuals with disabilities, or to a particular class of individuals with disabilities beyond those required in this part"; 28 C.F.R. Sec. 35.130(c) (1999). "A public entity . . . may not . . . on the basis of disability . . . provide different or separate aids, benefits, or services to individuals with disabilities or to any class of individuals with disabilities than is provided to others unless such action is necessary to provide qualified individuals with disabilities with aids, benefits or services that are as effective as those provided to others"; 28 C.F.R. Sec. 35.130(b)(1)(iv) (1999).

196. 28 C.F.R. Pt. 35.130, App. 35.130(b)(2) (1999). A number of regulations emphasize this point, including the following: "A public entity may not deny a qualified individual with a disability the opportunity to participate in services, programs, or activities that are not separate or different, despite the existence of permissibly separate or different programs or activities," 28 C.F.R. Sec. 35.130(b)(2) (1999); "nothing in this part shall be construed to require an individual with a disability to accept an accommodation, aid, service, opportunity or benefit provided under the ADA or this part which such individual chooses not to accept," 28 C.F.R. Sec. 35.130(e)(1) (1999).

197. "Even when separate or different aids, benefits or services would be more effective, paragraph (b)(2) provides that a qualified individual with a disability still has the right to choose to participate in the program that is not designed to accommodate individuals with disabilities"; 28 C.F.R. Pt. 35.130, App. 35.130(b)(1)(iv) and (b)(2) (1999).

198. "Assuming that a separate program would be appropriate for a particular individual, the extent to which the individual must be provided with modifications in the integrated program will depend not only on what the individual needs but also on the limitations

and defenses of this part. For example, it may constitute an undue burden for a public accommodation, which provides a special full-time interpreter on its special guided tour for individuals with hearing impairments, to hire an additional interpreter for those individuals who choose to attend the integrated program. The Department cannot identify categorically the level of assistance or aid required in the integrated program." One thing is clear: If the individual does not request any accommodations in the integrated program, then he cannot be excluded from it on the basis of disability"; 28 C.F.R. Pt. 35.130, App. 35.130(b)(1)(iv) and (b)(2) (1999).

199. *Interpretive Guidance* to 28 C.F.R. Sec. 35.130 (1999).
200. Olmstead v. L. C., note 187 at 2188. *See also* Messier v. Southbury Training School, 1999 U.S. Dist. LEXIS*35 (D. Conn. Jan. 5, 1999). This principle has been held applicable to other settings as well. In Concerned Parents to Save Dreher Park v. City of West Palm Beach, 846 F.Supp. 986 (S.D. Fla. 1994), the Recreation Department of the city of West Palm Beach sought to defund its separate programs for citizens with disabilities to save money. These programs, which were attended and enjoyed by such citizens, were separate from the department's other programs, although many were conducted in the same locations.
201. C.A. No. 89–2038, *slip op.* (W.D. Pa. Sept. 29, 1999).
202. *Id.*
203. Olmstead v. L. C., 119 S.Ct. at 2188 ("the state's own professionals determined that community-based treatment would be appropriate for L. C. and E. W. and neither woman opposed such treatment," and "community based treatment will not be imposed on patients who do not desire it").
204. Lois A. Weithorn, "Mental Hospitalization of Troublesome Youth: An Analysis of Skyrocketing Admission Rates," *Stan. Law Rev.* 40 (1988):773; Ira M. Schwartz, "The U.S. Supreme Court Held That Due Process Did Not Require a Judicial Hearing—Or Any Hearing at All—Prior to the Commitment of a Minor by His or Her Parents," Parham v. J. R., 442 U.S. 584 (1979). The court assumed that the necessary protection of the liberty interest of the minor would be provided by the neutrality of the admitting physician. This is doubtful, particularly in the case of private, for-profit hospitals, *see* Louise Armstrong, *And They Call It Help* (Reading, MA: Addison-Wesley, 1993).
205. Bonnie S. v. Altman, 683 F.Supp. 100 (D. N.J. 1989); Heichelbech v. Evans, 798 F.Supp. 708 (M.D. Ga. 1992); Doe v. Austin, 848 F.2d 1386, 1392 (6th Cir. 1988). Many states preclude guardians from institutionalizing their wards without seeking consent of a court to do so, *see, e.g.*, VT. STAT. ANN. Title 111, Sec. 3074 (1989).
206. House of Representatives, Committee on the Judiciary, Rep. No. 101-485 Pt. 3, 49–50, 101st Cong., 2nd Sess. (May 15, 1990).
207. House of Representatives, Committee on Energy and Commerce, House Rep. 101-485 Pt. 4, 101st Cong., 2nd Sess. (May 15, 1990) at 38.
208. 28 C.F.R. Sec. 35.130(b)(7) (1999).
209. 28 C.F.R. Sec. 35.130(b)(1)(iv) (1999).
210. 28 C.F.R. Sec. 35.130(b)(2) (1999).
211. 28 C.F.R. Pt. 35.104, App. 35.104 (1999).
212. 28 C.F.R. Pt. 35.130, App. 35.130(b)(iv) (1999).
213. *See* discussion *infra* pp. 118–121.
214. Olmstead v. L. C., note 203 at 2185.
215. *Id.* at 2187 (emphasis added).
216. *Id.* at 2189.
217. *Id.* at 2185 (emphasis added).
218. *See* chapter 5 for a more thorough discussion of the home- and community-based services waiver programs on Medicaid.
219. Health Care Financing Administration, information on home- and community-based ser-

vice waivers [online], retreived Feb. 2, 2000, available on the World Wide Web: http://
www.hcfa.gov/medicaid/ltc8.htm.

220. Michelle Melden, "The Home- and Community-Based Waiver Program Under Medicaid: An Update," *Clearinghouse Rev.* 29 (1995):142; Jane Ellen Rein, "Misinformation
and Self-Deception in Recent Long-Term Care Policy Trends," *J. Law & Politics* 12
(1996):195, 209; National Association of State Medicaid Directors, American Public
Human Services Association (1999), *Medicaid Home and Community Based Services
Waivers* [online], retreived Apr. 24, 2000, available on the World Wide Web: http://
medicaid.aphsa.org/1915ctext.htm.

221. Cramer v. Chiles, 33 F.Supp. 2d 1342 (S.D. Fla. 1999).

222. "All States except Arizona have at least one [home- and community-based waiver]
program. Arizona is a technical exception, though, because it runs the equivalent of a
HCBS waiver program under [a different waiver authority]." "Medicaid Waivers" can
be found on the World Wide Web at the HCFA web site, http://www.hcfa.gov/medicaid/
hpg4.htm. *See* note 218.

223. Duc Van Le v. Ibarra, written opinion of trial court judge on file with author, 1992 Colo.
LEXIS 385 (Apr. 20, 1992) (reversing trial court), 1992 Colo. LEXIS 447 (May 28,
1992) (granting a request for rehearing *en banc*), 1992 Colo. LEXIS 1148 (Dec. 14,
1992) (affirming trial court). This decision is discussed in more detail in chapter 5. *See
also* Goebel v. Colorado Department of Institutions, 764 P.2d 785 (Colo. 1988), which
suggests that a state mental health agency cannot claim that it was financially unable to
provide services to people with mental disabilities unless it had made this condition
known to the state legislature, specifically asked for more funding, and been turned
down.

224. In Duc Van Le v. Ibarra, *id.*, the state's defense that to reapply for home- and community-
based services waiver for people with mental illness would cost $30,000 was rejected
as a defense by the trial court, whose order was ultimately affirmed by the Colorado
Supreme Court.

225. *See* Interpretive Guidance to 1630.2(p) Undue Hardship: "If the employer or other
covered entity can show that the cost of accommodation would impose an undue hardship, it would still be required to provide the accommodation if the funding is available
from another source, *e.g.*, a State vocational rehabilitation agency, or if Federal, State,
or local tax deductions or tax credits are available to offset the cost of the accommodation. If the employer or other covered entity receives, or is eligible to receive, monies
from an external source that would pay the entire cost of the accommodation, it cannot
claim cost as an undue hardship. . . . To the extent that such monies pay or would pay
for only part of the cost of the accommodation, only that portion of the cost of the
accommodation that could not be recovered—the final net cost to the entity—may be
considered in determining undue hardship; *see* S. Rep. 116, 101st Cong., 1st Sess. at
36; House Labor Rep. 485, 101st Cong., 2nd Sess. at 69.

226. L. C. v. Olmstead, 138 F.3d 904.

227. *See* Travis D. v. Eastmont, Civ. Action No. CV-96-63-H-CCL, plaintiff's motion for a
partial summary judgment (D. Mont., filed Apr. 24, 1998) at 28, referring to the Statement of Uncontroverted Facts No. 178.

228. Rolland v. Celluci, 52 F.Supp. 2d 231 (D. Mass. 1999).

229. Cramer v. Chiles, 33 F.Supp. 2d 1342, 1350 (S.D. Fla. 1999); *see also* Brown v. Chiles,
Civ. A. No. 98-673-CIV (S.D. Fla., complaint filed Mar. 24, 1998).

230. Leonard I. Stein and Leonard J. Ganser, "Wisconsin's System for Funding Mental Health
Services," in *Unified Mental Health Systems: Utopia Unrealized,* John A. Talbott, Ed.
(San Francisco: Jossey-Bass, 1983) at 23–25.

231. 10 F.Supp. 2d 476 (E.D. Pa. 1998) (refusing to reconsider the prior order).

232. *Id.* at 479.

233. 28 C.F.R. Pt. 35-130, App. 35.130(b)(3) (1999).

234. The defense is not available in claims of intentional discrimination, and there is some doubt as to whether this defense is available at all in these kinds of cases, *see below.*

235. In Rolland v. Celluci, the plaintiffs alleged that expenditures per person in Massachusetts under the home- and community-based services waiver program was $36,000 a year, compared with institutional expenditures of $150,000 a year and nursing facility expenditures of $40,000 a year; Rolland v. Celluci, No. 98-30208-KPN (D. Mass. amended complaint, filed Jan. 27, 1999) (on file with author).

236. House of Representatives, Committee on the Judiciary, Rep. No. 101-485 (Pt. 3) (May 15, 1990) at 49–50.

237. *E.g.,* simply fixing the doors on the DeKalb County Courthouse costs $40,000; "Panel Studying Local Governments Delays Divulging Results," ATLANTA CONSTITUTION (Nov. 13, 1996):C4. The cost of renovating the courthouse and county offices in Edgefield, SC, to conform to the ADA was funded "in part" by a $300,000 community development block grant; Pat Willis, "Edgefield Courthouse Rededication Sunday," AUGUSTA CHRONICLE (May 1, 1998):B2. In Tennessee, a courthouse put in "a connector building with an elevator that makes the second-floor courtroom and all bathrooms accessible" for $1.6 million; Catherine Trevison, "Fighting Physical Discrimination: Couple Sues for Access to Courthouses," THE TENNESSEEAN (Aug. 21, 1998):A1. An elevator and wheelchair ramp in Murray County, OK, alone cost $200,000; Mark A. Hutchison, "Courthouse in Sulphur to Improve Access," THE DAILY OKLAHOMAN (June 23, 1995): 17.

238. Olmstead v. L. C., 119 S.Ct. 2176 at 2189.

239. S. H. v. Edwards, 860 F.2d 1045, 1048–1049 (11th Cir. 1988) (*vacated* on other grounds).

240. *Id.* at 1054 (Clark, J., dissenting).

241. Charles Q. v. Houstoun, 1997 U.S. Dist. LEXIS 17305*26 (M.D. Pa., Jan. 15, 1997).

242. Pennsylvania Department of Corrections et al. v. Yeskey, 524 U.S. 206 (1998) (hypertension); Randolph v. Rogers, 170 F.3d 850 (8th Cir. 1999) (deafness); Bohannon v. Edwards, 1999 U.S. App. LEXIS 19885*1 (7th Cir. Aug. 19, 1999) (double amputee); Torcasio v. Murray, 57 F.3d 1340 (4th Cir. 1995) (obesity); Rivera v. Dyett, 1992 U.S. Dist. LEXIS 13464*5 (S.D. N.Y. Sept. 10, 1992) (an inmate in a wheelchair also claimed to be perceived as having a psychiatric disability).

243. A. Dahleen Glanton, "Bounds of Silence: Deaf Man Who Spent 29 Years in Mental Wards Hopes for New Start in Life With Settlement of Lawsuit," LOS ANGELES TIMES (June 12, 1988):Pt. 2, p. 1.

244. Doe v. Wilzack, No. N83-2409 (D. Md., first amended complaint filed July 5, 1983) at 14, para. 37.

245. Tugg v. Towey, 864 F.Supp. 1201 (S.D. Fla. 1994) (deaf clients of community mental health services are entitled to preliminary injunction prohibiting the termination of services of therapists who could sign under the ADA); Wilson v. North Carolina, 981 F.Supp. 397 (E.D. N.C. 1997) (the plaintiff was black, deaf, and possibly mentally retarded; he was held in a segregated institution for decades with no treatment and no provision was made to communicate with him); Cameron v. Tomes, 990 F.2d 14 (1st Cir. 1993) (a forensic mental health client in a wheelchair was entitled to certain structural accommodations as a matter of due process); Doe v. Wilzack, No. N83-2409 (D. Md., filed July 5, 1983, settled Feb. 26, 1986) (involving the failure to provide appropriate treatment to deaf patients in the Maryland mental health system), *but see* Rivera v. Dyett, 1992 WL 233882*31 (S.D. N.Y. Sept. 10, 1992) (a diabetic prisoner had no further claim after his diet was adjusted following his initial complaint).

246. *See* Wilson v. North Carolina, 981 F.Supp. 397 (E.D. N.C. 1997) (one of the injuries the plaintiff claimed was a lack of contact with other deaf people); complaint in W. G. v. Dvoskin, No. 95 Civ 2106 (CLB) (complaint filed Mar. 29, 1995) (Spanish-speaking

plaintiffs asked for contact with other plaintiffs who speak Spanish); Doe v. Wilzack, No. N83-2409 at 8 (the complaintent alleged that "defendants have not placed [the plaintiff] with other patients who know sign language").

247. There is one such ward in Springfield Hospital in Sykesville, Maryland. Although it provided good services initially, one attorney reported that "a lot of good people left out of frustration. The replacements don't sign and Springfield doesn't make much effort to train incoming staff," interview with Laura Cain, Maryland Disability Center (July 11, 2000).

248. People who spoke only Spanish were transferred from Rockland Psychiatric Center to a Spanish-speaking ward in the Bronx as a result of this litigation, W. G. v. Dvoskin, 95-Civ-2106 (CLB) (S.D. N.Y., complaint filed Mar. 29, 1995); the cultural-competence requirement of all state hospitals in Texas was created as a result of threatened litigation, Beth Mitchell, attorney for Advocacy Inc., Austin, TX (personal communication, Oct. 18, 1999).

249. Wilson v. North Carolina, 981 F.Supp. 397 (E.D. N.C. 1997). The case law out of the prison and jail system has also been successful; Hanson v. Sangamon County Sheriff's Office, 941 F.Supp. 1098 (C.D. Ill. 1998); Clarkson v. Coughlin, 783 F.Supp. 789, 796 (S.D. N.Y. 1992); Randolph v. Rogers, 170 F.3d 850 (8th Cir. 1999); Duffy v. Riveland, 98 F.3d 447 (9th Cir. 1996).

250. Id.

251. Wilson v. North Carolina, 981 F.Supp. at 400 (E.D. N.C. 1997).

252. Unless the U.S. Supreme Court decides that individuals cannot maintain damage actions against state defendants under the ADA, see pp. 74–75 and 99–100.

253. See Wilson v. North Carolina, 981 F.Supp. at 400, note 1.

254. Neely v. Feinstein, 50 F.3d 1502 (9th Cir. 1995).

255. Caroline C. v. Johnson, No. 4:CV95:22 (D. Neb., consent decree signed Oct. 28, 1998).

256. D. Sobsey and T. Doe, "Patterns of Sexual Abuse and Assualt," Sexuality and Disability 9 (1991):243.

257. Dick Sobsey and Peter Calder, "Violence Against People With Disabilities: A Conceptual Analysis," report prepared for the U.S. National Research Council's Committee on Law and Justice and presented at the Workshop on Crime Victims With Developmental Disabilities (Oct. 28–29, 1999), University of California at Irvine.

258. Ruth Luckasson, "Crimes Against People With Developmental Disabilities: An Overview," report prepared for the U.S. National Research Council's Committee on Law and Justice and presented at the Workshop on Crime Victims With Developmental Disabilities (Oct. 28–29, 1999), University of California at Irvine at 4 (the police refused to accept the rape report of a mentally disabled woman because they believed that people with mental retardation could not be witnesses in court); Leigh Ann Davis, "The Criminal Justice Reponses to Victims With Developmental Disabilities: Utilizing Effective ADA Accommodations" at 4 (the mother reported the rape of her 23-year-old daughter, but the police did not return her phone calls after the mother revealed her daughter was mentally retarded).

259. "Care of Institutionalized Mentally Disabled Person, 1985," joint hearing before the Subcommittee on the Handicapped of the Committee on Labor and Human Resources and the Subcommittee on Labor, Health and Human Services, Education, and Other Related Agencies of the Committee on Appropriations of the United States Senate, 99th Cong., 1st Sess. (1985) ("in one California jurisdiction, it is virtually impossible to get the local district attorney to file criminal charges or substantial rape allegations if the rape involved a psychiatric patient"); Binder, "Sex Between Psychiatric Inpatients," Psychiatric Quarterly 57 (1985):121, 123; Judith L. Musick, "Patterns of Institutional Sexual Assault," Response to Violence in the Fam. and Sex. Assault 7 (1984):3, 5.

260. One hospital conducted an investigation into the suspicious deaths of more than 12

infants with disabilities or medical problems, concluded that a staff member was intentionally causing the deaths and laid her off, but did not notify law enforcement or child welfare authorities; Richard Elkind, *Death Shift: The True Story of Genene Jones and the Texas Baby Murders* (New York: Onyx Press, 1989). In another case, an institution had a client who died of multiple stab wounds and reported the death as due to "cardiac arrest"; Alvarado and Pope, "Agnew's Doctors Called Negligent in Patient's Slaying," SAN JOSE MERCURY NEWS (Sept. 28, 1994):B1. Another study reported by a newspaper shows that staff do not report criminal abuse of patients by other staff members for fear of retribution from administrators; Helm, "Study Finds Abusers of Disabled Often Their Helpers," EDMONTON JOURNAL (Oct. 27, 1990):C3.

261. Laura Mansnerus, "Watching the People Who Watch Over the Mentally Ill: Questions Disturb State Health Officials After Guard Admits Raping Four in His Care," NEW YORK TIMES 216 (Apr. 18, 1999):Sec. N14, p. 1 (the patient collected $675,000 in the suit after showing that the guard was reported for at least 11 assaults and had only one disciplinary hearing; the same story details years of reports of sexual assaults at other facilities, with no action taken).

262. Powers, Mooney, and Nunno, "Institutional Abuse: A Report of the Literature," *J. of Child and Youth Care* 4 (1990):81.

263. Youngberg v. Romeo, 457 U.S. 307 (1982).

264. Caroline C. v. Johnson, 1996 U.S. Dist. LEXIS 21358 (D. Neb. 1996) (*class certified*) (the settlement agreement signed by the attorneys on Oct. 28–30, 1998, is available from Bruce Mason, 1505 S. 108th St., Omaha NE 68144 or the Nebraska Advocacy Assn.).

265. The settlement agrement provides that "a class member who makes an allegation of rape, sexual assault or sexual abuse shall not, at any time after making the report/ incident, be punished or retaliated against, or be placed on ward restriction, in the quiet room, in seclusion or in restraints or denied privileges, or prevented from attending programs or groups, unless otherwise clinically necessary," Settlement Agreement, *id.*, IV(G)(14) at 12.

266. "No staff person, who has been the subject of a pending complaint of sexual molestation, harassment or abuse shall be in attendance of a class member who is in restraint or seclusion or 1:1 staffing," Settlement Agreement IV(G)(9) at 11.

267. Cornell v. State of New York, 389 N.E.2d 1064 (N.Y. 1979) (a 14-year-old boy raped in a psychiatric institution cannot sue the state in tort because "the relationship between the State and patients at state institutions is *sui generis,* and is not aptly compared to the type of voluntarily assumed relationship which may carry with it the imposition of absolute liability").

268. Patricia S. v. Waterbury Hospital, No. CV-97-0137073S (Conn. Super. Ct., complaint filed Dec. 9, 1996).

269. Maxine Harris, "Modifications in Service Delivery and Clinical Treatment for Women Who Are Diagnosed With Severe Mental Illness Who Are Also Survivors of Sexual Abuse Trauma," *J. of Mental Health Admin.* 21 (1994):396; Mary Ellen Fromuth and Barry Burkhart, "Recovery or Recapitulation? An Analysis of the Impact of Psychiatric Hospitalization on the Child Sexual Abuse Survivor," *Women and Therapy* 12 (1992): 81; Deborah Doob, "Female Sexual Abuse Survivors as Patients: Avoiding Retraumatization," *Archives of Psychiatric Nurs.* 6 (1992):245, 250; Sharon M. Valente, "Deliberating Self-Injury: Management in a Psychiatric Setting," *J. of Psychosocial Nurs.* 29 (1991):19, 24; Richard Schwartz, Peter Cohen, Norman Hoffman, and John E. Meeks, "Self-Harm Behaviors (Carving) in Female Adolescent Drug Abusers," *Clin. Ped.* 28 (1989):340, 341, 344 (noting that self-injuries increased after institutionalization and 20% of girls engaged in self-injury for the first time after institutionalization); R. R. Ross and H. B. McKay, *Self Mutilation* (Lexington, MA: Lexington Books, 1979) (all the girls in the study engaged in self-injury only after their institutionalization).

270. *See, e.g.*, Maxine Harris, Ed., *Sexual Abuse in the Lives of Women Diagnosed With Serious Mental Illness* (Amsterdam, The Netherlands: Harwood, 1997); Bruce L. Levin, Andrea K. Blanch, and Ann Jennings, *Women's Mental Health Services: A Public Health Perspective* (Thousand Oaks, CA: Sage, 1998); Sandra Bloom, *Creating Sanctuary: Toward an Evolution of Sane Societies* (New York: Routledge, 1997). This literature is not obscure. Judith Lewis Herman's *Trauma and Recovery* (New York: Basic Books, 1992) won the highest award bestowed by the American Psychiatric Association for a book in the field.

271. Armstead v. Coler, 914 F.2d 1464 (11th Cir. 1990); Martin v. Voinovich, 840 F.Supp. 1175, 1182 (S.D. Ohio 1993); Thomas S. by Brooks v. Flaherty, 902 F.2d 250 (4th Cir. 1990); Riffenburg v. State of Michigan, 1997 U.S. Dist. LEXIS 7073*12 and 15 (W.D. Mich., Apr. 24, 1997).

272. Riffenburg v. State of Michigan, *id.*

273. Garrity v. Gallen, 522 F.Supp. 171, 215–217 (D. N.H. 1981); Martin v. Voinovich, 840 F.Supp. 1175, 1192 (S.D. Ohio 1993).

274. Jackson v. Fort Stanton State Hospital, 757 F.Supp. 1243, 1299 (D. N.M. 1990); Garrity v. Gallen, 522 F.Supp. 171, 214–215 (D. N.H. 1981); Martin v. Voinovich, 840 F.Supp. 1175, 1192 (S.D. Ohio 1993); Homeward Bound v. Hissom No. 85-C-437 (N.D. Okla. July 24, 1987).

275. This issue is discussed in chapter 5.

276. Plummer v. Branstad, 731 F.2d 574, 578 (8th Cir. 1984); Messier v. Southbury Training School, 1999 U.S. Dist. LEXIS 1479*33 (D. Conn. Jan. 5, 1999); Garrity v. Gallen (D. N.H. 1981); Jackson v. Fort Stanton State Hospital, 757 F.Supp. 1243, 1299 (D. N.M. 1990), *rev'd* in part on other grounds, Lynch v. Maher, 507 F.Supp. 1268, 1278–1279 (D. Conn. 1981); Cable v. Department of Developmental Services of California, 973 F.Supp. 937, 942 (C.D. Ca. 1997); Goebel v. Colorado Department of Institutions, 764 P.2d 785 (Colo. 1988).

277. *See, e.g.*, Garrity v. Gallen, 522 F.Supp. at 171, 214–215.

278. Hopkins v. Digital Equipment, 1998 U.S. Dist. LEXIS 15762*11 (S.D. N.Y. Oct. 8, 1998); Hansborough v. City of Elkhart Parks and Recreation Department, 802 F.Supp. 199 (N.D. Ind. 1992); Walker v. Secretary of the Treasury, 713 F.Supp. 403 (N.D. Ga. 1989).

279. The U.S. Supreme Court approved, under limited circumstances and for limited periods of time, pretrial detention without bail for people charged with serious crimes who are deemed to present a serious danger to society, United States v. Salerno, 481 U.S. 739 (1987), and civil detention of juveniles under the delinquency systems, Schall v. Martin, 467 U.S. 253 (1984).

280. A few states provide for indefinite terms of commitment, although some courts have held that the U.S. Constitution requires state-initiated reviews of commitment; Streicher v. Prescott, 663 F.Supp. 335 (D.D.C. 1987); Fasulo v. Arafeh, 378 A.2d 553 (Conn. 1977). Other states provide for the review of commitment after 6 months, *see, e.g.*, Fla. Stat. ch. 394.467(6)(b) (1999). There is a great deal of evidence that these reviews are perfunctory.

281. *See* Kansas v. Hendricks, 521 U.S. 346 (1996).

282. In re Barbara H., 702 N.E.2d 555 (Ill. 1998).

283. *See* text and notes on pp. 132–133.

284. These states include Florida, West Virginia (26:5A-1), Arizona (ARIZ. REV. STAT. § 36-725–§ 36-738, 2000), and New Jersey (§ 30:9–57, 2000). In addition, New York city has a program permitting the involuntary confinement of people with tuberculosis; 24 R.C.N.Y. 11.47 (1993).

285. *See* Wendy Parmet, "AIDS and Quarantine: The Revival of an Archaic Doctrine," *Hofstra Law Rev.* 14 (1985):53, 54, notes 3 and 4 (describing, among other things, legis-

lation defeated in Colorado, California, and Texas and the proposal of Vernon Mark, identified only as "a Massachusetts neurosurgeon," to use a former leper colony to quarantine carriers of HIV who engaged in "irresponsible" behavior. Mark gained some notoriety after cowriting a letter to the *J. of the Amer. Med. Assn.* in the wake of urban riots, suggesting that brain abnormalities accounted for the rioters' behavior and recommending treatment for violent "slum dwellers."

286. *See, e.g.,* ARK. CODE ANN. Sec. 12-12-918 (Michie, 1997); CAL. WELF. & INST. CODE Secs. 6600 *et seq.* (1999); COLO. REV. STAT. Sec. 18-3-414.5 (1998).

287. 1994 IMHO Reference Tables, Table 14.1, and unpublished data from 1994 IMHO Survey, Center for Mental Health Services, Alcohol, Drug Abuse, and Mental Health Services Administration, Department of Health and Human Services, interview with Laura Sayres (July 11, 2000).

288. Whether commitments for sexual deviance would fall under the ADA, given Congress's exclusion of "pedophilia . . . or other sexual behavior disorders" from the ADA, 42 U.S.C. Sec. 12211(b)(1) (1999), is beyond the scope of this article.

289. City of Newark v. J. S., 652 A.2d 265 (N.J. Super. 1993).

290. 971 F.Supp. 1089 (S.D. Miss. 1997).

291. City of Newark v. J. S., 279 N.J. Super. 178, 652 A.2d 265 (1993).

292. One exception, as always, was Michael Perlin, who noted *J. S.*'s significance first in " 'Make Promises by the Hour': Sex, Drugs, the Americans With Disabilities Act and Psychiatric Hospitalization," *DePaul Law Rev.* 46 (1997):947, 974, 975.

293. *Id.* at 973.

294. *Id.*

295. This definition is taken from the DOJ's *Interpretive Guidance to Title II* but is also identical to the language in the statute of Title III.

296. 42 U.S.C. Secs. 12111(3), 12113(b)(Title I) (1999), and 42 U.S.C. Sec. 12182(b)(3)(Title III) (1999).

297. 524 U.S. 624 (1998).

298. *Id.*

299. *Id.*

300. *Id.*

301. City of Newark v. J. S., note 289, *supra* at 275.

302. Bragdon v. Abbott, *see* note 313, *id.*

303. *Id.* at 277.

304. *Id.*

305. The court mentioned the following witnesses: "J. S.'s admitting physician, pulmonary disease specialist, social worker, floor nurse, infectious control nurse, hospital vice president and chief of social work [making it unclear whether one person served the last two functions]" as well as the "chief of the Tuberculosis Program of the New Jersey Department of Health," *id.* at 268.

306. N.J. STAT. ANN. Sec. 30:4-27 (West 1997).

307. State v. Krol, 68 N.J. 236 (1975); State v. Fields, 77 N.J. 282 (1978). Almost all of these cases were brought by the Mental Health Division of the New Jersey Department of the Public Advocate, a forceful protector of the civil rights of people in New Jersey that was dissolved by Governor Christie Whitman in 1994.

308. Michael Perlin, "'Half-Wracked Prejudice Leaped Forth: Sanism, Pretextuality and Why and How Mental Health Law Developed as It Did," *J. of Contemp. Legal Issues* 10 (1999):3, 21.

309. *See* pp. 132–133, *infra.*

310. Parham v. J. R., 442 U.S. 584, 609, note 17 (1979); *see* text and notes at pp. 132–133, *infra.*

311. Grant Morris, "Defining Dangerousness: Risking a Dangerous Definition," *J. of Contemp. Legal Issues* 10 (1999):61.

312. City of Newark v. J. S., note 289 at 274. This caution is especially warranted in cases where a person is confined because of the fears of the community about his or her release—a fairly common occurrence in well-publicized cases, especially those involving criminal offenses.
313. Bragdon v. Abbott, 524 U.S. 624, 118 S. Ct. 2196, 141 L.Ed.2d 540, 564 (1998) ("Because few, if any, activities in life are risk free, *Arline* and the ADA require that the risk be significant").
314. The U.S. Supreme Court emphasized that the good-faith belief of a health care professional that an individual is a direct threat is not sufficient; the conclusion that a person is a direct threat must be based on objective facts: "Scientific evidence and expert testimony must have a traceable analytical basis in objective fact before it may be considered on summary judgment," *id.*
315. The EEOC interprets Title I's use of direct threat to include danger to self. In addition to adding a term not in the statute that significantly expands the exception to the statutory antidiscrimination mandate and for which there is no Congressional authority, EEOC's interpretation is not binding on Title II or Title III claims; DOJ is the appropriate interpretive authority for claims involving segregation and civil commitment for only danger to others cases.
316. In Hendricks v. Kansas, 521 U.S. 346 (1996), the U.S. Supreme Court held that a person could be institutionalized without the violation of substantive due process required by the U.S. Constitution if he or she were dangerous as a result of a mental condition that impaired the ability to control his or her actions. The court in *Hendricks* underscored the importance of the finding of dangerousness and was somewhat more vague about the definition or parameters of the mental condition that caused the dangerousness.
317. Wyo. Stat. Ann. Sec. 25-10-101(ii)(C) (Michie 1999).
318. City of Newark v. J. S., note 289 at 274.
319. *See* Foucha v. Louisiana, 504 U.S. 71 (1992).
320. It was only through an enormous effort of public education and political pressure that advocates for people with AIDS avoided the imposition of quarantines and other preventive detention for people with AIDS.
321. This is particularly true of the segregation imposed by nursing homes and institutions for people with mental retardation. In those cases, of course, the voluntary–involuntary nature of the institutionalization is more problematic, and troubling issues are raised by the question of whether guardians can "voluntarily" segregate their disabled wards if more appropriate placements exist in the community.
322. Amirault v. City of Roswell, 1996 WL 391986, 8 NDLR 212 (D. N.M. July 11, 1996).
323. *See, e.g.,* Greist v. Norristown State Hospital et al., No. 96-CV-8495, 1997 U.S. Dist. LEXIS 16320*5 (E.D. Pa. Oct. 16, 1997). In certain limited circumstances, an individual may appeal to a federal court after appealing an adverse decision all the way up the state court system, but it is virtually axiomatic that a lower federal court may not reverse a lower state court on any case filed initially in state court. In other cases challenging individual commitment proceedings under the ADA, courts have dismissed cases because the claims were too vague; Bodor v. Horsham Clinic, 1995 U.S. Dist. LEXIS 10006*27 (E.D. Pa., July 19, 1995).
324. Musko v. McCandless, 1995 U.S. Dist. LEXIS 5911*2 (E.D. Pa. May 1, 1995) (a man alleged that county officials committed him because of his frustration with a failure to abide by zoning regulations).
325. Public defender's offices are also public entities under Title II of the ADA.
326. Virginia Hiday, "The Attorney's Role in Involuntary Civil Commitment Proceedings," *N. C. Law Rev.* 60 (1982):1027, 1044, 1045; Fitch, "Involuntary Commitment of the Mentally Disabled: Implementation of the Law in Winston-Salem, North Carolina," *N C. Cent. Law J.* 14 (1984):406; Charles D. H. Parry et al., "A Comparison of Com-

mitment and Recommitment Hearings," *Intl. J. of Law & Psychiatry* 15 (1992):25, 30; Eric Turkheimer and Charles D. H. Parry, "Practice and Policy in Civil Commitment Hearings," *Amer. Psychologist* 47 (1992):646–647; N. Leavitt and P. Maykuth, "Conformance to Attorney Performance Standards: Attorney Advocacy Behavior in a Maximum Security Hospital," *Law and Human Behavior* 13 (1989):217; James Holstein, *Court Ordered Insanity* (New York: Aldine de Gruyter, 1993) at 47–53; Keilitz, Fitch, and McGraw, "A Study of Involuntary Civil Commitment in Los Angeles County," *Sw. Univ Law Rev.* 14 (1984):238; Keilitz and Roach, "A Study of Defense Counsel and the Involuntary Civil Commitment System in Columbus, Ohio," *Cap. Univ. Law Rev.* 13 (1983):175; McGraw, Fitch, Buckley, and Marvell, "Civil Commitment in New York City: An Analysis of Practice," *Pace Law Rev.* 5 (1985):259; D. Lelos, "Courtroom Observation Study of Civil Commitment," in *Civil Commitment and Social Policy,* A. L. McGarry, R. K. Scwhitzgebel, and P. L. Lipsitt, Eds. (1981) at 102–125; S. D. Stier and K. J. Stobe, "Involuntary Hospitalization in Iowa: The Failure of the 1975 Legislation," *Iowa Law Rev.* 64 (1979):1284, 1377; E. Andalman and D. L. Chambers, "Effective Counsel for Persons Facing Civil Commitment: A Survey, a Polemic, and a Proposal," *Miss. Law J.* 45 (1974):43; Fred Cohen, "The Function of the Attorney and the Commitment of the Mentally Ill," *Texas Law Rev.* 44 (1966):424.

327. Eric Turkheimer and Charles D. H. Parry, "Practice and Policy in Civil Commitment Hearings," *Amer. Psychologist* 47 (1992):646–647.

328. Sydeman, Cascardi, Poythress, and Ritterband, "Procedural Justice in the Context of Civil Commitment: A Critique of Tyler's Analysis," *Psychology, Pub. Policy, & Law* 3 (1997):207, 216.

329. *Id.* at 216. In an older study of the Chicago area, a single public defender was assigned to handle all the civil commitments in the city of Chicago—a caseload of 40–60 commitments per week and 200–3,000 commitments per year. Although the situation has improved, it is still far from ideal.

330. Charles D. H. Parry et al., "A Comparison of Commitment and Recommitment Hearings," *Intl. J. Law & Psychiatry* 15 (1992):25, 30.

331. Norman Poythress, "Psychiatric Expertise in Civil Commitment: Training Attorneys to Cope With Expert Testimony," *Law & Human Beh.* 2 (1978):1.

332. In re Barbara H., 702 N.E.2d 555 (Ill. 1998).

333. Sydeman, Cascardi, Poythress, and Ritterband, *supra* at 325, finding that "respondents' attorneys in civil commitment hearings in Virginia did not review the respondent's file in 62.1 percent and did not confer with respondents in 46.3 percent of 190 initial commitment hearings observed." *See also* Matter of Brazelton, 604 N.E.2d 376–377 (Ill. App. 1992) (the attorney representing the client with a mental disability was unaware of a burden of proof in the commitment hearing, which was established by the U.S. Supreme Court in 1979).

334. Survey No. 6.

335. The court of appeals in Lynch v. Baxley, 744 F.2d 1452 (11th Cir. 1984) declared that holding people prior to civil commitment hearings in jail cells violated the U.S. Constitution. Fifteen years later, the practice continued in many states; *see, e.g.,* Alice Doe v. Northeast Texas Mental Health and Mental Retardation, CA No. 5-96-CV-329 (E.D. Tx. Oct. 7, 1998) (a jury verdict of liability against the defendant for holding a mentally ill woman in a jail cell as she awaited her commitment hearing).

336. *See* Doe v. Public Health Trust of Dade County, 696 F.2d 901 (11th Cir. 1983).

337. Roe v. County Commission of Monongalia County, 926 F.Supp. 74 (N.D. W.Va. 1996).

338. *Id.* at 76.

339. *Id.* at 78.

340. *Id.* at 78.

341. Roe sued both the county commissioner and the sheriff's department, *id.* at 75.

342. Judge Ginger Lerner-Wren, *Mental Health Court Progress Report* (Ft. Lauderdale, FL: Mental Health Task Force, Fiscal and Data Committee, July 1997–June 1998) at 3.

343. Henry Fitzgerald, Sr., "Court a Safety Net for Mentally Ill," SUN-SENTINEL (Dec. 28, 1998):B3.

344. Judge Ginger Lerner-Wren, *id.* at note 342.

345. One woman, e.g., was arrested for trespassing on what had until very recently been her own property. After being evicted from her house, she was trying to reclaim her furniture, other property, and personal documents. She has not succeeded in doing so. She is now living in a cottage on the grounds of South Florida State Hospital.

346. Note that in a few cases, the state offered a time-served deal to several defendants in the Mental Health Court and was turned down; Canaan Goldman, *Summary of Observations of Broward County Mental Health Court* (Oct. 1–Nov. 14, 1998) (on file with the author).

347. *Id.*

348. Bennett Brummer, remarks made at the University of Miami–University of Nebraska Conference on Mental Health Law, Ft. Lauderdale, FL (Nov. 14, 1998). The public defender of Broward County supports the program; indeed, assistant public defender Howard Finckelstein was instrumental in its creation, Howard Finckelstein, remarks made at the University of Miami–University of Nebraska Conference, *id.*

349. Fitzgerald, "Court a Safety Net," note 343.

350. *Id.*

351. State courts are subject to Title II, *see* cited cases. DOJ already initiated several investigations and brought litigation against various court systems in the state of Florida for failing to comply with accessibility requirements under the ADA.

352. 42 U.S.C. Sec. 12132 (2000).

353. The court system was also in violation of many of the implementing regulations of Title II, including the regulation requiring that "a public entity shall not impose or apply eligibility criteria that screen out or tend to screen out an individual with a disability or any class of individuals with disabilities from fully and equally enjoying any," 28 C.F.R. Sec. 35.130(b)(8) (2000).

354. 28 C.F.R. Sec. 35.130(e)(1) provides that "nothing in this part shall be construed to require an individual with a disability to accept an accommodation, aid, service, opportunity or benefit under the ADA or this part which the individual chooses not to accept" (2000).

355. 28 C.F.R. Sec. 35.130(c) (2000).

356. B. Bard and J. Fletcher, "The Right to Die," *Atlantic Monthly* (Apr. 1968):59–64.

357. Raymond Duff and A. G. M. Campbell, "Moral and Ethical Dilemmas in the Special Care Nursery," *New Eng. J. of Med.* 289 (1973):890–891.

358. The facts of the case are synopsized in Bowen v. American Hospital Association, 476 U.S. 610 (1986).

359. The Child Abuse Amendments of 1984, 42 U.S.C. Sec. 5106 (1984), ensure the rights of incompetent individuals with disabilities to receive food, water, and medical treatment.

360. 476 U.S. 610 (1986).

361. 729 F.2d 144 (2nd Cir. 1984).

362. 476 U.S. 610 (1986).

363. Public Law 404, 79th Cong., 1st Sess.

364. Bowen v. American Hospital Association, *see* note 358.

365. *Id.*

366. In re Baby K, 832 F.Supp. 1022 (E.D. Va. 1993), *aff'd* on other grounds, 16 F.3d 1590 (4th Cir. 1994), where the mother of a severely handicapped child engaged in a legal dispute with a hospital that did not wish to provide respiratory support to the anence-

phalic child when she was taken to the hospital with respiratory distress. *See also* Causey v. St. Francis Medical Center, 719 S.2d 1072 (La. App. 1998) (the physician and the hospital withdrew life-sustaining care over the strongly expressed objections of the patient's family; the court suggested that "the Americans with Disability Act . . . preempts state law and does not recognize a health care provider's right to withdraw life-sustaining care deemed medically inappropriate," *id.* at 1075, note 2).

367. 28 C.F.R. Sec. 35.131(e)(2) (2000).
368. 442 U.S. 397 (1979).
369. *See* discussion on pp. 112–114 about whether a disfavored characteristic must be irrelevant to a decision or action for the decision or action to be deemed discriminatory.
370. United States v. University Hospital, 729 F.2d 144, 156 (2nd Cir. 1984).
371. *Id.* 144, 156.
372. The requirement of being a "qualified individual with a disability" remains in Title II, however.
373. Robert Jay Lifton, *The Nazi Doctors* (New York: Basic Books, 1986) at 62.
374. This was the crux of the dissent of Judge Winter in United States v. University Hospital, 729 F.2d 144, 162 (2nd Cir. 1984).
375. U.S. v. Morvant, 898 F.Supp. 1157 (E.D. La. 1995).
376. Glanz v. Vernick, 756 F.Supp. 632 (D. Mass. 1991) (the Rehabilitation Act).
377. Howe v. Hull, 873 F.Supp. 72 (N.D. Ohio 1994).
378. Woolfolk v. Duncan, 872 F.Supp. 1381, 1388–1389 (E.D. Pa. 1995).
379. 42 U.S.C. Sec. 12101(a)(3) (1999).
380. This testimony was particularly vivid in the context of people with AIDS and HIV seropositivity, but it also was a thread running through the testimony of people with mental disabilities.
381. *See* Woolfolk v. Duncan, 872 F.Supp. 72 at 1388, note 8.
382. L. C. v. Olmstead, 138 F.3d 893 (11th Cir. 1998).
383. P. L. 88-164.
384. P. L. 93-154.
385. Ellen Bassuk, Richard Winter, and Robert Apsler, "Cross-Cultural Comparison of British and American Psychiatric Emergencies," *Amer. J. of Psychiatry* 140 (1983):180–183.
386. Stephen M. Soreff, *Management of the Psychiatric Emergency* (New York: Wiley, 1981) at 7.
387. Samuel Gerson and Ellen Bassuk, "Psychiatric Emergencies: An Overview," *Amer. J. of Psych* 137(1) (1980):2; David H. Gustafson, Francois Sainfort, Sandra Johnson, and Michael Sateia, "Measuring Quality of Care in Psychiatric Emergencies: Construction and Evaluation of a Bayesian Index," *Foundation of the American College of Health Care Executives Health Services Research* 28(2) (June 1993):131. It is the author's experience that ERs are anything but "fast paced" and the slow pace of receiving assistance is one of the problems with psychiatric assistance in ER settings.
388. Samuel Gerson and Ellen Bassuk, *id.* at 3–4.
389. Soreff, *Management of the Psychiatric Emergency*, note 386, at 10 ("when one patient came to the ED for the eighth time in two months, staff totally ignored her for several hours").
390. Bryan Yates, Carol R. Nordquist, and R. Andrew Schultz-Ross, "Feigned Psychiatric Symptoms in the Emergency Room," *Psychiatric Services* 47 (Sept. 1996):998–999 (In 16% of cases, the resident "mildly" suspected the patient of malingering. The psychiatric residents "moderately" suspected malingering in 13% of presentations, "strongly" suspected malingering in 7% of presentations and were certain that individuals were malingering in 6% of cases. Thus, residents suspected almost half the patients they saw of malingering).
391. *See* Patricia Scherer v. Waterbury Hospital, No. CV-97-0137073S (complaint filed Dec.

9, 1996); Waterbury Hospital Holding Room Policy, Waterbury, CT (on file with the author).

392. Patricia Scherer v. Waterbury Hospital, No. CV-97-0137073 (Waterbury Sup. Ct. Feb. 22, 2000) at 1.

393. *Id.*

394. *Id.* at 2.

395. *Id.* at 5.

396. *Id.* at 6.

397. Herbert N. Wigder and Jeffrey C. Moffat, *Standards of Care in Emergency Medicine: A Practical Guide to Emergency Procedures and Legal Liability* (Gaithersburg, MD: Aspen, 1999).

398. J. R. Hillard, D. Ramm, W. W. K. Zung, and J. M. Holland, "Suicide in a Psychiatric Emergency Room Population," *Amer. J. of Psych.* 140 (1983):459.

399. The diagnosis made its first appearance in American Psychiatric Association's *Diagnostic and Statistical Manual of Mental Disorders* 3rd ed. (Washington, DC: Author, 1980).

400. Michael Magill and Robert W. Garrett, "Borderline Personality Disorder," *Amer. Fam. Physician* 35 (1987):187–195.

401. H. Russell Searight, "Borderline Personality Disorder: Diagnosis and Management in Primary Care," *J. of Fam. Practice* 34 (1992):605 ("These patients may be disruptive, demanding, and noncompliant. They often successfully provoke conflicts between physicians and their nursing staff").

402. *Id.*

403. William Ryan, *Blaming the Victim* rev. ed. (New York: Vintage Books, 1976); Clark Freshman, "Whatever Happened to Anti-Semitism? How Social Science Theories Identify Discrimination and Promote Coalitions Between 'Different' Minorities," *Cornell Law Rev.* 85 (2000):313.

404. Searight at note 401.

405. *Id.*; David Dawson and Harriet MacMillan, *Relationship Management of the Borderline Patient: From Understanding to Treatment* (New York: Brunner Mazell, 1993) (despite its title, this book is a very sound and commendable text).

406. Searight, *see* note 401.

407. *Id. See also* R. Anstett, "The Difficult Patient and the Physician–Patient Relationship," *J. of Fam. Practice* 11 (1980):281–286; D. E. Reiser and H. Levenson, "Abuses of the Borderline Diagnosis: A Clinical Problem With Teaching Opportunities," *Amer. J. of Psychiatry* 141 (1984):1528–1532.

408. George Vaillant, "The Beginning of Wisdom Is Never Calling a Patient a Borderline, or the Clinical Management of Immature Defenses in the Treatment of People With Personality Disorders," *J. of Psychotherapy and Research* 1 (1992):117.

409. Reiser and Levenson, "Abuses of the Borderline Diagnosis: A Clinical Problem With Teaching Opportunities."

410. Searight, *see* note 401, *supra.*

411. Magill and Garrett, "Borderline Personality Disorder," at note 400.

412. Ruth Gallop, W. J. Lance, and Paul Garfinkel, "How Nursing Staff Respond to the Label 'Borderline Personality Disorder,'" *Hosp. and Comm. Psychiatry* 40 (1989):815.

413. Department of Justice, 28 C.F.R. 35.130, App. § 35.130(b)(2).

414. *Impeachment* is the legal term for attacking a person's credibility. *The Federal Rules of Evidence* do not permit an individual's character to be introduced, Rule 404(a). They do, however, permit the opinion or reputation evidence of an individual's character for untruthfulness, Rule 608(a), and they permit experts to testify "if scientific, technical, or other specialized knowledge will assist the trier of fact to understand the evidence or determine a fact in issue," Rule 702. Experts are not permitted to testify as to whether they think a witness or victim is telling the truth, United States v. Binder, 769 F.2d. 595,

602 (9th Cir. 1985); United States v. Azure, 801 F.2d 336, 340–341 (8th Cir. 1986); Snowden v. Secretary, 135 F.3d 732, 737 (11th Cir. 1998). However, psychiatric experts have been permitted to testify that people with a BPD diagnosis often lie or cheat, which is impermissible character and credibility testimony with no scientific basis; Susan Stefan, "Impact of the Law on Women With Diagnoses of Borderline Personality Disorder Related to Childhood Sexual Abuse," in *Women's Mental Health Services: A Public Health Perspective,* Bruce Levin, Andrea K. Blanch, and Ann Jennings, Eds. (Thousand Oaks, CA: Sage, 1998) at 240, 246–248.

415. Susan Stefan, *id.*

416. Michael Sean Quinn, "Memory, Repression and Expertise: Civilly Actionable Sexual Misconduct in Texas and Individual Rights," *Tex. Forum in Civ. Lib. & Civ. Rights* 3(1) (1997):65 ("all three of these diagnoses [BPD, multiple personality disorder, and somatization disorder] are charged with pejorative meaning").

417. Although attacks on multiple personality disorder and learning disabilities may be seen as directed primarily at the mental health profession, which is seen as having created them, people who claim to have these disabilities are protrayed as either credulous victims of profiteering therapists, Joan Acocella, *Creating Hysteria: Women and Multiple Personality Disorder* (New York: Jossey-Bass, 1999); Ethan Watters and Richard Ofshe, *Therapy's Delusions: The Myth of the Unconscious and the Exploitation of Today's Walking Worried* (New York: Scribner, 1999), or manipulators of a victim-oriented system, Lowery v. Young, 1992 U.S. App. LEXIS 18205*5 (7th Cir. July 28, 1992).

418. *See* discussion *supra* at p. 109.

419. Most of these lawsuits allege employment discrimination, *e.g.,* Doe v. Region 13 MHMR, 704 F.2d 1402 (5th Cir. 1983).

420. Olmstead v. L. C., *see* discussion *supra* at pp. 110–114.

421. DeLong v. Mansfield, 1994 U.S. Dist. LEXIS 13202*8 (N.D. Ca. Aug. 30, 1994).

422. 674 N.E. 2d 731 (Ohio App. 1996).

423. In law, if one party delays unreasonably in asserting a claim and the delay works to the disadvantage of the party against whom the claim is made, the claim may be barred by the doctrine of "laches." Thus, in this case, the claim that a client was not eligible for services because of an inability to serve her needs made 9 years after providing her with services might be barred.

424. She could have sued the center as a public accommodation under Title III. Her argument that the receipt of substantial federal funds converted the center into a Title II entity was not accepted by the court.

425. Doe v. Adkins, 674 N.E.2d 731, 736 (Ohio App. 1996).

426. Kathleen Harris v. Oregon Health Sciences University, 1999 U.S. Dist. LEXIS 16231 (D. Ore. Sept. 15, 1999).

427. *Id.* *11.

428. *Id.*

429. *Id.* *13.

430. *Id.* *16.

431. *Id.*

432. *Id.* *18.

433. *Id.*

434. ADA Title II Interpretive Guidance to 28 C.F.R. Sec. 35.104, "Qualified Individual With a Disability."

435. U.S. Department of Justice, policy letter to David L. Rollison, Texas Department of Mental Health and Mental Retardation, San Antonio State Schools (June 15, 1993), quoted in U.S. Commission on Civil Rights, *Helping State and Local Governments Comply With the ADA: An Assessment of How the Department of Justice Is Enforcing Title II, Subpart A of the Americans With Disabilities Act* (Washington, DC: Author, Sept. 1998) at 94.

436. Anonymous v. Goddard Riverside Community Center, 1997 U.S. Dist. LEXIS 9724*1 (S.D. N.Y. July 10, 1997).
437. O'Neal v. Alabama Department of Public Health, 826 F.Supp. 1368 (M.D. Ala. 1993).
438. 19 F.Supp. 2d 567 (N.D. W.Va. 1998).
439. *Id.* at 570.
440. Phillip Hallie, *Tales of Good and Evil, Help and Harm* (New York: HarperCollins, 1997).
441. 521 U.S. 793 (1997).
442. 521 U.S. 702 (1997).
443. Bouvia v. Superior Court, 179 Cal. App. 3d 1127, 1141 (1986).
444. The ACLU represented Elizabeth Bouvia, which deeply angered many disability rights groups; *see* Nat Hentoff, "Elizabeth Bouvia and the ACLU: 'I Used to Go to the ACLU for Help. Now They're Killing Us,'" THE VILLAGE VOICE (July 30, 1996):10.
445. *See, e.g.,* Brief in support of the respondents, filed by the Gay Men's Health Crisis and Lambda Legal Defense and Education Fund on behalf of their members with terminal illnesses and five prominent Americans with disabilities. The five prominent Americans were Evan Davis, "a partner with a major national law firm"; Hugh Gallagher, "one of the leading historians on disability in this country"; Michael Stein, "former president of the National Disability Bar Association"; Barbara Swartz, a professor; and Susan Webb, a director of an independent living center for people with disabilities.
446. *See* Brief in support of petitioners filed on behalf of the National Legal Center for the Medically Dependent and Disabled and the Michigan Handicapper Caucus, *inter alia*; brief in support of petitioners filed by Not Dead Yet and Americans Disabled for Attendant Programs Today (ADAPT); brief in support of petitioners filed on behalf of seven present and former commissioners of the U.S. Commission on Civil Rights and a former chairman of the Equal Employment Opportunity Commission.
447. Sandy Banisky, "Protesters Fear Ruling Could Be Death Sentence: Disabled Urge Upholding Ban on Assisted Suicide," BALTIMORE SUN (Jan. 9, 1997):A13A; Evan Kemp, "Could You Please Die Now? Disabled People Like Me Have Good Reason to Fear the Push for Assisted Suicide," THE WASHINGTON POST (Jan. 5, 1997):C1.
448. United States v. Tennessee, 1995 U.S. Dist. LEXIS 21090*86 and *92 (W.D. Tenn. 1995) (note that although the decision is published by West at 925 F.Supp. 1292, the court order relating to DNR appearing in an appendix is not published by West but available on LEXIS); Connecticut ARC v. Thorne, No. H-78-653 (JAC)*19 (D. Conn. Feb. 12, 1993). The facts of this case are recounted in Connecticut ARC v. Thorne, 30 F.3d 367 (2nd Cir. 1994), which considers whether the postconsent decree joinder of the Department of Public Health and Addiction Services was appropriate.
449. Connecticut ARC v. Thorne, see note 448.
450. *Id.* at 23–24.
451. Laura Prescott, former human rights officer for western Massachusetts (personal communication, Oct. 18, 1999); Prescott speculated that a combination of circumstances explained the people to whom this happened—poverty, psychiatric label, medical conditions, and being "difficult to serve" in any of a number of different ways—angry clients or clients for whom no solution seemed to work.
452. Sheku G. Kamara, Paul D. Peterson, and Jerry L. Dennis, "Prevalence of Physical Illness Among Psychiatric Inpatients Who Die of Natural Causes," *Psychiatric Services* 49 (June 1998):788.
453. Catherine Odette, "Suicide: A Verb," in *Beyond Bedlam: Contemporary Women Psychiatric Survivors Speak Out,* Jeannie Grobe, Ed. (Chicago: Third Side Press, 1995) at 183.
454. Sheku G. Kamara, Paul D. Peterson, and Jerry L. Dennis (July 1998):788, 792.
455. 891 F.Supp. 1429, 1433 (D. Ore. 1995), *rev'd* on other grounds, 107 F.3d 1382 (9th Cir. 1997).

456. 28 U.S.C. 35.130(e)(2) (Title II) and 28 C.F.R. 36.203(c)(1) (Title III).

457. 28 C.F.R., 35.130, App. (2000).

458. Brophy v. New England Sinai Hospital, 497 N.E.2d 626 (Mass. 1986); Guardianship of Grant, 747 P.2d 445 (Wash. 1987); Childs v. Abramovice, 206 Cal. App. 3d 304 (1988).

459. Causey v. St. Francis Medical Center, 719 S.2d 1072, 1075, and note 2 (La. App. 1998).

460. So far only Oregon recognizes this right by statute, and the statute is limited to people who are terminally ill. There is federal legislation proposed to override Oregon voters' choice in this matter, *see* Alissa J. Rubin, "Oregon Assisted Suicide Law at Risk," L. A. TIMES (Sept. 14, 1999):Pt. A, p. 13. California courts have intimated that they recognized the right to commit suicide, Donaldson v. Lundgren, 2 Cal. App. 4th 1614 (1992) (implying such a right exists); Klein v. Bia Hotel Corp., 41 Cal. App. 4th 1133 (1996) (refusing to decide whether such a right exists and noting the association between suicide and mental illness).

461. P. L. 101-508, codified in scattered sections at 42 U.S.C., primarily 42 U.S.C. 1395cc and 1396a (1999).

462. 652 A.2d 265 (N.J. Super. 1993).

463. *Id.* at 278.

464. *Id.* at 279.

465. *Id.* at 43, note 12.

466. Thomas J. Moore, "No Prescription for Happiness: Could It Be That Antidepressants Do Little More Than Placebos?" BOSTON GLOBE (Oct., 1999):E1.

467. In 6 out of 10 trials conducted by Eli Lilly for the Food and Drug Administration (FDA), no measurable overall difference could be detected between those treated with Prozac and those who got a placebo. One trial deemed "successful" involved eight people. Another was dismissed by the FDA because no one could explain why one investigator got radically more successful results than anyone else. Serzone, a drug for depression, was tested in eight clinical trials and produced a measurable benefit in only two. Paxil was tested in six identical protocols and failed to produce a measurable effect in three of them. As Thomas J. Moore expounded, there is "no prescription for happiness: Could it be that antidepressants do little more than placebos?"

468. Compare Norman L. Cantor, "Making Advance Directives Meaningful," *Psychology, Public Policy, and Law* 4 (1998):629, with Robert Miller, "Advance Directives for Psychiatric Treatment: A View From the Trenches," *Psychology, Public Policy, and Law* 4 (1998):728.

469. 42 U.S.C. Sec. 12101(a)(5) (2000).

470. FLA. STAT. ANN. 394.4598(1) (West, 1999).

471. FLA. STAT. ANN. 394.4598(3) (West, 1999).

472. *Id.*

473. FLA. STAT. ANN. 744.331(3)(a) (West, 1999).

474. FLA. STAT. ANN. 744.331(3)(b) (West, 1999).

475. FLA. STAT. ANN. 744.331(3)(c) (West, 1999).

476. *See, e.g.,* in re Peterson, 446 N.W.2d 669, 673 (Minn. App. 1989); Maul v. Constan, 1989 U.S. Dist. LEXIS 18377*4 (N.D. Ind. Oct. 30, 1989) ("Dr. Constan believes that Mr. Maul's schizophrenia and paranoia render him incapable of making rational choices"); Adele S. v. Kingsboro Psychiatric Center, 539 N.Y.S.2d 769 (N.Y. App. 1989) ("The hospital's expert witness testified that the appellant has been diagnosed as a chronic paranoid schizophrenic as manifested by social withdrawal and absorption in fantasy. Moreover, the patient's evaluation statement confirms the expert's testimony that the appellant has denied that she requires medication and maintains a delusional belief that her condition is improving. For these reasons, the expert's opinion that the appellant is unable to make a reasoned decision with respect to her treatment is amply

supported by the record"); in the Matter of Andrew J., 607 N.Y.S.2d 83 (N.Y. App. 1994) ("The appellant's treating psychiatrist testified that the appellant has been diagnosed as a chronic paranoid schizophrenic, as manifested by a social personality disorder. The appellant's testimony confirms the expert's testimony that the appellant has denied that he requires medication because there is nothing wrong with him. The expert's opinion that the appellant is unable to make a reasoned decision with respect to his treatment is amply supported by the record").

477. The MacArthur Study of Competence concludes that findings of incompetence could not be correlated with any particular psychiatric diagnosis; Thomas Grisso and Paul S. Appelbaum, "The MacArthur Treatment Competence Study III: Abilities of Patients to Consent to Psychiatric and Medical Treatments," *Law and Human Behavior* 19 (1995): 149; *see also* Thomas Grisso et al., "The MacArthur Treatment Competence Study II: Measure of Abilities Related to Competence to Consent to Treatment," *Law and Human Behavior* 19 (1995):127.

478. FLA. STAT. ANN. 765.204(1) (1999); 405 ILCS 5/2-101 (West, 1996); N.J. STAT. 30: 6D-4 (2000).

479. *See, e.g.,* In re Phyllis, P., et al., 695 N.E.2d 851 (Ill. 1998); Lewellen v. Sullivan, 949 F.2d 1015, 1016 (8th Cir. 1991); Rennie v. Klein, 653 F.2d 836, 846 (3rd Cir. 1981) (*en banc vacated* for other reasons); 458 U.S. 1119 (1982); Dans v. Hubbard, 506 F.Supp. 915, 935 (N.D. Ohio 1980).

480. *See, e.g.,* OCGA 9-3-73(b) (creating an exception within a statute of limitations to limit tolling for people who are incompetent because of mental retardation and mental illness to 5 years).

481. Kumar v. Hall and Chaya v. Hall, 423 S.E.2d 653 (Ga. 1992) (refusing to decide an ADA issue because it was not raised in a lower court) (note that it could not have been raised in a lower court because the ADA became effective after the date of the lower court's decision but before the date of the U.S. Supreme Court's appeal). The dissenting opinion in these cases was not based on the discriminatory treatment of people with mental retardation and mental illness but on the argument that the plaintiff, who had a traumatic brain injury, was neither mentally ill nor mentally retarded.

482. *See, e.g.,* FLA. STAT. 744.3215(j).

483. Gerben v. Holsclaw, 692 F.Supp. 557 (E.D. Pa. 1988). According to this case, the mistreatment included "repeatedly forcing hypodermic needles through Erika's abdomen without any anesthetic in order to obtain a sterile sample of her urine, when such a sample had minimal treatment value in the context of Erika's life; refusing to permit Erika to have Tylenol for discomfort, despite the fact that she had literally worn the hair off the back of her head while crying in pain, and other procedures and medications, such as repetitive withdrawals of blood for blood samples and repetitive insertions of intravenous tubes under circumstances leading to the collapse of the affected veins and the infliction of substantial pain., *id.* at 559.

484. *Id.* at 560.

485. Other commentators and lawyers have as well, *see, e.g.,* Steven Schwartz, "Abolishing Competency as a Construction of Difference: A Radical Proposal to Promote the Equality of Persons With Disabilities," *Univ. of Miami Law Rev.* 47 (1993):867, 869 ("although not all persons with disabilities are incompetent, no one can be declared to lack the ability to make decisions without simultaneously qualifying as 'an individual with a disability' under federal law").

486. Thomas Grisso and Paul S. Appelbaum, note 477 at 172. I can confirm this from 15 years of my own experience representing clients in institutional settings around the country.

487. *Id.*

488. Bethesda Lutheran Homes and Services v. Leean, 122 F.3d 443, 449–450 (7th Cir. 1997)

(the regulations were struck down as unconstitutionally impeding the patient's right to travel).

489. *See, e.g.,* Kumar v. Hall, 423 S.E.2d 653 (Ga. 1992) (a 2-year statute of limitations on medical malpractice applies to people who are incompetent because of mental retardation or mental illness; for people who are incompetent because of other reasons, a statute of limitations may toll).

490. State *ex. rel.* McCormick v. Burson, 894 S.W.2d 739, 740 (Tenn. App. 1994), *appeal den.* (1995).

491. *Id.* at 747.

492. *Id.*

493. *Id.*

494. 14 VT. STAT. ANN. 2671(a) (1999).

495. 14 VT. STAT. ANN. 2671(b)(1) and 2671(d)(1) (1999).

496. MASS. ANN. LAWS ch. 201D § 1 defines *health care* to include the treatment of the mental condition of a patient.

497. "Personal Declaration of Preferences for Mental Health Treatment," ALASKA STAT. Sec. 47.30.970 permits an individual to declare his or her preferences with regard to psychotropic medication, electroconvulsive therapy, and hospitalization.

498. ARIZ. REV. STAT. 36-3281 (1999).

499. HAW. REV. STAT. 327F-1 (1992).

500. IDAHO CODE SEC. 66-602 *et seq.* (1999).

501. 755 ILL. COMP. STAT. 43/1 (1999).

502. ME. REV. STAT. 34-B sec. 3831, 3862 (1999).

503. MINN. STAT. 253B.03–6d (1991).

504. N.C. GEN. STAT. Sec. 122C-77 (1999).

505. 43A OKLA. STAT. 11-101 *et seq.* (1998).

506. OR. REV. STAT. Sec. 127.010 *et seq.* (1997).

507. S.D. CODIFIED LAWS Sec. 27A-16-18.

508. TEX. CIV. PRAC. & REM. CODE Sec. 137.001 (1999).

509. UTAH STAT. 62A-12-501 (1996).

510. 18 VT. STAT. ANN. Sec. 7626 (1999).

511. WYO. STAT. ANN. Sec. 35-22-301 (1999).

512. Hargrove v. State of Vermont, CA No. 2: 99-CV-128 (D. Vt., filed Apr. 28, 1999).

513. 42 U.S.C. Sec. 1395 cc(f) (West 1999).

514. Steven K. Hoge, "The Patient Self-Determination Act and Psychiatric Care," *Bulletin of the Amer. Acad. of Psychiatry & Law* 22 (1994):577 ("anecdotally it seems that psychiatrists and administrators of psychiatric hospitals may be particularly uninformed about the existence of the PSDA and its provisions").

515. 42 C.F.R. 489.102(e) (2000).

516. Jeffrey Geller, "The Use of Advance Directives by Persons With Serious Mental Illness for Psychiatric Treatment," *Psychiatric Quarterly* 71 (2000):1.

517. Lester Perling, "Health Care Advance Directives: Implications for Florida Mental Health Patients," *Univ. of Miami Law Rev.* 48 (1993):193.

518. In re Rosa M., 597 N.Y.S.2d 544 (1991) (honoring advance directive refusing ECT).

519. Diana Rickard, letter (personal communication, Oct. 20, 1998).

520. After significant protests, the University of Cincinnati discontinued such experiments. Anne Michaud, "UC Drops Controversial Psychoses Tests: Critics Contend Studies Unethical," CINCINNATI ENQUIRER (May 6, 1999):A1.

521. National Bioethics Advisory Commission, *Research Involving Persons With Mental Disorders That May Affect Decision-Making Capacity I* (Rockville, MD: Author, Dec. 1998). Available on the commission's web site: http://www.bioethics.gov. The commission made 21 recommendations to improve protections for people with mental disabilities in experimental research, *id.*

522. R. Levine, *Ethics and Regulations of Clinical Research* (Baltimore: Urban & Schwarzenberg, 1981).

523. Scott Allen, "Kennedy Opens Probe of Fernald Testing: Two Participants in Experiments Due to Testify," BOSTON GLOBE (Jan. 13, 1994):28 (120 children at Fernald State School in Massachusetts); Sarah Talaly, "State Agencies Search Past for Radiation Tests," CHICAGO TRIBUNE (Jan. 22, 1994):A1 (the residents of Elgin Mental Health Center in Illinois were subjected to radiation tests).

524. *See* Orlikow v. United States, 682 F.Supp. 77 (D.D.C. 1988). For other cases involving the CIA and the U.S. Army's deliberate administration of LSD to unknowing servicemen and Army personnel, *see* United States v. Stanley, 483 U.S. 669 (1987); Glickman v. United States, 626 F.Supp. 171, 175 (S.D. N.Y. 1985); and CIA v. Sims, 471 U.S. 159 (1985).

525. *See* Orlikow v. United States, 682 F.Supp. 77, *id.*

526. 45 C.F.R. Sec. 46.101–46.409 (2000).

527. Diaz v. Hillsborough County Hospital, 165 F.R.D. 689 (M.D. Fla. 1996). This case was recently settled for $3.8 million; see Peter Aronson, "A Medical Indignity," *Natl. Law J.* (Mar. 27, 2000):A1.

528. Nina Bernstein, "Two Institutions Faulted for Tests on Children," NEW YORK TIMES (June 12, 1999):B5 (the Office for Protection From Research Risk found that Mount Sinai's experiments involving the injection of hyperactive children with fenfluoramine exceeded the limit of minimal risk to the child, failed to sufficiently inform the parents of the foreseeable risks, and was not properly reviewed by Mount Sinai's IRB and similar deficiencies in similar City University of New York [CUNY] experiments).

529. Tracy Weber, "1997 Drug Test on Teenage Inmates Probed," LOS ANGELES TIMES (Aug. 16, 1999):A1 (the experimental use of Depakote, an anti-epileptic drug, on teenagers from 14 to 18 years old to see if it would prevent violence, although none of the teenagers had a condition for which the drug had been approved by the FDA; the California Youth Authority admitted that this experiment violated state laws).

530. T. D. v. New York State Office of Mental Health et al., 91 N.Y.S.2d 860 (N.Y. 1997).

531. 971 F.2d 1487 (10th Cir. 1992).

532. *See* T. D. v. New York State Office of Mental Health et al. (1997).

533. Vera Hassner Sharaz (personal communication, Aug. 30, 1999).

534. Al Guart, "Drug-Test Kid's Kin File Suit for $60M," N. Y. POST (May 12, 1999):3.

535. *See* Vera Hassner Sharaz at note 533 (1999).

536. National Bioethics Advisory Commission, Recommendation 3 (Dec. 1998), *see* note 521.

537. National Bioethics Advisory Commission, Recommendation 8 (Dec. 1998), *see* note 521.

Chapter 5
DISCRIMINATION IN THE DELIVERY OF SERVICES
TO PEOPLE WITH PSYCHIATRIC DISABILITIES

This chapter examines the application of the Americans With Disabilities Act (ADA) of 1990 to the complex systems that provide medical and health care services and income maintenance to people with mental disabilities. Some of these service delivery systems are private, such as disability and health insurance obtained as employment benefits; these are discussed in chapter 6. Some have historically been publicly funded and administered, such as the state mental health programs discussed in chapter 4 and the Medicaid and vocational rehabilitation programs discussed in this chapter. Some major service delivery systems for people with mental disabilities involve a mixture of public and private funding, administration, and service provision, including Social Security, Medicare, and workers' compensation. In the last 5 years, state have been increasingly contracting with the private sector to provide traditional state services, such as health care for the indigent and mental health care.

The ways in which all of these service delivery programs intersect—the linking of income benefits under Temporary Assistance to Needy Families (TANF)[1] and the current Supplemental Security Insurance (SSI) program with medical and health benefits under Medicaid—have enormous cost and policy implications for people with disabilities and society at large. These programs are expensive and generate a tremendous bureaucracy. Social Security Disability Insurance (SSDI) and SSI serve more than 11 million people with disabilities each year,[2] paying out more than $5 billion per month in benefits. Despite these sums, the individual benefit amounts are barely enough to live on. The average SSI benefit is $379.43 a month; the average SSDI benefit is about $740.[3] Approximately 59% of the people receiving SSI who are under the age of 65 are receiving benefits because of mental disabilities.[4]

Every health care provider in the country, "including all State and municipally managed hospitals, nursing homes, health plans, health care programs, health insurance, and all health care services, direct or contractual,"[5] falls under the scope of either Title II or Title III of the ADA. Most health care organizations also fall under Section 504 of the Rehabilitation Act of 1973 as entities receiving federal funds.

The ADA does not permit plaintiffs to sue federal defendants.[6] Most service delivery systems for people with mental disabilities, however, involve either joint federal–state ventures, such as Medicaid, which are subject to Title II of the ADA,[7] or private entities, such as insurance carriers or health maintenance organizations (HMOs), which are subject to Title III of the ADA.

The coexistence of disability benefits and the right to be free from discrimination on the basis of disability has been seen as dissonant by commentators,[8] courts,[9] congressional representatives, and members of the general public.[10] As discussed in chapter 3, it it not seen as incongruent when other groups receive benefits on the basis of a certain characteristic and protection from false stereotypes about that characteristic. Women may be entitled to maternity leave and freedom from discrimination on the basis of pregnancy. Military personnel may receive housing and medical benefits as well as protection from discrimination on the basis of their status. Likewise, some people with disabilities may be entitled to receive benefits on the basis of their disability. All should be free of unwarranted stereotypes and over-generalizations—even by the organizations providing the disability benefits.

Many aspects of service delivery systems have been subject to litigation under the ADA. Lawsuits under either Section 504 or the ADA have challenged budget choices and budget cuts,[11] age limits for welfare assistance and other forms of state welfare "reform,"[12] the inadequate provision of family reunification services by state social service agencies,[13] the operation of juvenile justice systems,[14] prison release programs,[15] and the structuring of workers' compensation systems.[16]

The ADA and the Rehabilitation Act have been applied to programs like SSI and SSDI, challenging complex application or appeal processes,[17] the failure to independently inquire into mental disability when evidence of mental disability is obvious,[18] inaccessible service delivery sites,[19] and Social Security regulations regarding deeming income or eligibility for benefits that explicitly or implicitly discriminate on the basis of disability.[20]

The Medicaid program has also been the subject of litigation. The most famous application of the ADA to the Medicaid program was not the result of litigation. It occurred when Dr. Louis Sullivan, Secretary of the U.S. Department of Health and Human Services (DHHS) in the Bush administration, relied on the Rehabilitation Act and the ADA to reject Oregon's Medicaid reform proposal. After conducting a poll of its citizens, Oregon had ranked medical services in order of priority and wanted to reimburse Medicaid services according to these priorities. DHHS refused to approve the proposal because some of the choices about who would receive medical services and who would not were overtly discriminatory and because the methodology of the poll resulted in the incorporation of discriminatory assumptions about the correlation between disability and quality of life into the rationing choices under the plan. Sullivan's Democrat successor shared both the assumption that the ADA was applicable to the Oregon plan and the belief that the plan discriminated on the basis of disability. This decision and its implications are discussed in detail below.

Discrimination in the Provision of Health Care Services

People with mental disabilies are often denied health care or get substandard health care. This happens to people with mental disabilities in part because they are often poor and poor people tend to receive substandard health care. It happens in part because state mental hospitals do not provide good medical care.

People with mental disabilities also avoid seeking medical care. Women with histories of physical and sexual abuse, who make up a staggeringly high percentage of women with diagnoses of serious mental illness,[21] avoid gynecological care and are less likely to receive mammograms and pap smears.[22] Women with mental illness generally receive inadequate gynecological care.[23] But middle- and upper-income people with psychiatric diagnoses who do seek medical assistance often fail to receive it because of the diminution of credibility associated with psychiatric disability and the tendency of medical professionals to interpret all reported symptoms through the lens of the individual's perceived mental illnses. This especially is the case for women.[24]

Several people who testified before Congress in support of the ADA raised this issue. The following story is one typical example:

> Carolyn from Hyannis reported to her mental health workers that she was pregnant. She was assumed to be delusional and ignored. Later, she sought services at the Cape Cod [ER] with what was thought to be delusional [*sic*] and was ignored, and later that evening, while wandering the streets, she miscarried with serious hemorrhaging.[25]

Emergency rooms (ERs) often deny medical care to people with mental illness, as described above, or interpret their physical symptoms as symptoms of mental illness and inappropriately transfer them to psychiatric hospitals.[26]

Nursing homes also have refused to admit or tried to discharge troublesome clients with mental disabilities, or provided residents with mental illness with inferior treatment. This is a complex issue because nursing homes are prohibited by federal statute from inappropriately admitting patients with mental disabilities who do not need skilled nursing care. However, they are prohibited by the ADA and Section 504 of the Rehabilitation Act and often by local licensure regulations from rejecting or discharging patients who need nursing care simply because those patients also have psychiatric diagnoses or behavioral difficulties.[27] In addition, they are required to provide "specialized services" to residents with mental retardation who do not need a high level of medical care but who do need specialized services in connection with their mental retardation.[28]

There are various legal causes of action for the denial of health care that are distinct from discrimination claims. For example, people covered by benefit plans through their employers who believe that they have been wrongly denied benefits can—and in many cases must[29]—bring an action under the Employment Retirement Income Security Act (ERISA).[30] People needing emergency care who are turned away from an ER or transferred before they have been stabilized can file a claim under the Emergency Medical Treatment and Active Labor Act (EMTALA),[31] although plaintiffs with diagnoses of mental illness have not done well in this area.[32] Nursing homes are covered by state licensing requirements, the Nursing Home Reform Act,[33] and a number of Medicaid regulations. In several egregious cases, courts have approved tort suits for the intentional infliction of emotional distress by ER staff and physicians who ignored patients in need.[34]

People with mental disabilities report many different kinds of discrimination in trying to access health care:[35]

1. the refusal of health care professionals to credit the report of physical symptoms, which leads to people being turned away without receiving the medical care they need
2. the interpretation of reports of physical symptoms as psychiatric symptoms, so that seeking medical treatment results in the commitment to a psychiatric facility
3. the provision of necessary services with blatant, overt hostility: Many women who inflict cuts on themselves report that medical personnel refuse to use anaesthetic when stitching the wounds, saying that this provides an incentive for the women to cease their behavior[36]
4. the failure of psychiatric institutions to provide their residents with adequate medical care

5. the disproportionate placement of do not resuscitate (DNR) orders in the
    files of patients with mental disabilities
6. "dumping"—the inappropriate transfer by hospitals of disproportionate
    numbers of psychiatric patients.

Emergency Rooms[37]

Both the research literature and anecdotal evidence are clear that people who have
or are perceived as having psychiatric disabilities are treated differentially and disadvantageously in ERs.[38] Although cases challenging this treatment have been filed
for some time,[39] the first case brought under the ADA seeking equal access to and
equal treatment in ERs under Title III of the ADA on behalf of a client with a
psychiatric disability was only recently filed and survived a motion to dismiss.[40]

There are a number of ways in which people with psychiatric disabilities are
discriminated against in ERs. First, their reports of medical problems are likely to
be minimized. As one woman wrote,

> you have severe abdominal pains again in the middle of the night. The last time the
> Emergency Room (ER) doctor said to come over right away when you get the pains
> to better diagnose them. So you go. A different ER doctor is there. He asks you the
> preliminary questions. Then he comes to, "Are you taking any medications?" After
> you name the psychotropic drugs you're on, his face changes to one of skepticism.
> Suddenly he doesn't believe the pains are real. He finds nothing in his examination.
> And he says he doesn't have any notes from any other ER doctor (though your last
> visit was only a week ago). He doesn't believe you. You're malingering, or hypo-
> chondriachal, or psychotic, or worse.[41]

There is abundant documentation that people with psychiatric disabilities frequently suffer serious and substantial medical problems. Over the past 20 years, the
medical literature has consistently and explicitly called for careful medical workups
of people presenting psychiatric crises in ERs.[42] Both mental health professionals
and ER professionals have acknowledged that the medical complaints of people with
psychiatric disabilities are not taken seriously. The failure to take seriously the medical complaints of people with psychiatric disabilities has resulted in serious injuries
that could have been avoided, a tragic number of known deaths[43] (sometimes as a
side effect of the medication prescribed for their mental condition), and any number
of silent, buried mistakes—poor people with no relatives, no advocates, and few to
mourn their unnecessary deaths. This is the essence of discrimination on the basis
of psychiatric disability: the loss of credibility simply because of a diagnosis, the
minimization of complaints of pain, and the interpretation of all attempts at communication through the lens of diagnosis and disability.

Another facet of discrimination in ERs is that even when people with psychiatric
disabilities receive needed medical treatment, it is often given with overt hostility
and blame. People with psychiatric disabilities who frequently come into ER are
known as "habitual offenders."[44] Women who have histories of sexual abuse and
cut themselves, or who try to kill themselves, and who often receive a diagnosis of
borderline personality disorder are often treated by the ER personnel with hostility
and contempt. This kind of treatment is a consistent theme in both the writings of

people with psychiatric disabilities and in the writings of the health care professionals who treat them.

> I went to the hospital last night. Such a weird experience going to a place that is supposed to help people who are suffering or sick. Some of the doctors and nurses are kind. However, their attitudes ooze with condescension and hostility most of the time. I have been stitched up without freezing because if I can do "this" to myself, I don't need anything for pain. . . . Some of them say, "Why would an intelligent person like you do 'this'?" or "Why would anyone as smart as you want to die?" or "What you need is a boyfriend (husband)." When I tell them I'm a lesbian, they say "Oh" in a knowing voice, like that explains everything.[45]

One man with a mental disability and a hearing and speech impairment described the worst discrimination he had encountered: "When I was being treated at an emergency room and the physician's assistant and nurse made fun of my speech. . . . I am very uncomfortable to this day when I go into emergency rooms."[46] Hospital staff were characterized by one respondent as "treat[ing] me harshly and rudely in ways that they would not if they did not feel I have a 'disability.' "[47] Even when people are not treated with overt hostility, they report being treated with indifference or disrespect.

> I went to the emergency room of a neighborhood hospital to ask for a 3-day supply of Prolixin to last until I could get a new prescription. The ER doctor interviewed me about my symptoms and I did not feel well enough to insist he interview me in private, not in the public hall. My apartment building superintendent came in with his son, who had hurt his hand, and when I turned around I said hello and realized he had heard everything I said.[48]

Some people with psychiatric diagnoses are afraid to go to ERs or even hospitals for tests because they fear that they could be institutionalized: "My psych history means . . . anytime I might go to a hospital for any purpose at all, an emergency or a test, they will see my psych history and I could be forced into psych treatment against my will."[49] This fear was repeated in many of the survey responses: "I never tell my doctors my psychiatric history for fear of having my physical problems mentally pathologized and/or finding myself on the psych ward (or in court) for normally crazy behavior."[50] The fear is not unreasonable. At least one case has been brought on behalf of individuals who went to the ER for treatment of physical illnesses and were detained for psychiatric treatment on the basis of histories of psychiatric treatment.[51]

ER personnel have also been sued (unsuccessfully) for not responding to the psychiatric symptoms of individuals who appeared for medical care.[52] Some of the problems surrounding the fear of forced commitment could be addressed by amending EMTALA on the federal level to clarify that no medical or mental health professional would be held liable under EMTALA for a failure to involuntarily commit any individual.[53] Similar legislation could be passed on a state level, immunizing physicians from tort claims for failure to involuntarily commit individuals presenting at the ER. Some states already have such legislation.[54] In other states, courts have held that this immunity exists as a matter of law.[55] As a practical matter, most tort cases charging doctors for the failure to commit already end with this result, but statutory clarification would dispose of the cases on a motion to dismiss and would give medical professionals the message that they could attend to the medical problem presented by psychiatric patients without fear of liability for not forcing psychiatric treatment on the individual.

Medical Settings

Although some authors have attributed the substandard care received by people with psychiatric disabilities in ER settings to the urgent time pressures of the ER and the fact that the doctor is less likely to know the individual, the kinds of discrimination identified in ER settings are replicated in regular medical settings. Having more time to spend with a patient or a longer history with a patient does not seem to mitigate the common practices of discrimination.

As in emergency care, in regular medical settings one of the most common complaints is that physical problems are ignored or interpreted as psychiatric symptoms. One survey respondent wrote that the worst discrimination she had experienced was "Medical—thought real physical problems were in my head. Such as a herniated disc that I had two back operations on."[56] Another wrote, "I had mononucleosis and the VA [Veteran's Administration] doctor told me it was a psych problem."[57] Several people responded to the survey question "Are you vulnerable to abuse because you have or are perceived as having a disability?" with references to the medical profession: "Providers of mental health and physical health services have disregarded my needs because of my diagnosis (they consider the diagnosis and sometimes disregard a physical ailment)."[58] Case law backs up these reports. In one case, a man with Ormond's disease[59] who had been mistakenly treated as having a mental illness had his doctor draft a notice of his diagnosis and proper treatment, as well as a warning of the dangers of misdiagnosing his condition as psychiatric.[60] This notice was supposed to be the first page of his medical charts. Despite seeing the notice from the doctor, the VA continued to treat the man as though he had a mental illness. The 10th Circuit refused to overturn an award of over $5 million, including punitive damages.[61]

The concern that people with psychiatric disabilities have about going to ERs for medical care and ending up in the psychiatric ward exists for hospital admissions as well. One survey respondent wrote that hospital treatment had been the worst form of discrimination experienced: "Taken for pneumonia, driven by surprise and force to a so-called psych ward . . . frustrated, appoverished [sic], time lost, lungs' situation aggravated."[62] Several cases involve situations where patients went to a doctor for such routine medical care as physicals and ended up in psychiatric wards.[63]

Treatment by medical professionals can be discriminatory because of doctors' stereotypes about people with mental illness. One respondent complained that a doctor refused to reveal the side effects of a medication even when asked: "I've been told if I know them [the side effects], I'll get them."[64] Another respondent, a lawyer, wrote, "Health care for physical problems has become more difficult since my disability has become known. I receive unsolicited advice and feel I receive a lower standard of care."[65]

Litigation under the ADA against medical and dental professionals has so far been almost completely limited to the outright refusal to treat a patient because of his or her disability. Most of these cases involve patients who were HIV positive or who had AIDS.[66] A small subset of cases challenge the failure of doctors or hospitals to provide interpreters for patients or patients' family members who are deaf.[67] A handful of other cases involve different claims: a doctor who angrily refused to treat a child with lesions and ejected him and his parents from the premises, shouting at them,[68] and a hospital charged with mistreating a patient with epilepsy.[69] Only one survey respondent indicated that some doctors refused to treat her medical problems at all when they learned she had a psychiatric history.[70] So far, the ADA has not been used to challenge medical doctors' failure to treat, or the inappropriate treatment of, patients with psychiatric diagnoses.

Hospital "Dumping" of Psychiatric Patients

One of the greatest difficulties with trying to assess discrimination against people with mental disabilities is that data are rarely collected about the ways in which they are treated. The "first national look at psychiatric patient-dumping," reported in late 1997,[71] showed that "sixty-five percent of U.S. hospitals that treat mental patients 'dump' those who are unable to pay on other facilities." *Dumping* in this study is defined as the "economically motivated transfer" of patients, usually to a publicly funded facility, rather than a transfer motivated by clinical concerns.[72]

The data in this study are preliminary and subject to various limitations, but nevertheless they represent the first nationwide attempt to measure economically motivated transfers of mental patients from private hospitals. In almost 20% of areas surveyed in the study, private, nonprofit hospitals—who receive tax breaks premised in part on providing service to indigent patients—were the worst offenders.[73] It is clear that "transfers from private to public inpatient facilities, when insurance benefits are exhausted, are more common for patients with ADM [alcohol, drug abuse, and mental health] disorders than for general medical and surgical patients."[74]

One reason advanced for the fact that mental patients appear more likely to be transferred to public facilities is that they are deemed not to be in "medically unstable" conditions; therefore, the transfers do not implicate EMTALA. However, this conclusion itself raises interesting questions regarding the possibility of discrimination. Is it discrimination to assume that psychiatric patients do not meet EMTALA's definition of medical instability? Could it be that the very conclusion that they are not medically unstable is itself a form of discrimination? If they are not medically unstable, what are these patients doing in hospitals anyway?

Denial of Nursing Home Care

Privately operated nursing homes[75] are covered under Title III of the ADA, as well as under Section 504 of the Rehabilitation Act, because all receive Medicaid and Medicare benefits. State-operated nursing homes are covered by Title II of the ADA. Both private and state-operated nursing homes are subject to a variety of different forms of federal and state oversight under the federal Omnibus Budget Reconciliation Act (OBRA) of 1987 and Medicaid and Medicare requirements.[76]

In 1987, Congress dramatically altered the legal obligations of nursing homes toward their clients, especially in the areas of intake and discharge.[77] The new laws required screening at intake to prevent nursing homes from inappropriately accepting patients from psychiatric and retardation facilities where the patients did not have the need for the intensive medical services and supervision provided by nursing homes.[78] At the same time, the laws protected people who were already in nursing homes from involuntary transfers or discharges unless certain conditions were met and required opportunities for notice or appeal.

Discrimination against people with mental disabilities, or behavioral manifestations of physical disabilities, is present in the nursing home setting in a variety of ways.[79] One discriminatory practice is the denial of nursing home admission to individuals in need of nursing home care on the basis of psychiatric disability or behavioral manifestations.[80] A second is the attempt to discharge existing patients because of these aspects of their condition or behavior.[81] One emerging issue is the increasing use of segregated units, wards, or floors for people with particular disabilities, such as Alzheimer's disease.

The laws under OBRA permit a patient to be transferred involuntarily or discharged if he or she endangers the safety of other residents.[82] One of the most frequent grounds for the discharge or transfer of a nursing home patient is that he or she is disruptive or endangers the safety of other residents.[83] A frequent technique is to send a resident to a psychiatric hospital for evaluation and then refuse to take the patient back.[84] Nursing homes take the position that sending people for a psychiatric evaluation is neither a discharge nor a transfer triggering the procedural rights of notice and due process; in practice, however, once the person is out the door without notice to his or her relatives, it is easier for the nursing home to fill the bed and refuse to readmit that person.

Some of these attempts to discharge a nursing home resident have been challenged as discriminatory under Section 504 of the Rehabilitation Act[85] or the ADA. The obvious questions under the ADA are the extent to which the OBRA standard permitting transfer on grounds of safety relates to the "direct threat" exception to the ADA and how the OBRA requirement that services be offered to ameliorate the behavioral problem relates to the ADA requirement of reasonable accommodation. Under the ADA, "direct threat" is only a defense if the facility can show that no reasonable accommodation could have ameliorated the threat. Because an entity is required to offer reasonable accommodations unless such accommodation fundamentally alters the nature of the entity, one could argued that the ADA requires more than OBRA. The cases are mixed on the extent to which it is part of the fundamental mission of nursing homes to provide services to clients with behavioral problems. The 3rd Circuit in *Wagner v. Fair Acres*[86] rejected the claim of a nursing home that it could not serve a prospective client with behavioral problems related to Alzheimer's disease. Indeed, behavioral problems are among the most common manifestations of Alzheimer's disease, and people with Alzheimer's make up a substantial proportion of the population of nursing homes.[87] Therefore, it seems fair to require that nursing homes develop the expertise to work with these individuals rather than discharging them.

Denial of Organ Transplants[88]

Although it is not widely known or discussed, people with certain kinds of disabilities, such as psychiatric disabilities, rarely receive organ transplants. A patient's poverty may play a part in the decisions never to refer him or her for a transplant,[89] to provide less treatment,[90] or to reject him or her for an organ transplant. It is difficult to parse out the effects of discrimination on the basis of economic status from discrimination on the basis of disability. But the standards used to make organ transplant decisions result in the screening out of people whose economic status is equivalent to other candidates and whose health is otherwise good, simply on the basis of perceived mental disability.

"Kidney transplant candidates undergo an evaluation process in order to identify medical, social, and psychological factors that may affect successful outcomes,"[91] for example. Every transplantation center in the country has both psychologists and psychiatrists on its evaluation team, and although different transplantation centers have different policies on issues such as age, cardiac and gastrointestinal testing of transplantation candidates, and the impact of drug abuse or a history of drug abuse on approval for a transplant, the "most uniform" consideration adopted by "eighty percent of the responding centers" involves "those with a history of psychosis."[92] Responding centers require a psychiatric evaluation when considering such a candidate for organ transplant.

What emerges from articles about transplantation is that compliance with medication, diet, and various regimens after transplantation is vital to the success of the transplant, and people with psychiatric diagnoses are simply assumed to be much more likely to be noncompliant. One typical article recommended a much greater emphasis on the likelihood of compliance in selecting transplant recipients and stated that a crucial component of such a strategy would involve "determining the existence of any prior or current history of mental health disorders or diminished intellectual capacity, prior or current history of substance abuse."[93] In an article reporting the decision of a transplant center to become the second in the country to perform transplants for people who are HIV positive, the reporter discussed the perception that there is a "sin test" used in deciding who gets organ transplants. In denying the allegation of a sin test, "transplant experts" cited the fact that "people with *some forms* of mental illness or mild mental impairments such as Down Syndrome received transplants."[94]

This was technically correct, although just barely. At the time the article was published, two people with Down syndrome had received heart transplants in the United States.[95] In both cases, threats of legal action under the ADA were necessary to persuade doctors to even consider the people for transplant purposes. Sandra Jensen, the first mentally retarded recipient of an organ transplant, was an activist with Down syndrome who held a job in a cafeteria, campaigned for greater awareness of the rights of people with disabilities, was present on the White House lawn for the signing of the ADA, and had an IQ of 45.[96] Jodi Riddle was the second recipient. "Riddle's cardiologist told [her mother] that there was no transplant list for Jodi. 'He said it was because she wasn't a productive person. That hurt and angered me.'"[97] The mother went to a lawyer with the California Protection and Advocacy Agency, who drafted a letter explaining to the cardiologist that the ADA did not permit these kinds of judgments to be made.[98]

After Sandra Jensen received the first heart transplant given to a person with Down syndrome, the California legislature passed a law the prohibits discrimination in the selection of transplant recipients on the basis of disability. Since 1996, Stanford Medical Center "no longer turns away mentally disabled people without first examining them."[99] Arthur Kaplan, a well-known bioethicist professor, noted that the passage of the ADA has increased the "pressure to be more inclusive."[100] But with doctors generally responsible for the initial referral to transplant centers and transplant centers still doing psychiatric evaluations, there may need to be more investigation on the impact that having a psychiatric history has on a person's chances of receiving an organ transplant. In addition, there are still many organ transplant centers with overt, blanket policies that exclude people explicitly on the basis of disability unrelated to the transplant. Just over one quarter of the transplant centers in this country would not consider someone with an IQ under 70 for a transplant.[101]

In the case of the Oregon Medicaid experiment, the discrimination was also overt. In its initial attempt to reform its Medicaid system, Oregon opted to fund liver transplants for all people with cirrhosis of the liver, except people whose cirrhosis was the result of alcoholism. This distinction was ruled to violate the requirements of the ADA by DHHS Secretary Sullivan,[102] and even those most critical of the rejection of the Oregon plan conceded that this particular choice did violate the ADA.[103]

However, some people with disabilities have expressed fear of a different form of discrimination: being too readily selected as donors. One woman's experiences with society's treatment of her physical disability "has kept me from signing the organ-donor card, despite many reassurances from medical people. Between being older, female, not physically prime, and not even anyone's mother, I'm afraid of being more valued for my very efficient internal organs than as a human being."[104]

Both the policies and practices of organ transplant centers are ripe for examination by advocates for people with psychiatric disabilities. Of course, in such an examination, advocates should be aware of the multiple factors that operate to screen many people with psychiatric disabilities from ever making it to the organ transplant centers, ranging from the prejudices of physicians to the pressures of poverty.

Medicaid and the ADA

The Medicaid program is a federal–state program in which the federal government reimburses a certain percentage of state expenditures for services that are deemed medically necessary for individuals who are qualified for the Medicaid program. In return for the federal reimbursement, the state must certify that these services are delivered promptly and equitably throughout the state. Despite these requirements, many mentally disabled individuals eligible for Medicaid are put on a waiting list —sometimes for years.[105] Federal courts have ordered the states to provide services to individuals on the waiting list in a number of cases.[106]

The emphasis in the ADA on integrating people with disabilities into the community and providing services in as integrated a setting as possible is ironic because Congress itself has created enormous fiscal incentives through the Medicaid program to support segregation and institutionalization in psychiatric hospitals and nursing homes. These incentives make it virtually impossible in some cases for people to receive care in their community or in their own home. Congress has structured Medicaid reimbursement to encourage placement in institutions, nursing homes, and private hospitals rather than to use home health care, personal attendants, and respite care.[107]

As currently structured, states are required to cover nursing home care under Medicaid, but Medicaid pays for most home- and community-based support services for people with mental disabilities only if the state applies for and is granted a home- and community-based services waiver, which permits the state to provide services in the community for people who would otherwise be institutionalized if the community services cost the same as or less than institutional services.[108] This waiver could, in fact, be used to remove all inappropriately institutionalized people, as long as the community services were not more expensive than their institutional counterparts. The requirement that the cost of the community services not exceed that of institutional services is known as "cost neutrality." Because Medicaid does not reimburse states for dollars spent on people in state psychiatric institutions,[109] however, the cost-neutrality requirement makes it difficult to use the home- and community-based services waiver for people with psychiatric disabilities.

The Medicaid program pays for care in nursing facilities, hospitals, and institutions but has, since its inception, excluded "services in an institution for tuberculosis or mental disease" except for people over age 65 and (since 1972) under age 21.[110] Native Americans, whose mental health services are paid for through Indian Health Service contracts, are not subject to the institution for mental disease (IMD) exclusion. Given the fiscal incentives, it is not surprising that people over age 65 and Native Americans are institutionalized in disproportionately large numbers in state mental hospitals. The rationale for the IMD exclusion, which dates back to the pre-Medicaid era of the first federal assistance program for medical care in 1950, appears to have been that because the institutionalization of people with mental illnesses was traditionally a state function, Medicaid reimbursement in this area would give states an undeserved windfall of federal funds.[111]

The exclusion of mental hospitals from Medicaid reimbursement can be seen as discriminating against people with mental illness. Indeed, several cases were brought to make this assertion.[112] The U.S. Supreme Court rejected a similar challenge under the equal protection clause of the 14th Amendment to the denial of SSI benefits to residents of IMDs.[113]

Although the IMD exclusion encouraged many states to discharge people to the community where they could receive federally funded SSI payments and federally matched Medicaid payments, it did not provide states with funds to support community-based treatment programs for these people. Rather, it created an incentive to transinstitutionalize people from IMDs into nursing facilities. This incentive was so great, in fact, that it induced a virtual tidal wave of transinstitutionalization, including the transfer of many younger adults to nursing homes.[114] Ultimately, the federal government, acting through the Health Care Financing Administration (HCFA), cracked down on the practice.[115] Congress later further limited this incentive by passing the Nursing Home Reform Amendments as part of the Omnibus Budget Reconciliation Act of 1987, which required nursing homes to screen patients to prevent inappropriate admission of people with psychiatric and developmental disabilities.[116]

Congress and the executive branch have taken some steps to reduce the states' use of institutions. In 1981, the same year that Congress passed the home- and community-based services waiver option, HCFA issued *Interpretive Guidance for ICF/MR* [Intermediate Care Facilities for the Mentally Retarded] *Serving 15 or Fewer Persons,* which was intended to indicate to the states that Medicaid ICF/MR funds could be used to pay for care in facilities of 4 to 15 people. In 1990 Congress amended Title XIX to permit states to pay for community-supported living arrangements under Medicaid for people with developmental disabilities (although not for people with psychiatric disabilities).[117] Beginning in 1995, all states were given the option of providing personal care services as part of Medicaid-supported services.[118] On June 24, 1997, Rep. Newt Gingrich (R-GA) and 76 cosponsors introduced in the House, and Sen. Russell D. Feingold (D-WI) introduced in the Senate, the Medicaid Community Attendant Services Act of 1997[119] (popularly known as "MiCasa") to permit Medicaid to cover community-based attendant care services for anyone entitled to nursing facility or intermediate care facility services. Although this legislation failed, its provisions were reintroduced by Sen. Arlen Specter (R-PA) and Sen. Tom Harkin (D-Iowa) in the Medicaid Community Attendant Services and Support Act (MiCassa; S.1935) and were referred to the Senate Finance Committee, where it languishes without cosponsors.

However, Medicaid and Medicare *do* reimburse for mental health care provided in general hospital settings. One study found that Medicaid and Medicare paid for about one-third of all days spent for mental disorders in general hospitals in 1985.[120] Not surprisingly, the locus of treatment of mental disorders has been shifting sharply from state psychiatric institutions to general hospital settings.[121] Indeed, "it was not until the passage of the Medicaid and Medicare legislation that psychiatric inpatient treatment in general hospitals outside the formal unit began to explode."[122]

Not only is the federal funding incentive structure still powerfully skewed in favor of institutionalization, but most states also have a mental health funding structure that reinforces institutionalization.[123] Bills in Congress attempting to create equality between funding for institutional and community treatment, even when supported by the majority of the professional community, have not succeeded.[124]

It is, of course, hardly unprecedented for Congress to pass civil rights bills extolling integration with one hand while continuing to appropriate funds to support discriminatory and segregationist structures with the other.[125] Litigation under the former may make only minor dents in discrimination and segregation as long as the fiscal structures remain undisturbed.[126] However, the existence of a federal funding mechanism—the home- and community-based services waiver program—to accomplish the transfer of people from institutions into the community means that states do have access to significant sources of funds to place unnecessarily segregated people into appropriate community placements. Because many states permit their mental health departments to shift funding between line items as necessary, most states also have the internal administrative structure to facilitate moving people from institutions into the community.

Of course, to benefit from Medicaid, a person with mental disabilities must first apply and be approved for the program. The process of applying for benefits is difficult for someone without mental disabilities, and the delay in processing the applications and receiving the benefits has been the subject of numerous lawsuits.[127] Recently, numerous class action suits charge that states are violating the Medicaid Act by discouraging people from applying for Medicaid,[128] not acting on Medicaid referrals from other agencies,[129] arbitrarily reducing Medicaid services such as personal care services without notice or hearing,[130] and conducting the "fair hearings" appeals unfairly.[131] These actions, which have been successful, suggest that courts are more receptive to claims involving violations of the Medicaid Act and of procedural due process claims than they have been for some time. Success in these cases depends on a finding that recipients have a right to enforce provisions of the Medicaid statute and its regulations that benefit them. Although results are mixed on whether and when Medicaid confers such a private right of action, a number of courts have held that recipients can enforce certain provisions of the Medicaid statute.[132]

Finally, if people are denied care for which the government is being billed, especially on a systemic basis, there is the possibility of a *qui tam* action under the False Claims Act,[133] which permits an individual who has knowledge of false claims being presented to the government to bring an action on behalf of the government and to receive up to 30% of any money recovered for the government if the case is proven.[134] Because the government pays billions of dollars in Medicare and Medicaid claims each year and estimates that it loses about $20 billion a year (10% of its budget) to fraudulent claims,[135] a citizen's recovery under this act could be—and has been—substantial.[136] The citizen is not limited to exposing claims made for his or her own care that are false. In fact, the *qui tam* claim of one accountant that Columbia Health Care Systems used a system of "double books" in charging the government involved thousands of people and potentially hundreds of millions of dollars.[137]

MCO–HMO Responsibilities

Given the importance of health care in the lives of people with disabilities, surprisingly few cases have been brought challenging discrimination practices by the newly emerging health care systems: managed care organizations (MCOs) and health maintenance organizations (HMOs). Some commentators have explained this phenomenon by reference to the difficulty of understanding how the health care system operates: "Because the health care system is so vast and complex, the number of civil rights challenges to its conduct have been few in relation to civil rights efforts in other human service areas with similar histories of de jure segregation, such as education."[138]

Nearly three-quarters of U.S. workers with health insurance receive coverage through an HMO, a preferred provider organization, or a point-of-service plan.[139] In the public sector, HCFA is now the largest purchaser of managed care in the country, accounting for coverage through Medicaid and Medicare of about 19 million Americans.[140] To understand the nature of litigation involving HMOs one has to understand procedural concepts, such as preemption and complex federal statutes like ERISA; for many lawyers, let alone ordinary citizens, this is a difficult task.

The final layer of complexity is added by the fast-growing trend of states' contracting out their Medicaid services to private HMOs and MCOs.[141] Almost every state in the country has adopted managed care in the provision of some or all of its health care services. Some states have different managed care programs for mental health services than they do for other medical services;[142] others include mental health services in the general program but provide an enhanced package of benefits for adults with serious mental illnesses, children with serious emotional disturbances, and children in or at risk of state custody. The ADA mandates that the state continues to be ultimately responsible for any discrimination in the policies and practices of those with whom it contracts to provide services.[143] Nor does receipt of a Medicaid waiver from the HCFA permit a state to waive the antidiscrimination requirements of the ADA.[144]

Potential discrimination against people with psychiatric disabilities in the provision of mental health services through managed care has been described in myriad and often paradoxical ways, depending on one's perspectives about managed care. For example, are "carve outs" for mental health care a form of discrimination or a provision of extra protection? Do managed care plans devoted solely to what is now called "behavioral health" constitute impermissible segregation or a way of providing needed expertise and specialized services?

Some scholars of health law have suggested that public mental health services should be gradually integrated into the larger health maintenance system[145] because the prevalence of medical problems among people with diagnoses of severe mental illness makes it more sensible and efficient for the same system to serve both.[146] Others have maintained that only through separate carve outs can people with serious mental illnesses be adequately served,[147] warning of the tendency of MCOs to disenroll people with serious mental illnesses, provide them with inadequate mental health services (referred to as HMO "skimping"),[148] or to underserve clients with the most severe mental disabilities.[149]

Attitudes among mental health lawyers are similarly mixed. Patient advocates in Montana opposed the state's attempt to exclude the State Hospital and Mental Health Nursing Care Center from the managed care contract to provide mental health services.[150] Their position was that the hospital was wasteful, inefficient, and served primarily as an employment resource for the Town of Anaconda, which was economically devastated after being abandoned by the copper interests that created it. However, the patient advocates welcomed managed care at the State Hospital because they assumed it would reduce both admissions and the length of stay for patients: "Every other person in the system, and Medicaid itself, will be protected from unnecessary or inappropriate medical treatment services by the oversight of the MCO, except these individuals who are institutionalized."[151] The advocates eventually sued in *Small v. Montana* to prevent the state from excluding the institutions from the managed care contract.[152]

Although *Small* succeeded in forcing the state to reword its managed care contract, lawyers in the case were not satisfied: "The State made very clear to the MCO that they needed a certain number of hospital beds filled to keep the contract—if the beds weren't filled, they'd lose the contract."[153] Thus, even though changes were made to the language of the contract, the practical realities of the relationship between the state and the MCO were viewed as creating considerable incentives for the MCO to keep state hospital beds filled.

In New Mexico, however, the managed care system has been charged in litigation with refusing to provide the most basic of services to Medicaid clients, refusing to provide legally required grievance hearings, and funneling adolescents with treatment needs into the juvenile justice and criminal justice systems in order to avoid its responsibility to pay for needed treatment.[154]

It could be that both perspectives are correct. Managed care may be the better approach in the context of hospitalization where it seems clear that utilization review has resulted in shorter hospitalizations than under traditional approaches.[155] However, state mental health systems may be preferable for community treatment. State mental health programs increasingly serve as the umbrella for the provision of a vast number of "psychosocial" services from employment and transportation assistance to drop-in centers and peer support groups. These approaches are more broadly targeted at the needs of people with mental diagnoses and are preferable to managed care's more strictly medically oriented model in the community. In the alternative, it may be, as has been suggested by some studies, that the differences in practices between different HMOs make generalizations about managed care difficult and unproductive. As one doctor said, "When you've seen one HMO, you've seen one HMO."[156]

One answer, of course, is to look to the contracts between the states and the MCOs to see just what services will be provided and to whom. Contracts between states and managed care companies comprise hundreds of pages of dense and hardly comprehensible prose. It is essential for advocates to participate in the creation of those contracts where possible and to at least be familiar with their contents, because, as contracts, they create legal rights for the clients who will benefit from them.

To be familiar with the states' contracts with MCOs under Medicaid waiver programs, advocates and consumers must first be able to obtain both the contract (including appendices and attachments)[157] and the request for proposals (RFP) that resulted in the contract. Although these contracts obviously have an enormous impact on public welfare, states and MCOs have sometimes been reluctant to share price provisions or even the contract itself. These agreements are subject to disclosure under state public records acts,[158] and some are available at Internet sites. Several cases have found that MCOs in these circumstances are state actors.[159]

Unfortunately, many contracts contain provisions that could have a disparate impact on individuals with psychiatric disabilities. For example,

> many Medicaid contracts with managed care plans permit plans to seek disenrollment for "noncompliant" patients, commonly defined as patients who fail to keep appointments, do not follow instructions, or threaten providers. It is not unheard of for states to allow plans to avoid certain patients altogether.[160]

Wisconsin's contract provides that

> the HMO shall not be liable, at the point in time commencing with the month for which the recipient's voluntary exemption becomes effective . . . for providing contract services to Medicaid cases in which there is an HMO enrollee who meets one or more of the following criteria: a. persons with recurrent or persistent psychosis and/or a major disruption in mood, cognition or perception; b. a person with a major impairment in functioning in personal or social role, *e.g.*, self care/activities of daily living, and who has extraordinary human service programming needs including extensive non-medical programming, which community agencies . . . and social/human service systems are typically best equipped to provide or coordinate, and who is or will be receiving these medical and non-medical services with a need for a comprehensive and coordinated program.[161]

However, some states, such as New York, provide in their RFPs that

> health plans may not refuse an assignment or seek to disenroll a member or otherwise discriminate against a member on the basis of age, sex, race, physical or mental handicap/developmental disability . . . except when that condition can be better treated by another provider type.[162]

It is not yet clear how these nondiscrimination clauses are being interpreted or even whether they are being monitored or enforced to ensure compliance. So far the record of the states in monitoring to ensure that services are actually provided by the MCOs with which they have contracted and that clients are being fairly dealt with has been woefully inadequate.[163]

There are signs, however, that both states and the managed care companies with which they contract may be subject to increasing litigation under the ADA. In one recent case, the Pennsylvania Department of Public Welfare was sued because it had contracted to provide Medicaid services with a number of HMOs, many of whose provider's offices were inaccessible to people in wheelchairs.[164] Although the court found that the ADA did not require that each provider's office be accessible, it did require the Department of Public Welfare to establish and enforce a number of distinct requirements regarding accessibility of provider offices, and it implied that the HMO's means of communicating with its disabled clients might not be adequate under the ADA. In another instance, the Maryland Disability Law Center recently filed a complaint with the U.S. Department of Justice (DOJ) about the accessibility of health care providers' offices under the state's program, and complaints by advocacy groups indicate that the problem is widespread and litigation may be just beginning.[165]

The judge in a different case implied that the discriminatory denial of care to patients by a primary care physician might receive particularly strong scrutiny in a managed care context because the degree of control exercised by a primary care physician over the patient's access to a variety of medical benefits, from referrals to specialty care, was so great. In that case, a primary care physician was charged with refusing to provide care, referrals, or even authorization for hospitalization after being informed that his patient was HIV positive.[166] Even when his patient developed active symptoms of AIDS, including vomiting, fever, shortness of breath, and breathing pain, the doctor refused to authorize hospitalization.[167] The plaintiff sued the physician, the hospital where he worked, and HealthPASS, the managed care medical assistance program created by the State of Pennsylvania in partnership with a private MCO. HealthPASS was sued for punitive damages on a variety of counts, including negligent hiring of the doctor, breach of contract, discrimination, and intentional infliction of emotional distress.

The court denied a motion to dismiss the claim for punitive damages on the ground that there was evidence in the record to support the contention that the physician was the employee of the MCO rather than an independent contractor. The court also denied the motion to dismiss the discrimination claim, holding that

> disability alone is not a permissible ground for withholding medical benefits. This principle is particularly acute where the plaintiff seeks medical benefits from a primary care physician in a managed health care system. In such a system, the participant depends on the primary care physician not only for medical treatment, but also for other benefits, such as authorization for hospitalization and referrals to specialty care.[168]

The court developed a burden-shifting analysis. If the plaintiff can show that he or she satisfies the plan eligibility requirements, "the focus appropriately shifts to the defendant's reasons for withholding the benefits."[169] The court held that a plan "may not withhold benefits . . . based on a particular disability but may act only pursuant to a bona fide medical reason."[170] Whether these two possibilities are really dichotomous rather than overlapping remains to be seen.

Litigation against states for discrimination in the delivery of Medicaid services under managed care is not limited to cases of individuals. *Taylor v. Johnson*,[171] a class-action suit, charged the state of New Mexico with having "established a managed care system for Medicaid recipients in New Mexico which does not meet the needs of children with serious, chronic, medical and/or mental health conditions."[172] The complaint stated claims under the New Mexico statutes, as well as the ADA, the U.S. Constitution, and the federal Medicaid statute.

The *Taylor* case will inevitably raise the question of the applicability of *Alexander v. Choate*[173] to ADA claims by managed care companies. Although not a case involving either mental disabilities or the ADA, *Alexander v. Choate* is arguably the most influential disability discrimination decision involving Medicaid. The plaintiffs in *Alexander* challenged the state of Tennessee's decision to limit the number of in-hospital days that would be reimbursable under its Medicaid program. The plaintiffs charged that the new regulation unlawfully discriminated against them as people with disabilities because the limitation on hospital days fell far more severely on disabled Medicaid recipients than on recipients who were not disabled.

Because the regulation was neutral on its face, the case raised the question of whether the Rehabilitation Act of 1973 permitted claims of discrimination on the basis of disparate impact. Finding that the Rehabilitation Act covered at least some claims of disparate impact discrimination, the court held that as long as the plaintiffs retained "meaningful access" to the "program or benefit" they sought, their challenge to the regulation should be rejected.[174] Because disabled recipients were not denied access to or excluded from the package of Medicaid services offered by Tennessee, plaintiffs could not sustain a disparate impact challenge to the change in regulations.[175]

It can be argued that *Alexander* is a misreading and dilution of the Rehabilitation Act, transforming it from a statute against discrimination into a statute that grants the affirmative right of "meaningful" access to programs for people with disabilities. In this sense, *Alexander's* tepid "meaningful access" requirement is similar to *Rowley's*[176] right to an educational program that is "reasonably calculated to enable [the disabled student] to receive education benefits."[177] But the 1990 Individuals With Disabilities Education Act (IDEA)[178] is a statute that gives substantive rights. The Rehabilitation Act and the ADA are discrimination statutes. Disparate impact has never been interpreted in the past to grant "meaningful" as opposed to "equal" access. The court's articulated concern that disparate impact claims by people with disabilities would open the floodgates of litigation because many social measures could be construed as having an adverse, disparate impact on people with disabilities could have been better addressed by the fundamental-alteration defense, available to states under the Rehabilitation Act just as under the ADA.

In addition, the scope of *Alexander's* applicability is uncertain. The case involved difficult decisions by a state in allocating scarce resources to assist its indigent and disabled citizens in securing state-financed health care. It is clear that in *Alexander* the Supreme Court was concerned, as in other cases,[179] with the specter of states operating under the burden of limited resources, facing systemic challenges at every step. It is not clear whether the reasoning of *Alexander* should be applied to cases challenging decisions by private companies whose principal mission is to maximize profits.[180] There may be policy reasons to extend some latitude to states that are trying to design programs to benefit large populations of needy people, even though

such reasons are irrelevant to the operations of for-profit, private corporations. For
that matter, these concerns are also inapplicable to state policies where the expen-
diture of scarce resources is not at issue.

How this applies to a situation in which the state contracts with a private, for-
profit organization to provide health care benefits that the state has obligated itself
to provide under the Medicaid program is unclear. First, the "program" at issue
needs to be defined. Is it the MCO, or the partnership between the state and the
MCO? Is it the MCO's division that administers the benefits in question? *Alexander*
puts a premium on how the "program" or "benefit" is defined. The U.S. Supreme
Court admonished that

> the benefit itself, of course, cannot be defined in a way that effectively denies other-
> wise qualified individuals the access to which they are entitled; to ensure meaningful
> access, reasonable accommodations in the grantee's programs or benefits may have
> to be made.[181]

The applicability of *Alexander* may also be undermined by a number of developments subsequent to the decision. Of course, the principal development was the
passage of the ADA, which was passed in part because of the failure of the Rehabilitation Act to accomplish the goal of equality for people with disabilities.[182] The
legislative history makes it plain that the ADA was enacted because the Rehabilitation Act was perceived as having failed to provide the necessary protection against
disability discrimination, not only in terms of its scope of coverage but also in terms
of the courts' interpretation and application of its standards. It is true that there are
positive references in the legislative history of the ADA to the precedential value of
Rehabilitation Act cases in general and to *Alexander* in particular.[183] However, the
legislative history's approving citations to *Alexander* were primarily, if not solely, to
support the proposition that claims for disparate impact were absolutely critical to
accomplishing the purposes of the ADA.[184]

The statutory language of the ADA makes it clear that Congress intended that
the ADA never be construed to grant less protection than the Rehabilitation Act.[185]
Clearly Congress saw the ADA as granting more protection than the Rehabilitation
Act, in light of its perspective on the inadequacies of the Rehabilitation Act. Thus,
the Rehabilitation Act standards are meant as a floor, not a ceiling, for the protections
of the ADA.

The second post-*Alexander* development was the congressionally mandated
promulgation of regulations by the DOJ. Although parts of the regulations prohibiting
disparate impact discrimination were clearly taken from *Alexander*, as instructed by
Congress, other aspects of the regulations appear to create a greater scope for complaints of discrimination and certainly a clearer set of guidelines, than does *Alexander's* confusing formula of "meaningful access." For example, the DOJ prohibits
the imposition or application of

> eligibility criteria that screen out or tend to screen out an individual with a disability
> or any class of individuals with disabilities from fully and equally enjoying any ser-
> vice, program, or activity, unless such criteria can be shown to be necessary for the
> provision of the service, program, or activity being offered.[186]

The DOJ made it clear that this regulation prohibits policies that "unnecessarily impose requirements or burdens on individuals with disabilities that are not placed on others."[187]

The third development, which involved the actual subject matter of *Alexander*, that is, the latitude accorded to states in their development of Medicaid programs, and the impact of the ADA, was the denial of Oregon's application for a Medicaid waiver on the basis that its proposed program discriminated on the basis of disability.

DHHS Secretary Sullivan gave three reasons for rejecting the proposal. First, in measuring quality of life, Oregon had assumed that quality of life with a disability was lower than quality of life without a disability. Second, its measurement of quality of life for a person with disabilities was based on the attitudes of the general population about the quality of life of people with disabilities, rather than any interviews with people with disabilities.[188] Third, some of the rankings of treatments were facially discriminatory on the basis of disability, such as providing liver transplants for people who did not have cirrhosis but refusing transplants for those who did or refusing life support for extremely low birthweight infants. Secretary Sullivan made it clear that the Medicaid program required "content neutral factor[s]" that did not have a "particular exclusionary effect on persons with disabilities" and that "did not take disability into account."[189]

These decisions, made by a Republican administration, were endorsed by the Democrat administration that followed it. Neither administration viewed the ADA as simply requiring that Oregon provide "meaningful access" to Medicaid for people with disabilities. Although the DHHS official under President Bush who drafted Sullivan's letter believed that he was simply following *Alexander*,[190] it seems fairly clear that both the Bush and Clinton administration DHHS and DOJ[191] believe that the ADA's application to Medicaid is more comprehensive than simply a prohibition against exclusion or denial of "meaningful access."

The fourth development undermining the applicability of *Alexander* to the ADA context is the fact that a majority of the U.S. Supreme Court pointedly ignored it when they decided in *Olmstead v. L. C.*[192] that the ADA prohibits inappropriately institutionalization, although the dissent referred to *Alexander* and other Rehabilitation Act cases in arguing for a narrower interpretation of prohibited discrimination under the ADA.

In summary, *Alexander* is, at most, a case involving facially neutral regulations by a state agency providing free services from limited resources. Its holding under Section 504 of the Rehabilitation Act that "meaningful access" to a program is all that is required under such circumstances may have been undermined by subsequent interpretations of the ADA, particularly in the context of the Oregon Medicaid proposal.

Home- and Community-Based Service Programs

The most far-reaching and arguably the most beneficial Medicaid programs are those that prevent institutionalization in psychiatric hospitals or nursing homes. The best known of these is the home- and community-based services waiver, which permits states to design their own programs to assist people who would otherwise be institutionalized. Because Medicaid does not pay for services in IMDs, the Medicaid waiver program has been far less useful for people with psychiatric disabilities than for people with mental retardation as a means of funding treatment in the community. The waiver requires states to show that Medicaid would otherwise be paying more money for an individual's care in an institutional setting than in community care. Because Medicaid does not pay for the individual's care in a state mental hospital at all, it is difficult to meet the cost-neutrality requirement for people with psychiatric disabilities.[193]

There are signs, however, that the exclusion of people with psychiatric disabilities may be the result of discrimination as well. Although the IMD exclusion applies neither to children nor to adults over age 65, only four states—New York, Vermont, Colorado, and Kansas—have applied for a waiver to serve children with emotional disturbances in the community, and not a single state serves adults who are over age 65 with psychiatric disabilities in the community.[194] The applications for waivers show that states are applying for behavioral management services in the community for people with developmental disabilities, traumatic brain injuries, or mental retardation but not for people with mental illness.[195] Many of these waivers involve services for individuals under 21, services that people with psychiatric disabilities would be eligible to receive if the states would apply for the waivers.

Because programs in which care is provided in the home and community are so desirable, everyone wants to be included in them. Because Congress is cutting rather than increasing assistance to poor, vulnerable, and disabled populations and because of inertia and underfinancing in states that do not use all of the funding for home- and community-based services available to them, there are never enough home- and community-based services to meet the demand. The desire to be included in these programs has spawned a fair amount of litigation involving states' definitions of eligibility for various home-based programs, including at-home supervision and attendants.[196]

In some cases, the challenges have been based on the charge that the state unreasonably excludes people with certain disabilities, or with the characteristics of certain disabilities, from its home-based service programs. Courts have rejected ADA challenges to programs that require an individual to be mentally alert[197] and challenges to programs of in-home supervision that require an individual *not* to be mentally alert or, as the court put it, "incapable of observing his own behavior."[198] One court permitted a challenge to proceed against the implementation of task-based assessment programs used to determine the amount of personal care service hours authorized for eligible Medicaid applicants and recipients that excluded "safety monitoring" as a separate task.[199]

The reasons that courts have given for rejecting the challenges to these programs have varied. One unnecessarily broad response is that the ADA permits discrimination as between people with different disabilities and that its protections only extend to situations in which people without disabilities are treated better than those with disabilities.[200] This very statement is a confused conflation of two separate issues. The first is whether discrimination is confined to disadvantageous treatment vis-à-vis people who are not disabled. The second is whether it is discriminatory to disadvantage an individual with a certain disability or a group of individuals with a certain disability vis-à-vis an individual with a different disability or group of individuals with a different disability. The first question is discussed in detail in chapter 4. The reasons why discrimination against a person or group of people with one kind of disability cannot be justified by reference to the nondiscriminatory treatment of another group of people with disabilities are discussed below.[201]

Other cases involving claims of discrimination relating to the provision of home- and community-based services include *Hodges v. Smith*, which challenged a Georgia policy that paid for enteral products for adults in nursing homes but not for those receiving home health care. The court upheld the policy, in part because the plaintiff had not shown that he would be institutionalized as a result of the operation of the policy.[202] Likewise, in *Cameron v. Alander*,[203] the state's refusal to pay benefits to a woman with a mental disability whose husband was providing services that would have been covered by state funds had she been institutionalized was held not to state a claim under the ADA.

People With Different Disabilities

The question of whether the ADA prohibits discrimination between groups of people with different disabilities is one of particular significance to people with psychiatric disabilities, who are often in the group that is being disadvantaged relative to other groups of people with disabilities. However underfunded or inadequate state pro- grams or social services may be, they will often be even more poorly funded and even more inadequate if the recipients of those services have psychiatric disabilities.

Although courts are almost unanimous that people may not be discriminated against on the basis of the severity of their disability,[204] they are divided on whether people with a particular disability may be disadvantaged in favor of people with another disability.[205] It seems clear that with two exceptions—health and disability insurance[206] and actions by legislatures intended to benefit a particular group (not actions to exclude or burden a particular group[207])—the ADA does prohibit discrim- ination against an individual or class of individuals on the basis of disability, even if the disadvantageous treatment on the basis of disability is by comparison to other individuals with different kinds of disabilities.

The language of the ADA, its legislative history, the regulations, most agency interpretations of those regulations, and case law under both the Rehabilitation Act and the ADA all strongly support this conclusion. In addition, policy reasons and common sense also counsel in favor of finding that the ADA prohibits discrimination between people with different disabilities. First, there is nothing in the statutory language of either the Rehabilitation Act or the ADA to suggest that their prohibition of discrimination on the basis of disability contains an exception insulating discrim- ination among different disabilities. Rather, the language of the ADA suggests the contrary in several ways. In addition to the standard rule of statutory construction that remedial statutes should be broadly construed to accomplish their purpose, the specific language of the ADA underscores the congressional intent "to provide a clear and comprehensive national mandate for the elimination of discrimination against individuals with disabilities."[208] In the face of this language, courts should hesitate to read in limitations that are not present in the statute itself, particularly because Congress has shown itself able in the ADA to write in limitations where it wishes them (e.g., in the case of claims against private insurance companies).

Second, as a number of courts have pointed out, the ADA's explicit statutory references to eliminating discrimination in institutionalization and health care services make little sense if discrimination can only occur in the context of benefits or services offered to people without disabilities.[209] The fact that the ADA mentions health services suggests that Congress was concerned about discrimination in that area, and even a glance at the testimony supporting the ADA justifies this concern. The outpouring of testimony—particularly on behalf of people who were HIV positive or had AIDS—regarding the refusal of physicians to treat a patient with AIDS or unequal medical treatment because of a disability was eloquent testimony to discrimination against people with certain kinds of disabilities by health care professionals who were presumably willing to treat people with other disabilities. Surveys show that this kind of discrimination continues.[210] Congress made clear that it intended these kinds of practices to be prohibited.

Third, Congress's explicitly stated purpose in passing both the Rehabilitation Act and the ADA was to provide Americans with disabilities with the same kinds of civil rights protections as were provided by statutes prohibiting discrimination on the basis of race, national origin, and gender.[211] Interpretation of these civil rights statutes by the Supreme Court and Courts of Appeals has made clear that it is no defense to a charge of individual discrimination to show that the defendant has treated other members of the minority group well. The Supreme Court recently held that "the fact that one person in the protected class has lost out to another person in the protected class is thus irrelevant so long as he has lost out because of his [protected status]."[212] These cases were cited favorably in the Supreme Court's decision in *Olmstead v. L. C.*,[213] underscoring that the focus of antidiscrimination cases should be on the basis for the defendant's actions toward the plaintiff rather than on comparisons between the plaintiff and some other person or group.

Showing that a defendant has treated members of another minority group fairly is even less of a defense to a charge of race or sex discrimination.[214] In a recent race–national origin discrimination claim by a woman of Vietnamese and French descent, the 9th Circuit gave short shrift to an employer's defense that it had favorably considered an Asian male and a white woman, noting the importance of the singular myths and stereotypes specifically associated with Asian women.[215]

Singular myths and stereotypes are also associated with some of the disabilities covered under the ADA. In different ways, people who suffer from chronic fatigue syndrome or cancer; people who have vision or hearing impairments; people who are morbidly obese or who have mobility impairments; and people with dwarfism, epilepsy, Tourette's syndrome, or learning disabilities all face certain specific kinds of misconceptions and stereotypes. In particular, mental illness, alcoholism, substance abuse, and HIV seropositivity have extraordinarily negative connotations in society and are associated with character defects and immorality. People with disabilities that have singular kinds of negative stereotypes associated with them are subject to the greatest discrimination and need the most protection.

It is these misconceptions and stereotypes that antidiscrimination legislation is meant to combat. Disability discrimination, as Congress has repeatedly underscored, is unfavorable treatment, neglect, misguided paternalism, fear, segregation, limitation, revulsion, or lowered expectations based on misunderstandings and misapprehensions about the nature of a particular disability.[216] An employer is not permitted to make "a preconceived and often erroneous judgment about an individual's capabilities based on 'labeling' of that person as having a *particular kind of disability*."[217] If a person is fired when his employer discovers his psychiatric diagnosis because his employer fears mentally ill people, it is irrelevant that the employer has no adverse preconceptions about people who are blind or deaf or have a mobility impairment and has hired a number of people with those characteristics. A number of courts have held that

> courts must be careful not to group all handicapped persons into one class, or even into broad sub-classes. This is because "the fact that an employer employs fifteen epileptics is not necessarily probative of whether he or she has discriminated against a blind person."[218]

Rather, as one court wrote in the context of Section 504, "the relevant inquiry is whether the application of 504 between persons with different or varying degrees of disability furthers the goal of eliminating disability-based discrimination."[219]

Many cases involving discrimination between people with different disabilities have not been brought against employers but against government entities under Title II. In this regard it is worth distinguishing between challenges to decisions by the legislative branch apportioning scarce resources—which should be upheld if they benefit a particular group of people with disabilities but struck down if they discriminatorily exclude or burden a particular group[220]—and decisions or actions by executive agencies, which should be scrutinized far more carefully. Congress intended Title II public entity defendants to be subject to a higher standard than Title I or Title III defendants because the Title II defendants, supported by taxpayer dollars, were supposed to provide a model of inclusion and integration for the latter.[221]

Other than health and disability insurance cases, decisions holding that the Rehabilitation Act and the ADA do not cover discrimination between people with different disabilities have rarely followed traditional sources of legal analysis—statutory language, legislative history, regulatory direction—or included much in the way of thoughtful consideration of these factors. Generally, there is a citation to a sentence or two taken out of context from the much-misunderstood case of *Traynor v. Turnage*[222] and an otherwise unsupported conclusive statement that discrimination between groups of people with different disabilities is permissible. It is astonishing that *Traynor*, a Supreme Court decision signed by four justices in a fact-specific case under the Rehabilitation Act, has apparently been seen as trumping conventional statutory analysis of the ADA.

Traynor involved the question of whether veterans were excluded from a benefit provided to all disabled veterans under an exception when the disability was caused by "willful misconduct" stated a disability discrimination claim under Section 504. Veterans who are honorably discharged from the military have 10 years to apply for benefits under the GI Bill. The 10-year limit is tolled if the veteran did not apply for benefits due to a mental or physical disability, as long as that disability was not the result of the veteran's "willful misconduct."[223]

In an elaborate interpretation that tells much about the curious intertwining of moral judgments and disability in this country, the VA decided in 1964 that when alcoholism was a symptom of mental illness, it was not misconduct; "primary" alcoholism did constitute willful misconduct.[224] However, organic diseases or disabilities that were the result of alcoholism were not excluded as the result of willful misconduct. Again, although alcoholism as "secondary to and a manifestation of an acquired psychiatric disorder" was not willful misconduct, attempted suicide ("deliberate drinking of a known poisonous substance"[225]) was willful misconduct without regard to whether it might be "secondary to and a manifestation of an acquired psychiatric disorder."[226]

Two veterans who missed the 10-year deadline for applying for benefits because of so-called primary alcoholism were denied benefits. They sued, claiming that the equation of primary alcoholism with misconduct violated the Rehabilitation Act. After the seven judges who decided the case[227] agreed unanimously that this policy of the VA was in fact susceptible to challenge under the Rehabilitation Act, a plurality of four judges rejected the veterans' challenge.

Justice Byron White, writing for himself and three other justices, strongly emphasized the fact-specific nature of the interpretive task before the court, noting that the Rehabilitation Act Amendments of 1978[228] had been passed only 1 year after the same Congress had passed the challenged provision and concluding that this made it less likely that the Rehabilitation Act was intended to implicitly overrule the prior year's legislation. Although he wrote that "the central purpose of 504 is to assure that handicapped individuals receive even-handed treatment in relation to non-handicapped individuals,"[229] he also recognized a potential cause of action for discrimination between categories of disabled individuals but held that the requirements to make out such a claim had not been met in this case: "It would arguably be inconsistent with §504 for Congress to distinguish between categories of disabled veterans according to generalized determinations that lack any substantial basis."[230]

However, Justice White found a "substantial basis" in the medical literature for the proposition that alcoholism was not a disease and, therefore, could be equated with misconduct. Regardless of whether one agrees with him about the body of literature, the requirement of a substantial basis in the medical literature supporting legislative distinction among disabilities is an important part of *Traynor* that has been completely lost in its later interpretations. In addition, Justice White insisted that in this particular case, the plaintiffs were not "denied benefits by virtue of their handicap, but because they engaged with some degree of willfulness in the conduct that caused them to become disabled."[231]

Finally, *Traynor* contains the unexceptionable statement that "there is nothing in the Rehabilitation Act that requires any benefit extended to one category of handicapped persons also be extended to all other categories of handicapped persons." This is true, but hardly supports a conclusion that Congress clearly intended the Rehabilitation Act to foreclose actions challenging discrimination between different kinds of disabilities that had predated *Traynor*[232] and that would continue after *Traynor*.[233] Although this statement has often been used to support the concept of permissible discrimination among different disabilities, it is, ironically, inapposite in *Traynor* itself.

In *Traynor*, primary alcoholism was equated with willful misconduct; on that basis, the plaintiffs were deprived of a benefit that they otherwise would have been entitled to receive as disabled veterans. If this is a decision based on an inaccurate generalized stereotype, as the three dissenting justices in *Traynor* insist it is,[234] then it is discrimination. If it is a statement based on a generalization supported by substantial medical evidence, as the four justices in the plurality argue, it may be a permissible distinction, but the central inquiry is nevertheless about whether the disadvantage arising from this distinction constitutes discrimination against people with primary alcoholism. *Traynor* is simply not about the extension of a benefit to a distinct group of people with disabilities. For example, Congress could permissibly create a scholarship program or college primarily for blind people (a benefit to a distinct group of people with disabilities) without being liable for discrimination. Or Congress could create a scholarship program for all people with disabilities. The analogous situation to *Traynor* is whether Congress can fund educational scholarships for all people with disabilities, except people with injuries from motorcycle accidents who were not wearing helmets, on the grounds that those people were morally blameworthy. This would raise issues of discrimination, which is the issue in *Traynor*.

Traynor involved deliberate exclusion from a benefit otherwise generally available to disabled people and, thus, implicated discrimination. At the very least, *Traynor* permits challenges to such actions and requires that those challenges be upheld in the absence of substantial medical evidence to sustain them. Arguably, *Traynor*'s reasoning is invalid in cases involving the ADA because those cases do not require that the discrimination be based solely on disability.

One of the reasons these questions are so troubling is their potential impact on states' ability to target certain kinds of assistance to certain groups of people with disabilities. Much of the confusion about discrimination between people with different disabilities has arisen from the concededly difficult question of when permissible government beneficence toward one group of people with disabilities turns into discrimination against another group of people with a different set of disabilities. This issue raises some extremely complex questions about the tension between the right of legislatures to make choices and the obligation of courts to protect politically powerless minorities against those choices. However difficult the resolution of this question may be at the margins, it certainly does not justify a wholesale conclusion that the ADA permits discrimination among people with different disabilities simply to avoid dealing with it.

The ADA does permit states to grant specific benefits to one minority group or a particular class of people with disabilities without having to donate equivalent largesse to all other groups, but this is not an authorization of discrimination. To give just a few examples, a state legislature can appropriate money to predominantly black colleges without having to equally fund predominantly Hispanic colleges, just as Congress can appropriate money to Gallaudet without obligating itself to appropriate money to any other institution of higher education focused on a particular disability group. These are not decisions to exclude people with a particular disability from a generally available benefit for all people or all people with disabilities. The appropriation decisions may be based on politics and clout, but they are not based on stereotypes, myths, or generalizations about the inability of Hispanics to benefit from a college education or the ineducability of people with disabilities other than deafness.

The ADA permits states to enact beneficial programs targeted at people with particular disabilities. The DOJ enacted a regulation that permits public entities to provide "benefits, services or advantages to individuals with disabilities, or to a particular class of individuals with disabilities beyond those required by this part."[235] In explaining the meaning of this regulation, the DOJ noted that it is based on a provision in regulations governing Section 504 of the Rehabilitation Act, and that Section 504 thus

> ensures that federally assisted programs are made available to all individuals, without regard to disabilities, unless the Federal program under which the assistance is provided is specifically limited to individuals with disabilities or a particular class of

individuals with disabilities. Because coverage under [the ADA] is not limited to federally assisted programs, paragraph (c) has been revised to clarify that State and local governments may provide special benefits, beyond those required by the non-discrimination requirements of this part, that are limited to individuals with disabilities or a particular class of individuals with disabilities, without thereby incurring additional obligations to persons without disabilities or to other classes of individuals with disabilities.[236]

The DOJ interpreted this regulation as permitting a provision in the California Health and Safety Code that requires health insurance plans to continue coverage of dependent children with mental retardation or physical disabilities but not to continue coverage for dependent children with psychiatric disabilities.[237] Although the theoretical basis cited by the DOJ is correct—that a particular class of individuals with disabilities can be granted benefits not granted to all other people with disabilities—the theory does not fit the facts in this specific case, which appear to mandate continued coverage of almost every disability except psychiatric disabilities. In this case, it appears that a particular disability is being selectively disadvantaged from a benefit made generally to children with physical disabilities and mental retardation. Thus, the California statute should have been found to be discriminatory under the ADA. However, this interpretation by the department was made only one month after the date that Title II of the ADA went into effect by a section in the DOJ that no longer has the authority to interpret the ADA, and perhaps it should not be regarded as authoritative.

As a theoretical matter, the distinction between permitting programs that benefit a discrete, identifiable population of people with disabilities (such as Gallaudet College) and prohibiting the exclusion of people with disabilities from programs intended for everyone (such as creating a right of access to all treatment records except mental health treatment records)[238] is a sensible one and easy to make.[239] On the margins, however, the question of what constitutes a choice to benefit certain groups of people with disabilities and what amounts to an irrational exclusion of a group of people based on disability becomes more difficult.

This is illustrated by a case brought under Section 504 of the Rehabilitation Act in which people with mental illnesses challenged Colorado's failure to apply for home- and community-based services for people with mental illness, when the state had applied for these services for people with mental retardation, developmental disabilities, AIDS, and people who were elderly.[240] Colorado had provided funding for services in the community under the waiver program until the DHHS terminated the waiver because Colorado was using funds to assist people who had recently been in psychiatric institutions, thus violating the program's requirement that home- and community-based services be less expensive than what Medicaid would otherwise have paid.[241] Colorado never reapplied for waiver funding for people with mental illness, although it continued to receive such funding for people with mental retardation or developmental disabilities and for people with AIDS.

The trial court found that the waiver program was a single unified program of community services, for which people with mental illness were eligible but excluded by the department's failure to reapply for funding, failure to work with the DHHS to determine how it could once again receive the waiver and failure to use excess funds from the waiver program on behalf of people with mental illness. In addition, the court found that because the Colorado Department of Social Services received funding under the waiver program, it was subject to the requirements of Section 504.

The Supreme Court of Colorado initially reversed the trial court decision, finding that the home- and community-based services program was divisible into separate programs, each serving people with different disabilities. Because the department no longer received funding for community services for people with mental illness, that program did not receive federal funding and, therefore, was not subject to Section 504 of the Rehabilitation Act.[242] The case boiled down to whether the home- and community-based services waiver program involved one program or several programs and whether Colorado had an obligation to pursue funding under the program for people with mental illness after its initial application for a waiver had been denied.

Is this a case of Colorado providing special benefits to people with developmental disabilities and AIDS, protected under 28 C.F.R. Sec. 35.130(c), or a case of prohibited exclusion of people with psychiatric disabilities from the benefits of a federally assisted program? The answer given by the regulations and followed by the cases requires an inquiry into whom the program was "designed to benefit." The first step in this inquiry is to examine the legislation that created the program.[243] If the program were solely a state program, the relevant legislation would be easy to identify. But what about a state-created program that springs from federal legislation? The home- and community-based services program was designed to permit states "to develop and implement creative alternatives to institutionalizing Medicaid-eligible individuals."[244] The statute does not distinguish among groups of Medicaid-eligible individuals. The regulations implementing the statute, however, require distinct, separate waiver requests to be submitted for "aged or disabled or both," "mentally retarded or developmentally disabled or both," and "mentally ill."[245] Do these requirements of separate waiver applications create, as the first Colorado Supreme Court panel thought, three separate programs, each of which could be described as an individual program designed to benefit a specific disability group, or are they all part of one waiver program designed to create alternatives to institutionalization for Medicaid-eligible individuals?[246]

In either case, does the motive of the legislature or relevant agency for choosing not to apply for services for one group of individuals with disabilities while applying for funding for other groups matter? The state claimed that it failed to reapply for services for people with mental illness because it considered such a reapplication futile and the cost of reapplying would be $30,000. The lower court specifically rejected this reason as providing an insufficient basis for failing to at least attempt to reapply for the waiver. Does the foreseeable consequence to the group of people with disabilities—in this case, unnecessary institutionalization—matter in determining whether an action is discriminatory?

One way of resolving these questions is to decide that the problem presented by this situation may not be that the Department of Institutions chose to apply for the waiver for a number of target populations, whereas excluding people with psychiatric disabilities. Rather, the problem may be that a number of Colorado citizens with mental illness were unnecessarily segregated in institutions. Under the integration mandate, the state could not keep these Colorado citizens in institutions if it could provide them with services in a more integrated setting.[247] Colorado could, if it chose to, ameliorate this situation without using federal funds. It could not, however, claim undue hardship or lack of money as a defense for inappropriately institutionalizing people if federal funding that might have been available for the purpose was not pursued. This brings us full circle back to the integration mandate. Ultimately, of course, all of these questions are interrelated, and their answers depend in large part on how antidiscrimination law is conceptualized.

The ADA and SSI–SSDI

The SSI and SSDI programs provide income for people who are deemed to be so disabled that they are unable to be gainfully employed in the national economy.

The Application for Benefits

The process of applying for disability benefits under either SSDI or SSI requires finding the appropriate office and getting to it, determining the appropriate application forms and retrieving them, filling out page and pages of forms[248] with questions such as "Do you (either alone or jointly with any other person) own any life estates or ownership interest in an unprobated estate?"[249] arranging for a medical examination, collecting medical reports, and responding to any requests by the Social Security Office for more information. In other words, it is a process that requires attention, concentration, focus, organization, access to one's records, patience, determination, and stamina.

Depending on the nature of the clerks at the Social Security Office and the mental health professionals who perform the evaluation, it may require substantial personal interaction, some of it possibly difficult or even hostile.[250] It is not surprising to learn that in one study of people receiving SSI or SSDI benefits because of mental illness, only 13.75% of applications were initiated by the individual. The vast majority of applications for benefits were initiated by either family members or mental health staff.[251] One of the primary factors that predict whether a person with a psychiatric disability is receiving Social Security benefits is not the severity of his or her disability but whether he or she had a parent, relative, or caseworker to fill out the forms and navigate the process of application for benefits.[252]

Many people with severe psychiatric disabilities do not have interested parents, relatives, or caseworkers to fill out the forms. They may not be able to independently navigate the process of applying for disability benefits.[253] Therefore, it also is not surprising that a substantial number of lawsuits have been brought challenging both the application process and the appeals process for the denial of Social Security disability benefits.[254] Not all of these cases have been brought under the rubric of disability discrimination; some have relied on the Social Security Act itself[255] or on constitutional claims.[256] These obstacles can only continue to arise in the context of managed care and the complex documents associated with receiving services from an HMO.

The Appeal of the Denial of Benefits

Anyone who knows people receiving disability benefits is familiar with the scenario. The person achieves a measure of stability in a life that has been wracked with homelessness, hospitalizations, and poverty and sometime thereafter receives a letter informing him that his disability status is subject to review. The panic and anxiety lead to depression, deterioration, and often hospitalization. This has been noted by researchers, courts,[257] and people with psychiatric disabilities.

The process by which unsuccessful applicants for SSI are supposed to appeal is, if anything, even more daunting than the process of application itself. Although federal law requires the Social Security Administration to clearly state the reason for denial of the application,[258] denial notices are simply form notices that are difficult to understand.[259] The General Accounting Office, Office of the Inspector General, and internal HHS reviews have for over 5 years unsuccessfully recommended revisions of these notices so that they could convey meaningful and understandable information.

Although the Social Security Administration provides a toll-free number to answer questions about denials of benefits, callers often do not get through. The following sequence tells the tale.

> In 1997, claimants placed 75.3 million calls to the toll-free number. Of those, 19.8 million calls, 26.3%, were met with a busy signal or terminated by the SSA [Social Security Administration] or the caller before conducting a conversation with [a] representative. In 1996, claimants placed 94.2 million calls to the toll-free number. Of those, 46.2 million calls, 49%, were met with a busy signal or terminated before a conversation with a representative [was conducted]. In 1995, claimants placed 121.4 million calls to the toll-free number. Of these, 64.7%, 78.6 million calls, were met with a busy signal or terminated before a conservation [was conducted].[260]

Even if the applicant manages to get through, the people answering the phones do not have access to the individual's application file and can only answer general questions about SSI.

The notice also lists various legal services numbers, but the Legal Services Corporation has not yet recovered from the enormous budgetary losses in the Reagan administration. Although Social Security rules permit the administration to deduct a portion of an SSDI award to pay a private attorney successful in appealing a denial of SSDI benefits, it may not do so in the case of SSI benefits. Thus, SSI clients are generally not assisted by counsel in appealing their denials of benefits. Only 2.8% of adverse notices are appealed, and only 1.0% of adverse notices result in appeals hearings. Of these, 0.2% make it to the second level of appeal provided by the SSA. More than one court has inferred that "many, many erroneous decisions are simply not appealed."[261]

A federal court recently held that SSI's notification of the denial of benefits violated both federal statutes and the due process clause of the 14th Amendment. Although the court rejected an equal protection claim on the basis of the assertion that welfare recipients receive more individualized and informative notification of the denial of benefits, the court repeatedly recognized that disability was relevant to the need for more understandable and simple procedures. It seems plausible that the kind of notification and appeals procedure described in *Ford v. Apfel* would also constitute discrimination on the basis of disparate impact on people with mental disabilities.

Even if the applicant understands the appeals process and the notice sufficiently to prepare an appeal, the average time for review of an adverse decision in Fiscal

Year 1998 was 850 days, which is almost 2½ years. Even this compares favorably with a practice held by a court in Florida to violate both federal law and the U.S. Constitution: The Florida agency with the federal statutory responsibility of assessing Medicaid eligibility of people denied SSI would "take absolutely no action; i.e. it does not notify applicants of the referral and/or their federal appeal rights, or request any additional information requisite to the processing of these applications, nor does it make eligibility determination on a timely basis."[262]

These practices underscore Congress's wisdom to ensure that the ADA includes disparate impact in discrimination prohibited by the ADA. Some of the practices that harm people with disabilities most are the result of bureaucracies that seem to exist for their own sake rather than to actually provide the assistance the law requires to the people they are mandated to serve. More litigation needs to be brought emphasizing the effect on people with disabilities of these practices.

Disabilities in the SSI Program

Often programs such as SSI give preferential benefits to people who are blind over people with other kinds of disabilities. Courts have uniformly upheld such preferential treatment under challenge. In *Vaughn v. Sullivan*,[263] for instance, the court found that a state does not violate Section 504 by disregarding earnings under a PASS program—which allows earnings from new employment to be disregarded for a time in computing income for purposes of SSI—when determining Medicaid benefits for people who are blind but counting those earnings for everyone else. The court held that the statutes in question do not require states to provide identical benefits, and because the plaintiffs had not shown that their total package of benefits was lower than that of comparable groups, they could not show discrimination. However, even if the plaintiffs did prove disparity in the benefit packages, neither Section 504 nor the ADA repeals the provisions of 42 U.S.C. Sec. 1396a(f) permits distinctions in public welfare benefits on the basis of physical condition.

Mentally Ill People With SSI Benefits Based on Legal Status

Congress denied SSI benefits to convicted criminals in 1980.[264] In 1994, Congress acted to further deny SSI benefits to people who had been accused of crimes punishable by imprisonment for more than 1 year but were found not guilty by reason of insanity.[265] A class of individuals denied benefits under the new provision sued under the ADA, charging that they were no different from people with mental disabilities who had not been charged with crimes and that the language used by Congress in passing the legislation showed invidious intent to discriminate on the basis of their disability.[266]

In *Milner v. Apfel,* Judge Posner wrote that there was nothing wrong with society drawing moral distinctions between people with mental illness who have been found not guilty by reason of insanity and all other people with mental illness.

> The moral difference between the criminal insane and the noncriminal insane, though a difference based on consequences rather than state of mind, reflects a moral intuition that is deeply rooted in the traditions of the American people . . . and being so rooted

it furnishes a rational basis for Congress' being less generous toward insane criminals.[267]

It is a little frightening to turn to a concept like "deeply rooted moral intuitions" as a legal justification for differential, disadvantageous treatment of a loathed and disfavored category of people. Not long ago, the notion that the races should not mix or disabled people should not procreate could have been described in identical terms. The equal protection claims were rebuffed so vigorously by Judge Posner that Judge Ripple felt compelled to write a concurrence dissociating himself from the tone and attitude of the majority opinion.[268]

Welfare and General Assistance Programs

The passage of the ADA coincided with renewed interest in reforming the Aid to Families With Dependent Childen (AFDC) program, popularly known as welfare. Well before the demise of AFDC,[269] states had been given permission to experiment with various innovations, usually including some kind of work requirement. Those work requirements, however, sprang from the perception that people on welfare could work but simply did not want to. This perception is undercut by the consistent finding that a substantial proportion of women on welfare have physical or mental health problems, with "estimates of the proportion of adult welfare recipients with a mental health condition—usually some form of depression—ranging from a low of 4% to as high as 28%."[270]

Welfare reforms have often been met by legal challenges. For example, an experiment that cut the benefits of those who did not work and gave incentives to those who did find employment was challenged as discriminating against people with disabilities on welfare who could not work.[271] Because the ADA forbids states to use "methods of administration" of a program that exclude qualified people with disabilities or give them lesser benefits and provides that states must give people with disabilities equal opportunity to obtain the same benefit received by people who are not disabled, the plaintiffs argued that the work incentive program discriminated against qualified welfare recipients who were disabled and could not work.

The district court upheld the reform proposals against these challenges. The Court of Appeals reversed on different grounds and did not reach the district court's reasoning on the ADA claims. Because the district court's analysis follows a familiar pattern, it is worth reviewing in some detail.

The district court acknowledged that the plaintiffs' arguments had "some force"[272] because "the effect of the Project on those disabled recipients who are unable to work appears unintended and serves no stated goal of the project. It appears harsh to cut the benefits of those who cannot work, and of their dependents, as part of a work incentive experiment."[273] Nevertheless, the court found that the program did not violate the ADA because (1) the state could have cut all benefits to all recipients without violating the ADA, and (2) having reduced everyone's benefits, the state could then create a work incentive program with extra benefits for which recipients with disabilities were not "qualified individuals" as required by the ADA, and thus recipients with disabilities could be excluded from the program. Thus, the state was permitted to accomplish the same goal in one step rather than two.

It is not clear that the court's second assumption was correct, but certainly its analytical sleight of hand helped the court transform the "benefit, service, or program" from welfare to the work incentive program, predetermining the result of the inquiry. The court disjoined the receipt of welfare benefits from the imposition of the work incentives and then considered the plaintiffs' qualifications for each in turn. Had the court considered whether the plaintiffs were qualified for welfare, it could not have escaped the conclusion that they were. They met all of the program requirements to receive welfare. Having found them qualified for welfare, the court could have proceeded in a variety of different ways.

For example, it could have looked to ADA regulations, which prohibit public entities from providing lesser benefits to individuals with disabilities,[274] or from using criteria or methods of administration that have the effect of defeating or substantially impairing the accomplishment of the objectives of the public entity's program with respect to individuals with disabilities,[275] or from using screening or eligibility requirements.

In the alternative, if the court wanted to uphold the work incentive requirement, an analytically more honest approach would have been to find the plaintiffs qualified individuals with disabilities and hold that because the work incentive program had a disparate impact on them, it could be analyzed under *Alexander v. Choate*. The court could then conclude that because the plaintiffs still received some benefits, they retained "meaningful access" to the welfare program.[276]

It is not clear how cases such as this one should be resolved. It should be clear that simply because a woman has a disability does not mean that she cannot work. Women with disabilities who are making the transition from welfare to work have the same rights to reasonable accommodations of their disabilities as other employees in America. However, it is also clearly true that people with disabilities have a great need for the health care coverage that often accompanied welfare. The Presidential Task Force on Employment of Adults With Disabilities recommended that

> creating access to affordable, comprehensive health care coverage is a vital prerequisite for enabling individuals with disabilities on TANF [Temporary Assistance to Needy Families] gain and sustain employment at living wages. The unique health care needs of disabled and chronically ill individuals frequently necessitate a continuity of health care coverage to maintain self-sufficiency.[277]

Whether such health care coverage could be considered a reasonable accommodation to enable people with disabilities to work and whether it would be the state TANF program or the employer's responsibility to provide health care coverage is an open question. Because the DOJ has opined that a state mental health agency has the responsibility to ensure that the community group homes with which it contracts are accessible to people with physical disabilities, perhaps some analogy could be drawn to state welfare-to-work programs.

The question of whether changes in state welfare programs illegally discriminated against people with disabilities came up again in *Does 1–5 v. Chandler*.[278] The plaintiffs challenged cuts in general assistance that capped benefits to people with disabilities but allowed unlimited benefits to needy families with children. The court found that aid to families with children and aid to disabled people were two distinct programs. Therefore, discrimination could occur only if funds under the program for children were not provided to parents with disabilities or children with disabilities.

States cannot, however, simply eliminate or limit the eligibility of people with disabilities within general welfare programs while continuing to pay the same benefits to other groups receiving welfare.[279] Not only have states that have attempted to do this been rebuffed by the courts, but plaintiffs in those case have also collected money damages, a relatively rare occurrence in Title II cases.

Both the question of what kinds of conditions a state may place on welfare benefit recipients and the proper analysis to be applied when these conditions are challenged, however, remains open. In *Hunsaker v. Contra Costa County,*[280] a case with profound and troubling implications, the Court of Appeals reversed a lower court's injunction forbidding Contra Costa County from using an interview form designed to identify substance abusers (whose receipt of welfare benefits would be conditioned on undergoing treatment) where the form concededly had significant false-positive results for former substance abusers who were now rehabilitated. The lower court had found that this unduly burdened the former substance abusers and prohibited the use of the form. The 9th Circuit held that as long as the disabled plaintiffs had "meaningful access" under *Choate* to welfare benefits, the undue burden on them was irrelevant. In effect, the Court of Appeals incorrectly interpreted the DOJ prohibition on government program placing undue burdens on disabled people as applying only to cases of intentional discrimination, when a glance at the regulations makes it clear that this analysis was specifically intended for disparate impact cases.

Workers' Compensation

Workers' compensation programs are found in every state, and there are a number of different programs at the federal level as well. These programs pay benefits to workers whose injuries or diseases arise out of or occur in the course of employment. There have been a number of individual and class action challenges under the ADA to the way in which workers' compensation benefits are administered.[281] Not one has been successful, although in some cases the arguments appear fairly persuasive.

Emotional Disabilities as Work-Related Injuries or Diseases

Different states use elaborate distinctions in deciding whether emotional injuries or illnesses are covered under workers' compensation statutes. Coverage decisions are contradictory across states: In some states, emotional conditions arising from predictably stressful jobs are covered because they are job related,[282] whereas in other states the same emotional condition arising out of the same job is not covered precisely because stress is an inherent part of the job.[283]

Almost all workers' compensation cases mirror the ADA employment discrimination cases in finding that emotional conditions caused by stress arising from interpersonal difficulties on the job are not employment related and, therefore, are not covered under workers' compensation.[284] Employees have unsuccessfully challenged this exclusion of benefits for emotional disabilities.[285]

Impairment Ratings Systems

In addition to individual challenges to exclusions or denials of workers' compensation payments as violations of the ADA,[286] there have been several systemic challenges to the operation of the workers' compensation system as a whole. These challenges have been based on a number of premises.

In deciding how to compensate workers who are permanently but partially disabled, many states rely on impairment schedules, usually based on the American Medical Association's *Guides to the Evaluation of Permanent Impairment*, which purports to offer an objective means of rating disabilities. Although the guides caution that "it must be emphasized and clearly understood that impairment percentages derived according to the Guides criteria should not be used to make direct financial awards or direct estimates of vocational disabilities," many states do just that. The general articulation of the challenge to impairment ratings is that they classify individuals with disabilities arbitrarily,[287] do not accurately reflect disabilities, are not individualized as required by the ADA,[288] and result in workers with more severe disabilities receiving less compensation than workers with less severe disabilities.

The use of the AMA guides may well be vulnerable to a thoroughly investigated and documented attack,[289] although it is not clear that the legal basis for this kind of challenge would be the ADA. In any event, questioning the system on which every state in the country bases an entrenched system of income replacement would require extensive investigation, fieldwork, and research, and the employment of a number of expert witnesses. Unfortunately, almost all ADA challenges to the workers' compensation scheme of ordering impairment ratings have been made by one Florida law firm[290] and do not appear to involve the kind of discovery and investigation that would be required. In addition, the firm has engaged in sanctionable conduct that may have adversely reflected on the substance of the claims.[291] A far more thoughtfully framed challenge has gone virtually unnoticed in the case law.[292]

The Equal Employment Opportunity Commission has specifically stated that the ADA supersedes any conflicting state workers' compensation laws,[293] and all courts have held that workers' compensation statutes and schemes are indeed subject to the ADA.[294] In each case, however, the court has held that the workers' compensation structure survives challenge. One court held that the impairment ratings system is sufficiently individualized to meet the requirements of the ADA.[295] Some courts have used the argument that the ADA does not prohibit discrimination between disabilities,[296] which I argue misinterprets Congress's intent in passing the ADA. Some courts have held that the purposes of the ADA—preventing discrimination—and the workers' compensation statutes—income replacement to workers with disabilities—are not in conflict, and therefore the latter is not preempted by the former. This is facile. Laws that discriminate incidentally to their purpose may be challenged just as easily as laws whose only purpose is to discriminate.

If the workers' compensation structure does result in a disparate impact on people with disabilities, by what standard should a court judge that discrimination? A number of the courts adjudicating these challenges have referred to *Griggs v. Duke Power Co.*,[297] which would suggest that if plaintiffs could point to an equally efficient and effective method of administering the workers' compensation program that resulted in more accurate assessments of people's disabilities, they might succeed. However, several courts have decided the challenge to the workers' compensation scheme under

Alexander v. Choate, in which the plaintiffs had done precisely that—presented the court with procedures by which the Tennessee Medicaid program could accomplish its goals with less of a disparate impact on disabled recipients—to no avail. Even the most thoughtful decisions conclude that all the workers' compensation program must do is provide workers with disabilities with "meaningful access" to disability benefits, and this is accomplished by the impairment ratings.[298] Of course, it is not true that workers with emotional injuries have "meaningful access" to workers' compensation benefits, and state workers' compensation programs do not have the "safe-harbor" provision accorded by the ADA to insurance companies.

Vocational Rehabilitation

People with all kinds of disabilities who testified in support of the ADA saved some of their most bitter and angry testimony for descriptions of their treatment at the hands of vocational rehabilitation agencies.[299] In one case, a woman who needed her van modified to be able to drive was denied the requested modifications until she could produce a driver's license.[300] Another woman testified that "if consumers of mental health services contact vocational rehabilitation on their own, they are put through the same testing and training as people with mental retardation."[301] The flavor of the testimony is summarized by the following excerpt from the testimony of Catherine Marshall.

> Most handicapped people who want an education or a job must deal with vocational rehabilitation. To start with, you have to have a physical to determine if you are eligible. If you are, your problems really start because you must be in touch with your assigned counselor. Fully 75 percent of the time, he or she is in conference, unavailable, on another line, out sick, or on vacation. When you leave a message, you very rarely get your call returned. When you do get in touch, then you have to deal with being told . . . what kind of medical equipment is best for you—usually the cheapest and most ineffective—and how little money is available. If you try to tell your counselor what your needs are, what you can do and what you would like to accomplish, you are told what is best for you, to be a realist, and then you are ignored. In July 1982, my counselor told me I was unsaivageable and that I would no longer receive the funds to finish my college education, nor would I receive any help to go to work. . . . Anyone who is successful in dealing with vocational rehabilitation should be canonized.[302]

The surveys were also replete with stories about being blocked by vocational rehabilitation agencies from jobs for which the respondents were suited by virtue of education and experience and steered toward manual labor or no labor at all.[303] One respondent wrote

> when I quit taking mental health medicines I applied to DVR [Department of Vocational Resources] for a small start-up loan to open a small business. . . . Finally I was denied based on a doctor's report (who saw me for three minutes but had my mental health records) that I didn't have any formal education, I was so severely disabled by mental illness that I would require months and months of special training to even enter the job market at the entry level. He said I didn't have any communication skills and I would need a lot of supervision at work and would never have it together enough

to operate a small business. I went to the private sector (where I should have gone in the first place) and had the money (with no credit or cosigners) in less than two weeks. I got the money because the folks in the private sector were not poisoned in their perception of me like the mental health people. They could see me as I really was.[304]

Another survey respondent, a self-described "conservative" with a master's degree in business administration, wrote about the reaction of the vocational rehabilitation agency to his stated goal of being a business executive.

They tried to arrange a psychiatric assessment to ensure I was not being grandiose. The only way I got in the door, was through a few people in the business department at the university I went to, who helped me refinance a new business and assisted me in building myself as an executive.[305]

The testimony to Congress and the surveys convey the impression that many employers never even get the opportunity to discriminate against people with disabilities because that discrimination is accomplished for them by the agencies statutorily mandated and paid with federal funds to help people with disabilities get jobs.[306] Many federal agencies and independent think tanks have also strongly criticized vocational rehabilitation, noting that people receiving disability insurance rarely return to work.[307]

First, the reported conduct of vocational rehabilitation agencies makes one of the most compelling cases for the proposition that discrimination exists, even with no comparison group of people without disabilities. According to testimony before Congress and the results of the survey, vocational rehabilitation agencies do not want to help those with psychiatric disabilities until they have resolved the problems caused by their disability, at which time, of course, they will no longer need the assistance of vocational rehabilitation.

Second, critics charge the vocational rehabilitation agencies do not want to provide the kinds of services that people with psychiatric disabilities need. They do not advocate for their clients with psychiatric disabilities, but shrink from them.[308] Third, vocational rehabilitation agencies make prospective clients take and "pass" psychiatric tests before the agencies will give services.[309] Fourth, vocational rehabilitation agencies require their clients with psychiatric disabilities to take medication, go to therapy, and submit to other intrusive measures as a condition of providing vocational rehabilitation services, conditions that are not imposed on other people with disabilities.

Now that the Supreme Court has declared in *Olmstead v. L. C.*[310] that the ADA covers adverse and disadvantageous acts based on a person's disability without any need for a comparison group, these discriminatory actions of vocational rehabilitation agencies are open to legal challenge. This makes sense. There must be some way to challenge vocational rehabilitation agencies if they embody the very stereotyping that the ADA was meant to prohibit. Because these agencies are meant to be the gateway to employment, it cannot be that they are not subject to the same kinds of prohibitions against discrimination to which an employer would be subject. Before *Olmstead*, case law on discrimination against people with psychiatric disabilities by vocational rehabilitation agencies was uneven. Absolute, articulated barriers to services were open to challenge, but de facto barriers to services were generally upheld.

For example, a man who had been trying to get vocational rehabilitation services for 20 years but was denied because he refused to submit to psychological testing was found to have stated a cause of action under the ADA on the basis that Title I precludes employers from requiring psychological exams before making job offers, and a parallel requirement might be found to apply to entities offering assistance in obtaining employment.[311]

However, a man with mental illness who initially received outstanding evaluations at his work placement but was fired for inappropriate behavior was informed by the vocational rehabilitation agency that he could not receive further services until he had "gained insight into appropriate work behavior" through counseling.[312] In other words, he was ineligible for help because of his mental illness, unless he overcame that illness, at which point he would no longer need their services.

The court decided that the purpose of the ADA was to ensure that people with disabilities received equal treatment vis-à-vis people without disabilities but not to safeguard evenhanded treatment of different classes of individuals with disabilities.[313] As discussed at length above, this is an incorrect interpretation of the ADA. Such an interpretation would effectively insulate vocational rehabilitation agencies from refusing to provide services to people with certain kinds of disabilities simply because it provided services to people with other disabilities. This would be analogous to protecting a doctor who refused to treat patients with AIDS because he treated patients with other disabilities.

A better approach to litigation is that both the ADA and Section 504 prohibit vocational rehabilitation agencies from acting in an "arbitrarily discriminatory manner."[314] In *McGuire*, a man with paraplegia sued vocational rehabilitation services for discrimination vis-à-vis other clients. He demanded the same level of tuition and maintenance benefits given to individuals with visual impairments, which was significantly higher than that available to any other class of individuals. The defendant agency argued that Congress meant to provide more services for people with visual impairments than for members of other disabled groups. The court held that while the "state may limit funding for vocational rehabilitation services, it may not do so in an arbitrarily discriminatory manner."[315] Because the plaintiff's disability was as severe as blindness and the sole reason that the state placed a lower cap on his services was because he was not visually impaired, the court ruled that the aid limits were arbitrary and discriminatory.

The court then pointed out that the DHHS regulations specifically stated that no qualified disabled person or class should receive differential treatment with regard to others. The defendant responded that the regulations were intended only to prevent discrimination as compared with people without disabilities. The court rejected this argument, noting that the defendant could cite no text or evidence to support that notion. It then emphasized that the regulation meant that no one should be denied benefits solely because of a particular disability and that the limits here had no rational basis.[316]

A number of the cases raise the issue of whether a vocational rehabilitation agency's refusal to fund a law school or graduate school education states a claim under Section 504 or the ADA. Almost universally, courts have correctly held that it does not, although for the wrong reasons.[317] The refusal to fund a graduate or law school education may or may not run afoul of the terms of the Vocational Rehabilitation Act itself, but unless a plaintiff can show that the vocational rehabilitation agency refused to fund such education on the basis of stereotypes about a particular disability or disabilities rather than on its understanding of the requirements of the act, there is no discrimination.

Conclusion

By far the most significant federal programs for people with disabilities—probably more significant than the ADA—are the SSI and SSDI and Medicaid programs. These permit a minimal life outside an institutional setting for many—whatever life can be lived on less than $500 a month, in the case of people who receive SSI.[318] If the federal budget surplus were used to even moderately increase SSI, it would probably do more for people's quality of life than any antidiscrimination law. But this book is not a work of fiction, so we will move on.

The operations of Medicaid, SSI, and SSDI, however, undermine many of the articulated goals of the programs and can have a profoundly negative impact on the very people they are supposedly designed to help. Many of these difficulties in fact arise out of disparate impact discrimination.

First, the application process is so complex that few people with mental disabilities can actually manage it on their own. The complexity of the application process serves as a barrier to the access to benefits to which a person with mental disabilities may be entitled, and accommodations should be made that would permit a person with mental disabilities to negotiate applications for benefits. In addition, as former welfare recipients are falling off the Medicaid rolls, states are violating their legal obligations to notify people who are no longer eligible for welfare that they may still be eligible for Medicaid and may even be actively discouraging people from applying for Medicaid, food stamps, or both.

Second, the rules about when and how much an individual can work without losing eligibility are even more complex and are an obstacle to employment that might alleviate the disability and provide needed additional income. To call simplifying these rules an "accommodation" for people with mental disabilities would suggest that people without disabilities could understand them, which would be largely inaccurate. These rules should be simplified so that they make sense to all ordinary people.

The linking of health care benefits under Medicaid to determinations of disability under SSI and SSDI and the linking of Medicaid benefits to institutional care are the two most significant reasons that people with mental disabilities remain segregated, islolated, and unemployed. If the states work to implement the Ticket to Work and Work Incentives Improvement Act[319] and Congress passes the the Health Care Assurance Act of 1999,[320] many of these difficulties could be resolved. As the Supreme Court pointed out in *Olmstead v. L. C.*, the structure of the Medicaid program has been changing over the years to support and encourage treatment in the community rather than institutional settings. The provision of home health care, respite, and personal care services through understandable and navigable SSI and Medicaid programs are essential to dismantling institutional segregation and providing treatment in the most integrated setting.

Endnotes

1. The Personal Responsibility and Work Opportunity Act of 1996, P. L. 104-193, replaced the Aid to Families With Dependent Children Program with TANF.
2. The most recent figures are 5,173,550 people with disabilities receiving SSI and 6,250,156 receiving SSDI. These figures can be obtained in updated form from the Social Security's web site: for SSI, http://ftp.ssa.gov/pub/statistics/2a1; for SSDI, http://ftp.ssa.gov/pub/statistics/1b1.
3. *Id.*
4. Ford v. Apfel, 2000 U.S. Dist. LEXIS 2898*9 (E.D. N.Y. Jan. 13, 2000).
5. U.S. Commission on Civil Rights, *Helping State and Local Governments Comply With the ADA: An Assessment of How the United States Department of Justice Is Enforcing Title II, Subpart A, of the Americans With Disabilities Act* (Washington, DC: Author, Sept. 1998) at 92.
6. Federal defendants may, however, be sued under Section 504 of the Rehabilitation Act for acts of discrimination that do not arise out of employment, which is covered by Section 501 of the Rehabilitation Act. One of the most notorious instances of systematic federal discrimination against people with psychiatric disabilities, the deliberate plan by the Social Security Administration (SSA) under Margaret Heckler to rid its rolls of psychiatrically disabled people, was the subject of a great deal of litigation, leading finally to a unanimous U.S. Supreme Court decision roundly condemning SSA's actions; Bowen v. City of New York, 476 U.S. 467 (1986). None of this litigation, however, was brought in the form of antidiscrimination claims.
7. As noted in chapter 4, the U.S. Supreme Court has agreed to decide whether individuals can bring damage actions against states under the ADA. The decision in University of Alabama v. Garrett should be issued in 2001.
8. Matthew Diller, "Dissonant Disability Policies: The Tensions Between the ADA and Federal Disability Benefit Programs," *Tex. Law Rev. 73* (1998); Christopher G. Bell, "The Americans With Disabilities Act, Mental Disabilities, and Work," in Richard Bonnie and John Monahan, Eds., *Mental Disorder, Work Disability and the Law* (Chicago: University of Chicago, 1997) at 217–218.
9. Harris v. Chater, 998 F.Supp. 223 (S.D. N.Y. 1998).
10. *See* chapter 3 for further details.
11. Philadelphia Police and Fire Association for Handicapped Children v. City of Philadelphia, 699 F.Supp. 1106 (E.D. Pa. 1988), *rev'd,* 874 F.2d 156 (3rd Cir. 1989); McNamara v. Dukakis, U.S. Dist. LEXIS 17565 (D. Mass. Dec. 27, 1990); Rodriguez v. DeBuono, 44 F.Supp. 2d 601 (S.D. N.Y. 1999), *rev'd sub nom,* Rodriguez v. City of New York, 197 F.3d 611 (2nd Cir. 1999).
12. Beno v. Shalala, 853 F.Supp. 1195, 1212 (1993), *rev'd,* 30 F.3d 1057 (9th Cir. 1994); Weaver v. New Mexico Department of Human Services, 945 P.2d 70 (N.M. 1997); Does 1–5 v. Chandler, 83 F.3d 1150 (9th Cir. 1996); Santana v. Hammons, 673 N.Y.S.2d 882 (N.Y. Sup. Ct. July 8, 1998).
13. J. B. v. Valdez, 1999 U.S. App. LEXIS 20169 (10th Cir. Aug. 12, 1999); In re Jonathan Burrows, 1996 Ohio App. LEXIS 2346 (May 30, 1996); In re B. K. F., 704 S.2d 314 (Ca. App. 1997); In re Torrance P., 522 N.W.2d 243 (Wisc. App. 1994); In re B. S., 693 A.2d 716 (Vt. 1997); Stone v. Davies County, 656 N.E.2d 824 (Ind. App. 1995); In re John D., 934 P.2d 308 (N.M. App. 1997); In re Penny J., 890 P.2d 389 (N.M. App. 1994); In re Aisha Martin, 1997 Ohio App. LEXIS 5572 (Ohio App. Dec. 17, 1997); J. T. v. Arkansas Department of Human Services, 947 S.W.2d 761 (Ark. 1997); In re A. P., 728 A.2d 375 (Pa. Super. 1997); In re Terry, 2000 Mich. App. LEXIS 45 (Mich. App. Feb. 29, 2000).
14. Alexander S. v. Boyd, 876 F.Supp. 773, 803 (D.S.C. 1995).

15. Raines v. Florida, 983 F.Supp. 1362 (N.D. Fla. 1997).

16. Cramer v. Florida, 885 F.Supp. 1545 (M.D. Fla. 1995), *aff'd*, 117 F.3d 1268 (11th Cir. 1997); Harding v. Winn-Dixie Stores, 907 F.Supp. 386 (M.D. Fla. 1995); Brown v. Campbell County Board of Education, 915 S.W. 2d 407 (Tenn. 1996); Barry v. Burdines, 675 S. 587 (Fla. 1996); Hensley v. Punta Gorda, 686 S.2d 724 (Fla. App. 1997); In re Worker's Compensation Claim of Frantz, 932 P.2d 750 (Wyo. 1997); Barbara Brown v. A-Dec, Inc., 1998 Ore. App. LEXIS 756 (Ore. App. June 3, 1998).

17. J. L. v. Social Security Administration, 971 F.2d 260 (9th Cir. 1991).

18. Crayton v. Callahan, 120 F.3d 1217 (11th Cir. 1997).

19. Anderson v. Department of Public Welfare, F.Supp. 2d 456 (E.D. Pa. 1998).

20. Addis v. Whitburn, 1998 U.S. App. LEXIS 21601 (7th Cir. Sept. 4, 1998).

21. Estimates range from 46%, J. C. Beck and B. van der Kolk, "Reports of Childhood Incest and Current Behavior of Chronically Hospitalized Psychotic Women," *Amer. J. of Psychiatry* 144 (1987):1474; to 51%, L. S. Craine, C. E. Henson, J. A. Colliver, et al. "Prevalence of a History of Sexual Abuse Among Female Psychiatric Patients in a State Hospital," *Hosp. and Comm. Psychiatry* 39 (1988):300; to 59–63%, J. B. Bryer, B. A. Nelson, J. Baker Miller, and P. A. Krol, "Childhood Sexual and Physical Abuse as Factors in Adult Psychiatric Illness," *Amer. J. of Psychiatry* 144 (1987):1426; to 73%, R. E. Gallagher, B. L. Flye, S. W. Hurt, M. H. Stone, and J. W. Hull, "Retrospective Assessment of Traumatic Experiences," *J. of Personality Disorders* 6 (1992):99. Overall, it seems safe to say that at least half of the institutionalized women were sexually abused as children.

22. Jeanne L. Steiner, Rani A. Hoff, Cate Moffett, Heather Reynolds, Martha Mitchell, and Robert Rosenheck, "Preventive Health Care for Mentally Ill Women," *Psychiatric Services* 49 (1998):696; A. D'Ercole, A. E. Skodol, E. L. Struening, et al., "Diagnosis of Physical Illness in Psychiatry Patients Using Axis I Standardized Medical History," *Hosp. and Comm. Psychiatry* 42 (1984):395.

23. Mary Ellen Handel, "Deferred Pelvic Examinations: A Purposeful Omission in the Care of Mentally Ill Women," *Hosp. and Comm. Psychiatry* 36 (1985):1070, *see also* articles at note 22.

24. R. K. Heyding, "Providing Medical Care to Mentally Ill Women in the Community," *Comm. Mental Health J.* 26 (1990):373.

25. Testimony of Patricia Deegan, A&P Comm. Print 1990 (28B)*1251.

26. Baber v. Hosp. Corp. of America, 977 F.2d 872 (4th Cir. 1992); Cass v. St. Rita's Medical Center, 1991 WL 34900 (Ohio App. 3rd Dist. Mar. 14, 1991); Rubenstein v. Benedictine Hospital, 790 F.Supp. 396 (N.D. N.Y. 1992); Swanson v. United States by and through the Veterans Administration, 557 F.Supp. 1041 (D. Ida. 1983).

27. *See, e.g.*, Wagner v. Fair Acres, 49 F.3d 1002 (3rd Cir. 1995); In re of the Involuntary Transfer or Discharge of J. S., 512 N.W.2d 604 (Minn. App. 1994) (a nursing home could not discharge a resident diagnosed with schizophrenia because she refused medication when she had a right to refuse medication); O'Neal v. Alabama Department of Public Health, 826 F.Supp. 1368, 1371 (M.D. Ala. 1993). Other attempts to discharge or refuse to admit patients with conduct problems caused by disabilities include Grubbs v. Medical Facilities of America, 879 F.Supp. 588 (W.D. Va. 1995); Nichols v. St. Luke Center of Hyde Park, 800 F.Supp. 1564 (S.D. Ohio 1992). Nursing homes also have a history of discriminating against poor people receiving Medicaid in favor of private-pay clients, *see* Blum v. Yaretsky, 457 U.S. 991 (1982); and Edelman, "Discrimination by Nursing Homes Against Medicaid Recipients: Improving Access to Institutional Long-Term Care for Poor People," *Clearinghouse Rev.* 20 (1986):339.

28. 42 U.S.C. Sec. 1396r(e)(7)(C)(i)(IV) and (iii)(III). *See also* Rolland v. Celluci, 1999 U.S. Dist. LEXIS 9079 (D. Mass. June 4, 1999).

29. ERISA has been found to pre-empt many state negligence and medical malpractice

actions, and it thus constitutes an aggrieved individual's sole remedy at law. The alacrity with which courts have held that ERISA preempted state-created remedies led one judge to compare it with "Pac-Man"; Andrews v. Traveller's Insurance Company, 984 F.Supp. 49, 57 (D. Mass. 1997) ("this court has previously compared ERISA to a 'Pac Man' that runs around the legal landscape [somewhat indiscriminately] eating up other claims").

30. 29 U.S.C. Secs. 1001 *et seq.* (1994). ERISA regulates the rights of individuals under employer-sponsored benefit plans, such as health, disability, and pension benefits. *See* Appendix B.

31. EMTALA protects the rights of people in emergency medical situations to receive stabilizing care in hospital ERs without regard to their ability to pay, 42 U.S.C. Sec. 1395dd. For more information, *see* Appendix B.

32. Baber v. Hospital Corporation of America, 977 F.2d 872 (4th Cir. 1992); Phipps v. Bristol Regional Medical Center, 1997 U.S. App. LEXIS 17919 (6th Cir. July 14, 1997) (the plaintiff's EMTALA complaint relating to physical ailments, depression, and suicidal thoughts was dismissed summarily); Ward v. Presbyterian Healthcare Services et al., 72 F.Supp. 2d 1285 (D.N.M. 1999).

33. The Nursing Home Reform Act was part of the Omnibus Budget Reconciliation Act of 1987 (OBRA), 42 U.S.C. Secs. 1395i-3, 1396r (1994).

34. Hoffman v. Memorial Osteopathic Hospital, 492 A.2d 1382 (Pa. Super. Ct. 1985).

35. Some of these, such as the substandard treatment of psychiatric patients in the ER, and the hostile treatment accorded to people on the basis of diagnoses, such as borderline personality disorder, and the dispensing of psychiatric drugs with less concern for the side effects than accompanies the dispensation of drugs for other illnesses, are manifestations of discrimination in psychiatric rather than medical treatment and are discussed in chapter 4.

36. *The Cutting Edge: A Newsletter for Women Living With Self-Inflicted Violence* 4(4) (Winter 1993):5.

37. This book divides the discussion of discrimination in ER settings into two parts. First, ERs discriminate against people with psychiatric disabilities in the treatment of their medical and physical problems by minimizing their symptoms or not crediting their accounts of physical distress, which is discussed in this chapter. Second, ERs offer substandard care for psychiatric emergencies compared with medical emergencies. This form of discrimination is discussed in chapter 4.

38. *See, e.g.*, Stephen M. Soreff, *Management of the Psychiatric Emergency* (New York: Wiley, 1981).

39. *See, e.g.*, Baber v. Hospital Corporation of America, note 26 (raising a claim under EMTALA).

40. Patricia S. v. Waterbury Hospital, No. CV97-0137073-S (Conn. Super. Ct., complaint filed Dec. 9, 1996).

41. Betty Blaska, "What It Is Like to be Treated Like a CMI [Chronically Mentally Ill]," in *Beyond Bedlam*, Jeanine Grobe, Ed. (Chicago: Third Side Press, 1995) at 28–29.

42. R. C. W. Hall, M. K. Popkin, R. A. Devaul, et al., "Physical Illness Presenting as Psychiatric Disease," *Archives of General Psychiatry* 35 (1978):1315–1320; Stephen M. Soreff, *Management of the Psychiatric Emergency* (New York: Wiley, 1981) at 18, 40; Mark W. Viner, John Waite, and Ole J. Thienhaus, "Emergency Psychiatry: Comorbidity and the Need for Physical Examinations Among Patients Seen in the Psychiatric Emergency Service," *Psychiatric Services* 47 (1997):947.

43. Hopper v. Callahan, 562 N.E.2d 822 (Mass. 1990).

44. Stephen M. Soreff, *Management of the Psychiatric Emergency* (New York: Wiley, 1981) at 9.

45. *The Cutting Edge: A Newsletter for Women Living With Self-Inflicted Violence* (Winter 1993):5.

46. P. W. Survey, on file with author.

47. M. E. C. Survey.

48. Survey No. 78, on file with author. The apartment superintendent later denied the respondent's request to move to a better apartment when it became available, even though it was general practice to permit quiet, orderly tenants who paid their rent on time to do so.

49. V. B. Survey, on file with author.

50. Survey No. 150, on file with author.

51. Rubenstein v. Benedictine Hospital, 790 F.Supp. 396, 398 (N.D. N.Y. 1992) (a woman with a psychiatric history goes to the ER because of shortness of breath and is involuntarily committed).

52. Eberhardt v. City of Los Angeles, 62 F.3d 1253 (9th Cir. 1995); Gerber v. Northwest Hospital Center, 943 F.Supp. 571 (D. Md. 1996).

53. The implications of EMTALA for mental illness context are unclear. One commentator insisted that EMTALA does not require treatment of anyone deemed dangerous to others; Wayne Edward Ramage, "The Pariah Patient: Lack of Funding for Mental Health Care," *Vand. Law Rev.* 45 (1992):951, 961–962.

54. N.C. GEN. STAT. §122C-210.1 (2000).

55. Farwell v. Chong Un, 902 F.2d 282 (4th Cir. 1990); United States v. Currie, 836 F.2d 209, 210 (4th Cir. 1987); Paddock v. Chacko, 522 S.2d 410 (Fla. App. 88); *rev. denied,* 533 S.2d 168, 169 (Fla. 1989); Stepakoff v. Kantar, 473 N.E.2d 1131, 1135 (Mass. 1985); King v. Smith, 539 S.2d 262, 264 (Ala. 1989).

56. J.A.V., Survey No. 83, on file with author.

57. Survey No. 97.

58. T. T., Survey No. 100; *see also* Survey No. 101 (a similar response to the question).

59. Ormond's disease, otherwise known as idiopathic retroperitoneal fibrosis, is a rare condition that "causes scar tissues in the peritoneal cavity which can encase tubular organs or structures between organs such as veins or arteries"; Deasy v. United States, 99 F.3d 354, 356 (10th Cir. 1996).

60. *Id.*

61. Deasy v. United States, 99 F.3d 354 (10th Cir. 1996).

62. A. M. W., Survey No. 149.

63. Okunieff v. Rosenberg, 996 F.Supp. 343 (S.D. N.Y. 1998).

64. J. E., Survey No. 138.

65. Survey No. 160.

66. Bragdon v. Abbott, 118 S.Ct. 2196 (1998) (the refusal to fill the cavity of a HIV-positive patient in the dentist office); Jairath v. Dyer, 154 F.3d 1280 (11th Cir. 1998) (a case brought under state law, not the ADA, involving the refusal to perform plastic surgery on a HIV-positive patient); Toney v. U.S. Health Care, 37 F.3d 1489 (3rd Cir. 1994) (affirming the holding below that a doctor's refusal to perform plastic surgery on a HIV-positive patient was due to the health maintenance organzation's termination of coverage, not discrimination); Hoepfl v. Barlow, 906 F.Supp. 317, 318 (E.D. Va. 1995) (a HIV-positive patient); Woolfolk v. Duncan, 872 F.Supp. 1381 (E.D. Pa. 1995); U.S. v. Morvant, 843 F.Supp. 1092 (E.D. La. 1994) (a dentist refused to treat HIV-positive patients); Howe v. Hull, 874 F.Supp. 779 (N.D. Ohio 1994).

67. Aikins v. St. Helena Hospital, 843 F.Supp. 1329 (N.D. Ca. 1994); New York v. Mid-Hudson Medical Group, 877 F.Supp. 143 (S.D. N.Y. 1995); Schroedel v. New York Medical Center, 885 F.Supp. 594 (S.D. N.Y. 1995); Mayberry v. Von Valtier, 843 F.Supp. 1160 (E.D. Mich. 1994).

68. Simenson v. Hoffman, 1995 U.S.Dist. LEXIS 15777 (N.D. Ill. Oct. 20, 1995).

69. Asselin v. Shawnee Mission Medical Center, 894 F.Supp. 1479 (D. Kan. 1995).

70. M. R., Survey No. 196.

71. Brenda C. Coleman, "Study Sees Most Hospitals 'Dumping' Mental Patients" (*AP*), reproduced in BUFFALO NEWS (Dec. 10, 1997):A5; 1997 WL 6479635, reporting on Mark Schlesinger, Robert Dowart, Claudia Hoover, and Sherrie Epstein, "The Determinants of Dumping: A National Study of Economically Motivated Transfers Involving Mental Health Care," *Health Services Res.* 32 (Dec. 1, 1997):561, a study by the Health Research and Educational Trust of the American Hospital Association.

72. *Id.* Mark Schlesinger, Robert Dowart, Claudia Hoover, and Sherrie Epstein (Dec. 1, 1997).

73. *Id.*

74. M. Susan Ridgely and Howard Goldman, "Symposium: Putting the 'Failure' of National Health Care Reform in Perspective: Mental Health Benefits and the 'Benefit' of Incrementalism," *St. Louis Law J.* 40 (1996):407, 416; *see also* M. Long, S. Fleming, and J. Chesney, "The Impact of Diagnosis Related Group Profitability on the Skimming and Dumping of Psychiatric Diagnosis Related Groups," *Intl. J. of Soc. Psychiatry* 39 (1993):108–121.

75. Nursing homes are often referred to in litigation and research literature by the technical terminology of the Medicare and Medicaid statutes: Under Medicare, nursing homes are called "skilled nursing facilities" (SNFs); under Medicaid, they are simply called "nursing facilities."

76. *E.g.,* state-operated nursing homes that violate the federal rights of their residents come under the jurisdiction of the Civil Rights of Institutionalized Persons Act, which permits DOJ to investigate conditions in state-operated institutions, such as prisons and psychiatric institutions, and bring litigation in its own name if those conditions violate federal constitutional and statutory rights. DOJ has in fact sued several states over the conditions in their nursing homes.

77. As part of the Omnibus Budget Reconciliation Act (OBRA), 42 U.S.C. Sec. 1395i-3(a)–(h) (changes in Medicare regulation) and Sec. 1396r(a)–(h) (changes in Medicaid regulation).

78. The screening process, known as PASARR, is imposed under 42 U.S.C. Sec. 1396e(e)(7)(B)(iv).

79. Although over 1 million people with disabilities are in nursing home settings, relatively little litigation or scholarship has been devoted to the application of the ADA to nursing home settings and even less to discrimination against people with psychiatric disabilities in nursing home settings. One nursing home case is, of course, Helen L. v. Didario, discussed in chapter 4; others include Wagner v. Fair Acres, 49 F.3d 1002 (3rd Cir. 1995); and Grubbs v. Medical Facilities of America, 879 F.Supp. 588 (W.D. Va. 1995). The only law review article specifically dealing with the ADA in a nursing home context is Elizabeth K. Schneider's "The ADA: A Little Used Tool to Remedy Nursing Home Discrimination," *Univ. of Tol. Law Rev.* 28 (1997):27489.

80. Wagner v. Fair Acres, 49 F.3d 1002 (3rd Cir. 1995).

81. Nichols v. St. Luke Center of Hyde Park, 800 F.Supp. 1564 (S.D. Ohio 1992); In re of the Involuntary Transfer or Discharge of J. S., 512 N.W.2d 604 (Minn. App. 1994).

82. 42 U.S.C. Secs. 1395i-3(c)(2)(A) (Medicare) and 1396r(c)(2)(A) (Medicaid).

83. Michael Schuster et al., "Nursing Home Transfer and Discharge Protections: Rights Not Fully Recognized," *Clearinghouse Rev.* 26 (1992):619, 620; *see, e.g.,* Nichols v. St. Luke's Center of Hyde Park, 800 F.Supp. 1564 (S.D. Ohio 1992).

84. *See* Kathleen Knepper, "Involuntary Transfers and Discharges of Nursing Home Residents Under Federal and State Law," *J. of Legal Med.* 17 (1996):215, 243–244, 259, 269.

85. Nichols v. St. Luke's Center of Hyde Park, 800 F.Supp. 1564 (S.D. Ohio 1992).

86. 49 F.3d 1002 (3rd Cir. 1995).

87. The figures on the proportion of nursing home clients with Alzheimer's disease vary

from around 50% to over 70%; *see* Lori A. Nicholson, "Hedonic Damages in Wrongful Death and Survival Actions: The Impact of Alzheimer's Disease," *Elder Law J.* 2 (1994): 249, 252; Nina J. Crimm, "Tax Plans for the 21st Century: Medical Incentive Vouchers Address the Needs of the Academic Health Care Centers and the Elderly, *Tulane Law Rev.* 71 (1997):653, 673.

88. An interesting question is whether a person with an organ transplant is disabled, has a history of disability, or is perceived as being disabled for purposes of disability discrimination law. *See* Chmielewski v. Xermac, 1998 Mich. LEXIS 1326 (June 9, 1998) (holding that the determination as to whether a liver transplant patient is disabled should take into consideration the mitigating effect of his antirejection medicine).

89. Transplants are so extraordinarily expensive that under ordinary circumstances, they can only be afforded by the wealthy, people whose private insurance covers transplants, and those states that have opted to include transplants in the package of service covered by the state Medicaid program. Coverage of organ transplants is optional under the Medicaid program, *see* Ellis by Ellis v. Patterson, 859 F.2d 52, 53 (8th Cir. 1988).

90. Johnson v. Thompson, 971 F.2d 1487 (10th Cir. 1992) (finding that the research study of children born with spina bifida in which the poorer infants received no treatment—and almost all died—whereas infants from higher income families received intensive treatment—and almost all lived—did not state a claim of disability discrimination because the decision was made on the basis of economic status).

91. Eleanor Ramos et al., "The Evaluation of Candidates for Renal Transplantation: The Current Practice," *Transplantation* 57 (1994):490.

92. *Id.*

93. Ingrid Kinkopf-Zagac, "Assessing Patient Compliance in the Selection of Organ Transplant Recipients," *Health Matrix* 6 (1996):503, 526.

94. Lisa M. Krieger, "HIV and Transplants," Chicago Tribune (Sept. 17, 1997, emphasis added):C7.

95. Peter Noah, "Woman, 22, Is Rare Patient for Surgery," Los Angeles Times (Feb. 28, 1997):B5.

96. Celeste Fremon, "I Wanted to Live: Woman Who Was Denied Heart and Lung Transplant Because She Is Retarded," *Good Housekeeping* 224 (1997):90.

97. Peter Noah (1997), *see* note 95.

98. *Id.*

99. Sheryl Gay Stolberg, "The Unlisted: Live and Let Die Over Transplants," New York Times (Apr. 5, 1998):Sec. 4, p. 3, col. 1.

100. *Id.*

101. M. E. Olbrisch and J. L. Levenson, "Psychological Evaluation of Heart Transplant Candidates," *J. of Heart and Lung Transplant* 10 (1991):948–955.

102. A letter from Dr. Louis Sullivan to Governor Barbara Roberts (Aug. 3, 1992), with an accompanying memorandum from the Department of Health and Human Services, Analysis Under the ADA of the Oregon Reform Demonstration.

103. "The Oregon Health Care Proposal and the Americans With Disabilities Act," *Harv. Law Rev.* 106 (1993):1296.

104. Survey No. 150.

105. Joe Fahy, "Disabled Hoosiers Suing for Better Options," Indianapolis Star (July 14, 2000):A1 (7,000 on waiting list in Indiana); Peter Pochna, "Suit Faults Mental Health Services," Portland Press Herald (June 13, 2000):A1; "Judge Shakes Off State in Disabilities Lawsuit," Albuquerque Tribune (Apr. 27, 2000):A3 (New Mexicans spend 9 years on waiting list).

106. Doe v. Chiles, 136 F.3d 709 (11th Cir. 1998); Rolland v. Celluci, 52 F.Supp. 2d 231 (D. Mass. 1999); Barthelemy et al. v. Louisiana Department of Health and Hospitals et al., No. 00-1083 (E.D. La., complaint filed Apr. 11, 2000).

107. Robert B. Friedland and Alison Evans, "People With Disabilities: Access to Health Care and Related Benefits," in Jerry L. Mashaw, Virginia Reno, Richard V. Burkhauser, and Monroe Berkowitz, Eds., *Disability, Work and Cash Benefits* (Kalamazoo, MI: Upjohn Institute, 1996):369 ("Medicaid financing for mental health has historically been skewed toward institutional care").

108. The home- and community-based services waiver program, Sec. 1915(c) of the Social Security Act, was first passed in 1981, 42 U.S.C. Sec. 1396n(c). Individuals eligible for home- and community-based service waivers include older people, people with mental retardation or developmental disabilities, physically disabled people, and people with psychiatric disabilities as well as "technology-dependent children" and people with AIDS. *See* the Health Care Financing Administration web page's information on home- and community-based service waivers at http://www.hcfa.gov/medicaid/ltc8.htm.

109. The institution for mental disease (IMD) exclusion provides that the federal government does not reimburse states for psychiatric care in a state mental hospital or other institution of mental disease if the recipient is over age 21 or under age 64; *also see* the discussion in chapter 3, p. 79.

110. *See* discussion in chapter 3, p. 79.

111. Schweiker v. Wilson, 450 U.S. 221, 236–237 (1981).

112. Legion v. Richardson, 354 F.Supp. 456 (S.D. N.Y. 1973), summarily affirmed *sub nom, Legion v. Weinberger,* 414 U.S. 1058 (1973); Kantrowitz v. Weinberger, 530 F.2d 1034, *cert. den.,* 429 U.S. 819 (1976).

113. Schweiker v. Wilson, 450 U.S. 221 (1981). The ADA, even though applicable to state Medicaid programs because states are public entities, is not applicable to federal statutory language. Although Congress's employment practices are covered under the ADA, 42 U.S.C. Sec. 12209, and "matters other than employment," it is clear that federal statutes must be attacked under the Rehabilitation Act, if at all.

114. *See* Richard Warner, *Recovery From Schizophrenia: Psychiatry and Political Economy* 2nd ed. (London: Routledge, 1994) at 89; Charles Kiesler, *The Unnoticed Majority in Psychiatric Inpatient Care* (New York: Plenum Press, 1993); *see also* Thomas S. v. Morrow, 781 F.2d 367 (4th Cir. 1986), *cert. den.,* 476 U.S. 1124 (1986).

115. *See, e.g.,* Connecticut Department of Income Maintenance v. Heckler, 471 U.S. 524, 526 (1985). Not only Connecticut but also Illinois, Minnesota, and California were investigated by HCFA for this practice, *id.* at 528. In these cases, the U.S. Supreme Court supported HCFA's position that nursing homes that overwhelmingly served people with psychiatric disabilities should be considered "institutions for mental disease" and thus states should not be reimbursed under Medicaid for payments to these nursing homes.

116. Nevertheless, in 1992 at the time of the litigation in Duc Van Le v. Ibarra, 635 people in Colorado with primary diagnoses of mental illness were living in nursing homes; 1992 Colo. LEXIS 385*7 (Apr. 20, 1992). In a case currently being litigated in Massachusetts, at the time of the filing of the complaint, 1,473 people with mental retardation and other developmental disabilities were living in nursing homes, Rolland v. Celluci, 52 F.Supp. 2d 231 (D. Mass. 1999).

117. 42 C.F.R. Sec. 441.400, implementing Sec. 1905(a)(24) of the Social Security Act. At the time, the home- and community-based services waiver was limited to eight states and limited the amount of Medicaid money that could go to these waiver programs to $5 million in Fiscal Year 1991, $10 million in Fiscal Year 1992, $20 million in Fiscal Year 1993, $30 million in Fiscal Year 1994, and $35 million in Fiscal Year 1995.

118. P. L. 101-508, enacting H.R.5835.

119. H.R.2020. This bill died in July 1997.

120. Charles Kiesler and Celeste Simpkins, *The Unnoticed Majority in Psychiatric Inpatient Care* (New York: Plenum Press, 1993) at 32.

121. *Id.* at 5–6.

122. *Id.* at 196 (the author's emphasis on the word *treatment* was omitted).

123. In most states, local entities pay for local community mental health services, but the state picks up the entire cost of caring for a citizen who is institutionalized in a state psychiatric facilities. States that have adopted a system of billing communities for the costs of caring for their citizens in state facilities, such as Ohio and Wisconsin, have experienced a substantial drop in the use of state facilities.

124. Senator John Chafee (R-RI) introduced a bill every year for many years that would have restructured fiscal incentives in a way that provided equal incentives for treatment in community-based settings as for treatment in institutional settings. Introduced originally in 1983 as S.2053, the Community and Family Living Amendments Act of 1983, the Chafee bill was modified, redrafted, and resubmitted every year through 1989, when it was introduced as S.384, the Medicaid Home and Community Quality Services Act.

125. Although Congress passed the Fair Housing Act in 1968 prohibiting discrimination in housing on the basis of race, "the historic and continuing governmental maintenance and intensification of residential racial segregation is crucial," and Housing and Urban Development policies have succeeded in creating and perpetuating housing segregation, *see* Florence Wagman Roisman, "The Lessons of American Apartheid: The Necessity and Means of Promoting Residential Racial Integration," *Iowa Law Rev.* 81 (1995):479, 490–493.

126. For the potential of litigation aimed at fiscal structures that result in discrimination and segregation, *see* chapter 4, pp. 120–123.

127. *See, e.g.,* Blanchard v. Forrest, 1994 U.S. Dist. LEXIS 10336 (E.D. La. 1994); Chapman v. Luna, 1991 U.S. App. LEXIS 15074 (6th Cir. 1991); Alexander v. Britt, 89 F.3d 194 (4th Cir. 1996).

128. Reynolds v. Guiliani, 35 F.Supp. 2d 331 (S.D. N.Y. 1999).

129. Padron v. Feaver, 180 F.R.D. 448 (S.D. Fla. 1998).

130. Mayer v. Wing, 922 F.Supp. 902 (S.D. N.Y. 1996).

131. Meachem v. Wing, 77 F.Supp. 2d 431 (S.D. N.Y. 1999).

132. In the area of mental disabilities in particular, these cases include Martin v. Voinovich, 840 F.Supp. 1175 (S.D. Ohio 199); and J. K. v. Dillenberg, 836 F.Supp. 694 (D. Az. 1993) (also rejecting the argument that a managed care entity was not a state actor for the purpose of a suit); Visser v. Taylor, 756 F.Supp. 501 (D. Kan. 1990). *See also* Homeward Bound v. Hissom, 1987 WL 27104 (N.D. Okla. July 24, 1987).

133. 31 U.S.C. 3729, 3730.

134. 31 U.S.C. 3730(d)(2) (2000). The U.S. Supreme Court held that an individual may not sue a state under the False Claims Act, Vermont Agency of Natural Resources v. United States, 120 S.Ct. 1858 (2000).

135. John T. Dauner and Julius A. Karash, "Four Convicted in Medicare Kickback Case: Crackdown Has Prompted Hospitals to Change the Way They Do Business," KANSAS CITY STAR (Apr. 6, 1999):A1.

136. Margaret Cronin Fisk, "The Whistleblower Juggernaut," *Natl. Law J.* (Aug. 9, 1999): A1 (profiling a woman who recovered $29 million and noting that it could be "dwarfed" by current cases).

137. Kurt Eichenwald, "He Blew the Whistle—And Health Giants Quaked," NEW YORK TIMES (Oct. 19, 1998):Sec. 3, p. 1.

138. Sara Rosenbaum, Rafael Serrano, Michele Magar, and Gillian Stern, "Civil Rights in a Changing Health Care System," *Health Affairs* 16 (Jan/Feb. 1997):90.

139. Gail A. Jensen, Michael A. Morrisey, Shannon Gaffney, and Derek Liston, "The New Dominance of Managed Care: Insurance Trends in the 1990s," *Health Affairs* 16 (Jan.– Feb. 1997):125.

140. Health Care Financing Administration, "Managed Care in Medicare and Medicaid,"

Fact Sheet (Washington, DC: Author, Aug. 19, 1997), available on the World Wide Web at http://www.hhs.gov/news/press/1997/pres/970819e.html.

141. The Balanced Budget Act of 1997 enables states to convert their Medicaid programs into managed care programs without the necessity of obtaining a federal waiver and permits states to require that Medicaid recipients enroll in a managed care program.

142. States with Medicaid waivers to permit them to "carve out" "behavioral health" for managed care include California, Colorado, Florida, Georgia, Hawaii, Indiana, Iowa, Massachusetts, Minnesota, Montana, Nebraska, North Carolina, Oregon, Texas, Utah, and Washington. Arkansas, Kansas, Kentucky, Mississippi, Missouri, New Mexico, New York, Pennsylvania, and West Virginia have waivers pending as of this book goes to press. By October 2000, the number will undoubtedly have grown.

143. Regulations issued by DOJ provide that "a public entity, in providing any aid, benefit, or service, may not, directly or through contractual licensing or other arrangements," discriminate on the basis of disability; 28 C.F.R. Sec. 35.130(b)(1).

144. Burns-Vidlak v. Chandler, 939 F.Supp. 765, 772 (D. Haw. 1996).

145. David Mechanic, "Integrating Mental Health Care into a General Health Care System," *Hosp. and Comm. Psychiatry* 45 (1994):893–897.

146. Bentson H. McFarland, Richard E. Johnson, and Mark C. Hornbrook, "Enrollment Duration, Service Use and Costs of Care for Severely Mentally Ill Members of a Health Maintenance Organization," *Archives of Gen. Psychiatry* 53 (Oct. 1996):938, 943.

147. R. Scheffler, C. Grogan, B. Cuffel, and S. Penner, "A Specialized Mental Health Plan for Persons With Severe Mental Illness Under Managed Competition," *Hosp. and Comm. Psychiatry* 44 (1993):937–942.

148. R. Sturm, C. A. Jackson, L. S. Meredith, W. Yip, et al., "Mental Health Care Utilization in Pre-Paid and Fee-for-Service Plans Among Depressed Patients in the Medical Outcomes Study," *Health Serv. Res.* 30 (1995):319–340.

149. W. H. Rogers et al., "Outcomes for Adult Outpatients With Depression Under Prepaid or Fee for Service Financing," *Archives of Gen. Psychiatry* 50 (1993):517; M. K. Popking et al., "Changes in Process of Care for Medicaid Patients With Schizophrenia in Utah's Prepaid Mental Health Plan," *Psychiatric Services* 49 (1998):518.

150. *See* the Letter from the Montana Advocacy Project to Beth Sullivan, Office of Managed Care, Health Care Financing Administration (June 13, 1996) (on file with author). This letter states that Montana's proposal to exclude patients at Montana State Hospital and the Montana Mental Health Nursing Care Center from the managed care plan "discriminates against persons institutionalized at [those institutions because] they are not to be accorded the rights of other persons under the plan."

151. *Id.*

152. Small v. Montana, No. CV-96-49-H-CCL (filed D. Mont. July 15, 1996).

153. Interview with Ira A. Burnim, Bazelon Center for Mental Health Law (Jan. 28, 1999).

154. Taylor v. Johnson, No. CV-98-09776 (Dist. Ct. Bernalillo County, filed Oct. 8, 1998).

155. Thomas M. Wizicker, Daniel Lessler, and Karen M. Travis, "Controlling Inpatient Psychiatric Utilization Through Managed Care," *Amer. J. of Psychiatry* 153 (1996):339.

156. Judith Feldman, quoted in Bentson H. McFarland, Richard E. Johnson, and Mark C. Hornbrook, "Enrollment Duration, Service Use, and Costs of Care for Severely Mentally Ill Members of a Health Maintenance Organization," *Archives of Gen. Psychiatry* 53 (Oct. 1996):938, 943.

157. "Advocates in more than one state have noted that appendices may need to be specifically requested from the State Medicaid agency. . . . [T]hese appendices can describe some very important aspects of the contractual arrangement." Jane Perkins and Kristi Olson, "An Advocate's Primer on Medicaid Managed Care Contracting," *Clearinghouse Rev.* (May/June 1997):29. *See also* the letter from Montana Advocacy Project to Beth Sullivan, Office of Managed Care, Health Care Financing Administration (June 13, 1996)

at 4, which states that "the State has provided interested parties with its [Montana Mental Health Access Plan] and RFP, however at numerous places within the RFP reference is made to 'attachments' that are not provided" (on file with author).

158. Wilmington Star-News v. New Hanover Regional Medical Center, 480 S.E.2d 53 (N.C.App. 1997).

159. Daniels v. Wadley, 926 F.Supp. 1305, 1311 (M.D. Tenn. 1996), *rev'd,* Daniels v. Menke, 145 F.3d 1330 (table case), 1998 U.S. App. LEXIS 7973 (6th Cir. Apr. 22, 1998); Catazo v. Wing, 992 F.Supp. 593, 596 (W.D. N.Y. 1998).

160. Sara Rosenbaum, Rafael Serrano, Michele Magar, and Gillian Stern, "Civil Rights in a Changing Health Care System," *Health Affairs* 16(1) (Jan.–Feb. 1997):90–105, note 14. Missouri's plan, e.g., permits disenrollment because of "a persistent refusal of the patient to follow prescribed treatments" or for "abusive or threatening conduct." The state, however, retains sole authority to approve or disapprove of the disenrollment, and the managed care plan must make at least three efforts to resolve the problem first. *See* Center for Health Policy Research, *A Nationwide Study of Medicaid Managed Care Contracts* 2nd ed. (June 8, 1998), available on the Internet at http://www.chcs.org/oview.htm at 23.

161. Center for Health Care Strategies, *A Nationwide Study of Medicaid Managed Care Contracts* 2nd ed. (Princeton, NJ: Author, 1998), available on the World Wide Web at http://www.chcs.org.

162. *Id.*

163. Jane Perkins and Kristi Olson, "An Advocate's Primer on Medicaid Managed Care Contracting," *Clearinghouse Rev.* 31 (May–June 1997):19, 21.

164. Anderson v. Department of Public Welfare, 1 F.Supp. 2d 456 (E.D. Pa. 1998).

165. Avram Goldstein, "Is Managed Care Equipped for the Disabled?" THE WASHINGTON POST (Apr. 22, 1998):B1, B5. This article quotes complaints by the National Health Law Program that the HCFA did not respond adequately to numerous complaints about problems affecting people with disabilities in state Medicaid managed care programs.

166. Woolfolk v. Duncan, 872 F.Supp. 1381 (E.D. Pa. 1995).

167. *Id.* at 1386.

168. *Id.* at 1388–1389.

169. *Id.* at 1390.

170. *Id.*

171. No. CV-98-0976 (filed on Oct. 8, 1998), 2nd Judicial District, Bernalillo County, N.M. (state court).

172. Complaint at 2, *id.*

173. Alexander v. Choate, 469 U.S. 287 (1985).

174. *Id.* at 302.

175. 469 U.S. 287, 309 (1985).

176. Rowley v. Board of Education, 458 U.S. 176 (1982) (interpreting the scope of the right to a "free appropriate education" under the Education for All Handicapped Children Act, now the Individuals With Disabilities in Education Act).

177. *Id.* at 206–207.

178. P. L. 101-476.

179. Youngberg v. Romeo, 457 U.S. 307 (1982); Parham v. J. R., 442 U.S. 584 (1979); Rhodes v. Chapman, 452 U.S. 337, 357 (1981).

180. Some courts have tended to rely on *Alexander* in cases involving private, for-profit insurance companies, which may be an unwarranted expansion of the scope of the case. *See, e.g.,* Weyer v. Twentieth Century Fox Film Corp., 198 F.3d 1104, 1118 (9th Cir. 2000); Lenox v. Healthwise of Kentucky, 149 F.3d 453, 457 (6th Cir. 1998); Ford v. Schering-Plough, 145 F.3d 601, 608 (3rd Cir. 1998); Parker v. Metropolitan Life, 121 F.3d 1006 (6th Cir. 1997) (*en banc*).

181. Alexander v. Choate, 469 U.S. 287, 300 (1985).
182. Congress concluded that the Rehabilitation Act provides inadequate protections to people with disabilities in terms of its scope, language, and the courts' interpretation of its protections; *see* Helen L. v. Didario, 46 F.3d at 331; *see also* Robert L. Burgdorf, Jr., "The Americans With Disabilities Act: Analysis and Implications of a Second-Generation Civil Rights Statute," *Harv. Civil Rights–Civil Liberties Law Rev.* 26 (1991): 413, 441–445.
183. H.R.101-485 (Pt. II) at 61, 84 *reprinted in* 1992 U.S.C.C.A.N. 343, 367 (May 15, 1990).
184. *Id.*
185. "Except as otherwise provided in this chapter, nothing in this chapter shall be construed to apply a lesser standard than the standards applied under Title V of the Rehabilitation Act of 1973 (29 U.S.C. Secs. 790 *et seq.*) or the regulations issued by Federal agencies pursuant to such title"; 42 U.S.C. Sec. 12201(a). The U.S. Supreme Court, in its second ADA decision, reaffirmed this statutory provision as guaranteeing that the ADA must be interpreted to provide at least as much protection as the Rehabilitation Act; Bragdon v. Abbott, 524 U.S. 624, 118 S.Ct. 2196, 141 L.Ed.2d 540, 563–564 (1998).
186. 28 C.F.R. § 35.130(b)(8) (2000).
187. 28 C.F.R. § 35.130(b)(8) (Interpretive Guidance).
188. It is not clear that interviews with disabled people would have ameliorated this problem because people with one disability cannot speak for those with other or multiple disabilities, with more extreme or lesser versions of the same disability, or indeed for anyone but themselves.
189. M. J. Mehlman, M. R. Durchslag, and D. Neuhauser, "When Do Health Care Decisions Discriminate Against Persons With Disabilities?" *Health Policy & Law* 22 (Apr. 1998): 1385, 1389.
190. Michael J. Astrue, "Pseudoscience and the Law: The Case of the Oregon Rationing Experiment," *Issues in Law & Med.* 9 (1994):375.
191. *See* the letter from Timothy Flanagan, assistant attorney general, Department of Justice, to Susan K. Zagame, acting general counsel, Department of Health and Human Services (Jan. 19, 1993), *Issues in Law & Med.* 9 (1994):418–422.
192. 527 U.S. 581 (1999).
193. The "frail elderly" population was added as a potential population for home- and community-based services in 1990, and states rapidly took advantage of this option. Only four states—Colorado, Kansas, New York, and Ohio—have waivers that specifically serve people with psychiatric disabilities (Missouri has such a waiver pending). Over half of all states have waivers permitting them to provide mental health and behavioral services to other populations, such as older people, people with brain damage, and children.
194. Interview with Mary Kay Mullen, Health Care Financing Administration (Apr. 25, 2000).
195. *See* Georgia Waiver no. 40170.90 ("behavior management to severely disabled adults between the ages of 21 and 64"); Idaho Waiver Application no. 40187 ("behavior consultation/crisis management to MR/DD [mentally retarded developmentally disabled] age 21 and older who are currently living in a State owned and operated ICF/MR [Intermediate Care Facility for the Mentally Retarded]"); Idaho Application no. 40189 ("behavior consultation/crisis management for individuals with TBI [traumatic brain injury]"); Mississippi Waiver no. 40119.90R1 ("didactic [psychosocial] svcs., psychological/behavior treatment to MR/DD under [age] 26"); Missouri Waiver no. 40185 ("behavior therapy and crisis intervention to MR/DD individuals up to [age] 18 years").
196. Helen L. v. Didario, 46 F.3d 325 (3rd Cir. 1995), was discussed at length in the previous chapter. *See* other cases such as Easley v. Snider, 36 F.3d 297 (3rd Cir. 1994); and Marshall v. McMahon, 17 Cal. App. 4th 1841 (Cal. App. 1993).
197. Easley v. Snider, 36 F.3d 297 (3rd Cir. 1994), *reh'g denied,* 1994 U.S. App. LEXIS 29663.

198. Marshall v. McMahon, 17 Cal. App. 4th 1841 (Cal. App. 1993).
199. Rodriguez v. DeBuono, 177 F.R.D. 143 (S.D. N.Y. 1997), *vac.* in part and remanding order granting preliminary injunction, 162 F.3d 56 (2nd Cir. 1998), amended by 175 F.3d 227 (2nd Cir. 1999), on remand, 44 F.Supp. 2d 601 (S.D. N.Y. 1999), *rev'd,* 197 F.3d 611 (2nd Cir. 1999).
200. Easley v. Snider, *see* note 197. *See* chapter 4 for a discussion of this argument.
201. The question of discrimination as to between groups of people with different disabilities is different than the question of whether the ADA prohibits discrimination as to between people with the same disability, which has usually been framed in terms of discrimination on the basis of severity of disability. This question is discussed in chapter 4.
202. Hodges v. Smith, 910 F.Supp. 646 (N.D. Ga. 1995).
203. Cameron v. Alander, 39 Conn. App. 216 (1995).
204. Messier v. Southbury Training School, 916 F.Supp. 133 D. Conn. 1996); Martin v. Voinovich, 840 F.Supp. 1175 (S.D. Ohio 1993); Garrity v. Gallen, 522 F.Supp. 171 (D. N.H. 1981); Jackson v. Fort Stanton State Hospital, 757 F.Supp. 1243, 1299 (D. N.M. 1990), *rev'd* in part on other grounds, 964 F.2d 980 (10th Cir. 1992).
205. *E.g.,* people who are blind are favored over people with other disabilites in numerous government disability benefits programs. Challenges to this kind of differential treatment have been uniformly rejected by the courts under both the ADA, Vaughn v. Sullivan, 83 F.3d 907 (7th Cir. 1996), and the Rehabilitation Act, Eva N. v. Brock, 741 F.Supp. 626 (E.D. Ky. 1990). However, numerous circuit courts have also held that the ADA and Section 504 prohibit discrimination among people with disabilities on the basis of the type of disability; Wagner v. Fair Acres Geriatric Center, 49 F.3d 1002, 1016, note 15 (3rd Cir. 1995); Doe v. Colautti, 592 F.2d 704, 708 (3rd Cir. 1979); McGuire v. Switzer, 734 F.Supp. 99, 114, note 16 (S.D. N.Y. 1990).
206. The statutory language of the ADA, legislative history, relevant regulations, and case law under the Rehabilitation Act all suggest that Congress intended for private insurance to be analyzed in a different way than the Medicaid program or other state health programs, *see* 42 U.S.C. Sec. 12201(c), setting up a ''safe harbor'' for private insurance coverage under certain circumstances. Congress undoubtedly intended to provide insurance companies a unique set of defenses to charges of discrimination under the ADA. The exact nature of these defenses remains unclear, and they may or may not save the disparities, but they require a different kind of analysis. As a matter of policy, special protection for private insurance companies may be unwise because subjecting public entities such as states to the full requirements of the ADA in Medicaid and other programs, while insulating private insurers to some extent from these requirements, simply gives preference to private, market-based discriminatory action whereas applying different standards to state entities. This underscores the fiction of the ''free market'': Insurance companies do not reject all regulations but lobby for and embrace regulations that limit their free market to more profitable clients, while freeing them from the constraints of antidiscrimination law. This leaves the states to serve the ''rejects'' of the free market while remaining fully bound by more restrictive regulations. Congress has chosen to pursue a different policy, however, and the courts must follow it.
207. These include such typical legislative actions as endowing a state school for the deaf and blind, *see* FLA. STAT. 242.3305 (1999); funding a statewide black leadership conference on HIV and AIDS, FLA. STAT. 381.0046(3) (1999); and the creation of an Alzheimer's disease advisory committee, FLA. STAT. 430.501 (1999).
208. 42 U.S.C. Sec. 12101(b)(1).
209. Helen L. v. Didario, 46 F.3d at 336; L. C. v. Olmstead, 138 F.3d at 900 (11th Cir. 1998), *cert. granted,* 119 S.Ct. 617 (Dec. 14, 1998), amended to limit grant to Q1 of Petition, 119 S.Ct. 633 (Dec, 17, 1998).
210. Mary A. Crossly, ''Of Diagnoses and Discrimination: Discriminatory Nontreatment of

Infants With HIV Infection," *Colum. Law Rev.* 93 (1993):1581, 1602 (48% of primary care physicians in Los Angeles reported that they had elected not to care for or said they would not provide care for patients with HIV infection).

211. House Judiciary Committee Report, Rep. No. 101–485 (Pt. III) at 26 ("the Americans with Disabilities Act completes the circle begun in 1973 with respect to persons with disabilities by extending to them the same civil rights protections provided to women and minorities beginning in 1964").

212. O'Connor v. Consolidated Coin Caterer's Corp., 517 U.S. 308, 312 (1996) (age discrimination).

213. 527 U.S. 581 (1999).

214. Jefferies v. Harris County Community Action Association, 615 F.2d 1025 (5th Cir. 1980) ("evidence of non-discriminatory treatment of black males and white females is irrelevant to the question of discrimination against a black female claiming bias on both racial and gender grounds").

215. Lam v. University of Hawaii, 40 F.3d 1551, 1561 (9th Cir. 1994).

216. This definition comes from an amalgamation of terms used by Congress in its statutory findings at the beginning of the ADA and in congressional reports and hearings.

217. House Rep. 101-485 (Pt. II) at 58 (emphasis added).

218. Prewitt v. U.S. Postal Service, 662 F.2d 292, 307 (5th Cir. 1981), *quoting* Amy Gittler, "Fair Employment and the Handicapped: A Legal Perspective," *De Paul Law Rev.* 27 (1978):953, 972 (the Rehabilitation Act).

219. Martin v. Voinovich, 840 F.Supp. 1175, 1192 (S.D. Ohio 1993).

220. *See* pp. 217–218 *infra* for a discussion of how to make this distinction.

221. H.Rep. 101-485, Pt. III, 101st Cong., 2nd Sess. (May 15, 1990) at 58–59.

222. 485 U.S. 535 (1988).

223. *Id.* at 538.

224. *Id.*

225. *Id.* at 538, note 2.

226. *Id.* at 538.

227. Justices Scalia and Rehnquist took no part in the decision in the case.

228. P. L. 95-602.

229. *See* note 222 at 548.

230. *Id.* at 550.

231. *Id.* at 549–550.

232. *See, e.g.,* Riley v. Ambach, 508 F.Supp. 1222 (E.D. N.Y. 1980), *rev'd* for other reasons, 668 F.2d 635 (2nd Cir. 1981); Garrity v. Gallen, 522 F.Supp. 171 at 215–217 (finding that the defendants had discriminated against physically disabled people with mental retardation by treating ambulatory mentally retarded people more favorably).

233. *See, e.g.,* Martin v. Voinovich, 840 F.Supp. 1175 (S.D. Ohio 1993); McGuire v. Switzer, 734 F.Supp. 99, 114–115 (S.D. N.Y. 1990), *but see* Flight v. Goeckler, 878 F.Supp. 424 (N.D. N.Y), *aff'd,* 68 F.3d 61 (2nd Cir. 1995).

234. 485 U.S. 535, 561–564 (1988).

235. 28 C.F.R. Sec. 35.130(c).

236. Department of Justice, Interpretive Guidance, 28 C.F.R. Sec. 35.130, explaining 28 C.F.R. Sec. 35.130(c).

237. Department of Justice, Civil Rights Division, Coordination and Review Section, Policy Letter of Finding to Unknown Complainant, California, Re: Healthcare, Feb. 3, 1992, cited in *U.S. Commission on Civil Rights, Helping State and Local Governments Comply With the ADA: An Assessment of How the United States Department of Justice is Enforcing Title II, Subpart A of the Americans With Disabilities Act* (Washington, DC: Author, Sept. 1998) at 94.

238. *See* Chris Doe v. Stincer, 990 F.Supp. 1427 (S.D. Fla. 1997), *vac.* on other grounds, 175 F.3d 879 (11th Cir. 1999).

239. Some people have suggested making the distinction in terms of the service provided; Braille services, e.g., can only assist blind people. Conversation with Mary Giliberti, Bazelon Center for Mental Health Law (Feb. 1999). However, "services provided" are subject to different levels of abstraction in defining them, so that the distinction becomes less helpful. Is the service provided by Gallaudet College an education, primarily through sign language, beneficial only to people who are deaf or hearing impaired, or is the service provided "education," which would benefit all people with disabilities?

240. Duc Van Le v. Ibarra (a written opinion of a trial court judge) (on file with author). The process by which the challenge was successful is more procedurally complex than usual. The plaintiffs won at trial. The U.S. Supreme Court took jurisdiction of the appeal and reversed the trial court, 1992 Colo. LEXIS 385 (Apr. 20, 1992). The Supreme Court then granted a request for rehearing *en banc*, 1992 Colo. LEXIS 447 (May 28, 1992). Because three justices of the Colorado Supreme Court would affirm the trial court, three would reverse, and the seventh judge recused himself, the trial court's judgment was affirmed, 1992 Colo. LEXIS 1148 (Dec. 14, 1992). The Supreme Court refused to reconsider this decision, 1993 Colo. LEXIS 4 (Jan. 11, 1993). Although the U.S. Supreme Court stayed the decision pending consideration of a petition for certiorari, it ultimately denied *certiorari*.

241. Because Medicaid does not cover services provided in psychiatric institutions, paying for community services for individuals who would otherwise be in a psychiatric institution was not considered to be a savings; *see* 42 C.F.R. Sec. 441(j).

242. Under the ADA, this issue would not arise because the department would be subject to Title II.

243. Easley v. Snider, 36 F.3d 297 (3rd Cir. 1994); Marshall v. McMahon, 17 Cal. App. 4th 1841, 1844–1845 (1993), *rev. den'd,* 1993 Cal. LEXIS 6086 (Ca. Nov. 17, 1993).

244. *See* the Health Care Financing Administration (HCFA) web site at http://www.hcfa.gov/medicaid.

245. 42 C.F.R. 441.301(b)(6) (2000).

246. This is assuming that the people with psychiatric disabilities were Medicaid eligible. HCVA found that the people served by the Colorado program were not Medicaid eligible because they would otherwise have been institutionalized and subject to the IMD exclusion.

247. L. C. v. Olmstead, 527 U.S. 581 (1999).

248. The current application for SSI involves one 15-page form, Form SSA-8000-BK (5-90), which concerns only the financial aspect of eligibility, and an additional 6-page form, SSA-3368-F6, the Disability Report, relating the claimant's disability.

249. SSA-8000-BK, question 24(a). To be fair, it is difficult for the SSA to comply with congressional admonitions designed to ensure that only the most needy people receive SSI while making their application forms brief and understandable. The Disability Report, which was recently redrafted, is admirably straightforward.

250. *See, e.g.,* Ford v. Apfel, 2000 U.S. Dist. LEXIS 2898*43 (E.D. N.Y. Jan. 13, 2000) (the claimant dropped her application for benefits because the Social Security Adminstration employee "left her 'very upset' and 'humiliated' ").

251. Sue E. Estroff, Catherine Zimmer, William S. Lachicotte, Julia Benoit, and Donald L. Patrick, " 'No Other Way to Go': Pathways to Disability Income Assistance Among Persons With Severe, Persistent Mental Illness," in Richard Bonnie and John Monahan, Eds., *Mental Disorder, Work Disability and the Law* (Chicago: University of Chicago Press, 1997) at 78.

252. Sue E. Estroff et al., *id.*

253. Numerous manuals are devoted to helping disabled people and their advocates navigate the benefits system. These unfortunately become rapidly outdated as regulations and laws change. One of the best is Edwin J. Lopez-Soto and James R. Sheldon, Jr., *Benefits*

Management for Working People With Disabilities (Rochester, NY: Greater Upstate Law Project, 1998).

254. J. L. v. Social Security Administration, 971 F.2d 260 (9th Cir. 1992).

255. Bowen v. City of New York, 476 U.S. 467 (1986).

256. Stieberger v. Apfel, 134 F.3d 37, 40 (2nd Cir. 1997) (the notice of administrative appellate time limits to appeal adverse determination of eligibility for mental disability benefits may be constitutionally defective when received by a person too mentally ill to understand the notice); Penner v. Schweiker, 701 F.2d 256, 260–261 (3rd Cir. 1983) (same); Young v. Bowen, 858 F.2d 951, 955 (4th Cir. 1988); Parker v. Califano, 644 F.2d 1199, 1203 (6th Cir. 1981); Evans v. Chater, 110 F.3d 1480, 1483 (9th Cir. 1997); Elchediak v. Heckler, 750 F.2d 892, 894 (11th Cir. 1985).

257. Bowen v. City of New York, 476 U.S. 467, 483 (1986); Ford v. Apfel, 2000 U.S. Dist. LEXIS 2898*42–43 (E.D. N.Y. Jan. 13, 2000) (describing the "tremendous trauma" and "thoughts of suicide" in response to the notices of termination of benefits).

258. *See, e.g.,* 42 U.S.C. 405(b) (1999); 20 C.F.R. 416.1404 (1999).

259. *See* Ford v. Apfel, note 250 *21.

260. *Id.* *23.

261. *Id.* *50; David v. Heckler, 591 F.Supp. 1033, 1044 (E.D. N.Y. 1984).

262. Padron v. Feaver, 180 F.R.D. 448, 450 (S.D. Fla. 1998).

263. Vaughn v. Sullivan, 83 F.3d 907 (7th Cir. 1996).

264. 42 U.S.C. Sec. 423(f).

265. 42 U.S.C. Sec. 402(x)(1)(A)(ii)(II).

266. Milner v. Apfel, 148 F.3d 812 (7th Cir. 1998).

267. *Id.* at 815.

268. *Id.* at 817.

269. Personal Responsibility and Work Opportunity Reconciliation Act, P. L. 104-193. Federal welfare reform is, of course, not subject to challenge under the ADA because the activities of the federal government are not covered by the ADA.

270. Presidential Task Force on Employment of Adults With Disabilities, Work Group on the Personal Responsibility and Work Opportunity Reconciliation Act (Nov. 1998) at 14. World Wide Web at http://www.dol.gov/_sec/public/programs/ptfead/rechart/sat5PTFEADfinalwp-16.htm. The report shows that "approximately 20% of female welfare recipients have either a work limitation due to a physical, mental or other health problem or a functional disability."

271. Beno v. Shalala, 853 F.Supp. 1195, 1212 (E.D. Ca. 1993), *rev'd,* 30 F.3d 1057 (9th Cir. 1994). The 9th Circuit reversed on grounds other than the ADA and did not consider the ADA claims in its decision.

272. *Id.* at 1213.

273. *Id.*

274. 28 C.F.R. Sec. 35.130(b)(1)(iii) (2000).

275. 28 C.F.R. Sec. 35.130(b)(3)(ii) (2000).

276. This would have required a factual inquiry into the impact of the cuts on the plaintiffs' ability to sustain themselves and a particularly difficult conclusion on when already inadequate welfare benefits reach the point of no meaningful access. Because many courts have found that small cuts in AFDC constitute irreparable harm—Moore v. Miller, 579 F.Supp. 1188, 1191–1192 (N.D. Ill. 1983) ("for those in the grip of poverty, living on the financial edge, even a small decrease in payments can cause irreparable harm"); Crane v. Mathews, 417 F.Supp. 532, 539–540 (N.D. Ga. 1976) (imposition of $2 co-payment for medical treatment is irreparable harm to welfare recipients living at subsistence level)—it might be argued that these much more substantial cuts deprived the plaintiffs of meaningful access to AFDC benefits.

277. Presidential Task Force on Employment of Adults With Disabilities, Work Group on the Personal Responsibility and Work Opportunity Reconciliation Act (Nov. 1998) at 19.

278. Does 1–5 v. Chandler, 83 F.3d 1150 (9th Cir. 1996).
279. Burns-Vidlak v. Chandler, 939 F.Supp. 765 (D. Haw. 1996) (in this case, the plaintiffs sued for damages and the restoration of benefits); Weaver v. N.M. Department of Human Services, 945 P.2d 70 (N.M. 1997).
280. 1998 U.S. App. LEXIS 16424 (9th Cir. July 20, 1998).
281. Brown v. Campbell County Board of Education, 915 S.W.2d 407 (Tenn. 1996); Cramer v. Florida, 885 F.Supp. 1545 (M.D. Fla. 1995), *aff'd*, Harding v. Winn-Dixie Stores, 907 F.Supp. 386 (M.D. Fla. 1995); Oregon state case, In re Bailey, 959 P.2d 84, 86 (Ore. App. 1998); Barry v. Burdines, 675 S.2d 587 (Fla. 1996); Hensley v. Punta Gorda, 686 S.2d 724 (Fla. App. 1997); Barbara Brown v. A-Dec, Inc., 961 P.2d 280 (Ore. App. 1998); In re Worker's Compensation Claim of Frantz, 932 P.2d 750 (Wyo. 1997) (challenged under the equal protection clauses of the state and federal constitutions).
282. Means v. Baltimore County, 689 A.2d 1238 (Md. 1997) (a paramedic's posttraumatic stress disorder may be compensable as an occupational disease).
283. Collado v. City of Albuquerque, 904 P.2d 57 (N.M. App. 1995).
284. Davis v. Dyncorps, 647 A.2d 446 (Md. 1994); *see, e.g.*, FLA. STAT. 440.02(1), excluding coverage for "mental or nervous injury due to stress, fright or excitement").
285. In re Worker's Compensation Claim of Frantz, 932 P.2d 750 (Wyo. 1997). Other cases unsuccessfully challenging the differential treatment of emotional and physical disabilities under constitutional equal protection provisions include Williams v. Alaska Department of Revenue, 895 P.2d 99 (Alaska 1995); Hansen v. Worker's Compensation Appeal Board, 23 Cal. Rptr. 2d 30 (Cal. App. 1993); and Hensley v. Punta Gorda, 686 S.2d 724 (Fla. App. 1997).
286. The Rehabilitation Act usually does not apply because the state workers' compensation statute neither is administered by a federal agency nor receives federal funds; Brown v. Campbell County Board of Education, 915 S.W.2d 407 (Tenn. 1996).
287. Barry v. Burdine's, 675 S.2d 587 (Fla. 1996).
288. *Id.*
289. *See* Ellen Smith Pryor, "Book Review: Flawed Promises: A Critical Evaluation of the AMA's Guides to the Evaluation of Permanent Impairment," *Harv. Law Rev.* 103 (1990): 964.
290. Cramer v. Florida, 117 F.3d 1258 (11th Cir. 1997); Hensley v. Punta Gorda, 686 S.2d 724 (Fla. App. 1997).
291. *See* Cramer v. Florida (1997) (an appellate court was apoplectic because the law firm pursued a challenge to the workers' compensation scheme under the ADA, which went up to the Florida Supreme Court, received adverse decision, and refiled the same challenge in federal court, without notifying either the federal district court or the court of appeals).
292. Brown v. Campbell County Board of Education, 915 S.W.2d 407 (Tenn. 1996). This case has not been cited outside of Tennessee.
293. *EEOC Technical Assistance Manual* 9.6.b (1992); *see* EEOC Enforcement Guidance re Workers' Compensation and the Americans With Disabilities Act, *EEOC Compliance Manual* 915.002 (Sept. 3, 1996).
294. Barry v. Burdine's, 675 S.2d 587, 589 (Fla. 1996).
295. *Id.* at 589.
296. Harding v. Winn-Dixie Stores, 907 F.Supp. 386 (M.D. Fla. 1995).
297. 401 U.S. 424 (1971).
298. Brown v. Campbell Board of Education, 915 SW2d 407 (Tenn. 1996).
299. *See, e.g.*, the testimony of Linda Mills, A&P Comm. Print 1990 (28B)*1186; Lisa Lyons, A&P Comm. Print (28B)*1158; Ilona Durkin, A&P Comm. Print (28B)*1081; Catherine Marshall, *id.* *1150–1151; Donald Levine, *id.* *1071; Lelia Batten, *id.* *1023.
300. Testimony of Linda Mills A&P Comm. Print (28B)*1186 (1990).

301. Testimony of Lelia Batten, A&P Comm. Print (28B)*1023 (1990).
302. Testimony of Catherine Marshall, A&P Comm. Print 1990 (28B)*1150–1151.
303. Survey No. 100 (a vocational agency undervalued her abilities); Survey No. 108 (a former CPA was not permitted to return to his prior field of employment through vocational rehabilitation); Survey No. 157 (see text below); Survey No. 158 (see text below); Survey No. 179; Survey No. 204 (the Office of Vocational Rehabilitation suggested that the respondent go on welfare; subsequently she arranged for her own employment); *but see* Jean Campbell and Ron Schraiberg, *The Well-Being Project* (Sacramento: California Department of Mental Health, 1989) at 179 (60% of people with psychiatric diagnoses in California who were surveyed reported that they had been in a vocational rehabilitation program that was "very beneficial" or "somewhat beneficial." This may be an artifact of the unique appointment by Gov. Jerry Brown of Ed Roberts, the founder of Independent Living Centers, to be the director of vocational rehabilitation for the state of California).
304. Survey No. 157 (on file with author).
305. Survey No. 158.
306. Testimony of Donald Levine, A&P Comm. Print (1990) (2B)*1071; Lisa Lyons, note 299*1157.
307. Carolyn L. Weaver, "Incentives Versus Controls in Federal Disability Policy," in *Disability and Work Incentives, Rights and Opportunities*, Carolyn L. Weaver, Ed. (Washington, DC: American Enterprise Institute Press, 1991) at 4; L. S. Muller, "Disability Beneficianos Who Work and Their Experiences Under Program Work Incentives," *Social Security Bulletin* 55 (1989):2.
308. Richard Baron, "Establishing Employment Services as a Priority for Persons With Long-Term Mental Illness, *Amer. Rehab.* 21(1) (Mar. 22, 1995):32 (noting that "VR [vocational rehabilitation] counselors . . . remain dubious about the vocational potential of those with mental illness" and that "it has been the habit of the [VR] field to insist that all of these problems [i.e., medication, housing, and social and financial problems] be solved before work issues are addressed"); Judith A. Cook and Susan A. Pickett, "Recent Trends in Vocational Rehabilition for People With Psychiatric Disability," *Amer. Rehab.* 20(2) (Dec. 22, 1994):2 (noting that the rehabilitation field has always considered services for people with mental illness as the "last frontier"); Robert B. Harvey, "Enhancing Employment Options for Individuals With Severe and Persistent Mental Illnesses," *Amer. Rehab* 20(4) (June 22, 1994):2 ("the VR system, in contrast, is perceived by many consumers [with mental illness] as cumbersome and/or unresponsive"); *see also* J. H. Noble, Jr., "Policy Reform Dilemmas in Promoting Employment of Persons With Severe Mental Illnesses," *Psychiatric Services* 49 (1998):775 (a federal–state VR program largely wastes an estimated $490 million annually on time-limited services to consumers with mental illnesses).
309. Kent v. Director of Missouri Department of Elementary and Secondary Education, 792 F.Supp. 59 (E.D. Mo. 1992).
310. 527 U.S. 581 (1999).
311. Kent v. Director of Missouri Department of Elementary and Secondary Education, *id.*
312. Doe v. Pfrommer, 148 F.3d 73, 76 (2nd Cir. 1998).
313. *Id.*
314. McGuire v. Switzer, 734 F.Supp. 99, 114 (S.D. N.Y. 1990). The holding in *McGuire* was put in some doubt by the 2nd Circuit's subsequent affirmance of Flight v. Goeckler, 68 F.3d 61 (2nd Cir. 1995). The continuing validity of *Flight*, in turn, is put in doubt by the U.S. Supreme Court's holding in Olmstead v. L. C. that the ADA does not require a nondisabled "comparison class" for a plaintiff to state a claim.
315. *Id.*
316. *Id.*

317. Berg v. Florida Department of Labor & Employment Security, Division of Vocational Rehabilitation, 163 F.3d 1251 (11th Cir. 1998); Mallett v. Wisconsin Division of Vocational Rehabilitation, 130 F.3d 1245 (7th Cir. 1997).
318. *See* note 2.
319. P. L. 106-170.
320. 119 S.Ct. 2176, 2187 (1999).

Chapter 6
PRIVATE INSURANCE AND THE
AMERICANS WITH DISABILITIES ACT

The most explicit discrimination on the basis of mental disabilities is done by private insurance companies, which provide differential and distinctly disadvantageous coverage for mental health conditions in both health insurance and disability benefits. In addition, private insurance companies deny people with histories of mental health treatment insurance for life, disability, and property or charge them substantially inflated rates, simply because they are receiving mental health treatment or even counseling or therapy. The Americans With Disabilities Act (ADA) of 1990 has a delphic section that purports to prohibit certain actions by insurance companies as discriminatory while insulating other actions from liability.

From 1987, when the National Council on the Handicapped began proposing a federal civil rights bill on behalf of people with disabilities,[1] until the last congressional hearing was held in 1989, hundreds of people testified before both the council and Congress about their experiences as disabled Americans. Much of that testimony detailed discriminatory insurance practices. Witnesses told of being denied insurance,[2] having insurance cancelled or withdrawn,[3] or being placed in a higher risk category or charged extremely high premiums[4] on the basis of disability; others told of having needed services categorically excluded or provided only once in an individual's lifetime.[5] Still other witnesses related that employers told them that they were being denied jobs because hiring a person with disabilities would lead to higher insurance rates.[6] There was also testimony that insurance companies refused to insure employers who hired too many people with disabilities.[7]

People with psychiatric disabilities also testified regarding discriminatory insurance practices. William Cavanaugh, the executive director of Ad Lib, an independent living center, testified that

> other discriminatory practices are sanctioned by law or traditional policies or regulations. One such example is the accepted practice of insurance firms being allowed to practice discriminatory policies that regularly deny medical insurance to individuals who are disabled based on possibilities of medical needs.[8]

Cavanaugh's testimony, however, was unusual. Although insurance companies treat people with psychiatric disabilities in many of the ways that they treat people with physical disabilities, insurance practices were not the principal focus of most testimony by people with psychiatric disabilities regarding the ADA. This may have been because, as one witness noted, "Most psychiatric clients do not have insurance because of their poverty levels."[9] However, it may also have been because Rep. Major Owens (D-NY), in a burst of candor, discouraged such testimony. When the House Subcommittee on Select Education of the House Committee on Education and Labor took testimony in Boston, the overwhelming condemnation of the insurance industry by witnesses with disabilities and their demands that discriminatory insurance practices be curtailed produced the following illuminating dialogue between Rep. Owens and the witness about the power of the insurance lobby:

> *Mr. Owens*: We deliberately, as you know, it was a consensus that the best political strategy was not to tackle the insurance issue in this bill head on. So, it is the kind of thing that we should be preparing legislation for in another bill and start that fight rolling.
> *Mr. Dorfer*: Why is that?
> *Mr. Owens*: We can discuss it in detail later. In terms of strategy, to take on the insurance industry, to put it bluntly, to take on the insurance industry might guarantee far more difficulty, double or triple the difficulty that we are going to encounter at this time to take on the insurance industry. But we understand the need. And, as a matter of strategy, let us move ahead with this and perhaps we should have the insurance bill—the bill to confront the insurance industry in the works, now, as a proposition for tomorrow. Thank you very much.[10]

The next two witnesses after Dorfer said that they had planned to testify about discrimination by insurance companies but would not address the issue in light of the exchange; finally, Rep. Owens encouraged them to speak out anyway.[11]

Once the ADA was passed, however, a number of discriminatory insurance practices were quickly challenged by people with psychiatric disabilities. These included refusing life, homeowner's, and other forms of insurance to people with psychiatric disabilities and the cancellation of coverage, both on the basis of psychiatric disability and discrimination in the terms and conditions of coverage in health and disability insurance policies and retirement plans. The results of the survey also document current practices by insurance companies. One man who was severely injured in a car accident illustrated those practices when he dictated the following through his sister:

> The day of the accident everyone assumed I would die—my eyes were pushed into my brain. . . . I had to have a third of the front part of my brain removed along with my eyes. . . . I have no eyes—just open sockets—the insurance considers prothetic [*sic*] eyes as cosmetic surgery.[12]

The most common complaint by far, however, involves the distinction made by insurance companies in both health and disability benefit plans between physical conditions and "mental," "psychiatric," "emotional," or "behavioral" conditions. These distinctions affected every aspect of coverage, from the duration of benefits to copayments to lifetime caps. The passage of the Mental Health Parity Act of 1996, which prohibited a few of these discriminatory practices in the context of health insurance,[13] has not stemmed the tide of ADA litigation in this area, which has so far concentrated principally in the area of disability benefits, to which the Mental Health Parity Act does not apply.

In deciding whether the challenged insurance company practices are prohibited under the ADA, courts have been faced with the task of interpreting Section 501(c) of the ADA,[14] a cryptic provision that appears to exempt most private insurance practices from the reach of the ADA. The exact language of the ADA relating to insurance companies is

> Section 501(c) Titles I–IV of the Act shall not be construed to prohibit or restrict—
> (1) an insurer, hospital or medical service company, health maintenance organization,

or any agent, or entity that administers benefit plans, or similar organizations from underwriting risks, classifying risks, or administering such risks that are based on or not inconsistent with State law; (2) a person or organization covered by this Act from establishing, sponsoring, observing or administering the terms of a bona fide benefit plan that are based on underwriting risks, classifying risks, or administering such risks that are based on or not inconsistent with State law; (3) a person or organization covered by this Act from establishing, sponsoring, observing, or administering the terms of a bona fide plan that is not subject to State laws that regulate insurance; Paragraphs (1), (2), and (3) shall not be used as a subterfuge to evade the purpose of subchapters I and III of this chapter.[15]

Despite a plethora of interpretive sources and guidance,[16] the task of understanding what Congress meant by Section 501(c) has proven to be difficult, and courts have devised a number of competing and contradictory interpretations of the ADA's application to insurance benefits.

Although there have been over 30 cases under the ADA challenging various aspects of insurance practices toward people who are perceived to have psychiatric disabilities,[17] few of these cases have actually examined the basis for insurance decision making in the area of psychiatric disabilities.[18] The paucity of critical examination by the judiciary of the proffered insurance rationales for the denial of policies, or for the greatly disproportionate charges or limitations of policies for people with psychiatric disabilities, contrasts with cases challenging insurance practices related to other disabilities, especially those related to AIDS, where courts have engaged in searching and skeptical examination of the rationale for insurance denials of individual coverage.[19]

Insurance companies deny life, disability, property, mortgage, and health insurance to individual applicants with psychiatric disabilities, and group disability and health policies contain grossly disparate terms and conditions of coverage for mental and physical conditions. The companies claim to have actuarial data supporting these decisions, and they argue that because mental conditions are extremely difficult to define and diagnose, caps are necessary because otherwise people would overuse the benefits, raising the cost of insurance for everyone.[20]

These claims and arguments have been treated with deference by courts, when in fact the data used by insurance companies to support disparate access and terms of coverage for psychiatric disabilities are open to serious question, especially in the area of individual underwriting decisions, but also in group coverage terms. Although there is a strong theoretical basis for the concept of risk classification, as an empirical matter, the basis for the risk classifications that are being made, particularly in the area of psychiatric disability, rests on shaky ground.

Studies by a host of respected independent organizations, including the Congressional Research Service,[21] the U.S. General Accounting Office, the Office of Technology Assessment, the Rand Corporation, and the University of California–Los Angeles,[22] have failed to substantiate that the degree of difference between insurance companies' coverage of mental and physical conditions is supported by corresponding degrees of economic exposure and risk. To the extent that insurance policies are based on insurance companies' own experience, those results are distorted because the experience is based on historical practices that are changing in the era of managed care and is predetermined by the structural biases of the coverage initially offered by insurance companies.

For example, if an insurance company offered—as most do—more generous coverage for hospitalization and inpatient care for mental illnesses than outpatient visits to therapists[23] and offered equally generous outpatient and inpatient coverage for physical illnesses, it would create an incentive favoring inpatient care for mental illnesses rather than favoring treatment in the most appropriate setting. Because inpatient care is more expensive than outpatient care, an insurance company that had structured its policies in this way would experience mental health care as proportionally more expensive than treatment for physical illnesses, but the insurance company itself would have guaranteed this result by the way it structured its policies. The more appropriate expense comparison would be between medical care in hospital settings and the mental health care covered by the insurance company.

Despite this, insurance companies are winning most ADA discrimination cases involving psychiatric disabilities, primarily because the courts fail to probe into the basis for their contention that psychiatric disabilities are more costly to insure than physical disabilities. This stands in contrast to discrimination cases involving coverage for HIV seropositivity and AIDS, where insurance companies have often lost because judges scrutinize the justification for insurance discrimination against people with those conditions.[24]

Therefore, this chapter examines the actual basis for insurance company policies and underwriting practices directed toward people with psychiatric disabilities, or who are perceived to have psychiatric disabilities, and argues that it is insufficient to justify the degree of discriminatory treatment reflected in insurance company policies and practices.

Summary of Insurance Practices

Courts interpret Section 501(c) in the context of existing federal legislation relating to the insurance industry. The McCarran–Ferguson Act[25] provides that regulation of the insurance industry is left up to the states, unless federal legislation explicitly regulates the insurance industry.[26] In addition to being essentially exempt from the antitrust laws,[27] for example, the insurance industry is also exempt from regulation by the Federal Trade Commission.[28] Although there was a flurry of congressional activity in the 1980s that almost resulted in federal regulation of the insurance industry, to date the federal government has never passed major legislation regulating insurance.

States have generally regulated the insurance industry under what is commonly called a "fair discrimination model." Under this model, insurance companies are allowed to classify, or discriminate, as long as the classifications correspond to "sound actuarial principles" or to "actual or reasonably anticipated experience,"[29] and as long as the difference in rate structure corresponds to differences in risk.[30]

As the Civil Rights Movement gained force, an "antidiscrimination" model (rather than "fair" discrimination) was used with some success to challenge insurance company practices that adversely affected suspect or quasisuspect classifications, such as ethnic minorities and women. More recently, the antidiscrimination model has been invoked to restrict the widespread practice of refusing to sell life, health, or disability insurance to women who are victims of domestic violence. Another example of the success of the antidiscrimination model has been the prohibition against insurers using genetic screening to deny coverage to individuals shown to have a high likelihood of developing breast and colon cancer, Huntington's chorea, and other diseases for which genetic markers exist or are being discovered.

The fair discrimination and antidiscrimination models generally share the assumption that insurance companies' conclusions are actuarially sound. Thus, both fair discrimination and antidiscrimination proponents would concur that black people have shorter life expectancies than white people and generally experience more health conditions and disabilities and that redlined neighborhoods may in fact present actuarially greater risks to insure, that women live longer than men, that battered women are more subject to injury, and that genetic markers effectively screen for certain health conditions. The models differ only in the conclusions to be drawn from these facts. The antidiscrimination model holds that it is fundamentally unfair to punish individuals for circumstances over which they have little or no control, or that are the results of different forms of discrimination, and that these values should trump the competing value of economic efficiency and optimal risk allocation. The fair discrimination model, however, permits difference in insurance coverage or charges as long as they are based on actual distinctions in health or longevity for which there is an evidentiary basis.

Parity between mental health and physical illness coverage is often spoken of in antidiscrimination terms, with the underlying assumption that the insurance companies' actuarial basis for discrimination is valid. A more thorough examination of that assumption, however, shows that insurance company practices toward people with psychiatric disabilities—from individual underwriting decisions to policies, such as the mental–physical distinction, that pervade the industry—are often based on outdated studies, draw the wrong conclusions from good studies, or even rely on precisely the sorts of irrational stereotypes that are typically associated with "unfair" discrimination. More important, the experience of insurance industries with costs related to psychiatric disabilities has been dictated by the structure of existing insurance coverage to become a self-fulfilling prophecy.

Insurance practices based on invalid assumptions are hardly unique to psychiatric disabilities. For example, insurance industry underwriting directives order agents not to sell insurance or to sell insurance at higher rates to men who are hairdressers or florists because of the assumption that these men are gay and thus present a greater risk of AIDS.[31] Insurers have denied coverage to people because they carry a single gene for sickle-cell anemia or Goucher's disease, in spite of the basic medical fact that such individuals have absolutely no chance of developing the disease.[32] A high official at State Farm Insurance justified denying coverage to battered women by saying that insuring a battered woman is like insuring a person with diabetes who refuses to take insulin.[33] It should not be surprising that social stereotypes and prejudice carry over into the individual assessments and decision making of insurance agents or even high-level executives.

What is surprising, however, is the tenacity of the stereotypes. Insurance companies historically have relied on manuals and actuarial research precisely to have an objective basis for decision making. Yet in many cases under the ADA, insurance companies refusing coverage to people with psychiatric disabilities were acting against the recommendations of their own manuals.[34] Sometimes these decisions could be seen as driven by the profit motive—charging more for insurance coverage than recommended by the manual[35]—but often they were not, as when companies denied coverage altogether to individuals whom the manuals considered to be reasonable risks for coverage.[36] Insurance decisions are often arbitrary, discretionary, and not necessarily based in actuarially sound data: "Underwriting decisions in particular tend to be made on the basis of very informal loss 'statistics,' that is 'personal judgment based on experience.'"[37]

This has been particularly true in the area of psychiatric disabilities or what the insurance industry typically calls "mental, nervous, and emotional disorders." An Office of Technology Assessment study in 1988 listed conditions that insurance companies had determined would result in higher premiums, exclusion waivers,[38] or an outright denial of coverage. People with "mild psychoneurosis" were subject to higher premiums, and people with schizophrenia, like people with AIDS, leukemia, and severe angina, were excluded from insurance coverage altogether.[39]

A book on underwriting produced by the Insurance Institute of America grouped "mental impairment" with "a criminal record" and "use of drugs" in describing risks that should be looked at "very closely."[40] One case challenged an insurer's uniform policy of denying disability insurance to anyone who had received any mental health services, including simply seeing a therapist, within 2 years of applying for the insurance.[41] In another case, an insurance company refused to provide landlord insurance to any landlord who rented to handicapped tenants.[42] Yet another case challenged a policy precluding coverage of anyone with "an occurrence" of bipolar disorder more than twice in a lifetime, or once within 5 years of the date of application for the policy. The insurance companies' own research and supporting materials do not justify these decisions. Although the standard texts relied on by insurance companies to assist in underwriting decisions contain major flaws,[43] none of them advocate or support any of the policies described above.

Although the fair discrimination model refers to "sound actuarial principles" and "experience or reasonably anticipated experience" as though they represent equally acceptable ways of reaching fair conclusions as to rates and policies, the latter is far less sound. Insurance companies that have consistently denied coverage to people with psychiatric disabilities do not have experience with such coverage, and the constantly changing world of new treatments and managed care undermines the validity of the experience other companies do have. As one insurance text acknowledges,

> in practice, it is quite difficult to find experience tables which forecast future claims costs. Claims rates change. Past experience does not necessarily represent future expectations. The characteristics of the policy for which premiums are being calculated usually differ from those reflected in the existing table. Frequently, only a single table exists, where theoretically a whole family of tables is required. A good deal of judgment is required in deciding on the table to be used.[44]

Insurance policies that do extend coverage to psychiatric disabilities reflect gross disparities between coverage of physical and psychiatric conditions. In one typical case, for example, the lifetime benefits for major medical expenses was $1 million, whereas the "eligible expenses incurred because of mental illness or 'functional nervous disorders' was limited to an annual maximum of $10,000 and a lifetime maximum of $20,000."[45] It is highly unlikely that these disparities are based on any sound actuarial principles or experience. In a recent case involving similar disparities in coverage for AIDS-related conditions, the insurer stipulated that "it has not shown and cannot show that its AIDS caps are or ever have been consistent with sound actuarial principles, actual or reasonably anticipated experience, bona fide risk classification, or state law."[46]

Furthermore, insurance coverage of psychiatric conditions has actually been drastically reduced in the past 10 years. Whereas "the total value of employer provided health care benefits, in constant dollars, decreased by 10.2 percent over the last ten years . . . the value of behavioral health care benefits decreased by 54.1 percent."[47] Some of this decrease in value may be attributable to relatively salutary trends, like a decrease in resorting to institutional care, but there has also been a dramatic increase in limitations on the number of outpatient visits.[48]

As will be described more fully below, the actual research, studies, and data that form the basis for the differentiation between physical disabilities and "mental, nervous, and emotional" disabilities do not appear to support the gross disparities in coverage between physical and psychiatric disabilities offered by most insurance coverage, nor the astonishingly high surcharges some insurance companies are requiring for "parity" coverage, nor the frequent practice of denying insurance coverage to people with a history of diagnosis or treatment for psychiatric disabilities.

Applicability of the ADA to Insurance Practices

When the National Council on the Handicapped (now the National Council on Disability; NCD) first suggested a broad, federal disability rights statute in 1986, it specifically recommended prohibiting discrimination by "all persons, companies, and agencies that make use of the mails or interstate communications and telecommunications services for the business of selling, arranging, or providing insurance."[49] This language was included because the council found that "individuals with disabilities have encountered discrimination in the availability of insurance; frequently individuals are denied certain types of insurance coverage because of presumptions about their increased risks and deficits, even though there may be no adequate actuarial data supporting such presumptions."[50]

A Safe Harbor for Private Insurance: The History of Section 501(c)

By the time that the ADA, drafted by the NCD, was introduced in Congress in 1988, "disability lobbyists and congressional staff convinced the Council to remove"[51] the provision concerning insurance companies because of concerns that insurance company opposition would doom the bill.[52] The subsequent Senate and House versions of the ADA, introduced in 1989, also did not contain any such language.[53]

This was not sufficient to calm the fears of the insurance industry and business lobbyists, however. As ADA legislation gathered steam, business and insurance interests formed the Disability Rights Working Group, whose comments on and objections to the draft ADA legislation were taken very seriously by Congress. In response to business and insurance industry concerns that the prohibition against disparate impact discrimination would force employers to purchase additional insurance coverage for disabled employees,[54] new language regarding insurance was added by congressional committees to the ADA.

This language, which appears in Title V, the "Miscellaneous" title of the ADA, appeared to exempt certain insurance activities from the mandate of the ADA. The exemption applied to insurance companies and the various organizations that sell health and disability insurance,[55] and to employers who offer those plans.[56] The language also provided that insurance and disability benefits regulated under federal rather than state law would also enjoy the same exemption from the requirements of the ADA.[57]

Although the Senate bill reported out of the Labor and Human Resources Committee did not include the latter provision, by October 1989, when the Senate passed S. 933, the only distinction between the Senate and House versions of Section 501(c) was a minute drafting difference.[58] Although numerous provisions of the ADA sparked controversy, debate, and minority statements, the new insurance provisions sailed through without controversy.

The lack of controversy did not mean that the language was clear or that insurance practices were uncontroversial. As numerous courts and commentators have noted, the statutory language regarding insurance practices is "ambiguous" and "confusing";[59] one judge described Section 501(c) as "totally ambiguous on its face."[60] Even some members of Congress were concerned about the vagueness of Section 501(c). Rep. Chuck Douglas (R-NH) complained that

> there are sections of the [ADA] which either have not been explained carefully or are incapable of being understood. A good example comes in Section 501(c) which deals with insurance. After spending a great deal of time explaining what insurance plans are permissible, the Act seems to say that these same plans which were previously approved are not permissible if they act as a subterfuge to the purposes of the Act. What does that mean? How does an employer or employee know when a subterfuge has been created?[61]

Insurance practices were also clearly open to challenge: In the 19 months after the effective date of Title I of the ADA,[62] 842 complaints about health insurance limitations and exclusions were filed with the Equal Employment Opportunity Commission (EEOC) alone.[63]

Meaning of Section 501(c)

When attempting to apply a statutory provision, the canons of legal interpretation instruct judges to first look to "the plain meaning of the statute."[64] If the statutory language is ambiguous, courts can look to legislative history, regulations by the agencies responsible for administering the law, and arguably analogous case precedent, as well as to the purpose of the statute and to public policy.

Statutory Language

The first part of Section 501(c) states that the provisions of the ADA "shall not be construed to prohibit or restrict" insurers from offering insurance plans that are legal under state law or employers from establishing or administering bona fide benefit plans. A plan is "bona fide" within the meaning of the ADA if it has been communicated to covered employees, exists, and pays benefits.[65] After describing plans subject to the exemption in three paragraphs, Section 501(c) limits the exemption with the last line by providing that "Paragraphs (1), (2) and (3) shall not be used as a subterfuge to evade the purposes of Titles I and III."[66]

The canons of statutory construction dictate that words cannot be redundant or surplusage. Therefore, first, the existence of Section 501(c) itself indicates that Congress believed that the contents of insurance policies would otherwise be covered by the language of the ADA. If the ADA did not cover the language of insurance plans, there would be no need for a "safe-harbor" provision articulating an exemption for the contents of bona fide benefit plans and for insurance coverage "based on or not inconsistent with" state law. Even the insurance companies themselves appear to concede that the provisions of their policies are covered under the ADA,[67] although their interpretation of Section 501(c) differs considerably from that of the EEOC.[68]

Second, the exemption represented by the opening language and the first three paragraphs is subject to two separate limitations. The first is that the insurance plans must be "based on or not inconsistent with state law."[69] The second is that the insurance plans shall not be used as a subterfuge to evade the purposes of Titles I and III. Congress must have meant to indicate both (a) that insurance plans could be illegal under the ADA because they evaded the purposes of Titles I and III and (b) that there could be circumstances under which plans evaded the purposes of Titles I and III but did not run afoul of state law. If the only circumstance under which a plan could be a subterfuge for discrimination was when it was not based on state law, there would have been no need to add the final provision of Section 501(c). Therefore, *subterfuge* must mean something different than "not based on state law."

One case presents an example of an insurance practice that passed muster under state law and yet could well be described as a subterfuge for discrimination. South Carolina had created a nonprofit state entity to assist "uninsurable but non-indigent persons in securing reimbursements for costs of their medical care,"[70] but in 1989, the South Carolina Legislature completely excluded AIDS and HIV infection from coverage under the plan. When the plan was challenged as discriminatory, a district court held that because the "underwriting risk" was "based on, or not inconsistent with state law"—because the South Carolina Legislature itself had enacted the exclusion—the ADA was not violated.[71] The exclusion was "written into the law casually, with no debate or actuarial studies."[72] South Carolina ultimately repealed the exclusion.[73]

Several cases support the approach of bifurcating the ADA's proscription on insurance practices into a prohibition of both (a) practices that discriminate on the basis of disability that have no sound actuarial basis or support and (b) practices engaged in as a subterfuge to avoid the requirements of Titles I and III.[74] Thus, it would appear that perhaps Section 501(c) prohibits a greater range of insurance practices than would be illegal under governing state law. It is clear that plans that do not pass muster under state law standards would not be covered under the exemption and would thus be fully exposed to liability under the ADA.

Judge Richard Posner of the 7th Circuit offered a different interpretation of Section 501(c), arguing that the ADA cannot regulate the contents of insurance policies any more than it can regulate the contents of stores' inventories to make either as useful to people with disabilities as to people without. Therefore, he posited that Section 501(c) exists to allow a defense to insurance companies for the denial of coverage to individuals, or for challenges to higher premiums.[75]

Generally, challenges to insurance practices have been mounted under either Title I, prohibiting discrimination in employment, or Title III, prohibiting discrimination by public accommodations. Only one case has attempted to use the provisions of Section 501 itself as the basis for recovery.[76] In *Baker v. Hartford Life Insurance*,[77] a plaintiff claimed that the denial of insurance coverage for his son was based on his son's disability; therefore it "violates Title V of the ADA because the denial was based on disability and not on state law," and "the defendant did not follow its own written procedure for appeal."[78] The court denied the defendant's motion to dismiss in this case, holding that the plaintiff had stated two separate viable claims: (a) that "the decision to deny plaintiff coverage was not based on considerations of underwriting or classifying risks," and (b) that, even if underwriting or classifying risks were the basis of the denial of coverage, the defendant was using Section 501(c) (1) "as a subterfuge."[79]

Thus, we come to the essence of Rep. Charles Douglas's (R-NH) complaint: What does the language regarding subterfuge mean? Courts have come to conflicting interpretations of the meaning of "subterfuge," corresponding to four basic theories. The first theory holds that Congress wrote the exception in language that suggests it intended to apply the fair discrimination model: Discrimination is permitted as long as it can be shown to be based on actuarially sound and objective data that demonstrate a difference in risk based on the classification. The legislative history strongly supports this interpretation, and the EEOC and Department of Justice (DOJ) adopted this approach to interpreting Section 501(c). Under this model, insurance practices would fail if they were not supported under the models that insurance companies themselves purport to use, that is, if the challenged classification bore an insufficient relationship to increased risk of exposure for the insurance companies.

There are two objections to this approach: The first is that the requirement that insurance policies meet the requirements of state law already imposes the fair discrimination model on insurance companies, and the subterfuge language must mean something else or be redundant. The second argument is that "subterfuge" is a term with a certain specific meaning, because Congress had originally used it in a similar context in the Age Discrimination in Employment Act (ADEA) of 1967.[80] *Subterfuge* under the ADEA was interpreted by the U.S. Supreme Court to have a different meaning from the fair discrimination model, requiring intentional discrimination on the basis of age for insurance companies to be liable. Therefore, the second argument runs, *subterfuge* must mean "intentional discrimination" in the same way that the Supreme Court interpreted it under the ADEA, an interpretation that Congress was aware of when it passed the ADA.

This argument is open to one major objection: Congress swiftly rejected the Supreme Court's interpretation that *subterfuge* meant intentional discrimination and, shortly after the decision in question, amended the ADEA to remove the term *subterfuge* entirely. Thus, there is reason to believe that Congress intended to send the message to the Supreme Court that its interpretation had been mistaken. Nevertheless, some courts continue to hold that the Supreme Court interpretation of *subterfuge* in the ADEA context—now no longer applicable to the ADEA—should be applied to ADA litigation.[81]

The third theory analogizes insurance company discrimination on the basis of disability to company discrimination on the basis of gender. The Supreme Court, applying Title VII, has held that it is discrimination on the basis of gender to make assumptions about an individual based on generalizations about the group to which she belongs, regardless of how true those generalizations might be.[82] In other words, the fair discrimination model has been explicitly held to be inapplicable to employers' insurance policies for their employees, at least in the context of sex discrimination. Because, as this theory holds, Congress made it clear that the ADA was to be interpreted as an analogue to the Civil Rights Acts of 1964,[83] there is some confusion about the applicability of prior lines of case law relating to discrimination against protected classes in insurance policies.

Judge Posner of the 7th Circuit theorized in a fourth interpretation that if an insurance company were to structure the contents of its policies to specifically discourage people with certain kinds of disabilities, for example, AIDS, from purchasing those policies, it would be engaging in prohibited subterfuge:

> For Mutual of Omaha to take the position that people with AIDS are so unhealthy that it won't sell them health insurance would be a prima facie violation of section 302(a).[84] But the insurance company just might be able to steer into the safe harbor provided by section 501(c), provided it didn't run afoul of the "subterfuge" limitation, as it would do if, for example, it had adopted the AIDS caps to deter people who know they are HIV positive from buying the policies at all.[85]

The subterfuge exception forces Judge Posner to retreat from his previously held position that the ADA does not cover the contents of insurance policies at all. He appears to say that the ADA prohibits insurance companies to write policies intended to deter people with certain kinds of disabilities from purchasing the policy, yet it is difficult to imagine any other reason for Mutual of Omaha to adopt a provision in its policies limiting lifetime benefits for AIDS or AIDS-related conditions to $25,000 when all other conditions are subject to a limit of $1 million—a provision that Mutual of Omaha concedes is not actuarially sound or based on any experience and is inconsistent with risk classification.[86] The language of Section 501(c) is ambiguous. No court has held otherwise.[87] Therefore, other sources of interpretive guidance must be examined.

Legislative History

The legislative history of the ADA includes committee reports and comments made by members of Congress in debating the legislation. Because the ADA was referred to so many different committees,[88] the legislative history is voluminous, if occasionally duplicative. The Senate and House reports contain a substantial amount of explanatory material about Section 501(c), which may, as Rep. Douglas noted, be open to some charges of inconsistency.

Several things do appear to be clear from the legislative history. First, Section 501(c) is an exemption for insurance discrimination, not employment discrimination arising from or derivative of insurance discrimination. Employers cannot "deny a qualified applicant a job because the employer's current insurance plan does not cover the person's disability or because of the increased costs of the insurance."[89]

In addition, it is clear that Congress did not intend "subterfuge" to be interpreted in the way that the same term had been interpreted by the Supreme Court under the ADEA: as a deliberate attempt to avoid the statute.[90] Under that interpretation, any plan passed prior to the statute could not be a subterfuge because a company could not have deliberately intended to avoid a statute not yet in existence. The legislative history makes clear that

> the decision to include [Section 501(c)] may not be used to evade the protections of Title I pertaining to employment, Title II pertaining to public services and Title III pertaining to public accommodations beyond the terms of points (1), (2) and (3) *regardless of the date an insurance plan . . . was adopted.*[91]

It is also clear that "a person with a disability cannot be denied insurance or be subject to different terms or conditions of insurance based on disability alone, if the disability does not pose increased risks."[92] As an example, the Committee on Labor and Human Resources noted that "a blind person may not be denied coverage based on blindness independent of actuarial risk classification."[93]

At the same time, however, the committee reports made clear their assumption that state regulatory activities were sufficient to ensure that insurance practices were carried out in a fair and nondiscriminatory manner:[94]

> The Committee does not intend that any provisions of this legislation should affect the way the insurance industry does business in accordance with the State laws and regulations under which it is regulated; the Committee added Section 501(c) to make it clear that this legislation will not disrupt the current nature of insurance underwriting or the current regulatory structure for self-insured employers of the insurance industry in sales, underwriting, pricing, administrative and other services, claims, and similar insurance regulated activities based on classification of risks as regulated by the States.[95]

Thus, although the legislative history seems clear that "subterfuge" means more than an intentional attempt to avoid the legislation, it does not go much further in explaining just what the term was intended to mean.

Regulations and Other Agency Guidance

Regulations and their interpretations, including Enforcement Guidance and *Technical Assistance Manuals,* promulgated by the EEOC[96] and DOJ[97] provide even more voluminous guidance than the legislative history, although the increased volume does not necessarily mean increased clarity. The EEOC in particular is open to the criticism that its interpretations appear internally contradictory.

In general, both agencies have concluded that " 'subterfuge' refers to disability-based disparate treatment that is not justified by the risks or costs associated with the disability."[98] Not all differences in insurance coverage, however, constitute "disability-based disparate treatment," and the distinctions between permissible disparate treatment and prohibited disability-based treatment are sometimes hard to fathom.

In addition to regulations, both the DOJ and the EEOC issued additional materials specifically answering questions regarding the application of the ADA in the insurance context. The EEOC, for example, has issued Enforcement Guidelines on how the ADA affects health insurance. The DOJ addressed insurance questions in its *Technical Assistance Manual.*

EEOC interpretation of Section 501(c).   There are some aspects of the EEOC regulations and the interpretation of the applicability of the ADA to insurance practices in employment that are quite clear. An employer cannot refuse to hire an employee because of concerns about the effect the hiring would have on insurance costs.[99] The EEOC also makes it clear that the ADA requires that "employees with disabilities be accorded equal access to whatever health insurance coverage the employer provides to other employees,"[100] and they cannot be subjected to different terms or conditions of participation in the employer's insurance program or of the insurance itself based solely on the disability.[101] If an employee becomes disabled while working, or the if employer learns of an employee's disability after hiring him or her, the employer is prohibited from either firing the employee[102] or changing insurance carriers to obtain coverage less favorable to the employee and less expensive to the employer.[103]

Adding to the confusion about the meaning of *subterfuge*, the EEOC in its *Technical Assistance Manual* noted that pre-existing-conditions clauses are acceptable under the ADA, "unless these exclusions are being used as a subterfuge to evade the purposes of the ADA."[104] Later, however, the EEOC defined *subterfuge* as "disability-based disparate treatment that is not justified by the risks or costs associated with the disability."[105]

It is important to note that because an adverse employment action based on concerns that the individual's disability would increase insurance costs would constitute disparate treatment, rather than disparate impact discrimination, defenses related to increased costs such as undue hardship, which is only a defense to the failure to make reasonable accommodations, would not be available.[106] The EEOC, however, has also issued a number of confusing and apparently internally contradictory interpretations of Section 501(c). For example, although the EEOC has indicated that the distinction between mental and physical disabilities is permissible in health insurance,[107] it has filed a substantial number of lawsuits and amicus briefs attacking the distinction as violating the ADA in the disability benefits context.[108] However, the differences between health insurance and disability benefits can be seen as justifying such differential treatment.[109]

More problematic, and possibly invalid as an unjustified limitation on the statutory language of the ADA, is the EEOC's nullification of the disparate impact theory of discrimination as it pertains to the disparity between coverage of psychiatric and physical conditions in health insurance benefits. The EEOC stated that "the adverse impact theory of discrimination is unavailable in this context."[110] It is not at all clear why the disparate impact theory would be available to challenge disparities in long-term disability programs but not in health insurance programs, or, more fundamentally, why the EEOC has the authority to wipe out a theory of recovery that Congress indicated repeatedly was central to the function of the ADA.[111]

Even if the interpretation that disparities in health insurance coverage do not violate the ADA is correct, the EEOC's explication of how to determine which disparities in coverage do violate the ADA and which do not is difficult to follow. For example, the EEOC has issued materials indicating that the adverse treatment of a discrete disability, such as schizophrenia or deafness, or a group of disabilities, such as cancers, in a health insurance policy would be considered discriminatory,[112] whereas adverse treatment of "eye care" or "mental/nervous conditions" is not discriminatory.[113] Also according to the EEOC, health insurance policies may contain limitations on coverage for certain procedures or treatments, pre-existing-conditions clauses, or reimbursements for certain kinds of drugs without violating the ADA.[114]

DOJ interpretations of Section 501(c). The DOJ regulations for Title III repeat verbatim the statutory provisions regarding insurance, with one addition. The regulations underscore that a public accommodation cannot refuse to admit or serve someone with a disability simply "because its insurance company conditions coverage or rates on the absence of individuals with disabilities."[115] No mention is made in the regulations of liability of the insurance company for containing such blatantly discriminatory provisions in its policies.

As the DOJ noted, it "received numerous comments" on this proposed regulation. Most commentators posited that "it did not go far enough in protecting individuals with disabilities and persons associated with them from discrimination."[116] Commentators asked for "strong" language and "stringent" standards because of "pervasive problems in the availability and cost of insurance for individuals with disabilities and parents of children with disabilities."[117]

The department declined to add more stringent standards, even though it noted that despite its requests for statistical support justifying these kinds of exclusionary practices, no such data were forthcoming. Rather, commentators associated with insurance companies argued that " 'hard data and actuarial statistics are not available to provide precise numerical justifications for every underwriting determination' but argued that decisions may be based on 'logical principles generally accepted by actuarial science and fully consistent with state insurance laws.' "[118] The department did not comment further on this suggestion. It did make clear that "all types of insurance are covered" and that "a public accommodation . . . may not entirely deny coverage to a person with a disability."[119]

The DOJ also made clear that its interpretation of the congressional intent in passing Section 501(c) was to permit insurance policies to engage in disparate treatment only when such treatment is supported by "sound actuarial data." A casual reader of the department's preamble might think it was clear on this issue; however, the remarks of the commentators associated with the insurance company served as predictions of the kinds of distinctions that would later divide the courts. There is actually a substantial difference among decisions reflecting "statistically sound correlations," "sound actuarial data," "sound actuarial principles," and "related to actual or reasonably anticipated experience," and this difference can be crucial in the outcome of a case, as shown later.

Challenging Insurance Practices as Discriminatory

Many practices of insurance companies have been successfully challenged as being discriminatory on the basis of race and gender. Challenges of disability discrimination, however, have been less successful.

Race discrimination. Race discrimination in insurance practices historically took two forms: (a) higher premiums for blacks for life, health, and disability insurance and (b) higher premiums or outright exclusion from property, automobile, and homeowner's insurance. The differential rates for life and health insurance were justified under the fair discrimination model because the life expectancies of black people were (and continue to be) substantially lower than white people in this country, and their health was (and continues to be) worse.

Regardless of the fair discrimination model and that black people continue to have a shorter life span, have more health problems, and report being disabled at a greater rate, there is no question in society that regardless of actuarial data or experience, black people should not be charged more for life, health, or disability insurance. In part, courts and insurance scholars attribute this consensus to a conclusion that the reasons for this disparity are not biological but social: that the disparities are the products of bigotry and adverse social conditions whose cost should not be passed on to the black consumer.[120] These cases and articles distinguish race disparities from gender and disability disparities, which they believe are real and biologically based, as opposed to socially constructed.[121] In addition, insurance companies have been charged with disparate impact discrimination against black and Hispanic people by the use of so-called insurance redlining, or the charging of higher property and automobile insurance rates to people living in zip codes that are heavily dominated by minority residents, and have been the target of much commentary and litigation.[122]

The final form of race discrimination that insurance companies have undertaken is discrimination in marketing and underwriting, that is, "avoiding nonwhite markets" for insurance[123] and refusing to sell policies to black people. That practice continues to this day and is the subject of investigation and enforcement by the Civil Rights Division of the DOJ.[124]

Gender discrimination. Gender discrimination has been the field in which the fair discrimination model has been most widely debated and, despite significant losses,[125] has been successfully attacked. The Supreme Court has heard three cases on gender discrimination in insurance practices[126] and has concluded that at least as to insurance provided through employers, Title VII of the Civil Rights Act prevents employers from providing insurance based on generalizations about gender, even if they are true as generalizations.[127]

Age discrimination. Neither the ADA nor the regulations issued pursuant to it define *subterfuge* or explain what a policy or practice adopted as a subterfuge might be. As noted above, however, the word was originally used in a similar context in the ADEA.[128]

The Supreme Court first interpreted the meaning of *subterfuge* in the ADEA in *United Airlines Inc. v. McMann,*[129] holding that engaging in subterfuge required an intention to subvert the act, and it, therefore, could not, by definition, apply to any plans or policies in place before the passage of the act. Thus, the court concluded, the plaintiff's forced retirement at age 60 was pursuant to a plan enacted before the ADEA and could not be a subterfuge. Congress reacted by passing legislation making it clear that forced retirement on the basis of age was a violation of the ADEA.

In *Public Employees Retirement System of Ohio v. Betts,*[130] the Supreme Court's next case involving the interpretation of subterfuge, it noted that whereas Congress had overruled the outcome in *McMann*, it had not defined nor changed the word *subterfuge*.[131] Therefore, the court held that its interpretation of the word in *McMann* was still good law, and it reaffirmed that no practice adopted before the passage of the ADEA could be considered a subterfuge. As to practices adopted after the ADEA, however, the court held that a plan was a subterfuge if "it discriminates in a manner forbidden by the substantive provisions of the Act."[132] The court then held that the ADEA did not apply to fringe benefits, such as pension plans. In doing so, the Supreme Court found that the EEOC's interpretation of subterfuge was contrary to the purposes of the ADEA and, therefore, invalid.

Congress reacted to this decision by passing the Older Workers Benefits Protection Act of 1990,[133] which made it clear that the ADEA did apply to fringe benefits, and Congress eliminated the use of *subterfuge* altogether.[134] In passing the Older Workers Benefits Protection Act, Congress reinstated the EEOC regulation that the Supreme Court had held invalid.

At least some members of Congress were clearly aware of the potential implications of the *Betts* decision, which was issued close in time to the ADA debates, to the ADA language regarding discrimination in insurance policies. On the floors of the House and Senate, sponsors of the ADA rose to "note that the term 'subterfuge' as used in the ADA, should not be interpreted in the manner in which the Supreme Court interpreted the term [in *Betts*]."[135] Rep. Don Edwards (D-CA) noted that Congress was moving speedily to reverse the interpretation of subterfuge in *Betts* and emphasized that the Supreme Court's language should not be applied to the ADA.[136]

Notwithstanding these remarks, when the EEOC sought comments to its proposed regulations, many commentators requested a definition of subterfuge, and some specifically suggested that the EEOC adopt the *McMann/Betts* definition. The EEOC did not ultimately define subterfuge, although it responded to *McMann/Betts* by noting in its regulations that "whether or not [insurance] activities are being used as a subterfuge is to be determined without regard to the date the insurance plan or employee benefit plan was adopted."[137] Still, insurance defendants have urged courts to adopt the *Betts* Court's definition of subterfuge as applicable to the ADA.

Courts' interpretations of the meaning of subterfuge have been widely divergent. Despite the clear language of the legislative history, some courts have specifically interpreted subterfuge in the same sense as used in *McMann* and *Betts*—an actual intent to avoid the strictures of the statute—and have upheld policies on the ground that they predated the adoption of the ADA and, therefore, could not constitute subterfuge within the meaning of *Betts*.[138] Other courts reject the requirement of intentional malice and simply find that the insurer must have sought to evade the purposes of the ADA.[139]

Challenges under Section 504 of the Rehabilitation Act. The insurance companies may have worried unnecessarily about their vulnerability under the ADA. Even without the benefit of protection under Section 501(c), courts proved remarkably inhospitable to claims of discrimination against insurance companies under Section 504 of the Rehabilitation Act of 1973.

In the years before the passage of the ADA, there were three attempts to challenge discrepancies in public and private insurance coverage between mental and physical disabilities.[140] The judges in these cases did not seem to take the claims seriously.[141] In one case, the judge characterized "the necessary consequence" of ruling in the plaintiffs' favor as the "end [of] all medical insurance" or "drastic reduction[s] in the amount of allowable benefits for those risks of primary concern to employers."[142]

More significant, in 1988 the Supreme Court ruled on *Alexander v. Choate*,[143] which concerned whether facially neutral changes to Medicaid coverage in Tennessee violated Section 504 of the Rehabilitation Act because they fell disparately on people with disabilities. Although *Alexander* involved facially neutral limitations of a resource-scarce state health program, it has been relied on by a number of appellate courts in justifying facially disparate treatment by private, for-profit insurance companies under the ADA.[144] The policy considerations underlying *Alexander* are not present in these cases, nor are the challenged provisions similar in any respect, yet *Alexander* is used as support for decisions in favor of insurance companies.[145]

Scope of Coverage and Standing to Sue

Both the EEOC and the DOJ have brought a number of cases directly related to discrimination in the provision of insurance benefits. The EEOC has challenged the total exclusion of benefits for AIDS and HIV-related illnesses in a health insurance plan; the suit, along with a companion suit by plan members, was successfully resolved with monetary settlements for the plaintiffs and the creation of a fund to pay medical expenses.[146] The EEOC has also brought a number of cases challenging differential treatment of mental and physical illnesses in disability benefit plans, *see infra*, although it also has stated that such distinctions in health insurance plans do not violate the ADA.

Title III and Insurance Offices

Although it is clear that insurance offices are covered under Title III of the ADA,[147] some insurance companies have argued that this simply means that the physical insurance office itself must be accessible to people with disabilities, rather than applying the term to the content of the policies.[148] This interpretation is inconsistent with the language of Title III, which makes it clear that more than physical accessibility is required. The statute explicitly addresses physical barriers and communication barriers as one, and only one, form of discrimination.[149] Other forms of discrimination include using "standards or criteria or methods of administration that have the effect of discriminating on the basis of disability; or [that] perpetuate the discrimination of others who are subject to common administrative control,"[150] as well as using "eligibility criteria that screen out or tend to screen out an individual with a disability or any class of individuals with disabilities from fully and equally enjoying any ... services" offered by the public accommodation unless the criteria are "necessary" for the provision of the services.[151]

The legislative history noted that lack of physical access to facilities was the first area of discrimination that needed to be addressed under Title III; however, it then described the other areas: "Additional areas of discrimination that witnesses identified included the imposition or application of standards or criteria that limit or exclude people with disabilities, the failure to make reasonable modifications in policies to allow participation, and a failure to provide auxiliary aids and services."[152] Examples of this form of discrimination under Title III include a credit application for a department store that inquired into history of mental illness, the refusal to treat burn victims because of HIV seropositivity, and a policy of refusing to accept checks without the presentation of a driver's license.[153]

Discrimination can occur not only in the "place" where examinations and courses related to applications, licensing, certification, or credentialing are offered but also in the "manner" in which the courses are offered,[154] and it includes the failure to make reasonable modifications to "policies, practices or procedures"[155] if those modifications are necessary for the enjoyment of the services by people with disabilities, unless the modifications requested would fundamentally alter the very nature of the services being offered.

None of these statutory definitions of discrimination can plausibly be interpreted as referring solely to physical accessibility. Furthermore, the testimony before Congress, the legislative history, and subsequent case law make it clear that citizens who are disabled are concerned about a great deal more than physical accessibility in their interactions with public accommodations: The denial of treatment for people with AIDS by doctors' offices and the failure to provide interpreters in hospitals and course accommodations that are required by college and graduate students are examples of issues raised under Title III that are not related to simple physical accessibility. This argument is a reflection of the discrimination that considers the only "valid" form of disability to be mobility impairment (preferably in a wheelchair); certainly if Title III were limited to physical accessibility issues only, it would make no sense to define *disability* for the purpose of Title III to include mental impairments of any kind. For that matter, Title III would also be irrelevant for people who were deaf, blind, or had many other kinds of disabilities.

In addition, Congress underscored that the purpose of Title III was to extend the protections of Section 504 of the Rehabilitation Act to the private sector. Insurance coverage had been challenged a number of times under Section 504, and although the challenges were unsuccessful, all of the courts involved assumed that the challenges stated a claim under Section 504.[156] Both the EEOC and the DOJ reject this argument, and the DOJ has said that the contents of insurance policies are covered under Title III:

> Insurance offices are places of public accommodation and as such may not discriminate on the basis of disability in the sale of insurance contracts or in the terms and conditions of the insurance contracts they offer. Because of the nature of the insurance industry, however, consideration of disability in the sale of insurance contracts does not always constitute "discrimination." An insurer or other public accommodation may underwrite, classify, or administer risks that are based on and not inconsistent with state law, provided that such practices are not used to evade the purposes of the ADA.[157]

For the most part, the courts have now adopted this interpretation, holding that any discriminatory practice by insurance companies is covered under Title III of the ADA, including discrimination in accepting or denying applications for insurance and discrimination in the terms and provisions of insurance policies.[158]

There are a number of reasons for finding that Title III does not simply require insurance companies to make their offices physically accessible. First, Title III prohibits discrimination in "the full and equal enjoyment of the goods, services, facilities, privileges, advantages, or accommodations of any place of public accommodation."[159] It is difficult to imagine that an insurance office would be required to install safety bars and accessible bathroom stalls, wider doors, ramps, and teletypewriter phones while being permitted to deny all people who are deaf or who have mobility impairments insurance coverage explicitly on the basis of their disability without fear of liability. As numerous courts have noted, Title III contains no language that supports such an interpretation.[160] The ADA's broad purpose of "providing a clear and comprehensive national mandate for the elimination of discrimination against individuals with disabilities"[161] and its broad definition of disability make clear that the discrimination prohibited under Title III is not limited to obstructing physical access to office buildings. In addition, Title III explicitly prohibits the use of "eligibility criteria to screen out individuals with disabilities,"[162] which underscores the mistake of holding that the ADA applies only to physical accessibility issues.

Finally, at least one court has held that the safe-harbor clause of Title V, holding that insurance companies would only be liable if their practices were a subterfuge to evade the purposes of Titles I and III, shows that under some circumstances at least, Congress contemplated that insurance companies could be liable under Title III for the contents of their policies or for their practices.[163]

Title III and the Contents of Insurance Policies

Many employees receive insurance coverage through their employers rather than purchasing such coverage directly for themselves from an insurance office. The 6th Circuit decided that the contents of insurance policies are covered by Title III only if the policy was a service provided to the plaintiff by an insurance office rather than by the employer:

> While we agree that an insurance office is a public accommodation . . . [the] plaintiff did not seek the goods and services of an insurance office. Rather, Parker accessed a benefit plan provided by her private employer and issued by MetLife. A benefit plan offered by an employer is not a good offered by a place of public accommodation.[164]

In this conclusion, the 6th Circuit was joined by the 3rd Circuit, which held that an employer-provided disability benefit is a term and condition of employment; discrimination is actionable under Title I against the employer but not against the insurer under Title III.[165] The 1st Circuit, however, disagreed with the requirement of a physical nexus between the plaintiff and the public accommodation, pointing out by way of example that Title III listed "travel services" as public accommodations and noting that travel services do a great deal of their business by telephone.[166] It would be absurd, the court reasoned, to cover services that a client obtained by walking in the door but not services obtained over the telephone.[167]

Essentially, the 1st Circuit now stands alone in holding that Title III governs the content of insurance policies, absent any nexus between the defendant insurance office and the plaintiff. If the insurance policy in which the contents were being challenged was provided by the employer rather than the result of a direct contact between the plaintiff and the insurance company, virtually every circuit court would hold that the plaintiff may not sue the insurance company under Title III of the ADA.[168] The 3rd and 6th Circuit Courts appear to hold that Title III simply requires the physical structures of public accommodations to be accessible. However, both the 7th and 2nd Circuit Courts have held that absent an affirmative defense, insurance companies may not discriminate in the sale of insurance policies to people with disabilities, refusing to limit Title III to the requirement that the insurance office be physically accessible.[169] In *EEOC v. Aramark*,[170] the Court of Appeals for the D.C.

Circuit noted the split in the circuits on this question, and the question of whether former employees can sue under Title I of the ADA, and refused to commit itself to either side. This question will probably be decided by the U.S. Supreme Court in the next few years.

Challenging Disability Benefits Plans

Although employers are clearly liable if they discriminate in the provision of fringe benefits to their employees, it has been relatively difficult for employees to file Title I cases once they begin receiving disability benefits. This is because many employers have successfully argued that Title I requires either (a) that the plaintiff must be a current employee or (b) that the "qualified individual with a disability"[171] requirement means that the plaintiff must be qualified for employment rather than qualified for the fringe benefit at issue. If "qualified individual" means the individual is qualified for the job that the plaintiff held, employers argue, then the former employee's receipt of disability benefits indicates conclusively that the employee is not qualified for the position.[172]

The EEOC, however, has adopted the position that the plaintiff need only be qualified for the fringe benefit whose provisions he or she is challenging as discriminatory. As long as the individual satisfies all of the nondiscriminatory criteria for eligibility for disability insurance, he or she should have standing to sue.

A number of courts have avoided examining the contents of insurance policies entirely by finding that the plaintiff had no standing to challenge the insurance policy as a fringe benefit under Title I because the plaintiff was, by definition, not qualified for the job that he or she formerly held or that he or she simply was not an employee or seeking employment. If this holding is made in tandem with a finding that Title III only covers the physical locations of insurance offices, or does not cover the contents of insurance policies, or does not cover the contents of insurance policies obtained through employers,[173] then insurance companies and employers are effectively completely immune from suit for the contents of their insurance policies, regardless of how discriminatory those policies might be.

This outcome has troubled a number of courts, both those that have held that former employees can sue under Title I of the ADA[174] and those that have barred such suits.[175] Those courts that have granted former employees standing have cited a number of reasons: The principal reason is that because the ADA prohibits discrimination in the provision of fringe benefits, and because no one disputes that disability insurance is a fringe benefit, Congress must have intended that there be an avenue available for litigation regarding this form of fringe benefit. Because this fringe benefit, by its nature, becomes meaningful only postemployment, Congress must have intended to give former employees standing to sue challenging discriminatory provisions of disability benefits. Indeed, if employees attempted to sue about provisions of disability benefit plans while they were still employed and not disabled, they would have clear standing problems, because it would be difficult to allege that the disparity in disability benefit plans constituted an actual injury to them. Other arguments include that Title VII, the model for the ADA, permits former employees standing to sue[176] and that the broad remedial purposes of the ADA would be defeated by a construction of the statute, which permits employers to discriminate on the basis of disability in providing postemployment benefits.

Litigation Involving Insurance Discrimination Against People With Psychiatric Disabilities

As mentioned at the beginning of this chapter, there has been considerable litigation against the insurance industry on behalf of people with mental disabilities. The greatest proportion of this litigation has been devoted to challenging disparities in mental health coverage compared with physical illness coverage. These challenges have uniformly failed. However, there have also been cases challenging the exclusion from coverage or denial of coverage to individuals because of their histories of receiving treatment for various mental health problems. These cases also have been far from successful.

What has not happened in any litigation to date is a sustained examination of and challenge to the underlying basis for discriminatory treatment of people with mental disabilities by insurance companies. In this chapter, I propose to discuss whether there is a solid basis for the conclusion that people who have received various kinds of mental health treatment represent higher risks for life and disability insurance.

Life Insurance

The legislative history and regulations make clear that the outright denial of insurance coverage to individuals with psychiatric disabilities is illegal under the ADA. As the DOJ underscores in its Interpretive Guidance, "a public accommodation may offer insurance policies that limit coverage for certain procedures or treatments, but may not entirely deny coverage to a person with a disability."[177] Several cases have adopted this position.[178]

In addition to being illegal, denial of coverage makes no sense for two basic reasons. First, one of the principal reasons that people with psychiatric disabilities are considered bad life insurance risks is that they are considered heightened suicide risks,[179] but most life insurance policies (and disability insurance policies, too) exclude suicide or injuries incurred as a result of self-inflicted injury or attempted suicide.[180]

Second, although insurance companies claim to rely on authoritative texts in making their coverage decisions, no standard text recommends denying people with psychiatric disabilities life insurance coverage outright; the most that is recommended is deferral for a few years or substantially higher premiums.[181]

Insurance companies base their decisions regarding life insurance on a number of factors. Individual underwriting decisions tend to made by individual insurance agents, based on both subjective impressions and texts in the field. Examination of case law shows that although these texts have serious methodological flaws, insurance company policies and underwriting decisions are almost universally more restrictive than those recommended by the texts, premiums charged when insurance is made available are higher than those recommended by the texts, and the texts often do not cover the specific disability or combination of disabilities at issue, and therefore, insurance company decisions regarding these disabilities are entirely subjective and not based on actuarial data or experience.[182]

Most life insurance companies use underwriting manuals, which contain mortality tables applicable to various conditions. These manuals include *Medical Selection of Life Risks*[183] and *Medical Risks: Patterns of Age and Mortality by Time Elapsed*.[184] As stated in the introduction to the latter text, "in insurance medicine comparative mortality tables are indispensable for risk selection (underwriting)."[185]

Medical Risks, however, is careful to point out its own limitations in its chapter on methodology:

> Virtually all of the mortality studies in this volume have dealt with selected populations and not random samples. Hence, statistical tests that assume independence of a study population from such total population or a control population are theoretically not appropriate. For practical purposes, nevertheless, such tests have been used to judge differences in mortality between the population under study and a standard or a control population.[186]

Even these cautions, however, do not capture the limitations that are inherent in the studies on mortality rates of people with mental disabilities on which *Medical Risks* relies. The limitations cast serious doubt on the reliability of the studies to support the proposition that diagnoses of mental illness by themselves are risk factors for excess mortality.

The Studies Are Old

The groups represented in the studies on which *Medical Risks* bases its conclusions are generally people who were institutionalized between the late 1960s and mid-1970s. Other studies look at data from the 1930s, 1940s, and 1950s. The latest date at which any individual was studied was in the early 1980s. *Medical Selection of Life Risks*, published in 1992, cites 35 articles published before 1980 out of 89 total articles; even this figure is low, however, because 5 of the articles published after 1980 are based on a single study.[187]

Although *Medical Risks* was published in 1990, the latest study relied on by its author was written in 1985.[188] Although the American Psychiatric Association adopted the *Diagnostic and Statistical Manual of Mental Disorders,* 3rd edition revised (*DSM-III-R*) in 1986,[189] with considerable changes from *DSM-III,* the Medical Risks chapter on psychiatric disability cites to *DSM-III* as authoritative. In one case, where the only clinical study in *Medical Selection of Life Risks* supporting United of Omaha's calculation of its premium was published in 1970, a court granted summary judgment to the plaintiff.[190] The court concluded as a matter of law that "the record is devoid of actuarial data regarding the mortality rate associated with [plaintiff's condition]."[191]

Insurance companies' reliance on these manuals is all the more problematic because comprehensive and recent mortality studies do exist.[192] Nor is the age of the studies in the underwriting manuals unproblematic. The people who were institutionalized and received diagnoses from institutions in the principal time period covered by the studies in these texts is simply not representative of the current population of people diagnosed with mental disabilities. The development of more effective therapies and medications in the past 10 years is completely missed in studies conducted before the mid-1980s. In addition, a number of people in the older studies may have been misdiagnosed. Several more recent studies show that diagnoses in state institutions tended to be mistaken and that those mistakes tended to be in the overdiagnosis of schizophrenia and the underdiagnosis of affective disorders. The mistakes were made significantly more often with diagnoses of African American men.[193] Because schizophrenia is the diagnosis most likely to result in adverse treatment by insurers, including the denial of insurance altogether, the reliance on these studies to show correlations between diagnosis and mortality, especially the diagnosis of schizophrenia, is suspect.

In addition, a substantial number of the studies cited in *Medical Selection of Life Risks* involved research on populations outside the United States. There are sufficient recent studies involving U.S. populations that insurance companies should not rely on data from countries whose social situations and medical coverage are markedly different from ours.

Finally, the appearance of a relatively large number of clinical studies in *Medical Selection of Life Risks* is deceptive, because many publications can be generated from a single study. The famous Iowa Record-Linkage Study, for instance, which looked at patients admitted to the University of Iowa Psychiatric Hospital between January 1, 1972, and December 31, 1981, has generated articles from 1985 to 1998, even longer than the longitudinal study period.[194] Insurance manuals cite these studies, creating an impression of a plethora of scholarship that actually represents the results of only one rather old investigation.

The Studies Are Based on Institutionalized Populations

Nearly all of the studies relied on by insurance manuals rely on institutionalized people as subjects; for experimental purposes, institutionalized people were a convenient sample to follow. Even more recent studies that link mental illness to excess mortality generally involve populations of institutionalized or recently discharged people. For example, the Center for Mental Health Services, in its "Facts About Mental Illness" cites a single study to support the "fact" that depression results in higher mortality rate. This study involves a population of people recently admitted to a nursing home.[195] The study itself is well done, but as its title indicates, it does nothing more than claim to have studied depression and mortality in nursing home populations.

The Mortality Rates May be Explained by Study Age or Effects of Institutionalization

For a variety of reasons, insurance company decisions about life insurance coverage for people diagnosed with psychiatric disabilities should not be based on the results of 20-year-old studies of institutionalized people. People who are institutionalized in psychiatric institutions are a highly unrepresentative population of all people with mental disabilities. The one conclusion that researchers have unanimously reached is that most people with mental disabilities—even serious ones—go untreated altogether.[196] Of those who seek treatment, the majority seek treatment from general practitioners or are treated in general hospitals.[197] Only a small percentage of people with mental disabilities seek, or are forced into, treatment from the specialized mental health sector, and of that small percentage, an even smaller percentage are institutionalized. The fact that the institutionalized population is a convenient captive population to study[198] is reminiscent of the man who lost his keys at night and looked for them under the streetlight because that was where the light was best. For insurance companies to base their coverage decisions for all people with disabilities on the findings of studies of people who are institutionalized is like basing coverage decisions for African American men on studies conducted with black prison populations.

The manuals relied on by insurance companies do recognize how institutionalization conflated the reasons for high mortality rates, even when relying almost entirely on studies conducted with institutionalized people. *Medical Selection of Life Risks* summarizes the reasons for the decline in excess mortality associated with mental illness, which it finds

> partly attributed to deinstitutionalization: in the era of protracted hospitalization the excess of natural deaths in psychiatric patients was mainly due to infection. . . . The high death rates previously recorded for psychiatric patients . . . are now less marked with reduction in duration of hospitalization and improvements in the provision of general medical care.[199]

Numerous recent mortality studies connect excess mortality of people with diagnoses of mental illness with factors other than the diagnosis itself, including institutionalization, poverty, and alcohol abuse. One study that examined psychiatric patients in both community and institutional settings found that excess mortality was due mainly to deaths of inpatients and deaths of people with psychotic diagnoses.[200] Another found that excess mortality of psychiatric patients in shelter care was virtually identical to excess mortality in a subsample of very low income California citizens without diagnoses of mental illness; the study speculated that the excess mortality might be associated more with poverty than mental illness.[201] People with mental disorders are at increased risk for poverty,[202] and poverty raises mortality rates.[203] Therefore, insurers may be attributing causation to mental illness, which in reality is explainable by institutionalization, income, and social status.

A third study gives some support to the proposition that people who receive inpatient behavioral health care have higher mortality rates than people who receive such care on an outpatient basis. A 5-year follow-up was conducted comparing people who received inpatient psychiatric treatment in three settings: a general hospital, the Vermont State Hospital, and community programs for people with severe and persistent mental illness. The inpatient group in the general hospital setting had a higher mortality rate for people age 50 and older than people who had been served in community settings, and the Vermont State Hospital group showed higher mortality in the middle-age categories than people served in the community.[204]

One set of studies that partially contradicts these findings was of older subjects of the Epidemiological Catchment Area survey. They include a 9-year follow-up of people who were 40 or older and, in a different article, a comparative follow-up of people 55 or older at the time of the interview. The studies found excess mortality, associated especially with diagnoses of alcohol abuse and depression, in a community sample.[205] The articles did not disclose whether the individuals were poor, but none of the individuals in the latter study committed suicide or died from "external causes."

Another reason insurance decisions should not be based on studies of people who are institutionalized is that institutions are dangerous places. Even with the ostensibly greater supervision provided by institutional personnel, accidents, injuries, and deaths occur in institutions at a far higher rate than in the community.[206] For people with certain diagnoses, such as borderline personality disorder, the reports from both patients and many treating professionals are that hospitalization increases rather than decreases the likelihood of suicide.[207]

In fact, one of the most consistent findings across all studies, old and new, in this country and abroad, is that the time of greatest risk for suicide in people with mental disabilities is in the first year or two after discharge from an institutional setting.[208] There are a number of possible explanations for this. Some have to do with the shock and damage of institutionalization, others with the failure to provide adequate transitional or discharge planning, others with the loss of the safety net provided by the institution, but no one has conducted any research to try to figure out the underlying reason or reasons. The real explanations might tell us a lot about the rationality or irrationality of equating suicidality with psychiatric disability rather than with institutionalization. Thus, it appears that people are being denied insurance because suicidality is equated with certain diagnoses. More careful research might show that the experience of hospitalization itself contributed substantially to the risk of suicide.

The real explanation is important because the principal reason given by insurance companies for denying life insurance to people with psychiatric disabilities is the risk of suicide.[209] Diagnosis of mental illness, however, is not nearly as powerful a predictor of successful suicide as are other factors, such as alcohol abuse, a previous history of suicide attempts, poverty, history of sexual abuse, and—in many cases— the experience of having been institutionalized.[210] There is strong support for the proposition that the most likely time that people who have been institutionalized will try to kill themselves is shortly after discharge.[211] No research has been uncovered to indicate that anyone has tried to find out why this might be so. There is strong anecdotal support in the writings of many, many people who have been institutionalized that the experience of institutionalization, especially for the first time, was so devastating to the individual's identity and sense of self that they became suicidal, not because of the diagnosis that got them put in the institution in the first place but because of the experiences they had when institutionalized.[212]

Still another reason the studies used in insurance decision making are suspect is that a number of other studies have associated risks of higher mortality with social factors, which are intrinsic components of institutionalization. High mortality is associated with isolation,[213] lack of social supports,[214] and unemployment, even in otherwise healthy individuals.[215] Institutionalization is isolating, results in a separation of the individual from his or her social supports, and by definition precludes employment. In a study involving people over 65, the increase in mortality associated with a perceived loss of social support—an increase of up to 400%[216]—is greater than any increase in mortality associated with psychiatric illness at any time of life. Some may argue that mental illness is the precursor of the unemployment, isolation, and lack of social support of institutionalization and indeed that those characteristics might have preceded and prompted the institutionalization. The response to this argument is that insurance companies can account for this by refusing to insure the unemployed—as they already do—rather than penalizing employed people for re-

ceiving psychiatric treatment. Although the studies that link mortality to unemployment and isolation have little to say directly about the effect of having a mental
illness on mortality, they lend circumstantial support to the hypothesis that being
institutionalized shortens one's life span.[217]

A number of conclusions follow from this discussion. First, insurance companies
whose basis for denying life insurance coverage to people with psychiatric disabilities
is the increased risk of suicide, and whose policies do not cover suicide, should have
to explain what non-suicide-based actuarial support they have for refusing life insurance coverage to applicants with psychiatric diagnoses. Second, individuals who
have not been institutionalized in more than 2 years should not be discriminated
against in life insurance underwriting decisions. Although fair discrimination might
permit adverse underwriting decisions against those who had been institutionalized
in the past 2 years—only if the policies did not exclude coverage for death caused
by suicide—this seems fundamentally unfair. The fact that institutions are isolating
and sometimes dangerous places, like the fact that some men beat their wives, may
indeed make it a "rational" decision to deny institutionalized people and battered
wives life insurance, or charge them higher premiums, but it is exacting an additional
penalty from people whom society has failed to protect in the first place.

The problems with the studies used by the insurance companies may be almost
irrelevant, however, because insurance companies and underwriters do not in practice
follow the recommendations of these texts. Instead, they deny coverage where the
texts recommend charging higher premiums. In addition, people seeking coverage
often have conditions or combinations of conditions that are not found in the texts
and, therefore, have no recommendations associated with them. It appears that underwriters may simply refuse to insure in the absence of guidance, a decision that
hardly squares with actuarial data, experience, or market theory.

One of the few cases involving the denial of life insurance is *Pallozzi v Allstate
Life Insurance Co.*[218] In *Pallozzi*, a couple applied for a joint life insurance policy
and was denied, based explicitly on their psychiatric diagnoses.[219] The couple had
jobs, a home, cars, and insurance to cover the home and the cars.[220] Neither had
been hospitalized in 7 or 8 years. Both were subsequently were issued life insurance
by another company.

The district court granted the defendant's motion for summary judgment, finding
that "the very nature of insurance requires discrimination" and that "common sense"
would dictate that individuals with the plaintiffs' diagnoses would have "a significantly higher risk classification than two individuals who do not have a disability or
even two individuals who have a different type of disability."[221] The Court of Appeals
reversed the decision, finding, among of other things, that the district court had
imposed too much of a burden for the plaintiffs to meet in their initial pleading.

The basis of which insurance companies deny life insurance coverage to people
who have received treatment for mental health problems is open to serious questioning. First, most insurance companies do not pay benefits for death by suicide.
Second, conclusions about the mortality of people with mental disabilities are based
on outdated studies of institutionalized populations. Third, other factors seem far
more important in predicting either suicide or death from natural causes than psychiatric diagnosis. Some of these—unemployment and poverty—may be associated
with mental disabilities. Nevertheless, using these factors rather than diagnosis to

make underwriting decisions would not be discriminatory and would be more likely to be actuarially sound.

Finally, recent court decisions, such as *Pallozzi, Doe v. Mutual of Omaha Insurance Co.,*[222] and *Thanda Woi v. Allstate,*[223] suggest that outright denial of insurance on the basis of disability does violate the ADA. Although courts have indicated that insurance companies remain free to write their policies to offer the coverage mixture that they see fit, their freedom to exclude disabled people from purchasing those policies has been curtailed by the ADA.

Health or Disability Insurance

It is a commonplace assumption in the popular and medical press that an individual who seeks psychiatric treatment may later be denied health or disability insurance on that basis.[224] Case law bears out that these assumptions are correct. Some insurance companies deny disability insurance coverage to anyone who has received any kind of mental health services in the past 2 years, including seeing a therapist;[225] others deny coverage to anyone who has "received treatment for a mental or nervous condition, regardless of seriousness, within the twelve months prior to application."[226] As of 1997, Metropolitan Life denied disability coverage to anyone who had experienced a single occurrence of symptoms of bipolar disorder in the past 5 years, or more than one occurrence in their lifetime.[227]

Again, as in the case with life insurance, the companies' own research and underwriting manuals do not support the decisions made by the companies.[228] The Health Insurance Association of American surveyed its members about their experiences in offering short- and long-term disability insurance on a group basis and long-term disability insurance on an individual basis. The following categories explain the results.

1. Group short-term disability. Insurance company expenditures for psychiatric disorders and substance abuse claims represented only 1.0% of all claims in dollars paid. Of that amount, about a third went to claims involving depression, a quarter to claims involving "psychoses," and anxiety and bipolar disorders claimed 5.5% and 1.4%, respectively.[229]

2. Group long-term disability. Although only 9.0% of all group long-term disability claims involved mental and nervous disorders, 13.1% of all long-term disability dollars went to claims for these conditions. Claims involving depression constituted less than a fifth of all long-term claims. It is interesting to note that although there were more claims involving psychoses in the long-term disability category than for short-term disability (16.7% vs. 7.4% of claims),[230] they cost the insurance companies less money—26.9% of group short-term disability dollars paid for mental and nervous claims went to claims involving "psychoses" whereas only 16.5% of group long-term disability dollars paid for mental and nervous claims were paid for claims involving "psychoses."[231]

3. Individual long-term disability. Although claims involving mental disorders accounted for only 6.4% of all claims on individual long-term disability policies, they accounted for 18% of claim dollars spent. Surprisingly, the

lion's share of both claims and dollars spent went to pay for claims involving anxiety disorders, a much higher proportion in individual disability claims than in group claims (64.6% of individual long-term disability claims involving mental disorders were for anxiety disorders vs. 21.3% of group long-term disability claims).[232] Only 10% of the individual policy claims for mental disorders involved bipolar disorders; thus, only about 0.5% of all individual long-term disability claims related to bipolar disorder.[233] Yet at least one company, namely, Metropolitan Life Insurance, litigated for years to defend its policy of refusing to sell an individual long-term disability policy at any price to an individual who had more than two "occurrences" of bipolar disorder.

The most comprehensive case to address the denial of benefits on the basis of psychiatric disabilities is *Doukas v. Metropolitan Life Insurance Company*.[234] Metropolitan Life denied Susan Doukas an application for mortgage disability insurance because she was diagnosed with bipolar disorder and had been taking lithium for 8 years. Ironically, although Metropolitan Life would not sell Doukas disability insurance at any price, it also argued that she was not disabled under the ADA and that it did not regard her as disabled, because it did not regard her as presently disabled but only possibly disabled in the future.[235] The court rejected this argument, finding that the nature of the fear caused by a disability was a fear of some future occurrence.[236]

The *Doukas* court rejected the plaintiff's argument that Metropolitan Life should be forced to show that it had an actuarially sound basis for its decision. The company preferred to use the alternative of "experience or reasonably predictable experience," even though standard insurance texts counsel that experience does not assist very much in making these predictions. However, the court was sympathetic to Doukas's arguments that Metropolitan Life's reliance on "bipolar disorder" as a category cut too wide a swath, in the face of more sophisticated prognosticators of future disability related to bipolar disorder, such as treatment noncompliance or substance abuse.[237]

Since *Doukas,* two courts have considered denials of individual long-term disability insurance on the basis of mental disability. The plaintiff in *Winslow v. IDS*[238] was diagnosed with dysthymia, a mild depression, and was taking Zoloft. Her application was denied pursuant to IDS's policy of automatically denying coverage to any individual who has received any form of mental health treatment in the year prior to applying for benefits, regardless of the seriousness of the condition.[239]

The court held as a matter of law that to deny an individual insurance coverage under these circumstances meant that the insurance company perceived Winslow as potentially disabled and thus covered by the ADA. It is interesting to note that IDS defended this by insisting that the highest number of payments for mental health claims were for depression-related claims,[240] when the insurance industry's own data show clearly that the largest percentage of both claims and dollars spent under individual long-term disability policies are paid to individuals with anxiety disorders.[241]

The second case, *Goldman v. Standard Insurance*,[242] is an aberration of poor legal reasoning. In that case, Goldman, an attorney, was denied long-term disability coverage because she had been seeing a therapist for an adjustment disorder. The court found that even though Goldman had been denied coverage, the insurance company must regard her as currently disabled for her to qualify for the protections of the ADA.[243] This decision would leave insurance companies free to exclude completely applicants for any kind of insurance on the basis of inaccurate and totally unsupported stereotypes about mental disability, violating even the principles of fair discrimination.

The court completely missed the point that most discrimination on the basis of mental disability arises from baseless fears that an individual is on the brink of violence, collapse, or other unpredictable behavior. These stereotypes cannot be overcome by the strongest of evidence—even if the individual has been a practicing attorney for over 10 years, such as Patrice Goldman, or an employee who has never missed a day of work because of mental health problems, such as Susan Winslow. These women were denied insurance coverage because they had seen a therapist. In each case, the insurance companies admitted that this was their blanket policy. These policies represent a conclusion that applicants receiving mental health treatment are so unlikely to be able to continue working that they should be completely denied insurance coverage. If this were actually true, if the impairments represented by seeking therapy actually meant that a person had a significant chance of being unable to work a normal job, it would substantially limit individuals' ability to work; the same is true for people with HIV seropositivity who are substantially limited in their ability to reproduce, even when the limitation only applies to future decisions.[244]

Whether a limitation is substantial is determined by a comparison with the general population; the general population expects a normal and uninterrupted work life, absent of the kind of emergencies for which one purchases long-term disability insurance. At the point that they denied Winslow and Goldman coverage, the insurance companies regarded them as being substantially limited in the major life activity of working, as compared with the general population, or else (by definition) insurance coverage would have been extended to them.

The ADA was passed so that such unthinking and baseless stereotypes could be eliminated from this country's practices. To hold that an insurance company must regard someone as presently disabled for that person to have standing to challenge the insurance company's decisions is to insulate all insurance company decision making from scrutiny under the ADA. People buy insurance to ensure against disability in the future, and insurance companies are required by the ADA to base their risk assessments on real data and real evidence.

The Provision of Unequal Psychiatric and Medical Benefits

The area that has drawn the most litigation under the ADA is the distinction between coverage of mental and physical conditions. These distinctions typically appear in two insurance contexts: health insurance and long-term disability benefits.

Distinction Between Health and Disability Insurance

The distinction between mental and physical conditions in health insurance coverage is reflected in substantially lower lifetime and annual caps on mental health treatment,[245] higher deductibles or copayments, and limits on outpatient psychotherapy. The Mental Health Parity Act of 1996, discussed more fully below, requires equivalent annual and lifetime caps for mental and physical conditions but very little else and is due to expire soon. Health insurance plans are regulated almost entirely by state laws. Therefore, states can also enact their own parity legislation. Many have done so, imposing more stringent requirements than the federal Mental Health Parity Act.

Disability benefits, however, cover a worker who is completely disabled from working. Typically, these plans cover mental disability—usually defined as "mental or nervous disorders"[246]—for 24 months, and physical disabilities until age 65, when Social Security and Medicare take over. Disability plans are primarily regulated by a comprehensive federal statute, the Employee Retirement Income Security Act (ERISA), with certain exceptions. Whether covered by ERISA or not, Section 501(c) of the ADA applies to all long-term disability plans. Because a number of states have enacted parity requirements for health insurance,[247] in many states citizens are in the somewhat anomalous position of being guaranteed parity in health insurance but not in disability benefits.[248] The EEOC has taken the position that disparities in the area of health insurance is permissible under the ADA but that distinctions in disability benefits are prohibited.[249]

Does the distinction between health insurance and disability benefits make any sense for purposes of the ADA? Perhaps it does. First, the insurance company's actuarial studies have more limited application in the context of disability benefits. When insurance companies reimburse for health care, they are paying for actual treatment, which clearly varies in cost with the condition treated and the age and condition of the individual treated. Disability benefits, however, are typically paid as a proportion of the employee's salary. Variance in disability benefit costs depends on the salaries of affected employees. This distinction mirrors those in federal assistance programs. Whereas the federal government rations its health care program for the poor, Medicaid, covering some services and not others, there is no distinction between physical and mental disabilities in federal income replacement, such as SSI or SSDI, which are programs for people with disabilities.

The Mental Health Parity Act

Parity legislation passed by Congress applies to health insurance but not to disability benefits. The Mental Health Parity Act of 1996[250] was passed as a compromise between those who wanted full parity and those who argued that parity in coverage would bankrupt insurance companies.[251] The act provides that for plan years beginning January 1, 1998, and ending October 1, 2001, group health plans in companies with more than 50 employees[252] that provide coverage for mental health conditions must provide equal lifetime benefit caps, unless the issuing companies can show that this raises their health insurance costs by 1% or more a year. The 1% exception is most likely to favor employers whose plans contain the most egregious disparities in coverage: for example, if a current plan has a $1 million cap on physical illness expenses and a $1,000 cap on mental health expenses, it is far more likely that it will cost that employer more than 1% of its costs to establish parity than it would if the existing mental illness cap were, for example, $750,000.

Because the opposition to this modest proposal has been so vocal, one would assume that the benefits would be great in scope; however, the real benefits have been largely illusory. Because plans are still free to limit actual office visits and to limit reimbursement for each visit, the lifetime benefit cap may well never be reached. In addition, plans may still vary copayment charges for mental health and physical illness and provide disparate coverage for inpatient and outpatient care.

The act also had unexpected repercussions that adversely influenced interpretations of the ADA. The passage of parity legislation has been used by courts to support holdings that the ADA does not apply to health insurance, because otherwise Congress would not have needed to legislate in the area.[253] Ironically, the passage of parity legislation in the area of health insurance has also been used to support the contention that the ADA does not apply to disability benefits, even though the parity legislation itself does not cover disability benefits.[254]

Challenges to Coverage Distinctions

Whereas a substantial number of cases have been brought under the ADA challenging differential coverage of mental and physical disabilities as discriminatory, litigation preceding and parallel to ADA litigation has sought to challenge the classification of various conditions as "mental" rather than "physical." Because the classification of a condition as mental has such dire consequences in terms of caps on lifetime benefits and because so many conditions have both physical and mental aspects, there has been extensive litigation on how to determine precisely what makes an illness, condition, or disorder mental.

For the most part, these cases have been litigated under ERISA.[255] This complicated statute permits employees to challenge the denial of disability benefits by their employers' insurance companies. However, court review is severely limited—if the plan administrator has discretionary authority to determine eligibility for benefits, a court will overturn the administrator's decision only if it is "arbitrary and capricious."[256] In addition, ERISA preempts most other causes of action relating to the denial of benefits, including state negligence claims.

ERISA challenges. Plaintiffs who are initially denied medical or surgical coverage in health insurance or disability benefits on the grounds that they have a mental, nervous, or emotional disorder have been diagnosed with a wide variety of conditions, including major depression,[257] obsessive–compulsive disorder,[258] congenital encephalopathy,[259] autism,[260] manic depression (or bipolar disorder),[261] cerebral arteriosclerosis,[262] anorexia,[263] chronic fatigue syndrome,[264] organic brain defects,[265] depression caused by Interferon treatment for hepatitis,[266] Alzheimer's disease,[267] depression and mild dementia secondary to diabetes,[268] and postpartum psychosis.[269] In one case, a plaintiff who had been hospitalized with a heart condition was denied coverage because the insurance company determined that his disability resulted from a mental or emotional condition; the plaintiff argued that the emotional condition was a secondary response to the heart condition and the medication he was forced to take for it.[270]

What makes something a mental illness as opposed to a physical illness? Essentially, courts have followed three distinct approaches in developing a substantive standard for determining what is a physical illness. The three substantive approaches concentrate on (a) the cause of the condition, (b) the nature of the symptoms treated, and (b) the modality of the treatment associated with the condition. Some courts have avoided the substantive question entirely by resorting to interpretative strategies.

The two interpretive devices most often used by the courts are to defer to the determination of the plan administrator, a mandate of ERISA law, and thus rule in favor of the defendants;[271] or, for those courts inclined to the plaintiff's position, to use the well-known insurance doctrine of construing an ambiguous policy in favor of the insured.[272] The very multiplicity of strategies by which courts determine whether a condition is *mental* appears to support the conclusion that the term is ambiguous, a conclusion also supported by the fact that in many cases, especially earlier cases, the insurance companies did not define the terms relating to mental conditions.

The cause. A number of courts have looked to whether the condition at issue results from a known physical cause, regardless of whether its manifestations are identical to those of conditions with no known physical cause.[273] In many cases of both physical and mental illness, however, no one is certain as to the cause of the illness.[274]

In deciding what causes a condition, these courts look to psychiatric and medical experts. This, too, has its own difficulties because there is little consensus among experts about what causes most forms of what is considered mental illness and even less agreement about other conditions, such as chronic fatigue syndrome or anorexia. In addition, political cross-currents affect both the construction of diagnoses and the course and conclusions of research in ways that courts do not like to acknowledge.[275]

The symptoms. The 8th and 5th Circuits declared that the dichotomy of mental and physical illness is (for insurance purposes at least) whatever the lay public believes that it is.[276] The rationale for this approach is that because ERISA requires insurance companies to write their plans "in a manner calculated to be understood by the average plan participant" and because the court concluded (without citation) that "laypersons are inclined to focus on the symptoms of an illness," then the meaning of a term should be derived from the interpretation that the court concludes that laypeople would ascribe to it. The court decided (again without citation) that "illness whose primary symptoms are depression, mood swings, and aberrational behavior are commonly characterized as mental illnesses, regardless of their cause.[277] Whether the public is mistaken is immaterial, and the courts evidently believe that they can discern the public mind as a matter of intuition or common sense or judicial notice without evidence.[278]

Other courts have decided that a mental illness is what an insurance company says it is, again regardless of the accuracy of the definition.[279] Congress may resolve this particular issue as a practical matter by legislating that mental and physical illnesses must be covered equally, but the issue will not go away. The 8th Circuit decided that "illnesses whose primary symptoms are depression, mood swings and unusual behavior are commonly characterized as mental illnesses regardless of their cause."[280] This would make thyroid imbalances mental illnesses, as well as brain tumors, Alzheimer's disease, AIDS, dementia, and hypoglycemia, all of which result in bizarre behavior and apparent mood swings. An even larger number of illnesses include depression as a symptom.

The treatment. One court has looked to the treatment actually received by the patient to determine whether or not it is covered as a physical or medical condition. In *Simons v. Blue Cross–Blue Shield of Greater New York*,[281] Amy Simons was admitted to the hospital after losing a considerable amount of weight in a 2-week period due to anorexia nervosa. She was fed on a nasal–gastric tube, and various tests were conducted to rule out brain tumors as an explanation for her eating disorder and severe headaches. The court ruled that "the plain, ordinary meaning of 'psychiatric' care is the sort of treatment, such as electroshock therapy and psychotropic medication, rendered to a patient who has been admitted to a psychiatric ward to attend to his or her psychiatric disorder."[282]

The court held that Amy Simons had received medical treatment, not psychiatric treatment. The fact that "Amy's physical disability was the result of the psychiatric condition known as anorexia nervosa does not transform what is customarily medical treatment into psychiatric treatment."[283] However, this perspective is not held by all courts. Some courts have held that medical treatment for difficulties caused by psychiatric conditions are subject to the "mental illness" limitation in disability coverage.[284] It is absolutely clear, however, that treatment for the mental health consequences of medical conditions is subject to the mental illness limitation.[285]

This parsing between physical and mental causes, symptoms, manifestations, and treatments quickly reaches the point of absurd. The 9th Circuit, using the interpretive doctrine that ambiguous phrases in a policy are to be construed in favor of the policyholder, has held that if the underlying cause is physical, or if the manifestation is physical, or if the manifestation is the result of a combination of physical and mental causes, then the policyholder will be covered.[286]

Some insurance companies have in fact begun to rewrite their own definitions of "mental or nervous disorders." One plan distinguishes between "medically determinable physical impairments" and all other impairments.[287] The company defined *medically determinable physical impairment* as "a physical impairment which results from anatomical or physiological abnormalities which are exclusively organic and non-psychiatric in nature and which are demonstrated by medically acceptable clinical and laboratory techniques."[288]

This definition, such as those promulgated by the insurance carriers of Unum, Cigna, Standard, and Fortis Benefits that exclude "self-reported" or "self-diagnosed" conditions,[289] is aimed not only at people with relatively better known psychiatric illnesses but also at the explosive growth of claims involving chronic fatigue syndrome.[290]

As long as definitions such as these are written in relatively abstract terms, they are open to the determination that they are ambiguous. The attempt to avoid ambiguity, however, in the decision by insurance carrier MetDisAbility to specifically limit coverage for chronic fatigue syndrome and back and joint sprains to 2 years[291] is subject to invalidation under the EEOC's regulations and interim guidance as selecting a specific disability for exclusion.

ADA challenges. Dozens of cases have been filed challenging the distinction between coverage for mental conditions and physical conditions in health insurance or long-term disability benefits.[292] Every case that has not been settled has lost, if not in the district court, then at the court of appeals level. There are two basic defenses that have been used to these challenges.

The first, which has been favored by a number of courts, is that differential coverage does not constitute discrimination because everyone who is covered by the insurance policy receives the same coverage. The fact that the differential coverage has a crushingly adverse impact on people with mental disabilities has been dismissed. Often courts cite the U.S. Supreme Court's decision in *Alexander v. Choate*,[293] without regard to the fact that the circumstances in *Alexander* were markedly different from the circumstances in these cases. It is important to note that

Alexander involved a state government providing free medical care to its poor and disabled citizens from a limited pot of resources, not a for-profit company selling insurance as a commercial transaction. In addition, the restrictions at issue in *Alexander*—limiting the number of days for hospital stays—were neutral on the face, in that they did not specifically refer to a disability or kind of disability, whereas the restrictions discussed here are specific to mental disabilities and, therefore, hardly neutral on the face.

The argument that everyone receives the same coverage is reminiscent of Anatole France's ironic comment on the majestic equality of the law that prohibits both rich and poor people from sleeping under a bridge[294] and—more chilling—of the U.S. Supreme Court's formulation of the equal protection doctrine in *Plessy v. Ferguson.*[295] Indeed, under the logic that immunizes any law that disadvantages members of a disfavored group simply because the law applies to members of both the disfavored group and the favored group, the Supreme Court wrongly decided *Loving v. Virginia,*[296] which prohibited both whites and blacks alike from intermarriage.

A different version of the same argument relies on the Supreme Court case of *Traynor v. Turnage*[297] for the argument that disability discrimination law does not prohibit discrimination between people with different disabilities. Again, this is based on a complete misreading of the meaning of *Traynor.*[298]

The disfavoring of mental disability coverage is clearly discriminatory against people with mental disabilities. The fallback position of the insurance industry is that the discrimination between coverage of mental or behavioral conditions and medical conditions is justified for objective, neutral reasons because mental conditions, "unlike most physical ailments . . . are extremely difficult to define, much less diagnose; as a consequence, benefits for these conditions are particularly subject to abuse and overutilization."[299] Even if this were the case, it would not justify discrimination against a group whose higher risk factors are at least partially due to the way they are treated in society. The fact that black people get sicker and die sooner than whites does not permit discrimination in insurance coverage of black people. This argument, however, need not be made because the insurance companies' arguments about mental health coverage are open to dispute on their own terms. Each part of this claim is subject to empirical investigation; each part fails the test of empirical investigation.

Physical ailments are "extremely difficult to define, much less diagnose." There are a number of physical ailments, of which chronic fatigue syndrome is only the best-known example, that are extremely difficult to define. Diagnoses of a number of other illnesses, such as lupus, are acknowledged by medical professions as simply the result of eliminating other possible diagnoses. There are any number of physical conditions, from back conditions to whiplash to migraines, for which medical professionals essentially have to rely on the reports of patients to make diagnoses.

However, some diagnoses of mental illness, such as bipolar disorder, are relatively easy to make, and their accuracy is relatively easy to check because, for example, lithium has been shown to be effective for most cases of bipolar disorder. Diagnoses of depression, anxiety disorder, panic disorder, obsessive–compulsive disorder, anorexia, bulimia, and other disorders also are fairly easy to make. Some diagnoses, such as dissociative identity disorder, are far more difficult, but they represent a tiny fraction of mental health conditions.

Mental disabilities are not necessarily difficult to define or diagnose. A number of mental disorders, such as bipolar disorder, depression and, in many cases, schizophrenia, are relatively easy to recognize. The widely respected Epidemiological Catchment Area Survey, which is universally cited as a reliable source of data about the prevalence of mental disorders, accomplished its mission by asking people questions, in many cases fewer than 50, and its findings are considered conclusive.[300] The World Health Organization has been classifying psychiatric disorders for almost 50 years. Indicia of the major psychiatric conditions are so clear that many cross-cultural studies have been conducted, confirming that schizophrenia, bipolar disorder, and depression exist across cultures.[301] In addition, historical accounts confirm that they have existed across time.[302]

There is no connection between the ease of definition or diagnosis of a condition and the number of claims or the expense of insuring it. Although mental health claims are expensive, there are certainly ways of cutting back on that expense, and insurance companies have failed to take advantage of many of them. Inpatient care is far more expensive than outpatient care, yet most insurance companies still allow far more generous benefits for inpatient treatment than for outpatient treatment. Psychotherapy, which is one form of treatment that is highly responsive to copayments,[303] could be regulated by progressively raising the copayment over time, thus encouraging early visits and discouraging unnecessarily extended services.

There is no actuarial basis supporting the massive distinction between mental health benefits and medical benefits. The insurance industry has also taken the position that the ADA does not require the industry to "justify coverage decisions with 'sound actuarial principles, reasonably anticipated experience, and bona fide risk classification.'"[304] In its successful argument against the 6th Circuit panel's decision in *Parker*,[305] the American Council of Life Insurance and Health Insurance Associations of America strongly protested the requirement that their decisions must be supported by sound actuarial data:

> The Panel effectively and impermissibly attempted to rewrite the statute by adding a third requirement—proof of sound actuarial data—to the already existing elements set forth by Congress in the statute: consistency with state law and absence of subterfuge. If the Panel's holding were followed by the Court, insurers would be required to justify affirmatively—in court—each and every challenged coverage distinction with reams of actuarial data.[306]

The argument made by the insurance industry in support of this proposition is that the requirement for sound actuarial data appears nowhere in the statutory language of the ADA.[307] Clearly, however, it does. The requirement that the insurance industry conform its practices to state law is another way of requiring that its distinctions be the product of fair discrimination, the model on which states regulate the insurance industry. For discrimination to be "fair," it requires sound actuarial data to support the distinctions being made. There are some good reasons to suppose that this actuarial data either do not exist or are not sound.

First of all, the proportion of an insurance company's business that corresponds to behavioral health expenses is so small that it is not economical for the companies to do many sophisticated actuarial analyses.[308] Because the overall behavioral health proportion is so low, it is even less likely that a sound actuarial basis exists for discrimination on the basis of particular disabilities, such as schizophrenia, depression, or bipolar disorder. Most companies do not keep data by diagnosis or even data concerning the percentage of claims relating to mental disabilities or dollars that went to mental health claims.[309]

Second, the introduction of managed care practices into the mental health arena is relatively new, but its effects are substantial in terms of costs to the insurance companies. Therefore, any analyses that do not take into consideration these effects are probably not as complete or as useful as they could be. Third, as mentioned earlier, the outside data and studies relied on by the insurance companies in making determinations about mental health coverage are out-of-date and do not necessarily differentiate between the impact of mental disability and the impact of institutionalization. Fourth, no studies have been conducted on the impact that insurance companies' skewed reimbursement policies favoring inpatient care over outpatient care have on the cost of providing mental health coverage.

None of the published cases even consider these questions The cases tell us nothing about what actuarial data the insurance industry relies on to support the extreme distinctions between coverage for mental and physical illness and disabilities. Nor do the cases reveal the basis for capping lifetime benefits for mental health coverage at $10,000 or $25,000 compared with caps of $1 million for medical or surgical benefits. What objective research, study, or experience supports more generous benefits for outpatient treatment for physical illnesses than for mental illnesses? What is the justification for the termination of disability benefits after 2 years rather than paying benefits until the disabled person turns age 65?

As a practical matter, insurance company practices in setting these differential coverages have rarely been closely scrutinized. As noted above, most litigation over the refusal to cover certain conditions involves the argument that the conditions are in fact physical rather than a challenge to the underlying premise involved in differentiating physical health coverage from mental health coverage.

Even when the differential between mental health coverage and physical coverage is directly challenged as discriminatory under the ADA or the Rehabilitation Act, the underlying justification for the distinction has not been examined. The insurance industry's major victories tend to be on threshold issues: The plaintiff is not a qualified individual with a disability and, therefore, has no standing to challenge the distinction,[310] or the contents of insurance policies are simply not regulated by the ADA or the Rehabilitation Act.[311] Plaintiff victories in these—increasingly rare —cases are usually the result of settlements.[312] Thus, the basis for insurance companies' decisions regarding benefit capping, rate setting, inpatient versus outpatient coverage, and other decisions that distinctly disadvantage people with mental disabilities has never been closely examined.

Mental Health Parity and Insurance

Arguments for and against parity of insurance coverage are weakened by a lack of research and by strong biases in extant studies. During the yearlong congressional debate about parity and after the passage of the Mental Health Parity Act of 1996,[313] a number of research studies were cited and commissioned to pinpoint precisely what kind of cost increase in insurance premiums would result if the federal government were to mandate parity of mental health benefits. Although insurance companies that provide parity of coverage for disability benefits charge between 7.5% and 21% more than standard premium costs,[314] the actual cost increase for providing full parity appears to be far lower, especially for those companies that use managed care in the provision of mental health benefits.

There are a number of studies available regarding the extra cost of providing parity in mental health coverage. Some of these are based on predictions of cost increases if various congressional proposals were adopted, some are based on the experience of insurance companies that provide coverage options that include partial and full parity,[315] some are based on the experience of the growing number of states that already require parity in coverage for mental health and medical or surgical benefits, and some have looked at more than one of these methods of predicting cost increases.[316]

The cost increase predicted by the studies varied substantially. Although the studies were conducted by respected actuarial organizations, it is nonetheless true that studies funded by organizations opposed to parity predicted far a greater cost impact than studies funded by organizations that favored parity.[317] The explanation for the differences in the predicted premium increases is primarily due to different assumptions about the degree to which companies will use managed care and the degree to which private coverage would shift costs from the public to the private sector.[318]

The predictions of the Congressional Budget Office fell almost exactly halfway in between the predictions of the studies commissioned by the various interest groups.[319] None of the studies, however, reported that premium costs would increase by as much as the percentage difference between nonparity and full-parity plans charged by most insurance companies that offer full parity.

One important fact to bear in mind is that even if full parity were to trigger a greatly increased use of mental health services, the effect on policy premiums would be relatively small because mental health treatment expenditures represent a relatively small fraction of all health expenditures. For example, one Maryland insurer experienced an increase in expenditures for mental health care of 22% in the first 6–8 months after parity was implemented, but because mental health and substance abuse treatment constituted only about 5% of total health care costs, the total premium increase attributable to parity was just over 1%.[320] The studies report that the cost of full parity for mental health benefits would be 3.2%,[321] 3.4%,[322] or 3.6%[323] —not an enormous increase, on the face of it, and certainly less than insurance companies have been claiming.

Experience of insurance companies providing parity coverage. Most insurance companies do not have records indicating that the provision of parity coverage greatly increases costs. This is precisely "because MH/SA [mental health/substance abuse] expenditures are generally a small portion of a health insurer's total premium, many insurers do not allocate resources to collect these data."[324]

Experience of states, counties, and cities mandating parity coverage. Some states have mandated as part of their regulation of insurance practices some form of parity between coverage offered for medical and physical illnesses and for mental illnesses. Of these, 22 states provide greater benefits in some form than those mandated by the Mental Health Parity Act.[325] Of that number, some provide full parity only for state government employees,[326] whereas others exclude employers of fewer than 50 employees.[327] Some states cover only serious mental illness or certain kinds of treatment.[328] In all states, the statutory parity mandate does not impact private employers who self-insure and are, thus, subject to regulation under ERISA.[329]

The experience of the states that mandate parity has been that costs have increased very little—generally about 1% or less.[330] Many of the state statutes that mandate parity have exceptions, however, such as exemptions for small businesses, and they do not include companies that self-insure. Some define *mental illnesses* to include only so-called serious mental illnesses,[331] although the evidence is that these illnesses are responsible for almost 90% of mental health care costs,[332] so that adopting a broad definition of mental illness is not likely to add a great deal to costs.

The experience of counties and cities in providing parity appears to be mixed. Whereas San Diego eliminated disability coverage for people with mental health benefits in 1994 because of the volume of claims[333] (and was promptly sued),[334] Phoenix settled a similar lawsuit by agreeing to institute parity in disability benefits, and it reports little in the way of rising costs: "Economically, I don't think it had much of an impact at all," said Don Erickson, Phoenix's personnel fiscal specialist. "Mental claims were a small amount of the total that applied for long-term disability, less than ten percent, and there haven't been any more claims than we had before."[335] When the defendant in *Leonard F. v. Israel Discount Bank*[336] settled the case, agreeing to provide parity in disability benefits, it explained the decision to settle on the basis that paying the differential was less expensive than litigating the case.[337]

A cautionary note: Parity policy issues.   Parity may not cost much more, but that is not necessarily a reason to embrace it. Parity of coverage raises a number of complex issues: Would it apply to involuntary treatment? Would parity under managed care cost less simply because very little care was being provided? Would parity encourage private hospitals to keep psychiatric patients with insurance coverage unnecessarily?[338] Private hospitals have been so eager to recruit psychiatric patients that they have hired "bounty hunters"; one of the largest civil settlements ever in a case brought by the DOJ involved National Medical Enterprise's (now Tenet's) unjustified retention of people against their will to maximize payments from insurance companies.[339] Some people in the survey raised issues of insurance parity, but relatively few. What most people seem to want is outpatient therapy, which is a low priority for almost everyone except the people who need it.

Conclusion

Insurance coverage raises many seemingly related but conceptually distinct categories of issues under the ADA. The first category is the discriminatory behavior of insurance companies toward individual applicants: denial of coverage, exclusion of coverage for certain conditions, and charging excessive premiums. Denying coverage entirely on the basis of a disability is clearly illegal under the ADA: Even Judge Posner agrees.[340] The pre-existing-condition exclusion, however, is clearly allowed: The legislative history makes this plain. Courts have not yet faced the question of charging excessive premiums; this may either be interpreted as illegal under the ADA because it violates the fair discrimination principle, or as a violation of the McCarran–Ferguson doctrine forbidding courts from entering the business of state regulation of insurance. Presumably each of these conclusions would apply to an insurance company refusing to insure an employer because it employed too many employees with disabilities, which would be illegal, or charging excessive premiums, which might be illegal.

A second distinct area involves the contents of insurance policies that are offered to employers and to the public. Litigation under the ADA challenging both caps on coverage and grossly unequal coverage for mental disabilities has proven to be a failure. Greater success has come from seeking legislative solutions, on a federal level in the form of the Mental Health Parity Act, and increasingly on the state level as well. Parity laws, however, raise complicated questions of their own: Does the drive to medicalize psychiatric disability mean that only the "medical" treatment of psychiatric disability will be covered, leaving psychotherapy out in the cold? Is involuntary treatment subject to parity? Private hospitals have a propensity to keep insured psychiatric patients too long anyway. Will parity simply fuel this trend?

One thing is clear: The basis on which insurance companies make underwriting decisions about psychiatric disabilities should be investigated further. Insurance companies that rely on 20-year-old studies of impoverished and institutionalized people to deny coverage or to charge exorbitant premiums must be challenged. Advocates should seek to enforce the fair discrimination requirements at the state level; some state insurance commissioners will be more sympathetic than others. There are more sophisticated means of making actuarial predictions available today, and insurance companies should be required to follow them.

Endnotes

1. National Council on the Handicapped, *Towards Independence* (Washington, DC: Author, 1987). The National Council on the Handicapped, established under the Rehabilitation Act of 1973, is an independent federal agency composed of 15 members in charge of advising the President and Congress about issues relating to Americans with disabilities. Congress changed the name to the National Council on Disability in 1988, in the Handicapped Programs Technical Amendments Act of 1988, P. L. 100-630. The first recipient of psychiatric services to serve on the council, Rae Unzicker, was appointed by President Clinton in Apr. 1995.

2. On Oct. 24, 1988, the Subcommittee on Select Education held a hearing on H. R.4498, the ADA. The testimony has been preserved by the law firm of Arnold and Porter, *see* note 5 of chapter 1. Testimony of William Dorfer (who was denied life insurance because of his muscular dystrophy), A&P Comm. Print 1990 (28B)*1098; testimony of Melissa Marshall, A&P Comm. Print 1990 (28B)*1102; testimony of Eileen Healy Horndt ("because disability is seen as an illness, the life and medical and disability insurance companies do not want to insure us . . . despite working consistently for the last 12 years I cannot get disability insurance"), A&P Comm. Print (28A)*1119; testimony of Rima Sutton, service coordinator, National Multiple Sclerosis Society ("another major problem disabled people face is the inability to obtain health or life insurance . . . a man [with MS] wanted to buy life insurance . . . but could not find one carrier in the whole state of New Hampshire to offer him a policy") (Boston testimony); testimony of Marcie Roth, supervising advocate at WeCAHR, an organization offering advocacy services to people with disabilities, A&P Comm. Print (28A)*1108 ("people with disabilities experience the most blatant discrimination of all at the hands of the insurance industry. Not only is private insurance generally denied most folks with disabilities, but those lucky enough to obtain private insurance find that items crucial to [the] maintenance of function and optimal health are categorically denied or provided only once over a per-

son's lifetime"); testimony of Nancy E. Durkin, A&P Comm. Print (28A)*1108; testimony of Barbara Johnson, A&P Comm. Print (28A)*1212; testimony of Stephen B. Fawcett, professor of human development and research associate of the Research and Training Center on Independent Living, and Barbara Bradford, training associate (after having collected data from over 17,000 people in 12 states, unavailable or unaffordable automobile, life, and liability insurance was considered an important issue by 89% of people; satisfaction with insurance was reported at 35%; both rates represent extremes among issues considered important and satisfaction reported by disabled consumers).

3. Testimony of Rep. Tony Coelho, A&P Comm. Print (1990) (28B)*940 (his insurance was cancelled when he was diagnosed with epilepsy); testimony of Barbara Johnson, A&P Comm. Print (28B)*1212; testimony of Scott Allen, A&P Comm. Print (1990) (28B)*1996 (people who are HIV positive lose their medical insurance because of discrimination about their disability).

4. Testimony of Melissa Marshall, A&P Comm. Print 1990 (28B)*1102; testimony of Eileen Healy Horndt, A&P Comm. Print (28B)*1119 (the insurance industry "is an area that has traditionally been a major problem for people with disabilities. Many people are paying exorbitant amounts of car, life, and medical insurance if we can get the insurance at all").

5. Testimony of Marcie Roth, A&P Comm. Print 1990 (28B)*1110 (for an infant girl born without arms, the insurance company will only pay for one set of prosthetic arms in her lifetime).

6. Statement of Laura Cooper, A&P Comm. Print (28B)*1980 ("I can recall representatives from law firms who told me, among other things, that they would not hire me because of what I would do to their insurance rates").

7. Testimony of Eileen Healy Horndt, A&P Comm. Print (28B)*1119, *1124 (independent living centers cannot get insurance because half the staff are people with disabilities; insurance companies deny employers liability insurance on the basis of the types of people they hire).

8. Testimony of William Cavanaugh, A&P Comm. Print (28B)*1067, Lafayette Hotel, Boston, MA, Oct. 24, 1988.

9. Testimony of Lelia Batten, A&P Comm. Print (28B)*1205 (noting that "most private therapists do not take Medicaid, and most clinics do not promote any treatment besides medication").

10. Colloquy between Rep. Owens and Bill Dorfer, A&P Comm. Print 1990 (28B)*1102.

11. Testimony of Nancy Durkin, A&P Comm. Print 1990 (28B)*1107; testimony of Marcie Roth at 1110. Rep. Owens then urged Roth to continue with her remarks.

12. Survey No. 94 (B. I. by sister S. S.) (on file with author).

13. The Mental Health Parity Act was Title VII of P. L. 104-204, 110 Stat. 2944; 29 U.S.C. 1185a and 42 U.S.C. 3000gg-f. For a discussion of the requirements and limitations of the Mental Health Parity Act, see notes 250–254 and text on pp. 278–279 and Appendix B.

14. 42 U.S.C. Sec. 12201(c).

15. 42 U.S.C. Sec. 12201(c). The "subchapters" language refers to Titles I (employment) and III (public accommodations) of the ADA.

16. In addition to the legislative history, which comprises the Committee Reports of the Senate Committee on Labor and Human Resources, at 84–86; the House Committee on Education and Labor, at 136–138; the House Committee on the Judiciary; the House Committee on Energy and Commerce at 70, each of which contains fairly extensive commentary about Section 501(c), both the EEOC and DOJ have published regulations and interpretive commentary relating to the ADA's coverage of insurance practices. In addition, the EEOC discussed insurance in its Technical Assistance Manual and issued an interim Interpretive Guidance specifically focused on Health Insurance and the ADA

(the final version has not been published and is not expected, *see* note 250). The EEOC also issued an EEOC Notice, *Questions and Answers About Disability and Service Retirement Plans Under the ADA* No. 915.002 (Washington, DC: Author, May 15, 1995). DOJ also addressed insurance practices in its *Technical Assistance Manual.*

17. These cases constitute the plurality of cases brought regarding insurance coverage under the ADA; EEOC v. Staten Island Savings Bank, 2000 U.S. LEXIS 4633 (2nd Cir. Mar. 23, 2000); Pallozzi v. Allstate Insurance Co., 2000 U.S. App. LEXIS 589 (2nd Cir. Jan. 13, 2000); Pallozzi v. Allstate Insurance Co., 198 F.3d 28 (2nd Cir. 1999); Leonard F. v. Israel Discount Bank, 199 F.3d 99 (2nd Cir. 1999); Weyer v. Twentieth Century Fox, 198 F.3d 1104 (9th Cir. 2000); Kimber v. Thiokol Corp., 196 F.3d 1092 (10th Cir. 1999); Lewis v. K-Mart, 180 F.3d 166 (4th Cir. 1999); Rogers v. Department of Health and Environmental Control, 174 F.3d 431 (4th Cir. 1999); Ford v. Schering-Plough, 145 F.3d 601 (3rd Cir. 1998); Leonard F. v. Israel Discount Bank, 101 F.3d 687 (2nd Cir. 1996) (table case); Baker v. Hartford Life, 1995 U.S. Dist. LEXIS 14103, Parker v. Metropolitan Life, 121 F.3d 1006 (6th Cir. 1997) (*en banc*); EEOC v. CNA, 96 F.3d 1039 (7th Cir. 1996); Whaley v. United States, 82 F.Supp. 2d 1060 (D.D.C. 2000); Goldman v. Standard Insurance Co., 1999 U.S. Dist. LEXIS 20191 (N.D. Ca. Dec. 20, 1999); Fennell v. Aetna, 1999 U.S. Dist. LEXIS 2358 (D.D.C. Feb. 26, 1999); Fitts v. Federal National Mortgage Association, 44 F.Supp. 2d 317 (D.D.C. 1999); Connors v. Maine Medical Center, 42 F.Supp. 2d 34 (D. Me. 1999); Muller v. First Unum Life Insurance Corp., 23 F.Supp. 2d 231 (N.D. N.Y. 1998); Leonard F. v. Israel Discount Bank, 967 F.Supp. 802 (S.D. N.Y. 1997); Erwin v. Northwestern Mutual Life Insurance Co., S.D. Ind. 1998); Doukas v. Metropolitan Life, 950 F.Supp. 422 (D. N.H. 1997); Brewster v. Cooley Associates/Counselling and Consulting, 1997 U.S. Dist. LEXIS 21433 (D. N.M. 1997); Berta Bril v. Dean Witter/Discover, 986 F.Supp. 171 (S.D. N.Y. 1997); Pappas v. Bethesda Hospital Association, 861 F.Supp. 616 (S.D. Ohio 1994); Bennett v. State Farm Mutual Automobile Insurance Co., 1994 WL 728282, 3 A.D. Cases 1477 (N.D. Ohio Oct. 19, 1994); Esfahani v. Medical College of Pennsylvania, 919 F.Supp. 832 (E.D. Pa. 1996); Schroeder v. Connecticut General Life Insurance Co., No. 93-M-2433 1994 WL 909636 (D. Colo. Apr. 22, 1994); EEOC v. Aramark Corp. et al., Civ. No. 97-734 (RMV) (D.D.C. 1997); EEOC v. Chase Manhattan Bank et. al., Civ. No. 97-6620 (S.D. N.Y. filed Sept. 9, 1997); Goldman v. Standard Insurance Co., No. C-98-0662 (N.D. Ca. Feb. 19, 1998); EEOC v. Cigna and Insurance Co. of North America, No 2:98-CV-259 (E.D. Pa. Jan. 16, 1998); Harris v. City of Phoenix, No. CIV 95-0361 (D. Ariz. filed Oct. 1995), *Disability Compliance Bull.* 7 (Mar. 28, 1996):7; Badua v. City of San Diego, 189 F.3d 472 (9th Cir. 1999) (table case), 1999 U.S. App. LEXIS 18442 (9th Cir. Aug. 5, 1999); EEOC v. Bath Iron Works and Fortis Insurance Corp., 1999 U.S. Dist. LEXIS 10600 (D. Me. Feb. 8, 1999).

18. The case that comes closest to real scrutiny is Doukas v. Metropolitan Life, 950 F.Supp. 422 (D. N.H. 1997).

19. *See, e.g.,* Chabner v. Mutual of Omaha Life Insurance Co., 994 F.Supp. 1185 (N.D. Ca. 1998), (fascioscapulohumeral muscular dystrophy); Anderson v. Gus Mayer Stores, 924 F.Supp. 763 (E.D. Tx. 1993).

20. *See* Brief of American Council of Life Insurance, filed in Parker v. Metropolitan Life Insurance Co., 121 F.3d 1006 (6th Cir. 1997) (*en banc*); *see also* Benjamin W. Boley, Thomas J. Mikula, and Timothy G. Lynch, "Legislative and Judicial Efforts to Mandate Parity Between Health Care and Disability Income Benefits for Physical and Mental Illnesses," *J. of Pension Planning and Compliance* 24 (Spring 1998):1.

21. M. J. O'Grady, "Mental Health Parity: Issues and Options in Developing Benefits and Premiums," Rep. No. 96-466 EPW (Washington, DC: Congressional Research Service, 1996).

22. Roland Sturm, "How Expensive Is Unlimited Mental Health Care Coverage Under Managed Care?" *J. of the Amer. Med. Assn.* 278 (Nov. 12, 1997):1533.

23. Some insurance companies cover only mental health expenses due to hospitalization; *see* Tolson v. Avondale Industries, Inc., 1998 U.S. App. LEXIS 11708 (5th Cir. June 3, 1998).

24. *But see* Doe v. Mutual of Omaha Life Insurance Co., 179 F.3d 557 (7th Cir. 1999) (the insurance company won, despite the admission that its AIDS caps have no actuarial basis whatsoever).

25. P. L. 79-33, 79-34, 59 Stat. 33.

26. The relevant text of the McCarran–Ferguson Act, 15 U.S.C. Sec. 1012(b), reads "no Act of Congress shall be construed to invalidate, impair, or supersede any laws enacted by any State for the purpose of regulating the business of insurance . . . unless such Act specifically relates to the business of insurance."

27. This exclusion is mandated by the McCarran–Ferguson Act, 15 U.S.C. Secs. 1011–1015 (1994).

28. 15 U.S.C. Sec. 1012(b) (1994).

29. National Association of Insurance Commissioners, "Model Regulation on Unfair Discrimination in Life and Health Insurance on the Basis of Physical or Mental Impairment," adopted 1993. As of Oct. 1995, 10 states had adopted this regulation (Arkansas, California, Iowa, Maine, Massachusetts, Missouri, New Jersey, Texas, Utah, and Wisconsin); and 14 had related legislation (Arizona, Florida, Georgia, Illinois, Kansas, Maryland, Michigan, Minnesota, North Carolina, Ohio, Oregon, Rhode Island, Virginia, and Washington).

30. Examples of statutory language incorporating fair discrimination principles in the context of disability include provisions such as "no insurer issuing, providing, or administering any contract of individual or group insurance providing life, annuity, or disability benefits applied for and issued on or after January 1, 1984, shall refuse to insure, or refuse to continue to insure, or limit the amount, extent, or kind of coverage available to an individual, or charge a different rate for the same coverage solely because of a mental or physical impairment, except where the refusal, limitation or rate differential is based on sound actuarial principles or is related to actual and reasonably anticipated experience"; Calif. Insur. C Sec. 10144 (West, 1998).

31. Katy Chi-Wen Li, "The Private Insurance Industry's Tactics Against Suspected Homosexuals: Redlining Based on Occupation, Residency and Marital Status," *Amer. J. of Law & Med.* 22(1996):477, 479–480 (noting also that Great Republic Life Insurance also warned its agents about men who were in the jewelry and fashion industries, interior decorators, or antique dealers).

32. Jill Gaulding, "Race, Sex, and Genetic Discrimination in Insurance: What's Fair?" *Cornell Law Rev.* 80 (1995):1646, 1687, quoting Larry Gostin, "Genetic Discrimination: The Use of Genetically Based Diagnostic and Prognostic Tests by Employers and Insurers," *Amer. J. of Law & Med.* 17 (1991):109, 118.

33. Deborah Hellman, "Is Actuarially Fair Insurance Pricing Actually Fair? A Case Study in Insuring Battered Women," *Harv. C. R.–C. L. Law Rev.* 32 (1997):355, 361 (quoting "Morning Edition: New Law to Make Insurance Companies Cover Abused Women," National Public Radio radio broadcast, Mar. 8, 1995).

34. Winslow v. IDS Life Insurance Co., 29 F.Supp. 2d 557, 559 (D. Minn. 1998); Doukas v. Metropolitan Life, 950 F.Supp. 422, 429 (D. N.H. 1996).

35. Chabner v. Mutual of Omaha, 994 F.Supp. 1185, 1187 (N.D. Ca. 1998).

36. Doukas v. Metropolitan Life, 950 F.Supp. 422 (D. N.H. 1996); Pallozzi v. Allstate Insurance Co., 198 F.3d 28 (2nd Cir. 1999); Goldman v. Standard Insurance Co., 1999 U.S. Dist. LEXIS 20191 (N.D. Ca. Dec. 20, 1999) (the attorney denied the disability insurance because she had been seeing a psychotherapist for adjustment disorder).

37. Jill Gaulding, "Race, Sex and Genetic Discrimination in Insurance: What's Fair?" *Cornell Law Rev.* 80 (1995):1646, 1652, quoting Robert B. Holtom, *Restraints on Under-*

writing: Risk Selection, Discrimination and the Law 6–7 (Cincinnati, OH: National Underwriting, 1979). The author described underwriting as "an art which was passed down from one underwriter to another," *id.* at 5.

38. An *exclusion waiver* refers to a decision to provide insurance to the individual except for the condition covered by the exclusion waiver.

39. Office of Technology Assessment, *Medical Testing and Health Insurance* OTA-H-384 (Washington, DC: U.S. Government Printing Office, Aug. 1988) at 60, Table 2-5.

40. G. William Glendenning and Robert B. Holtom, *Personal Lines Underwriting* 2d ed. (Malvern, PA: Insurance Institute of America, 1982) at 74.

41. Goldman v. Standard Insurance Co., 1999 U.S. Dist. LEXIS 20191 (N.D. Ca. Dec. 20, 1999). The plaintiff lost this case because the court held that she was not disabled; despite the insurance company's refusal to provide her with coverage, it did not regard her as disabled either.

42. Doukas v. Metropolitan Life, 950 F.Supp. 422, 429 (D. N.H. 1996).

43. *See* discussion *infra* at pp. 269–273.

44. T. H. Kirkpatrick, "Premiums and Reserves," in Davis W. Gregg and Vane B. Lucas, Eds., *Life and Health Insurance Handbook* 3d ed. (Homewood, IL: Richard D. Irwin, 1973) at 328.

45. Heaton v. State Health Benefits Commission, 624 A.2d 69, 71 (Sup. Ct. N.J. 1993). Under the Mental Health Parity Act of 1996, the lifetime benefit would have to be the same for psychiatric as major medical expenses, but the company could still limit the annual maximum to $10,000, thus permitting someone to reach the lifetime cap if they had the maximum permitted psychiatric expenses for 100 years.

46. Doe v. Mutual of Omaha Insurance Co., 179 F.3d 557, 558 (7th Cir. 1999).

47. The Hay Group Study, "Health Care Plan Design and Cost Trends—1988–1997" (May 1998) at 2, available at http://www.naphs.org/News/HayGroupReport.html.

48. In 1988, 26% of plans imposed a limit on outpatient visits; in 1997, 48% of plans imposed such a limit. *Id.* at 10.

49. National Council on the Handicapped, *Toward Independence* (Washington, DC: Author, 1986) at 19.

50. *Id.* at 14.

51. Robert L. Burgdorf, Jr., "The ADA: Analysis and Implications of a Second Generation Civil Rights Statute," *Harv. C. R.–C. L. Law Rev.* 26 (1991):413, 508. Apparently, disability advocates and Sen. Lowell Weicker, at that time the chief proponent of the ADA, pressured the National Council on Disabilities to remove the section regarding insurance because of "the fear that the insurance industry would oppose the bill as originally drafted and prevent its enactment"; H. Miriam Farber, "Subterfuge: Do Coverage Limitations and Exclusions in Employer-Provided Health Care Plans Violate the Americans With Disabilities Act?" *N.Y. Univ. Law Rev.* 69 (1994):850, 861, note 49.

52. S.2345, 100th Cong., 2nd Sess., introduced by Sen. Lowell Weicker and others on Apr. 28, 1988, and H.R.4498, introduced by Rep. Tony Coelho on Apr. 29, 1988. Although insurance companies were not explicitly covered, they were covered by implication because the bills covered "any public accommodation covered by Title II of the Civil Rights Act of 1964," Section 4(a)(3).

53. S.933, 101st Cong., 1st Sess. (May 9, 1989), was introduced by Sen. Harkin and others; the companion bill in the House, H.R.2273, was introduced by Rep. Coehlo and others.

54. Disability Rights Working Group, Working Paper No. 1, "Concerns With the Americans With Disabilities Act," A&P Comm. Print (1990) (28B)*1376. The Disability Rights Working Group complained that "the language in Title I creates incredible new liabilities for employers if they provide disabled persons with a benefit which is 'less effective than' or 'is different or separate' from that provided to others [citation omitted]." Group health insurance benefits, which are offered under the same terms and conditions to all

employees, may still be "less effective" or "separate or different" for a person with disabilities, *id.*

55. This provision now appears at 42 U.S.C. Sec. 12201(c)(1).

56. This provision now appears at 42 U.S.C. Sec. 11201(c)(2).

57. This provision now appears at 42 U.S.C. Sec. 12201(c)(3).

58. The Senate language for the last sentence was "except that paragraphs (1), (2), and (3) are not used as a subterfuge to evade the purpose of Title I and III." Although the language on insurance in the House bill voted out of the Judiciary and Education and Labor Committees was identical to the Senate language as passed, the House Committee on Energy and Commerce substituted for the last line of Section 501(c): "Paragraphs (1), (2) and (3) shall not be used as a subterfuge to evade the purposes of Titles I and III." This was the language of the House bill as finally passed. In the conference committee, the Senate receded, and the House language became law.

59. H. Miriam Farber, *supra* at note 45, at 855 (characterizing Section 501(c) as having "a great deal of ambiguity"); Christopher Aaron Jones, "Legislative 'Subterfuge?': Failing to Insure Persons With Mental Illness Under the Mental Health Parity Act and the Americans With Disabilities Act," *Vand. Law Rev.* 50 (1997):753, 757 (calling Section 501(c) a "confusing statutory provision").

60. Parker v. Metropolitan Life Insurance Co., 99 F.3d 181 at 190 (6th Cir. 1996).

61. Rep. Douglas was referring specifically to Sec. 501(c), H. R. Rep. No 101-485, Pt. 3 at 94.

62. Title I of the ADA, prohibiting discrimination in employment, went into effect for employers of more than 25 employees on July 26, 1992, and for employers of 15 employees or more on July 26, 1994, 42 U.S.C. Sec. 12111(5) (A).

63. H. Miriam Farber, *supra* note 51, at 850.

64. K-Mart Corporation v. Cartier, Inc., et al., 486 U.S. 281 (1988).

65. Krauel v. Iowa Methodist Medical Center, 95 F.3d 674, 678 (8th Cir. 1996) (relying on the language from the U.S. Supreme Court's decision in Public Employees Retirement System v. Betts, 492 U.S. 158, 166 [1989]; and Piquard v. City of East Peoria, 887 F.Supp. 1106 [N.D. Ill. 1995]).

66. 42 U.S.C. 12201(c).

67. The Brief of *amici* American Council of Life Insurance and Health Insurance Association of America in the 6th Circuit's *en banc* reconsideration of Parker v. Metropolitan Life (hereafter called the "American Council of Life Insurance Brief") asserted that "the purpose [of Section 501(c)] is to preserve prevailing insurance practices except where it can be proven that a distinction in coverage is inconsistent with state law or a subterfuge for unlawful discrimination," at 7.

68. The American Council of Life Insurance Brief asserts that insurance companies are not required by the ADA to prove any actuarial basis for limitations or distinctions in coverage, at 10.

69. One court held that this phrase is itself ambiguous and subject to different interpretations; Doukas v. Metropolitan Life, 950 F.Supp. 422, 428 (D. N.H. 1996).

70. "South Carolina 'High Risk' Pool Sued," *Disability Compliance Bull.* 3(20) (Apr. 28, 1993):3.

71. "Court Allows State's High-Risk Insurance Pool to Exclude Persons With HIV," *Disability Compliance Bull.* 7(5) (Dec. 21, 1995) (reporting on Givens v. South Carolina Health Insurance Pool). Although the 4th Circuit heard arguments on appeal in the case, Givens v. South Carolina Health Insurance Pool, No. 95-2791 (4th Cir.), no decision was ever reported in the case.

72. "Court Allows State's High-Risk Insurance Pool to Exclude Persons With HIV" (Dec. 21, 1995):10.

73. "South Carolina Prepared to Implement the Health Insurance Portability and Account-

ability Act of 1996," *South Carolina Department of Insurance Newsletter* 2(2) (Mar.–Apr. 1997):1.

74. Doukas, 950 F.Supp. at 432; Baker v. Hartford Life, 1995 U.S. Dist. LEXIS 14103 (28B)*10, 1995 WL 573430*4 ("even though an insurer may claim to be basing a denial of coverage on actuarial or classification of risk considerations, that claim is not conclusive as the question of whether section 12201(c) is being used as a subterfuge would remain"). One case following this reasoning was vacated as moot without comment on the ADA analysis used, World Insurance Co. v. Branch, 996 F.Supp. 1203, 1209 note 6 (N.D. Ga. 1997), *vac.*, 156 F.3d 1142 (11th Cir. 1998).

75. John Doe v. Mutual of Omaha, 179 F.3d 557, 562 (7th Cir. 1999).

76. One court explicitly held that Title V does not create a private right of action, Doukas, 950 F.Supp. at 422, 425 note 2.

77. Baker v. Hartford Life, 1995 U.S. Dist. LEXIS 14103 (N.D. Ill. 1995).

78. *Id.* *8.

79. *Id.*

80. P. L. 90-202, 29 U.S.C. 623(f)(2). Originally exempted from the definition of discrimination were age-based employment decisions pursuant to "any bona-fide employment benefit plan . . . which is not a subterfuge to evade the purposes of" the ADEA.

81. Parker v. Metropolitan Life, 121 F.3d 1006 (6th Cir. 1997) (*en banc*).

82. Arizona Governing Committee v. Norris, 463 U.S. 1073 (1983).

83. "The Americans With Disabilities Act completes the circle begun in 1973 with respect to persons with disabilities by extending to them the same civil rights protections provided to women and minorities in 1964," House Jud. Comm. Rep. 101-485, Pt. 3 (May 15, 1990), 101st Cong., 2nd Sess., at 26.

84. Section 302(a) is Title III's general prohibition against discrimination on the basis of disability by a public accommodation.

85. Doe v. Mutual of Omaha, 179 F.3d at 562.

86. *Id.* at 558.

87. Even the *Parker* court noted what it called a "discrepancy" among the statute, regulations, and agency interpretation of the term *subterfuge,* 121 F.3d 1006, 1014 (6th Cir. 1997) (*en banc*).

88. The House Education and Labor, Judiciary, Public Works and Transportation, and Energy Committees all considered the bill; in the Senate, only the Committee on Labor and Human Resources considered it.

89. Senate Committee on Labor and Human Resources, ADA of 1989, S. Rep. 116, 101st Cong., 1st Sess., at 85. Some employers continue to engage in this practice, however, *see* Sawinski v. Bill Currie Ford, 866 F.Supp. 1383 (M.D. Fla. 1994); and Gonzales v. Garner Foods, 89 F.3d 1523, 1524 (11th Cir. 1996).

90. United Airlines v. McMann, 434 U.S. 192 (1977).

91. Committee on Education and Labor, 101st Cong., 2nd Sess. Rep. No. 101-485 (Pt. II) at 135–137 (May 15, 1990; emphasis added).

92. Senate Committee on Labor and Human Resources, Rep. 101-116, 101st Cong., 1st Sess., Aug. 2 (legislative day Jan. 3, 1989) at 84.

93. Senate Rep. 101-116 at 85.

94. There is substantial evidence to the contrary, *see supra* at pp. 253–254.

95. Senate Rep. 101-116 at 84.

96. EEOC is the agency authorized to interpret and enforce Title I of the ADA, which prohibits discrimination in employment. Its regulations related to insurance in the employment context are found at 29 C.F.R. Secs. 1630.5 and 1630.16(f).

97. DOJ is the agency authorized to interpret and enforce Titles II and III of the ADA. Regulations of Title III referring to insurance are found at 28 CFR Sec. 36.212.

98. *EEOC Interim Guidance on Application of the ADA to Health Insurance,* 1993 DLR 109 d22 (June 9, 1993).

99. "The fact that the individual's disability is not covered by the employer's current insurance plan or would cause the employer's insurance premiums or workers' compensation costs to increase would not be a legitimate nondiscriminatory reason justifying disparate treatment of an individual with a disability." EEOC, Title I Interpretive Guidance Section to 1630.15(a), *citing* Senate Report at 85; House Labor Report at 136, and House Judiciary Report at 70. Employers' explicit reference to insurance costs when rejecting a disabled applicant for a job was a frequent complaint of witnesses with disabilities who testified in support of the ADA, *see* testimony of Laura Cooper, A&P Comm. Print (1990) (28B)*1980–1981; and testimony of Steve Beebe, A&P Comm. Print (1990) (28B)*1802–1803.

100. 29 C.F.R. Sec. 1630.5 Interpretive Guidance.

101. EEOC Title I Interpretive Guidance to 29 C.F.R. Sec. 1630.16(f).

102. U.S. Employment Opportunity Commission v. AIC Security Investigations Ltd., 1996 WL 48587 (N.D. Ill. 1996).

103. Anderson v. Gus Mayer Boston Store of Delaware, 924 F.Supp. 763 (E.D. Tx. 1996).

104. *EEOC Technical Assistance Manual,* I-7.09 (Jan. 1992) (EEOC-M-1A).

105. "EEOC Interim Enforcement Guidance on the Application of the Americans With Disabilities Act of 1990 to Disability-Based Distinctions in Employer-Provided Health Insurance," EEOC Notice No. 915.002 (June 8, 1993).

106. The EEOC's regulations make it clear that the only defense to a charge of disparate treatment is a legitimate, nondiscriminatory reason for the adverse employment action. Compare 29 C.F.R. Sec. 1630.15(a) and Interpretive Guidance with 29 C.F.R. Sec. 1630.15(b) and Interpretive Guidance.

107. "EEOC Interim Enforcement Guidance on the Application of the Americans With Disabilities Act of 1990 to Disability-Based Distinctions in Employer-Provided Health Insurance" (June 8, 1993).

108. CarParts Distribution Center v. Automotive Wholesaler's Association of New England, 37 F.3d 12 (1st Cir. 1994); Leonard F. v. Israel Discount Bank of New York, 101 F.3d 687 (2nd Cir. 1996); Parker v. Metropolitan Life Insurance Co. et al., 121 F.3d 1006 (6th Cir. 1997) (*en banc*); Equal Employment Opportunity Commission v. CNA Insurance Cos., 96 F.3d 1039 (7th Cir. 1996); Modderno v. King, 82 F.3d 1059 (D.C.C. 1996) (the Rehabilitation Act), *cert. den.,* 519 U.S. 1064 (1997); Esfahani v. Medical College of Pennsylvania, 919 F.Supp. 832 (E.D. Pa. 1996); Lewis v. Aetna Life Insurance Co., 982 F.Supp. 1158 (E.D. Va. Oct. 24, 1997); Schroeder v. Connecticut General Life Insurance Co., No. 93-M-2433, 1994 WL 909636 (D. Colo. Apr. 22, 1994). In addition to the CNA case, the EEOC has filed EEOC v. Aramark Corp. et al., Civ. No. 97-734 (RMV) (D.D.C. 1997) and EEOC v. Chase Manhattan Bank et al., Civ. No. 97-6620 (S.D. N.Y. filed Sept. 9, 1997). For a discussion of whether health insurance and disability benefits should be treated differently, *see* pp. 277–278, *infra*.

109. *See* text on pp. 277–278, *infra.*

110. EEOC Interim Guidance at 5, note 7.

111. The legislative history of the ADA states that "discrimination results from actions or inactions that discriminate by effect as well as by intent or design." Report of the Senate Committee on Labor and Human Resources Accompanying S.933, Senate Rep. 101-116, 101st Cong., 1st Sess. (Aug. 30, 1989) at 6. *See also* identical language in the House Committee on Education and Labor accompanying H.R.2273, House Rep. No. 101-485, Pt. 2 (May 15, 1990) at 29. Specifically, the Senate Committee Report explains the meaning of *discrimination* as defined in Title I declared: "Subparagraphs (B) and (C) incorporate a disparate-impact standard to ensure that the legislative mandate to end discrimination does not ring hollow." This standard is consistent with the interpretation of Section 504 by the U.S. Supreme Court in Alexander v. Choate, 469 U.S. 287 (1985), Senate Rep. 101-116 at 30, and identical language in the House report, *supra* at note 92 at 61.

112. EEOC Interim Guidance on the Application of the ADA to Health Insurance, 1993 Daily Labor Rep. 109 d22 at 4 (June 9, 1993). Although the guidelines are labeled *interim* guidelines, the EEOC has not moved to adopt permanent guidelines and indicated informally its intention to retain the interim guidelines for the indefinite future.

113. *Id.* at 3.

114. *Id.*

115. 28 C.F.R. Sec. 36.212 (c).

116. Preamble to Regulation on Non-Discrimination, Comment on Sec. 36.212.

117. *Id.*

118. *Id.*

119. *Id.*

120. Leah Wortham, "Insurance Classification: Too Important to be Left to the Actuaries," *Univ. of Mich. J. of Law Ref.* 19 (1986):349, 368–369.

121. *See* Lange v. Rancher, 56 N.W.2d 542 (Wisc. 1953) (invalidating the decision of the insurance commissioner supporting a refusal to offer life insurance to black people because there was no evidence of biological difference between the races); Jill Gaulding, "Race, Sex, and Genetic Discrimination in Insurance: What's Fair?" *Cornell Law Rev.* 80 (1995):1446.

122. Willy E. Rice, "Race, Gender, 'Redlining' and Discriminatory Access to Loans, Credits and Insurance: An Historical and Empirical Analysis of Consumers Who Sued Lenders and Insurers in Federal and State Courts, 1950–1995," *San Diego Law Rev.* 33 (1996): 583; *see also* Abdullah v. Commonwealth of Massachusetts, 84 F.3d 18 (1st Cir. 1996) (upholding the division of Massachusetts into 15 territories for insurance risk purposes, even though prices were higher in minority-dominated areas).

123. A former insurance commissioner discussed an American Academy of Actuaries study in testimony before Congress showing that "many insurers avoid non-White markets," Herbert Denenberg, "Insurance Competition Improvement Act: Hearings on S.2474 Before the Senate Subcommittee on Antitrust, Monopoly and Business Rights of the Senate Committee on the Judiciary," 96th Cong., 2nd Sess. 153 (1980); *see also* Leah Wortham, "Insurance Classification: Too Important to be Left to the Actuaries," *Univ. of Mich. J. of Law* 19 (1986):349, 354.

124. The Civil Rights Division of DOJ sued American Family Insurance Co. and Nationwide Insurance Co. for race discrimination in the area of property insurance during the 1990s. Both cases settled for monetary relief in the neighborhood of $13.2 million and injunctive relief aimed at increasing the availability of property insurance in minority neighborhoods. Prepared statement of Bill Lann Lee, acting assistant attorney general, Civil Rights Division, DOJ, before the House Judiciary Comm., Constitution Subcommittee (Feb. 25, 1998), available on LEXIS through the Federal News Service.

125. Telles v. Commissioner of Insurance, 574 N.E.2d 359 (Mass. 1991).

126. General Electric Co. v. Gilbert et al., 429 U.S. 125 (1976); Geduldig v. Aiello, 417 U.S. 484 (1974); Arizona Governing Committee et al. v. Norris, 463 U.S. 1073 (1983).

127. *Id.,* Arizona Governing Committee et al. v. Norris (1983).

128. The ADEA provides that "it shall not be unlawful for an employer, employment agency, or labor organization . . . (2) to observe the terms of a bona-fide seniority system or any bona-fide employee benefit plan such as a retirement, pension or insurance plan, which is not a subterfuge to evade the purposes of this chapter."

129. United Airlines Inc. v. McMann, 434 U.S. 192 (1977).

130. Public Employees Retirement System of Ohio v. Betts, 492 U.S. 158, at 167–169 (1989).

131. *Id.*

132. *Id.* at 176.

133. P. L. 101-433 (1990).

134. Instead, Congress provided that it would not be illegal to observe the terms of a bona fide seniority system "that is not intended to evade the purposes of this Act . . . or (B)

to observe the terms of a bona fide employee benefit plan—(i) where, for each benefit
or benefit package, the actual amount of payment made or cost incurred on behalf of
an older worker is not less than that made or incurred on behalf of a younger worker,
as permissible under section 1625.10, title 29 Code of Federal Regulation (as in effect
on June 22, 1989)."

135. 136 Cong. Rec. S9, 967 (daily ed. July 13, 1990) (statement of Sen. Edward Kennedy).
     See also 136 Cong. Rec. H4, 626 (daily ed. May 17, 1990) (statement of Rep. Waxman)
     and 136 Cong. Rec. H4, 624 (daily ed. May 17, 1990) (statement of Rep. Edwards).
136. 136 Cong. Rec. H4, 624 (daily ed. May 17, 1990) (statement of Rep. Edwards).
137. Interpretive Guidance to Sec. 1630.16(f).
138. Krauel v. Iowa Methodist Medical Center, 95 F.3d 674 (8th Cir. 1996) (discrimination
     must be both intentional and related to discrimination in a nonfringe benefit aspect);
     Modderno v. King, 82 F.3d 1059, 1065 (D.C.C. 1996); Tenbrink v. Federal Home Loan
     Bank, 920 F.Supp. 1156 (D. Kan. 1996); Piquard v. City of East Peoria, 887 F.Supp.
     1106 (C.D. Ill. 1996).
139. Anderson v. Gus Mayer, 924 F.Supp. 763, 780 (E.D. Tx. 1996).
140. Doe v. Colautti, 592 F.2d 704, 708-10 (3rd Cir. 1979); Doe v. Devine, 545 F.Supp. 576,
     585 (D.D.C. 1982); Bernard B. v. Blue Cross–Blue Shield, 528 F.Supp. 125, 132-33
     (S.D. N.Y. 1981) (challenging the exclusion of psychiatric inpatient care in city hospitals
     from basic Blue Cross–Blue Shield health insurance coverage under the Rehabilitation
     Act). For an excellent discussion of these cases and critique of their reasoning, *see*
     Leonard Rubenstein, "Ending Discrimination Against Mental Health Treatment in Pub-
     licly Financed Health Care," *St. Louis Law J.* 40 (1996):315.
141. *E.g.,* the plaintiffs were denied discovery aimed at establishing discriminatory intent and
     then faulted for producing no evidence of discriminatory intent; Bernard B. v. Blue
     Cross–Blue Shield, 528 F.Supp. (S.D. N.Y. 1981) at 132–133.
142. *Id.* at 125, 133.
143. 469 U.S. 287 (1988).
144. *See, e.g.,* Ford v. Schering-Plough, 145 F.3d 601 (3rd Cir. 1998).
145. For extensive discussion of the decision in Alexander v. Choate, *see* chapter 5.
146. EEOC v. Mason Tenders District Council Welfare Fund et al., 93-CIV-3865JES (S.D.
     N.Y.); *see also* Donaghey et al. v. Mason Tenders et al., a companion case, 93-CIV-
     1154JES, which was settled at the same time.
147. 42 U.S.C. Sec. 12181(7)(F) specifically lists "insurance offices" as places of public
     accommodations.
148. Pappas v. Bethesda Hospital Association, 861 F.Supp. 616 (S.D. Ohio 1994); CarParts
     Distribution Center, Inc. v. Automotive Wholesaler's Association of New England, Inc.,
     37 F.3d 12 (1st Cir. 1994); Parker v. Metropolitan Life Insurance, 121 F.3d 1006 (6th
     Cir. 1997); Kotev v. First Colony Life Insurance Co., 927 F.Supp. at 1320; Pallozzi v.
     Allstate Life Insurance Co., 998 F.Supp. 204 (N.D. N.Y. 1998), *rev'd,* 198 F.3d 28 (2nd
     Cir. 1999); Chabner v. Mutual of Omaha Life Insurance Co., 994 F.Supp. 1185 (N.D.
     Ca. 1998); Doukas v. Metropolitan Life, 950 F.Supp. 422, 426 (D. N.H. 1996).
149. 42 U.S.C. § 12182(b)(2)(A)(iv) and (v).
150. 42 U.S.C. § 12182(b)(1)(D).
151. 42 U.S.C. § 12182(b)(2)(A)(i).
152. Comm. on Education and Labor, House Rep. 101-485 (Pt. 2), 101st Cong., 2nd Sess.,
     at 35–36 (May 15, 1990).
153. *Id.* at 105–106.
154. 42 U.S.C. § 12189.
155. *Id.*
156. Doe v. Devine, 545 F.Supp. 576, 585 (D.D.C. 1982); Doe v. Colautti, 592 F.2d 704,
     708 (3rd Cir. 1979).

157. *Department of Justice Technical Assistance Manual*, III-3.11000, reprinted in *Americans With Disabilities Act Manual* (Washington, DC: BNA, 1992) at 90:0917. Note that DOJ uses "evasion" rather than "subterfuge" language, consistent with the language of the ADEA, *see* p. 258 *supra.*

158. CarParts Dist. Center Inc. v. Automotive Wholesaler's Assn of New England, Inc., 37 F.3d 12 (1st Cir. 1994); Doukas v. Metropolitan Life Insurance Co., 950 F.Supp. 422, 426 (D. N.H. 1996); Kotev v. First Colony Life Insurance Co., 927 F.Supp. 1316 (C.D. Ca. 1996); Baker v. Hartford Life Ins. Co., 1995 WL 573430 (N.D. Ill. 1995); World Insurance Co. v. Branch, 966 F.Supp. 1203 (N.D. Ga 1997) (later *vac.* as moot); Cloutier v. Prudential Insurance Co., 964 F.Supp. 299 (N.D. Ca. 1997).

159. 42 U.S.C. Sec. 12182(a).

160. *CarParts, see* note 158; Kotev, *see* note 158.

161. 42 U.S.C. Sec. 12101(b)(1).

162. 42 U.S.C. Sec. 12182(b)(2)(A)(ii).

163. Kotev v. First Colony Life Insurance, 927 F.Supp. 1316 (C.D. Ca. 1996).

164. Parker v. Metropolitan Life, 121 F.3d at 1011–1012.

165. Ford v. Schering-Plough, 145 F.3d 601 (3rd Cir. 1998).

166. CarParts Distribution Center, Inc. v. Automotive Wholesaler's Association of New England, 37 F.3d 12 (1st Cir. 1994).

167. *Id.* at 19.

168. McNeil v. Time Insurance Co., 205 F.3d 179 (5th Cir. 2000); Weyer v. 20th Century Fox Film, 198 F.3d 1104, 1115 (9th Cir. 2000); Ford v. Schering-Plough, 145 F.3d 601 (3rd Cir. 1998); Parker v. Metropolitan Life, 121 F.3d 1006 (6th Cir. 1997) (*en banc*), *cert. den.,* 522 U.S. 1084 (1998).

169. Pallozzi v. Allstate Life Insurance Co., 198 F.3d 28 (2nd Cir. 2000); Doe v. Mutual of Omaha Insurance Co., 179 F.3d 557 (7th Cir. 1999).

170. 208 F.3d 266, 268 (D.D.C. 2000).

171. 42 U.S.C. 12112(a).

172. Berta Bril v. Dean Witter, 986 F.Supp. 171 (S.D. N.Y. 1997); EEOC v. CNA, 96 F.3d 1039 (7th Cir. 1996); Pappas v. Bethesda Hospital Association, 861 F.Supp. 616 (S.D. Ohio 1994); Hollander v. Paul Revere Life Insurance Co., 1997 WL 811531 (S.D. N.Y. Apr. 18, 1997); Gonzales v. Garner Food Services, 89 F.3d 1523 (11th Cir. 1996) (there was no standing once the employee was no longer employed).

173. Parker v. Metropolitan Life, 121 F.3d 1006 (6th Cir. 1997) (*en banc*).

174. Castellano v. City of New York, 1998 U.S. App. LEXIS 3646 (2nd Cir. Feb. 24, 1998); Graboski v. Giuliani, 937 F.Supp. 258 (S.D. N.Y. 1996) (disability retirees may sue under Title I of the ADA).

175. *See, e.g.,* Parker v. Metropolitan Life Insurance Co., 875 F.Supp. 1321, 1326 (W.D. Tenn. 1995) and Castellano v. City of New York, 946 F.Supp. 249, 253 (S.D. N.Y. 1996), which both called the denial of standing "undesirable and perhaps unpalatable."

176. Robinson v. Shell Oil, 117 S.Ct. 843 (1997).

177. DOJ, *Interpretive Guidance to Regulations,* Sec. 36.212.

178. Winslow v. IDS Life Insurance, 29 F.Supp. 2d 557 (D. Minn. 1998).

179. R. D. C. Brackenridge and W. John Elder, *Medical Selection of Life Risks* (New York: Stockton Press, 1992); Edward E. Lew et al., Eds., *Medical Risks: Trends in Mortality by Age and Time Elapsed: A Reference Volume* (New York: Praeger, 1990).

180. Health Insurance Association of America, *Disability Income Insurance: An Overview of Income Protection Insurance* 2nd ed. (Washington, DC: Author, 1994) at 14; Davis W. Gregg and Vane B. Lucas, *Life and Health Insurance Handbook* 3rd ed. (Homewood, IL: Richard D. Irwin, 1973) at 118–119.

181. See notes 179 and 180.

182. Although companies sometimes claim to be making decisions on the basis of company experience, "because mental health/substance abuse expenditures are generally a small portion of a health insurer's total premium, many insurers do not allocate resources to collect this data"; Merrile Sing, Steven Hill, Suzanne Smolkin, and Nancy Heiser, *The Costs and Effects of Parity for Mental Health and Substance Abuse Insurance Benefits* (Washington, DC: U.S. Department of Health and Human Services, Public Health Service, Substance Abuse and Mental Health Services Administration, 1998) at 12. When companies such as Price Waterhouse and Coopers Lybrand developed estimates of the cost of full parity between physical and mental health coverage, they were forced to use predictive models because there was a paucity of existing data about the costs of mental health coverage. It is also difficult to understand how a company with a long-standing policy of refusing to underwrite insurance at all for certain conditions can accumulate experience.

183. Richard D. Brackenridge and John C. Elder, *Medical Selection of Life Risks* 3rd ed. (New York: Stockton Press, 1992). *Also* cited in *Chabner* as a basis for Mutual of Omaha's underwriting decisions.

184. E. A. Lew and J. Gajewski, Eds., *Medical Risks: Patterns of Age and Mortality by Time Elapsed: A Reference Volume Sponsored by the Association of Life Insurance Medical Directors of America and the Society of Actuaries* (New York: Praeger, 1990).

185. *Id.* at viii.

186. *Id.* at 1–6.

187. *See* text at note 194.

188. There is one reference to a *Statistical Bulletin* in 1986, but this does not appear to be a study.

189. The *DSM* was created to categorize and describe mental disorders. The 1st edition, published in 1952, contained 60 disorders. By the time the 4th edition was issued in 1994, it contained 374 diagnoses.

190. Chabner v. Mutual of Omaha, 994 F.Supp. 1185, 1194-95 (N.D. Ca. 1998).

191. *Id.*

192. Bruce P. Dembling, Donna T. Chen, and Louis Vachon, "Life Expectancy and Causes of Death in a Population Treated for Severe Mental Illness," *Psychiatric Services* 50 (1999): 1036; P. Prior, E. Hassall, and K. W. Cross, "Causes of Death Associated With Psychiatric Illness," *J. of Pub. Health* 18 (1996):381–389; S. P. Segal and P. L Kotler, "A Ten-Year Perspective of Mortality Risk Among Mentally Ill Patients in Sheltered Care," *Hosp. and Comm. Psychiatry* 42 (1991):708–713; John A. Pandiani, *Mortality Rates for People Served by Behavioral Health Care Programs in Vermont* (**city:** Vermont MHSIP Indicator Project, Mar. 31, 1997), copies available from Pandiani at 802/241-2639.

193. Alan A. Lipton and Franklin S. Simon, "Psychiatric Diagnosis in a State Hospital: Manhattan State Revisited," *Hosp. & Comm. Psychiatry* 36 (1985):368; Billy E. Jones and Beverly Gray, "Problems in Diagnosing Schizophrenia and Affective Disorder Among Blacks," *Hosp. & Comm. Psychiatry* 37 (1986):61. These studies have been going on for a long time. See Herbert S. Gross et al., "The Effect of Race and Sex on the Variation of Diagnosis and Disposition in a Psychiatric Emergency Room," *J. of Nervous & Mental Dis.* 148 (1969):638. They were collected in Susan Stefan, "Issues Relating to Women and Ethnic Minorities in Mental Health Treatment and Law," in Bruce Sales and Dan Shuman, Eds., *Law, Mental Health and Mental Disorder* (Pacific Grove, CA: Brooks/Cole, 1996) at 250.

194. D. W. Black, G. Warrack, and G. Winokur, "Excess Mortality Among Psychiatric Patients," *J. of the Amer. Medical Assn.* 253 (1985):58–61; D. W. Black, G. Winokur, and G. Warrack, "Suicide in Schizophrenia: The Iowa Record-Linkage Study," *J. of Clin. Psychiatry* 46 (1985):14–17; D. W. Black, G. Warrack, and G. Winokur, "The Iowa

Record-Linkage Study: Suicides and Accidental Deaths Among Psychiatric Inpatients," *Archives of Gen. Psychiatry* 42 (1985):71–75 (the first of a series of three articles on the study in the same journal, ending at 88); D. W. Black and G. Winokur, "Cancer Mortality in Psychiatric Patients," *Intl. J. of Psychiatry and Med.* 16 (1986–1987):189–197; D. W. Black, "Mortality in Schizophrenia: The Iowa Record-Linkage Study," *Psychosomatics* 29 (1988):55–60; D. W. Black, "Iowa Record-Linkage Study: Death Rates in Psychiatric Patients," *J. of Affective Disorders* 50 (1998):277–282.

195. B. W. Rovner, P. S. German, L. J. Brant, R. Clark, L. Burton, and M. F. Folstein, "Depression and Mortality in Nursing Homes," *J. of the Amer. Med. Assn.* 265 (1991): 2672.

196. Lee N. Robins and Darrell A. Regier, *Psychiatric Disorders in America: The Epidemiological Catchment Area Survey* (New York: Free Press, 1990).

197. *Id.*

198. Institutionalized people have been subject to a variety of unpleasant and nontherapeutic experiments. In the future, such activity may prove vulnerable under the ADA, *see* chapter 4.

199. Maurice Lipsedge, "Psychiatric Disorders," in *Medical Selection of Life Risks* at 723.

200. P. Prior, E. Hassall, and K. W. Cross, "Causes of Death Associated With Psychiatric Illness," *J. of Pub. Health* 18 (1996):381–389.

201. S. P. Segal and P. L. Kotler, "A Ten-Year Perspective of Mortality Risk Among Mentally Ill Patients in Sheltered Care," *Hosp. and Comm. Psychiatry* 42 (1991):708–713.

202. M. L. Bruce, D. T. Takeuchi, and P. J. Leaf, "Poverty and Psychiatric Status," *Archives of Gen. Psychiatry* 48 (May 1991):470–474.

203. Norman J. Waitzman and Ken R. Smith, "Separate But Lethal: The Effects of Economic Segregation on Mortality in Metropolitan America," *Milbank Q.* 76 (1998):341.

204. John A. Pandiani, *Mortality Rates for People Served by Behavioral Health Care Programs in Vermont* (Mar. 31, 1997).

205. M. L. Bruce, P. J. Leaf, G. P. M. Rozal, L. Florio, and R. A. Hoff, "Psychiatric Status and 9-Year Mortality Data in the New Haven ECA Study," *Amer. J. of Psychiatry* 151 (1994):716–721; M. L. Bruce and P. J. Leaf, "Psychiatric Disorders and 15-Month Mortality in a Community Sample of Older Adults," *Amer. J. of Pub. Health* 79 (1989): 727–730.

206. *See* chapter 4 for further discussion of this issue.

207. *See* Lynn Williams, David Dawson and Harriet MacMillan, *Relationship Management of the Borderline Patient: From Understanding to Treatment* (New York: Brunner/Mazel, 1993).

208. D. W. Black and G. Winokur, "Prospective Studies of Suicide and Mortality in Psychiatric Patients," *Annals of New York Academy of Science* 481 (1986):106–113.

209. As discussed more fully below, there is some reason to believe that this is pretextual because almost all policies do not cover suicide in any event.

210. Michael F. Gliatto and Anil K. Rai, "Evaluation and Treatment of Patients With Suicidal Ideation," *Amer. Fam. Physician* 59 (Mar. 15, 1999) (noting that "those who go on to commit suicide rarely have 'pure' depression, but usually depression that is comorbid with alcohol abuse" and cautioning that "it is not the psychiatric disorder itself that increases the risk of completed suicide, but the combination of the psychiatric disorder and a recent stressor, such as the death of a loved one, separation, divorce, or unemployment"). *See also* J. Brown, P. Cohen, and J. G. Johnson, "Childhood Abuse and Neglect: Specificity of Effects on Adolescent and Young Adult Depression and Suicidality," *J. of Amer. Acad. of Child & Adoles. Psychiatry* 38 (1999):1490 (a prospective study over a 17-year period shows the risk of repeated suicide attempts was eight times higher for youths with a sexual abuse history).

211. Black and Winokur (1986); R. E. Leitman, "Predicting and Preventing Hospital and Clinic Suicides," *Suicide & Life Threatening Beh.* 21 (1991):56. Some studies suggest

that this holds true with adolescents as well; D. B. Goldston, S. S. Daniel, D. M. Reboussin, B. A. Reboussin, et al., "Suicide Attempts Among Formerly Hospitalized Adolescents: A Prospective Naturalistic Study of Risk During the First Five Years After Discharge," *J. of Amer. Acad. of Child. & Adolesc.* 38 (1999):660.

212. *See, e.g.,* Daphne Scholinski, *The Last Time I Wore a Dress* (New York: Riverhead Books, 1997) at 77 ("I told Heather [that] I was going to kill myself . . . if I was always going to be locked up in some hospital I might as well kill myself and get it over with"); Janet and Paul Gotkin, *Too Much Anger, Too Many Tears* (New York: HarperPerennial, 1992) at 102 ("each time you venture out [of the institution] and see the widening gap between your world and theirs, between inside and outside, you come back to the hospital feeling so bad you want to kill yourself").

213. Ronald D. Garson, "Stress, Behavior, Social Support Systems," in *Medical Risks: Trends in Mortality by Age and Time Elapsed* Vol. 1 (New York: Praeger, 1990) at 3–25 ("Loneliness [and] isolation . . . have been identified as risk factors for mortality").

214. There is substantial empirical research supporting "an increase in mortality with a decrease in social supports," with social supports defined as "marital status, contact with friends and relatives, church memberships, and memberships in various group associations"; J. S. House, C. Robbins, and H. L. Metzner, "The Association of Social Relationships and Activities With Mortality: Prospective Evidence From the Tecumseh Community Study," *Amer. J. of Epidemiology* 116 (1982):123–140; L. F. Berkman and S. L. Syme, "Social Networks, Host Resistance and Mortality: A Nine-Year Follow-Up Study of Alameda County Residents," *Amer. J. of Epidemiology* 109 (1979):186–204.

215. J. Fox and P. Goldblatt, "Socio-Demographic Differences in Mortality," *Population Trends* (1982):27.

216. D. G. Blazer, "Social Support and Mortality in an Elderly Community Population," *Amer. J. of Epidemiology* 115 (1982):684.

217. *See* notes 214–216 for J. S. House, C. Robbins, and H. L. Metzner (1982); L. F. Berkman and S. L. Syme, (1979); J. Fox and P. Goldblatt (1982); and D. G. Blazer (1982).

218. 998 F.Supp. 204 (N.D. N.Y. 1998), *rev'd*, 198 F.3d 28 (2nd Cir. 1999).

219. Both had a diagnosis of depression; he had an additional diagnosis of agoraphobia, and she had an additional diagnosis of borderline personality disorder.

220. Pallozzi v. Allstate Life Insurance Co. of New York, No. 97-CV-0236 (N.D. N.Y. filed Feb. 2, 1997), complaint, paragraph 8.

221. *Id.* at 207. The court quoted another opinion in which the chief underwriter of an insurance company testified under oath that if the company had been aware that an individual had "mild to moderate" depression, the company would not issue a policy to that individual"; Aguilar v. United States Life Insurance Co., 556 N.Y. S.2d 584, 585 (1st Dept. 1990).

222. 179 F.3d 557, 559 (7th Cir. 1999) (refusing to sell a policy and charging higher rates for policies on the basis of the purchaser's disability was potentially discriminatory, whereas placing a cap on the benefits for a particular condition was not).

223. 75 F.Supp. 2d 1 (D.D.C. 1999) (the refusal to sell landlord insurance because the tenant was disabled stated a claim under the ADA).

224. Michael Kiefer, "Bottom Line Coverage: The Policy of Dropping Sick People from Health Insurance Rolls Isn't Called a 'Death Spiral' for Nothing," NEW YORK TIMES (Mar. 10, 1993):10 ("Nowadays . . . past psychological counselling, however minor [, is] reason enough for denying insurance coverage"); Pippa Wysong, "The Catch-22 of Mental Disability Coverage: Insurance Industry Standards Have Some Doctors Thinking Twice About Seeking Psychiatric Care," *Medical Post* 34 (Feb. 3, 1998):9 ("it is widely recognized that individuals treated for depression or other psychiatric problems could later be considered 'high-risk' by insurers and denied disability insurance").

225. *See* Goldman v. Standard Insurance Co., C98-0662 (N.D. Ca. filed Feb. 19, 1998).

226. Winslow v. IDS Life Insurance Co., 29 F.Supp. 2d 557 (D. Minn. 1998).

227. Doukas v. Metropolitan Life, 950 F.Supp. 422 (D. N.H. 1996).

228. Winslow v. IDS Life Insurance Co. (D. Minn. 1997) (Paul Revere underwriting manual does not require the automatic rejection of an applicant but a longer exclusion period; nevertheless, the company rejected the applicant); Health Insurance Association of America, *Disability Claims for Mental and Nervous Disorders* (Washington, DC: Author, 1995).

229. Health Insurance Association of America (1995) at 4.

230. *Id.*

231. *Id.*

232. *Id.* at 7.

233. *Id.* at 4.

234. Doukas, 1997 U.S. Dist. LEXIS 21757 (D. N.H. Oct. 21, 1997) (denying the defendant's motion for summary judgment on the grounds that Doukas was not disabled); 950 F.Supp. 422 (D. N.H. 1996) (denying the defendant's motion for summary judgment on ADA claims); 882 F.Supp. 1197 (D. N.H. 1995) (granting the motion to dismiss the Fair Housing Act claim but denying motion to dismiss on the basis of statute of limitations).

235. Doukas, 1997 U.S. Dist. LEXIS 21757 (D. N.H. Oct. 21, 1997).

236. *Id.* *12–13.

237. Doukas, 950 F.Supp. 422, 429–430 (D. N.H. 1996).

238. 29 F.Supp. 2d 557 (D. Minn. 1998).

239. IDS also denied her application for a policy that excluded coverage for disabilities caused by mental problems, *id.* at 558.

240. *Id.* at 559.

241. *See* note 232, *supra.*

242. 1999 U.S. Dist. LEXIS 20191 (N.D. Ca. Dec. 20, 1999).

243. *Id.* *12.

244. Bragdon v. Abbott, 524 U.S. 624, 637–643.

245. Lifetime treatment caps are usually either $50,000 or $100,000 for mental illness, compared with $1 million for physical illnesses, although some caps for mental illness are as low as $20,000.

246. Lynd v. Reliance Insurance 94 F.3d 976, 985, note 1 (5th Cir. 1996) (Dennis J., dissenting).

247. As of Sept. 1999, Arizona, Arkansas, California, Colorado, Connecticut, Delaware, Georgia, Indiana, Maine, Louisiana, Maryland, Massachusetts, Minnesota, Missouri, New Hampshire, New Jersey, North Carolina, Rhode Island, South Carolina, South Dakota, Tennessee, and Vermont had statutes that in some way granted more benefits than the Mental Health Parity Act, although in other respects were more limited. Florida, Illinois, New York, Nevada, and Utah considered and rejected such bills. Other states passed bills to bring state laws into conformity with the federal requirements under the Mental Health Parity Act. For example, these parity bills have been strongly opposed by some organizations of current and former psychiatric patients on the grounds that parity will increase the rate of involuntary commitment.

248. *See, e.g.,* Lynd v. Reliance Insurance, 94 F.3d 976, 985, note 1 (5th Cir. 1996) (Dennis J., dissenting).

249. EEOC, *Interim Enforcement Guidance on the Application of the ADA to Health Insurance* Doc. No. N-915-002 (June 8, 1993).

250. P. L. 104-204, 110 Stat. 2874; 42 U.S.C. Sec. 300gg-5 (1996). Interim rules with request for comments issued by the Internal Revenue Service, the Pension and Welfare Benefits Administration, and the Health Care Financing Administration can be found at 26 C.F.R. Pt. 54, 29 C.F.R. Pt. 2590 and 45 C.F.R. Pt. 146, respectively (Dec. 22, 1997). Apparently, no final regulations were ever adopted.

251. *See* Brian D. Shannon, "Paving the Path to Parity in Health Insurance Coverage for Mental Illness: New Law or Merely Good Intentions?" *Univ. of Colo. Law Rev.* 68 (1997):63.

252. Less than 10% of companies in this country employ more than 50 employees, U.S. Census Bureau, *Statistical Abstract of the United States* (Washington, DC: U.S. Government Printing Office, 1998) at Table 870.

253. Modderno v. King, 82 F.3d 1059 (D.C.C. 1996).

254. Ford v. Schering-Plough, 145 F.3d 601, 610 (3rd Cir. 1998); EEOC v. CNA, 96 F.3d 1039, 1044 (7th Cir. 1996); Parker v. Metropolitan Life, 121 F.3d at 1017–1018 (1997); Rogers v. Department of Health and Environmental Control, 174 F.3d 431, 436 (4th Cir. 1999); Conners v. Maine Medical Center, 42 F.Supp. 2d 34 (D. Me. 1999).

255. 29 U.S.C. 1001 (West, 1999).

256. 29 U.S.C. 1132(a)(1)(B). *See* Firestone Tire and Rubber v. Bruch, 489 U.S. 101, 115 (1989). If the administrator is operating under a conflict of interest, the court will be less deferential; Chambers v. Family Health Plan, 100 F.3d 818, 825 (10th Cir. 1996).

257. Weyer v. Twentieth Century Fox, 198 F.3d 1104 (9th Cir. 2000); Parker v. Metropolitan Life Insurance Co. (1997); Lynd v. Reliance Standard Life Insurance Co., 94 F.3d 976 (5th Cir. 1996). The plaintiff in Leonard F. v. Israel Discount Bank of New York, 101 F.3d 687 (2nd Cir. 1996), was also apparently suffering from major depression.

258. Dorsk v. Unum Life, 8 F.Supp. 2d 19 (D. Me. 1998).

259. Phillips v. Lincoln National Life Insurance, 978 F.2d 302 (7th Cir. 1992).

260. Kunin v. Benefit Trust Life Insurance, 910 F.2d 534 (9th Cir.), *cert. denied,* 498 U.S. 1013 (1990) (autism was not considered a mental illness).

261. Arkansas Blue Cross–Blue Shield v. Doe, 733 S.W.2d 429 (Ark. 1987) (not a mental illness); Esfahani v. Medical College of Pennsylvania, 919 F.Supp. 832 (E.D. Pa. 1996) (survives motion to dismiss); Rosenthal v. Mutual Life Insurance Co. of New York, 732 F.Supp. 108 (S.D. Fla. 1990); John Doe I et al. v. Guardian Life Insurance Co. of America, 145 F.R.D. 466 (N.D. Ill. 1992); Equitable Life Assurance Society v. Berry, 212 Cal. App. 3d 832 (1989); Fitts v. Fannie Mae and Unum Life Insurance, 44 F.Supp. 2d 317 (D.D.C. 1999); Attar v. Unum Life Insurance, 1997 U.S. Dist. LEXIS 23254 (N.D. Tx. July 19, 1997).

262. Sachs v. Commercial Insurance Co., 290 A.2d 760 (N.J. Super. 1972), *aff'd o.b.,* 306 A.2d 83 (1973) (cerebral arteriosclerosis not considered a mental illness).

263. Simons v. Blue Cross–Blue Shield of Greater New York, 536 N.Y.S.2d 431 (N.Y. App. Div. 1989) (the hospitalization to treat malnutrition due to anorexia was not considered "mental").

264. Rock v. Unum Life, 1999 U.S. App. LEXIS 29859 (10th Cir. Nov. 15, 1999).

265. Malerbi v. Central Reserve Life Insurance of America, 407 N.W.2d 157 (Neb. 1987) (mental illness limitation does not apply to behavioral abnormalities caused by an organic brain defect).

266. Tolson v. Avondale Industries, 141 F.3d 604 (5th Cir. 1998).

267. Heaton v. State Health Benefits Commission, 624 A.2d 69, 71 (N.J. Super. 1993).

268. Kimber v. Thiokol Corp., 196 F.3d 1092 (10th Cir. 1999).

269. Blake v. Union Mutual Stock Life Insurance Co. of America, 906 F.2d 1525 (11th Cir. 1990) (postpartum psychosis is considered mental).

270. Schroeder v. Connecticut General Life Insurance Co., 1994 U.S. Dist. LEXIS 21298 (D. Colo. Apr. 22, 1994).

271. Tolson v. Avondale Industries, 141 F.3d 604 (5th Cir. 1998).

272. This is known as the doctrine of *contra proferendum.* The reasoning behind adopting this approach is that the primary purpose of ERISA is to protect the plan participants; insurance companies are in the best position to write clear plan definitions; Phillips v. Lincoln Natl. Life Insurance Co., 978 F.2d 302 (7th Cir. 1992); Simons v. Blue Cross– Blue Shield of Greater New York, 536 N.Y.S. 2d 431 (Sup. Ct. 1989).

273. Heaton v. State Health Benefits Commission, 624 A.2d 69, 72 (N.J. App. 1993) (Alzheimer's disease is considered to be a physical illness); Blake v. Union Mutual v. Stock Life Insurance Co. of America, 906 F.2d 1525 (11th Cir. 1990) (postpartum depression is considered to be a mental illness); Kunin v. Benefit Trust Life Insurance, 910 F.2d 534 (9th Cir. 1990) (autism is considered to be a physical illness); Dorsk v. Unum Life Insurance, 8 F.Supp. 2d 19 (D. Me. 1998) (obsessive–complusive disorder may be a physical illness).

274. Brewer v. Lincoln Natl. Life Insurance, 921 F.2d 150, 152 (8th Cir. 1990) (three experts testified that the precise cause of affective disorder was unknown); Hughes v. Boston Life, 26 F.3d 264 (1st Cir. 1994) (the causes of multiple sclerosis are "shrouded in mystery").

275. *See, e.g.,* Paula Caplan, *They Say You're Crazy: How the World's Most Powerful Psychiatrists Decide Who's Normal* (Reading, MA: Addison-Wesley, 1995) at 86–167 (recounting the political maneuvering around the attempt to introduce self-defeating personality disorder and late luteal phase of dysphoric disorder into the *Diagnostic and Statistical Manual of Mental Disorders* [Washington, DC: American Psychiatric Assn., 1994]).

276. Brewer v. Lincoln Natl. Life Insurance, 921 F.2d 150, 154 (8th Cir. 1990); Tolson v. Avondale Industries, 141 F.3d 604 (5th Cir. 1998).

277. Brewer v. Lincoln Natl. Life Insurance, *id.* at 154.

278. *Id.* ("Robert C. Brewer's illness manifested itself in terms of mood swings and aberrant behavior. Regardless of the cause of his disorder, it is abundantly clear that he suffered from what laypersons would consider to be a 'mental illness'").

279. Torre v. Federated Mutual Insurance Co., 897 F.Supp. 1332, 1362 (D. Kan. 1995).

280. *Brewer* (1990) at 154; *see also* Stauch v. Unisys, 24 F.3d 1054, 1056 (8th Cir. 1994).

281. Simons v. Blue Cross–Blue Shield of Greater New York, 536 N.Y.S.2d 431 (Sup. Ct. App. Div. 1989).

282. *Id.* at 434.

283. *Id.*

284. Hancock v. Montgomery Ward, 787 F.2d 1302 (9th Cir. 1986) (holding that physical problems caused by stress would fall under the exclusion for mental illness); Dames v. Paul Revere Life, 2000 U.S. Dist. LEXIS 2268 (D. Ore. Feb. 16, 2000) (fibromyalgia is caused by psychiatric conditions that fall under the 24-month limitations).

285. Kimber v. Thiokol, 196 F.3d 1092 (10th Cir. 1999).

286. Patterson v. Hughes Aircraft, 11 F.3d 948, 950 (9th Cir. 1993).

287. Lewis v. Aetna Life Insurance Co., 1997 WL 671815 (E.D. Va. 1997). This new definition did not, however, prove successful in assisting the defendant to avoid the plaintiff's ADA claim.

288. Randazzo v. Federal Express Corp. Long-Term Disability Plan, 2000 U.S. Dist. LEXIS 159 (S.D. N.Y. Jan. 11, 2000); Aetna Life, 982 F.Supp. 1158 (E.D. Va. 1997).

289. Russell v. Unum Life Insurance Co., 40 F.Supp. 2d 747 (D. S.C. 1999)

290. Nancy Ann Jeffrey, "Insurers Curb Some Benefits for Disability," *Wall St. J.* (July 25, 1996):A3.

291. *Id.*

292. Leonard F. v. Israel Discount Bank of New York, 101 F.3d 687 (2nd Cir. 1996); Parker v. Metropolitan Life Insurance Co. et al., 121 F.3d 1006 (6th Cir. 1997) (*en banc*); EEOC v. CNA Insurance Cos., 96 F.3d 1039 (7th Cir. 1996); Lewis v. K-Mart Corp., 180 F.3d 166 (4th Cir. 1999); Modderno v. King (D.C. Cir. 1996) (Rehabilitation Act); Esfahani v. Medical College of Pennsylvania, 919 F.Supp. 832 (E.D. Pa.1996); Schroeder v. Connecticut General Life Insurance Co., No. 93-M-2433, 1994 WL 909636 (D. Colo. Apr. 22, 1994); Harris v. City of Phoenix, No. Civ. 95-0361 (D. Ariz. filed Oct. 1995). In addition to the CNA case, the EEOC has filed EEOC v. Aramark Corp. et al.,

Civ. No. 97-734 (RMV) (D.D.C. 1997); EEOC v. Chase Manhattan Bank et al., Civ. No. 9-6620 (S.D. N.Y. filed Sept. 9, 1997); EEOC v. CIGNA, No. 2:98-CV-259 (E.D. Pa. filed Jan. 18, 1998); and EEOC v. Bath Iron Works and Fortis Insurance Corp., 1999 U.S. Dist. LEXIS 10596 (D. Me. 1999).

293. 469 U.S. 287 (1985).

294. "The majestic equality of the laws, which forbid rich and poor alike to sleep under bridges, to beg in the streets, and to steal their bread"; Anatole France, "Le Lys Rouge" [The Red Lily], in Winifred Stevens (Trans.), *The Works of Anatole France* 5 (New York: Wells, 1924) at 91 (original written 1894).

295. 163 U.S. 537 (1896).

296. 388 U.S. 1 (1967).

297. 485 U.S. 535 (1988).

298. *Traynor* is discussed at length in chapter 5.

299. *Amicus* brief for American Council of Life Insurance and Health Insurance Association of America at 5; Parker v. Metropolitan Life, 121 F.3d 1006 (6th Cir. 1997) (*en banc*).

300. Lee N. Robins and Darrel A. Regier, *Psychiatric Disorders in America: The Epidemiological Catchment Area Survey* (New York: Free Press, 1991).

301. M. Birchwood, R. Cochrane, F. MacMillan, et al., "The Influence of Ethnicity and Family Structure on Relapse in First Episode Schizophrenia," *Brit. J. of Psychiatry* 161 (Nov. 18, 1999):783.

302. D. V. Jeste, R. Del Carmen, J. B. Lohr, and R. J. Wyatt, "Did Schizophrenia Exist Before the Eighteenth Century?" *Compr. Psychiatry* 26 (1985):493–503.

303. S. S. Scharfstein and C. A. Taube, "Reductions in Insurance for Mental Disorders: Adverse Selection, Moral Hazard, and Consumer Demand," *Amer. J. of Psychiatry* 139 (Nov. 1982):1425.

304. Brief of the American Council on Life Insurance at 13.

305. Parker v. Metropolitan Life, 121 F.3d 1006 (6th Cir. 1997) (*en banc*).

306. Brief of the American Council on Life Insurance at 13.

307. *Id.*

308. The Hay Study Group, "Health Care Plan Design and Cost Trends: Executive Summary" (May 1998):4, available at http://www.naphs.org/News/HayGroupReport.html (in 1997, behavioral health expenses were 3.1% of the total health care benefit costs of employer health benefits).

309. Health Insurance Association of America, "Disability Claims for Mental and Nervous Disorders" (Washington, DC: Author, 1995) at 1. *See also* the Hay Group Study at note 308.

310. EEOC v. CNA, 96 F.3d 1039 (7th Cir. 1996).

311. *See* text at pp. 267–268.

312. "Bank's Accord With EEOC Eliminates Distinctions in Long-Term Disability Plans," U.S.L.W. 66(33) (Mar. 3, 1998):2519 (announcing the settlement of Leonard F. v. Israel Discount Bank of New York, No. 95-CV-6964) (S.D. N.Y. settlement filed Feb. 17, 1998).

313. *See* Brian D. Shannon, "Paving the Path to Parity in Health Insurance Coverage for Mental Illness: New Law or Merely Good Intentions?" *Univ. of Colo. Law Rev.* 68 (1997):63, for a thorough exploration of the history of the congressional debate.

314. "Achieving Parity," *Mental Health Law Reporter,* 16(3) (Mar. 1998):17 (quoting EEOC trial attorney Gerald Letwin).

315. Willard Manning, Kenneth Wells, Joan Buchanan, et al., *Effects of Mental Health Insurance Experiment* (Santa Monica, CA: RAND Corp., 1989).

316. Merrile Sing, Steven Hill, Suzanne Smolkin, and Nancy Heiser, *The Costs and Effects of Parity for Mental Health and Substance Abuse Insurance Benefits* DHHS Pub. No. (SMA) 98-3205 (Washington, DC: U.S. Department of Health and Human Services,

Public Health Service, Substance Abuse and Mental Health Services Administration, Mar. 1998). This study looks at the experience of the states with parity laws and develops a prediction model based on assumptions about parity.

317. *Cf., e.g.,* Ronald Bachman, "An Actuarial Analysis of the Domenici–Wellstone Amendment to S.1028, 'Health Insurance Reform Act,' to Provide Parity for Mental Health Benefits Under Group and Individual Insurance Plans" (Atlanta, GA: Coopers & Lybrand, Apr. 1996) (a study commissioned by the American Psychological Association to examine the effects of full parity shows an increase in premiums of 3.2%); with Jack Rodgers, "Analysis of the Mental Health Parity Provision in S.1028" (Washington, DC: Price Waterhouse LLP, May 31, 1996) (a study commissioned by the Association of Private Pension and Welfare Plans Business Roundtable, the ERISA Industry Committee, and the National Association of Manufacturers shows that full parity would increase premiums by 8.7%).

318. Sing et al., *see* note 316, at 22.

319. Congressional Budget Office, *CBO's Estimate of the Impact on Employers of the Mental Health Parity Amendment in H.R.3101* (Washington, DC: Author, May 13, 1996) (predicting a 4.0% increase for a composite of indemnity and managed care plans and a 5.3% increase for indemnity plans).

320. Sing et al., *see* note 316, at 13.

321. Ronald Bachman, "An Actuarial Analysis of the Domenici–Wellstone Amendment to S.1028, 'Health Insurance Reform Act,' to Provide Parity for Mental Health Benefits Under Group and Individual Insurance Plans" (1996).

322. Sing et al., *The Costs and Effects of Parity for Mental Health and Substance Abuse Insurance Benefits,* also available from the Knowledge Exchange Network, 800/789-2647 or on the World Wide Web at http://www.mentalhealth.org at ii. The cost of parity in cost sharing would be 0.3% and parity in service limits would be 1.1%, *id.* If companies offered parity in fee for service or preferred provider plans, the premium increase would be 5.0%; "health maintenance organizations that tightly manage care would have only a .6% premium increase," *id.*

323. *Id.*

324. Sing et al., *see* note 316, at 12.

325. As of Sept. 1999, Arizona, Arkansas, California, Colorado, Connecticut, Delaware, Georgia, Indiana, Maine, Maryland, Massachusetts, Minnesota, Missouri, New Hampshire, New Jersey, North Carolina, Rhode Island, South Carolina, South Dakota, Tennessee, and Vermont had statutes that in some way granted greater benefits than the Mental Health Parity Act, although in most of these states benefits were limited either by employers covered or conditions covered.

326. These states are Massachusetts, Indiana, North Carolina, and Texas; Sing et al., note 316.

327. Arkansas, Maine, Maryland, and Minnesota have such exceptions; Sing et al., note 316 at 4.

328. Rhode Island, for example, covers only "medical treatment" of mental illness, meaning inpatient hospitalization and outpatient medication visits. Psychotherapy may be limited to $1,000 a year. National Advisory Mental Health Council, *Parity in Coverage of Mental Health Services in an Era of Managed Care: An Interim Report to Congress by the National Advisory Mental Health Council* (Rockville, MD: Author, Apr. 1997) at 20.

329. The Mental Health Parity Act applies to all employers, regardless of whether they self-insure or not.

330. Sing et al., note 316, at 16–17; National Advisory Mental Health Council, *see* note 328, at 20–21.

331. Colorado, Connecticut, Maine, New Hampshire, Rhode Island, and Texas cover only "serious" or "biologically based" mental illnesses.

332. Sing et al., note 316 at 30. Sing et al. came to this conclusion by comparing a study that estimated increases attributable to full parity for coverage of all mental health diagnoses at 2.8%, Stephen Melek and Bruce Pyenson, "Premium Rate Estimates for a Mental Illness Parity Provision to S.1028: 'The Health Insurance Reform Act of 1995' " (Denver, CO: Milliman & Robertson, Apr. 11, 1996), with a study by the same authors indicating increases for coverage of serious mental illnesses at 2.5%, Stephen Melek and Bruce Pyenson, "The Costs of Non-Discriminatory Health Insurance Coverage for Mental Illness" (Denver, CO: Milliman & Robertson, Apr. 11, 1996).

333. "Of the 831 disability claims filed in 1992 and 1993, 111 were for mental disorders, including stress. . . . Psychological benefits accounted for $757,940 of the $3.7 million paid out during those two years"; Clark Brooks, "Unfair Disability Coverage Alleged; San Diego Sued Over Insurance Benefits for Mental Illnesses," SAN DIEGO UNION TRIBUNE (Feb. 15, 1998):B1.

334. *Id.* The district court's denial of a preliminary injunction was upheld by the 9th Circuit; Badua v. City of San Diego, 1999 U.S. App. LEXIS 18442 (9th Cir. August 5, 1999).

335. *Id.*

336. Frank Palmieri, "Firm Settles ADA Case Involving Mental Health," *Employee Benefit News* (Apr. 1, 1998).

337. *Disability Compliance Bull.* 11(6) (Mar. 12, 1998):1, 5.

338. However, even an involuntary commitment order by a judge has not been enough to convince some companies under managed care that inpatient treatment was warranted; Andrews-Clarke v. Traveler's Insurance, 984 F.Supp. 49 (D. Mass. 1997) (the patient was sent to a facility for the people who are criminally insane where he was raped and sodomized; he later committed suicide). There is obviously a tension here between the insurance companies and the hospitals, with the patient being caught in the middle and having very little say.

339. Kevin Murphy, "Lawsuit by Ontario Alleges Unneeded Care: Provider Kept Patients in Mental Health Facilities for Excessive Periods, Complaint Says," MILWAUKEE JOURNAL SENTINEL (Apr. 20, 1998):17; Maria Glod, "Lawsuits Allege Abuses by Psychiatric Hospitals; More Than 30 Area Cases Grow Out of Federal Investigation That Broke Up National Chain," THE WASHINGTON POST (Jan. 10, 1998):C3.

340. Doe v. Mutual of Omaha Life Insurance Co., 179 F.3d 557 (7th Cir. 1999).

Chapter 7
PROFESSIONAL EDUCATION, LICENSING, AND DISCIPLINE

Both history and modern case law confirm that people in all walks of life and all professions can be diagnosed with or have mental illnesses, including those thought of as severe mental illnesses. Mental health professionals and lawyers have diagnoses of attention deficit hyperactivity disorder (ADHD), bipolar disorder, and major depression.[1] Indeed, doctors and lawyers are more likely to be severely depressed than the population in general.[2]

People with disabilities who aspire to careers in the medical and legal professions encounter substantial discrimination if their disabilities are obvious or disclosed. From universities that forbid students with diagnosed mental disabilities from living in student dormitories to licensing boards that demand that medical students with ADHD undergo a full psychiatric examination at their own expense before being given accommodations on examinations, the areas of education and licensing of medical and legal professionals are filled with barriers and burdens based on discriminatory stereotypes. Although some problems also exist with disciplinary functions of the professions, they are substantially fewer.

The areas of discrimination in professional education, licensing, and discipline have a number of issues unique to them. When a court decides whether a law or medical student is disabled, should it compare his or her limitations with the population as a whole, or to other law or medical students? How much deference should be granted to professional schools or professional associations in determinations of admission, dismissal, or discipline? What kinds of questions can licensing boards ask without violating the Americans With Disabilities Act (ADA) of 1990?

Cases involving professionals generally fall under Titles II and III of the ADA. Cases challenging the actions of state law or medical schools or of licensing boards fall under Title II, whereas cases challenging the actions of hospitals, doctors' offices, lawyers' offices, and private medical and law schools fall under Title III. Cases challenging the denial or revocation of private hospital privileges may fall through the cracks between Titles I and III and not be covered by the ADA at all.

The title under which a claim falls is important in a variety of practical ways. Individual plaintiffs cannot assert a claim for damages under Title III, for example, although they can receive attorney's fees. Title II appears to permit individual claims for damages without any cap, although few Title II cases have involved damages. Section 504 of the Rehabilitation Act of 1973, under which colleges and universities have been regulated since the 1970s, has been used most frequently by plaintiffs, in part because there are regulations directed specifically at postsecondary institutions[3] and there is extensive case law interpreting these regulations.

Discrimination

Colleges, Universities, and Professional Schools

Although mental health professionals and lawyers are subject to discrimination because of diagnoses of mental illness, it is equally true that mental health professionals and lawyers engage in a substantial amount of discrimination on the basis of disability themselves. Education and training, even in the so-called helping professions, are no prophylactic against the myths and stereotypes associated with mental illness.[4] Perhaps this is because discrimination is entrenched in the policy and practice of the institutions that educate and train the helping professionals, at both the undergraduate and graduate level.

Richard Scotch noted in his history of the disability rights movement that the greatest number of objections to the first regulations interpreting Section 504 of the Rehabilitation Act came from institutions of higher education. He quoted one staff member of the Office of Civil Rights as saying that

> the reactions to the proposed regulations were quite interesting, I think. The main screaming and yelling was done by the higher education institutions, and that's interesting, because the basic thrust of the regulations is much less intrusive to higher education than it is to elementary and secondary, or even employment. And I have the feeling that, for whatever reasons, the American Council on Education and its disciples, minions would be the more pejorative term, decided to take on the handicapped as the best political place to make their overregulation fight.[5]

Ten years after the fight over the Section 504 regulations, little had changed. Witnesses testifying before Congress in support of the ADA repeatedly described acts of deliberate, intentional discrimination by institutions of higher education based solely on their disability.[6] These included denials of educational opportunity by universities and professional schools. One woman testified that although she had an *A* average she was not permitted to major in human services when her history of psychiatric hospitalization was discovered, because students were required to be "psychologically fit."[7] Another witness told of a nursing school that refused to admit someone with a psychiatric history because "nursing was a very stressful profession and her psychiatric history would indicate she would not be able to deal with stress."[8]

These complaints of discrimination are echoed by people with mental disabilities in every forum available to them. When asked to describe the worst discrimination they had ever experienced, a substantial percentage of respondents to the survey cited conduct by institutions of higher education and professional schools.[9] As one woman wrote,

> find out about people's experiences of being denied entry into graduate schools of social work, psychology, and other advanced degree programs—like psychiatry. In 1974 my husband at the time who is black had to advocate for my acceptance into the School of Social Work at Portland State University. At that time he told me there was an unwritten rule rejecting applicants who mentioned having psychiatric histories. He spoke directly to the Admissions Officer who at first thought I was black, too, and was eager to expand his minority student population.[10]

The U.S. Department of Education's Office of Civil Rights, which investigates reports of discrimination in higher education,[11] reported that "more than 10 percent of all complaints received between Oct. 1, 1993, and Sept. 30, 1994, alleged disability discrimination at a postsecondary institution."[12] Of 551 complaints, investigation led the agency to raise ADA or Section 504 "compliance concerns" in 173 of the cases. The number of compliance concerns did not necessarily track states with high populations of students; whereas California had 20 and Florida 17, New York had only 4, the same as Tennessee and 5 fewer than Arizona.[13]

These accounts of discrimination are particularly telling because colleges, universities, and professional schools are subject to Section 504 of the Rehabilitation Act, were fully aware of these regulations, and had been prohibited from discriminating on the basis of disability for more than 10 years at the time the ADA was passed.[14] Indeed, two of the first Supreme Court cases involving discrimination under the Rehabilitation Act involved educational institutions as defendants.[15]

Ten years after the passage of the ADA and more than 20 years after universities and professional schools were first prohibited from discriminating on the basis of disability,[16] discrimination in higher education and among the professions remains a substantial source of complaint and litigation. In 1999, students and faculty at California State University at Northridge conducted a protest, "forcing the creation of a committee to study implementation of the Americans with Disabilities Act."[17] Reports from protection and advocacy agencies[18] abound with cases involving higher education and the professions: the refusal of colleges to permit people with recent histories of psychiatric treatment to live in dormitories,[19] the refusal to permit people with mental disabilities to complete clinical programs and therefore their exclusion from graduate educational studies,[20] and the refusal to provide accommodations in the classroom. Litigated discrimination cases include a substantial number against well-known and less-famous institutions of higher education.[21]

Law schools have been the defendants in a substantial number of disability discrimination cases brought by students involving admission,[22] expulsion,[23] failure to provide accommodations,[24] creation of a hostile environment,[25] and discriminatory letters regarding students to State Boards of Bar Examiners.[26] Professors occasionally sue for disability discrimination as well.[27]

Medical schools are sued even more frequently than law schools for disability discrimination. There may be a number of reasons for this. First, medical school requires two standardized tests, the MCAT for admission and the U.S. Medical Licensing Examination after successful completion of 2 years of medical school, and a number of the cases involve these tests as they relate to students' learning disabilities. Second, cases involve both medical students[28] and residents,[29] and medical school and residency last longer than law school. Third, some disabilities may appear to be more salient obstacles to accomplishing the essential functions of being a medical student or doctor.[30] Finally, medical schools may simply be less attuned to legal rights than law schools; more disability discrimination cases against medical schools are brought by faculty members as well as students.[31] However, that at least some law students litigate more tenaciously.[32]

Licensing and Discipline of Professionals

It is not only the training grounds for professionals that are the sources of discrimination. Modern discrimination cases involving mental disabilities also involve a substantial number of cases challenging questions on professional licensure[33] and relicensure[34] applications, applications for the judiciary,[35] failure to grant accommodations in licensure exams,[36] denial of hospital privileges,[37] and professional discipline.[38] Litigants under the ADA and Rehabilitation Act raising these issues include not only doctors and lawyers, but pilots[39] and college professors[40] as well.

It is important to note that these cases are *not* necessarily brought by the same group of people. Cases involving professional schools, bar admissions, and requests for accommodations in the practice of law or medicine are, with very few exceptions, brought by different kinds of people than cases involving professional discipline. It is ironic that public apprehensions surround disability discrimination laws and the possibility of their use to excuse misbehavior and misconduct in employment, when the reality is that this is far more likely in the case of doctors and lawyers seeking to escape the consequences of misconduct than in the average employment discrimination case.

The consistent argument of those seeking to remove questions regarding psychiatric treatment from licensure applications is that there is no inherent link between psychiatric diagnosis or treatment and fitness to practice law or medicine. The small amount of available research tends to support this claim,[41] and the American Psychiatric Association and American Bar Association have taken positions in support of it. For every doctor or lawyer with ADHD or depression seeking to mitigate punishment for theft from clients or sex with patients, there are thousands of competent and caring lawyers and doctors with these diagnoses who go about their work every day without missing deadlines or embezzling funds.

Courts often take a hands-off, deferential approach to most discrimination claims involving the professions, and this approach appears to be generally (although not always) sensible in professional discipline cases. Disciplinary bodies investigate only on receiving complaints, and those complaints always involve behavior or (more often) its absence–failure to file cases, failure to turn over money due to the client. As noted,

> in the vast majority of disciplinary cases involving an attorney's mental health, it is acts and/or omissions of the attorney, which acts themselves would be grounds for disbarment or suspension, that bring to light the possibility of mental or emotional problems.[42]

The focus of disciplinary bodies is therefore necessarily and appropriately on conduct. Disciplinary proceedings are more individualized and involve more due process protections than decisions by licensing boards or institutions of higher education. People subject to professional discipline are more often represented by counsel and more often have the resources to appeal these decisions to the courts. Case law, research, and experience suggest that courts should, however, inquire more carefully into the decisions of professional schools about their students and that concern should be at its highest in reviewing the policies and procedures of licensing authorities.[43]

Licensing bodies oversee the applications of every student who wishes to practice law or medicine. Because they conduct a much higher volume of business than disciplinary bodies, their approaches are necessarily less individualized. Licensing bodies rely more on standard questions, record release, and assumptions that streamline procedures. These assumptions often include using psychiatric diagnoses and treatment as proxies for questionable character or predictors of future misconduct, although there is no proof that either psychiatric diagnosis or treatment serves as any kind of proxy for future misconduct. Licensing bodies have also been known to respond to requests for accommodations, such as extended time on an examination, with a demand that the applicant submit to a full medical and psychiatric examination at his or her own expense.[44] Requests for accommodations are rarely factors in disciplinary hearings. Licensing cases often, although not always, challenge existing blanket questions, policies, and procedures regarding people with disabilities.

Although both disciplinary bodies and licensing bodies operate with citizen membership and almost no other form of oversight, and therefore enjoy a great deal of discretion, applicants for licensure are often unwilling to sue or even complain about licensing boards for fear of jeopardizing their chances at ultimately obtaining licensure. Thus, it is more realistic to assume that professionals subject to discipline will raise any issues of discrimination that ought to be raised, and thus subject disciplinary boards to court oversight, than it is to assume that people wishing to be admitted to the practice of law or medicine will challenge the policies of state licensing boards.

Professional schools also have a great deal of discretion, but their operations generally are considerably more public than those of bar and medical examiners. Within the school itself, more people are usually involved in decision making. Unlike licensing and disciplinary bodies, there are often personnel or offices in professional schools whose function it is to advocate for the student, and federal law requires a grievance process for a student who believes that he or she has been discriminated against on the basis of disability. Also, individuals with disabilities are more willing to sue professional schools than either licensing boards or disciplinary boards. This is because professional schools are—and have been for over 20 years—governed by a substantial and specific set of federal regulations, which set out a number of concrete obligations that professional schools have to their disabled students. No such body of law exists in regard to licensing or discipline, although case law is beginning to establish certain guidelines.

It is interesting to note that the discipline, licensing, and professional school cases have each developed a body of legal doctrine, conceptually distinct from the others, focusing on different issues and coming to different conclusions. Disability discrimination law is at its clearest in the licensing cases and is at its most doctrinally confused and distorted in cases involving professional schools.

Legal Issues of Relevance to Professionals

Allegations of discrimination on the basis of disability raise unique questions in the context of professional education, licensure, and discipline. They include issues such as the level of deference, if any, courts should grant to professional bodies in making determinations about the impact of an individual's disability on his or her professional capacities and whether disabilities should be determined to exist by comparison with other professionals in the field or by comparison with society at large.

Meaning of Disability in the Professional Environment

A recurring issue in litigation brought by professionals and would-be professionals such as medical students and law students is whether and how the definition of *disability* should be adjusted in professional school settings. Although the ADA and Rehabilitation Act regulations recognize "learning" as a major life activity that may be substantially limited by an impairment,[45] law students and medical students frequently have learning disabilities that substantially limit learning in a professional school environment but not in the world at large.[46] Is such a person disabled? The Interpretive Guidance to the Title II regulations state that the person's important life activities must be "restricted as to the conditions, manner, or duration under which they can be performed in comparison to most people."[47] However, when the claim is that a person is substantially limited in the major life activity of working, "a person's expertise, background, and job expectations are relevant factors in defining the class of jobs used to determine whether an individual is disabled."[48] Thus, whether the major life activity limited by the impairment is "working," "learning," or "academic functioning" may have significant bearing on whether an individual is considered disabled for the purposes of the ADA.[49] If learning is the major life activity, will it be divided into component parts? Some cases have held reading is a major life activity,[50] and many courts have found "concentrating" to be a major life activity.[51]

Two cases in particular present opposite sides of the dilemma of defining disability in the professional setting: *Bartlett v. New York State Board of Law Examiners*[52] and *Price v. National Board of Medical Examiners*.[53] Marilyn Bartlett successfully completed a master's degree in education despite a severe reading disability before she went to law school. She received accommodations for her disability while in law school, but the New State Board of Law Examiners refused to provide her with accommodations on the grounds that she was not disabled. She took and failed the New York Bar five times—only once with any kind of accommodations—before she finally prevailed in federal district court and (on different grounds) in the 2nd Circuit.

The New York State Board of Law Examiners that argued that Bartlett was not disabled because their expert, Dr. Frank Vellutino, concluded that only individuals who scored below the 30th percentile on two subtests in the Woodcock Reading Mastery Test, Revised, could be considered disabled. Bartlett argued that her reading disability could not be measured solely by the Woodcock Test. Because the Woodcock test was untimed, it did not measure the detrimental effect of her extreme slowness and hesitation in reading, and because it was designed primarily for children, it was not suitable to consider it in isolation from other factors. A host of clinicians had diagnosed her as having a severe reading disability. She argued that she was disabled in reading, learning, and working as a result of this reading disability.

The district judge concluded that because Bartlett, as a result of a number of self-accommodations, could probably read as well as an average member of the public, she could not be said to be disabled in either reading or learning,[54] but because the relevant comparison group for working purposes was the group of people who had finished law school and were taking the Bar, her impairment substantially limited her in working when compared with them. The New York State Board of Law Examiners, which has a long history of fiercely litigating requests for accommodations,[55] appealed to the 2nd Circuit, arguing that its decisions regarding disability should be granted deference by courts (the appropriate degree of deference due to professional schools and boards is discussed in the next section), and that Bartlett was not disabled because she could work in a number of professions and had indeed already taught school.

On appeal, the 2nd Circuit substantially affirmed on different grounds, holding that the district judge erred in holding that Bartlett was not disabled in reading or learning and therefore should never have proceeded to the issue of whether she was disabled in working. Barlett used both conscious and unconscious compensations for her reading disability. The panel concluded that these self-accommodations, or ways that she had taught herself to try to get around or minimize the effects of her disability, were mitigating measures that should not be taken into account in determining whether she was disabled.[56]

This holding was of crucial importance to medical and law students with learning disabilities, who are the paradigmatic self-accommodators, and for people with psychiatric disabilities, for whom self-accommodation is also a familiar concept.[57] Indeed, it represents a significant breakthrough of social understanding of the nature of disability in general. Every time that we congratulate ourselves for feeling completely comfortable with or "not noticing" someone's disability, we may simply be unaware of how much that person has accommodated himself or herself to us, to our environment, and to our expectations.[58] The degree to which this self-accommodation is invisible or erased has a tremendously negative social impact because when people with disabilities do ask for accommodations, even reasonable accommodations, society often reacts as though it is being asked to do all the work of accommodation rather than understanding that the requested accommodation is probably just the tip of the accommodation iceberg.

The Supreme Court, however, vacated the 2nd District's decision in *Bartlett* and remanded for reconsideration in light of its decision that mitigating devices and medications must be considered in determining whether an individual is disabled. One question is whether self-accommodation is distinct from medical devices such as eyeglasses or prostheses. The answer is probably not because a companion case to *Sutton*, *Albertson's v. Kirkingburg*,[59] held that a man with monocular vision who effectively self-accommodated was not disabled. The U.S. Supreme Court's action opens the door for reinstatement of the original district court holding that compared with other law school graduates, Marilyn Bartlett was substantially limited in her ability to work.

A case reaching the opposite conclusion from the district court's holding in *Bartlett* is *Price v. National Board of Medical Examiners*.[60] In *Price*, medical students with ADHD requested accommodations on the first step of the National Medical Examination. The court in *Price* paraded the many accomplishments of the plaintiffs and concluded that they were not disabled within the meaning of the ADA because they were not substantially limited in the major life activity of learning compared with people in the general population. In fact, the court in *Price* proffered the following hypothetical situation:

> Take, for example, two hypothetical students. Student A has an average intellectual capacity and an impairment (dyslexia) that limits his ability to learn so that he can only learn as well as 10 percent of the general population. Therefore, Student A has a disability for purposes of the ADA. By contrast, Student B has superior intellectual capability, but her impairment (dyslexia) limits her ability so that she can learn as well as the average person. Her dyslexia qualifies as an impairment. However, Student B's impairment does not substantially limit the major life function of learning, because it does not restrict her ability to learn as compared with most people. Therefore, Student B is not a person with a disability under the ADA.[61]

Although this perspective has been adopted by at least two other courts,[62] it is an extraordinarily stigmatizing view of disability. To say that these students with learning disabilities are not disabled because of their superior achievement is to equate disability with inferiority, thus granting accommodations only to students who would fail without them.[63] Comparing medical students or law students with significant learning disabilities with the population as a whole rather than with other medical students or law students means that students with learning disabilities, who could successfully compete in medical school or law school with reasonable accommodations, are excluded from both education and career opportunities in law and medicine. As one court put it, "although Betts may well have a learning disorder that 'substantially limits' his ability to attend medical school, attending medical school is not a 'major life activity.'"[64] Those students with disabilities who do struggle through are not able to show their true potential.[65]

Finally, this perspective on disability serves as a perverse disincentive for students with disabilities to try to self-accommodate and learn ways to reduce the impact of their disabilities by sending the message that too much success in this area may cut off accommodations altogether. This is not what Congress had in mind when it passed the ADA: The purpose of the ADA is to open all facets of American society to people with disabilities, not just the nonprofessional jobs. As the judge in *Bartlett* noted, "by measuring a disability for purposes of professional examination against a reference population that would otherwise be totally unprepared and unqualified to take such an examination, the findings of such applicants' disability is [*sic*] necessarily skewed against a finding of disability,"[66] and such skewed measuring effectively operates as an absolute bar to any accommodations for virtually anyone with a learning disability in the professions.

Several other courts have concluded that defining disability in a way that results in the exclusion of qualified individuals from entry into a profession is permissible under the ADA. In one troubling case involving a dental student with visual difficulties, the court concluded that the plaintiff was not disabled because he could pursue careers other than dentistry.[67] The court did not even focus on whether the accommodations the student requested were reasonable or would enable him to get a professional education and become a dentist. In another case, a court dismissed a medical student's request for accommodations for his anxiety disorder, which manifested itself during math and science examinations, with the conclusion that it did not impede his performance in a wide variety of areas and therefore did not constitute a disability.[68] The clear intention of Congress in passing the ADA was to pave the way for the integration of people with disabilities into all aspects of society, including employment in the professions. If courts continue to use the availability of other occupational paths as a reason to find that an individual is not disabled, they will cut off entry into the professions for the vast majority of people with disabilities, who would not be on the threshold of professional education without having other occupational options open to them.

There are indeed difficult issues involved in accommodating people with psychiatric and learning disabilities in professional school, but they do not involve the appropriate reference population, which in the context of professional schools and examinations clearly should be the population with the same training, education, and preparation. The ADA makes it clear that people who are otherwise qualified should not be denied career opportunities because of their disabilities. The National Medical Examination and the New York Bar Examination are intended to measure knowledge of medicine and law.[69] If a medical or law student's disability impedes accurate measurement of that knowledge, and the requested accommodation results in a more valid measurement of that knowledge, it should be granted.

The more difficult issues involve ensuring a nexus between impairments caused by disability and the requested accommodation[70] and coming up with a valid way of measuring the point at which a limitation in the ability to do such things as "concentrate" and "focus" becomes substantial enough to constitute a disability. The New York Board of Law Examiners claimed that the court should grant them deference in deciding this latter question. Should defendants in cases involving education and regulation of the legal and medical professions be granted deference by the courts, and if so, in what areas, is a subject of considerable disagreement in the courts?

Level of Deference Courts Should Give to Academia and the Professions

Universities making academic dismissal decisions, licensing boards making admission decisions, and disciplinary arms of law and medicine often express outrage and astonishment that their decisions could be subject to oversight, especially court oversight, on the issue of whether their decisions violate laws prohibiting discrimination. Most defendants in these cases have argued in some way or another that courts should not review their decisions.

Initially, these arguments were made as a constitutional matter.[71] As these arguments failed, defendants deployed new legal theories to prevent courts from reviewing their decisions. They contended that a number of procedural doctrines precluded federal involvement: abstention,[72] the Rooker–Feldman doctrine,[73] and the *res judicata* effect of state administrative decisions. Furthermore, if courts did have the power to consider discrimination claims brought against professional schools and licensing entities, judges were told they should defer to defendants' conclusions regarding the qualifications of the plaintiffs and the necessity of defendants' requirements.[74]

Deference Due to Educational Institutions

These claims are typically made broadly, so it has been up to the courts to decide whether any deference should be granted at all and, if so, to parse out which decisions and policies should be granted deference, and under what circumstances. Some courts deciding discrimination cases against universities have confused the requirement of deference when a student claims that his or her constitutional due process rights have been violated by a university's decision to dismiss him or her with the test set out for statutory claims of discrimination under the Rehabilitation Act or the ADA. The U.S. Supreme Court made clear that in constitutional due process matters relating to student dismissals, the decisions of universities are to be given considerable deference, and the Court has applied the "professional-judgment" standard to such challenges.[75] It is clear that constitutional adjudication differs from statutory adjudication and that a constitutional due process standard is not the correct standard by which to measure a statutory discrimination claim.[76] Most courts understand the distinction.

As the 1st Circuit explained in *Wynne v. Tufts University*, discrimination statutes require something more of academic defendants than constitutional challenges:

> First, as we have noted, there is a real obligation on the academic institution to seek suitable means of reasonably accommodating a handicapped person and to submit a factual record indicating that it conscientiously carried out this statutory obligation. Second, the *Ewing* formulation, hinging judicial override on "a substantial departure from accepted academic norms" is not necessarily a helpful test in assessing whether professional judgment has been exercised in exploring reasonable alternatives for a handicapped person. We say this because such alternatives may involve new approaches or devices quite beyond "accepted academic norms."[77]

A claim of statutory discrimination resembles a constitutional equal protection claim far more than a constitutional due process claim, but it is equally clear that the "rational basis" constitutional test is not applicable to statutory discrimination claims. As the 10th Circuit explained,

> in other words, they [the defendants] say that the rational basis test of equal protection must be applied when considering §504. The rational basis test is not applicable where there is an alleged violation of a statute, §504, which prohibits discrimination on the basis of handicap. That statute by its very terms does not provide that a recipient of federal assistance may act in an unreasonable manner to promote legitimate governmental means, even if discrimination should result. Rather, the statute provides that a recipient of federal financial assistance may not discriminate on the basis of handicap, regardless of whether there is a rational basis for so discriminating.[78]

Although the few district court decisions relying on the constitutional due process standard[79] applied the law incorrectly, that does not mean that no deference is due to academic decision making in certain contexts. In fact, most of the circuits to consider the application of the ADA to institutions of higher education have ruled that if the academic institution's response to the disabled student's requests meets certain threshold standards, then the conclusions of the institution will be due some degree of deference.[80] It is clear that a university or professional school forfeits deference if it dismisses a student's request out of hand or fails to consider requested alternatives or to investigate the student's condition and concerns.[81] The decisions suggest that before reaching a decision, the responsible parties should discuss the issue with the student, his or her treatment professionals, the faculty involved, and their own disability issues coordinators and engage in "reasoned deliberations as to whether the modifications would change the essential academic standards" involved.[82] It seems difficult to reconcile these decisions with the statute's requirements of confidentiality for students with disabilities, but presumably a student who is on the verge of being dismissed academically has lost some aspects of confidentiality already.

Deference Due to Regulating and Licensing Agencies

Although the Rehabilitation Act and the ADA require more of an institution of higher education than the constitutional standard, it is true that academia, with its First Amendment–related concerns for intellectual freedom and autonomy, has always been an area that courts were reluctant to regulate. Courts have evinced far less hesitation in disposing of the claims to deference of licensing bodies.

Courts have emphasized that the decision of a state agency or regulating body is not due deference simply because it is a state agency or regulating body.[83] Rather, the entity seeking deference must have some expertise in the area in which it seeks deference, and that area must be one in which courts do not have equal expertise. Clearly, boards of bar examiners are not disability experts.[84] They are entitled to no particular deference in their decisions regarding whether an applicant is disabled. By the same token, boards of bar examiners are not experts in whether a given accommodation is sufficient to address a given disability.[85]

The Practice of Medicine and Law

The practice of law is supposed to center on the protection of rights, and medicine is known as the healing profession. It might therefore be expected that these professions would serve as models to the rest of society in their treatment of people with disabilities. However, the medical and legal professions are hardly examples of inclusion and accommodation when it comes to lawyers and doctors with disabilities. Rather, discrimination on the basis of disability begins in some cases with an application to professional school and continues on throughout professional life, including applications to the judiciary[86] or for clinical privileges.[87]

Applications to Medical and Law Schools

Inquiring as to an Applicant's Disability

The law has forbidden for many years inquiries about mental or physical disabilities on applications to graduate schools, including medical schools, that receive federal funds. Regulations applicable to postsecondary educational institutions forbid these institutions from making "preadmission inquiry as to whether an applicant for admission is a handicapped person."[88] The only exception permits institutions to allow, but not require, individuals with disabilities to volunteer their status for the purposes of remedying past discrimination. This purpose as well as the applicant's option not to answer the question must be made clear on the application.[89]

The law also prohibits the use of tests for admission that have a "disproportionate, adverse effect on handicapped persons or any class of handicapped persons"[90] unless the test has been "validated as a predictor of success in the academic program." The validation must be for success in the entire academic program, not just the first year, and validation tests must be repeated periodically.[91]

Flagging LSAT and MCAT Scores Under "Nonstandard" Conditions

The principal examination relied on by medical schools to assist in admission decisions is the MCAT, whereas most law schools require applicants to take the LSAT. When applicants receive accommodations on either examination, an asterisk is affixed to the score, and an annotation is made that the test was taken under "nonstandard conditions."

The practice of adding an asterisk to test scores if the test was taken under nonstandard conditions has resulted in some complaints to the Office of Civil Rights of the Department of Education. Currently, the Office's policy permits medical schools to use the asterisked test scores as long as scores are not the only criterion for admission and applicants are not denied admission because they took the test under nonstandard conditions.[92] The Office of Civil Rights will find discrimination, however, if members of the medical school admission committee acknowledge looking less favorably on asterisked test scores than on standard test scores.[93]

The Office of Civil Rights considers it beneficial for professional schools to include people with disabilities on their admissions committees.[94] Given the predominance of people with learning disabilities among complainants against medical schools, a medical school is well advised to include on their admissions committees[95] people with learning disabilities, people with knowledge of learning disabilities through training and experience (e.g., neurologists), and people with family members who have learning disabilities who can provide needed advice and expertise in admissions decisions.

There are continuing concerns about the permissibility under the ADA of identifying tests taken under accommodated conditions;[96] however, the use of asterisks to indicate test scores taken under nonstandard conditions is only the tip of the litigation iceberg. The MCAT and LSAT are subject to question in terms of the validity of their predictive abilities. A recent study compared medical students admitted to the University of California at Davis Medical School under "special considerations"—those whose grade point averages (GPAs) and MCAT scores were low enough to preclude admission absent special considerations such as race or poverty or disability—with matched medical students admitted under the regular program, whose MCATs and GPAs were much higher.[97] There was no significant difference between the two groups in rate of graduation, failure of courses in medical school, completion of residency, passage of licensing examinations, board certification, or entry into various medical specialties.[98] Under the regulations, if the MCAT or LSAT has a disparate impact on the admission of students with disabilities, it must be validated for success in the entire academic program. Clearly, further research needs to be done to explore both those questions in greater detail.

Refusing to Admit Based on Evaluation of Professional Rather Than Educational Potential

Both the ADA and Section 504 of the Rehabilitation Act require graduate schools to make reasonable modifications in any "policies, practices, or procedures" if modifications are necessary to ensure that these requirements do not "have the effect of discriminating, on the basis of handicap, against a qualified handicapped applicant or student."[99]

A key question in this area is whether a professional school can deny admission to a student who can, with accommodations, successfully complete his or her education on the grounds that the student will be unlikely to function as a professional in the field for which he or she is being trained. For example, a number of people go to law school simply for the background, with no intention of practicing law. If a student could, with accommodations, meet the essential requirements of the law school, could the law school legally base any decision making on its conclusion that the student could not practice law?

A related question is whether it is an "essential function" of a professional training school to require a student to demonstrate the skills necessary to practice in every area of the profession. Some students with learning disabilities might not be able to be tax lawyers but could be public defenders. Some medical students might be able to be psychiatrists but not surgeons. Can a professional school exclude the student if he or she would be unable, no matter what accommodations were granted, to practice in a given area of medicine or law?

Southeastern Community College v. Davis, the Supreme Court's only pronouncement so far on the issue of reasonable accommodations, gives a mixed message regarding whether professional schools may require students to be able to perform any aspect of the profession for which they are training. On the one hand, the Supreme Court noted that "training for all normal roles of an RN represents a legitimate academic policy";[100] on the other hand, the court commented that the insistence on continuing past requirements in the face of technological change might be unreasonable and discriminatory.[101]

The Office of Civil Rights has adopted the position that institutions of higher education may require a student to complete training for every possible application of his or her professional degree. This requirement seems unreasonable for a variety of reasons. As a practical matter, the very structure of the professions seems antithetical to the position of the Office of Civil Rights. It is not sufficient to graduate from a professional school to practice. Most professions have a licensing requirement that ostensibly screens applicants on the basis of whether they are qualified to practice in that profession. In addition, the existence in every state of "inactive" status for professionals, such as doctors and lawyers, suggests that one can be a doctor or lawyer without practicing the profession.

More important, the language and regulations of the ADA, issued after the Supreme Court interpreted the Rehabilitation Act, suggest that Congress intends a different result to be reached under the ADA. It seems clear from the language of the ADA and its regulations that professional schools may not exclude or fail to accommodate a student on the basis of the judgment that the student may not be able to practice in the profession. Title III of the ADA, which applies to private universities and graduate schools, simply provides that "no individual shall be discriminated against on the basis of disability," eliminating entirely the requirement of being qualified or otherwise qualified. Of course, this does not mean that schools must admit unqualified students, but schools can defend against charges of discrimination only by showing that eligibility criteria are "necessary for the provision of the goods, services, facilities, privileges, advantages, or accommodations being offered"[102] or that making the modifications requested would constitute a "fundamental alteration" of the program being offered or result in an "undue burden."[103]

It appears that the burden has shifted, at least under Title III, to the school to demonstrate that its criteria are necessary for the program being offered, which is clearly an educational one. If the student can meet the educational requirements, then the student should not be excluded from the school because of its doubts about the student's ability to be employed. After all, few graduate schools place 100% of their students in employment immediately, and surely no school would argue that the education by itself was a waste of time.

Accommodations in Professional School

Although the regulations to both Section 504 and the ADA envision a broad range of accommodations,[104] court interpretations and the practice of the Office of Civil Rights have been less liberal. The case of *Guckenberger v. Boston University*, which generated much interest from the press, suggests that universities (and by implication, graduate schools) have at the very least an affirmative duty to interact with students with disabilities.[105] Past a certain point, it is clearly illegal to fail to communicate policies regarding accommodations, ignore requests from students for reasonable accommodations, have inadequate or poorly trained staff, or unreasonably delay instituting agreed-on accommodations.[106] Beyond these requirements, accommodations vary from the controversial (course substitutions) to the mundane (taping classes) with an enormous variety of possibilities in between.

Course Substitutions

The case of *Guckenberger v. Boston University* focuses in large part on the question of whether waiving course requirements such as mathematics or foreign languages for graduation from a university was a reasonable accommodation. The district court's decision, following the 1st Circuit's guidance in *Wynne v. Tufts University*,[107] made clear that universities (and, by extension, professional schools) cannot simply reject out-of-hand requests for course substitutions or waivers by students with disabilities. Judge Patty Saris found that Boston University had improperly "relied on the status quo as a rationale for refusing to consider seriously a reasonable request for modification of its century old degree requirement."[108] The university had a duty to seek an appropriate reasonable accommodation for students with disabilities and to consider alternatives to requiring the suggested courses for graduation.

However, the student plaintiffs had an obligation (not met in the request to waive the mathematics requirement) to come forward with research demonstrating that their asserted disabilities precluded them from being able to successfully complete the course requirements. Judge Saris also found that "in general, federal law does not require a university to modify degree requirements that it determines are a fundamental part of its academic program." Universities and professional schools, however, must come forward with evidence that providing the reasonable accommodation would lower academic standards or require substantial program alteration.[109] *Wynne v. Tufts University* suggests that submitting an affidavit from the dean or president of the school stating in conclusory terms that the course requirement is necessary without showing why, and without indicating what reasonable accommodations were considered, and why they were rejected, will be insufficient.

One of the more notorious aspects of the *Guckenberger* case was President Jon Westling's articulated belief that students who claimed to have learning disabilities were "lazy fakers,"[110] and the professionals who evaluated them were "snake-oil salesmen,"[111] coconspirators in a quest to reduce academic standards. In particular, the revelation that Westling's reference in a speech to a student with a learning disability whom he called by the sobriquet of "Somnolent Samantha"[112] was entirely fabricated makes *Guckenberger* a particularly egregious case, not a particularly representative case.

Extended Time on Examinations

This area seems to be relatively uncontroversial. Many cases indicate in passing that medical or law students with disabilities such as dyslexia, ADHD,[113] other visual or learning disabilities, or physical disabilities[114] were given extra time to complete examinations.[115]

Forms of Examinations

One of the most famous and prolonged discrimination cases in higher education is *Wynne v. Tufts University*. This case involved Steven Wynne's ultimately unsuccessful quest to take his biochemistry exam orally rather than in a written multiple-choice format. Wynne, who had dyslexia and had difficulties with the passive-voice construction and triple-negative structure that accompanies many multiple-choice tests, insisted he could pass the only medical school course that he had failed[116] if the examination were given orally. Tufts refused to permit him to do so.

Initially, the district court granted Tufts summary judgment concluding that Wynne was not "otherwise qualified" to be a medical student, because he had clearly been unable to meet the requirements of medical school. Tufts' sole submission as to why the multiple-choice test was so imperative was an affidavit by the Dean of the Medical School, explaining why he believed that multiple-choice examinations were important.

A panel of the 1st Circuit reversed the district court's decision. The 1st Circuit then vacated the panel decision and convened *en banc* to render a decision, meaning that every judge in the 1st Circuit voted on the case. Although the *en banc* majority agreed that deference had to be paid to the judgment of the academic defendants, they underscored that this was not simply *Ewing* or *Horowitz* professional judgment deference.[117] The court held that the Rehabilitation Act required the medical school to at least consider possible alternatives to the multiple-choice format and to have legitimate pedagogical reasons for rejecting these alternatives. In other words, when a student with a disability makes a request for a reasonable accommodation, the school cannot simply reject the request out of hand, nor may it reject the request for reasons of administrative, or even faculty, convenience. The court stated that

> there is no indication of who took part in the decision or when it was made. Were the simple conclusory averment of the head of an institution to suffice, there would be no way of ascertaining whether the institution had made a professional effort to evaluate possible ways of accommodating a handicapped student or had simply embraced what was most convenient for faculty and administration.[118]

Three judges dissented from the *en banc* decision, including now Justice Stephen Breyer, who wrote the dissenting opinion. Judge Breyer wrote that "Mr. Wynne's particular disability, a psychological learning disadvantage, is closely related to the kind of characteristic, namely an inability to learn to become a good doctor, to which

Tufts reasonably and lawfully need not 'accommodate.' "[119] The equation of "learning disability" with "inability to learn" is the most common mistake made by people who do not understand the nature of learning disability, and in some ways an understandable one, given the unfortunate term "learning disability." People with learning disabilities are by definition of average or superior intelligence and can learn; they simply have problems learning in certain modalities and perform better when learning in other ways. To equate a learning disability with an inability to learn is similar to equating blindness or deafness with an inability to learn. In all three cases, both learning and accurate demonstrations of the knowledge and skills that have been acquired are possible, even though a student may learn in different ways and need testing in different modalities.

Miscellaneous Accommodations

Other accommodations that have been provided by medical schools include tutoring,[120] paying for disability testing,[121] being seated in the front of the class,[122] having taped lectures,[123] being allowed to retake examinations or repeat courses,[124] and taking examinations in a separate room[125] or at home,[126] taking leaves of absence,[127] taking modified course loads, and using modified examination formats including dictation.[128] Courts in cases involving reasonable accommodations seem to be following the "interactive process" guidance applicable to employment cases. That is, a university or graduate school that can show that it took a request for accommodations seriously and provided some or even many accommodations is in a much better legal position than an institution that simply dismissed a student without notice or attempt to resolve the issues that were of concern.[129]

Issues Relating to Psychiatric Disabilities in Professional School

Disclosure and Barriers to Seeking Treatment

I have been teaching law school for 10 years, and one of the most common stories of law students with diagnosed psychiatric disabilities is the degree to which friends and family tried to recast their difficulties as normal stress, in the face of the student's growing realization that something more serious was going on.[130] Often, the student was discouraged from seeking help until the difficulties become so overwhelming that he or she withdrew from school.

Friends and family mean well; they often want to protect the student from the difficulties of disclosure to bar and medical examiners[131] and perceive that any psychiatric diagnosis would impair career opportunities. However, an equally common story from law students is one of psychiatric hospitalization in the middle of a family crisis, usually the parents' divorce. Students view these hospitalizations as unnecessary, coercive, and frightening. What these two sets of stories have in common is that in neither case was the student's perception of his or her own situation and need for treatment honored; in both situations, students were unwilling to reveal their history for fear of being stigmatized. Thus, law students are frequently unaware that other students around them have been institutionalized and are now successfully pursuing legal careers.

Effects of Disabilities Versus Effects of Medication

A key issue for professional students with psychiatric disabilities, such as depression, anxiety or panic disorder, obsessive–compulsive disorder, or bipolar disorder, is that the medication prescribed for these conditions creates its own impairments, usually relating to fatigue, lower energy level, the need for more sleep, and sometimes difficulty concentrating. The Supreme Court has made it clear that medications themselves can cause disabilities and that the disabling effects of medications must be accommodated under the ADA.[132]

Involuntary Psychiatric Examinations

The question of whether and when a professional school can require its students to submit to psychiatric examinations was raised but not decided in *Boyle v. Brown University*.[133] In that case, a 4th-year medical student was, without her knowledge, referred to the impaired medical student committee (IMSC) of a state medical association, an organization outside a medical school. Although Boyle had chronic fatigue syndrome, she had not informed the administration and had privately worked out accommodations with several faculty members. Three faculty members had approached the dean because they believed that Boyle's reactions to her grades indicated emotional difficulties. The dean, on this basis alone, and without meeting with Boyle, decided he had three options: (a) request that Boyle undergo an independent psychiatric examination, (b) refer her to the IMSC, or (c) take unspecified administrative action himself.[134]

The first that Boyle learned of this was when she received a call from the IMSC, asking her to come before them. She refused and asked for a meeting with the dean. He reiterated that her only choices were to get an independent psychiatric examination, go before the IMSC, or be suspended from her fourth year of medical school for "psychological reasons." Boyle's ADA suit was dismissed because the ADA had not been in effect at the time of the threatened dismissal, and the statute of limitations had run on her Rehabilitation Act claims. *Boyle* serves as a potent reminder of the extent of power and discretion that a professional school has over the lives and futures of its students and the capricious way in which that power is sometimes exercised.

Dismissal From Medical School and Readmission

Boyle echoes the first Rehabilitation Act case ever brought involving a graduate student with psychiatric disabilities.[135] *Doe v. New York University* is worth exploring in detail because it is a profound illustration of the "catch-22" faced by many people with psychiatric disabilities.[136] This case concerned the refusal of New York University Medical School to readmit a student who had left after a series of escalating battles with the medical school over her psychiatric condition. It is also a classic example of overlapping issues involving gender, psychiatric disability, and the extraordinary deference paid by courts to medical institutions.

"Jane Doe" applied to New York University Medical School, which accepted 170 out of 5,000 applicants. The application asked (probably illegally[137]) whether she had any "chronic or recurrent illnesses, emotional problems, or bodily defects."[138] She indicated that she did not. In fact, Doe had a recent history of cutting herself severely and numerous brief psychiatric hospitalizations, which were notably unsuccessful in resolving her emotional problems and apparently only exacerbated them.

Doe was admitted to medical school. She did satisfactorily in school, although she kept postponing a required physical examination. She finally went for the examination on October 30 of her first year in medical school.[139] After being asked about the scars on her arms during a required physical examination, she told the doctor about "some of her problems." The doctor's immediate response was to tell her she should "undergo a psychiatric examination to determine whether she was fit to stay at the school."[140] Doe's reply was that "'it's my body and what I do to it is my concern. If I want to go out and [expletive] a cat I can.' She walked out without completing the examination."[141]

Soon after this incident, Doe was required to undergo a battery of psychiatric interviews by Associate Dean David S. Scotch. Although she had been doing satisfactorily in school, the associate dean asked her to withdraw. She appealed to the dean of the medical school, who permitted her to stay on the condition that she undergo psychiatric treatment. Three months passed uneventfully until Doe had to see Scotch to sort out a scheduling problem. He was not in his office when she arrived, and she became distressed and angry:

> She left the office and attempted to calm herself, but to no avail. She returned and told Dean Scotch that she would have to revert to her past habits in order to cope with the situation. She retreated to a bathroom, where she bled herself with a catheter.[142]

Doe was allowed to withdraw from medical school on the understanding that she could seek reinstatement. Her diagnosis was borderline personality disorder, which the court of appeals characterized in the following way:

> [Borderline personality disorder] is a serious condition. . . . A person suffering from it is likely to have it continue through most of his or her adult life, subject to modification only by treatment by well-trained therapists over a period of years and adoption of a lifestyle which avoids situations that subject the person to types of stress with which he or she cannot cope.[143]

After her withdrawal from New York University Medical School, Doe worked at an advertising agency, received a master's degree in science from Harvard's School of Public Health, and worked for the U.S. Department of Health, Education, and Welfare (HEW), where she received awards for outstanding work.

During this time she sought readmission to the medical school. When she was denied readmission, she sued, and after both the Office of Civil Rights and the district court judge found that she had been discriminated against, she was permitted to reenter in October 1981 while the court of appeals considered the school's appeal on an expedited basis. She had not cut herself or been hospitalized since March 1976, but as the district court noted, "based upon its acceptance of this diagnosis [borderline personality disorder], New York University has taken the position that there is nothing Jane Doe can do or prove (now, or in the future) that will convince them she is cured."[144] The district court, however, "finds the plaintiff's actual behavior and condition over the past five years to be more reliable criteria for predicting her future behavior."[145]

The court of appeals reversed, finding her not "otherwise qualified" to be a medical student. Although it did not erase her accomplishments, it minimized them, attributing her excellent record since leaving New York University to "the fact that the types of stress to which she has been subjected at the Harvard School of Public Health and as an HEW employee do not approximate the seriousness of those she would experience as a medical student and doctor."[146]

Rather than looking at Doe herself and her accomplishments, the court of appeals chose to listen to the psychiatric experts, many of whom testified that Doe could not possibly recover from her borderline personality disorder without more therapy than she had received, thus making her seeming recovery of the last 5 years appear fragile and dooming her to likely recurrence. Although the court noted that mental illness itself should not be seen as automatically rendering a person not otherwise qualified, it distinguished Doe's situation as one in which "long-term treatment has been prescribed by competent psychiatrists and Doe has declined to accept such treatment."[147] This is particularly ironic in the light of the fact that by the time of the decision, Doe had over 20 years of intermittent mental health treatment of all kinds, which for the most part was completely unsuccessful. The fault for this was laid by the court squarely at Doe's door.

There was no history of Doe's being unable to get along with fellow students, patients, or her faculty members at the medical school. Most of her violence was self-directed, with some violence directed at mental health professionals, often in the context of involuntary treatment. Her last attack on a mental health professional predated the court's decision by over 7 years. Nevertheless, the court found that "NYU is of necessity concerned with the safety of other students, faculty, and patients to whom Doe would be exposed."[148]

The appeals court disagreed with the lower court's standard, which would have granted Doe admission if it appeared more likely than not that she could complete her medical training and serve successfully as a physician. The appeals court outlined its own standard for decision in the case, which predetermined the outcome:

> if she presents any appreciable risk [of harm to herself or others], this factor could properly be taken into account in deciding whether, among qualified applicants, it rendered her less qualified than others for the limited number of places available. In view of the seriousness of the harm inflicted in prior episodes, NYU is not required to give preference to her over other qualified applicants who do not pose any such appreciable risk at all.[149]

It is clear from the facts presented in the case that Doe may have had a history of sexual abuse.[150] The violence she directed at herself usually came about in the context of confrontations with mental health professionals (and sometimes others) attempting to assert authority and control over her. If the experts and the court had understood the source and meaning of her behavior, the case would have looked completely different, both in terms of the determination of Doe's qualifications for medical school and in the discussion (which never occurred in either court) of what accommodations might be provided for her to enable her to succeed. Doe's cutting behavior could be explained in terms of its coping function by experts (the opinion notes that she herself explained it that way)[151] and perhaps would then seem less bizarre and more explicable and predictable. The dangers of medical school for Doe —not the stress, which was the focus of expert testimony and the court's opinion —but the powerlessness of the medical student and the authoritarian nature of medical education, could have been explored more carefully. The medical school's insistence on therapy that Doe did not want might have been seen not only as counterproductive, but as causing the very behavior the therapy was designed to address.

Instead, women in Doe's situation—a substantial number of professionally successful women who deteriorate badly when they interact with the mental health system, particularly involuntarily—are left with one of the most misguided legal decisions on record. The court has essentially imposed an impossible burden of proof on such a woman: She must prove that there is no appreciable risk that her difficulties will recur. This is impossible to prove, even with expert witnesses; Doe had expert witnesses, but as is usual in cases involving diagnoses of borderline personality disorder, her witnesses either testified that she no longer had borderline personality disorder or never had it.

The lesson of the appellate court in this case is a particularly searing one for women with histories of childhood sexual abuse: The past cannot be overcome. Nothing that Doe could testify about herself or that she accomplished was given as much credence as the predictions of psychiatrists who met with her for an hour. Rather than celebrating and praising her accomplishments as even more remarkable in the face of the pain and suffering that she obviously had survived, the court saw her as causing her own problems. This is the crux of both the clinical and legal treatment received by women who are diagnosed with borderline personality disorder: They are blamed for their own losses by the experts and courts that discount their accomplishments, erase their struggle, and deprive them of the control they need to survive.

Accommodations on the U.S. Medical Licensing Examination

After 2 years of medical school, every medical student in the United States must take and pass the U.S. Medical Licensing Examination before being permitted to continue. This test is administered by the National Board of Medical Examiners, which decides whether to grant accommodations on the examination to medical students. One medical student with a learning disability who had failed the examination by one point sued for additional time and a room free of distraction. The board agreed to provide these accommodations.[152]

The National Board of Medical Examiners allows a student to take this examination six times. If a student fails the sixth time, he or she is precluded from taking the examination again. However, the student must be a medical student to take the examination. In one case, a medical student sued her medical school for dismissing her after failing the exam three times, thus precluding her from taking the examination again.[153] The court held that she had sued the wrong entity, finding that she should have asked the board to allow her to retake the examination as a reasonable accommodation.

Admission to Residency Programs

One of the first cases brought under the Rehabilitation Act involved discrimination in admissions to a residency program in psychiatry.[154] *Pushkin v. University of Colorado Board of Regents*, a highly significant case[155] brought by a doctor with multiple sclerosis, established a number of significant foundations of discrimination law involving professional schools.

Pushkin, like *Guckenberger*, involved a fairly egregious set of circumstances. The articulated explanation for denying Pushkin admission to the psychiatry program was that his patients would get upset if they had to see him, and he in turn would be upset by their reaction to him.[156] Several members of the panel that interviewed him for admission to the residency program also noted that he was "unconsciously angry" about his disfigurement but was in denial about it.[157] His previous supervisor, who worked with him for over a year, had noted that he had "a pleasing personality, works well with his colleagues, and is able to handle the most difficult case in a satisfactory manner."[158] The court rejected the defendants' argument that they based Pushkin's rejection on his poor performance in the interviews and looked at the basis for the conclusion that he had done poorly in the interviews, which the court found "was inextricably involved with Dr. Pushkin's handicap and by the interviewer's perception of the problems the handicap would create."[159] Relatively few cases since this involve such overtly discriminatory behavior. One can only hope that it is as a result of education banishing such stereotypes rather than simply silencing their expression.

Applications for Medical Licensure

Questions on the Application

Courts universally have held that the ADA is implicated when questions regarding psychiatric illness or treatment are asked on professional applications.[160] Licensing boards are public entities, and therefore covered under Title II of the ADA. Although most of the cases involving these questions involve applications to practice law, the first case establishing the principle that the ADA is implicated involved the practice of medicine.[161] The plaintiff challenged, among other questions, the following inquiry: "Have you ever suffered or been treated for any mental illness or psychiatric problems?"[162] Anyone who answered in the affirmative to any of these questions was required to explain these answers in detail on a separate sheet, and was subject to further investigation as a result.[163] The court found that the questions served as screening devices to select out applicants who would be subject to greater burdens of investigation, and that these greater burdens, which would fall on many applicants who were fully qualified to be doctors, constituted discrimination on the basis of disability.

This case was one of the first ADA cases in which the Department of Justice (DOJ) filed a brief as *amicus curiae*. The department supported the plaintiff and ultimately helped negotiate a settlement that resulted in limiting questions relating to psychiatric treatment on the New Jersey licensure and relicensure applications. The new question asks "Do you have a medical condition[164] which in any way impairs or limits your ability to practice medicine with reasonable skill and safety?" This question was approved by the DOJ in the context of professional licensing. It is interesting to note that in an employment setting, the question "Are you physically and mentally capable of performing your job?" triggered a lawsuit by the Equal Employment Opportunity Commission as violative of the ADA.[165]

Despite the result in *Medical Society of New Jersey*, these questions have increased rather than decreased since the enactment of the ADA.[166] In 1995, Jerry Weiner, then president of the American Psychiatric Association, wrote to state medical boards to express concern about the nature of questions regarding psychiatric treatment on licensure applications.[167] Although medical boards are less likely to ask about mental illness and treatment in relicensure applications than licensure applications, almost half of all medical boards (47%) still do ask those questions.[168] Medical boards are also far less likely to ask about physical impairment or disability than mental impairment.[169] These questions are clearly not necessary, for 13 boards of medical examiners do not ask any questions about mental illness or treatment on their licensure applications.

Even though the questions are not necessary, not all of these types of questions are illegal. The key is that there must be a nexus between the information sought by the question and actual present impairment or inability to function as a doctor. Inquiries about whether an applicant sought psychotherapy in the past are illegal because there is no demonstrable connection between seeking psychotherapy and competence as a physician. However, questions such as "Do you have or have you been diagnosed with any physical injury, disease, or mental condition which impairs your ability to practice medicine?" are legal because they directly relate the condition to an impairment of the ability to practice medicine. These kinds of questions have been criticized by some because they depend on self-assessment. Another type of question is "Have you ever been, or have you been told you are, personally or professionally impaired as a result of your medical, surgical or psychiatric condition other than substance abuse?" This question is problematic because it asks for an applicant's lifetime history of impairment. The American Psychiatric Association and the American Psychological Association have urged licensing boards to concentrate on the present condition of the applicant. Most states limit their questions to the past 5 or 10 years.

Questions that raise ADA issues but so far have not been challenged include questions about histories of hospitalization or institutionalization. Some states, such as New York, have voluntarily removed such questions, and others such as Massachusetts, never had them. Some states limit these questions to involuntary commitment. In addition, there are doubts about how far back in time questions can legally inquire. Generally, questions should ask about the present and not the past, about actual functioning and not about diagnosis or treatment, and about conduct and not conditions. There is no research showing any difference in the number of disciplinary cases attributed to mental illness as between states that ask for mental health information and states that do not.

Accommodations on the Medical Licensing Examination

Title III of the ADA specifically requires that "any person[170] that offers examinations or courses ... related to applications, licensing, certification, or credentialing for

... professional or trade purposes shall offer such examinations in a place and manner accessible to persons with disabilities."[171] The DOJ has implemented this requirement with two different sets of regulations: one for entities that offer examinations and the other for entities that offer courses. The regulation relating to entities that offer examinations may well be invalid because it substantially limits the scope of the statutory provision. Although the statutory language refers to accessibility of examinations for "people with disabilities," the implementing regulations related to examinations narrow the scope to individuals "with a disability that impairs sensory, manual or speaking skills,"[172] thus excluding all mental, psychiatric, and learning disabilities.[173] The companion regulations relating to "courses" contain no such limitations.[174] Both sets of regulations require the entities to provide appropriate auxiliary aids and services for people with disabilities. The DOJ sued Harcourt Brace, which owns the Bar-Bri preparatory course for the bar exam, for not making auxiliary aids and services available and for charging students with disabilities for the auxiliary aids and services that were available.[175] This litigation was recently settled.

Again, there has been far more litigation brought on behalf of applicants to the bar than applicants to the practice of medicine in the area of accommodations on the examination. Two cases have been brought in the area of accommodations on medical examinations: one settled favorably to the plaintiffs;[176] the other, *Price v. National Board of Medical Examiners*, was decided against the plaintiffs by the court.[177] First and foremost, those who rely on examinations should "be able to articulate what skills the exam is seeking to test, and if possible offer validation studies that the test actually accomplishes this goal."[178] It is not clear whether these validation studies have been done on the National Medical Examination.

Obstacles to Medical Licensure

Relatively few decisions to exclude an applicant from the practice of medicine on the basis of mental illness are appealed to courts. In one case,[179] the Medical Board of Colorado initially decided to exclude an applicant[180] for two reasons. First, it concluded that her ingestion of codeine in two suicide attempts, one 16 years prior to her application and the other 7 years prior to her application, constituted proof that she "engaged in an excessive use of drugs." Second, it concluded that she behaved unprofessionally in making numerous attempts to draw blood from a patient.[181] The court concurred with the board, finding that any past history of mental illness that rendered an applicant unable to perform medical services could be considered by the board in withholding a license to practice medicine. This case was not brought under the ADA, and the court's conclusions might be altered by application of the ADA.[182] Courts have found that it is discriminatory under the ADA to consider an applicant's history without any limitation as to relevant time periods.[183]

Accommodations While in Practice

The existing case law suggests that although doctors with physical disabilities tend to do well in litigation challenging the failure of hospitals to accommodate their disabilities,[184] physicians with disabilities that are "mental" or perceived to be "mental" uniformly lose their cases.[185]

Professional Discipline and the ADA

Disciplinary proceedings raise the most complex procedural questions in ADA cases involving the professions. These procedural issues include abstention, *res judicata*, and immunity.[186] Because professional disciplinary proceedings are state proceedings, federal courts are generally reluctant to intervene in them and often abstain.[187] Nothing in the ADA, however, precludes raising a discrimination claim based on the ADA in state court, and some doctors subject to professional discipline have appealed either the procedures of disciplinary boards or their sanctions, claiming that the boards have violated the ADA.

Doctors who attempt suicide or attempt to harm themselves are often women.[188] There is little evidence that these behaviors have an impact on their professional treatment of patients. No tolerance is shown them in disciplinary proceedings, however, and they are summarily dismissed from the practice of medicine. However, doctors who are alcoholics, substance abusers,[189] or who become sexually involved with their patients[190] are often men, and case law reveals extraordinary attempts by colleagues, hospitals, and sometimes by disciplinary boards to cover for these individuals.[191]

It is interesting to note that many of the cases involving professional discipline and the ADA were brought by women or minorities;[192] in one, *Alexander v. Margolis*, the plaintiff explicitly accused the medical boards of selective prosecution by race.[193] *Alexander* contains the most extreme language by any court, both equating psychiatric disability with danger and risk and granting disciplinary boards power to act without fear of discrimination litigation liability, if the "plaintiff's mental condition exposes the public to some measure of risk." The court found that the board was not only empowered but "duty bound" to consider his mental condition when deciding whether to reinstate the plaintiff's license.

The Power of Disciplinary Boards to Order Psychiatric Examinations

Almost every state in the country has a statute that provides as a condition of licensure to practice medicine that physicians must agree in advance to submit to a mental or physical examination if directed to do so by the licensing board.[194] In one case, a psychiatrist subject to such an examination challenged the statute, which permitted the Board of Medical Practice to require the examination if it had "probable cause to believe that a physician is unable to practice medicine with reasonable skill and safety to patients because of a mental or physical condition." The psychiatrist argued that the statute violated both the Constitution and the ADA.[195]

The court rejected both challenges. It found that the term "mental condition" was not unconstitutionally vague, although it conceded that the "legislature could have lessened the possibility of confusion by including a definition for the term 'mental condition.'" Most important, the court noted that the statute only "authorizes licensure inquiries in response to specific conduct; the central inquiry is whether the physician can practice medicine with reasonable skill and safety to patients. Humenansky's mental condition is only relevant if it precludes skillful and safe practice."[196]

If licensing or disciplinary boards only require mental or physical examinations when they have good cause to believe that substantial claims of specific conduct raise significant questions about a professional's ability to safely practice and if the examinations are narrowly tailored to achieve the purposes of the inquiry, then they are likely to be permissible under the ADA. Examinations should not be ordered solely on the basis of unsubstantiated claims or without considering other, less intrusive methods of inquiry.

Reporting Requirements

Does the ADA conflict with reporting requirements involving substance abuse? The limited case law suggests that the answer is no, even if the report turns out to be mistaken.[197] The decision is probably correct, although reached for the wrong reasons. In *Morgan v. NW Permanente, P.C.*, a professional was reported because the reporter believed he had alcohol on his breath, which he claimed was caused by his diabetes. The court held that the ADA was not violated because there was no showing of a reasonable accommodation that the reporter failed to offer. Of course, however, discrimination can occur without regard to requests for reasonable accommodations; indeed, that form of discrimination is the model with which we are most familiar. Rather, the ADA should not interfere with reporting requirements if the requirements only apply to situations in which the reporter has an objective basis for believing that the professional constitutes a direct threat to the health and safety of others. Presumably, professionals are not reported unless this is the case; frivolous or baseless reporting based on myths and stereotypes about psychiatric disabilities should be barred by the ADA.

Contingent Admission to Practice

In some cases, doctors receive their licenses on a conditional or probationary basis, usually contingent on completing a number of years of therapy. Whether these conditional admission programs violate the ADA or constitute reasonable accommodations under the ADA is an interesting question, which probably must be resolved on a case-by-case basis.[198] For example, in one case, a resident with a diagnosis of dyslexia and ADHD simply asked for accommodations in the third test of the U.S. Medical Licensing Examination and was ordered by the Board of Medicine to tell them what accommodations she would need to practice medicine and to submit to a complete psychiatric and physical examination, to determine if any "protections" for herself or the public were necessary before she was granted her license. She sued under the ADA, protesting that the board was attempting to impose "accommodations" on her that she did not want and for which she had not asked and that to do so was a form of segregation prohibited by the ADA.[199] Unfortunately, this case was dismissed on procedural grounds.[200] It might have served as the vehicle to remind states that the imposition of unwanted accommodations or special programs is specifically prohibited by the ADA.[201]

Revocation of Hospital Privileges

The threshold question to be resolved in cases challenging the denial of hospital privileges is whether they can be brought under the ADA at all. Courts are divided on this issue. The 6th Circuit has rejected such claims, reasoning that Title III, prohibiting discrimination by public accommodations, does not apply to employment claims; and that Title I, the employment title, does not apply to the revocation of hospital privileges because doctors are independent contractors of the hospital rather than its employees.[202] The 3rd Circuit has held that Title III does apply to revocation of hospital privileges,[203] and its approach appears more sensible. Congress expressly instructed that the ADA was to be interpreted as providing at least the same rights as the Rehabilitation Act, and the Rehabilitation Act has been interpreted to permit claims of discrimination based on the denial of hospital privileges.[204] In addition, the DOJ, which was entrusted by Congress with interpretation of Title III of the ADA, has taken a strong position that hospital privileges are covered by Title III and presented this position to the Court in *Menkowitz*. As the Court in *Menkowitz* noted, the ADA is a remedial statute, intended to be construed broadly for the protection of the citizens of this country.

Doctors depend on hospital privileges for their livelihood, yet hospitals do not use them in the sense intended by Title I of the ADA. If discriminatory denial of hospital privileges was not covered by Title III, then doctors could be denied their livelihood on a discriminatory basis without any protection from the ADA.

Conclusion

The first generation of children to have fully benefited from the requirements of the Education for all Handicapped Children Act (now the Individuals With Disabilities in Education Act[205]) graduated from college during the years that the ADA was passed and took effect. Although these children benefited from new understandings of disabilities and new teaching techniques at the primary and secondary level, they now aspire to education in universities and professional schools that may be reluctant to change their ways and resentful about being asked to do so.

Unless these institutions manifest egregious indifference or intentional discrimination, as in the cases of *Pushkin* and *Guckenberger*, courts have tended to be protective of institutional prerogatives and practices. There is a great need for high-quality research to parse out which educational assumptions and testing methods are supported and which are not, from the MCAT to multiple-choice examinations. The most important need in this area is for the DOJ, and Congress if necessary, to clarify that the appropriate comparison class in determining disability are people with equivalent skills, experience, and training and that exclusion from a profession such as law, medicine, or dentistry cannot be excused with the observation that other career paths remain open to a student. The *Bartlett* cases should be studied as model understandings of the meaning and interpretation of disability discrimination law in the context of professional education, testing, and accommodations.

In addition, the accommodations requested by students with learning disabilities and psychiatric disabilities tend to cause the greatest resentment. Just as in the area of employment, the accommodations requested by people with psychiatric disabilities are seen by other students as advantages they themselves could use. No one resents a sign language interpreter or Braille texts, but everyone wants extra time on an examination. To minimize student resentment, universities and professional schools must be careful to insist on a nexus between the disability and the requested accommodation and on careful documentation of the disability. In addition, further research and education would be useful to support existing data that extra time does not materially assist students without disabilities on examinations.

Those medical and law examiners that retain questions about mental health treatment should have to show the research on which they base their claims that these questions are relevant. Such questions discourage students from seeking needed mental health treatment and are clearly unnecessary, because a number of states do without them altogether. Examiners should also make public the standards by which they grant and refuse accommodations, so students have a better idea at the beginning of professional school whether they will receive accommodations on the bar or National Medical Examination. From the published cases, disciplinary boards seem to concentrate appropriately on conduct. Perhaps further research should be done to understand better the process by which these boards operate, but the published cases reveal little that appears alarming or discriminatory.

Endnotes

1. *See* chapters 1 and 2.
2. A recent study found lawyers to have the highest rate of depression among 104 occupational groups, William Eaton et al., "Occupations and the Prevalence of Major Depressive Disorder," *J. of Occup. Med.* 32 (1990):1079. See also Susan Daicoff, "Lawyer Know Thyself: A Review of Empirical Research on Attorney Attributes Bearing on Professionalism," *Amer. Univ. Law Rev.* 46 (1997):1337–1338; C. S. North and J. E. M. Ryall, "Psychiatric Illness in Female Physicians: Are High Rates of Depression an Occupational Hazard?" *Post Grad. Med.* 101 (1997):233, 240, 242.
3. In prohibiting discrimination on the basis of disability in any program or activity receiving federal financial assistance, the Rehabilitation Act specifically defines "program or activity" to include "all the operations" of "a college, university, or other postsecondary institution, or a public system of higher education"; 29 U.S.C. Sec. 794(b)(2)(A). Regulations specifically directed at postsecondary institutions are found at 34 C.F.R. Secs. 104.41–104.48.
4. That is why calls for education will never be as effective as calls for integration in ending discrimination. Reading, hearing, or studying about disability is no substitute for having a disabled person as a friend.
5. Richard Scotch, *From Good Will to Civil Rights: Transforming Federal Disability Policy* (Philadelphia: Temple University Press, 1984) at 100, 101.
6. People who were deaf, were blind, or had epilepsy complained of an outright denial of admission to school on the basis of their disability, statement of Janet M. Kyricos, A&P Comm. Print 1990 (28B)*1138–1139; these people were also asked to withdraw from school because of their disabilities, statement of Barbara Waters, A&P Comm. Print 1990 (28B)*1162–1163. One witness with a mobility impairment was denied admission to a dormitory, statement of Judy Heumann, A&P Comm. Print 1990 (28B)*1002–1003. Discrimination was also described in the form of total refusal of accommodations, statement of Denise Karuth, A&P Comm. Print 1990 (28B)*1227. In addition, people with mobility impairments complained of inaccessible buildings, statement of Mellissa Marshall, A&P Comm. Print 1990 (28B)*1103 (this disabled law student must enter the law

school through the back door and meet with deans in the Disabled Students Conference Area "where they keep the sports equipment," and the library is inaccessible); statement of Bonnie O'Day, A&P Comm. Print (1990) (28B)*1076 (recounting the death of a student in a wheelchair at the University of Virginia because of dangerous and inaccessible conditions); statement of Eric Griffin, A&P Comm. Print (1990) (28B)*1062 ("disability diaries" submitted included one stating that a man could not attend certain reunion activities at Middlebury College because they were inaccessible to him).

7. Statement of Eleanor Blake, A&P Comm. Print (1990) (28B)*1260.

8. Statement of Lawrence Urban, A&P Comm. Print (1990) (28B)*1234.

9. *See* chapter 1.

10. Survey No. 151 (the respondent, who is white, was admitted and "did very well academically").

11. Although public institutions of higher education are subject to Title II of the ADA and private institutions are subject to Title III of the ADA, and therefore complaints against them can be directed to the U.S. Department of Justice (DOJ), in practice, DOJ turns these complaints over to the U.S. Department of Education's Office of Civil Rights to investigate. The Office of Civil Rights has divided the country into regions for the purposes of investigating complaints of discrimination.

12. "College Officials Say Disability Complaints Will Continue to Rise," *Disability Compliance Bull.* 7(14) (May 9, 1996):1.

13. *Id.* at 5.

14. Although Section 504 of the Rehabilitation Act was passed in 1973, regulations implementing the prohibition against discrimination as to colleges, universities, and professional schools were not in place until 1979.

15. Southeastern Community College v. Davis, 442 U.S. 397 (1979), discussed further at p. 319; Camenisch v. University of Texas, 451 U.S. 390 (1981) (dismissing the challenge to a preliminary injunction ordering the university to provide accommodations to a disabled student as moot but remanding for trial as to whether the university would be obligated to pay the cost of the accommodations).

16. Section 504 of the Rehabilitation Act of 1973 applies to all entities receiving federal funds, which include virtually every college, university, and professional school in the country. Applicable regulations, first by the Department of Health, Education, and Welfare and then by the Department of Education, specifically address the obligations of institutions of higher education. Nevertheless, very few of these institutions took appreciable action until the passage of the ADA. As a matter of demographics, the first class of students whose entire school lives had been subject to the Education for All Handicapped Children Act (now the Individuals With Disabilities in Education Act) graduated from high school in 1988 and college in 1992, so the passage of the ADA coincided nicely with the first generation of disabled college and graduate school students with an understanding of their rights.

17. Jennifer Barrios, "Our Sixth Annual Roundup of Campus Activism," *Mother Jones* 24 (1999):20.

18. These agencies operate in every state by an act of Congress, dedicated to protecting and advocating for people with disabilities, people with mental retardation, and institutionalized or recently institutionalized people with diagnoses of mental illness. *See* Appendix B for more information.

19. Bob Fleischner, Center for Public Representation, Northampton, MA (personal communication, Oct. 16, 1998), on file with author.

20. O'Brien v. University of Massachusetts and Bay State Community Services, No. 94-CV-12094-RFK (D. Mass. 1995) (on file with author).

21. Doe v. New York University, 666 F.2d 761 (2nd Cir 1981); Doe v. Vanderbilt University,

1997 U.S. App. LEXIS 34104 (6th Cir. Nov. 26, 1987); Boyle v. Brown University, 881 F.Supp. 747 (D. R.I. 1995); Doe v. Harvard University, 1994 U.S. App. LEXIS 28320 (1st Cir. Oct. 12, 1994); Wynne v. Tufts University, 976 F.2d 791 (1st Cir 1992) (called "Wynne II").

22. Norris v. Seattle University School of Law, 112 F.3d 517, 1997 WL 205977 (9th Cir. Apr. 21, 1997) (a summary judgment was affirmed because there was no evidence in the record of the appellant's disability); Homola v. Southern Illinois University at Carbondale School of Law, 1995 U.S. App. LEXIS 4204 (7th Cir. Mar. 1, 1995) (dismissed suit on *res judicata* grounds); Mallet v. Marquette University, 65 F.3d 170 (7th Cir. Aug. 25, 1995) (table case), 1995 U.S. App. LEXIS 24324.

23. Fetik v. New York University Law School, 1998 WL 651044 (S.D. N.Y. Sept. 23, 1998) (the dismissal of ADA and Rehabilitation Act claims on the basis that the plaintiff did not allege she had an impairment); Kenyon v. Hastings College of Law, 1997 WL 732525 (N.D. Ca. Nov. 13, 1997) (the rejection of the plaintiff's claim that he was fraudulently induced to abandon his previous ADA–Rehabilitation Act claims); Scott v. Western State University College of Law, 112 F.3d 517, 1997 WL 207599, 10 N.D.L.R. 38 (9th Cir. Apr. 21, 1997) (the summary judgment was affirmed when the law school did not know of the appellant's disability at the time he was dismissed for failing to maintain the required grade point average; additionally finding that the law school was not required to lower its standards to accommodate a person with a disability); Aloia v. New York Law School, 1998 WL 80236 (S.D. N.Y. July 27, 1988) (a summary judgment was granted because the law school was not aware of the student's disability and requiring a 2.0 grade point average is a reasonable requirement); Anderson v. University of Wisconsin, 841 F.2d 737 (7th Cir. 1988).

24. DeAngelis v. Widener University School of Law et al., No. 97-6254, 11 N.D.L.R. 272 (E.D. Pa. Jan. 13, 1998) (ADA and Rehabilitation Act claims were barred by the statute of limitations); McGregor v. Louisiana State University Board of Supervisors, 3 F.3d 850 (5th Cir. 1993), *cert. denied,* 510 U.S. 1131 (1994); Robinson v. Hamline University, 1994 WL 175019 (Minn. App. May 10, 1994).

25. Rothman v. Emory University, 123 F.3d 446 (7th Cir. 1997).

26. *Id.*; Martin v. Widener University School of Law, 625 F.Supp. 1288 (D. Del. 1985), *aff'd,* 884 F.2d 1384 (3rd Cir. 1989).

27. Redlich v. Albany Law School, 899 F.Supp. 100 (N.D. N.Y. 1995) (the professor did not establish that he was disabled under the Rehabilitation Act).

28. Ellis v. Morehouse School of Medicine, 925 F.Supp. 1529 (N.D. Ga. 1996); Lewin v. Medical College of Hampton Roads, 910 F.Supp. 1161 (E.D. Va. 1996); Boyle v. Brown University, 881 F.Supp. 747 (D. R.I. 1995) (the claims of the plaintiff with chronic fatigue syndrome were brought before the effective date of the ADA, and the court was unwilling to consider a Rehabilitation Act claim when it was not mentioned in her complaint); Wolsky v. Medical College of Hampton Roads, 1 F.3d 222 (4th Cir. 1993), *cert den.,* 510 U.S. 1073 (1994) (the claim of the medical student with panic disorder under the Rehabilitation Act was barred by a 1-year statue of limitations); Baker v. University of Kansas Medical School, 991 F.2d 628 (10th Cir. 1993) (the Rehabilitation Act claim was barred by a 2-year statute of limitations); Wynne v. Tufts University School of Medicine, 976 F.2d 791 (1st Cir. 1992); Nathanson v. Medical College of Pennsylvania, 926 F.2d 1368 (3rd Cir. 1991); Doe v. Vanderbilt University, 1997 U.S. App. LEXIS 34104 (6th Cir. Nov. 26, 1997) (the appeals of the student with bipolar disorder were dismissed); Repp v. Oregon Health Sciences University, 972 F.Supp. 546 (D. Ore. 1997) (the disability was not disclosed in the decision that dismissed a complaint on the statute of limitations grounds); Betts v. Rectors of the University of Virginia, 967 F.Supp. 882 (W.D. Va. 1997); Leacock v. Temple University School of Medicine, 1998 U.S. Dist. LEXIS 18871 (E.D. Pa. Nov. 27, 1998) (dismissed in part on the grounds of the expiration of the statute of limitations).

29. Lee v. Trustees of Dartmouth College, 958 F.Supp. 37 (D. N.H. 1997) (refusing to grant summary judgment for the defendant when there were material issues of fact as to whether the defendant had perceived the plaintiff as being disabled and discriminated against him on that basis); Sherman v. State of Washington, 905 P.2d 355 (Washington 1996) (*en banc*) (reversing lower court's grant of summary judgment in favor of the plaintiff and remanding for trial); Doe v. University of Maryland Medical System Corporation, 50 F.3d 1261 (4th Cir. 1995) (upholding the termination of the neurosurgical resident who was HIV positive); Roth v. Lutheran General Hospital, 57 F.3d 1446 (7th Cir. 1995); Pushkin v. Board of Regents of Colorado, 658 F.2d 1372 (10th Cir. 1981).

30. Ohio Civil Rights Commission v. Case Western, 666 N.E.2d 1376 (Ohio 1996). In another case, an applicant who used a wheelchair and was impaired in the use of his hands and arms was turned down by a medical school, although he indicated that he wished to practice psychiatry, Thomas Jefferson University, Complaint No. 03-90-2049, *N.D. Law Rev.* 1 (Nov. 30, 1990):229 (the determination of the Office of Civil Rights, U.S. Department of Education). There are, by contrast, blind law students, blind lawyers, and even an association of blind judges as well as mobility impaired and quadriplegic law students and lawyers. In their first Rehabilitation Act case decision, the U.S. Supreme Court found that the exclusion of a hearing-impaired nurse from nursing school was proper, Southeastern Community College v. Davis, 442 U.S. 397 (1979). By contrast, there are deaf lawyers and deaf law school professors, although deaf students have had to sue law schools to obtain accommodations, see Lisa Green Markoff, "One Disabled Student's Lawsuit Sheds Light on Issues of Access," *Natl. J.* 12(12) (Dec. 4, 1989):4. The same is true of students with mobility impairment.

31. Gertler v. Goodgold, 487 N.Y.S.2d 565 (Sup. Ct. App. Div. 1995); Wagner v. Texas A&M University, 939 F.Supp. 1297 (S.D. Tx. 1996); Esfahani v. Medical College of Pennsylvania, 919 F.Supp. 832 (E.D. Pa. 1996).

32. *See* the saga of Martin v. Widener University School of Law, 625 F.Supp. 1288 (D. Del. 1985), *aff'd*, 884 F.2d 1384 (3rd Cir. 1989), *cert. den.*, 110 S.Ct. 422, *reh'g denied*, 110 S.Ct. 766 (1990); Martin v. Pennsylvania Board of Bar Examiners, No. C-86-1363 (E.D. Pa. June 19, 1986); Martin v. Widener University School of Law, No. 88-0768 (D.D.C. July 22, 1988); Martin v. Walmer, 1990 WL 145759 (E.D. Pa. Sept. 26, 1990); Martin v. Delaware Law School of Widener University; Martin v. Widener University School of Law, 1992 WL 153540 (Sup. Ct. New Castle County June 17, 1992). As a review of these cases indicates, this list does not begin to exhaust the actual number of cases filed by Martin.

33. In re Underwood, 1993 WL 649283 (Supreme Judicial Ct. Me. Dec. 7, 1993); In re Application of Frickey, 515 N.W.2d 741 (Minn. 1994); Campbell v. Greisberger, 80 F.3d 703 (2nd Cir. 1996); Ellen S. v. Florida Board of Bar Examiners, 859 F.Supp. 1489 (S.D. Fla. 1994); Applicants v. Texas State Board of Law Examiners, 1994 WL 923404 (W.D. Tx. Oct. 11, 1994).

34. Medical Society of New Jersey v. Jacobs, 1993 WL 413016 (D. N.J. Oct. 5, 1993).

35. Pat Doe v. Judicial Nominating Commission of the 15th Judicial District of Florida, 906 F.Supp. 1534 (S.D. Fla. 1995).

36. Bartlett v. New York State Board of Law Examiners 156 F.3d 321 (2nd Cir.), *vac. and remanded,* 119 S.Ct. 2388 (1999); D'Amico v. New York State Board of Law Examiners, 813 F.Supp. 217 (W.D. N.Y. 1993) (visual impairment); Christian v. New York State Board of Law Examiners, 1994 WL 62797 (S.D. N.Y. Feb. 23, 1994) (dyslexia and dysgraphia); Argen v. New York State Board of Law Examiners, No. 93-CV-586H (W.D. N.Y. Aug. 11, 1994) (learning disability); Pazer v. New York State Board of Law Examiners, 849 F.Supp. 284 (S.D. N.Y. 1994); Fowler v. New York State Board of Law Examiners, 885 F.Supp. 66 (W.D. N.Y. 1994); Price v. National Board of Medical Ex-

aminers, 966 F.Supp. 419 (S.D. W.Va. 1997); Kotz v. Florida Board of Medicine, 33 F.Supp. 2d 1019 (M.D. Fla. 1998); Doe v. National Board of Medical Examiners, 199 F.3d 146 (3rd Cir. 1999); Clement v. Virginia Board of Law Examiners, 1997 U.S. App. LEXIS 27951 (4th Cir. Oct. 10, 1997).

37. Landefeld v. Marion General Hospital, 994 F.2d 1178 (6th Cir. 1993); Judice v. Hospital Serv. Dist. No. 1, *N.D. Law Rev.* 7 (E.D. La. 1996):458 (alcoholism); Altman v. New York City Health and Hospitals Corp., 100 F.3d 1054 (2nd Cir. 1996); *see also* Doe v. Maryland Medical System Corp., 50 F.3d 1261 (4th Cir. 1995) (the resident with HIV was permanently suspended from surgical practice).

38. Ramachandar v. Sobol, 5 AD Cases 295 (1993); Alexander v. Margolis, 921 F.Supp. 482 (W.D. Mich. 1995); Doe v. Connecticut, 75 F.3d 81 (2nd Cir. 1995).

39. Witter v. Delta Airlines, 138 F.3d 1366 (11th Cir. 1998); Bullwinkel v. U.S. Department of Transportation, 787 F.2d 254 (7th Cir. 1986) (National Transportation Safety Board decision was affirmed by a 7th Circuit court; there were no attorney's fees charged under the Equal Access to Justice Act).

40. Esfahani v. Medical College of Pennsylvania, 919 F.Supp. 832 (E.D. Pa. 1996).

41. Carl Baer and Peg Corneille, "Character and Fitness Inquiry: From Bar Admission to Professional Discipline," *The Bar Examiner* 61 (Nov. 1992).

42. Robert A. Brazener, "Validity and Application of Regulations Requiring Suspension or Disbarment of Attorney Because of Mental or Emotional Illness," 50 A.L.R.3d 1259 (1996).

43. The individual licensing decisions of these authorities cannot be challenged in federal court because of the Rooker–Feldman doctrine, which precludes a challenge of a final state court determination in federal court, Rooker v. Fidelity Trust Co., 263 U.S. 413 (1923), and District of Columbia Court of Appeals v. Feldman, 460 U.S. 462 (1983).

44. *See, e.g.,* Kotz v. Florida Board of Medical Examiners, 33 F.Supp. 2d 1019 (M.D. Fla. 1998).

45. 28 U.S.C. Sec. 35.104 (under definition of *disability*), Title II; 28 C.F.R. Sec. 36.104 (under the definition of *disability*), Title III.

46. *See* Price v. National Board of Medical Examiners, 966 F.Supp. 419 (S.D. W.Va. 1997); Bartlett v. New York Board of Law Examiners, 970 F.Supp. 1094 (S.D. N.Y. 1997), *aff'd* in major part on other grounds, 156 F.3d 321 (2nd Cir. 1998), *vac. and remanded,* 119 S.Ct. 2388 (June 24, 1999). *See* Kevin H. Smith, "Disabilities, Law Schools, and Law Students, *Akron Law Rev.* 32 (1999):1.

47. 28 C.F.R., Pt. 35, App. A (interpretation of "substantial limitation of a major life activity").

48. Webb v. Garelick Manufacturing Co., 94 F.2d 484, 487 (8th Cir. 1996); *see* 29 C.F.R. Sec. 1630.2(j)(3)(i). This regulation by the Equal Employment Opportunity Commission has been held by some courts to be relevant in Title II cases, Bartlett v. New York Board of Law Examiners, 2 F.Supp. 3d 388 (S.D. N.Y. 1998).

49. Lee v. Trustees of Dartmouth College, 958 F.Supp. 37, 42 (D. N.H. 1997); McGuinness v. University of New Mexico School of Medicine, 170 F.3d 974 (10th Cir. 1998).

50. Several courts either have held that reading is a major life activity, Barlett v. New York Board of Law Examiners, 156 F.3d 321, 324, 328, note 3 (2nd Cir. 1998), *vac.* on other grounds, 527 U.S. 1031 (1999); Sweet v. Electronic Data Systems, 1996 U.S. Dist. LEXIS 5544*16 (S.D. N.Y. Apr. 26, 1996), or have implied that it is, Pridemore v. Rural Legal Aid Society, 625 F.Supp. 1180, 1184 (S.D. Ohio 1985) (a Rehabilitation Act case). In at least one case, the defendant conceded that reading is a major life activity for purposes of a motion for summary judgment, Gonzalez v. National Board of Medical Examiners, 60 F.Supp. 2d 703, 707 (E.D. Mich. 1999).

51. Taylor v. Phoenixville School Dist., 184 F.3d 296, 307 (3rd Cir. 1999); Herbst v. General Accident Insurance Co., 1999 U.S. Dist. LEXIS 15807 (E.D. Pa. Sept. 30, 1999); *but*

see Pack v. Kmart Corp., 166 F.3d 1300 (10th Cir. 1999) (concentration was considered not a major life activity).

52. *See* note 45. Because the 2nd Circuit held that the plaintiff's self-accommodation need not be considered in determining whether she was disabled, the Supreme Court vacated *Bartlett,* 119 S.Ct. 2388 (June 24, 1999), in the light of its decision that mitigating medications and devices must be considered in determining disability under the ADA, *see* Sutton v. United Airlines 119 S.Ct. 2139 (June 22, 1999). The issue under discussion in this section—what the relevant field of comparison should be in defining disability in a professional setting—is very different from and was not discussed or decided by the Supreme Court in *Sutton.*

53. 966 F.Supp. 419 (S.D. W.Va. 1997).

54. The regulations of the EEOC require that substantial limitations in other life activities be considered before considering whether an individual is substantially limited in working, 29 C.F.R. Pt. 1630, App. at 1630.2(j) ("If an individual is not substantially limited with respect to any other major life activity, the individual's ability to perform the major life activity of working should be considered"). Although DOJ regulations provide that EEOC regulations are followed as to employment discrimination cases brought under Title II, 28 C.F.R. Sec. 35.140(b)(1), it is unclear whether this structure governs in a nonemployment case. Nevertheless, both the district court and the court of appeals followed this method of analysis in *Bartlett.*

55. D'Amico v. New York State Board of Law Examiners, 813 F.Supp. 217 (W.D. N.Y. 1993); Christian v. New York State Board of Law Examiners, 1994 WL 62797 (S.D. N.Y. Feb. 24, 1994); Argen v. New York State Board of Law Examiners, No 93-CV-586H (W.D. N.Y. Aug. 11, 1994); Pazer v. New York State Board of Law Examiners, 849 F.Supp. 284 (S.D. N.Y. 1994); Bartlett v. New York State Board of Law Examiners, 156 F.3d 321 (2nd Cir. 1998); Fowler v. New York State Board of Law Examiners, 885 F.Supp. 66 (W.D. N.Y. 1994). Considering that the Florida Board of Bar Examiners asked to raise the application fee for taking the bar after litigating only one major case, *see* Florida Board of Bar Examiners Re: Amendments to the Rules of the Supreme Court of Florida Relating to Admissions to the Bar, 676 S.2d 372, 392 (Fla. 1996) ("other higher than expected expenses included the costs associated with compliance with the Americans with Disabilities Act . . . the significant costs associated with federal ADA litigation"), one can only surmise who is actually paying for the cost of litigating these New York cases.

56. A number of other courts have held that an individual's self-accommodations (although not denominating them as such) should not be considered in determining disability. In one case, a court found that the unconscious adjustments of the brain after a policeman lost sight in one eye that enabled him to visually compensate did not mean he was not disabled. In another case, the conscious adaptations of a man with only one arm should not be considered in determining disability, Doane v. City of Omaha, 115 F.3d 624 (8th Cir. 1997).

57. *See* Jean Campbell and Caroline L. Kaufman, "Equality and Difference in the ADA: Unintended Consequences for Employment of People With Mental Health Disabilities," in *Mental Disorder, Work·Disability and the Law*, Richard Bonnie and John D. Monahan, Eds. (Chicago: University of Chicago Press, 1997) at 230.

58. *Id.* (quoting a blind man, "people frequently say, 'I don't consider you disabled.' That's because I make accommodations to my disability. . . . I'm accommodating all the time, but they don't know it or realize it").

59. 119 S.Ct. 2133 (June 22, 1999).

60. 966 F.Supp. 419 (S.D. W.Va. 1997).

61. *Id.* at 427.

62. Betts v. Rectors of the University of Virginia, 1999 U.S. App. LEXIS 23105 (4th Cir.

Sept. 22, 1999); Gonzalez v. National Board of Medical Examiners, 60 F.Supp. 2d 703 (E.D. Mich. 1999).

63. This fits with Deborah Piltcher's explanation of the two myths that licensing boards subscribe to about people with learning disabilities: They are not bright enough to pass the pertinent examination, or they are simply slow readers without impairments, Deborah Piltcher et al., "The ADA and Professional Licensing," *Mental and Physical Disability Law Reporter* 17 (Sept.–Oct. 1993):556, 558.

64. Betts v. Rectors of the University of Virginia (1999).

65. Imagine that the NCAA forbade all swimmers to use inhalers that enable patients with asthma to breathe. Under the *Price* court's reasoning, Tom Dolan, the swimmer with asthma who won the gold medal at the 1996 Olympics, would not be allowed to protest this rule, even though it discriminated on the basis of disability because without the inhaler, he is still a very good swimmer. Using the inhaler to overcome his asthma enabled him to swim to his true potential and win a gold medal.

66. Bartlett v. New York State Board of Law Examiners, 2 F.Supp. 2d 388 (S.D. N.Y. 1998).

67. Pacella v. Tufts University, 1999 U.S. Dist. LEXIS 14781 (D. Mass. Sept. 21, 1999).

68. McGuinness v. University of New Mexico School of Medicine, 170 F.3d 974, 979 (10th Cir. 1998).

69. The New York Board of Law Examiners acknowledged that the New York Bar does not seek to test, *see* Bartlett v. New York Board of Law Examiners, 156 F.3d 321 (2nd Cir. 1998).

70. Thus, I believe that the district court judge in *Bartlett* erred when she distinguished *Price* by saying that the medical students were claiming a learning disability as opposed to a reading disability, thus posing the question of whether they could learn as well or better than the general population. ADHD affects one's ability to focus and concentrate, which does impede learning but whose obstacle to learning was not necessarily at issue in *Price*. By the time one is taking an examination, the time for learning the material is over. The question was whether disabilities in concentration and focus would block accurate measurement of what the students had learned, just as whether Bartlett's disability in reading would impede accurate measurement of what she had learned.

71. *See* Ellen S. v. Florida Board of Bar Examiners 859 F.Supp. 1489 (S.D. Fla. 1994); Pat Doe v. Judicial Nominating Commission of the 15th Judicial District of Florida, 906 F.Supp. 1534 (S.D. Fla. 1995).

72. The abstention doctrine is a generally discretionary doctrine that counsels federal courts to exercise caution in deciding cases that may interfere with the states' abilities to exercise their sovereignty. There are three kinds of abstention: Younger abstention, Pullman abstention, and Burford abstention. Younger abstention states that a federal court may not enjoin ongoing state proceedings. It is generally applicable to criminal proceedings but has been held applicable to certain civil proceedings. Defendants successfully invoked Younger abstention in disciplinary proceedings against the doctor in Doe v. Connecticut, 75 F.3d 81 (1st Cir. 1996), and in a challenge to a Board of Medical Examiner's insistence that the doctor asking for accommodations for ADHD pay for a full psychiatric examination, Kotz v. Fla. Board of Medicine, 33 F.Supp. 2d 1019 (M.D. Fla. 1998); *see also* Campbell v. Greisberger, 865 F.Supp. 115 (W.D. N.Y. 1994) (implying abstention concerns). Pullman abstention counsels federal courts against deciding cases that raise novel issues of state laws that have not been construed by state courts; if the federal court can defer to a state court construction of its own statute, that might be preferred. Burford abstention is invoked when the exercise of federal jurisdiction would cause needless and avoidable conflict with important state polices and the states have provided a method for judicial review of the policies or decisions being challenged.

73. The Rooker–Feldman doctrine is a nondiscretionary mandate that a federal court may not properly review a final state court decision on merits. The federal courts are not

supposed to act as appellate courts for state decisions. Thus, individual decisions by boards of bar and medical examiners to deny individuals a license to practice are not reviewable by federal courts, although the general policies and practices of the boards are subject to such review; Dale v. Moore, 121 F.3d 624 (11th Cir. 1997); Johnson v. Kansas, 888 F.Supp. 1073 (D. Kan. 1995). A court has also used the Rooker–Feldman doctrine inappropriately to deny the review of the final decision by the university, Childress v. Clement, 5 F.Supp. 2d 384 (E.D. Va. 1998), whose decisions are not equivalent to state court decisions.

74. D'Amico v. New York State Board of Law Examiners, 813 F.Supp. 217 (W.D. N.Y. 1993); Ellis v. Morehouse School of Medicine, 925 F.Supp. 1529 (N.D. Ga. 1996).

75. Regents of the University of Michigan v. Ewing, 474 U.S. 214, 225 (1985). It is interesting to contemplate that the standard originally devised for due process challenges to decisions of the administrators of mental institutions was transferred with hardly any change in the wording to the academic setting. For a critique of the importation of this standard into due process law involving higher education, *see* Susan Stefan, "Leaving Civil Rights to the Experts: From Deference to Abdication Under the Professional Judgment Standard," *Yale Law J.*, 102 (1992):639.

76. *See* Pushkin v. Board of Regents of the University of Colorado (rejecting the defendants' suggestion to use the "rational basis" test in a Rehabilitation Act case); Bangerter v. City of Orem, 46 F.3d 1491, 1503 (10th Cir. 1995) (rejecting the defendant's suggestion to use the "rational basis" test in a Fair Housing Act case).

77. *Wynne*, 932 F.2d at 25.

78. Pushkin v. Board of Regents of the University of Colorado, 658 F.2d 1372, 1383 (10th Cir. 1981).

79. Ellis v. Morehouse, 925 F.Supp. 1529 (N.D. Ga. 1996); Doherty v. Southern College of Optometry, 862 F.2d 570 (6th Cir. 1988); *see also* Robinson v. Hamline University, 1994 WL 175019*4 (Minn. App. May 10, 1994) (finding that the defendant "presented undisputed facts demonstrating that it had rationally exercised professional judgment").

80. Wynne v. Tufts University, 932 F.2d 19 (1st Cir. 1991); Doe v. New York University, 666 F.2d 761 (2nd Cir. 1981); McGregor v. Louisiana State University Board of Supervisors, 3 F.3d 850 (5th Cir. 1993); Zukle v. University of California Board of Regents, 166 F.3d 1041 (9th Cir. 1999); Wong v. Board of Regents of the University of California, 1999 U.S. App. LEXIS 22353 (9th Cir. Sept. 16, 1999). The 10th Circuit ruled that the decisions of a university and graduate school are not entitled to deference when challenged as discriminatory under Section 504 of the Rehabilitation Act, Pushkin v. Board of Regents of the University of Colorado, 658 F.2d 1372 (10th Cir. 1981).

81. Guckenberger v. Boston University, 974 F.Supp. 106 (D. Mass. 1997); Wong v. Board of Regents of the University of California, 1999 U.S. App. LEXIS 22353 (9th Cir. Sept. 16, 1999) (the institution was not entitled to deference when the dean made the decision without conducting an inquiry into the proposed accommodation and whether it was feasible to implement and without learning about the nature of the student's disability or discussing the issue with the disability services coordinator on campus).

82. Guckenberger v. Boston University, 8 F.Supp. 2d at 82, 89.

83. D'Amico v. New York Board of Law Examiners, 813 F.Supp. 217 (W.D. N.Y. 1993); Bartlett v. New York State Board of Law Examiners, 156 F.3d 321 (2nd Cir. 1998), *vac.* and *remanded* on other grounds, 119 S.Ct. 2388 (1999); *but see* Doe v. Connecticut, 75 F.3d 81 (2nd Cir. 1995) (implying that disciplinary boards should be granted deference in abstention context).

84. *D'Amico, id.*; *Bartlett, id.*

85. *D'Amico, id.*

86. Pat Doe v. Judicial Nominating Commission, 906 F.Supp. 1534 (S.D. Fla. 1995).

87. Kay Redfield Jamison, *An Unquiet Mind: A Memoir of Moods and Madness* (New York: Vintage Books, 1995) at 204–206.

88. 34 C.F.R. Sec. 104.42(b)(4).

89. 34 C.F.R. Sec. 104.42 (c).

90. 34 C.F.R. Sec. 104.42(b)(2).

91. 34 C.F.R. Sec. 104.42(d).

92. In re SUNY Health Science Center at Brooklyn, Complaint No. 02-92-2004, 5 N.D.L.R. 77 (Aug. 18, 1993) (Office of Civil Rights, U.S. Department of Education).

93. *Id.*

94. In re University of Massachusetts Medical Center, Complaint No. 01-93-2051, 4 N.D.L.R. 314 (Aug. 6, 1993) (U.S. Department of Education, Office of Civil Rights).

95. *Id.*

96. *See, e.g.,* Kristan S. Mayer, "Flagging Non-Standard Test Scores in Admissions to Institutions of Higher Education," *Stanford Law Rev.* 50 (1998):469. *See also* Joseph Slobodzian, "Disabled Test-Takers and LSAC Reach Agreement on Readers," *Natl. J.* 20(15) (Dec. 8, 1997) ("Unresolved by the settlement, but left open to further negotiations between the LSAC [Law School Admissions Council] and NFB [National Federation of the Blind] officials, is the council's policy of notifying law schools that the blind or visually impaired require extra time or special accommodations when taking exams").

97. Robert C. Davidson and Ernest L. Lewis, "Affirmative Action and Other Special Consideration Admissions at University of California, Davis, School of Medicine," *J. of the Amer. Med. Assn.* 278(14) (Oct. 8, 1997):1153–1154.

98. *Id.* at 1155–1157.

99. 34 C.F.R. Sec. 104.44. This regulation applies to all postsecondary education.

100. *Southeastern Community College,* 442 U.S. 397, at 413, note 12. (1979).

101. *Id.* at 412–413.

102. 42 U.S.C. Sec. 12182(b)(2)(A)(i).

103. 42 U.S.C. Sec. 12182(b)(2)(A)(ii) and (iii).

104. The Section 504 regulations include as examples of accommodations varying the length of time permitted to complete degree requirements, substitution of specific courses required to complete a degree, adaptation of the manner in which specific courses are conducted, taped texts, and readers in libraries; note that neither taping in class nor guide dogs may be prohibited to disabled students, 34 C.F.R. Sec. 104.44(A),(B), and (C). Title III regulations include as examples of reasonable accommodations to be provided by public accommodations "qualified interpreters, notetakers, computer-aided transcription services, written materials, telephone handset amplifiers, assistive listening devices, assistive listening systems, telephones compatible with hearing aids, closed caption decoders, open and closed captioning, telephone devices for deaf persons (TDDs), videotext displays, . . . qualified readers, taped texts, audio recordings, Brailled materials, [and] large print materials," 28 C.F.R. Sec. 36.303(b)(1) and (2). Accommodations actually offered to students with disabilities are even more varied.

105. Guckenberger v. Boston University, 974 F.Supp. 106 (D. Mass. 1997); *see also* Wynne v. Tufts Medical School, 932 F.2d at 25.

106. Guckenberger, *id.*

107. Wynne sued Tufts University in 1988. The district court granted summary judgment for Tufts on the basis of a single affidavit by the Dean of Tufts. A panel of the 1st Circuit reversed the original decision, the panel's decision was vacated, and the case was considered by the 1st Circuit, 932 F.2d 19 (1st Cir. 1991) (*en banc*), which vacated and remanded on different grounds than the original panel decision. On remand, the district court once again awarded summary judgment to Tufts on an expanded record. This decision was affirmed by a 1st Circuit panel, which included two judges who would have upheld the district court's granting of summary judgment in the first place, 976 F.2d 791 (1st Cir. 1992).

108. Guckenberger v. Boston University, 974 F.Supp. 106, 115 (D. Mass. 1997).

109. Wynne v. Tufts University, 976 F.2d 791, 794–795 (1st Cir. 1992); McGregor v. Louisiana State University, 3 F.3d 850, 860 (5th Cir. 1993).

110. *Id.* at 115, 140.

111. *Id.*

112. *Id.* at 115.

113. Kaltenberger v. Ohio College of Podiatric Medicine, 162 F.3d 432 (6th Cir. 1998).

114. Wynne v. Tufts University, 976 F.2d 791 (1st Cir. 1992); Betts v. Rectors of the University of Virginia, 1999 U.S. App. LEXIS 23105 (4th Cir. Sept. 22, 1999) (the defendant conceded double time is a reasonable accommodation); Zukle v. Board of Regents, U.S. 166 F.3d 1041 (9th Cir. 1999); McGregor v. Louisiana State University Board of Supervisors, 3 F.3d 850, 855 (5th Cir. 1993).

115. Ellis v. Morehouse, 925 F.Supp. 1529 (N.D. Ga. 1996); Herdman v. University of Illinois, 1998 U.S. Dist. LEXIS 17447 (N.D. Ill. Oct. 28, 1998).

116. Initially, Wynne failed 8 of 15 courses. He was permitted to repeat these courses and passed all but 2. He took makeup exams on those 2 and passed 1 of them. The remaining course was the biochemistry course that became the focus of the litigation.

117. *See* discussion *supra* at pp. 315–316.

118. Wynne, 932 F.2d 19, 28 (1st Cir 1991).

119. *Id.* at 30.

120. Kaltenberger v. Ohio College of Podiatric Medicine, 162 F.3d 432 (6th Cir. 1998); Robinson v. Hamline University, 1994 WL 175019*4 (Minn. App. May 10, 1994).

121. Wynne, 932 F.2d 19, 28 (1st Cir. 1991).

122. Kaltenberger, 162 F.3d at 432.

123. *Id.*; Wynne v. Tufts University, 976 F.2d 791, 795 (1st Cir. 1992).

124. Wynne v. Tufts University, 976 F.2d 791, 795 (1st Cir. 1992).

125. Kaltenberger, 162 F.3d at 432.

126. McGregor v. Louisiana State University Board of Supervisors, 3 F.3d 850, 856 (5th Cir. 1993).

127. Herdman v. University of Illinois, 1998 U.S. Dist. LEXIS 17447 (N.D. Ill. Oct. 28, 1998); Wong v. Board of Regents of University of California, 1999 U.S. App. LEXIS 22353 (9th Cir. Sept. 16, 1999).

128. *McGregor* at 856. Students taking longer examinations and students with diabetes are also routinely permitted to bring food and drink with them into an examination.

129. *Cf.* Robinson v. Hamline University, 1994 WL 175019*4 (Minn. App. May 10, 1994), with O'Brien v. University of Massachusetts and Bay State Community Services, No. 94-CV-12094 C.F.R. (D. Ma. 1995) (the training program dismissed the student immediately on discovering her diagnosis of multiple personality disorder) (the case was settled after the adverse district court's decision on the defendant's motion to dismiss and for summary judgment).

130. *See* chapter 2 for a discussion on discrimination manifesting itself through a minimizing of a person's symptoms and struggles. This kind of discrimination is felt by people who are perceived as successful in the world.

131. *See* the discussion later for litigation to prevent bar examiners from asking questions about mental health treatment.

132. Sutton v. United Airlines, 119 S.Ct. 2139 (June 22, 1999).

133. Boyle v. Brown University, 881 F.Supp. 747 (DRI 1995), *aff'd,* 70 F.3d 110 (1st Cir 1995) (table case).

134. *Id.* at 749.

135. Doe v. New York University, 666 F.2d 761 (2nd Cir. 1981).

136. This discussion is largely taken from Susan Stefan, "Impact of the Law on Women With Diagnosis of Borderline Personality Disorder Related to Childhood Sexual Abuse," in *Women's Mental Health Services: A Public Health Perspective,* Bruce Levin, Andrea Blanch, and Ann Jennings, Eds. (Thousand Oaks, CA: Sage, 1998) at 263–268.

137. Although the court of appeals found that New York University "was entitled, in determining whether she was qualified, to be advised of and to take into account her mental impairment," *id.* at 777, the U.S. Department of Education's Office of Civil Rights and the regulations governing Section 504 indicated that an institution of higher education cannot ask about disabilities or histories of disabilities on their applications, 34 C.F.R. Sec. 104.42 (b)(4).

138. Doe v. New York University (1981).

139. *Id.*

140. *Id.*

141. *Id.* (deletion in original).

142. *Id.*

143. *Id.* at 768.

144. Doe v. New York University, No. 77-Civ-6285 (GLG) (S.D. N.Y. Oct. 2, 1981).

145. *Id.*

146. *Id.* at 778.

147. *Id.* at 779.

148. *Id.* at 777. The district court more perceptively noted that if Doe were a danger, it would be to herself or to authority figures, not to her fellow students or her patients.

149. *Id.*

150. There is a significant correlation between self-injurious behavior of the type exhibited by Doe and a history of sexual abuse, *see* Heather Y. Swanston, Jennifer S. Tebbutt, et al., "Sexually Abused Children 5 Years After Presentation: A Case-Control Study," *Pediatrics* 100 (Oct. 1997):600; B. A. Vanderkolk, J. C. Perry, and J. L. Herman, "Childhood Origins of Self-Destructive Behavior," *Amer. J. of Psychiatry* 148 (1991):1665.

151. Doe v. New York University at 767.

152. *See* "Medical Testing Board Settles Suit by Granting Accommodation," *Disability Compliance Bull.* 10(1) (June 19, 1997):7. The lawsuit was brought by Equip for Equality, the Illinois Protection and Advocacy Agency.

153. Ferrell v. Howard University, 1999 U.S. Dist. LEXIS 20900 (D.D.C. Dec. 2, 1999).

154. Pushkin v. Regents of the University of Colorado, 658 F.2d 1372 (10th Cir. 1981).

155. *Pushkin* has been cited 678 times, with only a few courts questioning its holdings. In addition, Congress cited *Pushkin* with approval in the legislative history, Senate Labor and Human Resources Rep. at 45; House Committee on Education and Labor, Rep. No. 101-485 (Pt. II) at 85.

156. *Pushkin*, 658 F.2d at 1386.

157. *Id.* at 1387.

158. *Id.*

159. *Id.*

160. Bartlett v. New York State Board of Law Examiners 156 F.3d 321 (2nd Cir. 1998), *vac.* and *remanded,* 119 S.Ct. 2388 (1999); D'Amico v. New York State Board of Law Examiners, 813 F.Supp. 217 (W.D. N.Y. 1993) (visual impairment); Christian v. New York State Board of Law Examiners, 1994 WL 62797 (S.D. N.Y. Feb. 23, 1994) (dyslexia and dysgraphia); Argen v. New York State Board of Law Examiners, No. 93-CV-586H (W.D. N.Y. Aug. 11, 1994) (learning disability); Pazer v. New York State Board of Law Examiners, 849 F.Supp. 284 (S.D. N.Y. 1994); Fowler v. New York State Board of Law Examiners, 885 F.Supp. 66 (W.D. N.Y. 1994); Price v. National Board of Medical Examiners, 966 F.Supp. 419 (S.D. W.Va. 1997); Kotz v. Florida Board of Medicine, 33 F.Supp. 2d 1019 (M.D. Fla. 1998); In re Underwood, 1993 WL 649283 (Supreme Judicial Ct. of Me., Dec. 7, 1993); In re Application of Frickey, 515 N.W.2d 741 (Minn. 1994); Campbell v. Greisberger, 80 F.3d 703 (2nd Cir. 1996); Ellen S. v. Florida Board of Bar Examiners, 859 F.Supp. 1489 (S.D. Fla. 1994); Applicants v. Texas State Board

of Law Examiners, 1994 WL 923404 (W.D. Tx. Oct. 11, 1994); Mueller v. Committee of Bar Examiners of California, *see* Tamar Lewin, "Dyslexic Law Student Sues on Exam's Time Limit," NEW YORK TIMES 167(50,094) (Oct. 23, 1997):A14.

161. Medical Society of New Jersey v. Jacobs, No. 93-3670 (WGB), 1993 WL 413016, 62 U.S.L.W. 2238, 2 A.D. Cases 1318, 3 A.D.D. 207 (D. N.J. Oct. 5, 1993).

162. *Id.* *1. The plaintiffs also challenged the following questions on the application for renewal of medical licenses: "Are you presently or have you previously suffered from or been in treatment for any psychiatric illness?" and "Have you suffered from or been treated for any mental or psychiatric illness?"; *id.* *2.

163. *Id.* *7.

164. "Medical" condition is defined to include "emotional or mental illness."

165. "Consent Decree Between the Equal Employment Opportunity Commission and Glenn View Manor," *Mental and Physical Disability Law Reporter* 22 (Jan.–Feb. 1998):62.

166. Thomas E. Hansen, Rupert R. Goetz, Joseph D. Bloom, and Darien S. Fenn, "Changes in Questions About Psychiatric Illness Asked on Medical Licensure Applications Between 1993 and 1996," *Psychiatric Services* 49 (1998):202.

167. *Id., supra* note 166 at 203.

168. *Id.*

169. *Id.* at 204.

170. The regulations make it clear that a "person" includes private entities, 28 C.F.R. Sec. 36.309(a).

171. 42 U.S.C. Sec. 12189 (LEXIS 2000).

172. 28 C.F.R. Sec. 36. 309(b)(1) and (3).

173. It might be possible to argue that some learning disabilities are disabilities related to impairment of sensory skills; for example, reading disability is related to the impairment of visual skills. Properly understood, however, these kinds of learning disabilities relate to cognitive function or brain function rather than visual abilities.

174. 28 C.F.R. Sec. 36.309(c) (LEXIS 2000).

175. William Claiborne, "Bar Review Course Agrees to Aid Disabled Students: U.S. Accused Harcourt Brace of Violating the ADA," THE WASHINGTON POST (174) (May 28, 1994): A2.

176. The National Board of Medical Examiners settled a case brought by Equip for Equality, the Illinois Protection and Advocacy organization. Joseph Perry was lead counsel in this case.

177. *See* pp. 313–315 *supra.*

178. Deborah Piltcher, Jamie W. Katz, and Janine Valles, "The Americans With Disabilities Act and Professional Licensing," *Mental and Physical Disability Law Reporter* 17 (1993):556, 559.

179. Hall v. Colorado State Board of Medical Examiners, 876 P.2d 77 (Colo. App. 1994).

180. Their later decision was to grant her a probationary license to practice medicine for 5 years, with mandatory psychotherapy by a practitioner acceptable to the board and practice in a group setting also acceptable to the board, *id.* at 78.

181. *Id.*

182. Many courts have found that inquiries or conclusions that were permissible under the applicable state constitutions nevertheless violated the ADA. For example, *Jacobs* was the second attack on mental health inquiries after a challenge based on the state constitution failed; similarly, questions on the application to the Florida Bar were upheld by the Florida Supreme Court on constitutional grounds but invalidated by a federal court under the ADA, Ellen S. v. Florida Board of Bar Examiners, 859 F.Supp. 1489 (S.D. Fla. 1994).

183. Doe v. Judicial Nominating Commission, 906 F.Supp. 1534, 1545 (S.D. Fla. 1995).

184. Mark v. Burke Rehabilitation Hospital, No. 94 Civ. 3596 RLC, 1999 U.S. Dist. LEXIS 5159, Mental and Physical Disability Law Reporter 21 (S.D. N.Y. April 17, 1997):332 (lymphoma); Lee v. Trustees of Dartmouth College, 958 F.Supp. 37 (D. N.H. 1997) (perceived multiple sclerosis).

185. Robertson v. Neuromedical Center, 161 F.3d 292 (1st Cir. 1998) (ADHD); Landefeld v. Marion General Hospital, 997 F.2d 1178 (6th Cir. 1993).

186. In addition to these issues, other procedural questions include the Rooker–Feldman doctrine, *res judicata* implications of state administrative decisions, collateral estoppel arising out of state proceedings, and 11th and even 10th Amendment challenges to federal court jurisdiction. *See* Doe v. Connecticut, 75 F.3d 81 (2nd Cir. 1995); Kotz v. Florida Board of Medicine, 33 F.Supp. 2d 1019 (M.D. Fla. 1998).

187. *Id.*

188. *But see* Arkansas State Medical Board v. Young, 1994 Ark. App. LEXIS 407 (Ark. App. Sept. 7, 1994) (1-year probation for the doctor's attempted suicide).

189. Hill v. State Medical Board of Ohio, 1996 Ohio App. LEXIS 5470*18 (Ohio App. Dec. 5, 1996); Alexander v. Margolis, 921 F.Supp. 482, 487 (W.D. Mich. 1995), *aff'd,* 98 F.3d 1341 (6th Cir. 1996).

190. *Doe* at 81.

191. Altman v. New York City Health and Hospitals Corporations, 100 F.3d 1054–1056 (2nd Cir. 1996).

192. Alexander v. Margolis, 921 F.Supp. 482, 487 (W.D. Mich. 1995) (a black physician); Diane Bay Humenansky v. Minnesota Board of Medical Examiners, 525 N.W.2d 559 (Minn. App. 1995).

193. *Alexander,* 921 F.Supp. at 482, 487.

194. *See* Humenansky v. Minnesota Board of Medical Examiners, 525 N.S.2d 559, 563, note 1 (Minn. App. 1994) (collecting statutes).

195. *Id.*

196. *Id.* at 564.

197. Morgan v. NW Permanente, P. C., 989 F.Supp. 1330 (D. Ore. 1997).

198. For an excellent article dealing in part with "impaired physician" programs, *see* Phyllis Coleman and Ronald A. Shellow, "Restricting Medical Licenses Based on Illness in Wrong-Reporting Makes It Worse," *J. of Law & Health* 9 (1994–1995):273.

199. Kotz v. Florida Board of Medicine, 33 F.Supp. 2d 1019 (M.D. Fla. 1998).

200. The court abstained on Younger v. Harris abstention grounds, which means that a federal court is counseled to avoid interfering with ongoing state proceedings. The case includes an interesting discussion by the court implying that licensure decisions might be subject to different abstention analysis than disciplinary decisions and refusing to apply the Rooker–Feldman doctrine to licensing decisions at all. *See* later in this chapter for a further discussion of the Rooker–Feldman doctrine.

201. *See* 28 C.F.R. Sec. 35.130(b)(2) and *Interpretive Guidance to Title II Regulations.*

202. Krasnopolsky v. Appalachian Regional Healthcare, 1999 U.S. App. LEXIS 7237 (6th Cir. Apr. 7, 1999).

203. Menkowitz v. Pottstown Memorial Hospital, 154 F.3d 113 (3rd Cir. 1998).

204. Landefeld v. Marion General Hospital, 994 F.2d 1178 (6th Cir. 1993).

205. P. L. 101-476.

CONCLUSION:
From Segregation to Transformation

> The point is this: even in the most ideal of cases, the law is only one of several imperfect and more or less external ways of defending what is better in life against what is worse. By itself, the law can never create anything better.[1]

My husband and I are vegetarians, and we like to eat in restaurants. Some places have nothing on the menu for us. Others will try to put something together if we tell the waiter that we are vegetarians, although usually we have to ask them to do that. Sometimes the dish is wonderful and imaginative; other times, it is a plate of limp steamed vegetables on a bed of rice. Our favorite places to eat are Italian, Indian, and Mexican restaurants, where we can simply order something from the menu without ever having to identify ourselves as being vegetarians, who are singled out as customers with special needs to be accommodated.

It is better to identify oneself as different (and implicitly burdensome) and be accommodated than to go hungry, but it is best of all to simply be another customer ordering a meal. Even better, I sometimes think wistfully, would be to live in a world where being a vegetarian was treated neither as a self-indulgent affectation nor as a burden on hosts and restaurateurs. My parents and my husband's parents understand, but then they care about us as people and do not consider our differences burdensome. That is the point.

Like us, people with mental disabilities do not want to be singled out and treated differently, whether the treatment is adverse and hostile or allegedly beneficial and "special." People with psychiatric disabilities want to be part of the world, not shut away from it. My survey asked "What do you want other people to know about psychiatric disability, perceptions of psychiatric disability, discrimination, or law that I should include?" The overwhelming majority of responses spoke to the desire to simply be perceived and treated as human beings:

> As Louise Wahl used to say, "We are part of the human condition and we want to build satisfactory lives. We want to work and contribute, create, have friendships, and enjoy life!"[2]

> * * *

> We just want a chance to take back control of our lives. We want to live outside of institutions. We want to live.[3]

> * * *

> That we are not the subhuman monsters that the media makes us out to be—that it really hurts to be treated that way.[4]

> * * *

> Mental illness has been around for centuries. It has not changed. What has and what needs to is the vision of what it means. We are still after all, humans with dreams,

goals, and hopes. That side of our story is never told. When we are diagnosed we become a label and lose our personhood. The saddest part of this illness, the worst to overcome, is the stigma (far worse than any symptom I ever experienced).[5]

One person, asked what the world should know about psychiatric disability, simply wrote, "I would make a good neighbor."[6]

The first message, therefore, is the crucial importance of integration rather than exclusion. At the most basic level, my husband and I should not be denied entrance into a restaurant just because we are vegetarians. Although blanket exclusions on the basis of mental illness or a history of hospitalization are receding, they are still very much a part of the country's fabric. Blanket exclusions should be eliminated root and branch from the country's laws, policies, and programs; that is, any exclusion based on a current or past diagnosis of mental illness, history of hospitalization or mental health treatment, or prescription for medication should be struck down. This includes outright denial of insurance on the basis of a history of or treatment for mental illness; differential access to treatment records; differential rights in the execution and enforcement of advance directives; exclusion from the military; and denial of security clearances. Advocacy projects can bring these cases to light, although a more efficient and consciousness-raising method to eliminate these laws might be to identify all such state laws and bring them to legislatures and ask for their repeal. Those laws that were not repealed through this process could then be challenged in court.

Since the Americans With Disabilities Act (ADA) of 1990 was passed, the trend has been away from blanket exclusion and toward the retention or addition of psychiatric diagnosis or treatment history as a factor to be considered in decision making. Many medical and legal licensing boards follow this trend, as do organ transplant centers. Consideration of psychiatric diagnosis or treatment history in decision making should be assessed through a two-step process.

First, entities that include a history of psychiatric diagnosis or treatment as a factor in decision making should be prepared to produce a rational justification for doing so. These entities should clearly articulate the assumptions underlying the choice of a history of psychiatric treatment or a diagnosis of mental illness as a factor in decision making. Does psychiatric diagnosis or treatment serve as a proxy for some other undesirable characteristic, such as unreliability or poor judgment, for example? Is the decision to use these factors on the basis of substantial, high-quality research or on any research at all? Or is it just the result of centuries of stereotypes and myths?

Second, can the entity do without the question? How necessary is considering diagnosis or treatment for mental illness to accomplishing the goals of the entity? Would it fundamentally alter the program to remove those factors from consideration? Advocacy groups should negotiate and lobby with these organizations to remove issues of diagnosis and treatment, as opposed to conduct, as factors of consideration. If no one with psychiatric disabilities is ultimately excluded as a result of questions about diagnosis and treatment, as is often the case with professional licensing, it may be a reason to discontinue asking those questions and requiring the provision of treatment histories. If everyone is excluded (as is probably the case with organ transplant centers), that indicates de facto blanket exclusion masquerading as discretion. Many personnel of such programs might be uncomfortable with the continued oversight required to determine if they are applying the diagnosis and treatment factors discriminatorily and might prefer to simply eliminate them.

The emphasis on integration rather than exclusion as a policy has direct implications in a wide variety of areas. In housing, it means a preference for integrated housing in the community (improving Section 8 access and ensuring that landlords accept Section 8 certificates) rather than board-and-care settings shared with other residents with disabilities that often operate as small-scale and less closely monitored segregated settings. Most obviously, the preference for integration means a concerted social policy to phase out large-scale segregated psychiatric institutions while taking care not to simply re-create those facilities by transferring their occupants to nursing homes, jails, and board-and-care facilities.[7]

These recommendations are not abstractions. They entail support and passage of MiCasa,[8] legislation that would partially eliminate the billion-dollar fiscal advantage enjoyed by nursing homes under Medicaid and Medicare and make home health care a reality for more Americans with disabilities. They mean that when states like Virginia, Pennsylvania, and New Jersey confront obsolete state institutional facilities, they commit the state's resources to strengthening its community treatment rather than building new state institutions. They mean that "community facilities" on the grounds of state hospitals are not permitted. They mean that "mental health courts" are not preferable alternatives to police practices and an integrated judicial system whose employees—servants of citizens with psychiatric disabilities as much as any other citizens—are trained in recognizing and assisting people with psychiatric disabilities and providing them with the reasonable accommodations that they need.

Unlike race and gender discrimination, there are enormous fiscal incentives that underlie disability segregation and inequality. Three of the strongest lobbies in Washington, DC, are those for nursing homes, the insurance industry, and the drug companies—the so-called Segregation Three. People in the first world of psychiatric disabilities discussed in chapter 2—people with jobs and families whose primary identities do not revolve around their psychiatric diagnoses—have been battling the Segregation Three on a variety of issues: lack of coverage for mental health treatment by private insurance, the stranglehold of nursing homes as the only alternative to independent living, and the skyrocketing price of prescription drugs. As a result of these battles, a feeble federal requirement that private insurance provide parity of coverage of mental health conditions has emerged, which is scheduled to expire by the time this book is published, and stronger state parity laws have been adopted in more than half the states. Assisted-living facilities, home health care, and personal care assistants are emerging as alternatives to segregation in nursing homes. Congress is moving to expand Medicare reimbursement for drugs, but not to cap the prices.[9]

These battles have relatively little significance for the second world of people with psychiatric disabilities—those who have no private insurance, who cannot afford the astronomical prices of assisted-living facilities and personal care attendants, and often do not want the prescription drugs anyway. However, state mental health agencies are less subject to the fiscal incentives described above and, when they set their minds to it, can greatly improve the quality and integration of the services that they provide. State mental health agencies were moving toward working with their clients in designing services and often support client advocacy and self-help groups. The states face opposition in closing institutions from labor unions and parent groups, whose influence is relatively less significant (a sad comment) than the influence of insurance companies, nursing homes, and drug companies in the private sector.

This is one reason to be suspicious of the tidal wave of privatization that is hitting the state mental health systems. Privatization can only mean the introduction of fiscal incentives and private for-profit megacorporations. The idea of "empowering consumers" is foreign to these organizations. Satisfied customers, yes; quality assurance, certainly. But working to transform their clients from a politically disenfranchised and marginalized group to an organized constituency with shared decision-making authority is not the language of managed care.

The emphasis on integration also has a variety of less-direct but equally important implications for social policy. If the restaurant is open to my husband and me, but we cannot afford it because we are unemployed due to discrimination against vegetarians, we may have an empty right to a seat in the restaurant. The key to true integration in American society is work. I have written a companion volume[10] to this book that deals solely with discrimination in employment. For the purposes of the subjects discussed here, the major obstacle preventing disabled Americans from working is the fear of losing health care benefits. The Ticket to Work and Work Incentives Improvement Act of 1999,[11] which is a first step toward permitting people with disabilities to work without losing health care benefits, is key to solving this problem. However, integrating into today's America—integrating into the existing community and social structure—means integrating into burgeoning work stress, deteriorating health care, evaporating social services, with their attendant racism, violence against women and children, and indifference to elderly people.

It seems paradoxical to call for integration into a society so toxic that it drove some of these people "crazy" in the first place. It is clear that for most people with psychiatric disabilities, their injuries and suffering are not encapsulated neatly in diagnoses or in moments of discrimination: that acknowledgment of their sexual abuse, experiences of war, violence, or criminal victimization is crucial to understanding their lives as well as their legal claims; that their poverty, race, and gender shape and exacerbate the discriminatory ways in which others behave toward them in ways that we as a society should understand but instead have tried to erase.[12] Because the "characteristics on the basis of which they suffer discrimination" are "more complex than many of the stigmatized characteristics that have been raised in the past," however, they are "more complex than legal doctrine seems prepared to accommodate."[13]

As Dr. Robert Coles wrote in praise of Harry Stack Sullivan, "Sullivan was one psychiatrist who knew that poverty and injustice could undo even fairly solid minds."[14] This is all the more true of violence and sexual abuse that children cannot make sense of, have no words for, and sometimes do not survive. One survey respondent identified as his "substantial limitation on major life activities" that "I cannot understand the world I live in."[15] He responded that he did not feel part of the community where he lived, writing that "peaceful environments that do not single out harmless, well-meaning people for the satisfaction of hatred are places where it is possible to live."[16]

America is a very difficult place in which to live. We have always had more of a talent for absorption than for real integration. There is a connection between the conditions of society and the disabilities of that society. Just as lead paint and mercury poisoning cause mental retardation and chemicals in the Love Canal caused cancer, stress, downsizing, and sexual abuse cause psychiatric breakdowns. It should surprise no one that when poor women were asked about their mental health problems, their answers were filled with references to violence, lack of job security, and single parenthood because

> at the core of many of these responses was concern with lack of money and related problems in paying bills, finding a decent place to live, putting food on the table, and getting adequate medical care . . . respondents in the study find it impossible to separate [emotional] problems from the disturbing conditions in which [they] live.[17]

As one survey respondent wrote,

> most of what you see going on in prison, death row, and psychiatric garbage pits are the poor, uneducated, uncared for, and unloved. If competition is what people feel makes our society great, then maybe euthanasia is the answer now and genetic engineering the answer later. It would be a much more honest approach than the medical and governmental crap going on now. Personally I hope I get to be somewhere where variations in consciousness are tolerated and nurturing is valued.[18]

If rather than having an array of special programs targeted at mental illness, blindness, or drug abuse, society had better health care and labor legislation, if all workers were protected from excessive hours of work or abusive work environments, if basic health care and preventive services were readily available, if adequate housing were easily affordable, then people with psychiatric disabilities would probably benefit more than they do from the presence of community mental health centers or laws aimed at protecting "patients' rights." Likewise, in terms of affirmatively improving the conditions of people's lives, people with psychiatric disabilities generally benefit more from broad-based laws designed to protect a larger group. The ADA, designed to protect all citizens with disabilities, is generally better than statutes designed specifically to protect people with psychiatric disabilities.

Case after case, however, reflects the reality that people with psychiatric disabilities are better off securing leave under the Family and Medical Leave Act of 1993 than as a reasonable accommodation for their disability under the ADA or challenging "personality test" requirements for jobs under state labor statutes than under the ADA.[19] People with psychiatric disabilities are better off writing health care proxies under statutes that grant all citizens the right to enforceable advance directives than under statutes specifically drafted to cover the advance directives of people with psychiatric disabilities. They are better off trying to make the vocational rehabilitation agencies do their jobs by litigating under the Vocational Rehabilitation Act itself than under disability discrimination law.[20] They are better off if unions secure more civil workplaces and shorter hours for all workers than by trying to change those conditions only as to themselves and incurring the resentment of other workers. As David Oaks wrote,

> I think it's valuable that someone who feels they are diagnosed "depressed" can get a reasonable accommodation to have flexible hours, and a private room where they can cry and call their counselor. But I think that is a reasonable demand for EVERYONE to have, if there was a good union: that all workers can have some flexibility on hours (if it's reasonable), and a room for peer support. EVERYONE.[21]

This conclusion makes sense for a number of reasons. First, it is based on the premise of antidiscrimination law itself: that people are more alike than different, at least when it comes to basic human needs for shelter, security, and dignified treatment. Second, it makes sense because people who are thought to have psychiatric disabilities are among the most despised and misunderstood of all people with disabilities: programs and statutes that are specifically designed for them are not as likely to be generous, and much less likely to be interpreted generously than programs that cover all citizens, or even all people with disabilities. Third, the conditions of life for people with psychiatric disabilities are affected by their economic status, race, age, and gender. Therefore, policy initiatives, including antidiscrimination laws, that are focused solely on the psychiatric disability will inevitably fail to effectively solve many of the problems. In some ways, the more focused the program on psychiatric disability, the less effective it will be.

These observations, too, translate into a number of concrete suggestions. People with psychiatric disabilities from the first group—Tipper Gore, Mike Wallace, and others—need to open up a dialogue with people from the second group—but not by inviting one or two people as the token "psychiatric consumers" at a conference where people from the first group do not identify themselves in the same way. Currently, there is an abyss between the two groups that may at least be potentially bridged with such broad issues as support for the ADA and wider public education. In addition, people with psychiatric disabilities must do a better job organizing themselves as a group to be considered politically and must ally with groups such as people with physical disabilities, with labor organizations, and with other constituencies to push for the passage of legislation that will be of benefit to all.

There are some areas, however, in which disability discrimination law is crucial. The ADA has already benefited a number of people in a range of ways that are documented in survey responses and interviews. For example, one respondent told of events that could not happen now because of the ADA:

> When my arms and I weren't getting along so well, I learned not to say I'd need special equipment to keep working . . . . I was quite shocked at how easily a job that I thought valued me was willing to get along without me. This was pre-ADA.[22]

* * *

> I worked as a temp for a large publishing company, and during the two years I temped I worked a full-time schedule with several deadlines in each work week. I had no holiday pay, no vacation pay (and took no vacations), no medical insurance, and I was not absent from work one day in two years. Several bosses approached me about taking a permanent job, and when I would accept, the personnel department would tell them I could not be hired on the permanent payroll because they did not want to provide me with medical insurance. I knew that the discussion with the medical department after my employment physical (as a temp!) was about the fact that it was Prolixin they detected in my blood test, not a street drug, but most people I worked with assumed I had something like a heart condition, and I said nothing.[23]

The ADA is also needed to attack segregation in institutional settings and in the community. Disability discrimination law is also vital to ensure that people with psychiatric disabilities are not intentionally excluded from the general laws that benefit citizens at large—still a common occurrence in American law.

By itself, however, the law can never be sufficient. Laws are not self-enforcing; they are in human hands. Lawyers who are wary of people with mental disabilities will not take them as clients; judges will not believe their evidence; juries will doubt their claims. The existence of the ADA provides an opportunity for equality and justice, nothing more. "Human progress never rolls in on the wheels of inevitability";[24] it is the work of exhausted, wounded, struggling people. Equality and justice are our work, and the law is only one way to do it. However difficult, we cannot cease to work for the world envisioned by those who responded to the survey: a world open to difference and to all the different languages of suffering. Only by striving to understand these languages and their meanings can we work to make the suffering cease.

Endnotes

1. Valclav Havel, *Living in Truth* (Boston: Faber & Faber, 1990) at 99.
2. Survey No. 78, on file with author.
3. E. H., Survey No. 178.
4. Survey No. 104, on file with author.
5. J. A. V., Survey No. 83, on file with author.
6. M. M., Survey No. 163.
7. There are other direct implications not covered in the subject matter of this book, including a preference for mainstreaming in classrooms rather than placement in special trailers on school grounds or in segregated residential settings. This will only succeed if teachers receive the training that they need to deal with children with various disabilities.
8. See chapter 5.
9. In the last year alone, over 30 bills have been introduced to Congress to enhance Medicare coverage of prescription drugs or permit income tax credits for prescription drug purposes. *See, e.g.,* S.2541, 106 Cong., 2nd Sess., introduced May 10, 2000; S.2342, 106th Cong., 2nd Sess., introduced Apr. 4, 2000; S.2319, 106th Cong., 2nd Sess., introduced Mar. 29, 2000; H.R.4375, 106th Cong., 2nd Sess., introduced May 3, 2000; H.R.4234, 106th Cong., 2nd Sess., introduced Apr. 11, 2000.
10. Susan Stefan, tentatively titled *Hollow Promises: The Americans Disability Act and Employment Discrimination Against People With Mental Disablities* (Washington, DC: American Psychological Association, in press).
11. P. L. 106-170.
12. This is also true of people with disabilities in general, who are more often members of racial minorities, women, poor, and with lower levels of education than people who are not disabled; Matthew Diller, "Dissonant Disability Policies: The Tensions Between the Americans With Disabilities Act and Federal Disability Benefit Programs," *Tex. Law Rev.* 76 (1998):1003, 1013.
13. Kathryn Abrams, "The Pursuit of Social and Political Equality: Complex Claimants and Reductive Moral Judgments: New Patterns in the Search for Equality," *Univ. of Pitt. Law Rev.* 57 (1996):337. *See also* Clark Freeman, "Whatever Happened to Anti-Semitism?" *Cornell Law Rev.* 85 (2000):313, 321–324.
14. Robert Coles, "Harry Stack Sullivan," in *The Mind's Fate: A Psychiatrist Looks at His Profession*, 2nd ed., Robert Coles, Ed. (New York: Little Brown, 1995) at 218.
15. *Id.*
16. D. E., Survey No. 201.
17. Deborah Belle, Ed., *Lives in Stress: Women and Depression* (Beverly Hills, CA: Sage, 1982) at 198.
18. Survey No. 179.
19. Thompson v. Borg-Warner, 1996 U.S. Dist. LEXIS 4781*21, *28 (N.D. Ca. Mar. 11,

1996) (finding no claim under the ADA for discrimination but finding a cause of action under California labor law).

20. Doe v. Pfrommer, 148 F.3d 73, 78, 83 (2nd Cir. 1998) (denying the ADA and Rehabilitation Act claims but permitting the plaintiff to proceed with his claim under Section 1983 for the violation of his rights under the Vocational Rehabilitation Act).

21. David Oaks, Survey No. 168 (specifically requesting to be quoted by name: "I think people should be encouraged to come out of the darn closet[;] it's too crowded in there").

22. Survey No. 150.

23. Survey No. 78, on file with author.

24. Martin Luther King Jr., "Letter From the Birmingham Jail," in *Why We Can't Wait* (New York: Harper & Row, 1964) at 89.

APPENDIX A
Survey

Susan Stefan is writing a book about discrimination against people with diagnoses or labels of psychiatric disability. She would like to learn more about the perspectives and experiences of people who have these diagnoses and labels. Please take a few minutes to fill out this form. As you can see, it is anonymous, and it will help her a great deal. Please return the survey to Susan Stefan, University of Miami School of Law, P.O. Box 248087, Coral Gables, FL 33124-8087. Thank you very much.

1.   Do you believe you have a disability?
        _____ Yes   _____ No

1a. How would you define or describe "having a disability"? _____

_____

_____

2.   Do you believe that other people regard you as having a disability?
        _____ Yes   _____ No

3.   Do you believe that you have a physical or mental impairment?
        _____ Yes   _____ No

3a. If yes, does the impairment substantially limit you in one or more major life activities?
        _____ Yes   _____ No

3b. If you answered yes to 3a, please describe: _____

_____

_____

4.   Are you vulnerable to abuse because you have or are perceived as having a disability?
        _____ Yes   _____ No
        If yes, explain and/or give examples. _____

_____

_____

5. Have you ever been discriminated against?
   _____ Yes _____ No

5a. If yes, please check all the categories that apply:
   ____ housing   ____ access to stores, movies, etc.
   ____ access to medical care   ____ how people treated you
   ____ employment   ____ courtroom situations
   ____ insurance   ____ institutional settings
   ____ education   ____ other (specify below)

   _____

   _____

5b. Did you feel as though you were discriminated against because of
   ____ race   ____ religion
   ____ sex   ____ sexual preference
   ____ age   ____ psychiatric diability orperceived disability
   ____ physical disability ____ a combination of one or more of the above

6. In what areas of your life have you experienced the worst discrimination?

   _____

   _____

   _____

7. Please give examples of the worst discrimination you have encountered.

   _____

   _____

   _____

8. Please explain how you felt afterward, for how long this effect lasted, and what
   impact it had on the way you lived your life after that. _____

   _____

   _____

9. What do you think is the best thing that can be done to make sure these kinds
   of things don't keep happening? _____

   _____

   _____

10. Do you think the Americans With Disabilities Act can prevent these things
    from happening to people?
    _____ Yes _____ No _____Yes, if _____

    _____

11. Do you know anyone who sued or was sued under the Americans With Disa-
    bilities Act?
    _____ Yes _____ No
    If yes, what was the case about? What happened? _____

    _____

    _____

12. Do you feel part of the community where you live? Why or why not? _____

    _____

13. I am writing a book about discrimination, law, and psychiatric disability, in-
    cluding perceptions of psychiatric disability. What do you want to know about
    that I should include?

    _____

    _____

    _____

14. What do you want other people to know about psychiatric disability, percep-
    tions of psychiatric disability, discrimination, or law that I should include?

    _____

    _____

    _____

May I quote from your responses to this survey in my book? The quote would be
anonymous. Unless you want me to use initials, I will simply number all the survey
responses and cite the response by its number.

        _____ Yes, you may quote from this.
        _____ I would like you to use my initials, which are _____.
        _____ I prefer that you cite my survey by its number.

APPENDIX B
Statutes Providing Disability Rights and Benefits

The Americans With Disabilities Act

The Americans With Disabilities Act (ADA) was signed by President Bush on July 26, 1990. Its effective date was January 26, 1992, for all titles, except that employers with more than 15 but fewer than 25 employees were not covered until January 26, 1994.

Title I

Title I of the ADA prohibits discrimination in employment on the basis of disability by any employer with 15 employees or more. Discrimination includes asking questions about disability on job applications or in job interviews. Employers may not ask an applicant about a history of psychiatric hospitalization or institutionalization, nor may they ask about any medication the applicant is taking. After a job is offered, employers may require health testing, as long as they require it of all employees and keep the results confidential in a file separate from the employee's personnel file.

The phone number of the Equal Employment Opportunity Commission (EEOC) office that serves a particular area can be obtained by calling 800/669-4000 (voice) or 800/669-6820 (TDD). Information on EEOC-enforced laws can be obtained by calling 800/669-EEOC (voice) or 800/800-3302 (TDD).

Information on specific accommodations in employment can be obtained from the Job Accommodation Network, 800/526-7234 or 800/ADA-WORK (both numbers accommodate both voice and TDD callers).

General information can be obtained from the President's Committee on Employment of People With Disabilities, Suite 636, 1111 20th St. NW, Washington, DC 20036-3470, 202/653-5044 (voice), 202/653-5050 (TDD).

Title II

Title II of the ADA prohibits discrimination by state and local governments or by state and local government entities. This includes the courts, boards of bar examiners, judicial nominating commissions, prisons and jails, city police pension fund trustees, city zoning boards, and others. Title II has been held to apply to employment discrimination by public entities in some circuits[1] but not in others.[2] In this case, a person would not have to file an administrative complaint before filing a lawsuit. Title II also applies to discrimination by public providers of transportation—an issue that seldom arises for people with psychiatric disabilities. The U.S. Supreme Court will decide in 2001 whether states can be sued under the ADA for damages.[3]

The Disability Rights Section of the Civil Rights Division of the Department of

Justice (DOJ) enforces Title II of the Americans With Disabilities Act; its address is Disability Rights Section, P.O. Box 66738, Washington, DC 20035-6738, and the phone number is 800/514-0301. DOJ maintains an ADA Information Line at 800/ 514-0301 (voice) or 800/514-0383 (TDD). In addition, DOJ publications relating to the ADA are available at the DOJ web site at http://www.usdoj.gov/crt/ada/ adahom1.htm.

Title III

Title III of the ADA prohibits discrimination by "public accommodations," which include hospitals, doctors' offices, insurance offices, private schools and universities, movie theatres, and restaurants. There is some controversy about whether Title III applies only to physical accessibility. The majority view is that it prohibits all discrimination on the basis of disability by a public accommodation. Unlike Titles I and II of the ADA and Section 504 of the Rehabilitation Act, individual plaintiffs cannot seek damages as a remedy under Title III of the ADA. DOJ can bring an action for damages when there is a pattern or practice of discrimination. So far, DOJ has filed relatively few cases using this authority.

The Disability Rights section of the Civil Rights Division of the DOJ enforces Title III of the ADA.

See Title II for information about DOJ.

The Rehabilitation Act of 1973

Section 501

This provision forbids discrimination on the basis of disability in the employment practices of the federal government. The federal government is required to undertake affirmative action to ensure hiring, placement, and advancement of individuals with disabilities. Aggrieved individuals must first file a complaint with the Merit Systems Protection Board. If dissatisfied with the outcome of administrative proceedings, individuals can file an action in federal district court.

Section 503

This section requires any party entering into a contract in excess of $10,000 with the federal government to have an affirmative action plan in place to promote employment of people with disabilities. If a disabled person believes he or she has been discriminated against by a federal contractor, he or she may file a complaint with the Department of Labor. Almost every circuit court has held that there is no private right of action under Section 503 of the Rehabilitation Act, that is, that people who are discriminated against by federal contractors cannot sue to vindicate their rights.[4] In fact, one court even held that the Department of Labor itself could not bring a complaint against a federal contractor for disability discrimination, holding that Section 503 only required the government to place affirmative action language in its contracts.[5] The one certain remedy available is for the government to delay or suspend payments to the contractor or to cancel the contract with the contractee.[6] This does happen,[7] although very rarely.

Section 504

Any entity that receives federal assistance is subject to the Rehabilitation Act of 1973. "Federal assistance" is differentiated from federal funds paid in satisfaction of a contract for goods or labor covered in Section 503. Federal assistance has been interpreted very broadly, including sending federal personnel to provide free training; in addition, railroads,[8] hospitals, airlines (under some circumstances),[9] sports arenas, and telephone companies[10] have been held to receive federal assistance. Each federal agency that distributes federal funds has regulations prohibiting disability discrimination and has internal offices to which complaints about disability discrimination can be addressed for investigation (although unlike employment discrimination, a person may go directly to federal or state court with a discrimination claim without having to first make an administrative complaint).

The Individuals With Disabilities in Education Act

This statute was first passed as the Education for the Handicapped Act in 1973, and it is still best known as the Education for All Handicapped Children Act. The Act was in large part the result of two lawsuits brought by mental health lawyers,[11] using the same constitutional claims—due process and equal protection—that had been used in attacking commitment processes and fighting for the right to treatment. The language of the Act, however, with its attention to integration and mainstreaming, reflected the ideals of the disability rights movement.

Unlike the major antidiscrimination statutes, the Individuals With Disabilities in Education Act creates an entitlement to a free and appropriate education for all disabled children. Also unlike the antidiscrimination statutes, children do not have to be "qualified" for education—every child between the ages of 3 and 18 is entitled to free, appropriate public education.[12] This includes children in residential facilities, institutions, jails, foster care, homeless children, and children in long-term care for physical disability. The school district is required to pay for the educational services required. Because of overlap among Medicare, Medicaid, and state mental health agency responsibilities, school systems are sometimes able to evade their responsibilities. In addition, children with disabilities must comprise at least 10% of each Project Head Start program.

For more information, contact the Office of Special Education Programs, U.S. Department of Education, Room 3086, 330 C St. SW, Washington, D.C. 20202, 202/205-5507 (voice), 202/205-9754 (TDD).

The Air Carrier Access Act

This statute was passed in 1986.[13] It contains a provision prohibiting discrimination by any air carrier on the basis of disability, including the denial of boarding.[14] The act is enforced by the Department of Transportation, although an individual can also file a lawsuit directly in federal court. There is no specific statute of limitations provision in the act.

The statute has been held to create a private right of action for travelers who are discriminated against by airlines.[15] Courts are divided, however, on the kinds of remedies that plaintiffs may seek.[16]

For more information or to file a complaint, contact the Department Office of Civil Rights, Office of the Secretary, U.S. Department of Transportation, 400 Seventh St. SW, Washington, DC 20590, 202/366-4648 (voice), 202/366-8538 (TDD).

Individuals may also contact the Aviation Consumer Protection Division, C-75, U.S. Department of Transportation, 400 Seventh St. SW, Washington, DC 20590, 202/366-2220 (voice), 202/755-7687 (TDD).

The Fair Housing Amendments Act

This law, passed in 1988, applies to the sale and rental of private housing covered by Title VIII of the Civil Rights Act.[17] It forbids discrimination on the basis of disability in housing, although it exempts rooms or units in dwellings occupied by no more than four families if the owner also lives in the housing unit. Landlords may not inquire if prospective tenants have a disability. If a landlord inquires for the purpose of finding out if a person is qualified for priority housing available to people with disabilities, the landlord may inquire, as long the he or she makes this inquiry of all applicants.

The Housing and Civil Enforcement Section of DOJ litigates cases under the Fair Housing Act and can be reached at 202/514-4713 or P.O. Box 65998, Washington, DC 20035-5998.

Other Federal Statutes Relating to People With Mental Disabilities

Statutes Relating to Treatment–Services

The Emergency Medical Treatment and Active Labor Act (EMTALA)

EMTALA[18] requires that indigent people in emergency rooms receive the same screening as people who have insurance coverage, and it prohibits hospital emergency room personnel from turning away or transferring people with an emergency medical condition without giving them treatment to stabilize that condition, unless the transfer can be effected without danger of the condition deteriorating.

The Employment Retirement Income Security Act (ERISA)

Whereas EMTALA regulates the conduct of emergency rooms towards indigent patients, ERISA[19] regulates people's rights under employee benefit plans, including the right to receive treatment for mental illnesses or disabilities. Claims under ERISA involving people with mental disabilities cluster around two major issues: differential coverage of mental and physical conditions[20] and denial of authorization for treatment in a variety of contexts, including admission to inpatient units to people who then commit suicide.[21]

The Consolidated Omnibus Budget Reconciliation Act (COBRA)

This act requires employers with group health plans to offer continued health insurance coverage to individuals at the individual's expense (but paying the group health rate of coverage) for 18 months after the individual leaves the job.[22]

The Health Insurance Portability and Accountability Act

This statute forbids an insurer that offers group health plans from discriminating against any individual based on that individual's health status. People may not be denied coverage because of their medical condition, receipt of health care, genetic information, or disability, and the Act limits exclusion for preexisting medical conditions.[23]

The Mental Health Parity Act

Passed as an amendment to the Health Insurance Portability and Accountability Act, this legislation requires that all health insurance providers who provide insurance for mental health conditions must provide the same aggregate lifetime and annual coverage for mental disability as for physical conditions. This provision does not apply to businesses with fewer than 50 employees.[24]

The State Comprehensive Mental Health Services Plan Act

According to this statue, to receive federal block-grant funds for mental health services, each state must submit a plan that establishes a community-based system of care for seriously mentally ill individuals, describes the treatment available for such people, and lists ways to reduce the hospitalization rates of people with mental illness. If the state fails to achieve any of these objectives, its federal allotment may be reduced.[25]

The Federal Nursing Home Reform Act

Subtitle C of the Omnibus Reconciliation Act of 1987, entitled Nursing Home Reform,[26] requires any nursing home that receives Medicaid or Medicare payments to be subject to unannounced inspections at least once every 15 months by the state agency in charge of monitoring such facilities.[27] If a nursing home is found to be giving substandard care, then inspection teams must conduct a more extensive survey to determine the cause of the violations.[28]

The Nursing Home Reform Amendments of 1987 required that independent clinical teams screen people prior to admission to a nursing home to prevent inappropriate admissions of people with mental retardation, developmental disabilities, and psychiatric disabilities. This screening program, which must be repeated each year, is known as preadmission screening and annual resident review (PASARR).

If people with those disabilities are confined to nursing homes, they must be provided with specialized services to meet their particular needs.

The Technology-Related Assistance for Individuals With Disabilities Act of 1988

This act created funding for assistive-technology projects in all 50 states to provide people with disabilities with greater access to improvements in assistive technology or devices and to train disabled people and their family in the use of these devices.[29]

Statutes Relating to Rights

Voting

The Accessibility for Elderly and Handicapped Act. Passed in 1984, this statute directs state agencies in charge of carrying out elections to ensure that the polling stations for federal elections (which as a practical matter encompass polling stations for state elections) are accessible to older and handicapped voters.[30] In addition, these agencies must provide registration and voting aids, such as instructions printed in large type and telecommunications devices for deaf people.

The National Voter Registration Act. Known as the "Motor Voter Law" because one of its requirements is that all state Department of Motor Vehicle offices, and all forms for renewals of drivers' licenses by mail, include voter registration forms, the statute also requires states to "designate as voter registration agencies all offices . . . that provide State-funded programs primarily engaged in providing services to persons with disabilities."[31] Although it is clear that places such as community mental health centers must provide voter registration services, one court of appeals has recently held that offices providing services for disabled students in state universities and colleges must also provide voter registration services.[32]

The Patient Self Determination Act (PSDA)

This statute requires all facilities receiving federal Medicare–Medicaid funding, which includes almost all private and state hospitals providing psychiatric care, to inform patients of their state statutory rights regarding advance directives, living wills, and the right to refuse treatment. It forbids hospitals to deny care to patients because they have (or do not have) advance directives.[33]

The Civil Rights of Institutionalized Persons Act (CRIPA)

This statute gives DOJ's Civil Rights Division standing to bring litigation against states that are violating the rights of institutionalized people, whether those people are in institutions, prisons, or jails. This statute also applies to nursing homes on the rare occasions that such facilities are state run.[34]

People who wish to report violations of the civil rights of institutionalized people can call DOJ at 202/514-6255 or write to the Special Litigation Section, Civil Rights Division, U.S. Department of Justice, P.O. Box 66400, Washington, DC 20035-6400.

The Protection and Advocacy for Mentally Ill Individuals Act

This act gives federal funds to states to fund protection and advocacy agencies (called "P&As") to ensure that the legal rights of individuals in psychiatric institutions are protected, including their right to safety and freedom from abuse or neglect.[35] The protection and advocacy agency's jurisdiction also extends to individuals for 90 days after they have been discharged from an institution. The agency's representatives are authorized to have access to patients and their records when the agency receives a complaint of abuse or neglect or has probable cause to believe that abuse or neglect or violations of rights have taken place or are taking place. Protection and advocacy agencies may also bring litigation in their own names on behalf of their clients.

For the name and address of the protection and advocacy agency in each state, call the National Association of Protection and Advocacy Systems at 202/408-9514.

The Family Medical Leave Act

Enacted in 1993, this statute covers employers with more than 50 employees. It requires employers to permit up to 12 weeks of unpaid leave for "medical reasons, for the birth or adoption of a child, and for the care of a child, spouse, or parent who has a serious health condition."[36] The statute of limitations for bringing claims under this act runs 2 years after the date of the last event constituting the alleged violation for which the action is brought.[37] Damages recoverable include lost wages, salary, employment benefits, or other compensation denied as a result of the violation, with interest. Some courts have rejected the concept that damages for emotional distress count as "other compensation."[38] Punitive damages are not allowed, but if the employer intentionally violates the statute, damages may be doubled.

Conspiracy to Deprive of Civil Rights Based on Disability

Originally enacted after the Civil War, this statute prohibits conspiracies to deprive certain groups of their civil rights.[39] Although African Americans and women are clearly covered, the circuits are divided over whether people with disabilities are protected under this statute. At least one court has held that operators of a community mental health facility who conspired to deprive residents of their benefit checks were subject to an action under this title.[40]

The Client Assistance Program (CAP; Part of the Rehabilitation Act)

This legislation provides assistance and advocacy for clients of the Vocational Rehabilitation program. Generally, protection and advocacy agencies (see above) receive funding under this program for this work.

The False Claims Act

Under the *qui tam* provision of this statute, an individual who has information that the government is being defrauded can sue on behalf of the government. If the fraud is proven and the government recovers the money, the individual who filed the suit is entitled to up to 30% of the funds recovered.[41]

"Fraud" under the false claims act includes a number of activities relevant to people with psychiatric disabilities. For example, false claims for a Medicare or Medicaid reimbursement, or claims that federally supported Medicare or Medicaid health maintenance organizations (HMOs) denied treatment that the HMO promised to offer in its contract with the government, or false claims of compliance with the Individuals With Disabilities in Education Act or Rehabilitation Act to receive federal funds, and making false statements regarding human participant protections in research grants have all been the subject of *qui tam* actions.

There are some key requirements: The individual must provide the government with information about the fraud prior to filing the action; the government may dismiss the case if it sees fit; and the individual may not otherwise divulge the information to the media.

Endnotes

1. Bledsoe v. Palm Beach County Soil and Water Conservation District, 133 F.3d 816 (11th Cir. 1998).
2. Zimmerman v. Oregon Department of Justice, 170 F.3d 1169 (9th Cir. 1999), *see* chapter 4.
3. University of Alabama at Birmingham Board of Trustees v. Garrett, No. 99-1240, 68 U.S.L.W. 3654 (Apr. 17, 2000).
4. Davis v. United Air Lines, 662 F.2d 120 (2nd Cir. 1981); Beam v. Sun Shipbuilding & Dry Dock Co., 679 F.2d 1077 (3rd Cir. 1982); Painter v. Horne Brothers Inc., 710 F.2d 143 (4th Cir. 1983); Rogers v. Frito-Lay Inc., 611 F.2d 1074 (5th Cir. 1980); Hoopes v. Equifax, 611 F.2d 134 (6th Cir. 1979); Simpson v. Reynolds Metals Co., 629 F.2d 1226 (7th Cir. 1980); Simon v. St. Louis County Missouri, 656 F.2d 316 (8th Cir. 1981); Fisher v. City of Tucson, 663 F.2d 861 (9th Cir. 1981); Hodges v. Atchison Topeka and Santa Fe Railroad, 728 F.2d 414 (10th Cir. 1984).
5. American Airlines v. Cynthia Metzler, 958 F.Supp. 273, 275 (N.D. Tx. 1997); Wood v. Diamond State Tel. Co., 440 F.Supp. 1003, 1009 (D. Del. 1977).
6. 41 C.F.R. Sec. 60-741.66 (2000).
7. *See* Board of Governors of the University of North Carolina v. U.S. Department of Labor, 917 F.2d 812, 815 (4th Cir. 1990). This case is not about whether the University of North Carolina discriminated on the basis of disability but about whether the university was one unified system for these purposes or whether each of its campuses constituted a separate part. The Department of Labor prevailed in its contention that the former interpretation governed.
8. Moreno v. Consolidated Rail Corp., 99 F.3d 782 (6th Cir. 1996) (federal funds for railroad crossing improvements constitute federal assistance under the Rehabilitation Act); Sharrow v. Bailey, 910 F.Supp. 187 (M.D. Pa. 1995) (the hospital's acceptance of Medicare–Medicaid funds constitutes receipt of federal assistance under the Rehabilitation Act); Laconic v. City of St. Petersburg, 731 F.Supp. 1522 (M.D. Fla. 1990) (the stadium receiving federal funds was subject to the Rehabilitation Act); Rivera-Flores v. Puerto Rico

Telephone, 64 F.3d 742 (1st Cir. 1995) (federal emergency assistance to a telephone company constituted federal assistance for Rehabilitation Act purposes).

9. Most disability discrimination litigation against an airlines is covered by the Air Carrier Access Act, *infra*; *see, e.g.,* ADAPT v. Skywest Airlines, 762 F.Supp. 320, 322-325 (D. Utah 1991) and Jacobson v. Delta Airlines, 742 F.2d 1202 (9th Cir. 1984). The federal government subsidizes flights to some small communities under the Essential Air Services Program, 49 U.S.C. Sec. 1389, and those flights have been held to come within the gambit of the Rehabilitation Act.

10. Rivera-Flores v. Puerto Rico Telephone Co., 64 F.3d 742 (1st Cir. 1995).

11. Pennsylvania Association for Retarded Citizens v. Pennsylvania, 334 F.Supp. 1257 (E.D. Pa. 1971); Mills v. Board of Education of the District of Columbia, 348 F.Supp. 866 (D.D.C. 1972).

12. Courts have rejected the argument of states that only children who can "benefit" from education are entitled to it, *see* Timothy W. v. Rochester, 875 F.2d 954 (1st Cir. 1989).

13. 49 U.S.C. Secs. 40102 *et seq.*

14. 49 U.S.C. Sec. 41705.

15. Shinault v. American Airlines, 936 F.2d 796, 800 (5th Cir. 1991); Tallarico v. TWA, 881 F.2d 566, 570 (8th Cir. 1989).

16. *Compare* Shinault v. American Airlines, 936 F.2d 796, 800 (5th Cir. 1991) and ADAPT v. Skywest, 762 F.Supp. 320 (D. Utah 1991) (neither punitive damages nor damages for emotional distress were awarded) with Tallarico v. TWA, 881 F.2d 566, 570 (8th Cir. 1989) (damages for emotional distress and punitive damages were allowed but not injunctive relief).

17. 42 U.S.C. Secs. 3601, 3602, 3604-3608.

18. 42 U.S.C. Sec. 1395dd. EMTALA was enacted as part of the COBRA Act of 1985, *see below. See* Mellissa K. Stull, annotation, *Construction and Application of Emergency Medical Treatment and Active Labor Act,* 104 A.L.R. Fed. 166 (1991).

19. 29 U.S.C. Sec. 1144 , 1001 *et seq.* (2000).

20. *See* chapter 5.

21. Tolton v. American Biodyne, 48 F.3d 937 (6th Cir. 1995).

22. 29 U.S.C. Secs. 1161-1169.

23. 29 U.S.C. Sec. 1181.

24. 42 U.S.C. Sec. 300gg-5, 29 U.S.C. Sec. 1185(a).

25. 42 U.S.C. Secs. 300x-300x-9.

26. Passed as part of the Omnibus Reconciliation Act of 1987, 42 U.S.C. Secs. 1395i-3, 1396r.

27. 42 U.S.C. Sec. 1395i-3(g)(2)(A).

28. 42 U.S.C. Sec. 1395i-3(g)(2)(B).

29. 29 U.S.C. Secs. 2201–2288.

30. 42 U.S.C. Secs. 1973ee–1973ee-6.

31. 42 U.S.C. Sec. 1973gg.

32. National Coalition v. Allen, 152 F.3d 283 (4th Cir. 1998).

33. 42 U.S.C. Sec. 1395cc(f)(1)(A).

34. 42 U.S.C. Secs. 1997 *et seq.*

35. 42 U.S.C. 10801 *et seq.*

36. 29 U.S.C. Secs. 2601 *et seq.*

37. 29 U.S.C. Sec. 2617(c)(1).

38. McAnnally v. Wyn South Molded Products, 912 F.Supp. 512 (N.D. Ala. 1996).

39. 42 U.S.C. Sec. 1985.

40. Trautz v. Weisman, 819 F.Supp. 282 (S.D. N.Y. 1993).

41. 31 U.S.C. Sec. 3730.

TABLE OF AUTHORITIES

Numbers in italics refer to listings in endnote sections.

Laws

Cases

INDEX

Numbers in italics refer to listings in endnote sections.

ABOUT THE AUTHOR

Susan Stefan, JD, is a professor of law at the University of Miami School of Law. Prior to 1990, she worked as an attorney at the Mental Health Law Project (now the Bazelon Center for Mental Health Law) in Washington, DC. She graduated magna cum laude from Princeton University in 1980, received a master's in philosophy from Cambridge University in 1981, and received her law degree from Stanford University Law School in 1984. Ms. Stefan writes about disability and mental health law. She also continues to litigate cases involving the Americans With Disabilities Act and its application to people with psychiatric disabilities.